Microsoft® Visual C# 2005®

An Introduction to Object-Oriented Programming

Second Edition

Joyce Farrell

Microsoft® Visual C# 2005®:
An Introduction to Object-Oriented Programming, *Second Edition*
by Joyce Farrell

Vice President, Technology and Trades ABU:
Dave Garza

Director of Learning Solutions:
Sandy Clark

Acquisitions Editor:
Amy Jollymore

Managing Editor:
Tricia Coia

Development Editor:
Dan Seiter

Content Project Managers:
Danielle Chouhan, Philippa Lehar

Marketing Specialist:
Victoria Ortiz

Cover Designer:
Steve Deschene

Art Director:
Beth Paquin

Compositor:
International Typesetting and Composition

Manufacturing Coordinator:
Julio Esperas

Editorial Assistant:
Erin Kennedy

Copy Editor:
Mary Kemper

Proofreader:
Brandy Lilly

Indexer:
Rich Carlson

COPYRIGHT © 2008 Thomson Course Technology, a division of Thomson Learning, Inc. Thomson Learning™ is a trademark used herein under license.

Printed in Canada

1 2 3 4 5 6 7 8 9 EB 06 05 04 03 02

For more information,
contact Thomson Course Technology,
25 Thomson Place, Boston,
Massachusetts, 02210.

Or find us on the World Wide Web at:
www.course.com

ALL RIGHTS RESERVED. No part of this work covered by the copyright hereon may be reproduced or used in any form or by any means—graphic, electronic, or mechanical, including photocopying, recording, taping, Web distribution, or information storage and retrieval systems—without the written permission of the publisher.

For permission to use material from this text or product, contact us by
Tel.: (800) 730-2214
Fax: (800) 730-2215
www.thomsonrights.com

Disclaimer
Thomson Course Technology reserves the right to revise this publication and make changes from time to time in its content without notice.

ISBN-13: 978-14239-0151-8
ISBN-10: 1-4239-0151-7

BRIEF CONTENTS

PREFACE		XV
READ THIS BEFORE YOU BEGIN		XVIII
CHAPTER 1	A FIRST PROGRAM USING C#	1
CHAPTER 2	USING DATA	39
CHAPTER 3	MAKING DECISIONS	81
CHAPTER 4	LOOPING	115
CHAPTER 5	USING ARRAYS	139
CHAPTER 6	USING METHODS	171
CHAPTER 7	USING CLASSES AND OBJECTS	213
CHAPTER 8	INTRODUCTION TO INHERITANCE	271
CHAPTER 9	EXCEPTION HANDLING	321
CHAPTER 10	USING GUI OBJECTS AND THE VISUAL STUDIO IDE	365
CHAPTER 11	USING CONTROLS	413
CHAPTER 12	HANDLING EVENTS	473
CHAPTER 13	FILES AND STREAMS	515
APPENDIX A	OPERATOR PRECEDENCE AND ASSOCIATIVITY	557
APPENDIX B	CREATING A MULTIFILE ASSEMBLY	561
APPENDIX C	USING THE IDE EDITOR	565
INDEX		571

TABLE OF CONTENTS

PREFACE	XV
READ THIS BEFORE YOU BEGIN	XVIII

CHAPTER 1 A FIRST PROGRAM USING C# — 1

PROGRAMMING	2
OBJECT-ORIENTED PROGRAMMING	3
THE C# PROGRAMMING LANGUAGE	7
WRITING A C# PROGRAM THAT PRODUCES OUTPUT	8
SELECTING IDENTIFIERS	11
ADDING COMMENTS TO A PROGRAM	13
ELIMINATING THE REFERENCE TO Out BY USING THE System NAMESPACE	15
Not Recommended: Using an Alias	16
WRITING AND COMPILING A C# PROGRAM	16
Compiling Code from the Command Prompt	17
Compiling Code from within the Visual Studio IDE	19
ALTERNATE WAYS TO WRITE A Main() METHOD	20
YOU DO IT	21
Entering a Program into an Editor	22
Compiling and Executing a Program from the Command Line	23
Compiling and Executing a Program Using the Visual Studio IDE	24
Deciding Which Method to Use	29
Adding Comments to a Program	29
CHAPTER SUMMARY	31
KEY TERMS	31
REVIEW QUESTIONS	34
EXERCISES	37
Debugging Exercises	38
UP FOR DISCUSSION	38

CHAPTER 2 USING DATA — 39

DECLARING VARIABLES	40
DISPLAYING VARIABLE VALUES	43
USING THE INTEGRAL DATA TYPES	47
USING FLOATING-POINT DATA TYPES	47

MICROSOFT® VISUAL C# 2005®: AN INTRODUCTION TO OBJECT-ORIENTED PROGRAMMING

FORMATTING FLOATING-POINT VALUES	48
USING THE STANDARD BINARY ARITHMETIC OPERATORS	50
USING SHORTCUT ARITHMETIC OPERATORS	51
USING THE `bool` DATA TYPE	53
UNDERSTANDING NUMERIC TYPE CONVERSION	54
USING THE `char` DATA TYPE	55
USING THE `string` DATA TYPE	57
DEFINING NAMED CONSTANTS	60
ACCEPTING CONSOLE INPUT	61
YOU DO IT	63
Declaring and Using Variables	63
Performing Arithmetic	64
Working with Boolean Variables	66
Using Escape Sequences	67
Writing a Program That Accepts User Input	68
CHAPTER SUMMARY	69
KEY TERMS	70
REVIEW QUESTIONS	73
EXERCISES	76
Debugging Exercises	79
UP FOR DISCUSSION	79

CHAPTER 3 MAKING DECISIONS   81

UNDERSTANDING DECISION MAKING	82
MAKING DECISIONS USING THE `if` STATEMENT	83
MAKING DECISIONS USING THE `if-else` STATEMENT	86
USING COMPOUND EXPRESSIONS IN `if` STATEMENTS	88
Using the Conditional AND Operator	88
Using the Conditional OR Operator	90
Using the Logical AND and OR Operators	90
Combining AND and OR Operators	91
MAKING DECISIONS USING THE `switch` STATEMENT	92
USING THE CONDITIONAL OPERATOR	96
USING THE NOT OPERATOR	97
AVOIDING COMMON ERRORS WHEN MAKING DECISIONS	97
Performing Accurate and Efficient Range Checks	98
Using AND and OR Appropriately	99
Using NOT Correctly	100

TABLE OF CONTENTS

YOU DO IT	100
Using `if-else` Statements	100
Using AND and OR Logic	102
CHAPTER SUMMARY	104
KEY TERMS	105
REVIEW QUESTIONS	106
EXERCISES	111
Debugging Exercises	112
UP FOR DISCUSSION	113

CHAPTER 4 LOOPING   115

LEARNING ABOUT THE LOOP STRUCTURE	116
USING THE `while` LOOP	116
USING THE `for` LOOP	120
USING THE `do` LOOP	122
USING NESTED LOOPS	124
ACCUMULATING TOTALS	126
IMPROVING LOOP PERFORMANCE	128
YOU DO IT	128
Using a `while` Loop	128
Using `for` Loops	129
CHAPTER SUMMARY	131
KEY TERMS	132
REVIEW QUESTIONS	133
EXERCISES	136
Debugging Exercises	137
UP FOR DISCUSSION	137

CHAPTER 5 USING ARRAYS   139

DECLARING AN ARRAY AND ASSIGNING VALUES TO ARRAY ELEMENTS	140
INITIALIZING AN ARRAY	142
USING SUBSCRIPTS TO ACCESS ARRAY ELEMENTS	143
USING THE `Length` PROPERTY	144
USING `foreach` TO CONTROL ARRAY ACCESS	145
SEARCHING AN ARRAY FOR AN EXACT MATCH	146
Using a `for` Loop to Search an Array	146
Using a `while` Loop to Search an Array	148
SEARCHING AN ARRAY FOR A RANGE MATCH	150

USING THE `BinarySearch()` METHOD	151
USING THE `Sort()` AND `Reverse()` METHODS	153
USING MULTIDIMENSIONAL ARRAYS	155
YOU DO IT	159
Creating and Using an Array	159
Initializing an Array	160
Using a `for` Loop with an Array	160
Using the `Length` Property with an Array	161
Using the `Sort()` and `Reverse()` Methods	161
CHAPTER SUMMARY	163
KEY TERMS	164
REVIEW QUESTIONS	165
EXERCISES	168
Debugging Exercises	170
UP FOR DISCUSSION	170

CHAPTER 6 USING METHODS — 171

UNDERSTANDING METHODS	172
WRITING METHODS WITH NO PARAMETERS AND NO RETURN VALUE	173
HIDING IMPLEMENTATION	176
WRITING METHODS THAT REQUIRE A SINGLE ARGUMENT	177
WRITING METHODS THAT REQUIRE MULTIPLE ARGUMENTS	180
WRITING A METHOD THAT RETURNS A VALUE	183
PASSING AN ARRAY TO A METHOD	185
USING `ref`, `out`, AND `params` PARAMETERS WITHIN METHODS	189
Using Value Parameters	189
Using Reference and Output Parameters	191
Using Parameter Arrays	193
OVERLOADING METHODS	195
AVOIDING AMBIGUOUS METHODS	196
YOU DO IT	198
Calling a Method	198
Writing a Method That Receives Parameters and Returns a Value	199
Using Reference Parameters	201
Overloading Methods	202
CHAPTER SUMMARY	203
KEY TERMS	204
REVIEW QUESTIONS	206

TABLE OF CONTENTS

EXERCISES	210
Debugging Exercises	212
UP FOR DISCUSSION	212

CHAPTER 7 USING CLASSES AND OBJECTS — 213

UNDERSTANDING CLASS CONCEPTS	214
CREATING A CLASS FROM WHICH OBJECTS CAN BE INSTANTIATED	216
CREATING INSTANCE VARIABLES AND METHODS	217
DECLARING OBJECTS	218
CREATING PROPERTIES	221
STORING AND ORGANIZING YOUR CLASSES	224
UNUSUAL USE: `public` FIELDS AND `private` METHODS	226
UNDERSTANDING THE `this` REFERENCE	229
UNDERSTANDING CONSTRUCTORS	232
PASSING PARAMETERS TO CONSTRUCTORS	233
OVERLOADING CONSTRUCTORS	234
USING CONSTRUCTOR INITIALIZERS	236
PASSING OBJECTS TO METHODS	238
OVERLOADING OPERATORS	239
DECLARING AN ARRAY OF OBJECTS	244
Using the `Sort()` and `BinarySearch()` Methods with Arrays of Objects	245
UNDERSTANDING DESTRUCTORS	250
YOU DO IT	251
Creating a Class and Objects	251
Adding Overloaded Constructors to a Class	254
Creating an Array of Objects	255
CHAPTER SUMMARY	258
KEY TERMS	260
REVIEW QUESTIONS	262
EXERCISES	265
Debugging Exercises	269
UP FOR DISCUSSION	270

CHAPTER 8 INTRODUCTION TO INHERITANCE — 271

UNDERSTANDING THE CONCEPT OF INHERITANCE	272
UNDERSTANDING INHERITANCE TERMINOLOGY	274
EXTENDING CLASSES	276
USING THE `protected` ACCESS SPECIFIER	278

OVERRIDING BASE CLASS METHODS	282
ACCESSING BASE CLASS METHODS FROM A DERIVED CLASS	285
UNDERSTANDING HOW A DERIVED CLASS OBJECT "IS AN" INSTANCE OF THE BASE CLASS	286
USING THE Object CLASS	288
Using the Object Class's GetType() Method	289
Using the Object Class's ToString() Method	289
Using the Object Class's Equals() Method	290
Using the Object Class's GetHashCode() Method	290
WORKING WITH BASE CLASSES THAT HAVE CONSTRUCTORS	293
Using Base Class Constructors That Require Arguments	294
CREATING AND USING ABSTRACT CLASSES	295
CREATING AND USING INTERFACES	298
RECAPPING THE BENEFITS OF USING INHERITANCE	302
YOU DO IT	303
Extending a Class	305
Using Base Class Members in a Derived Class	306
Adding Constructors to Base and Derived Classes	309
CHAPTER SUMMARY	310
KEY TERMS	311
REVIEW QUESTIONS	312
EXERCISES	316
Debugging Exercises	319
UP FOR DISCUSSION	320

CHAPTER 9 EXCEPTION HANDLING — 321

UNDERSTANDING EXCEPTIONS	322
PURPOSELY GENERATING A SystemException	324
UNDERSTANDING TRADITIONAL ERROR-HANDLING METHODS	325
UNDERSTANDING OBJECT-ORIENTED EXCEPTION-HANDLING METHODS	326
USING THE Exception CLASS'S ToString() METHOD AND Message PROPERTY	329
CATCHING MULTIPLE ExceptionS	331
USING THE finally BLOCK	336
HANDLING AN Exception WITH A LOOP	338
THROWING ExceptionS BETWEEN METHODS	340
TRACING ExceptionS THROUGH THE CALL STACK	343
A Case Study: Using StackTrace	344
CREATING YOUR OWN Exception CLASSES	347

TABLE OF CONTENTS

RETHROWING AN Exception	350
YOU DO IT	352
Purposely Causing Exceptions	352
Handling Exceptions	354
Catching Various Exception Types	355
CHAPTER SUMMARY	356
KEY TERMS	358
REVIEW QUESTIONS	358
EXERCISES	362
Debugging Exercises	364
UP FOR DISCUSSION	364

CHAPTER 10 USING GUI OBJECTS AND THE VISUAL STUDIO IDE   365

CREATING A MessageBox	366
ADDING FUNCTIONALITY TO MessageBox BUTTONS	372
CREATING A Form	374
CREATING A Form THAT IS A PROGRAM'S MAIN WINDOW	378
PLACING A Button ON A Window	380
USING THE VISUAL STUDIO IDE TO DESIGN A Form	382
UNDERSTANDING THE CODE CREATED BY THE IDE	385
Comments	387
The Dispose() Method	388
Object Declarations	388
The InitializeComponent() Method	389
Preprocessor Directives	389
The Project's Main() Method	390
ADDING FUNCTIONALITY TO A Button ON A Form	390
USING VISUAL STUDIO HELP	392
YOU DO IT	394
Creating MessageBoxes	394
Working with the Visual Studio IDE	395
Providing Functionality for a Button	402
Adding a Second Button to a Form	403
CHAPTER SUMMARY	406
KEY TERMS	407
REVIEW QUESTIONS	408
EXERCISES	411
Debugging Exercises	412
UP FOR DISCUSSION	412

MICROSOFT® VISUAL C# 2005®: AN INTRODUCTION TO OBJECT-ORIENTED PROGRAMMING

CHAPTER 11 USING CONTROLS — 413
UNDERSTANDING Controls — 414
CREATING A Form WITH Labels — 417
SETTING A Label'S Font — 421
USING A LinkLabel — 423
ADDING COLOR TO A Form — 427
USING CheckBox AND RadioButton OBJECTS — 428
ADDING A PictureBox TO A Form — 433
ADDING ListBox, CheckedListBox, AND ComboBox Controls TO A Form — 435
ADDING MonthCalendar AND DateTimePicker Controls TO A Form — 439
WORKING WITH A Form'S LAYOUT — 443
UNDERSTANDING GroupBoxES AND PanelS — 445
ADDING A MenuStrip TO A Form — 445
USING OTHER Controls — 448
YOU DO IT — 448
   Adding Labels to a Form and Changing Their Properties — 448
   Examining the Code Generated by the IDE — 451
   Adding CheckBoxes to a Form — 453
   Adding RadioButtons to a Form — 457
   Adding a MonthCalendar to a Form — 461
CHAPTER SUMMARY — 465
KEY TERMS — 466
REVIEW QUESTIONS — 468
EXERCISES — 470
   Debugging Exercises — 472
UP FOR DISCUSSION — 472

CHAPTER 12 HANDLING EVENTS — 473
EVENT HANDLING — 474
UNDERSTANDING DELEGATES — 477
CREATING COMPOSED DELEGATES — 479
DECLARING YOUR OWN EVENTS AND HANDLERS — 480
USING THE BUILT-IN EventHandler — 483
HANDLING Control COMPONENT EVENTS — 485
HANDLING MOUSE EVENTS — 489
HANDLING KEYBOARD EVENTS — 492

TABLE OF CONTENTS

MANAGING MULTIPLE `Control`S	494
Defining Focus	494
Firing a Single Event from Multiple Controls	494
CONTINUING TO LEARN ABOUT `Control`S AND `Event`S	496
YOU DO IT	496
Creating Delegates	496
Creating a Composed Delegate	498
Creating a Delegate That Encapsulates Instance Methods	501
Creating an Event Listener	502
Using `TabStop` and `TabIndex`	504
Associating One Method with Multiple Events	505
Using the `sender` Object in an Event	506
CHAPTER SUMMARY	507
KEY TERMS	508
REVIEW QUESTIONS	509
EXERCISES	512
Debugging Exercises	513
UP FOR DISCUSSION	514

CHAPTER 13 FILES AND STREAMS — 515

UNDERSTANDING COMPUTER FILES AND HOW THEY ARE STORED	516
USING THE `File` AND `Directory` CLASSES	517
UNDERSTANDING DATA ORGANIZATION WITHIN A FILE	520
UNDERSTANDING STREAMS	522
WRITING TO A SEQUENTIAL ACCESS TEXT FILE	525
READING FROM A SEQUENTIAL ACCESS TEXT FILE	528
SEARCHING A SEQUENTIAL FILE	530
UNDERSTANDING SERIALIZATION AND DESERIALIZATION	532
YOU DO IT	536
Creating a File	536
Reading from a File	538
Using the `Seek()` Method	539
Creating a File in a GUI Environment	541
Reading Data from a File into a `Form`	544
CHAPTER SUMMARY	549
KEY TERMS	550
REVIEW QUESTIONS	551

EXERCISES	554
Debugging Exercises	556
UP FOR DISCUSSION	556

APPENDIX A OPERATOR PRECEDENCE AND ASSOCIATIVITY   **557**

APPENDIX B CREATING A MULTIFILE ASSEMBLY   **561**

APPENDIX C USING THE IDE EDITOR   **565**

INDEX   **571**

PREFACE

Microsoft Visual C# 2005, Second edition provides the beginning programmer with a guide to developing programs in C#, a language developed by the Microsoft Corporation as part of the .NET framework and Visual Studio platform. The .NET framework contains a wealth of libraries for developing applications for the Windows family of operating systems. You can write programs for .NET in many languages, but C# is the only language designed specifically for .NET. With C#, you can build small, reusable components that are well-suited to twenty-first century Web-based programming applications. Although similar to Java and C++, many features of C# make it easier to learn and ideal for the beginning programmer. You can program in C# using a simple text editor and the command prompt, or you can manipulate program components using Visual Studio's sophisticated Integrated Development Environment. This book provides you with the tools to use both techniques.

This textbook assumes that you have little or no programming experience. The writing is nontechnical and emphasizes good programming practices. The examples are business examples; they do not assume mathematical background beyond high school business math. Additionally, the examples illustrate one or two major points; they do not contain so many features that you become lost following irrelevant and extraneous details. This book provides you with a solid background in good object-oriented programming techniques and introduces you to object-oriented terminology using clear, familiar language.

ORGANIZATION AND COVERAGE

Microsoft Visual C# 2005 presents C# programming concepts, enforcing good style, logical thinking and the object-oriented paradigm. Chapter 1 introduces you to the language by letting you create working C# programs using both the simple command line and the Visual Studio environment. In Chapter 2 you learn about data and how to input, store, and output data in C#. In Chapters 3, 4, and 5, you learn about the classic programming structures and how to implement them in C#: making selections, looping, and manipulating arrays. Chapter 6 provides a thorough study of methods, including passing parameters into and out of methods and overloading them. Chapter 7 introduces the object-oriented concepts of classes, objects, data hiding, constructors, and destructors. After completing Chapters 8 and 9, you will be thoroughly grounded in the object-oriented concepts of inheritance and exception handling, and will be able to take advantage of both features in your C# programs. Chapters 10 and 11 introduce you to GUI objects. You will learn about controls, how to set their properties, and how to make attractive, useful, graphical, and interactive programs. Chapter 12 takes you further into the intricacies of handling events in your interactive GUI programs. In Chapter 13, you learn to save data to and retrieve data from files.

FEATURES

Microsoft Visual C# 2005 is a superior textbook because it also includes the following features:

» *Objectives*—Each chapter begins with a list of objectives so you know the topics that will be presented in the chapter. In addition to providing a quick reference to topics covered, this feature provides a useful study aid.

» *Notes*—These tips provide additional information—for example, an alternative method of performing a procedure, another term for a concept, background information on a technique, or a common error to avoid.

MICROSOFT® VISUAL C# 2005®: AN INTRODUCTION TO OBJECT-ORIENTED PROGRAMMING

NEW! » *Figures*—Each chapter contains many figures. Code figures are most frequently 25 lines long or shorter, illustrating one concept at a time. Frequently placed screen shots show exactly how program output appears. In this edition, all C# keywords that appear in figures are blue to help them stand out from programmer-created identifiers.

» *Summaries*—Following each chapter is a summary that recaps the programming concepts and techniques covered in the chapter. This feature helps you to recap and check your understanding of the main points in each chapter.

NEW! » *Key Terms*—Each chapter includes a list of newly introduced vocabulary, shown in the order of appearance in the text. The list of key terms provides a mini-review of the major concepts in the chapter.

NEW! » *You Do It*—In each chapter, step-by-step exercises help the student create multiple working programs that emphasize the logic a programmer uses in choosing statements. This section enables students to achieve success on their own—even students in online or distance learning classes.

» *Review Questions*—Each chapter contains 20 multiple-choice review questions that provide a review of the key concepts in the chapter.

» *Exercises*—Each chapter concludes with meaningful programming exercises that provide additional practice of the skills and concepts you learned in the chapter. These exercises increase in difficulty and allow you to explore logical programming concepts.

» *Debugging exercises*—Each chapter contains four programs that contain syntax and/or logical errors that you fix. Completing these exercises provides valuable experience in locating errors, interpreting code written by others, and observing how another programmer has approached a problem.

NEW! » *Up for Discussion*—Each chapter concludes with a few thought-provoking questions that concern programming in general or C# in particular. The questions can be used to start classroom or on-line discussions, or to develop and encourage research, writing, and language skills.

NEW! » *Program code*—The Student Disk provides code for each full program presented in the chapter figures. Providing the code on disk allows students to run it, view the results for themselves, and experiment with multiple input values. Having the code on disk also enables students to experiment with the code without a lot of typing.

» *Quality*—Every program example in the book, as well as every exercise, case project, and game solution, was tested by the author using Visual Studio 2005 Express Edition, and then tested again by a Quality Assurance team using Visual Studio 2005 Professional Edition, the most recent version available.

TEACHING TOOLS

The following supplemental materials are available when this book is used in a classroom setting. All of the teaching tools for this book are provided to the instructor on a single CD-ROM.

Electronic Instructor's Manual. The Instructor's Manual that accompanies this textbook includes:

» Additional instructional material to assist in class preparation, including suggestions for lecture topics.

» Solutions to Review Questions, end-of-chapter programming exercises, debugging exercises, and Up For Discussion questions.

PREFACE

ExamView®. This textbook is accompanied by ExamView, a powerful testing software package that allows instructors to create and administer printed, computer (LAN-based), and Internet exams. ExamView includes hundreds of questions that correspond to the topics covered in this text, enabling students to generate detailed study guides that include page references for further review. The computer-based and Internet testing components allow students to take exams at their computers, and save the instructor time by grading each exam automatically.

PowerPoint Presentations. This book comes with Microsoft PowerPoint slides for each chapter. These slides are included as a teaching aid for classroom presentation; teachers can make them available on the network for chapter review, or print them for classroom distribution. Instructors can add their own slides for additional topics they introduce to the class.

Solution Files. Solutions to all "You Do It" exercises and end-of chapter exercises are provided on the Teaching Tools CD-ROM and on the Course Technology Web site at *www.course.com*. The solutions are password protected.

Distance Learning. Course Technology is proud to present online test banks in WebCT and Blackboard to provide the most complete and dynamic learning experience possible. Instructors are encouraged to make the most of the course, both online and offline. For more information on how to access the online test bank, contact your local Course Technology sales representative.

ACKNOWLEDGMENTS

I would like to thank all of the people who helped to make this book a reality, especially Dan Seiter, the development editor, who worked against multiple, aggressive deadlines to make this book into a superior instructional tool. Thanks also to Tricia Coia, managing editor; Amy Jollymore, acquisitions editor; and Danielle Chouhan, content project manager. I am grateful to be able to work with so many fine people who are dedicated to producing good instructional materials.

I am also grateful to the many reviewers who provided helpful comments and encouragement during this book's development, including I-ping Chu, DePaul University; Phil Jalowiec, Maricopa County Community College; Jo Ann Smith, William Rainey Harper College (retired); and Judi Zaplatynsky, William Rainey Harper College.

Thanks, too, to my husband, Geoff, my companion and cheering section as the book was being written in Wisconsin, Illinois, Iowa, Oklahoma, and Texas.

Joyce Farrell

MICROSOFT® VISUAL C# 2005®: **AN INTRODUCTION TO OBJECT-ORIENTED PROGRAMMING**

READ THIS BEFORE YOU BEGIN

TO THE USER

To complete the exercises in this book, you will need data files that have been created specifically for the book. Your instructor will provide the data files to you. You also can obtain the files electronically from the Course Technology Web site by connecting to *www.course.com* and then searching for this book title. Note that you can use a computer in your school lab or your own computer to complete the exercises in this book.

The data files for this book are organized such that the examples and exercises are divided into folders named Chapter.*xx*, where *xx* is the chapter number. You can save these files in the same folders unless specifically instructed to do otherwise in the chapter.

USING YOUR OWN COMPUTER

To use your own computer to complete the steps and exercises, you will need the following:

- » **Software**. Microsoft Visual C# 2005 Express Edition or Professional Edition, including the Microsoft .NET Framework. If your book came with a copy of the software, you may install it on your computer and use it to complete the material.
- » **Hardware**. A Pentium II-class PC, 450 MHz or higher.
- » **Operating system**. Windows Vista, Windows NT, Windows 2000, or Windows XP.
- » **Data files**. You will not be able to complete the exercises in this book using your own computer unless you have the data files. You can get the data files from your instructor, or you can obtain them electronically from the Course Technology Web site by connecting to **www.course.com** and searching for this book title.

TO THE INSTRUCTOR

To complete all the exercises in this book, your users must work with a set of files called a data disk. These files are included in the Instructor's Resource Kit. You can also obtain these files electronically through the Course Technology Web site at **www.course.com**. Follow the instructions in the Help file to copy the user files to your server or stand-alone computer. You can view the Help file using a text editor such as WordPad or Notepad.

Once the files are copied, you can make data disks for the users yourself or tell them where to find the files so they can make their own data disks.

LICENSE TO USE DATA FILES

You are granted a license to copy the data files to any computer or computer network used by people who have purchased this book.

CHAPTER ONE

A FIRST PROGRAM USING C#

In this chapter you will:

Learn about programming
Explore object-oriented programming concepts
Learn about the C# programming language
Write a C# program that produces output
Learn how to select identifiers to use within your programs
Add comments to a C# program
Eliminate the reference to `Out` by using the `System` namespace
Write and compile a C# program using the command prompt and using Visual Studio
Learn alternate ways to write the `Main()` method

A FIRST PROGRAM USING C#

Programming a computer is an interesting, challenging, fun, and sometimes frustrating task. As a programmer, you must be precise and careful as well as creative. Learning to program is fascinating; learning a new programming language expands your horizons.

As new programming languages are developed and introduced, your job becomes easier and more difficult at the same time. Programming becomes easier because built-in capabilities are added to every new language that is developed, and tasks that might have taken you weeks or months to develop 20 years ago are now included in the language so you can add them to a program with a few keystrokes. Programming becomes more difficult for the same reason— new languages have so many features that you must devote a significant amount of time to learning them.

C# (pronounced "C Sharp") is a relatively new language that provides you with a wide range of options and features. As you work through this book, you will master many of them, one step at a time. If this is your first programming experience, you will learn new ways to approach and solve problems and to think logically. If you know how to program but are new to C#, you will be impressed by its capabilities.

In this chapter, you will learn about the background of programming that led to the development of C#, and you will write and execute your first C# programs.

PROGRAMMING

A computer **program** is a set of instructions that you write to tell a computer what to do. Internally, computers are constructed from circuitry that consists of small on/off switches; the most basic circuitry-level language that computers use to control the operation of those switches is called **machine language**. Machine language is expressed as a series of 1s and 0s—1s represent switches that are on, and 0s represent switches that are off. If programmers had to write computer programs using machine language, they would have to keep track of the hundreds of thousands of 1s and 0s involved in programming any worthwhile task. Not only would writing a program be a time-consuming and difficult task, but modifying programs, understanding others' programs, and locating errors within programs would also be cumbersome. Additionally, the number and location of switches vary from computer to computer, which means you would need to customize a machine-language program for every type of machine on which the program had to run.

Fortunately, programming has evolved into an easier task because of the development of high-level programming languages. A **high-level programming language** allows you to use a vocabulary of reasonable terms such as "read," "write," or "add" instead of the sequence of on/off switches that perform these tasks. High-level languages also allow you to assign reasonable names to areas of computer memory; you can use names such as "`HoursWorked`" or "`PayRate`," rather than having to remember the memory locations (switch numbers) of those values.

Each high-level language has its own **syntax**, or rules of the language. For example, to produce output, you might use the verb "print" in one language and "write" in another.

All languages have a specific, limited vocabulary, along with a set of rules for using that vocabulary. Programmers use a computer program called a **compiler** to translate their high-level language statements into machine code. The compiler issues an error message each time a programmer uses the language incorrectly; subsequently, the programmer can correct the error and attempt another translation by compiling the program again. When you learn a computer programming language such as C#, C++, Visual Basic, or Java, you really are learning the vocabulary and syntax rules for that language.

> **NOTE** In some languages, such as BASIC, the language translator is called an interpreter. In others, such as assembly language, it is called an assembler. These translators operate in different fashions, but the ultimate goal of each is to translate the higher-level language into machine language.

In addition to learning the correct syntax for a particular language, a programmer must understand computer programming logic. The **logic** behind any program involves executing the various statements and procedures in the correct order to produce the desired results. For example, you might be able to execute perfect individual notes on a musical instrument, but if you do not execute them in the proper order (or execute a B-flat when an F-sharp was expected), no one will enjoy your performance. Similarly, you might be able to use a computer language's syntax correctly, but be unable to execute a logically constructed, workable program. Examples of logical errors include multiplying two values when you should divide them, or attempting to calculate a paycheck before obtaining the appropriate payroll data.

> **NOTE** Programmers call some logical errors **semantic errors**. For example, if you misspell a programming language word, you commit a syntax error, but if you use a correct word in the wrong context, you commit a semantic error.

To achieve a working program that accomplishes the tasks it is meant to accomplish, you must remove all syntax and logical errors from the program. This process is called **debugging** the program.

> **NOTE** Since the early days of computer programming, program errors have been called "bugs." The term is often said to have originated from an actual moth that was discovered trapped in the circuitry of a computer at Harvard University in 1945. Actually, the term "bug" was in use prior to 1945 to mean trouble with any electrical apparatus; even during Thomas Edison's life, it meant an "industrial defect." In any case, the process of finding and correcting program errors has come to be known as debugging.

OBJECT-ORIENTED PROGRAMMING

There are two popular approaches to writing computer programs: procedural programming and object-oriented programming.

When you write a **procedural program**, you use your knowledge of a programming language to create and name computer memory locations that can hold values, and you write a series of steps or operations to manipulate those values. The named computer memory locations are called **variables** because they hold values that might vary. In programming languages, a variable is referenced by using a one-word name (an **identifier**) with no embedded spaces. For example, a company's payroll program might contain a variable named PayRate. The memory location referenced by the name PayRate might contain different values at different times.

A FIRST PROGRAM USING C#

For instance, an organization's payroll program might contain a different value for `PayRate` for each of 100 employees. Additionally, a single employee's `PayRate` variable might contain different values before or after a raise, or before or after surpassing 40 work hours in one week. During the execution of the payroll program, each value stored under the name `PayRate` might have many operations performed on it—for example, reading it from an input device, multiplying it by another variable representing hours worked, and printing it on paper.

> **» NOTE** When programmers do not capitalize the first letter of an identifier but do capitalize each new word, as in `payRate`, they call the style **camel casing**, because the identifier appears to have a hump in the middle. When programmers adopt the style of capitalizing the first letter of all new words in an identifier, even the first one, as in `PayRate`, they call the style **Pascal casing**. Most C# programmers use Pascal casing when creating method names, but this convention is not required to produce a workable program.

For convenience, the individual operations used in a computer program often are grouped into logical units called **procedures** or **methods**. For example, a series of four or five comparisons and calculations that together determine an employee's federal tax withholding value might be grouped as a method named `CalculateFederalWithholding()`. A procedural program defines the variable memory locations, then **calls** or **invokes** a series of procedures to input, manipulate, and output the values stored in those locations. A single procedural program often contains hundreds of variables and thousands of procedure calls.

> **» NOTE** In C#, all procedure names are followed by a set of parentheses. When you pronounce a procedure name, you ignore the parentheses. When this book refers to a procedure, the name will be followed with parentheses. This practice helps distinguish procedure names from variable and class names.

Object-oriented programming is an extension of procedural programming. Object-oriented programs contain variables, procedures, and six other features:

» Objects
» Classes
» Encapsulation
» Interfaces
» Polymorphism
» Inheritance

> **» NOTE** Although procedural and object-oriented programming techniques are somewhat similar, they raise different concerns in the design and development phase that occurs before programs are written.

The components called **objects** are similar to concrete objects in the real world. You create objects that contain their own variables and methods, and then you manipulate those objects to achieve a desired result. Writing object-oriented programs involves both creating objects and creating applications that use those objects.

If you've ever used a computer that has a command-line operating system (such as DOS), and if you've used a GUI (a graphical user interface, such as Microsoft Windows), then you already have an idea of the difference between procedural and object-oriented programs. If you want to move several files from a CD to a hard disk, you can accomplish the task using either a typed command at a prompt or command line (as in DOS), or using a mouse in a graphical environment (as in Windows). The difference lies in whether you issue a series of sequential commands to move the files (in DOS) or drag icons representing the files from one screen location to another (in Windows). You can move the files using either operating system, but the GUI system allows you to treat files as objects.

> **NOTE** The **command line** is the line on which you type a command in a system that uses a text interface. The **command prompt** is a request for input that appears at the beginning of the command line. In DOS, the command prompt indicates the disk drive and optional path, and ends with >.

Objects in both the real world and in object-oriented programming are made up of attributes and methods. The **attributes** of an object represent its characteristics. For example, some of your `Automobile`'s attributes are its make, model, year, and purchase price. Other attributes describe whether the `Automobile` is currently running, its gear, its speed, and whether it is dirty. All `Automobile`s possess the same attributes, but not the same values, or **states**, for those attributes. For example, some `Automobile`s currently are running, but some are not. The value of an attribute can change over time; for example, some `Automobile`s are running now, but will not be running in the future. Therefore, the states of an `Automobile` are variable. Similarly, your `Dog` has attributes that include its breed, name, age, and shot status (that is, whether its shots are current); the states for a particular dog might be "Labrador retriever", "Murphy", "7", and "yes".

> **NOTE** Programmers also call the values of an object's attributes the **properties** of the object. The **state of an object** is the collective value of all its attributes at any point in time.

A **class** is a category of objects or a type of object. A class describes the attributes and methods of every object that is an **instance**, or example, of that class. For example, `Automobile` is a class whose objects have a year, make, model, color, and current running status. Your 2001 red Chevrolet is an instance of the class that is made up of all `Automobile`s; so is my supervisor's 2007 black Porsche. Your Collie named Bosco is an instance of the class that is made up of all `Dog`s; so is my Labrador named Murphy. Thinking of items as instances of a class allows you to apply your general knowledge of the class to its individual members. The particular instances of these objects contain all of the attributes that their general category contains; only the states of those attributes vary. If your friend purchases an `Automobile`, you know it has some model name; if your friend gets a `Dog`, you know it has some breed. You probably don't know the current state of the `Automobile`'s speed or exact contents of the `Dog`'s shots, but you do know that those attributes exist for the `Automobile` and `Dog` classes. Similarly, in a GUI operating environment, you expect each window you open to have specific, consistent attributes, such as a menu bar and a title bar, because each window includes these attributes as a member of the general class of GUI Windows.

> **NOTE** By convention, programmers using C# begin their class names with an uppercase letter. Thus, the class that defines the attributes and methods of an automobile would probably be named `Automobile`, and the class that contains dogs would probably be named `Dog`. However, following this convention is not required to produce a workable program.

Besides attributes, objects possess methods or procedures that they use to accomplish tasks, including changing attributes and discovering the values of attributes. `Automobile`s, for example, have methods for moving forward and backward. They also can be filled with gasoline or be washed; both are methods that change some of an `Automobile`'s attributes. Methods also exist for ascertaining the status of certain attributes, such as the current speed of an `Automobile` and the status of its gas tank. Similarly, a `Dog` can walk or run, eat, and get a bath, and there are methods for determining whether it needs a walk, food, or a bath. GUI operating system components, such as windows, can be maximized, minimized, and dragged; depending on the component, they can also have their color or font style altered.

Like procedural programs, object-oriented programs have variables (attributes) and procedures (methods), but the attributes and methods are encapsulated into objects that are then used much like real-world objects. **Encapsulation** is the technique of packaging an object's attributes and methods into a cohesive unit that can be used as an undivided entity. Programmers sometimes refer to encapsulation as using a "**black box**," a device you use without regard for the internal mechanisms. If an object's methods are well written, the user is unaware of the low-level details of how the methods are executed; in such a case, the user must understand only the **interface** or interaction between the method and object. For example, if you can fill your `Automobile` with gasoline, it is because you understand the interface between the gas pump nozzle and the vehicle's gas tank opening. You don't need to understand how the pump works or where the gas tank is located inside your vehicle. If you can read your speedometer, it does not matter how the display figure is calculated. In fact, if someone produces a new, more accurate speedometer and inserts it into your `Automobile`, you don't have to know or care how it operates, as long as the interface remains the same as the previous one. The same principles apply to well-constructed objects used in object-oriented programs.

Object-oriented programming languages support two other distinguishing features in addition to organizing objects as members of classes. One feature, **polymorphism**, describes the ability to create methods that act appropriately depending on the context. For example, you are able to "fill" both a `Dog` and an `Automobile`, but you do so by very different means. A friend would have no trouble understanding your meaning if you said "I need to fill my `Automobile`" and distinguishing the process from that of "filling" your `Dog`, your `BankAccount`, or your `AppointmentCalendar`. Older, non-object-oriented languages could not make such distinctions, but object-oriented languages can.

Object-oriented languages also support inheritance. **Inheritance** provides the ability to extend a class so as to create a more specific class. The more specific class contains all the attributes and methods of the more general class, and usually contains new attributes or methods as well. For example, if you have created a `Dog` class, you might then create a more specific class named `ShowDog`. Each instance of the `ShowDog` class would contain all the attributes and methods of a `Dog`, along with additional methods or attributes. For example, a `ShowDog` might require an attribute to hold the number of ribbons won and a method for entering a dog show. Using polymorphism, you might need to specialize the `Dog`'s methods to be appropriate for a `ShowDog`. For example, the fill method might be different (perhaps using more expensive food). The advantage of inheritance is that when you need a class such as `ShowDog`, you often can extend an existing class, thereby saving a lot of time and work.

THE C# PROGRAMMING LANGUAGE

The **C# programming language** was developed as an object-oriented and component-oriented language. It is part of Microsoft Visual Studio 2005, a package designed for developing applications that run on Windows computers. Unlike other programming languages, C# allows every piece of data to be treated as an object and to employ the principles of object-oriented programming. C# provides constructs for creating components with properties, methods, and events, making it an ideal language for twenty-first-century programming, where building small, reusable components is more important than building huge, stand-alone applications.

>> **NOTE** Technically, you can use pointers in C#, but only in a mode called unsafe, which is rarely used.

C# contains a GUI interface that makes it similar to Visual Basic. C# is considered more concise than Visual Basic, and is modeled after the C++ programming language, but some of the most difficult features to understand in C++ have been eliminated in C#. For example, pointers are not used in C#, object destructors and forward declarations are not needed, and using `#include` files is not necessary. Multiple inheritance, which causes many C++ programming errors, is not allowed in C#.

C# is very similar to Java, because Java was also based on C++. In Java, simple data types are not objects; therefore, they do not work with built-in methods. In C#, every piece of data is an object, providing all data with the functionality of true objects. Additionally, in Java, simple parameters (also called primitive parameters) must be passed by value, which means a copy must be made of any data that is sent to a method for alteration, and the copy must be sent back to the original object. C# provides the convenience of passing primitive parameters by reference, which means the actual object can be altered by a method without a copy being passed back. If you have not programmed before, the difference between C# and other languages means little to you. However, experienced programmers will appreciate the thought that the developers of C# put into its features.

>> **NOTE** **Primitive data** is simple data, such as a number, as opposed to complex data, such as an `Employee`, a `BankAccount`, or an `Automobile`. In Chapter 2, you will learn about C#'s simple data types—those that are intrinsic to the language. In Chapter 7, you will create complex objects that are composed of primitive data types.

>> **NOTE** The C# programming language was standardized in 2002 by Ecma International. You can read or download this set of standards at *www.ecma-international.org/publication/standards/Ecma-334.htm*.

>> **NOTE** Microsoft Corporation refers to the current version of C# as C# 3.0. You can find Microsoft's C# specifications at *http://msdn2.microsoft.com/en-us/vcsharp/aa336809*

A FIRST PROGRAM USING C#

WRITING A C# PROGRAM THAT PRODUCES OUTPUT

> **NOTE**
> In code figures in this book, C# keywords appear in blue. You will learn about keywords in the next section.

At first glance, even the simplest C# program involves a fair amount of confusing syntax. Consider the simple program in Figure 1-1. This program is written on seven lines, and its only task is to display "This is my first C# program" on the screen.

```
public class FirstClass
{
    public static void Main()
    {
        System.Console.Out.WriteLine("This is my first C# program");
    }
}
```

Figure 1-1 `FirstClass` console application

The statement that does the actual work in this program is in the middle of the figure: `System.Console.Out.WriteLine("This is my first C# program");`. The statement ends with a semicolon because all C# statements do.

The text "This is my first C# program" is a **literal string** of characters—that is, a series of characters that will be used exactly as entered. Any literal string in C# appears between double quotation marks.

The string "This is my first C# program" appears within parentheses because the string is an argument to a method, and arguments to methods always appear within parentheses. **Arguments** represent information that a method needs to perform its task. For example, if making an appointment with a dentist's office was a C# method, you would write `MakeAppointment("September 10", "2 p.m.");`. Accepting and processing a dental appointment is a method that consists of a set of standard procedures. However, each appointment requires different information—the date and time—and this information can be considered the arguments of the `MakeAppointment()` method. If you make an appointment for September 8 at 2 p.m., you expect different results than if you make one for September 9 at 8 a.m. or December 25 at midnight. Likewise, if you pass the argument "Happy Holidays" to a method, you will expect different results than if you pass the argument "This is my first C# program."

> **NOTE** The words "argument" and "parameter" are often used interchangeably, although many programmers make a clear distinction between the two. An argument is the expression used when you call or invoke a method, while a **parameter** is an object or reference that is declared in a method definition; in other words, where the method instructions are written. You will learn more about the terms *call* and *invoke* in Chapter 6. Do not worry if you do not understand arguments and parameters at this point; their uses will become clearer when you write methods in Chapter 6.

Within the statement `System.Console.Out.WriteLine("This is my first C# program");`, the method to which you are passing the argument string "This is my first C#

program" is named `WriteLine()`. The **`WriteLine()` method** displays output on the screen, positions the cursor on the next line, and waits for additional output.

> **NOTE** In C#, you usually refer to method names by including their parentheses, as in `WriteLine()`. This practice makes it easy for you to distinguish method names from variable names.

> **NOTE** The **`Write()` method** is very similar to the `WriteLine()` method. With `WriteLine()`, the cursor is moved to the following line after the message is displayed. With `Write()`, the cursor does not advance to a new line; it remains on the same line as the output.

Within the statement `System.Console.Out.WriteLine("This is my first C# program");`, `Out` is an object. The `Out` object represents the screen on the terminal or computer where you are working. Of course, not all objects have a `WriteLine()` method (for instance, you can't write a line to a computer's mouse, your `Automobile`, or your `Dog`), but the creators of C# assumed that you frequently would want to display output on the screen at your terminal. For this reason, the `Out` object was created and endowed with the method named `WriteLine()`. Soon, you will create your own C# objects and endow them with your own methods.

> **NOTE** The C# programming language is case sensitive. Thus, the object named `Out` is a completely different object than one named `out`, `OUT`, or `oUt`.

Within the statement `System.Console.Out.WriteLine("This is my first C# program");`, `Console` is a class. It defines the attributes of a collection of similar "`Console`" objects, just as the `Dog` class defines the attributes of a collection of similar `Dog` objects. One of the `Console` objects is `Out`. (You might guess that another `Console` object is `In`, which represents the keyboard.)

Within the statement `System.Console.Out.WriteLine("This is my first C# program");`, `System` is a namespace. A **namespace** is a scheme or mechanism that provides a way to group similar classes. To organize your classes, you can (and will) create your own namespaces. The **`System` namespace**, which is built into your C# compiler, holds commonly used classes.

> **NOTE** You will create other namespaces when you create GUI objects in Chapter 10.

> **NOTE** An advantage to using Visual Studio is that all of its languages use the same namespaces. In other words, everything you learn about any namespace in C# is knowledge you can transfer to Visual C++ and Visual Basic.

The dots (periods) in the statement `System.Console.Out.WriteLine("This is my first C# program");` are used to separate the names of the namespace, class, object, and method. You will use this same namespace-dot-class-dot-object-dot-method format repeatedly in your C# programs.

The statement `System.Console.Out.WriteLine("This is my first C# program");` appears within a method named `Main()`. Every method in C# contains a header and a body. A **method header** includes the method name and information about what will pass into and be returned from a method. The **method body** of every method is contained within a pair of curly braces and includes all the instructions executed by the method.

A FIRST PROGRAM USING C#

The program in Figure 1-1 includes only one statement between the curly braces of the `Main()` method. Soon, you will write methods with many more statements. For every opening curly brace ({) in a C# program, there must be a corresponding closing curly brace (}). The precise position of the opening and closing curly braces is not important to the compiler. For example, the method in Figure 1-2 is executed exactly the same way as the one shown in Figure 1-1. The only difference is in the amount of whitespace used in the method. In general, whitespace is optional in C#. **Whitespace** is any combination of spaces, tabs, and carriage returns (blank lines). You use whitespace to organize your program code and make it easier to read; it does not affect your program. Usually, vertically aligning each pair of opening and closing curly braces, as in Figure 1-1, makes your code easier to read than the format shown in Figure 1-2.

```
public static void Main(){ System.Conscle.Out.WriteLine
("This is my first C# program");}
```

Figure 1-2 A `Main()` method with little whitespace

>> **NOTE**
If you do not use an access modifier within a method header, then by default the method is `private`. Other classes cannot use a `private` method. You will learn more about public and private access modifiers in Chapter 7.

The method header for the `Main()` method contains four words. Three of these words are **keywords**—predefined and reserved identifiers that have special meaning to the compiler. In the method header `public static void Main()`, the word `public` is an access modifier. When used in a method header, an **access modifier** defines the circumstances under which the method can be accessed. As opposed to cases in which a method is **private**, the access modifier **public** indicates that other classes may use this method.

In the English language, the word *static* means "showing little change" or "stationary." In C#, the reserved keyword **static** has a related meaning. It indicates that the `Main()` method will be executed through a class—not by a variety of objects. It means that you do not need to create an object of type `FirstClass` to use the `Main()` method defined within `FirstClass`. In C#, you will create many nonstatic methods within classes that are executed by objects. For example, you might create a `display()` method in an `Automobile` class that you use to display an `Automobile`'s attributes. If you create 100 `Automobile` objects, the `display()` method will operate differently and appropriately for each object, displaying different makes, models, and colors of `Automobiles`. (Programmers would say a nonstatic method is "invoked" by each instance of the object.) However, a `static` method does not require an object to be used to invoke it. Only one version of the `static` `Main()` method for `FirstClass` will ever be executed. Of course, other classes eventually might have their own, different `Main()` methods. You will learn the mechanics of how `static` and nonstatic methods differ in Chapter 6.

In English, the word *void* means empty. When the keyword **void** is used in the `Main()` method header, it does not indicate that the `Main()` method is empty, but rather that the method does not return any value when called. This doesn't mean that `Main()` doesn't produce output—it does. Instead, it means the `Main()` method does not send any value back to any other method that might call it. You will learn more about return values when you study methods in greater detail in Chapter 6.

In the method header, the name of the method is `Main()`. All C# applications must include a method named `Main()`, and most C# applications will have additional methods with other names. When you execute a C# application, the `Main()` method always executes first.

> **NOTE** You will write many C# *classes* that do not contain a `Main()` method. However, all executable *applications* (runnable programs) must contain a `Main()` method.

> **NOTE** You also can write the `Main()` method header as `public static int Main()`, `public static void Main(string[] args)`, or `public static int Main(string[] args)`. You will learn more about these alternative forms of `Main()` at the end of this chapter.

SELECTING IDENTIFIERS

Every method that you use within a C# program must be part of a class. To create a class, you use a class header and curly braces in much the same way you use a header and braces for a method within a class. When you write `public class FirstClass`, you are defining a class named `FirstClass`. A class name does not have to contain the word "Class" as `FirstClass` does. You can define a C# class using any name or identifier you need, as long as it meets the following requirements:

- An identifier must begin with an underscore, the at sign (@), or a letter. (Letters include foreign-alphabet letters such as Р and Ψ, which are contained in the set of characters known as Unicode.)
- An identifier can contain only letters or digits, not special characters such as #, $, or &.
- An identifier cannot be a C# reserved keyword, such as `public` or `class`. Table 1-1 provides a complete list of reserved keywords. (Actually, you can use a keyword as an identifier if you precede it with an "at" sign, as in `@class`. This feature allows you to use code written in other languages that do not have the same set of reserved keywords. However, when you write original C# programs, you should not use the keywords as identifiers.)

> **NOTE** In this book, all identifiers begin with a letter.

> **NOTE** An identifier with an @ prefix is a **verbatim identifier**.

A programming standard in C# is to begin class names with an uppercase letter and use other uppercase letters as needed to improve readability. Table 1-2 lists some valid and conventional class names you might use when creating classes in C#. Table 1-3 lists some class names that are valid, but unconventional; Table 1-4 lists some illegal class names.

In Figure 1-1, the line `public class FirstClass` contains the keyword `class`, which identifies `FirstClass` as a class. The reserved word `public` is an access modifier. Similar to the way an access modifier describes a method's accessibility, when used with a class, the access modifier defines the circumstances under which the class can be accessed; `public` access is the most liberal type of access.

The simple program shown in Figure 1-1 has many pieces to remember. For now, you can use the program shown in Figure 1-3 as a shell, where you replace the identifier `AnyLegalClassName` with any legal class name, and the line `/*********/` with any statements that you want to execute.

A FIRST PROGRAM USING C#

abstract	event	new	struct
as	explicit	null	switch
base	extern	object	this
bool	false	operator	throw
break	finally	out	true
byte	fixed	override	try
case	float	params	typeof
catch	for	private	uint
char	foreach	protected	ulong
checked	goto	public	unchecked
class	if	readonly	unsafe
const	implicit	ref	ushort
continue	in	return	using
decimal	int	sbyte	virtual
default	interface	sealed	void
delegate	internal	short	volatile
do	is	sizeof	while
double	lock	stackalloc	
else	long	static	
enum	namespace	string	

Table 1-1 Java reserved keywords

> **»NOTE**
> The following identifiers have special meaning in C# but are not keywords: add, alias, get, global, partial, remove, set, value, where, and yield. For clarity, you should avoid using these words as your own identifiers.

Class Name	Description
Employee	Begins with an uppercase letter
FirstClass	Begins with an uppercase letter, contains no spaces, and has an initial uppercase letter that indicates the start of the second word
PushButtonControl	Begins with an uppercase letter, contains no spaces, and has an initial uppercase letter that indicates the start of all subsequent words
Budget2008	Begins with an uppercase letter and contains no spaces

Table 1-2 Some valid and conventional class names in C#

CHAPTER ONE

Class Name	Description
employee	Begins with a lowercase letter
First_Class	Although legal, the underscore is not commonly used to indicate new words
Pushbuttoncontrol	No uppercase characters are used to indicate the start of a new word, making the name difficult to read
BUDGET2003	Appears with all uppercase letters
Public	Although this identifier is legal because it is different from the keyword public, which begins with a lowercase "p," the similarity could cause confusion

Table 1-3 Some unconventional (though legal) class names in C#

Class Name	Description
an employee	Space character is illegal
Push Button Control	Space characters are illegal
class	"class" is a reserved word
2003Budget	Class names cannot begin with a digit
phone#	The # symbol is not allowed; identifiers consist of letters and digits

Table 1-4 Some illegal class names in C#

»NOTE
You should follow established conventions for C# so that other programmers can interpret and follow your programs. This book uses established C# programming conventions.

```
public class AnyLegalClassName
{
    public static void Main()
    {
        /*********/;
    }
}
```

Figure 1-3 Shell program

ADDING COMMENTS TO A PROGRAM

As you can see, even the simplest C# program takes several lines of code and contains somewhat perplexing syntax. Large programs that perform many tasks include much more code. As you write longer programs, it becomes increasingly difficult to remember why you included steps and how you intended to use particular variables. **Program comments** are

13

A FIRST PROGRAM USING C#

nonexecuting statements that you add to document a program. Programmers use comments to leave notes for themselves and for others who might read their programs in the future.

> **NOTE** As you work through this book, you should add comments as the first few lines of every program file. The comments should contain your name, the date, and the name of the program. Your instructor might want you to include additional comments.

Comments also can be useful when you are developing a program. If a program is not performing as expected, you can **comment out** various statements and subsequently run the program to observe the effect. When you comment out a statement, you turn it into a comment so that the compiler will ignore it. This approach helps you pinpoint the location of errant statements in malfunctioning programs.

There are three types of comments in C#:

- **Line comments** start with two forward slashes (//) and continue to the end of the current line. Line comments can appear on a line by themselves, or at the end of a line following executable code.
- **Block comments** start with a forward slash and an asterisk (/*) and end with an asterisk and a forward slash (*/). Block comments can appear on a line by themselves, on a line before executable code, or after executable code. When a comment is long, block comments can extend across as many lines as needed.
- C# also supports a special type of comment used to create documentation from within a program. These comments, called **XML-documentation format comments**, use a special set of tags within angle brackets (<>). (XML stands for Extensible Markup Language.) You will learn more about this type of comment as you continue your study of C#.

> **NOTE** The forward slash (/) and the backslash (\) characters often are confused, but they are distinct characters. You cannot use them interchangeably.

Figure 1-4 shows how comments can be used in code. The program covers 12 lines of type, yet only seven are part of the executable C# program, and the only line that actually *does* anything is the one that displays "Message".

```
public class ClassWithOneExecutingLine
/* This class has only one line that executes */
{
    public static void Main()
    {
        // The next line writes the message
        System.Console.Out.WriteLine("Message");   // Comment
    }
    /* This program serves
       to demonstrate that a program
       can "look" a lot longer than it really is */
}
```

Figure 1-4 Using comments within a program

CHAPTER ONE

ELIMINATING THE REFERENCE TO Out BY USING THE System NAMESPACE

A program can contain as many statements as you want. For example, the program in Figure 1-5 produces the three lines of output shown in Figure 1-6. A semicolon separates each program statement.

```
public class ThreeLines
{
    public static void Main()
    {
        System.Console.Out.WriteLine("Line one");
        System.Console.Out.WriteLine("Line two");
        System.Console.Out.WriteLine("Line three");
    }
}
```

Figure 1-5 A program that produces three lines of output

Figure 1-6 Output of ThreeLines program

The program in Figure 1-5 shows a lot of repeated code—the phrase System.Console.Out.WriteLine appears three times. When you use the name of the object Out, you are indicating the console screen. However, Out is the default output object. That is, if you write System.Console.WriteLine("Hi"); without specifying a Console object, the message "Hi" goes to the default Console object, which is Out. Most C# programmers usually use the WriteLine() method without specifying the Out object.

When you need to repeatedly use a class from the same namespace, you can shorten the statements you type by using a clause that indicates a namespace where the class can be found. You use a namespace with a **using clause**, or **using directive**, as shown in the shaded statement in the program in Figure 1-7. If you type using System; prior to the class definition, the compiler knows to use the System namespace when it encounters the Console class. The output of the program in Figure 1-7 is identical to that in Figure 1-5, in which System and Out were both repeated with each WriteLine() statement.

15

A FIRST PROGRAM USING C#

```
using System;
public class ThreeLines
{
    public static void Main()
    {
        Console.WriteLine("Line one");
        Console.WriteLine("Line two");
        Console.WriteLine("Line three");
    }
}
```

Figure 1-7 A program that produces three lines of output with a `using System` clause and no explicit reference to the `Out` object

NOT RECOMMENDED: USING AN ALIAS

At this point, the clever programmer will say, "I'll shorten my typing tasks even further by typing `using System.Console;` at the top of my programs, and producing output with statements like `WriteLine("Hi");`." However, `using` cannot be used with a class name like `System.Console`—only with a namespace name like `System`. Another option is to assign an alias to a class with a `using` clause. An **alias** is an alternative name for a class. You might assign one as a convenience when a fully qualified class name is very long. For example, Figure 1-8 shows a program that uses an alias for `System.Console` (see shaded statement). The lines of code within the program are shorter, but more difficult for another programmer to read. In general, and especially while you are learning C#, you should avoid using aliases if your intention is simply to reduce typing.

```
using SC = System.Console;
public class ThreeLines
{
    public static void Main()
    {
        SC.WriteLine("Line one");
        SC.WriteLine("Line two");
        SC.WriteLine("Line three");
    }
}
```

Figure 1-8 Using an alias for `System.Console`—a technique that is not recommended

WRITING AND COMPILING A C# PROGRAM

After you write and save a program, two more steps must be performed before you can view the program output:

CHAPTER ONE

1. You must compile the program you wrote (called the **source code**) into **intermediate language (IL)**.
2. The C# **just in time (JIT)** compiler must translate the intermediate code into executable statements.

> **NOTE** When you compile a C# program, you translate your source code into intermediate language. The JIT compiler converts IL instructions into native code at the last moment, and appropriately for each different type of computer on which the code might eventually be executed. In other words, the same set of IL can be JIT-compiled and executed on any supported architecture.

> **NOTE** Some developers say that languages like C# are "semi-compiled." That is, instead of being translated immediately from source code to their final executable versions, programs are compiled into an intermediate version that is later translated into the correct executable statements for the machine on which the program is running.

You can perform these steps from the command line or within the Integrated Development Environment (IDE) that comes with Visual Studio. Both methods produce the same results; the one you use is a matter of preference. You might prefer the simplicity of the command line because you do not work with multiple menus and views. Additionally, if you want to pass command-line arguments to a program, you must compile from the command line. On the other hand, many programmers prefer using the IDE because it provides features such as color-coded keywords and automatic statement completion.

COMPILING CODE FROM THE COMMAND PROMPT

To compile your source code from the command line, you first locate the command prompt. For example, in Windows XP, you click Start, All Programs, Accessories, and Command Prompt. As shown in Figure 1-9, you type `csc` at the command prompt, followed by the name of the file that contains the source code. The command `csc` stands for "C Sharp compiler." For example, to compile a file named ThreeLines.cs, you would type `csc ThreeLines.cs` and then press the Enter key. One of three outcomes will occur:

» You receive an operating system error message such as "Bad command or file name" or "csc is not recognized as an internal or external command, operable program or batch file".

» You receive one or more program language error messages.

» You receive no error messages (only a copyright statement from Microsoft), indicating that the program has compiled successfully.

Figure 1-9 Compiling a program from the root directory at the command line

17

A FIRST PROGRAM USING C#

If you receive an operating system message such as "csc is not recognized...," or "Source file could not be found," it may mean that:

- You misspelled the command `csc`.
- You misspelled the filename.
- You forgot to include the extension .cs with the filename.
- You didn't use the correct case. If your filename is ThreeLines.cs, then `csc threelines.cs` will not compile.
- You are not within the correct subdirectory or folder on your command line. For example, Figure 1-9 shows the `csc` command typed in the root directory of the C drive. If the ThreeLines.cs file is stored in a folder on the C drive, then the command shown will not work.
- The C# compiler was not installed properly.
- You need to set a path command.

  To set a path command, you must locate the C# compiler on your hard disk. To locate the C# compiler whose name is csc.exe, use Explorer or click Start and then click Search, and choose All Files or Folders to look for the file named csc.exe. If your search fails to find csc.exe, you need to obtain and install a copy of the C# compiler.

  If you do find the csc.exe file, type `path =` at the command line, followed by the complete path name that describes where csc.exe is stored; then try to execute the `ThreeLines` program again. For example, you might type the following:

  `path = c:\Windows\Microsoft.NET\Framework\v2.0.50727`

  Press Enter. Next, type `csc ThreeLines.cs` and press Enter again.

If you receive a programming language error message, it means that the source code contains one or more syntax errors. A syntax error occurs when you introduce typing errors into your program. For example, if the first line of your program begins with "Public" (with an uppercase *P*), you will get an error message such as "`A namespace does not directly contain members such as fields or methods`" after compiling the program, because the compiler won't recognize `ThreeLines` as a class with a `Main()` method. If this problem occurs, you must reopen the text file that contains the source code, make the necessary corrections, save the file, and compile it again.

> **» NOTE** The C# compiler issues warnings as well as errors. A warning is less serious than an error; it means that the compiler has determined you have done something unusual, but not illegal. If you have purposely introduced a warning situation to test a program, then you can ignore the warning. Usually, however, you should treat a warning message just as you would an error message and attempt to remedy the situation.

If you receive no error messages after compiling the code, then the program compiled successfully and a file with the same name as the source code—but with an .exe extension—is created and saved in the same folder as the program text file. For example, if ThreeLines.cs compiles successfully, then a file named ThreeLines.exe is created.

CHAPTER ONE

To run the program from the command line, you simply type the program name—for example, `ThreeLines`. You can also type the full filename, ThreeLines.exe, but it is not necessary to do so.

COMPILING CODE FROM WITHIN THE VISUAL STUDIO IDE

As an alternative to using the command line, you can compile and write your program within the Visual Studio IDE. This approach has several advantages:

- » Some of the code you need is already created for you.
- » The code is displayed in color, so you can more easily identify parts of your program. Reserved words appear in blue, comments in green, and identifiers in black.
- » If error messages appear when you compile your program, you can double-click an error message and the cursor will move to the line of code that contains the error.
- » Other debugging tools are available. You will become more familiar with these tools as you develop more sophisticated programs.

Figure 1-10 shows a program written in the editor of the Visual Studio IDE. You can see that the environment looks like a word processor, containing menu options such as File, Edit, and Help, and buttons with icons representing options such as Save, Copy, and Paste. You will learn about some of these options later in this chapter and continue to learn about more of them as you work with C# in the IDE.

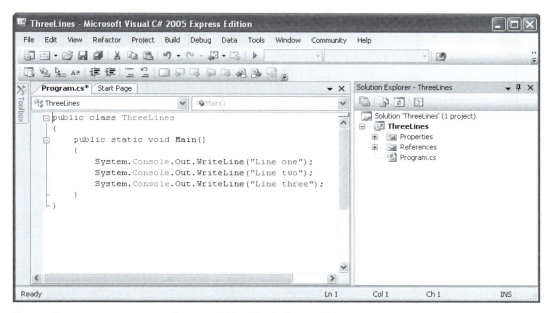

Figure 1-10 `ThreeLines` program as it appears in Visual Studio Express Edition

ALTERNATE WAYS TO WRITE A `Main()` METHOD

Figures 1-8 and 1-10 show a `Main()` method with the following header:

```
public static void Main()
```

Using the return type `void` and listing nothing between the parentheses that follow `Main` is just one way to write a `Main()` method header in a program. (However, it is the first way listed in the C# documentation, and it is the convention that this book uses.)

Figure 1-11 shows an alternate way to write the `Main()` method header in the `ThreeLines` class. The shaded phrase `string[ ] args` is a parameter to the `Main()` method. A **string** is a data type that can hold a series of characters. The square brackets indicate that you can

```
using System;
public class ThreeLines
{
    public static void Main(string[ ] args)
    {
        Console.WriteLine("Line one");
        Console.WriteLine("Line two");
        Console.WriteLine("Line three");
    }
}
```

Figure 1-11 A `Main()` method with a `string[ ] args` parameter

include a list or array of those strings. In Figure 1-11, `args` is a programmer-chosen name for the memory location where the list of `strings` is stored. Although you can use any identifier, `args` is traditional. Use this format for the `Main()` method header if you need to access command-line arguments passed in to your application. For example, if you issued the following command, then the `strings` "yes", "no", and "maybe" would be stored at the memory location named `args`:

```
cs ThreeLines yes, no, maybe
```

> **» NOTE** In Chapter 6, you will create other methods that can accept parameters.

> **» NOTE** You will learn more about the `string` data type in Chapter 2. You will learn more about how to use command-line arguments in Chapter 5 when you study arrays.

> **» NOTE** In particular, Java programmers might prefer the version of `Main()` that includes the `string[ ] args` parameter because, conventionally, they write their main methods with the same parameter.

CHAPTER ONE

Even if you do not need access to command-line arguments, you can still use the version of the `Main()` method header that references them. You should use this form for your `Main()` method headers if your instructor at school or supervisor at work indicates you should follow this convention.

Some programmers prefer to write the `ThreeLines` class `Main()` method as shown in Figure 1-12. The shaded keyword `int` replaces `void` in the method header, indicating that the method returns an integer value. If you use this form of method header, then the last statement in the `Main()` method must be a return statement that returns a number. By convention, a return value of 0 means an application ended without error. The value might be used by your operating system or another program that uses your program.

```
using System;
public class ThreeLines
{
    public static int Main(string[] args)
    {
        Console.WriteLine("Line one");
        Console.WriteLine("Line two");
        Console.WriteLine("Line three");
        return 0;
    }
}
```

Figure 1-12 A `Main()` method with an `int` return type

> **NOTE** You will learn more about the `int` data type in Chapter 2. You will learn more about how to return values from methods in Chapter 6.

> **NOTE** In particular, C++ programmers might prefer the version of `Main()` that returns an `int` because, conventionally, they write their main methods with an `int` return type.

Even if you do not need to use a return value from a `Main()` method, you can still use the version of the `Main()` method header that uses a return value. You should use this form for your `Main()` method headers if your instructor at school or supervisor at work indicates you should follow this convention.

YOU DO IT

Now that you understand the basic framework of a program written in C#, you are ready to enter your first C# program into a text editor so you can execute it. It is a tradition among programmers that the first program you write in any language produces "Hello, world!" as

A FIRST PROGRAM USING C#

its output. You will create such a program now. To create a C# program, you can use the editor that is included as part of the Microsoft Visual Studio IDE. (The C# compiler, other language compilers, and many development tools also are contained in the IDE, which is where you build, test, and debug your C# application.) Alternatively, you can use any text editor. There are advantages to using the C# editor to write your programs, but using a plain text editor is simpler when you are getting started.

ENTERING A PROGRAM INTO AN EDITOR
To write your first C# program:

1. Start any text editor, such as Notepad, WordPad, or any word-processing program. Open a new document, if necessary.
2. Type the class header **public class Hello**. In this example, the class name is `Hello`.
3. Press the **Enter** key and type the class-opening curly brace **{**.
4. Press **Enter** again, then type three spaces to indent.
5. Write the `Main()` method header:

   public static void Main()

   Press **Enter** and then press **Tab** or enter a few spaces to indent.

6. Type **{**, press **Enter**, and then press three spaces to indent. Type the one executing statement in this program:

   System.Console.Out.WriteLine("Hello, world!");

7. Press **Enter**, press three spaces, type a closing curly brace for the `Main()` method, press **Enter**, and type a closing curly brace for the class. Your code should look like Figure 1-13.

```
public class Hello
{
   public static void Main()
   {
      System.Console.Out.WriteLine("Hello, world!");
   }
}
```

Figure 1-13 The `Hello` class

8. Save the program as **Hello.cs** in the Chapter.01 folder on your Student Disk. It is important that the file extension be .cs, which stands for *C Sharp*. If the file has a different extension, the compiler for C# will not recognize the program as a C# program.

> **»NOTE** Many text editors attach their own filename extension (such as .txt or .doc) to a saved file. Double-check your saved file to ensure that it does not have a double extension (as in Hello.cs.txt). If the file has a double extension, rename it. If you type quotes surrounding a filename (as in "Hello.cs"), most editors will save the file as you specify, without adding their own extension. If you use a word-processing program as your editor, select the option to save the file as a plain text file.

CHAPTER ONE

COMPILING AND EXECUTING A PROGRAM FROM THE COMMAND LINE

To compile and execute your `Hello` program from the command line:

1. Go to the command prompt on your system. For example, in Windows XP, click **Start**, then point to **All Programs**, point to **Accessories**, and click **Command Prompt**. Change the current directory to the name of the folder that holds your program.

> **»NOTE** If your command prompt indicates a path other than the one you want, you can type `cd\` and then press Enter to return to the root directory. You can then type a command similar to `cd Chapter.01` or `cd C#\Chapter.01` to change the path to the one where your program resides. The command `cd` is short for *change directory*.

2. Type the command that compiles your program:

   `csc Hello.cs`

   If you receive no error messages and the prompt returns, it means that the compile operation was successful, that a file named Hello.exe has been created, and that you can execute the program. If you do receive error messages, check every character of the program you typed to make sure it matches Figure 1-13. Remember, C# is case sensitive, so all casing must match exactly. When you have corrected the errors, repeat this step to compile the program again.

3. You can verify that a file named Hello.exe was created in several ways:

   » At the command prompt, type **dir** to view a directory of the files stored in your Chapter.01 folder. Both Hello.cs and Hello.exe should appear in the list. See Figure 1-14.

Figure 1-14 Directory of Chapter.01 folder after compiling Hello.cs

   » Use Windows Explorer to view the contents of the Chapter.01 folder, verifying that two Hello files are listed.
   » Double-click the **My Computer** icon, find and double-click the **Chapter.01** folder, and verify that two Hello files are listed.

A FIRST PROGRAM USING C#

4. At the command prompt, type **Hello**, which is the name of the program (the name of the executable file), and then press **Enter**. Alternatively, you can type the full filename **Hello.exe**, but typing the .exe extension isn't necessary. The output should look like Figure 1-15.

Figure 1-15 Output of the `Hello` application

> **NOTE** You can use the `/out` compiler option between the `csc` command and the name of the .cs file to indicate the name of the output file. For example, if you type `csc /out:Hello.exe Hello.cs`, you create an output file named Hello.exe. By default, the name of the output file is the same as the name of the .cs file. Usually, this is your intention, so most often you omit the `/out` option.

COMPILING AND EXECUTING A PROGRAM USING THE VISUAL STUDIO IDE

Next, you will use the C# compiler environment to compile and execute the same `Hello` program you ran from the command line.

To compile and execute the `Hello` program in the Visual Studio IDE:

> **NOTE** Appendix C describes useful features of the Visual Studio text editor.

1. Within the text editor you used to write the `Hello` program, select the entire program text. In Notepad, for example, you can highlight all the lines of text with your mouse (or press **Ctrl+A**). Next, copy the text to the Clipboard for temporary storage by clicking **Edit** on the menu bar and then clicking **Copy** (or by pressing **Ctrl+C**). You will paste the text later.

> **NOTE** If you are using a version of Visual Studio other than Visual Studio Express, your steps might vary slightly from these.

2. Open Visual Studio. If there is a shortcut icon on your desktop, you can double-click it. Alternatively, in Windows XP, you can click the **Start** button, point to **All Programs**, point to Visual C# 2005, and click **Visual C# 2005**.

3. On the Start Page, click **File** on the menu bar, then click **New Project**, as shown in Figure 1-16.

4. In the New Project window, click **Console Application**. Enter **Hello** as the name for this project (see Figure 1-17). Click **OK**. Visual C# creates a new folder for your project named after the project title.

5. The `Hello` application editing window appears, as shown in Figure 1-18. A lot of code is already written for you in this window, including some `using` statements, a namespace named `Hello`, a class named `Program`, and a `Main()` method. You could leave the class header, `Main()` method header, and other features, and just add the specific statements you need. You would save a lot of typing and prevent typographical errors. In this case,

CHAPTER ONE

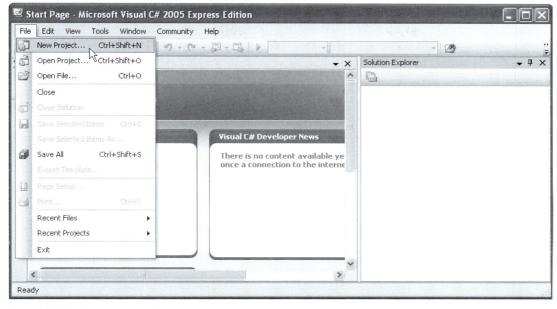

Figure 1-16 Selecting a new project

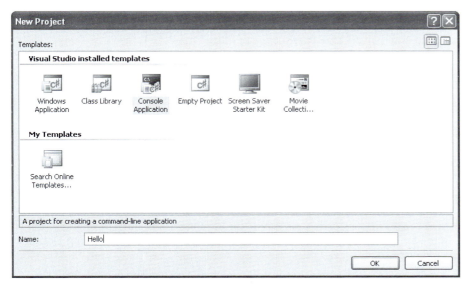

Figure 1-17 Entering the project name

25

A FIRST PROGRAM USING C#

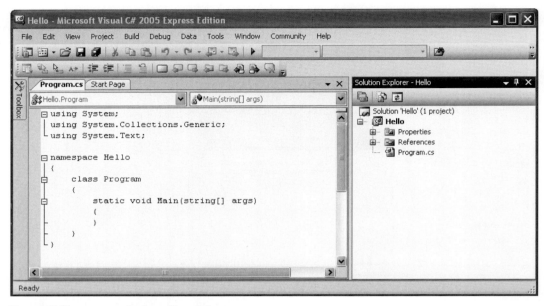

Figure 1-18 The `Hello` application editing window

however, you have already written a functioning `Hello` program, so you will replace the prewritten code with your `Hello` code. Select all the code in the editor window by highlighting it with your mouse (or by pressing **Ctrl+A**). Then press **Delete**. Paste the previously copied `Hello` program into the editor by pressing **Ctrl+V** (or by clicking **Edit** on the menu bar and then clicking **Paste**).

> **»NOTE**
> When you select the code in the editor window, be sure to delete it and not cut it. If you cut it, then the same text will be reinserted when you select Paste.

6. Save the file by clicking **File** on the menu bar and then clicking **Save Hello**, or by clicking the **Save** button on the toolbar. Your screen looks like Figure 1-19.

7. To compile the program, click **Build** on the menu bar and then click **Build Solution**. (Alternatively, you can press **F6**.) You should receive no error messages, and the words "Build succeeded" should appear near the lower-left edge of the window.

8. Click **Debug** on the menu bar and then click **Start Without Debugging**. The output appears in Figure 1-20; you see "Hello, world!" followed by the message "Press any key to continue". Press any key to dismiss the output screen.

9. Close Visual Studio by clicking **File** on the menu bar and then clicking **Exit**, or by clicking the **Close** box in the upper-right corner of the Visual Studio window. When you receive a message "Do you want to save or discard changes to the current solution?", click **Save**. In the Save Project window, you can select a folder location to save the project, as shown in Figure 1-21.

10. When you create a C# program using an editor such as Notepad and compile with the `csc` command, only two files are created—Hello.cs and Hello.exe. When you create a C#

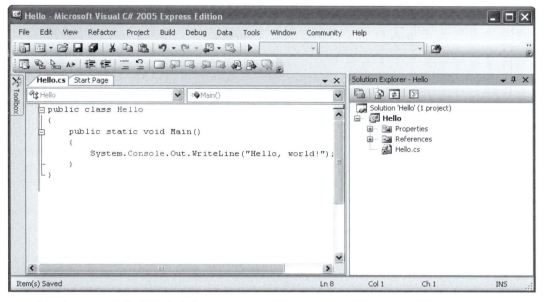

Figure 1-19 The `Hello` application in the IDE

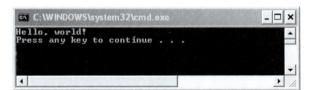

Figure 1-20 Output of the `Hello` application in Visual Studio

Figure 1-21 The Save Project window

program using the Visual Studio editor, many additional files are created. You can view their filenames in several ways:

» At the command prompt, type **dir** to view a directory of the files stored in your Chapter.01 folder. Within the Chapter.01 folder, a new folder named Hello has been created. Type the command **cd Hello** to change the current path to include this new folder,

A FIRST PROGRAM USING C#

then type **dir** again. You see another folder named Hello. Type **cd Hello** again, and **dir** again. Figure 1-22 shows the output using this method; it shows several folders and files.

```
C:\C#\Chapter.01\Hello\Hello>dir
 Volume in drive C has no label.
 Volume Serial Number is B057-44EB

 Directory of C:\C#\Chapter.01\Hello\Hello

09/12/2008  08:36 AM    <DIR>          .
09/12/2008  08:36 AM    <DIR>          ..
09/12/2008  08:36 AM    <DIR>          bin
09/12/2008  08:36 AM             1,991 Hello.csproj
09/12/2008  08:37 AM    <DIR>          obj
09/12/2008  08:36 AM    <DIR>          Properties
               1 File(s)          1,991 bytes
               5 Dir(s)  26,798,833,664 bytes free

C:\C#\Chapter.01\Hello\Hello>_
```

Figure 1-22 Directory listing for Hello folder

» Double-click the **My Computer** icon, find and double-click the correct drive and the **Chapter.01** folder, double-click the **Hello** folder, and view the contents. Double-click the second **Hello** folder and view the contents there too. Figure 1-23 shows the Hello folder contents.

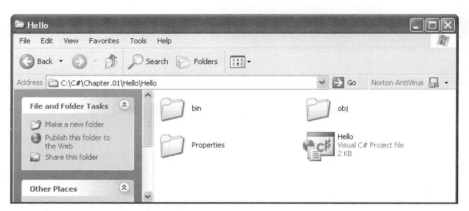

Figure 1-23 Contents of the C#/Chapter.01/Hello/Hello folder using My Computer

» Use Windows Explorer to view the contents of the Hello folders within the Chapter.01 folder.

The innermost Hello folder contains a bin folder, an obj folder, a Properties folder, and additional files. If you explore further, you will find that the bin folder contains Debug and Release folders, which include additional files. Using the Visual Studio editor to compile your programs creates a lot of overhead. These additional files become important as you create more sophisticated C# projects. For now, while you learn C# syntax, using the command line to compile programs is simpler.

>>**NOTE** If you followed the earlier instructions on compiling a program from the command line, and you used the same folder when using the IDE, you will see the additional Hello.cs and Hello.exe files in your folder. These files will have an earlier time stamp than the files you just created. If you were to execute a new program from within Visual Studio without saving and executing it from the command line first, you would not see these two additional files.

DECIDING WHICH METHOD TO USE

When you write, compile, and execute a C# program, you can use either the command line or the Visual Studio IDE. You would never need to use both. You might prefer using an editor with which you are already familiar (such as Notepad) and compiling from the command line because only two files are generated, saving disk space.

On the other hand, the IDE provides many useful features, such as automatic statement completion. For example, if you type System and a dot, then a list of choices is displayed, and you can click Console instead of typing it. Similarly, after the dot that follows Console, a list of choices is displayed from which you can select Out. Additionally, in the IDE, words are displayed using different colors based on their category; for example, one color is used for C# reserved words and a different color for literal strings. It is also easier to correct many errors using the IDE. When compiler errors or warnings are issued, you can double-click the message, and the cursor jumps to the location in the code where the error was detected. Another advantage to learning the IDE is that if you use another programming language in Visual Studio (C++ or Visual Basic), the environment will already be familiar to you.

The C# language works the same way, no matter what method you use to compile your programs. Everything you learn in the next chapters about input, output, decision making, loops, and arrays will work the same way, regardless of the compilation technique you use. You can use just one technique, or compile some programs in each environment as the mood strikes you. You can also mix and match techniques if you prefer. For example, you can use an editor you like to compose your programs, then paste them into the IDE to execute them.

Although any program can be written using either compilation technique, when you write graphical user interface (GUI) applications that use existing objects such as message boxes and buttons, you will find that the extensive amount of code automatically generated by the IDE is very helpful. For the first nine chapters of this book, you are encouraged to use whichever compilation technique you prefer. In Chapter 10, you will be encouraged to use the IDE to take advantage of its many time-saving features.

ADDING COMMENTS TO A PROGRAM
To add comments to your program:
1. If you prefer compiling programs from the command line, then open the **Hello.cs** file in your text editor. If you prefer compiling programs from within Visual Studio, then open

A FIRST PROGRAM USING C#

Visual Studio, click **File**, click **Open Project**, browse for the correct folder, double-click the **Hello** folder, and then double-click the **Hello** file. In the Solution Explorer at the side of the screen, double-click **Hello**, as shown in Figure 1-24.

»NOTE
If you do not see the Solution Explorer window in Visual Studio, click the Solution Explorer icon on the toolbar (shown below). Alternately, from the main menu, choose **View** and then **Solution Explorer**. The Solution Explorer displays the various files that make up a project.

Figure 1-24 Solution Explorer window

2. Position your cursor at the top of the file, press **Enter** to insert a new line, press the **Up** arrow key to go to that line, and then type the following comments at the top of the file. Press **Enter** after typing each line. Insert your name and today's date where indicated.

    ```
    // Filename Hello.cs
    // Written by <your name>
    // Written on <today's date>
    ```

3. Scroll to the line that reads `public static void Main()` and press **Enter** to start a new line. Then press the **Up** arrow; in the new blank line, aligned with the start of the `Main()` method header, type the following block comment in the program:

    ```
    /*  This program demonstrates the use of
    the WriteLine() method to print the
    message Hello, world!   */
    ```

4. Save the file, replacing the old Hello.cs file with this new, commented version.

5. If you prefer to compile programs from the command line, type **csc Hello.cs** at the command line. When the program compiles successfully, execute it with the command **Hello**. If you prefer compiling and executing programs from within Visual Studio, click **Debug** and **Start Without Debugging**. Adding program comments makes no difference in the execution of the program.

CHAPTER ONE

CHAPTER SUMMARY

» A computer program is a set of instructions that you write to tell a computer what to do. Programmers write their programs, then use a compiler to translate their high-level language statements into intermediate language and machine code. A program works correctly when both its syntax and logic are correct.

» Procedural programming involves creating computer memory locations, called variables, and sets of operations, called procedures. In object-oriented programming, you envision program components as objects that are similar to concrete objects in the real world; then you manipulate the objects to achieve a desired result. Objects exist as members of classes and are made up of states and methods.

» The C# programming language was developed as an object-oriented and component-oriented language. It contains many features similar to those in Visual Basic, Java, and C++.

» To write a C# program that produces a line of console output, you must pass a literal string as an argument to the `System.Console.Out.WriteLine()` method. `System` is a namespace, `Console` is a class, and `Out` is an object. The `WriteLine()` method call appears within the `Main()` method of a class you create.

» You can define a C# class or variable by using any name or identifier that begins with an underscore or a letter, contains only letters or digits, and is not a C# reserved keyword.

» Program comments are nonexecuting statements that you add to document a program or to disable statements when you test a program. There are three types of comments in C#: line comments that start with two forward slashes (//) and continue to the end of the current line, block comments that start with a forward slash and an asterisk (/*) and end with an asterisk and a forward slash (*/), and XML-documentation comments.

» When you need to repeatedly use a class from the same namespace, you can shorten the statements you type by using a clause that indicates a namespace where the class can be found.

» To create a C# program, you can use the Microsoft Visual Studio environment. You can also use any text editor, such as Notepad, WordPad, or any word-processing program. After you write and save a program, you must compile the source code into intermediate and machine language.

» You have multiple options for writing the `Main()` method header; the format you use depends on your need for command-line arguments and the conventions you prefer in your working environment.

KEY TERMS

A computer **program** is a set of instructions that you write to tell a computer what to do.

Machine language is the most basic circuitry-level language.

A **high-level programming language** allows you to use a vocabulary of reasonable terms such as "read," "write," or "add" instead of the sequence of on/off switches that perform these tasks.

A FIRST PROGRAM USING C#

A language's **syntax** is its set of rules.

A **compiler** is a computer program that translates high-level language statements into machine code.

The **logic** behind any program involves executing the various statements and procedures in the correct order to produce the desired results.

Semantic errors are the type of logical errors that occur when you use a correct word in the wrong context.

Debugging a program is the process of removing all syntax and logical errors from the program.

A **procedural program** is created by writing a series of steps or operations to manipulate values.

Variables are named computer memory locations that hold values that might vary.

An **identifier** is the name of a program component such as a variable, class, or method.

Camel casing is a style of creating identifiers in which the first letter is not capitalized, but each new word is.

Pascal casing is a style of creating identifiers in which the first letter of all new words in a variable name, even the first one, is capitalized.

Procedures or **methods** are compartmentalized program units that accomplish tasks.

A program **calls** or **invokes** procedures.

Object-oriented programming is a programming technique that features objects, classes, encapsulation, interfaces, polymorphism, and inheritance.

Objects are program elements that are instances of a class.

The **command line** is the line on which you type a command in a system that uses a text interface.

The **command prompt** is a request for input that appears at the beginning of the command line.

The **attributes** of an object represent its characteristics.

The **states** of an object are the values of its attributes.

The **properties** of an object are its values.

The **state of an object** is the collective value of all its attributes at any point in time.

A **class** is a category of objects or a type of object.

Each object is an **instance** of a class.

Encapsulation is the technique of packaging an object's attributes and methods into a cohesive unit that can be used as an undivided entity.

A **black box** is a device you use without regard for the internal mechanisms.

An **interface** is the interaction between a method and an object.

Polymorphism is the ability to create methods that act appropriately depending on the context.

CHAPTER ONE

Inheritance is the ability to extend a class so as to create a more specific class that contains all the attributes and methods of a more general class; the extended class usually contains new attributes or methods as well.

The **C# programming language** was developed as an object-oriented and component-oriented language. It exists as part of Visual Studio 2005, a package used for developing applications for the Windows family of operating systems.

Primitive data is simple data, such as a number.

A **literal string** of characters is a series of characters that is used exactly as entered.

An **argument** or a **parameter** to a method represents information that a method needs to perform its task. An argument is the expression used when you call a method, while a parameter is an object or reference that is declared in a method definition; that is, where the method instructions are written.

The `WriteLine()` **method** displays a line of output on the screen, positions the cursor on the next line, and waits for additional output.

The `Write()` **method** displays a line of output on the screen, but the cursor does not advance to a new line; it remains on the same line as the output.

A **namespace** is a scheme that provides a way to group similar classes.

The `System` **namespace**, which is built into your C# compiler, holds commonly used classes.

A **method header** includes the method name and information about what will pass into and be returned from a method.

The **method body** of every method is contained within a pair of curly braces and includes all the instructions executed by the method.

Whitespace is any combination of spaces, tabs, and carriage returns (blank lines). You use whitespace to organize your program code and make it easier to read.

Keywords are predefined and reserved identifiers that have special meaning to the compiler.

An **access modifier** defines the circumstances under which a method or class can be accessed; `public` access is the most liberal type of access.

In a method header, `public` is an access modifier that indicates other classes may use the method.

In a method header, `private` is an access modifier that indicates other classes may not use the method.

The reserved keyword `static` indicates that a method will be executed through a class and not by an object.

In a method header, the keyword `void` indicates that the method does not return any value when called.

A **verbatim identifier** is an identifier with an @ prefix.

Program comments are nonexecuting statements that you add to document a program.

When you **comment out** a statement, you turn it into a comment so that the compiler will not execute its command.

Line comments start with two forward slashes (//) and continue to the end of the current line. Line comments can appear on a line by themselves, or at the end of a line following executable code.

Block comments start with a forward slash and an asterisk (/*) and end with an asterisk and a forward slash (*/). Block comments can appear on a line by themselves, on a line before executable code, or after executable code. They can also extend across as many lines as needed.

XML-documentation format comments use a special set of tags within angle brackets to create documentation from within a program.

You use a namespace with a `using clause`, or `using directive`.

An **alias** is an alternative name for a class.

Source code is the statements you write when you create a program.

Intermediate language (IL) is the language into which source code statements are compiled.

The C# **just in time (JIT)** compiler translates intermediate code into executable statements.

A `string` is a data type that can hold a series of characters.

REVIEW QUESTIONS

1. A computer program written as a series of on and off switches is written in _____ .

    a. machine language

    b. a low-level language

    c. a high-level language

    d. a compiled language

2. A program that translates high-level programs into intermediate or machine code is a(n) _____ .

    a. mangler

    b. compiler

    c. analyst

    d. logician

3. The grammar and spelling rules of a programming language constitute its _____ .

    a. logic

    b. variables

    c. syntax

    d. vortex

4. Variables are _____ .

    a. procedures

    b. named memory locations

    c. grammar rules

    d. operations

CHAPTER ONE

5. Programs in which you create and use objects that have attributes similar to their real-world counterparts are known as _____ programs.
   a. procedural
   b. logical
   c. authentic
   d. object-oriented

6. Which of the following pairs is an example of a class and an object, in that order?
   a. robin and bird
   b. chair and desk
   c. university and Harvard
   d. oak and tree

7. The technique of packaging an object's attributes into a cohesive unit that can be used as an undivided entity is _____.
   a. inheritance
   b. encapsulation
   c. polymorphism
   d. interfacing

8. Of the following languages, which is least similar to C#?
   a. Java
   b. Visual Basic
   c. C++
   d. COBOL

9. A series of characters that appears within double quotation marks is a(n) _____.
   a. parameter
   b. interface
   c. argument
   d. literal string

10. The C# method that prints a line of output on the screen and then positions the cursor on the next line is _____.
    a. `WriteLine()`
    b. `PrintLine()`
    c. `DisplayLine()`
    d. `OutLine()`

11. Which of the following is an object?
    a. `System`
    b. `Console`
    c. `Out`
    d. `WriteLine`

12. In C#, a scheme that groups similar classes is a(n) _____.
    a. superclass
    b. method
    c. namespace
    d. identifier

13. Every method in C# contains a _____.
    a. header and a body
    b. header and a footer
    c. variable and a class
    d. class and an object

A FIRST PROGRAM USING C#

14. Which of the following is a method?
    a. `namespace`
    b. `public`
    c. `Main()`
    d. `static`

15. Which of the following statements is true?
    a. An identifier must begin with an underscore.
    b. An identifier can contain digits.
    c. An identifier must be no more than 16 characters long.
    d. An identifier can contain only lowercase letters.

16. Which of the following identifiers is not legal in C#?
    a. `per cent increase`
    b. `annualReview`
    c. `HTML`
    d. `alternativetaxcredit`

17. The text of a program you write is called _____.
    a. object code
    b. source code
    c. machine language
    d. executable documentation

18. Programming errors such as using incorrect punctuation or misspelling words are collectively known as _____ errors.
    a. syntax
    b. logical
    c. executable
    d. fatal

19. A comment in the form `/* this is a comment */` is a(n) _____.
    a. XML comment
    b. block comment
    c. executable comment
    d. line comment

20. If a programmer inserts `using System;` at the top of a C# program, which of the following can the programmer use as an alternative to `System.Console.Out.WriteLine("Hello");`?
    a. `System("Hello");`
    b. `WriteLine("Hello");`
    c. `Console.WriteLine("Hello");`
    d. `Console.Out("Hello");`

CHAPTER ONE

EXERCISES

1. Indicate whether each of the following C# programming language identifiers is legal or illegal.

   a. `WeeklySales`
   b. `last character`
   c. `class`
   d. `MathClass`
   e. `myfirstinitial`
   f. `phone#`
   g. `abcdefghijklmnop`
   h. `23jordan`
   i. `my_code`
   j. `90210`
   k. `year2008Budget`
   l. `abfSorority`

2. Name at least three attributes that might be appropriate for each of the following classes:

   a. `TelevisionSet`
   b. `EmployeePaycheck`
   c. `PatientMedicalRecord`

3. Name a class to which each of these objects might belong:

   a. your red bicycle
   b. Albert Einstein
   c. last month's credit card bill

4. Write, compile, and test a program that displays your first name on the screen. Save the program as **Name.cs** in the Chapter.01 folder on your Student Disk.

5. Write, compile, and test a program that displays your full name, street address, and city and state on three separate lines on the screen. Save the program as **Address.cs** in the Chapter.01 folder on your Student Disk.

6. Write, compile, and test a program that displays your favorite quotation on the screen. Include the name of the person to whom the quote is attributed. Use as many display lines as you feel are appropriate. Save the program as **Quotation.cs** in the Chapter.01 folder on your Student Disk.

7. Write, compile, and test a program that displays a pattern similar to the following on the screen:

   ```
        X
       XXX
      XXXXX
     XXXXXXX
        X
   ```

   Save the program as **Tree.cs** in the Chapter.01 folder on your Student Disk.

8. Write a program that displays your initials on the screen. Compose each initial with six lines of smaller initials, as in the following example:

```
        J     FFFFFF
        J     F
        J     FFF
        J     F
J       J     F
JJJJJ         F
```

Save the program as **Initials.cs** in the Chapter.01 folder on your Student Disk.

9. From 1925 through 1963, Burma Shave advertising signs appeared next to highways all across the United States. There were always four or five signs in a row containing pieces of a rhyme, followed by a final sign that read "Burma Shave." For example, one set of signs that has been preserved by the Smithsonian Institution reads as follows:

```
Shaving brushes
You'll soon see 'em
On a shelf
In some museum
Burma Shave
```

Find a classic Burma Shave rhyme on the Web and write a program that displays it. Save the program as **BurmaShave.cs** in the Chapter.01 folder on your Student Disk.

DEBUGGING EXERCISES

Each of the following files in the Chapter.01 folder on your Student Disk has syntax and/or logical errors. In each case, determine the problem and fix the program. After you correct the errors, save each file using the same filename preceded with "Fixed". For example, DebugOne1.cs will become FixedDebugOne1.cs.

a. DebugOne1.cs
b. DebugOne2.cs
c. DebugOne3.cs
d. DebugOne4.cs

UP FOR DISCUSSION

1. Using an Internet search engine, find at least three definitions for *object-oriented programming*. (Try searching with and without the hyphen in *object-oriented*.) Compare the definitions and compile them into one "best" definition.

2. What is the difference between a compiler and an interpreter? What programming languages use each? Under what conditions would you prefer to use one over the other?

3. What is the image of the computer programmer in popular culture? Is the image different in books than in TV shows and movies? Would you like a programmer's image for yourself, and if so, which one?

CHAPTER TWO

2

USING DATA

In this chapter you will:

Learn about declaring variables
Display variable values
Learn about the integral data types
Learn about floating-point data types
Format floating-point values
Use standard binary arithmetic operators
Use shortcut arithmetic operators
Learn about the `bool` data type
Learn about numeric type conversion
Learn about the `char` data type
Learn about the `string` data type
Define named constants
Accept console input

USING DATA

In Chapter 1, you learned about programming in general and the C# programming language in particular. You wrote, compiled, and ran a C# program that produces output. In this chapter, you build on your basic C# programming skills by learning how to manipulate data, including variables, data types, and constants. As you will see, using variables makes writing computer programs worth the effort.

DECLARING VARIABLES

> **NOTE**
> You will learn to create named constants later in this chapter.

You can categorize data as variable or constant. A data item is **constant** when it cannot be changed after a program is compiled—in other words, when it cannot vary. For example, if you use the number 347 within a C# program, then 347 is a constant, and every time you execute the program, the value 347 will be used. You can refer to the number 347 as a **literal constant**, because its value is taken literally at each use.

On the other hand, when you want a value to be able to change, you can create a variable. A **variable** is a named location in computer memory that can hold different values at different points in time. For example, if you create a variable named `heatingBill` and include it in a C# program, `heatingBill` might contain the value 347, or it might contain 200. Different values might be used when the program is executed multiple times, or different values might even be used at different times during the same execution of the program. Because you can use a variable to hold `heatingBill` within a utility company's billing system, you can write one set of instructions to compute `heatingBill`, yet use different `heatingBill` values for thousands of utility customers during one execution of the program.

> **NOTE**
> You learned about the `System` namespace in Chapter 1.

Whether it is stored as a constant or in a variable, each data item you use in a C# program has a data type. A **data type** describes the format and size of (amount of memory occupied by) a data item. C# provides for 14 basic or **intrinsic types** of data, as shown in Table 2-1. Of these built-in data types, the ones most commonly used are `int`, `double`, `char`, `string`, and `bool`. Each C# intrinsic type is an **alias**, or other name for, a class in the `System` namespace.

You name variables using the same rules for identifiers as you use for class names. Basically, variable names must start with a letter, cannot include embedded spaces, and cannot be a reserved keyword. You must declare all variables you want to use in a program. A **variable declaration** is the statement that names a variable and reserves storage for it; it includes:

» The data type that the variable will store
» The identifier that is the variable's name
» An optional assignment operator and assigned value when you want a variable to contain an initial value
» An ending semicolon

> **NOTE** You learned the rules for creating identifiers in Chapter 1. The C# reserved keywords are listed in Table 1-1 in Chapter 1.

> **NOTE** Variable names usually begin with lowercase letters to distinguish them from class names. You should follow this convention when naming your variables. However, variable names *can* begin with either an uppercase or lowercase letter.

Type	System Type	Bytes	Description	Largest Value	Smallest Value
byte	Byte	1	Unsigned byte	255	0
sbyte	Sbyte	1	Signed byte	127	−128
short	Int16	2	Signed short	32,767	−32,768
ushort	UInt16	2	Unsigned short	65,535	0
int	Int32	4	Signed integer	2,147,483,647	−2,147,483,648
uint	UInt32	4	Unsigned integer	4,294,967,295	0
long	Int64	8	Signed long integer	Greater than 9×10^{18}	Less than -9×10^{18}
ulong	UInt64	8	Unsigned long integer	Greater than 18×10^{18}	Less than -18×10^{18}
float	Single	4	Floating-point	Approximately 3.4×10^{38}	Approximately 1.5×10^{-45}
double	Double	8	Double-precision floating-point	Approximately 1.7×10^{308}	Approximately 5.0×10^{324}
decimal	Decimal	16	Fixed precision number	Exactly 1×10^{28}	Exactly 1×10^{-28}
string	String	NA	Unicode string	NA	NA
char	Char	2	Unicode character	0xFFFF	0x0000
bool	Boolean	1	Boolean value (true or false)	NA	NA

Table 2-1 C# data types

>> **NOTE** The highest `char` value, 0xFFFF, represents the character in which every bit is turned on. The lowest value, 0x0000, represents the character in which every bit is turned off. Any value that begins with "0x" represents a hexadecimal, or base 16, value.

>> **NOTE** For any two `String`s, the one with the higher Unicode character value in an earlier position is considered higher. For example, "AAB" is higher than "AAA". The `String` type has no true minimum. However, you can think of the empty string "" as being the lowest.

>> **NOTE** Although the `Boolean` type has no true maximum or minimum, you can think of `true` as the highest and `false` as the lowest.

USING DATA

For example, the variable declaration `int myAge = 25;` declares a variable of type `int` named `myAge` and assigns it an initial value of 25. In other words, four bytes of memory are reserved with the name `myInt` and the value 25 is stored there. The declaration is a complete statement that ends in a semicolon. The equal sign (=) is the **assignment operator**; any value to the right of the assignment operator is assigned to, or taken on by, the variable to the left. An assignment made when a variable is declared is an **initialization**; an assignment made later is simply an **assignment**. Thus, `int myAge = 25;` initializes `myAge` to 25, and a subsequent statement, such as `myAge = 42;`, assigns a new value to the variable. Note that the expression `25 = myAge;` is illegal because assignment always takes place from right to left. By definition, a constant cannot be altered, so it is illegal to place one (such as 25) on the left side of an assignment operator.

> **NOTE**
> The number 32 in the name `System.Int32` represents the number of bits of storage allowed for the data type. There are 8 bits in a byte, and an `int` occupies 4 bytes.

Instead of using a name from the Type column of Table 2-1, you can use the fully qualified type name from the `System` namespace that is listed in the System Type column. For example, instead of using the type name `int`, you can use the full name `System.Int32`. It's better to use the shorter alias `int`, however, for several reasons:

» The shorter alias is easier to type and read.
» The shorter alias resembles type names used in other languages such as Java and C++.
» Other C# programmers expect the shorter type names.

The variable declaration `int myAge;` declares a variable of type `int` named `myAge`, but no value is assigned at the time of creation. You can make an assignment later in the program, but you cannot use the variable in an arithmetic statement or display the value of the variable until you assign a value to it.

You can declare multiple variables of the same type in separate statements on different lines. For example, the following statements declare two variables. The first variable is named `myAge` and its value is 25. The second variable is named `yourAge` and its value is 19.

```
int myAge = 25;
int yourAge = 19;
```

You also can declare two variables of the same type in a single statement by using the type once and separating the variable declarations with a comma, as shown in the following statement:

```
int myAge = 25, yourAge = 19;
```

Some programmers prefer to use the data type once and break the declaration across multiple lines, as in the following example:

```
int myAge = 25,
    yourAge = 19;
```

> **NOTE**
> When a statement occupies more than one line, it is easier to read if lines after the first one are indented a few spaces. This book follows that convention.

When you declare multiple variables of the same type, a comma separates the variable names and a single semicolon appears at the end of the declaration statement, no matter how many lines the declaration occupies. However, when declaring variables of different types, you must use a separate statement for each type. The following statements declare two variables of type int (myAge and yourAge) and two variables of type double (mySalary and yourSalary), without assigning initial values to any of them:

```
int myAge, yourAge;
double mySalary, yourSalary;
```

Similarly, the following statements declare two ints and two doubles, assigning values to two of the four named variables:

```
int    numCarsIOwn = 2,
       numCarsYouOwn;
double myCarsMpg,
       yourCarsMpg = 31.5;
```

DISPLAYING VARIABLE VALUES

NOTE
You first used the WriteLine() method to display strings in Chapter 1.

You can display variable values by using the variable name within a WriteLine() method call. For example, Figure 2-1 shows a C# program that displays the value of the variable someMoney. Figure 2-2 shows the output of the program.

```
using System;
public class DisplaySomeMoney
{
    public static void Main()
    {
        double someMoney = 39.45;
        Console.WriteLine(someMoney);
    }
}
```

Figure 2-1 Program that displays a variable value

Figure 2-2 Output of DisplaySomeMoney program

The output shown in Figure 2-2 is rather stark—just a number with no explanation. The program in Figure 2-3 adds some explanation to the output; the result is shown in Figure 2-4. This program uses the Write() method to display the string "The money is $" before displaying the value of someMoney. Because the program uses Write() instead of WriteLine(), the second output appears on the same line as the first output.

USING DATA

```
using System;
public class DisplaySomeMoney2
{
   public static void Main()
   {
      double scmeMoney = 39.45;
      Console.Write("The money is $");
      Console.WriteLine(someMoney);
   }
}
```

Figure 2-3 Program that displays a string and a variable value

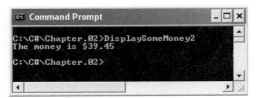

Figure 2-4 Output of `DisplaySomeMoney2` program

If you want to display several strings and several variables, you can end up with quite a few `Write()` and `WriteLine()` statements. To make producing output easier, you can combine strings and variable values into a single `Write()` or `WriteLine()` statement by using a format string. A **format string** is a string of characters that optionally contains fixed text and contains one or more format items or placeholders for variable values. A **placeholder** consists of a pair of curly braces containing a number that indicates the desired variable's position in a list that follows the string. The first position is always position 0. For example, if you remove the `Write()` and `WriteLine()` statements from the program in Figure 2-3 and replace them with the shaded statement in Figure 2-5, the program produces the output shown in Figure 2-6. The placeholder {0} holds a position into which the value of `someMoney` is inserted. Because `someMoney` is the first variable after the format string (as well as the only variable), its position is 0.

```
using System;
public class DisplaySomeMoney3
{
   public static void Main()
   {
      double someMoney = 39.45;
      Console.WriteLine("The money is ${0} exactly",
         someMoney);
   }
}
```

Figure 2-5 Using a format string

CHAPTER TWO

Figure 2-6 Output produced using format string

To display two variables within a single call to `Write()` or `WriteLine()`, you can use a statement like the following:

```
Console.WriteLine("The money is {0} and my age is {1}",
     someMoney, myAge);
```

The number within the curly braces in the format string must be less than the number of values you list after the format string. In other words, if you list six values to be displayed, valid format position numbers are 0 through 5. You do not have to use the positions in order. For example, you can choose to display the value in position 2, then 1, then 0. You also can display a specific value multiple times. For example, if `someMoney` has been assigned the value 439.75, the following code produces the output shown in Figure 2-7:

```
Console.WriteLine("I have ${0} . ${0}!! ${0}!!",
     someMoney);
```

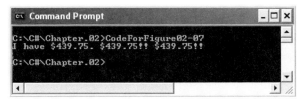

Figure 2-7 Displaying the same value multiple times

> **» NOTE**
> When C# program statements become lengthy, you might want to split them into multiple lines in your editor. However, you cannot split a statement in the middle of a string.

When you use a series of `WriteLine()` statements to display a list of variable values, the values are not right-aligned as you normally expect numbers to be. For example, the following code produces the output shown in Figure 2-8:

```
int num1 = 4, num2 = 56, num3 = 789;
Console.WriteLine("{0}", num1);
Console.WriteLine("{0}", num2);
Console.WriteLine("{0}", num3);
```

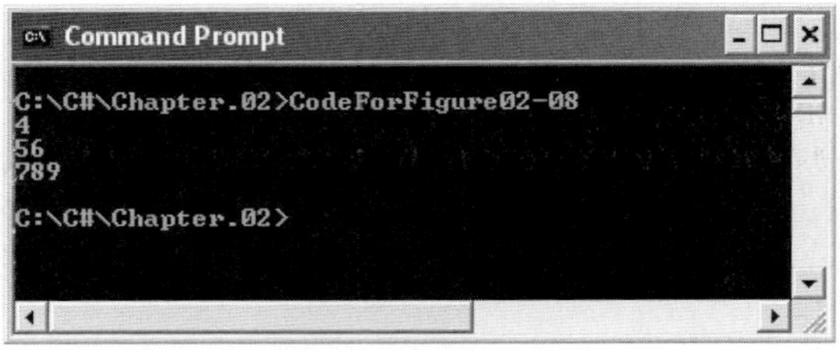

USING DATA

```
C:\C#\Chapter.02>CodeForFigure02-08
4
56
789

C:\C#\Chapter.02>
```

Figure 2-8 Displaying values with different numbers of digits without using field sizes

If you use a second number within the curly braces in a number format, you can specify alignment and field size. For example, the following code produces the output shown in Figure 2-9. The output created by each `WriteLine()` statement is right-aligned in a field that is five characters wide.

```
int num1 = 4, num2 = 56, num3 = 789;
Console.WriteLine("{ 0, 5} ", num1);
Console.WriteLine("{ 0, 5} ", num2);
Console.WriteLine("{ 0, 5} ", num3);
```

> **NOTE** By default, numbers are right-aligned in their fields. If you use a negative value for the field size in a `Write()` or `WriteLine()` statement, the value displayed will be left-aligned in the field.

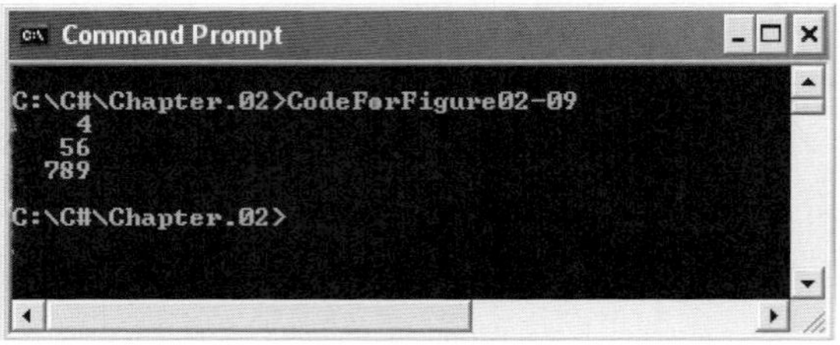

```
C:\C#\Chapter.02>CodeForFigure02-09
    4
   56
  789

C:\C#\Chapter.02>
```

Figure 2-9 Displaying values with different numbers of digits using field sizes

When you include a format string in a `Console.WriteLine()` statement, you cannot extend the string across multiple lines by pressing Enter. Instead, you can **concatenate** (join together in a chain) multiple strings into a single entity using a plus sign (+). For example, the following two statements produce identical results. In the second, the format string is broken into two parts and concatenated.

```
Console.WriteLine("I have ${ 0} . ${ 0} is a lot.",
    someMoney);
Console.WriteLine("I have ${ 0} . " +
    "${ 0} is a lot. ", someMoney);
```

> **NOTE** In this example, the + could go at the end of the first code line or the beginning of the second one. If the + is placed at the end of the first line, someone reading your code is more likely to notice that the statement is not yet complete. Because of the limitations of this book's page width, you will see examples of concatenation frequently in program code.

CHAPTER TWO

USING THE INTEGRAL DATA TYPES

In C#, nine data types are considered **integral data types**—that is, types that store whole numbers. The nine types are **byte**, **sbyte**, **short**, **ushort**, **int**, **uint**, **long**, **ulong**, and **char**. The first eight always represent whole numbers, and the ninth type, char, is used for characters like 'A' or 'a'. Actually, you can think of all nine types as numbers because every Unicode character, including the letters of the alphabet and punctuation marks, can be represented as a number. For example, the character 'A' is stored within your computer as a 65. Because you more commonly think of the char type as holding alphabetic characters instead of their numeric equivalents, the char type will be discussed in its own section later in this chapter.

> **NOTE**
> You first learned about Unicode in Chapter 1; you examine it further later in this chapter.

The most basic of the other eight integral types is int. You use variables of type int to store (or hold) **integers**, or whole numbers. An int uses four bytes of memory and can hold any whole number value ranging from 2,147,483,647 down to −2,147,483,648. If you want to save memory and know you need only a small value, you can use one of the shorter integer types—byte, sbyte (which stands for signed byte), short (short int), or ushort (unsigned short int). For example, a payroll program might contain a variable named numberOfDependents that is declared as type byte, because numberOfDependents will never need to hold a negative value or a value exceeding 255; for that reason, you can allocate just one byte of storage to hold the value.

> **NOTE** When you declare variables, you always make a judgment about which type to use. If you use a type that is too large, you waste storage. If you use a type that is too small, your program won't compile. Many programmers simply use int for most whole numbers.

When you assign a value to any numeric variable, you do not type any commas; you type only digits. You can also type a plus or minus sign to indicate a positive or negative integer.

USING FLOATING-POINT DATA TYPES

A **floating-point** number is one that contains decimal positions. C# supports three floating-point data types: float, double, and decimal. A **float** data type can hold as many as seven significant digits of accuracy. A **double** data type can hold 15 or 16 significant digits of accuracy. A value's number of **significant digits** specifies the mathematical accuracy of the value. For example, a double given the value 123456789.987654321 will appear as 123456789.987654 because it is accurate to only the seventh digit to the right of the decimal point. Compared to floats and doubles, the **decimal** type has a greater precision and a smaller range, which makes it suitable for financial and monetary calculations. For example, a decimal given the value 123456789.987654321 will appear as 123456789.987654321 (notice that it is accurate to the rightmost digit). A decimal cannot hold as large a value as a double can, but the decimal will be more accurate to more decimal places.

Just as an integer constant such as 178 is an int by default, a floating-point number constant such as 18.23 is a double by default. To explicitly store a constant as a float, you may place an *F* after the number, as in the following:

```
float pocketChange = 4.87F;
```

USING DATA

You can use either a lowercase or uppercase *F*. You can also place a *D* (or *d*) after a floating-point value to indicate that it is a `double`; even without the *D*, however, it will be stored as a `double` by default. To explicitly store a value as a `decimal`, use an *M* (or *m*) after the number. (*M* stands for monetary; *D* can't be used for `decimal`s because it indicates `double`.)

If you store a value that is too large in a floating-point variable, you will see output expressed in scientific notation. Values expressed in **scientific notation** include an *E* (for exponent). For example, if you declare `float f = 1234567890f;`, the value will appear as 1.234568E9, meaning that it is approximately 1.234568 times 10 to the ninth power, or 1.234568 with the decimal point moved nine positions to the right.

FORMATTING FLOATING-POINT VALUES

By default, C# always displays floating-point numbers in the most concise way it can while maintaining the correct value. For example, if you declare a variable and display it as in the following statements, the output will appear as "The amount is 14".

```
double myMoney = 14.00;
Console.WriteLine("The amount is {0}", myMoney);
```

The two zeros to the right of the decimal point in the value will not appear because they add no mathematical information. To see the decimal places, you can convert the floating-point value to a string using a standard numeric format string.

Standard numeric format strings are strings of characters expressed within double quotation marks that indicate a format for output. They take the form *X0*, where *X* is the format specifier and *0* is the precision specifier. The **format specifier** can be one of nine built-in format characters that define the most commonly used numeric format types. The **precision specifier** controls the number of significant digits or zeros to the right of the decimal point. Table 2-2 lists the nine format specifiers.

You can use a format specifier with the `ToString()` method to convert a number into a string that has the desired format. For example, you can use the *F* format specifier to insert a decimal point to the right of a nondecimal number, followed by the number of zeros indicated by the precision specifier. (If no precision specifier is supplied, two zeros are inserted.) For example, the first `WriteLine()` statement in the following code produces 123.00, and the second produces 123.000:

```
double someMoney = 123;
string moneyString;
moneyString = someMoney.ToString("F");
Console.WriteLine(moneyString);
moneyString = someMoney.ToString("F3");
Console.WriteLine(moneyString);
```

> **»NOTE**
> You will learn more about strings later in this chapter.

> **»NOTE**
> You will learn more about creating and using methods in Chapter 6.

You use *C* as the format specifier when you want to represent a number as a currency value. Currency values appear with a dollar sign and appropriate commas as well as the desired number of decimal places, and negative values appear within parentheses. The integer you use following the *C* indicates the number of decimal places. If you do not provide a value for

CHAPTER TWO

Format Character	Description	Default Format (if no precision is given)
C or c	Currency	$XX,XXX.XX ($XX,XXX.XX)
D or d	Decimal	[-]XXXXXXX
E or e	Scientific (exponential)	[-]X.XXXXXXE+xxx [-]X.XXXXXXe+xxx [-]X.XXXXXXE-xxx [-]X.XXXXXXe-xxx
F or f	Fixed-point	[-]XXXXXXX.XX
G or g	General	Variable; either general or scientific
N or n	Number	[-]XX,XXX.XX
P or p	Percent	Represents a passed numeric value as a percentage
R or r	Round trip	Ensures that numbers converted to strings will have the same values when they are converted back into numbers
X or x	Hexadecimal	Minimum hexadecimal (base 16) representation

Table 2-2 Format specifiers

the number of decimal places, then two digits are shown after the decimal separator by default. For example, both of the following `WriteLine()` statements produce $456,789.00:

```
double moneyValue = 456789;
string conversion;
conversion = moneyValue.ToString("C");
Console.WriteLine(conversion);
conversion = moneyValue.ToString("C2");
Console.WriteLine(conversion);
```

>> **NOTE** Currency appears with a dollar sign and commas in the English culture. A **culture** is a set of rules that determines how culturally dependent values such as money and dates are formatted. You can change a program's culture by using the `CultureInfoClass`. The .NET framework supports more than 200 culture settings, such as Japanese, French, Urdu, and Sanskrit.

To display a numeric value as a formatted string, you do not have to create a separate string object. You also can make the conversion in a single statement; for example, the following code displays $12,345.00:

```
double payAmount = 12345;
Console.WriteLine(payAmount.ToString("c2"));
```

49

USING THE STANDARD BINARY ARITHMETIC OPERATORS

>> **NOTE**
Several shortcut arithmetic operators will be discussed in the next section.

Table 2-3 describes the five most commonly used binary arithmetic operators. You use these operators to manipulate values in your programs. The operators are called **binary operators** because you use two arguments with each—one value to the left of the operator and another value to the right of it. The values that operators use in expressions are called **operands**; binary operators are surrounded by two operands.

Operator	Description	Example
+	Addition	45 + 2: the result is 47
−	Subtraction	45 − 2: the result is 43
*	Multiplication	45 * 2: the result is 90
/	Division	45 / 2: the result is 22 (not 22.5)
%	Remainder (modulus)	45 % 2: the result is 1 (that is, 45 / 2 = 22 with a remainder of 1)

Table 2-3 Binary arithmetic operators

The operators / and % deserve special consideration. When you divide two integers using the / operator, whether they are integer constants or integer variables, the result is an integer; in other words, any fractional part of the result is lost. For example, the result of 45 / 2 is 22, not 22.5. When you use the remainder (modulus) operator with two integers, the result is an integer with the value of the remainder after division takes place—so the result of 45 % 2 is 1 because 2 "goes into" 45 twenty-two times with a remainder of 1.

>> **NOTE** In older languages, such as assembler, you had to perform division before you could take a remainder. In C#, you do not need to perform a division operation before you can perform a remainder operation. In other words, a remainder operation can stand alone.

>> **NOTE** Even though you define a result variable as a floating-point type, integer division still results in an integer. For example, the statement `double d = 7 / 2;` results in d holding 3, not 3.5. If you want the result to hold 3.5, at least one of the operands in the calculation must be a floating-point number, or else you must perform a cast. You will learn about casting later in this chapter.

>> **NOTE** As with `int`s, you can add, subtract, multiply, and divide with floating-point numbers. Unlike with `int`s, however, you cannot perform modulus operations with such numbers. (Floating-point division results in a floating-point answer, so there is no remainder.)

When you combine mathematical operations in a single statement, you must understand **operator precedence**, or the rules that determine the order in which parts of a mathematical expression are evaluated. Multiplication, division, and remainder always take place prior to addition or subtraction in an expression. For example, the following expression results in 14:

```
int result = 2 + 3 * 4;
```

The result is 14 because the multiplication operation (3 * 4) occurs before adding 2. You can override normal operator precedence by putting the operation that should be performed first in parentheses. The following statement results in 20 because the addition within parentheses takes place first:

```
int result = (2 + 3) * 4;
```

In this statement, an intermediate result (5) is calculated before it is multiplied by 4.

> **NOTE** Operator precedence is also called **order of operation**. A closely linked term is **associativity**, which specifies the order in which a sequence of operations with the same precedence are evaluated. Appendix A contains a chart that describes the precedence and associativity of every C# operator.

USING SHORTCUT ARITHMETIC OPERATORS

Increasing the value held in a variable is a common programming task. Assume that you have declared a variable named `counter` that counts the number of times an event has occurred. Each time the event occurs, you want to execute a statement such as the following:

```
counter = counter + 1;
```

This type of statement looks incorrect to an algebra student, but the equal sign (=) is not used to compare values in C#; it is used to assign values. The statement `counter = counter + 1;` says "Take the value of `counter`, add 1 to it, and assign the result to `counter`."

Because increasing the value of a variable is so common, C# provides several shortcut ways to count and accumulate. The following two statements are identical in meaning:

```
counter += 1;
counter = counter + 1;
```

The += operator is the **add and assign operator**; it adds the operand on the right to the operand on the left and assigns it to the operand on the left in one step. Similarly, the following statement increases `bankBal` by a rate stored in `interestRate`:

```
bankBal += bankBal * interestRate;
```

Besides the shortcut operator +=, you can use -=, *=, and /=. Each of these operators is used to perform an operation and assign the result in one step. For example:

» `balanceDue -= payment;` subtracts a payment from `balanceDue` and assigns the result to `balanceDue`.

» `rate *= 100` multiplies `rate` by 100. For example, it converts a fractional value stored in `rate`, such as 0.27, to a whole number, such as 27.

» `payment /= 12` changes a payment value from an annual amount to a monthly amount due.

> **NOTE** You cannot place spaces between the two symbols used in any of the shortcut arithmetic operators. Spaces surrounding the operators are optional.

USING DATA

When you want to increase a variable's value by exactly 1, you can use either of two other shortcut operators—the **prefix increment operator** and the **postfix increment operator**. To use a prefix increment operator, you type two plus signs before the variable name. For example, these statements result in someValue holding 7:

```
int someValue = 6;
++someValue;
```

The variable someValue holds 1 more than it held before the ++ operator was applied. To use a postfix ++, you type two plus signs just after a variable name. Executing the following statements results in anotherValue holding 57:

```
int anotherValue = 56;
anotherValue++;
```

You can use the prefix ++ and postfix ++ with variables, but not with constants. An expression such as ++84 is illegal because 84 is constant and must always remain as 84. However, you can create a variable as in int val = 84;, and then write ++val or val++ to increase the variable's value to 85.

The prefix and postfix increment operators are **unary operators** because you use them with one operand. Most arithmetic operators, like those used for addition and multiplication, are binary operators that operate on two operands.

When you only want to increase a variable's value by 1, there is no apparent difference between using the prefix and postfix increment operators. However, these operators function differently. When you use the prefix ++, the result is calculated and stored, and then the variable is used. For example, in the following code, both b and c end up holding 5. The WriteLine() statement displays "5 5". In this example, 4 is assigned to b, then b becomes 5, and then 5 is assigned to c.

```
b = 4;
c = ++b;
Console.WriteLine("{0} {1}", b, c);
```

In contrast, when you use the postfix ++, the variable is used, and then the result is calculated and stored. For example, in the second line of the following code, 4 is assigned to c; then, *after* the assignment, b is increased and takes the value 5.

```
b = 4;
c = b++;
Console.WriteLine("{0} {1}", b, c);
```

This last WriteLine() statement displays "5 4". In other words, if b = 4, then the value of b++ is also 4, and that value is assigned to c. However, after the 4 is assigned to c, b is increased to 5.

Besides the prefix and postfix increment operators, you can use a prefix or postfix **decrement operator** (--) that reduces a variable's value by 1. For example, if s and t are both assigned the value 34, then --s has the value 33 and t-- has the value 34, but t becomes 33.

CHAPTER TWO

USING THE `bool` DATA TYPE

Boolean logic is based on true-or-false comparisons. An `int` variable can hold millions of different values at different times, but a **Boolean variable** can hold only one of two values—true or false. You declare a Boolean variable by using type **`bool`**. The following statements declare and assign appropriate values to two `bool` variables:

```
bool isItMonday = false;
bool areYouTired = true;
```

> **NOTE** If you begin a `bool` variable name with a form of the verb "to be" or "to do," such as "is" or "are," then you can more easily recognize the identifiers as Boolean variables when you encounter them within your programs.

> **NOTE** When you use "Boolean" as an adjective, as in "Boolean variable," you usually begin with an uppercase B because the data type is named for Sir George Boole, the founder of symbolic logic, who lived from 1815 to 1864. The C# data type `bool`, however, begins with a lowercase "b."

You also can assign values based on the result of comparisons to Boolean variables. A **comparison operator** compares two items; an expression containing a comparison operator has a Boolean value. Table 2-4 describes the six comparison operators that C# supports.

Operator	Description	true Example	false Example
<	Less than	3 < 8	8 < 3
>	Greater than	4 > 2	2 > 4
==	Equal to	7 == 7	3 == 9
<=	Less than or equal to	5 <= 5	8 <= 6
>=	Greater than or equal to	7 >= 3	1 >= 2
!=	Not equal to	5 != 6	3 != 3

Table 2-4 Comparison operators

When you use any of the operators that require two keystrokes (==, <=, >=, or !=), you cannot place any whitespace between the two symbols.

Legal (but somewhat useless) declaration statements might include the following, which compare two values directly:

```
bool isSixBigger = 6 > 5;   // Value stored would be true
bool isSevenSmallerOrEqual = 7 <= 4;
   // Value stored would be false
```

Using Boolean values is more meaningful when you use variables (that have been assigned values) rather than constants in the comparisons, as in the following examples:

```
bool doesEmployeeReceiveOvertime = hoursWorked > 40;
bool isEmployeeInHighTaxBracket = annualIncome > 100000;
```

USING DATA

> **» NOTE**
> Boolean variables become more useful after you learn to make decisions within C# programs. You learn about decision making in Chapter 3.

In the first statement, the `hoursWorked` variable is compared to a constant value of 40. If the `hoursWorked` variable holds a value less than or equal to 40, then the expression is evaluated as false. In the second statement, the `annualIncome` variable value must be greater than 100000 for the expression to be true.

> **» NOTE** When you display a `bool` variable's value with `Console.WriteLine()`, the displayed value is `True` or `False`. However, the values within your programs are `true` and `false`.

UNDERSTANDING NUMERIC TYPE CONVERSION

When you perform arithmetic with variables or constants of the same type, the result of the arithmetic retains the same type. For example, when you divide two `int`s, the result is an `int`; when you subtract two `double`s, the result is a `double`. Often, however, you need to perform mathematical operations on different types. For example, in the following code, you multiply an `int` by a `double`:

```
int hoursWorked = 36;
double payRate = 12.35;
double grossPay = hoursWorked * payRate;
```

When you perform arithmetic operations with operands of dissimilar types, C# chooses a **unifying type** for the result and **implicitly** (or automatically) converts nonconforming operands to the unifying type, which is the type with the higher **type precedence**. The conversion is called an **implicit cast**—the automatic transformation that occurs when a value is assigned to a type with higher precedence.

For example, if you multiply an `int` and a `double`, the result is implicitly a `double`. This requirement means the result must be stored in a `double`; if you attempt to assign the result to an `int`, you will receive a compiler error message.

The implicit numeric conversions are:

> **» NOTE**
> Conversions from `int`, `uint`, or `long` to `float` and from `long` to `double` may cause a loss of precision, but will never cause a loss of magnitude.

- » From `sbyte` to `short`, `int`, `long`, `float`, `double`, or `decimal`
- » From `byte` to `short`, `ushort`, `int`, `uint`, `long`, `ulong`, `float`, `double`, or `decimal`
- » From `short` to `int`, `long`, `float`, `double`, or `decimal`
- » From `ushort` to `int`, `uint`, `long`, `ulong`, `float`, `double`, or `decimal`
- » From `int` to `long`, `float`, `double`, or `decimal`
- » From `uint` to `long`, `ulong`, `float`, `double`, or `decimal`
- » From `long` to `float`, `double`, or `decimal`
- » From `ulong` to `float`, `double`, or `decimal`
- » From `char` to `ushort`, `int`, `uint`, `long`, `ulong`, `float`, `double`, or `decimal`
- » From `float` to `double`

> **NOTE** Implicit conversions are not always the result of arithmetic calculations; simple assignments often result in implicit conversions. For example, if money is declared as a double, then the following statement implicitly converts the integer 15 to a double:
> ```
> money = 15;
> ```

> **NOTE** A constant expression of type int, such as 25, can be converted to sbyte, byte, short, ushort, uint, or ulong. For example, sbyte age = 19; is legal. However, you must make sure that the value of the constant expression is within the range of the destination type, or the program will not compile.

You may **explicitly** (or purposefully) override the unifying type imposed by C# by performing an explicit cast. An **explicit cast** involves placing the desired result type in parentheses followed by the variable or constant to be cast. For example, two explicit casts are performed in the following code:

```
double bankBalance = 189.66;
float weeklyBudget = (float) bankBalance / 4;
      // weeklyBudget is 47.415, one-fourth of bankBalance
int dollars = (int) weeklyBudget;
      // dollars is 47, the integer part of weeklyBudget
```

The value of bankBalance / 4 is implicitly a double because a double divided by an int produces a double. The double result is then converted to a float before it is stored in weeklyBudget, and the float value weeklyBudget is converted to an int before it is stored in dollars. When the float value is converted to an int, the decimal-place values are lost.

> **NOTE** It is easy to lose data when performing a cast. For example, the largest byte value is 255, and the largest int value is 2,147,483,647, so the following statements produce distorted results:
> ```
> int anOkayInt = 345;
> byte aBadByte = (byte)anOkayInt;
> ```

> **NOTE** If you attempt to store 256 in a byte, you will receive an error message unless you place the statement in a section of code preceded by the keyword unchecked, which tells the compiler not to check for invalid data. If you use the unchecked mode and store 256 in a byte, the results will look the same as storing 0; if you store 257, the result will appear as 1. You will see 89 when you store 345 in a byte variable and display the results, because the value 89 is exactly 256 less than 345.

USING THE char DATA TYPE

You use the **char** data type to hold any single character. You place constant character values within single quotation marks because the computer stores characters and integers differently. For example, the following statements are both legal:

```
char aCharValue = '9';
int aNumValue = 9;
```

USING DATA

However, the following statements are both illegal:

```
char aCharValue = 9;
int aNumValue = '9';
```

A number can be a character, in which case it must be enclosed in single quotation marks and declared as a `char` type. An alphabetic letter, however, cannot be stored in a numeric type variable. The following code shows how you can store several characters using the `char` data type:

```
char myInitial = 'J';
char percentSign = '%';
char numThatIsAChar = '9';
```

> **NOTE**
> A variable of type `char` can hold only one character. To store a string of characters, such as a person's name, you must use a `string`. You will learn about `string`s later in this chapter.

You can store any character—including nonprinting characters, such as a backspace or a tab—in a `char` variable. To store these characters, you use two symbols in an **escape sequence**, which always begins with a backslash. The pair of symbols represents a single character. For example, the following code stores a backspace character and a tab character in the `char` variables `aBackspaceChar` and `aTabChar`, respectively:

```
char aBackspaceChar = '\b';
char aTabChar = '\t';
```

In the preceding code, the escape sequence indicates a unique value for each character—a backspace or tab instead of the letter *b* or *t*. Table 2-5 describes some common escape sequences that are used in C#.

Escape Sequence	Character Name
\'	Single quotation mark
\"	Double quotation mark
\\	Backslash
\0	Null
\a	Alert
\b	Backspace
\f	Form feed
\n	Newline
\r	Carriage return
\t	Horizontal tab
\v	Vertical tab

Table 2-5 Common escape sequences

The characters used in C# are represented in **Unicode**, which is a 16-bit coding scheme for characters. For example, the letter *A* actually is stored in computer memory as a set of 16

CHAPTER TWO

zeros and ones—namely, 0000 0000 0100 0001. (The spaces are inserted here after every set of four digits for readability.) Because 16-bit numbers are difficult to read, programmers often use a shorthand notation called **hexadecimal**, or **base 16**. In hexadecimal shorthand, 0000 becomes 0, 0100 becomes 4, and 0001 becomes 1. Thus, the letter A is represented in hexadecimal as 0041. You tell the compiler to treat the four-digit hexadecimal 0041 as a single character by preceding it with the \u escape sequence. Therefore, there are two ways to store the character *A*:

NOTE
For more information about Unicode, go to www.unicode.org.

```
char letter = 'A';
char letter = '\u0041';
```

The second option, using hexadecimal, is obviously more difficult and confusing than the first option, so it is not recommended that you store letters of the alphabet using the hexadecimal method. However, you can produce some interesting values using the Unicode format, and so you should know how to use it. For example, letters from foreign alphabets that use characters instead of letters (Greek, Hebrew, Chinese, and so on) and other special symbols (foreign currency symbols, mathematical symbols, geometric shapes, and so on) are not available on a standard keyboard, but they are available in Unicode.

USING THE string DATA TYPE

In C#, you use the **string** data type to hold a series of characters. The value of a string is always expressed within double quotation marks. For example, the following statement declares a string named firstName and assigns "Jane" to it:

```
string firstName = "Jane";
```

When you assign a literal (such as "Jane") to a string, you can compare the string to another string using the == and != operators in the same ways that you compare numeric or character variables. For example, the program in Figure 2-10 declares three string variables.

```
using System;
public class CompareNames1
{
    public static void Main()
    {
        string name1 = "Amy";
        string name2 = "Amy";
        string name3 = "Matthew";
        Console.WriteLine("compare {0} to {1} : {2}",
            name1, name2, name1 == name2);
        Console.WriteLine("compare {0} to {1} : {2}",
            name1, name3, name1 == name3);
    }
}
```

Figure 2-10 Program that compares two strings using == operator (not recommended)

USING DATA

Figure 2-11 shows the results: strings that contain "Amy" and "Amy" are considered equal, but strings that contain "Amy" and "Matthew" are not.

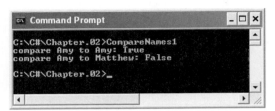

Figure 2-11 Output of CompareNames1 program

>> **NOTE**
Later in this chapter, you learn how to allow a user to enter data into a program from the keyboard.

Besides the == comparison operator, you can use several prewritten methods to compare strings. The advantage to using these other methods is that other classes you will eventually create use methods with the same names to compare their objects. You can compare strings with any of the following methods: Equals(), Compare(), and CompareTo().

The String class **Equals()** method requires two string arguments that you place within its parentheses, separated by a comma. As when you use the == operator, the Equals() method returns true or false.

The **Compare()** method also requires two string arguments. When it returns 0, the two strings are equivalent; when it returns a positive number, the first string is greater than the second; and when it returns a negative value, the first string is less than the second. A string is considered equal to, greater than, or less than another string **lexically**, which in the case of letter values means alphabetically. That is, when you compare two strings, you compare each character in turn from left to right. If each Unicode value is the same, then the strings are equivalent. If any corresponding character values are different, the string that has the greater Unicode value earlier in the string is considered greater.

The **CompareTo()** method uses a string, a dot, and the method name. The string to compare to is placed within parentheses. Like the Compare() method, it returns a 0 when the compared strings are equal, a negative number if the first string is less, and a positive number if the second string (the one in parentheses) is less. Figure 2-12 shows a program that makes several comparisons using the three methods; in each case the method name is shaded. Figure 2-13 shows the program's output.

>> **NOTE** The Equals(), Compare(), and CompareTo() methods are case sensitive. In other words, "Amy" does not equal "amy". In Unicode, the decimal value of each uppercase letter is exactly 32 less than its lowercase equivalent. For example, the decimal value of a Unicode 'a' is 97 and the value of 'A' is 65.

CHAPTER TWO

```
using System;
public class CompareTwoNames
{
    public static void Main()
    {
        string name1 = "Amy";
        string name2 = "Amy";
        string name3 = "Matthew";
        Console.WriteLine("compare {0} to {1}: {2}",
            name1, name2, String.Equals(name1, name2));
        Console.WriteLine("compare {0} to {1}: {2}",
            name1, name3, String.Equals(name1, name3));
        Console.WriteLine("compare {0} to {1}: {2}",
            name1, name2, String.Compare(name1, name2));
        Console.WriteLine("compare {0} to {1}: {2}",
            name1, name3, String.Compare(name1, name3));
        Console.WriteLine("compare {0} to {1}: {2}",
            name1, name3, name1.CompareTo(name2));
        Console.WriteLine("compare {0} to {1}: {2}",
            name1, name3, name1.CompareTo(name3));
    }
}
```

Figure 2-12 Program that compares two strings using three methods

Figure 2-13 Output of CompareTwoNames program

>>**NOTE** In C#, a string is **immutable**. That is, a string's value is not actually modified when you assign a new value to it. For example, when you write name = "Amy"; followed by name = "Donald";, the first characters "Amy" still exist in computer memory, but the name variable no longer refers to their memory address. The situation is different than with numbers; when you assign a new value to a numeric variable, the value at the named memory address actually changes.

>>**NOTE**
In Chapter 7, you will learn how to write your own CompareTo() methods for classes you create.

>>**NOTE** Another useful string method is **StartsWith()**. In the CompareTwoNames program, the expression name3.StartsWith("Ma") would be true.

59

DEFINING NAMED CONSTANTS

By definition, a variable's value can vary, or change. Sometimes you want to create a **named constant** (often simply called a constant), an identifier whose contents cannot change. You create a named constant similarly to the way you create a named variable, but by using the keyword `const`. Although there is no requirement to do so, programmers usually name constants using all uppercase letters, inserting underscores for readability. This convention makes constant names stand out so that the reader is less likely to confuse them with changeable variable names. For example, the following declares a constant named TAX_RATE that is assigned a value of 0.06:

```
const double TAX_RATE = 0.06;
```

You must assign a value to a constant when you create it. You can use a constant just as you would use a variable of the same type—for example, display it or use it in a mathematical equation—but you cannot assign any new value to it. Figure 2-14 shows a program that uses a TAX_RATE constant to calculate the tax on two different-priced items. Figure 2-15 shows the output.

It's good programming practice to declare constants for any value that should never change; doing so makes your programs clearer. For example, when you declare a constant `const int INCHES_IN_A_FOOT = 12;` within a program, then you can use a statement such as the following:

```
lengthInInches = lengthInFeet * INCHES_IN_A_FOOT;
```

This statement is **self-documenting**; that is, even without a program comment, it is easy for someone reading your program to tell why you performed the calculation in the way you did.

```
using System;
public class SalesTax
{
    public static void Main()
    {
        const double TAX_RATE = .06;
        double itemPrice = 3.99;
        double tax;
        tax = itemPrice * TAX_RATE;
        Console.WriteLine("With {0} tax, a {1} item costs {2} more",
            TAX_RATE, itemPrice.ToString("C"), tax.ToString("C"));
        itemPrice = 145.65;
        tax = itemPrice * TAX_RATE;
        Console.WriteLine("With {0} tax, a {1} item costs {2} more",
            TAX_RATE, itemPrice.ToString("C"), tax.ToString("C"));
    }
}
```

Figure 2-14 `SalesTax` program

CHAPTER TWO

Figure 2-15 Output of `SalesTax` program

ACCEPTING CONSOLE INPUT

When you write a program in which you assign values to variables and then manipulate those values, the output of the program is always the same. For example, no matter how many times you execute the `SalesTax` program in Figure 2-14, the two tax values are always calculated as $0.24 and $8.74. A more useful program would allow a user to input any price for which the tax could be calculated. A program that allows user input is an **interactive program**.

You can use the **`Console.ReadLine()`** method to accept user input from the keyboard. This method accepts all of the characters entered by a user until the user presses Enter. The characters can be assigned to a `string`. For example, the following statement accepts a user's input and stores it in the variable `myString`:

```
myString = Console.ReadLine();
```

If you want to use the data as a `string`—for example, if the input is a word or a name—then you simply use the variable to which you assigned the value. If you want to use the data as a number, then you must use a `Convert()` method to convert the input `string` to the proper type.

> **NOTE** The `Console.Read()` method is similar to the `Console.ReadLine()` method. `Console.Read()` reads just one character from the input stream, whereas `Console.ReadLine()` reads every character in the input stream until the user presses the Enter key.

Figure 2-16 shows an interactive program that prompts the user for a price and calculates a 6 percent sales tax. The program displays "Enter the price of an item" on the screen. Such an instruction to the user to enter data is called a **prompt**. After the prompt appears, the `Console.ReadLine()` statement accepts a string of characters and assigns them to the variable `itemPriceAsString`. Before the tax can be calculated, this value must be converted to a number. This conversion is accomplished in the shaded statement. Figure 2-17 shows a typical execution of the program in which the user typed 28.77 as the input value.

USING DATA

```
using System;
public class InteractiveSalesTax
{
    public static void Main()
    {
        const double TAX_RATE = 0.06;
        string itemPriceAsString;
        double itemPrice;
        double total;
        Console.WriteLine("Enter the price of an item");
        itemPriceAsString = Console.ReadLine();
        itemPrice = Convert.ToDouble(itemPriceAsString);
        total = itemPrice * TAX_RATE;
        Console.WriteLine("With a tax rate of {0}, a {1} item " +
            " costs {2} more.", TAX_RATE, itemPrice.ToString("C"),
            total.ToString("C"));
    }
}
```

Figure 2-16 InteractiveSalesTax program

Figure 2-17 Typical execution of InteractiveSalesTax program

Table 2-6 shows Convert class methods you can use to change strings into more useful data types. The methods use the class types (also called run-time types) in their names. For example, recall from Table 2-1 that the "formal" name for an int is Int32, so the method you use to convert a string to an int is named Convert.ToInt32().

CHAPTER TWO

Method	Description
ToBoolean()	Converts a specified value to an equivalent Boolean value
ToByte()	Converts a specified value to an 8-bit unsigned integer
ToChar()	Converts a specified value to a Unicode character
ToDecimal()	Converts a specified value to a decimal number
ToDouble()	Converts a specified value to a double-precision floating-point number
ToInt16()	Converts a specified value to a 16-bit signed integer
ToInt32()	Converts a specified value to a 32-bit signed integer
ToInt64()	Converts a specified value to a 64-bit signed integer
ToSByte()	Converts a specified value to an 8-bit signed integer
ToSingle()	Converts a specified value to a single-precision floating-point number
ToString()	Converts the specified value to its equivalent String representation
ToUInt16()	Converts a specified value to a 16-bit unsigned integer
ToUInt32()	Converts a specified value to a 32-bit unsigned integer
ToUInt64()	Converts a specified value to a 64-bit unsigned integer

Table 2-6 Selected Convert class methods

YOU DO IT
DECLARING AND USING VARIABLES
In the following steps, you will write a program that declares several integral variables, assigns values to them, and displays the results.

To write a program with integral variables:

1. Open a new file in the text editor you are using to write your C# programs. Create the beginning of a program that will demonstrate variable use. Use the System namespace, name the class **DemoVariables**, and type the class-opening curly brace.

   ```
   using System;
   public class DemoVariables
   {
   ```

   >>**NOTE**
   Recall from Chapter 1 that you can write C# programs in any editor with which you are comfortable.

2. In the Main() method, declare two variables (an integer and an unsigned integer) and assign values to them.

   ```
   public static void Main()
   {
       int anInt = -123;
       uint anUnsignedInt = 567;
   ```

USING DATA

3. Add a statement to display the two values.

   ```
   Console.WriteLine ("The int is {0} and the unsigned int
       is {1}.", anInt, anUnsignedInt);
   ```

4. Add two closing curly braces—one that closes the Main() method, and one that closes the DemoVariables class. Align each closing curly brace vertically with the opening brace that is its partner. In other words, the first closing brace aligns with the brace that opens Main(), and the second aligns with the brace that opens DemoVariables.

5. Save the program as **DemoVariables.cs** and compile it. If you receive any error messages, correct the errors and compile the program again. When the file is error-free, execute the program. The output should look like Figure 2-18.

Figure 2-18 Output of DemoVariables program

6. Experiment with the program by introducing invalid values for the named variables. For example, change the value of anUnsignedInt to **–567** by typing a minus sign in front of the constant value. Compile the program. You receive the following error message:

   Constant value '-567' cannot be converted to a 'uint'.

7. Correct the error either by removing the minus sign or by changing the data type of the variable to **int**, and compile the program again. You should not receive any error messages. Remember to save your program file after you make each change and before you compile.

8. Change the value of anInt from –123 to **–123456789000**. When you compile the program, the following error message appears:

   Cannot implicitly convert type 'long' to 'int'.

   The value is a long because it is greater than the highest allowed int value. Correct the error either by using a lower value or by changing the variable type to **long**, and compile the program again. You should not receive any error messages.

9. Experiment with other changes to the variables. Include some variables of type short, ushort, byte, and sbyte, and experiment with their values.

PERFORMING ARITHMETIC

In the following steps, you will add some arithmetic statements to the DemoVariables.cs program.

CHAPTER TWO

To use arithmetic statements in a program:

1. Open a new C# program file and enter the following statements to start a program that demonstrates arithmetic operations:

   ```
   using System;
   public class DemoVariables2
   {
      public static void Main()
      {
   ```

2. Write a statement that will declare seven integer variables. You will assign initial values to two of the variables; the values for the other five variables will be calculated. Because all of these variables are the same type, you can use a single statement to declare all seven integers. Recall that to do this, you insert commas between variable names and place a single semicolon at the end. You can place line breaks wherever you want for readability. (Alternatively, you could use as many as seven separate declarations.)

   ```
   int value1 = 43, value2 = 10,
         sum, diff, product, quotient, remainder;
   ```

3. Write the arithmetic statements that calculate the sum of, difference between, product of, quotient of, and remainder of the two assigned variables.

   ```
   sum = value1 + value2;
   diff = value1 - value2;
   product = value1 * value2;
   quotient = value1 / value2;
   remainder = value1 % value2;
   ```

   >> **NOTE** Instead of declaring the variables sum, diff, product, quotient, and remainder and assigning values later, you could declare and assign all of them at once, as in int sum = value1 + value2;. The only requirement is that value1 and value2 must be assigned values before you can use them in a calculation.

4. Include five WriteLine() statements to display the results.

   ```
   Console.WriteLine("The sum of {0} and {1} is {2}",
      value1, value2, sum);
   Console.WriteLine("The difference between {0} and {1}" +
      " is {2}", value1, value2, diff);
   Console.WriteLine("The product of {0} and {1} is {2}",
      value1, value2, product);
   Console.WriteLine("{0} divided by {1} is {2}", value1,
      value2, quotient);
   Console.WriteLine("and the remainder is {0}", remainder);
   ```

5. Add two closing curly braces—one for the Main() method and the other for the DemoVariables2 class.

65

USING DATA

6. Save the file as **DemoVariables2.cs**. Compile and execute the program. The output should look like Figure 2-19.

Figure 2-19 Output of DemoVariables2 program

7. Change the values of the value1 and value2 variables, save the program, and compile and run it again. Repeat this process several times. After each execution, analyze the output to make sure you understand the results of the arithmetic operations.

WORKING WITH BOOLEAN VARIABLES

Next, you will write a program that demonstrates how Boolean variables operate.

To write a program that uses Boolean variables:

1. Open a new file in your editor and name it **DemoVariables3.cs**.

2. Enter the following code. In the Main() method, you declare an integer value, then assign different values to a Boolean variable. Notice that when you declare value and isSixMore, you assign types. When you reassign values to these variables later in the program, you do not redeclare them by using a type name. Instead, you simply assign new values to the already declared variables.

```
using System;
public class DemoVariables3
{
   public static void Main()
   {
      int value = 4;
      bool isSixMore = 6 > value;
      Console.WriteLine("When value is {0} isSixMore is {1}",
         value, isSixMore);
      value = 35;
      isSixMore = 6 > value;
      Console.WriteLine("When value is {0} isSixMore is {1}",
         value, isSixMore);
   }
}
```

3. Save, compile, and run the program. The output looks like Figure 2-20.

Figure 2-20 Output of `DemoVariables3` program

4. Change the value of the variable named `value` and try to predict the outcome. Run the program to confirm your prediction.

USING ESCAPE SEQUENCES

Next, you will write a short program to demonstrate the use of escape sequences.

To write a program using escape sequences:

1. Open a new file in your text editor and name it **DemoEscapeSequences**.

2. Enter the following code. The three `WriteLine()` statements demonstrate using escape sequences for tabs, a new line, and alerts.

```
using System;
public class DemoEscapeSequences
{
   public static void Main()
   {
      Console.WriteLine("This line\tcontains two\ttabs");
      Console.WriteLine("This statement\ncontains a new line");
      Console.WriteLine("This statement sounds " +
         " three alerts\a\a\a");
   }
}
```

3. Save the program as **DemoEscapeSequences.cs**. Compile and test the program. Your output should look like Figure 2-21. Additionally, if your system has speakers and they are on, you should hear three "beep" sounds caused by the three alert characters: '\a'.

Figure 2-21 Output of `DemoEscapeSequences` program

USING DATA

WRITING A PROGRAM THAT ACCEPTS USER INPUT

In the next steps, you will write an interactive program that allows the user to enter two integer values. The program then calculates and displays their sum.

To write the interactive addition program:

1. Open a new file in your editor. Type the first few lines needed for the `Main()` method of an `InteractiveAddition` class:

   ```
   using System;
   public class InteractiveAddition
   {
      public static void Main()
      {
   ```

2. Add variable declarations for two `string`s that will accept the user's input values. Also, declare three integers for the numeric equivalents of the `string` input values and their sum.

   ```
   string name, firstString, secondString;
   int first, second, sum;
   ```

3. Prompt the user for his or her name, accept it into the `name` string, and then display a personalized greeting to the user, along with the prompt for the first integer value.

   ```
   Console.WriteLine("Enter your name");
   name = Console.ReadLine();
   Console.WriteLine("Hello {0}! Enter the first integer", name);
   ```

4. Accept the user's input as a `string`, and then convert the input `string` to an integer.

   ```
   firstString = Console.ReadLine();
   first = Convert.ToInt32(firstString);
   ```

5. Add statements that prompt for and accept the second `string` and convert it to an integer.

   ```
   Console.WriteLine("Enter the second integer");
   secondString = Console.ReadLine();
   second = Convert.ToInt32(secondString);
   ```

6. Assign the sum of the two integers to the `sum` variable and display all of the values. Add the closing curly brace for the `Main()` method and the closing curly brace for the class.

   ```
         sum = first + second;
         Console.WriteLine("{0}, the sum of {1} and {2} is {3}",
            name, first, second, sum);
      }
   }
   ```

7. Save the file as **InteractiveAddition.cs** in the Chapter.02 folder of your Student Disk. Compile and run the program. When prompted, supply your name and any integers you want, and confirm that the result appears correctly. Figure 2-22 shows a typical run of the program.

CHAPTER TWO

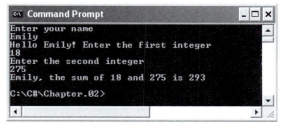

Figure 2-22 Typical execution of InteractiveAddition program

CHAPTER SUMMARY

» Data is constant when it cannot be changed after a program is compiled; data is variable when it might change. C# provides for 14 basic built-in types of data. A variable declaration includes a data type, an identifier, an optional assigned value, and a semicolon.

» You can display variable values by using the variable name within a WriteLine() or Write() method call. To make producing output easier, you can combine strings and variable values into a single Write() or WriteLine() statement by using a format string.

» In C#, nine data types are considered integral data types—byte, sbyte, short, ushort, int, uint, long, ulong, and char.

» C# supports three floating-point data types: float, double, and decimal. You can perform the mathematical operations of addition, subtraction, multiplication, and division with floating-point data, but not modulus. You can use format and precision specifiers to display floating-point data to a specified number of decimal places.

» You use the binary arithmetic operators +, −, *, /, and % to manipulate values in your programs. When you combine mathematical operations in a single statement, you must understand operator precedence, or the order in which parts of a mathematical expression are evaluated. Multiplication, division, and remainder always take place prior to addition or subtraction in an expression, unless you use parentheses to override the normal precedence.

» Because altering the value of a variable is a common task, C# provides you with several shortcut arithmetic operators. They include +=, −=, *=, /=, and the prefix and postfix increment (++) and decrement (−−) operators.

» A bool variable can hold only one of two values—true or false. C# supports six comparison operators: >, <, >=, <=, ==, and !=. An expression containing a comparison operator has a Boolean value.

» When you perform arithmetic with variables or constants of the same type, the result of the arithmetic retains the same type. When you perform arithmetic operations with operands of different types, C# chooses a unifying type for the result and implicitly converts nonconforming operands to the unifying type. You may explicitly override the unifying type imposed by C# by performing a cast.

USING DATA

» You use the `char` data type to hold any single character. You place constant character values within single quotation marks. You can store any character—including nonprinting characters such as a backspace or a tab—in a `char` variable. To store these characters, you must use an escape sequence, which always begins with a backslash.
» In C#, you use the `string` data type to hold a series of characters. The value of a `string` is always expressed within double quotation marks. Although the == and != comparison operators can be used with `string`s that are assigned literal values, you can also use the `Equals()`, `Compare()`, and `CompareTo()` methods that belong to the `String` class.
» Named constants are program identifiers you cannot change.
» You can use the `Console.ReadLine()` method to accept user input. Often, you must use a `Convert` class method to change the input string into a usable data type.

KEY TERMS

A data item is **constant** when it cannot be changed after a program is compiled—in other words, when it cannot vary.

A **literal constant** is a value that is taken literally at each use.

A **variable** is a named location in computer memory that can hold different values at different points in time.

A **data type** describes the format and size of a data item.

Intrinsic types of data are basic types; C# provides 14 intrinsic types.

An **alias** is another name for something.

A **variable declaration** is the statement that names a variable; it includes the data type that the variable will store, an identifier that is the variable's name, an optional assignment operator and assigned value when you want a variable to contain an initial value, and an ending semicolon.

The **assignment operator** is the equal sign (=); any value to the right of the assignment operator is assigned to, or taken on by, the variable to the left.

An **initialization** is an assignment made when a variable is declared.

An **assignment** is a statement that provides a variable with a value.

A **format string** is a string of characters that contains one or more placeholders for variable values.

A **placeholder** in a format string consists of a pair of curly braces containing a number that indicates the desired variable's position in a list that follows the string.

To **concatenate** strings is to join them together in a chain.

Integral data types are those that store whole numbers.

The nine integral types are **byte**, **sbyte**, **short**, **ushort**, **int**, **uint**, **long**, **ulong**, and **char**. The first eight always represent whole numbers, and the ninth type, `char`, is used for characters like 'A' or 'a'.

CHAPTER TWO

Integers are whole numbers.

A **floating-point** number is one that contains decimal positions.

A `float` data type can hold a floating-point number with as many as seven significant digits of accuracy.

A `double` data type can hold a floating-point number with 15 or 16 significant digits of accuracy.

A value's number of **significant digits** specifies the mathematical accuracy of the value.

The `decimal` data type is a floating-point type that has a greater precision and a smaller range than a `float` or `double`, which makes it suitable for financial and monetary calculations.

Values expressed in **scientific notation** include an *E* (for exponent).

Standard numeric format strings are strings of characters expressed within double quotation marks that indicate a format for output.

The **format specifier** in a format string can be one of nine built-in format characters that define the most commonly used numeric format types.

The **precision specifier** in a format string controls the number of significant digits or zeros to the right of the decimal point.

A **culture** is a set of rules that determines how culturally dependent values, such as money and dates, are formatted.

Binary operators use two arguments—one value to the left of the operator and another value to the right of it.

Operands are the values that operators use in expressions.

Operator precedence determines the order in which parts of a mathematical expression are evaluated.

Operator precedence is also called **order of operation**.

Associativity specifies the order in which a sequence of operations with the same precedence are evaluated.

The **add and assign operator** (+=) adds the operand on the right to the operand on the left and assigns it to the operand on the left in one step.

The **prefix increment operator** (++ before a variable) increases the variable's value by 1 and then evaluates it.

The **postfix increment operator** (++ after a variable) evaluates a variable and then adds 1 to it.

Unary operators are operators used with one operand.

The **decrement operator** (--) reduces a variable's value by 1. There is a prefix and a postfix version.

A **Boolean variable** can hold only one of two values—true or false.

The `bool` data type holds a Boolean value.

A **comparison operator** compares two items; an expression containing a comparison operator has a Boolean value.

USING DATA

A **unifying type** is the type chosen for an arithmetic result when operands are of dissimilar types.

Implicitly means automatically.

Type precedence is a hierarchy of data types used to determine the unifying type in arithmetic expressions containing dissimilar data types.

An **implicit cast** is the automatic transformation that occurs when a value is assigned to a type with higher precedence.

Explicitly means purposefully.

An **explicit cast** purposefully assigns a value to a different data type; it involves placing the desired result type in parentheses followed by the variable or constant to be cast.

The `char` data type can hold any single character.

An **escape sequence** is two symbols beginning with a backslash that represent a nonprinting character such as a tab.

Unicode is a 16-bit coding scheme for characters.

Hexadecimal, or **base 16**, is a mathematical system that uses 16 symbols to represent numbers.

The `string` data type is used to hold a series of characters.

The String class **Equals()** method determines if two strings have the same value; it requires two `string` arguments that you place within its parentheses, separated by a comma.

The `Compare()` method requires two `string` arguments. When it returns 0, the two `string`s are equivalent; when it returns a positive number, the first `string` is greater than the second; and when it returns a negative value, the first `string` is less than the second.

Lexically means alphabetically.

The `CompareTo()` method uses a `string`, a dot, and the method name. When it returns 0, the two `string`s are equivalent; when it returns a positive number, the first `string` is greater than the second; and when it returns a negative value, the first `string` is less than the second.

In C#, a `string` is **immutable**, or unchangeable. That is, a `string`'s value is not actually modified when you assign a new value to it; instead, the `string` refers to a new memory location.

The `StartsWith()` method is used with a `string` and a dot, and its parentheses contain another `string`. It returns true if the first `string` starts with the characters contained in the second `string`.

A **named constant** (often simply called a constant) is an identifier whose contents cannot change.

A **self-documenting** program element is one that is self-explanatory.

An **interactive program** is one that allows user input.

The `Console.ReadLine()` method accepts user input from the keyboard.

A **prompt** is an instruction to the user to enter data.

CHAPTER TWO

REVIEW QUESTIONS

1. When you use a number such as 45 in a C# program, the number is a _____.
   a. literal constant
   b. figurative constant
   c. literal variable
   d. figurative variable

2. A variable declaration must contain all of the following *except* a(n) _____.
   a. data type
   b. identifier
   c. assigned value
   d. ending semicolon

3. Which of the following is true of variable declarations?
   a. Two variables of the same type can be declared in the same statement.
   b. Two variables of different types can be declared in the same statement.
   c. Two variables of the same type must be declared in the same statement.
   d. Two variables of the same type cannot coexist in a program.

4. Assume you have two variables declared as `int var1 = 3;` and `int var2 = 8;`. Which of the following would display *838*?
   a. `Console.WriteLine("{0}{1}{2}", var1, var2);`
   b. `Console.WriteLine("{0}{1}{0}", var1, var2);`
   c. `Console.WriteLine("{0}{1}{2}", var2, var1);`
   d. `Console.WriteLine("{0}{1}{0}", var2, var1);`

5. Assume you have a variable declared as `int var1 = 3;`. Which of the following would display *X 3X*?
   a. `Console.WriteLine("X{0} X", var1);`
   b. `Console.WriteLine("X{0,2} X", var1);`
   c. `Console.WriteLine("X{2,0} X", var1);`
   d. `Console.WriteLine("X{0}{2} ", var1);`

6. Assume you have a variable declared as `int var1 = 3;`. What is the value of `22 % var1`?
   a. 0
   b. 1
   c. 7
   d. 21

73

USING DATA

7. Assume you have a variable declared as `int var1 = 3;`. What is the value of `22 / var1`?
   - a. 1
   - b. 7
   - c. 7.333
   - d. 21

8. What is the value of the expression `4 + 2 * 3`?
   - a. 0
   - b. 10
   - c. 18
   - d. 36

9. Assume you have a variable declared as `int var1 = 3;`. If `var2 = ++var1`, what is the value of `var2`?
   - a. 2
   - b. 3
   - c. 4
   - d. 5

10. Assume you have a variable declared as `int var1 = 3;`. If `var2 = var1++`, what is the value of `var2`?
    - a. 2
    - b. 3
    - c. 4
    - d. 5

11. A variable that can hold the two values `true` and `false` is of type _____.
    - a. `int`
    - b. `bool`
    - c. `char`
    - d. `double`

12. Which of the following is *not* a C# comparison operator?
    - a. `=>`
    - b. `!=`
    - c. `==`
    - d. `<`

13. What is the value of the expression `6 >= 7`?
    - a. 0
    - b. 1
    - c. true
    - d. false

14. Which of the following C# types *cannot* contain floating-point numbers?
    - a. `float`
    - b. `double`
    - c. `decimal`
    - d. `int`

15. Assume you have declared a variable as `double hourly = 13.00;`. What will the statement `Console.WriteLine(hourly);` display?
    - a. 13
    - b. 13.0
    - c. 13.00
    - d. 13.000000

16. Assume you have declared a variable as `double salary = 45000.00;`. Which of the following will display *$45,000*?

    a. `Console.WriteLine(salary.toString("f"));`

    b. `Console.WriteLine(salary.toString("c"));`

    c. `Console.WriteLine(salary);`

    d. two of these

17. When you perform arithmetic operations with operands of different types, such as adding an `int` and a `float`, _____.

    a. C# chooses a unifying type for the result

    b. you must choose a unifying type for the result

    c. you must provide a cast

    d. you receive an error message

18. Unicode is _____.

    a. an object-oriented language

    b. a subset of the C# language

    c. a 16-bit coding scheme

    d. another term for hexadecimal

19. Which of the following declares a variable that can hold the word *computer*?

    a. `string device = 'computer';`

    b. `string device = "computer";`

    c. `char device = 'computer';`

    d. `char device = "computer";`

20. Which of the following compares two string variables named `string1` and `string2` to determine if their contents are equal?

    a. `string1 = string2`

    b. `string1 == string2`

    c. `Equals.String(string1, string2)`

    d. Two of the above

USING DATA

EXERCISES

1. What is the numeric value of each of the following expressions, as evaluated by the C# programming language?

   a. 4 + 2 * 3

   b. 6 / 4 * 7

   c. 16 / 2 + 14 / 2

   d. 18 / 2

   e. 17 / 2

   f. 32 / 5

   g. 14 % 2

   h. 15 % 2

   i. 28 % 5

   j. 28 % 4 * 3 + 1

   k. (2 + 6) * 4

   l. 20 / (4 + 1)

2. What is the value of each of the following Boolean expressions?

   a. 5 > 2

   b. 6 <= 18

   c. 49 >= 49

   d. 2 == 3

   e. 2 + 6 == 7

   f. 3 + 7 <= 10

   g. 3 != 9

   h. 12 != 12

   i. –2 != 2

   j. 2 + 5 * 3 == 21

3. Are any of the following expressions illegal? For the legal expressions, what is the numeric value of each statement, as evaluated by the C# programming language?

   a. 2.2 * 1.4

   b. 6.78 – 2

   c. 24.0 / 6.0

   d. 7.0 % 3.0

   e. 9 % 2.0

4. Choose the best data type for each of the following, so that no memory storage is wasted. Give an example of a typical value that would be held by the variable and explain why you chose the type you did.

   a. your age

   b. the U.S. national debt

   c. your shoe size

   d. your middle initial

5. Write a C# program that declares variables to represent the length and width of a room in feet. Assign appropriate values to the variables, such as length = 15 and width = 25. Compute and display the floor space of the room in square feet (area = length * width). As output, do not display only a value; instead, display explanatory text with the value, such as *The floor space is 375 square feet*. Save the program as **Room.cs** in the Chapter.02 folder on your Student Disk.

6. Write a C# program that declares variables to represent the length and width of a room in feet and the price of carpeting *per square foot* in dollars and cents. Assign appropriate values to the variables. Compute and display, with explanatory text, the cost of carpeting the room. Save the program as **Carpet.cs** in the Chapter.02 folder on your Student Disk.

7. Write a program that declares variables to represent the length and width of a room in feet and the price of carpeting *per square yard* in dollars and cents. Assign the value 25 to the `length` variable and the value 42 to the `width` variable. Compute and display the cost of carpeting the room. (*Hint:* There are nine square feet in one square yard.) Save the program as **Yards.cs** in the Chapter.02 folder on your Student Disk.

8. Write a program that declares a `minutes` variable to represent minutes worked on a job, and assign a value to it. Display the value in hours and minutes. For example, 197 minutes becomes 3 hours and 17 minutes. Save the program as **HoursAndMinutes.cs** in the Chapter.02 folder on your Student Disk.

9. Write a program that declares four variables to hold the number of eggs produced in a month by each of four chickens, and assign a value to each variable. Sum the eggs, then display the total in dozens and eggs. For example, a total of 127 eggs is 10 dozen and 7 eggs. Save the program as **Eggs.cs** in the Chapter.02 folder on your Student Disk.

10. Modify the `Eggs` program in Exercise 9 so it prompts the user for and accepts a number of eggs for each chicken. Save the program as **EggsInteractive.cs** in the Chapter.02 folder on your Student Disk.

11. Write a program that declares five variables to hold scores for five tests you have taken, and assign a value to each variable. Display the average of the test scores to two decimal places. Save the program as **Tests.cs** in the Chapter.02 folder on your Student Disk.

12. Modify the `Tests` program in Exercise 11 so it accepts five test scores from a user. Save the program as **TestsInteractive.cs** in the Chapter.02 folder on your Student Disk.

13. Write a program that declares two variables to hold the names of two of your friends, and assign a value to each variable. Display the result of using the `String.Compare()` method with your friends' names. Save the program as **TwoFriends.cs** in the Chapter.02 folder on your Student Disk.

14. Modify the `TwoFriends` program in Exercise 13 so it accepts your friends' names from the keyboard. Save the program as **TwoFriendsInteractive.cs** in the Chapter.02 folder on your Student Disk.

USING DATA

15. Write a program that prompts the user for a name, Social Security number, hourly pay rate, and number of hours worked. In an attractive format (similar to Figure 2-23), display all the input data as well as the following:

    » Gross pay, defined as hourly pay rate times hours worked
    » Federal withholding tax, defined as 15% of the gross pay
    » State withholding tax, defined as 5% of the gross pay
    » Net pay, defined as gross pay minus taxes

    Save the program as **Payroll.cs** in the Chapter.02 folder on your Student Disk.

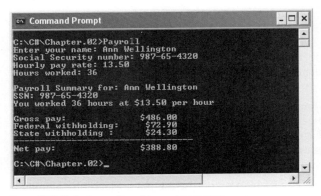

Figure 2-23 Typical execution of `Payroll` program

16. Write a program for the Magic Blender Company. The program prompts the user for a name, street address, city, state, zip code, and quantity of blenders ordered at $39.95 each. In an attractive format (similar to Figure 2-24), display all the input data as well as the following:

    » Amount due before tax, defined as number ordered times price each
    » Sales tax, defined as 7% of the amount due
    » Net due, defined as amount due before tax, plus tax

    Save the program as **OrderReceipt.cs** in the Chapter.02 folder on your Student Disk.

CHAPTER TWO

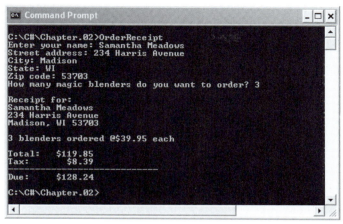

Figure 2-24 Typical execution of `OrderReceipt` program

DEBUGGING EXERCISES

Each of the following files in the Chapter.02 folder on your Student Disk has syntax and/or logical errors. In each case, determine the problem and fix the program. After you correct the errors, save each file using the same filename preceded with "Fixed". For example, DebugTwo1.cs will become FixedDebugTwo1.cs.

a. DebugTwo1.cs

b. DebugTwo2.cs

c. DebugTwo3.cs

d. DebugTwo4.cs

UP FOR DISCUSSION

1. What advantages are there to requiring variables to have a data type?

2. Some programmers use a system called Hungarian notation when naming their variables. What is Hungarian notation, and why do many object-oriented programmers feel it is not a valuable style to use?

3. Computers can perform millions of arithmetic calculations in an hour. How can we possibly know the results are correct?

CHAPTER THREE

3

MAKING DECISIONS

In this chapter you will:

Understand decision making
Learn how to make decisions using the `if` statement
Learn how to make decisions using the `if-else` statement
Use compound expressions in `if` statements
Make decisions using the `switch` statement
Use the conditional operator
Use the NOT operator
Learn to avoid common errors when making decisions

MAKING DECISIONS

A major reason that computer programs seem so powerful is their ability to make decisions. Programs that decide which travel route will afford the best weather conditions, which Web site will provide the closest match to search criteria, or which recommended medical treatment has the highest probability of success all rely on a program's decision making. In this chapter, you will learn to make decisions in C# programs.

UNDERSTANDING DECISION MAKING

When computer programmers write programs, they rarely just sit down at a keyboard and begin typing. Programmers must plan the complex portions of programs using paper and pencil. Programmers often use **pseudocode**, a tool that helps them plan a program's logic by writing plain English statements. Using pseudocode requires that you write down the steps needed to accomplish a given task. You write pseudocode in everyday language, not the syntax used in a programming language. In fact, a task you write in pseudocode does not have to be computer-related. If you have ever written a list of directions to your house—for example, (1) go west on Algonquin Road, (2) turn left on Roselle Road, (3) enter expressway heading east, and so on—you have written pseudocode. A **flowchart** is similar to pseudocode, but you write the steps in diagram form, as a series of shapes connected by arrows.

> **NOTE**
> You learned the difference between a program's logic and its syntax in Chapter 1.

Some programmers use a variety of shapes to represent different tasks in their flowcharts, but you can draw simple flowcharts that express very complex situations using just rectangles and diamonds. You use a rectangle to represent any unconditional step and a diamond to represent any decision. For example, Figure 3-1 shows a flowchart and pseudocode describing driving directions to a friend's house. Notice how the actions illustrated in the flowchart and the pseudocode statements correspond. The logic in Figure 3-1 is an example of a logical structure called a **sequence structure**—one step follows another unconditionally. A sequence structure might contain any number of steps, but when one task follows another with no chance to branch away or skip a step, you are using a sequence.

Sometimes, logical steps do not follow in an unconditional sequence—some tasks might or might not occur based on decisions you make. Flowchart creators use diamond shapes to indicate alternative courses of action, which are drawn starting from the sides of the diamonds. Figure 3-2 shows a flowchart describing directions in which the execution of some steps depends on decisions.

Figure 3-2 shows a **decision structure**—one that involves choosing between alternative courses of action based on some value within a program. For example, the program that produces your paycheck can make decisions about the proper amount to withhold for taxes, the program that guides a missile can alter its course, and a program that monitors your blood pressure during surgery can determine when to sound an alarm. Making decisions is what makes computer programs seem "smart."

When reduced to their most basic form, all computer decisions are yes-or-no decisions. That is, the answer to every computer question is "yes" or "no" (or "true" or "false," or "on" or "off"). This is because computer circuitry consists of millions of tiny switches that are either "on" or "off," and the result of every decision sets one of these switches in memory. The values `true` and `false` are Boolean values; every computer decision results in a Boolean value.

CHAPTER THREE

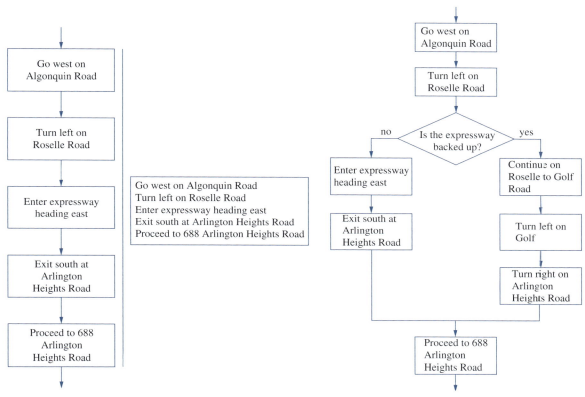

Figure 3-1 Flowchart and pseudocode of a series of sequential steps

Figure 3-2 Flowchart including a decision

Thus, internally, a program you write never asks, for example, "What number did the user enter?" Instead, the decisions might be "Did the user enter a 1?" "If not, did the user enter a 2?" "If not, did the user enter a 3?"

MAKING DECISIONS USING THE if STATEMENT

The `if` and `if-else` statements are the two most commonly used decision-making statements in C#. You use an **if statement** to make a single-alternative decision. In other words, you use an `if` statement to determine whether an action will occur. The `if` statement takes the following form:

```
if(expression)
    statement;
```

MAKING DECISIONS

where *expression* represents any C# expression that can be evaluated as true or false and *statement* represents the action that will take place if the expression evaluates as true. You must place the if statement's evaluated expression between parentheses.

Usable expressions in an if statement include Boolean expressions, such as amount > 5 and month == "May", as well as the value of bool variables, such as isValidIDNumber. If the expression evaluates as true, then the statement executes. Whether the expression evaluates as true or false, the program continues with the next statement following the complete if statement.

>> **NOTE** You learned about Boolean expressions and the bool data type in Chapter 2. Table 2-4 summarizes how you use the comparison operators.

>> **NOTE** Often, programmers mistakenly use a single equal sign rather than the double equal sign when attempting to determine equivalency. For example, the expression number = HIGH does not compare number to HIGH. Instead, it attempts to assign the value HIGH to the number variable. When it is part of an if statement, this assignment is illegal.

>> **NOTE** The only condition under which the assignment operator would work as part of an if statement is when the assignment is made to a bool variable. For example, suppose a dating-service program has defined two bool variables—doesSheSmoke and doesHeSmoke. Suppose you want to match smokers only with other smokers. The statement that uses a single = sign, if(doesSheSmoke = doesHeSmoke)..., compiles. However, it does not compare smoking preferences. Instead, it assigns the second value to the first, then makes the decision based on the single resulting value.

>> **NOTE** In some programming languages, such as C++, nonzero numbers evaluate as true and 0 evaluates as false. In C#, only Boolean expressions evaluate as true and false.

For example, the code segment written and diagrammed in Figure 3-3 displays "A" and "B" when number holds a value less than 5. The expression number < 5 evaluates as true, so the statement that displays "A" executes. Then the independent statement that displays "B" executes.

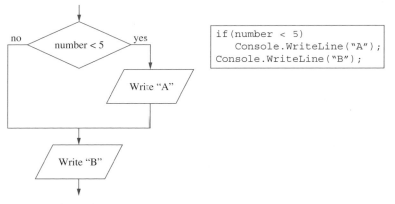

Figure 3-3 Flowchart and code including a typical if statement

>> **NOTE** You can leave a space between the keyword if and the opening parenthesis if you think that format is easier to read.

>> **NOTE** In Figure 3-3, notice there is no semicolon at the end of the line containing if(number < 5). The statement does not end at that point; it ends after Console.WriteLine("A");. If you incorrectly insert a semicolon at the end of if(number < 5), then the statement says, "If number is less than 5, do nothing; then, no matter what the value of number is, print 'A'."

When an evaluated expression is `false`, the rest of the statement does not execute. For example, when `number` is 5 or greater in Figure 3-3, only "B" is displayed. Because the expression `number < 5` is `false`, the statement that displays "A" never executes.

Although it is customary, and good style, to indent the statement that executes when an `if` Boolean expression evaluates as `true`, the C# compiler does not pay any attention to the indentation. Each of the following `if` statements displays "A" when `number` is less than 5. The first shows an `if` written on a single line; the second shows an `if` on two lines but with no indentation.

```
if(number < 5) Console.WriteLine("A");
if(number < 5)
Console.WriteLine("A");
```

When you want to execute two or more statements conditionally, you must place the statements within a block. A **block** is one or more statements contained within a pair of curly braces. For example, the code segment written and diagrammed in Figure 3-4 displays both "C" and "D" when `number` is less than 5, and it displays neither when `number` is not less than 5.

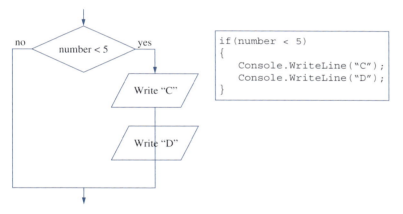

Figure 3-4 Flowchart and code including a typical `if` statement containing a block

> **NOTE** When you create a block using curly braces, you do not have to place multiple statements within it. It is perfectly legal to block a single statement. Blocking a single statement can be a useful technique to help prevent future errors. When a program later is modified to include multiple statements that depend on the `if`, it is easy to forget to add curly braces. You will naturally place the additional statements within the block if the braces are already in place.

> **NOTE** Indenting alone does not cause multiple statements to depend on the evaluation of a Boolean expression in an `if`. For multiple statements to depend on an `if`, they must be blocked with braces.

You can place any number of statements within the block contained by the curly braces, including another `if` statement. Figure 3-5 shows a **nested if** statement—one in which one decision structure is contained within another. With a nested `if` statement, a second `if`'s Boolean expression is tested only when the first `if`'s Boolean expression evaluates as `true`. When a user enters a number greater than 5 in the program in Figure 3-5, the first `if` expression evaluates as `true` and the `if` statement that tests whether the number is less than 10 executes. When the second `if` evaluates as `true`, the `Console.WriteLine()` statement executes. However, if the second `if` is `false`, no output occurs. When the user enters a

MAKING DECISIONS

number less than or equal to 5, the first `if` expression is `false` and the second `if` expression is never tested, and again no output occurs. Figure 3-6 shows the output after the program is executed three times using three different input values. Notice that when the value input by the user is not between 5 and 10, no output message appears; the message is displayed only when both `if` expressions are `true`.

```
using System;
public class NestedDecision
{
    public static void Main()
    {
        const int HIGH = 10, LOW = 5;
        string numberString;
        int number;
        Console.Write("Enter an integer ");
        numberString = Console.ReadLine();
        number = Convert.ToInt32(numberString);
        if(number > 5)
            if(number < 10)
                Conscle.WriteLine("{0} is between {1} and {2}",
                    number, LOW, HIGH);
    }
}
```

Figure 3-5 Program using nested `if`

Figure 3-6 Output of three executicns of the `NestedDecision` program

MAKING DECISIONS USING THE if-else STATEMENT

Some decisions you make are **dual-alternative decisions**; they have two possible outcomes. If you want to perform one action when a Boolean expression evaluates as `true` and an alternate action when it evaluates as `false`, you can use an **if-else statement**. The `if-else` statement takes the following form:

CHAPTER THREE

```
if(expression)
    statement1;
else
    statement2;
```

> **NOTE**
> You can code an if without an else, but it is illegal to code an else without an if.

For example, Figure 3-7 shows a program that contains an if-else statement. With every execution of the program, one or the other of the two WriteLine() statements executes. Figure 3-8 shows two executions of the program.

```
using System;
public class IfElseDecision
{
    public static void Main()
    {
        const int HIGH = 10;
        string numberString;
        int number;
        Console.Write("Enter an integer ");
        numberString = Console.ReadLine();
        number = Convert.ToInt32(numberString);
        if(number > HIGH)
            Console.WriteLine("{0} is greater than {1}",
                number, HIGH);
        else
            Console.WriteLine("{0} is not greater than {1}",
                number, HIGH);
    }
}
```

Figure 3-7 Program with a dual-alternative if-else statement

> **NOTE**
> The indentation shown in the if-else example in Figure 3-7 is not required, but is standard. You vertically align the keyword if with the keyword else, and then indent the action statements that depend on the evaluation.

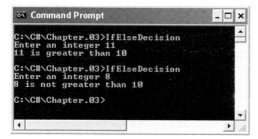

Figure 3-8 Output of two executions of the IfElseDecision program

> **NOTE** Just as you can block several statements so they all execute when an expression within an if is true, you can block multiple statements after an else so that they will all execute when the evaluated expression is false.

87

MAKING DECISIONS

When `if-else` statements are nested, each `else` always is paired with the most recent unpaired `if`. For example, in the following code, the `else` is paired with the second `if`.

```
if(saleAmount > 1000)
    if(saleAmount < 2000)
        bonus = 100;
    else
        bonus = 50;
```

In this example, the following bonuses are assigned:

» If `saleAmount` is between $1000 and $2000, `bonus` is $100 because both evaluated expressions are `true`.

» If `saleAmount` is $2000 or more, `bonus` is $50 because the first evaluated expression is `true` and the second one is `false`.

» If `saleAmount` is $1000 or less, `bonus` is unassigned because the first evaluated expression is `false` and there is no corresponding `else`.

USING COMPOUND EXPRESSIONS IN `if` STATEMENTS

In many programming situations you encounter, you need to make multiple decisions. For example, suppose a specific college scholarship is available:

» If your high school class rank is higher than 75 percent
» And if your grade-point average is higher than 3.0
» And if you are a state resident
» Or if you are a resident of a cooperating state
» Or if one of your parents went to the college

No matter how many decisions must be made, you can decide on the scholarship eligibility for any student by using a series of `if` statements to test the appropriate variables. For convenience and clarity, however, you can combine multiple decisions into a single `if` statement using a combination of AND and OR operators.

USING THE CONDITIONAL AND OPERATOR

As an alternative to nested `if` statements, you can use the **conditional AND operator** (or simply the **AND operator**) within a Boolean expression to determine whether two expressions are both `true`. The AND operator is written as two ampersands (`&&`). For example, the two code samples shown in Figure 3-9 work exactly the same way. The `age` variable is tested, and if it is greater than or equal to 0 and less than 120, a message prints to explain that the value is valid.

```
// using &&
 if(age >= 0 && age < 120)
    Console.Out.WriteLine("Age is valid");

// using nested ifs
 if(age >= 0)
    if(age < 120)
       Console.Out.WriteLine("Age is valid");
```

Figure 3-9 Comparing using the AND operator and nested `if` statements

You are never required to use the AND operator, because nested `if` statements achieve the same result, but using the AND operator often makes your code more concise, less error-prone, and easier to understand.

It is important to note that when you use the AND operator, you must include a complete Boolean expression on each side of the `&&` operator. If you want to set a bonus to $400 when a `saleAmount` is both over $1000 and under $5000, the correct statement is as follows:

```
if(saleAmount > 1000 && saleAmount < 5000)
   bonus = 400;
```

The following statement is incorrect and will not compile:

```
if(saleAmount > 1000 && < 5000)
   bonus = 400;
```

The statement is invalid because the numeric constant 5000 is used on the right side of the AND expression, and 5000 is not a Boolean expression.

> **NOTE** For clarity, many programmers prefer to surround each Boolean expression that is part of a compound Boolean expression with its own set of parentheses. For example:
>
> ```
> if((saleAmount > 1000) && (saleAmount < 5000))
>    bonus = 400;
> ```
>
> Use this format if it is clearer to you.

The expressions in each part of an AND expression are evaluated only as much as necessary to determine whether the entire expression is `true` or `false`. This feature is called **short-circuit evaluation**. With the AND operator, both Boolean expressions must be `true` before the action in the statement can occur. If the first expression is `false`, the second expression is never evaluated, because its value does not matter. For example, if `a` is not greater than `LIMIT` in the following `if` statement, then the evaluation is complete because there is no need to evaluate whether `b` is greater than `LIMIT`.

```
if(a > LIMIT && b > LIMIT)
   Console.WriteLine("Both are greater than LIMIT");
```

MAKING DECISIONS

USING THE CONDITIONAL OR OPERATOR

> **» NOTE**
> You create the OR operator by using two vertical pipes. On most keyboards, the pipe is found above the backslash key; typing it requires that you also hold down the Shift key.

You can use the **conditional OR operator** (or simply the **OR operator**) when you want some action to occur even if only one of two conditions is `true`. The OR operator is written as `||`. For example, if you want to print a message indicating an invalid age when the variable is less than 0 or is 120 or greater, you can use either code sample in Figure 3-10.

```
// using ||
  if(age < 0 || age >= 120)
     Console.Out.WriteLine("Age is not valid");

// using nested ifs
  if(age < 0)
     Console.Out.WriteLine("Age is not valid");
  else
     if(age >= 120)
        Console.Out.WriteLine("Age is not valid");
```

Figure 3-10 Using the OR operator or nested `if` statements

> **» NOTE** A common use of the OR operator is to decide to take action whether a character variable is uppercase or lowercase. For example, in the following decision, any subsequent action occurs whether the selection variable holds an uppercase or lowercase 'A':
>
> `if(selection == 'A' || selection == 'a') …;`

When the OR operator is used in an `if` statement, only one of the two Boolean expressions in the tested expression needs to be `true` for the resulting action to occur. As with the AND operator, this feature is called short-circuit evaluation. When you use the OR operator and the first Boolean expression is `true`, the second expression is never evaluated, because it doesn't matter whether it is `true` or `false`.

USING THE LOGICAL AND AND OR OPERATORS

The **Boolean logical AND** (&) and **Boolean logical inclusive OR** (|) operators work just like their && and || (*conditional* AND and OR) counterparts, except they do not support short-circuit evaluation. That is, they always evaluate both sides of the expression, no matter what the first evaluation is. This can lead to a **side effect**, or unintended consequence. For example, in the following statement that uses &&, if `salesAmountForYear` is not at least 10000, the first half of the expression is `false`, so the second half of the Boolean expression is never evaluated and `yearsOfService` is not increased.

```
if(salesAmountForYear >= 10000 && ++yearsOfService > 10)
   bonus = 200;
```

On the other hand, when a single & is used and `salesAmountForYear` is not at least 10000, then even though the first half of the expression is `false`, the second half is still evaluated, and `yearsOfService` is increased:

```
if(salesAmountForYear >= 10000 & ++yearsOfService > 10)
   bonus = 200;
```

Because the first half of the expression is `false`, the entire evaluation is `false`, and, as with `&&`, `bonus` is still not set to 200. However, a side effect has occurred: `yearsOfService` is incremented.

In general, you should avoid writing expressions that contain side effects. If you want `yearsOfService` to increase no matter what the `salesAmountForYear` is, then you should increase it in a stand-alone statement.

COMBINING AND AND OR OPERATORS

You can combine as many AND and OR operators in an expression as you need. For example, when three conditions must be `true` before performing an action, you can use an expression such as `if(a && b && c)`. When you combine AND and OR operators within the same Boolean expression, the AND operators take precedence, meaning their Boolean values are evaluated first.

For example, consider a program that determines whether a movie theater patron can purchase a discounted ticket. Assume discounts are allowed for children (age 12 and younger) and for senior citizens (age 65 and older) who attend G-rated movies. The following code looks reasonable, but it produces incorrect results because the `&&` evaluates before the `||`.

```
if(age <= 12 || age >= 65 && rating == 'G' )
   Console.Out.WriteLine("Discount applies");
```

For example, assume a movie patron is 10 years old and the movie rating is 'R'. The patron should not receive a discount (or be allowed to see the movie!). However, within the `if` statement above, the expression `age >= 65 && rating == 'G'` evaluates first. It is `false`, so the `if` becomes the equivalent of `if(age <= 12 || false)`. Because `age <= 12` is true, the `if` becomes the equivalent of `if(true || false)`, which evaluates as `true`, and the statement "Discount applies" incorrectly displays.

You can use parentheses to correct the logic and force the expression `age <= 12 || age >= 65` to evaluate first, as shown in the following code.

```
if((age <= 12 || age >= 65) && rating == 'G' )
   Console.Out.WriteLine("Discount applies");
```

With the added parentheses, if `age` is 12 or less OR 65 or greater, the expression is evaluated as `if(true && rating == 'G' )`. When the `age` value qualifies a patron for a discount, then the `rating` value must also be acceptable. Figure 3-11 shows the `if` within a complete program. Figure 3-12 shows the execution before the parentheses surrounding `age <= 12 || age >= 65` were added, and Figure 3-13 shows the output after the inclusion of the parentheses.

MAKING DECISIONS

> **» NOTE**
> You can use parentheses for clarity even when they are not required. For example, the following expressions both evaluate `a && b` first:
>
> `a && b || c`
> `(a && b) || c`
>
> If the version with parentheses makes your intentions clearer, you should use it.

```
using System;
public class MovieDiscount
{
    public static void Main()
    {
        int age = 10;
        char rating = 'R';
        if((age <= 12 || age >= 65) && rating == 'G')
            Console.Out.WriteLine("Disccount applies");
        else
            Console.Out.WriteLine("Full price");
    }
}
```

Figure 3-11 Movie ticket discount program using parentheses to alter precedence of Boolean evaluations

Figure 3-12 Incorrect results when `MovieDiscount` program is executed without added parentheses

Figure 3-13 Correct results when parentheses are added to `MovieDiscount` program

> **» NOTE** In Chapter 2, you controlled arithmetic operator precedence by using parentheses. Appendix A describes the precedence of every C# operator. For example, in Appendix A you can see that the comparison operators <= and >= have higher precedence than both && and ||.

MAKING DECISIONS USING THE `switch` STATEMENT

By nesting a series of `if` and `else` statements, you can choose from any number of alternatives. For example, suppose you want to print different strings based on a student's class year. Figure 3-14 shows the logic using nested `if` statements. The program segment tests the `year` variable four times and executes one of four statements, or displays an error message.

```
if(year == 1)
    Console.WriteLine("Freshman");
else
    if(year == 2)
        Console.WriteLine("Sophomore");
    else
        if(year == 3)
            Console.WriteLine("Junior");
        else
            if(year == 4)
                Console.WriteLine("Senior");
            else
                Console.WriteLine("Invalid year");
```

Figure 3-14 Executing multiple alternatives using a series of `if` statements

An alternative to the series of nested `if` statements in Figure 3-14 is to use the `switch` structure (see Figure 3-15). The **switch structure** tests a single variable against a series of exact matches. The `switch` structure in Figure 3-15 is easier to read and interpret than the series of nested `if` statements in Figure 3-14. The `if` statements would become harder to read if additional choices were required and if multiple statements had to execute in each case. These additional choices and statements might also make it easier to make mistakes.

>> **NOTE**
The `switch` statement is not as flexible as the `if` because you can test only one variable, and it must be tested for equality.

>> **NOTE**
You are not required to list the `case` label values in ascending order, as shown in Figure 3-15. It is most efficient to list the most common case first, instead of the case with the lowest value.

```
switch(year)
{
    case 1:
        Console.WriteLine("Freshman");
        break;
    case 2:
        Console.WriteLine("Sophomore");
        break;
    case 3:
        Console.WriteLine("Junior");
        break;
    case 4:
        Console.WriteLine("Senior");
        break;
    default:
        Console.WriteLine("Invalid year");
        break;
}
```

Figure 3-15 Executing multiple alternatives using a `switch` statement

MAKING DECISIONS

The `switch` structure uses four new keywords:

» The keyword **switch** starts the structure and is followed immediately by a test expression (called the **switch expression**) enclosed in parentheses.

» The keyword **case** is followed by one of the possible values that might equal the `switch` expression. A colon follows the value. The entire expression—for example, `case 1:`—is a `case` label. A **case label** identifies a course of action in a `switch` structure. Most `switch` structures contain several `case` labels.

» The keyword **break** usually terminates a `switch` structure at the end of each `case`. Although other statements can end a `case`, `break` is the most commonly used.

» The keyword **default** optionally is used prior to any action that should occur if the test expression does not match any `case`.

The `switch` structure shown in Figure 3-15 begins by evaluating the `year` variable shown in the `switch` statement. If `year` is equal to the first `case` label value, which is 1, then the statement that displays "Freshman" will execute. The `break` statement causes a bypass of the rest of the `switch` structure, and execution continues with any statement after the closing curly brace of the `switch` structure.

If the `year` variable is not equivalent to the first `case` label value of 1, then the next `case` label value is compared, and so on. If the `year` variable does not contain the same value as any of the `case` label expressions, then the `default` statement or statements execute.

In C#, an error occurs if you reach the end point of the statement list of a `switch` section. For example, the following code is not allowed, because when the `year` value is 1, "Freshman" is displayed, and the code reaches the end of the `case`.

```
switch(year)
{
    case 1:
        Console.WriteLine ("Freshman");
    case 2:
        Console.WriteLine ("Sophomore");
        break;
}
```

> **» NOTE**
> Besides `break`, you can use a `return` statement or a `throw` statement to end a `case`. You learn about `return` statements in Chapter 6 and `throw` statements in Chapter 9.

Not allowing code to reach the end of a `case` is known as the "no fall through rule" because in other programming languages, such as Java and C++, this syntax would be allowed; when `year` equals 1, both "Freshman" and "Sophomore" would be displayed. Falling through to the next `case` is not allowed in C#; the most common way to avoid this error is to use a `break` statement at the end of each `case`.

> **» NOTE** The **governing type** of a `switch` statement is established by the `switch` expression. The governing type can be `sbyte`, `byte`, `short`, `ushort`, `int`, `uint`, `long`, `ulong`, `char`, `string`, or an `enum` type. An **enum** is an enumeration—a programmer-defined type that declares a set of constants. You will use enumerations in Chapter 11.

A `switch` does not need to contain a `default` case. If the test expression in a `switch` does not match any of the `case` label values, and there is no `default` value, then the program simply continues with the next executable statement. However, it is good programming practice to include a `default` label in a `switch` structure; that way, you provide for actions when your data does not match any case. The `default` label does not have to appear last, although usually it does.

»NOTE
You receive a compiler error if two or more `case` label values in a `switch` statement are the same.

You can use multiple labels to govern a list of statements. For example, in the code in Figure 3-16, "`Upperclass`" is displayed whether the `year` value is 3 or 4.

```
switch(year)
{
    case 1:
        Console.WriteLine("Freshman");
        break;
    case 2:
        Console.WriteLine("Sophomore");
        break;
    case 3:
    case 4:
        Console.WriteLine("Upperclass");
        break;
    default:
        Console.WriteLine("Invalid year");
        break;
}
```

Figure 3-16 Example `switch` structure using multiple labels to execute a single statement block

You are never required to use a `switch` structure; you can always achieve the same results with nested `if` statements. The `switch` structure is simply a convenience you can use when there are several alternative courses of action depending on a match with a variable. Additionally, it makes sense to use a `switch` only when there are a reasonable number of specific matching values to be tested. For example, if every sale amount from $1 to $500 requires a 5 percent commission, it is not reasonable to test every possible dollar amount using the following code:

```
switch(saleAmount)
{
    case 1:
        commRate = .05;
        break;
    case 2:
        commRate = .05;
        break;
    case 3:
        commRate = .05;
        break;
// ...and so on for several hundred more cases
```

MAKING DECISIONS

With 500 different dollar values resulting in the same commission, one test—
`if(saleAmount <= 500)`—is far more reasonable than listing 500 separate cases.

USING THE CONDITIONAL OPERATOR

The **conditional operator** is used as an abbreviated version of the `if-else` statement; it requires three expressions separated with a question mark and a colon. Like the `switch` structure, you never are required to use the conditional operator. Rather, it is simply a convenient shortcut, especially when you want to use the result immediately as an expression. The syntax of the conditional operator is:

```
testExpression ? trueResult : falseResult;
```

> **NOTE** Unary operators use one operand; binary operators use two. The conditional operator ?: is **ternary** because it requires three arguments: a test expression and `true` and `false` result expressions. The conditional operator is the only ternary operator in C#.

The first expression, `testExpression`, is evaluated as `true` or `false`. If it is `true`, then the entire conditional expression takes on the value of the expression following the question mark (`trueResult`). If the value of the `testExpression` is `false`, then the entire expression takes on the value of `falseResult`. For example, consider the following statement:

```
biggerNum = (a > b) ? a : b;
```

This statement evaluates `a > b`. If `a` is greater than `b`, then the entire conditional expression takes the value of `a`, which then is assigned to `biggerNum`. If `a` is not greater than `b`, then the expression assumes the value of `b`, and `b` is assigned to `biggerNum`.

The conditional operator is most often used when you want to use the result as an expression without creating an intermediate variable. For example, suppose an income tax program has declared `double`s for tax owed when calculated using a standard formula and when calculated using an alternative minimum-tax formula. A taxpayer is required to make a quarterly payment that is one-fourth of the larger of the two values. A usable statement might be as follows:

```
double payment = ((altMinTax > stdTax) ? altMinTax : stdTax) / 4;
```

As another example, a conditional operator can be used directly in an output statement such as the following:

```
Console.WriteLine((testScore >= 60)) ? "Pass" : "Fail");
```

Conditional expressions are frequently more difficult to read than `if-else` statements, but they can be used in places where `if-else` statements cannot.

USING THE NOT OPERATOR

You use the **NOT operator**, which is written as an exclamation point (!), to negate the result of any Boolean expression. Any expression that evaluates as `true` becomes `false` when preceded by the NOT operator, and any `false` expression preceded by the NOT operator becomes `true`.

For example, suppose a monthly car insurance premium is $200 if the driver is younger than age 26 and $125 if the driver is age 26 or older. Each of the following `if` statements (which have been placed on single lines for convenience) correctly assigns the premium values.

```
if(age < 26) premium = 200;      else premium = 125;
if(!(age < 26)) premium = 125;   else premium = 200;
if(age >= 26) premium = 125;     else premium = 200;
if(!(age>= 26)) premium = 200;   else premium = 125;
```

The statements with the NOT operator are somewhat more difficult to read, particularly because they require the double set of parentheses, but the result is the same in each case. Using the NOT operator is clearer when the value of a Boolean variable is tested. For example, a variable initialized as `bool oldEnough = (age >= 25);` can become part of the relatively easy-to-read expression `if(!oldEnough)...`.

AVOIDING COMMON ERRORS WHEN MAKING DECISIONS

New programmers frequently make errors when they first learn to make decisions. As you have seen, the most frequent errors include the following:

- » Using the assignment operator instead of the comparison operator when testing for equality
- » Inserting a semicolon after the Boolean expression in an `if` statement instead of after the entire statement is completed
- » Failing to block a set of statements with curly braces when several statements depend on the `if` or the `else` statement
- » Failing to include a complete Boolean expression on each side of an `&&` or `||` operator in an `if` statement

In this section, you will learn to avoid other types of errors with `if` statements. Programmers often make errors at the following times:

- » When performing a range check incorrectly or inefficiently
- » When using the wrong operator with AND and OR
- » Using NOT incorrectly

MAKING DECISIONS

PERFORMING ACCURATE AND EFFICIENT RANGE CHECKS

When new programmers must make a range check, they often introduce incorrect or inefficient code into their programs. A **range check** is a series of `if` statements that determine whether a value falls within a specified range. Consider a situation in which salespeople can receive one of three possible commission rates based on their sales. For example, a sale totaling $1000 or more earns the salesperson an 8% commission, a sale totaling $500 through $999 earns 6% of the sale amount, and any sale totaling $499 or less earns 5%. Using three separate `if` statements to test single Boolean expressions might result in some incorrect commission assignments. For example, examine the following code:

```
if(saleAmount >= 1000)
   commissionRate = 0.08;
if(saleAmount >= 500)
   commissionRate = 0.06;
if(saleAmount <= 499)
   commissionRate = 0.05;
```

> **NOTE** In this example, `saleAmount` is assumed to be an integer. As long as you are dealing with whole dollar amounts, the expression `if(saleAmount >= 1000)` can be expressed just as well as `if(saleAmount > 999)`. If `saleAmount` was a floating-point variable, the preceding code would fail to assign a commission rate for sales from $499.01 through $499.99.

Using this code, if a `saleAmount` is $5000, the first `if` statement executes. The Boolean expression `(saleAmount >= 1000)` evaluates as `true`, and 0.08 is correctly assigned to `commissionRate`. However, when a `saleAmount` is $5000, the next `if` expression, `(saleAmount >= 500)`, also evaluates as `true`, so the `commissionRate`, which was 8%, is incorrectly reset to 6%.

A partial solution to this problem is to use an `else` statement following the `if(saleAmount >= 1000)` expression:

```
if(saleAmount >= 1000)
   commissionRate = 0.08;
else if(saleAmount >= 500)
   commissionRate = 0.06;
else if(saleAmount <= 499)
   commissionRate = 0.05;
```

With this code, when the `saleAmount` is $5000, the expression `(saleAmount >= 1000)` is `true` and the `commissionRate` becomes 8%; then the entire `if` structure ends. When the `saleAmount` is not greater than or equal to $1000 (for example, $800), the first `if` expression is `false` and the `else` statement executes and correctly sets the `commissionRate` to 6%.

This version of the code works, but it is somewhat inefficient. When the `saleAmount` is any amount that is at least $500, either the first `if` sets `commissionRate` to 8% for amounts of at least $1000, or its `else` sets `commissionRate` to 6% for amounts of at least $500. In either of these two cases, the Boolean value tested in the next statement, `if(saleAmount <= 499)`, is always `false`. After you know that the `saleAmount` is not at least $500, rather than asking `if(saleAmount <= 499)`, it's easier and more efficient to use an `else`. If the `saleAmount` is not at least $1000 and is also not at least $500, it must by default be less than or equal to $499. The improved code is as follows:

```
if(saleAmount >= 1000)
    commissionRate = 0.08;
else if(saleAmount >= 500)
    commissionRate = 0.06;
else commissionRate = 0.05;
```

In other words, because this example uses three commission rates, two boundaries should be checked. If there were four rates, there would be three boundaries, and so on.

Within a nested `if-else`, it is most efficient to ask the most likely question first. In other words, if you know that most `saleAmount` values are over $1000, compare `saleAmount` to that value first. That way, you most frequently avoid asking multiple questions. If, however, you know that most `saleAmount`s are small, you should ask `if(saleAmount < 500)` first.

USING AND AND OR APPROPRIATELY

Beginning programmers often use the AND operator when they mean to use OR, and often use OR when they should use AND. Part of the problem lies in the way we use the English language. For example, your boss might request, "Print an error message when an employee's hourly pay rate is under $5.65 and when an employee's hourly pay rate is over $60." Because your boss used the word "and" in the request, you might be tempted to write a program statement like the following:

```
if(payRate < 5.65 && payRate > 60)
   Console.WriteLine("Error in pay rate");
```

However, as a single variable, no `payRate` value can ever be both below 5.65 and over 60 at the same time, so the print statement can never execute, no matter what value the `payRate` has. In this case, you must write the following statement to print the error message under the correct circumstances:

```
if(payRate < 5.65 || payRate > 60)
    Console.WriteLine ("Error in pay rate");
```

Similarly, your boss might request, "Print the names of those employees in departments 1 and 2." Because the boss used the word "and" in the request, you might be tempted to write the following:

```
if(department == 1 && department == 2)
   Console.WriteLine ("Name is: {0}", name);
```

However, the variable `department` can never contain both a 1 and a 2 at the same time, so no employee name will ever be printed, no matter what department the employee is in.

USING NOT CORRECTLY

Whenever you use negatives, it is easy to make logical mistakes. For example, suppose your boss says, "Make sure if the sales code is not 'A' or 'B', the customer gets a 10% discount. You might be tempted to code the following:

```
if(salesCode != 'A' || salesCode != 'B')
    discount = 0.10;
```

However, this logic will result in every customer receiving the 10% discount because every `salesCode` is either not 'A' or not 'B'. For example, a `salesCode` of 'A' is not 'B'. The statement above is always `true`. The correct statement is one of the following:

```
if(salesCode != 'A' && salesCode != 'B')
    discount = 0.10;

if(!(salesCode == 'A' || salesCode == 'B'))
    discount = 0.10;
```

In the first example, if the `salesCode` is not 'A' and it also is not 'B', then the discount is applied correctly. In the second example, if the `salesCode` is 'A' or 'B', the inner Boolean expression is `true`, and the NOT operator (!) changes the evaluation to `false`, not applying the discount for 'A' or 'B' sales. You also could avoid the confusing negative situation by asking questions in a positive way, as in the following:

```
if(salesCode == 'A' || salesCode == 'B')
    discount = 0;
else
    discount = 0.10;
```

YOU DO IT

USING `if-else` STATEMENTS

In the next steps, you will write a program that requires using multiple, nested `if-else` statements to accomplish its goal—determining whether any of the three integers entered by a user are equal.

To create a program that uses nested `if-else` statements:

1. Open a new text file and write the first lines necessary for a `CompareThreeNumbers` class:

    ```
    using System;
    public class CompareThreeNumbers
    {
    ```

2. Begin a `Main()` method by declaring a string for input and three integers that will hold the input values.

    ```
    public static void Main()
    {
        string inputString;
        int num1, num2, num3;
    ```

3. Add the statements that retrieve the three integers from the user and assign them to the appropriate variables.

```
Console.Write("Enter an integer ");
numberString = Console.ReadLine();
num1 = Convert.ToInt32(numberString);
Console.Write("Enter an integer ");
numberString = Console.ReadLine();
num2 = Convert.ToInt32(numberString);
Console.Write("Enter an integer ");
numberString = Console.ReadLine();
num3 = Convert.ToInt32(numberString);
```

>> **NOTE**
In Chapter 6, you will learn to write methods, avoiding repetitive code like that shown here.

4. If the first number and the second number are equal, there are two possibilities: either the first is also equal to the third, in which case all three numbers are equal, or the first is not equal to the third, in which case only the first two numbers are equal. Insert the following code:

```
if(num1 == num2)
   if(num1 == num3)
      Console.Out.WriteLine("All three numbers are equal ");
   else
      Console.Out.WriteLine("First two are equal");
```

5. If the first two numbers are not equal, but the first and third are equal, print an appropriate message. For clarity, the `else` should vertically align under `if(num1 == num2)`.

```
else
   if(num1 == num3)
      Console.Out.WriteLine("First and last are equal");
```

6. When `num1` and `num2` are not equal, and `num1` and `num3` are not equal, but `num2` and `num3` are equal, display an appropriate message. For clarity, the `else` should vertically align under `if(num1 == num3)`.

```
   else
      if(num2 == num3)
         Console.Out.WriteLine("Last two are equal");
```

7. Finally, if none of the pairs (`num1` and `num2`, `num1` and `num3`, nor `num2` and `num3`) are equal, display an appropriate message. For clarity, the `else` should vertically align under `if(num2 == num3)`.

```
         else
            Console.Out.WriteLine
               ("No two numbers are equal");
```

8. Add a closing curly brace for the `Main()` method and a closing curly brace for the class.

MAKING DECISIONS

9. Save the file as **CompareThreeNumbers.cs** in the Chapter.03 folder on your Student Disk. Compile the program, then execute it several times, providing different combinations of equal and nonequal integers when prompted. Figure 3-17 shows several executions of the program.

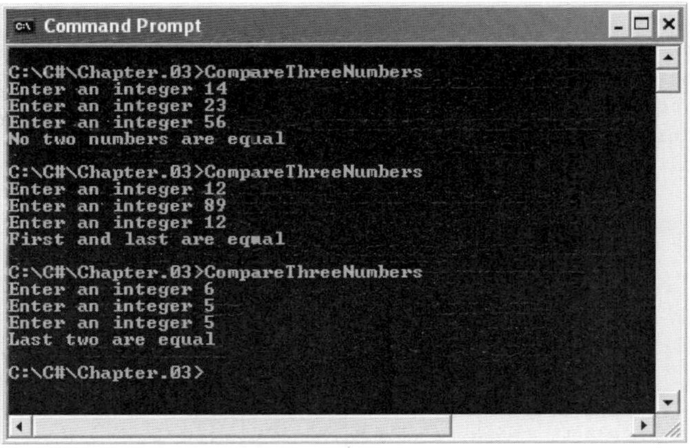

```
C:\C#\Chapter.03>CompareThreeNumbers
Enter an integer 14
Enter an integer 23
Enter an integer 56
No two numbers are equal

C:\C#\Chapter.03>CompareThreeNumbers
Enter an integer 12
Enter an integer 89
Enter an integer 12
First and last are equal

C:\C#\Chapter.03>CompareThreeNumbers
Enter an integer 6
Enter an integer 5
Enter an integer 5
Last two are equal

C:\C#\Chapter.03>
```

Figure 3-17 Several executions of the CompareThreeNumbers program

USING AND AND OR LOGIC

In the next steps, you will create an interactive program that allows you to test AND and OR logic for yourself. The program decides whether a delivery charge applies to a shipment. If the customer lives in Zone 1 or Zone 2, then shipping is free, as long as the order contains fewer than 10 boxes. If the customer lives in another zone or if the order is too large, then a delivery charge applies. First, you will create a program with incorrect logic; then you will fix it to demonstrate correct use of parentheses when combining ANDs and ORs.

To create the delivery charge program:

1. Open a new file in your text editor and enter the first few lines of the program. Define constants for ZONE1, ZONE2, and the LOWQUANTITY limit, as well as variables to hold the customer's input string, which will be converted to the zone and number of boxes in the shipment.

```
using System;
public class DemoORAndANDWrongLogic
{
    public static void Main()
    {
        const int ZONE1 = 1, ZONE2 = 2;
        const int LOWQUANTITY = 10;
        string inputString;
        int quantity;
        int deliveryZone;
```

2. Enter statements that describe the delivery charge criteria to the user and accept keyboard values for the customer's delivery zone and shipment size.

```
Console.Out.WriteLine("Delivery is free for zone {0} or {1}",
   ZONE1, ZONE2);
Console.WriteLine("when the number of boxes is less than {0}",
   LOWQUANTITY);
Console.WriteLine("Enter delivery zone ");
inputString = Console.ReadLine();
deliveryZone = Convert.ToInt32(inputString);
Console.WriteLine
   ("Enter the number of boxes in the shipment");
inputString = Console.ReadLine();
quantity = Convert.ToInt32(inputString);
```

3. Write a compound `if` statement that appears to test whether the customer lives in Zone 1 or 2 and has a shipment consisting of fewer than 10 boxes.

```
if(deliveryZone == ZONE1 || deliveryZone == ZONE2    &&
   quantity < LOWQUANTITY)
      Console.Out.WriteLine("Delivery is free");
else
   Console.Out.WriteLine("A delivery charge applies");
```

4. Add closing curly braces for the `Main()` method and for the class, and save the file as **DemoORAndANDWrongLogic.cs** in the Chapter.03 folder on your Student Disk. Compile and execute the program. Enter values for the zone and shipment size. The program appears to run correctly until you enter a shipment for Zone 1 that exceeds nine boxes. Such a shipment should not be free, but the output indicates that it is. Figure 3-18 shows the output.

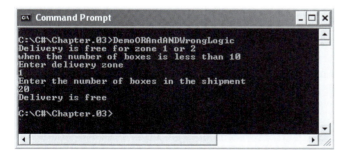

Figure 3-18 Sample execution of `DemoORAndANDWrongLogic` program

5. To remedy the problem, insert parentheses around the expression `deliveryZone == ZONE1 || deliveryZone == ZONE2` within the `if` statement in the `Main()` method. Change the class name to `DemoORAndAND` (removing *WrongLogic*). Save the new version of the program as **DemoORAndAND.cs**. When you compile and execute this version of the

program, every combination of zone and quantity values should work correctly. Figure 3-19 shows the output for a Zone 1 delivery of 20 boxes.

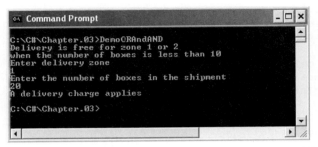

Figure 3-19 Output of DemoORAndAND program when user enters 1 and 20

CHAPTER SUMMARY

» A flowchart is a pictorial tool that helps you understand a program's logic. A decision structure is one that involves choosing between alternative courses of action based on some value within a program.

» You use an if statement to make a single-alternative decision. The if statement takes the form if(expression) statement;. When you want to execute multiple statements conditionally, you can place the statements within a block defined by curly braces.

» When you make a dual-alternative decision, you can use an if-else statement. The if-else statement takes the following form:

if(expression) statement1;
else statement2;

Just as you can block several statements so they all execute when an expression within an if is true, you can block multiple statements after an else so they all execute when the evaluated expression is false.

» You can use the conditional AND operator (or simply the AND operator) within a Boolean expression to determine whether two expressions are both true. The AND operator is written as two ampersands (&&). When you use the AND operator, you must include a complete Boolean expression on each side of the && operator.

» You can use the conditional OR operator (or simply the OR operator) when you want some action to occur when one or both of two conditions are true. The OR operator is written as ||.

» When you combine AND and OR operators within the same Boolean expression without parentheses, the AND operators take precedence, meaning their Boolean values are evaluated first.

» The switch statement tests a single variable against a series of exact matches.

» The conditional operator is used as an abbreviated version of the if-else statement. It requires three expressions separated with a question mark and a colon.

CHAPTER THREE

» You use the NOT operator, which is written as an exclamation point (!), to negate the result of any Boolean expression.

» Common errors when making decisions include using the assignment operator instead of the comparison operator, inserting a semicolon after the Boolean expression in an `if` statement, failing to block a set of statements when they should be blocked, failing to include a complete Boolean expression on each side of an `&&` or `||` operator in an `if` statement, performing a range check incorrectly or inefficiently, using the wrong operator with AND and OR, and using the NOT operator incorrectly.

KEY TERMS

Pseudocode is a tool that helps programmers plan a program's logic by writing plain English statements.

A **flowchart** is a tool that helps programmers plan a program's logic by writing program steps in diagram form, as a series of shapes connected by arrows.

A **sequence structure** is a unit of program logic in which one step follows another unconditionally.

A **decision structure** is a unit of program logic that involves choosing between alternative courses of action based on some value.

An **`if` statement** is used to make a single-alternative decision.

A **block** is one or more statements contained within a pair of curly braces.

A **nested `if`** statement is one in which one decision structure is contained within another.

Dual-alternative decisions have two possible outcomes.

An **`if-else` statement** performs a dual-alternative decision.

The **conditional AND operator** (or simply the **AND operator**) determines whether two expressions are both `true`; it is written using two ampersands (`&&`).

Short-circuit evaluation is the C# feature in which parts of an AND or OR expression are evaluated only as far as necessary to determine whether the entire expression is `true` or `false`.

The **conditional OR operator** (or simply the **OR operator**) determines whether at least one of two conditions is `true`; it is written using two pipes (`||`).

The **Boolean logical AND** operator determines whether two expressions are both `true`; it is written using a single ampersand (`&`). Unlike the conditional AND operator, it does not use short-circuit evaluation.

The **Boolean logical inclusive OR** operator determines whether at least one of two conditions is `true`; it is written using a single pipe (`|`). Unlike the conditional OR operator, it does not use short-circuit evaluation.

A **side effect** is an unintended consequence.

The **`switch` structure** tests a single variable against a series of exact matches.

105

MAKING DECISIONS

The keyword **switch** starts a `switch` structure.

The **switch expression** is a condition in a `switch` statement enclosed in parentheses.

The keyword **case** in a `switch` structure is followed by one of the possible values that might equal the `switch` expression.

A **case label** identifies a course of action in a `switch` structure.

The keyword **break** optionally terminates a `switch` structure at the end of each `case`.

The keyword **default** is used optionally prior to any action that should occur if the test expression in a `case` structure does not match any case.

The **governing type** of a `switch` statement is established by the `switch` expression. The governing type can be `sbyte`, `byte`, `short`, `ushort`, `int`, `uint`, `long`, `ulong`, `char`, `string`, or `enum`.

An **enum** is an enumeration—a programmer-defined type that declares a set of constants.

The **conditional operator** is used as an abbreviated version of the `if-else` statement; it requires three expressions separated by a question mark and a colon.

A **ternary** operator requires three arguments.

The **NOT operator** (!) negates the result of any Boolean expression.

A **range check** is a series of `if` statements that determine whether a value falls within a specified range.

REVIEW QUESTIONS

1. What is the output of the following code segment?

   ```
   int a = 3, b = 4;
   if(a == b)
      Console.Write("Black ");
      Console.WriteLine("White");
   ```

   a. Black   c. Black White
   b. White   d. nothing

2. What is the output of the following code segment?

   ```
   int a = 3, b = 4;
   if(a < b)
   {
      Console.Write("Black ");
      Console.WriteLine("White");
   }
   ```

   a. Black   c. Black White
   b. White   d. nothing

3. What is the output of the following code segment?
   ```
   int a = 3, b = 4;
   if(a > b)
      Console.Write("Black ");
   else
      Console.WriteLine("White");
   ```
   a. Black
   b. White
   c. Black White
   d. nothing

4. If the following code segment compiles correctly, what do you know about the variable x?
   ```
   if(x) Console.WriteLine("OK");
   ```
   a. x is an integer variable
   b. x is a Boolean variable
   c. x is greater than 0
   d. one of these

5. What is the output of the following code segment?
   ```
   int c = 6, d = 12;
   if(c > d);
      Console.Write("Green ");
      Console.WriteLine("Yellow");
   ```
   a. Green
   b. Yellow
   c. Green Yellow
   d. nothing

6. What is the output of the following code segment?
   ```
   int c = 6, d = 12;
   if(c < d)
      if(c > 8)
         Console.Write("Green");
      else
         Console.Write("Yellow");
   else
      Console.Write("Blue");
   ```
   a. Green
   b. Yellow
   c. Blue
   d. nothing

MAKING DECISIONS

7. What is the output of the following code segment?
   ```
   int e = 5, f = 10;
   if(e < f && f < 0)
      Console.Write("Red ");
   else
     Console.Write("Orange");
   ```

   a. Red
   b. Orange
   c. Red Orange
   d. nothing

8. What is the output of the following code segment?
   ```
   int e = 5, f = 10;
   if(e < f || f < 0)
      Console.Write("Red ");
   else
      Console.Write("Orange");
   ```

   a. Red
   b. Orange
   c. Red Orange
   d. nothing

9. Which of the following expressions is equivalent to the following code segment?
   ```
   if(g > h)
      if(g < k)
         Console.Write("Brown");
   ```

   a. if(g > h && g < k) Console.Write("Brown");
   b. if(g > h && < k) Console.Write("Brown");
   c. if(g > h || g < k) Console.Write("Brown");
   d. two of these

10. Which of the following expressions assigns true to a Boolean variable named isIDValid when the idNumber is greater than 1000, less than or equal to 9999, or equal to 123456?

    a. isIDValid = (idNumber > 1000 && idNumber <= 9999 && idNumber == 123456)
    b. isIDValid = (idNumber > 1000 && idNumber <= 9999 || idNumber == 123456)
    c. isIDValid = ((idNumber > 1000 && idNumber <= 9999) || idNumber == 123456)
    d. two of these

11. Which of the following expressions is equivalent to a || b && c || d?

    a. a && b || c && d
    b. (a || b) && (c || d)
    c. a || (b && c) || d
    d. two of these

12. How many case labels would a switch statement require to be equivalent to the following if statement?

    ```
    if(v == 1)
        Console.WriteLine("one");
    else
        Console.WriteLine("two");
    ```

    a. zero
    b. one
    c. two
    d. impossible to tell

13. Falling through a switch case is most often prevented by using the _____.

    a. break statement
    b. default statement
    c. case statement
    d. end statement

14. If the test expression in a switch does not match any of the case values, and there is no default value, then _____.

    a. a compiler error occurs
    b. a run-time error occurs
    c. the program continues with the next executable statement
    d. the expression is incremented and the case values are tested again

15. Which of the following is equivalent to the statement if (m == 0) d = 0 ; else d = 1;?

    a. ? m == 0 : d = 0, d = 1;
    b. m? d = 0; d = 1;
    c. m == 0 ; d = 0; d = 1?
    d. m == 0 ? d = 0 : d = 1;

16. Which of the following C# expressions is equivalent to a < b && b < c?

    a. c > b > a
    b. a < b && c >= b
    c. ! (b <= a) && b < c
    d. two of these

MAKING DECISIONS

17. Which of the following C# expressions means, "If `itemNumber` is not 8 or 9, add `TAX` to `price`"?

    a. `if(itemNumber != 8 || itemNumber != 9)`
        `price = price + TAX;`
    b. `if(itemNumber != 8 && itemNumber != 9)`
        `price = price + TAX;`
    c. `if(itemNumber != 8 && != 9)`
        `price = price + TAX;`
    d. two of these

18. Which of the following C# expressions means, "If `itemNumber` is 1 or 2 and `quantity` is 12 or more, add `TAX` to `price`"?

    a. `if(itemNumber = 1 || itemNumber = 2 && quantity >= 12)`
        `price = price + TAX;`
    b. `if(itemNumber == 1 || itemNumber == 2 || quantity >= 12)`
        `price = price + TAX;`
    c. `if(itemNumber == 1 && itemNumber == 2 && quantity >= 12)`
        `price = price + TAX;`
    d. none of these

19. Which of the following C# expressions means, "If `itemNumber` is 5 and `zone` is 1 or 3, add `TAX` to `price`"?

    a. `if(itemNumber == 5 && zone == 1 || zone == 3)`
        `price = price + TAX;`
    b. `if(itemNumber == 5 && (zone == 1 || zone == 3))`
        `price = price + TAX;`
    c. `if(itemNumber == 5 && (zone == 1 || 3))`
        `price = price + TAX;`
    d. two of these

20. Which of the following C# expressions means, "If `itemNumber` is not 100, add `TAX` to `price`"?

   a. `if(itemNumber != 100)`
      `price = price + TAX;`
   b. `if(!(itemNumber == 100))`
      `price = price + TAX;`
   c. `if(!(itemNumber <100) && !(itemNumber > 100))`
      `price = price + TAX;`
   d. all of these

EXERCISES

As you create each exercise, save the finished program in the Chapter.03 folder on your Student Disk.

1. Write a program that prompts the user for an hourly pay rate. If the value entered is less than $5.65, display an error message. Save the program as **CheckLowRate.cs**.

2. Write a program that prompts a user for an hourly pay rate. If the value entered is less than $5.65 or greater than $49.99, display an error message. Save the program as **CheckLowAndHighRate.cs**.

3. Write a program that prompts a user for an hourly pay rate. If the user enters values less than $5.65 or greater than $49.99, prompt the user again. If the user enters an invalid value again, display an appropriate error message. If the user enters a valid value on either the first or second attempt, display the pay rate as well as the weekly rate, which is calculated as 40 times the hourly rate. Save the program as **EnsureValidPayRate.cs**.

4. Write a program for a furniture company. Ask the user to choose *P* for pine, *O* for oak, or *M* for mahogany. Show the price of a table manufactured with the chosen wood. Pine tables cost $100, oak tables cost $225, and mahogany tables cost $310. (If the user enters something other than *P*, *O*, or *M*, set the price to 0.) Save the program as **Furniture.cs**.

5. Write a program for a college's admissions office. The user enters a numeric high school grade point average (for example, 3.2) and an admission test score. Print the message "Accept" if the student meets either of the following requirements:

   » A grade point average of 3.0 or higher and an admission test score of at least 60
   » A grade point average of less than 3.0 and an admission test score of at least 80

   If the student does not meet either of the qualification criteria, print "Reject". Save the program as **Admission.cs**.

MAKING DECISIONS

6. Write a program that prompts the user for an hourly pay rate and hours worked. Compute gross pay (hours times pay rate), withholding tax, and net pay (gross pay minus withholding tax). Withholding tax is computed as a percentage of gross pay based on the following:

Gross Pay	Withholding Percentage
Up to and including 300.00	10%
300.01 and up	12%

   Save the program as **Payroll.cs**.

7. Write a program that allows the user to enter two integers and a character. If the character is *A*, add the two integers. If it is *S*, subtract the second integer from the first. If it is *M*, multiply the integers. Display the results of the arithmetic. Save the file as **Calculate.cs**.

8. a. Write an application for a lawn-mowing service. The lawn-mowing season lasts 20 weeks. The weekly fee for mowing a lot under 400 square feet is $25. The fee for a lot that is 400 square feet or more, but under 600 square feet, is $35 per week. The fee for a lot that is 600 square feet or over is $50 per week. Prompt the user for the length and width of a lawn, and then print the weekly mowing fee, as well as the total fee for the 20-week season. Save the file as **Lawn.cs**.

   b. To the Lawn application you created in Exercise 8a, add a prompt that asks the user whether the customer wants to pay (1) once, (2) twice, or (3) 20 times per year. If the user enters 1 for once, the fee for the season is simply the seasonal total. If the customer requests two payments, each payment is half the seasonal fee plus a $5 service charge. If the user requests 20 separate payments, add a $3 service charge per week. Display the number of payments the customer must make, each payment amount, and the total for the season. Save the file as **Lawn2.cs**.

9. Write an application that asks a user to enter an IQ score. If the score is a number less than 0 or greater than 200, issue an error message; otherwise, issue an "above average", "average", or "below average" message for scores over, at, or under 100, respectively. Save the file as **IQ.cs**.

DEBUGGING EXERCISES

Each of the following files in the Chapter.03 folder on your Student Disk has syntax and/or logical errors. In each case, determine the problem and fix the program. After you correct the errors, save each file using the same filename preceded with *Fixed*. For example, save DebugThree1.cs as **FixedDebugThree1.cs**.

   a. DebugThree1.cs
   b. DebugThree2.cs
   c. DebugThree3.cs
   d. DebugThree4.cs

CHAPTER THREE

UP FOR DISCUSSION

1. In this chapter, you learned how computer programs make decisions. Insurance companies use programs to make decisions about your insurability, as well as the rates you will be charged for health and life insurance policies. For example, certain preexisting conditions may raise your insurance premiums considerably. Is it ethical for insurance companies to access your health records and then make insurance decisions about you?

2. Job applications are sometimes screened by software that makes decisions about a candidate's suitability based on keywords in the applications. For example, when a help-wanted ad lists "management experience," the presence of those exact words might determine which résumés are chosen for further scrutiny. Is such screening fair to applicants?

3. Medical facilities often have more patients waiting for organ transplants than there are available organs. Suppose you have been asked to write a computer program that selects which of several candidates should receive an available organ. What data would you want on file to use in your program, and what decisions would you make based on the data? What data do you think others might use that you would not use?

CHAPTER FOUR

4

LOOPING

In this chapter you will:

Learn about the loop structure
Learn how to create loops using the `while` statement
Learn how to create loops using the `for` statement
Learn how to create loops using the `do` statement
Use nested loops
Accumulate totals
Understand how to improve loop performance

LOOPING

In Chapter 3, you learned how computers make decisions. Looping allows a program to repeat tasks based on a decision. For example, programs that produce thousands of paychecks or invoices rely on the ability to loop to repeat instructions. Likewise, programs that repeatedly prompt you for a valid credit card number or for the correct answer to a tutorial question require the ability to loop to do their jobs efficiently. In this chapter, you will learn to create loops in C# programs.

LEARNING ABOUT THE LOOP STRUCTURE

> **NOTE**
> One execution of any loop is called an **iteration**.

If making decisions is what makes programs seem smart, looping is what makes programs seem powerful. A **loop** is a structure that allows repeated execution of a block of statements. Within a looping structure, a Boolean expression is evaluated. If it is `true`, a block of statements called the **loop body** executes, and the Boolean expression is evaluated again. As long as the expression is `true`, the statements in the loop body continue to execute. When the Boolean evaluation is `false`, the loop ends. Figure 4-1 shows a diagram of the logic of a loop.

> **NOTE**
> Recall from Chapter 3 that a block of statements might be a single statement with or without curly braces, or it might be multiple statements with curly braces.

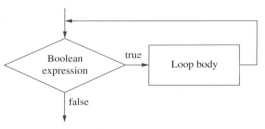

Figure 4-1 Flowchart of a loop structure

In C#, you can use several mechanisms to create loops. In this chapter, you will learn to use three types of loops:

» A `while` loop, in which the loop-controlling Boolean expression is the first statement in the loop
» A `for` loop, which is usually used as a concise format in which to execute loops
» A `do` loop (or `do-while` loop), in which the loop-controlling Boolean expression is the last statement in the loop

USING THE `while` LOOP

> **NOTE**
> The evaluated Boolean expression in a `while` statement can be a compound expression that uses ANDs and ORs (just as within an `if` statement).

You can use a **`while` loop** to execute a body of statements continuously as long as some condition continues to be `true`. A `while` loop consists of the keyword `while`, followed by a Boolean expression within parentheses, followed by the body of the loop. The body can be a single statement or a block of statements surrounded by curly braces.

For example, the following code shows an integer declaration followed by a loop that causes the message "Hello" to display (theoretically) forever because there is no code to end the loop. A loop that never ends is called an **infinite loop**.

```
int number = 1;
while (number > 0)
   Console.WriteLine("Hello");
```

In this loop, the expression `number > 0` evaluates as `true`, and "Hello" is displayed. The expression `number > 0` evaluates as `true` again and "Hello" is displayed again. Because nothing ever alters the value of `number`, the loop runs forever, evaluating the same Boolean expression and printing "Hello" (as long as computer memory and hardware allow).

> **» NOTE** An infinite loop does not actually execute infinitely. All programs run with the help of computer memory and hardware, both of which have finite capacities.

> **» NOTE** It is always a bad idea to write an infinite loop, although even experienced programmers write them by accident. If you ever find yourself in the midst of executing an infinite loop, you can break out by holding down the Ctrl key and pressing the C key or the Break (Pause) key.

To make a `while` loop end correctly, three separate actions should occur:

» A variable, the **loop control variable**, is initialized (before entering the loop).
» The loop control variable is tested in the `while` expression.
» The body of the `while` statement must take some action that alters the value of the loop control variable (so that the `while` expression eventually evaluates as `false`).

For example, the code in Figure 4-2 shows a loop that displays "Hello" four times. The variable `number` is initialized to 1. Then the shaded `while` expression compares `number` to 5, finds it is less than 5, and so the loop body executes. The loop body shown in Figure 4-2 consists of two statements made into a block by surrounding them with curly braces. The first statement prints "Hello" and the second statement adds 1 to `number`. The next time `number` is evaluated, its value is 2, which is still less than 5, so the loop body executes again. "Hello" prints a third time and the `number` becomes 4, then "Hello" prints a fourth time and the `number` becomes 5. Now when the expression `number < 5` evaluates, it is `false`, so the loop ends. If there were any subsequent statements following the `while` loop's closing curly brace, they would execute after the loop was finished.

```
using System;
public class FourHellos
{
   public static void Main()
   {
      int number = 1;
      while(number < 5)
      {
         Console.WriteLine("Hello");
         number = number + 1;
      }
   }
}
```

Figure 4-2 A program containing a `while` loop whose body executes four times

LOOPING

> **NOTE** To an algebra student, a statement such as number = number + 1; looks wrong—a value can never be one more than itself. In C# (and many other programming languages), however, the expression number = number + 1; isn't a mathematical equation; rather, it is a programming language statement that takes the value of number, adds 1 to it, and assigns the new value back into number.

The curly braces surrounding the body of the while loop in Figure 4-2 are important. If they are omitted, the while loop ends at the end of the "Hello" statement. Adding 1 to number would no longer be part of the loop body, so an infinite loop would be created. Even if the statement number = number + 1; was indented under the while statement, it would not be part of the loop without the surrounding curly braces.

Also, if a semicolon is mistakenly placed at the end of the partial statement, as in the following, then the loop is also infinite:

```
int number = 1;
while (number < 5);
{
       Console.WriteLine("Hello");
       number = number + 1;
}
```

This loop has an **empty body**, or a body with no statements in it. In this case, number is initialized to 1, the Boolean expression number < 5 evaluates, and because it is true, the loop body is entered. Because the loop body is empty, ending at the semicolon, no action takes place, and the Boolean expression evaluates again. It is still true (nothing has changed), so the empty body is entered again, and the infinite loop continues. The program can never progress to either the statement that displays "Hello" or the statement that increases the value of number. The fact that these two statements are blocked using curly braces has no effect because of the incorrectly placed semicolon.

Within a correctly functioning loop's body, you can change the value of the loop control variable in a number of ways. Many loop control variable values are altered by **incrementing**, or adding to them, as in Figure 4-2. Other loops are controlled by reducing, or **decrementing**, a variable and testing whether the value remains greater than some benchmark value. Such a loop, for which the number of iterations is predetermined, is called a **definite loop** or **counted loop**. Often, the value of a loop control variable is not altered by arithmetic, but instead is altered by user input. For example, perhaps you want to continue performing some task while the user indicates a desire to continue. In that case, you do not know when you write the program whether the loop will be executed two times, 200 times, or not at all. This type of loop is an **indefinite loop**.

Consider a program that displays a bank balance and asks if the user wants to see what the balance will be after one year of interest has accumulated. Each time the user indicates she wants to continue, an increased balance appears. When the user finally indicates she has had enough, the program ends. The program appears in Figure 4-3, and a typical execution appears in Figure 4-4.

CHAPTER FOUR

```
using System;
public class LoopingBankBal
{
    public static void Main()
    {
        double bankBal = 1000;
        double intRate = 0.04;
        string inputString;
        char response;
        Console.Write("Do you want to see your balance? Y or N ...");
        inputString = Console.ReadLine();
        response = Convert.ToChar(inputString);
        while(response == 'Y' )
        {
            Console.WriteLine("Bank balance is {0}", bankBal.ToString("C"));
            bankBal = bankBal + bankBal * intRate;
            Console.Write("Do you want to see next year's balance? Y or N ...");
            inputString = Console.ReadLine();
            response = Convert.ToChar(inputString);
        }
        Console.WriteLine("Have a nice day!");
    }
}
```

Figure 4-3 LoopingBankBal program

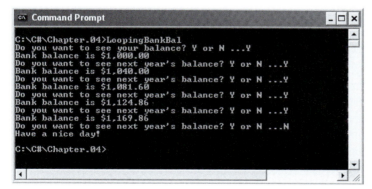

Figure 4-4 Typical execution of the LoopingBankBal program

>> **NOTE** The program shown in Figure 4-3 continues to display bank balances while the response is *Y*. It could also be written to display while the response is not *N*, as in while (response != 'N').... A value such as 'Y' or 'N' that a user must supply to stop a loop is called a **sentinel value**.

119

LOOPING

The program shown in Figure 4-3 contains three variables that are involved in the looping process: a bank balance, an interest rate, and a response. The `response` is the loop control variable. It is initialized when the program asks the user, "Do you want to see your balance?" and reads the response. The loop control variable is tested with `while(response == 'Y')`. If the user types any response other than Y, then the loop body never executes; instead, the next statement to execute is the display of "Have a nice day!". However, if the user enters Y, then all four statements within the loop body execute. The current balance is displayed, and the program increases the balance by the interest rate value; this value will not be displayed unless the user requests another loop repetition. Within the loop, the program prompts the user and reads in a new value for `response`. This is the statement that potentially alters the loop control variable. The loop ends with a closing curly brace, and program control returns to the top of the loop, where the Boolean expression in the `while` loop is tested again. If the user typed Y at the last prompt, then the loop is entered and the increased `bankBal` value that was calculated during the last loop cycle is finally displayed.

> **» NOTE**
> In C#, character data is case sensitive. If a program tests `response == 'Y'`, a user response of y will result in a `false` evaluation.

USING THE for LOOP

Each time the `LoopingBankBal` program in Figure 4-3 executes, the user might continue the loop a different number of times, which makes it an indefinite loop. You can use a `while` loop for either definite or indefinite loops. To write either type of `while` loop, you initialize a loop control variable, and as long as its test expression is `true`, you continue to execute the body of the `while` loop. To avoid an infinite loop, the body of the `while` loop must contain a statement that alters the loop control variable.

Because you need definite loops so frequently when you write programs, C# provides a shorthand way to create such a loop. This shorthand structure is called a **for loop**. With a `for` loop, you can indicate the starting value for the loop control variable, the test condition that controls loop entry, and the expression that alters the loop control variable, all in one convenient place.

You begin a `for` statement with the keyword `for` followed by a set of parentheses. Within the parentheses are three sections separated by exactly two semicolons. The three sections are usually used for:

» Initializing the loop control variable
» Testing the loop control variable
» Updating the loop control variable

The body of the `for` statement follows the parentheses. As with an `if` or a `while` statement, you can use a single statement as the body of a `for` loop, or you can use a block of statements enclosed in curly braces. The `while` and `for` statements shown in Figure 4-5 produce the same output—the integers 1 through 10.

Within the parentheses of the `for` statement shown in Figure 4-5, the initialization section prior to the first semicolon sets a variable named x to 1. The program will execute this statement once, no matter how many times the body of the `for` loop eventually executes.

> **» NOTE**
> Recall that `++x` increases the value of x by 1. You learned about the shortcut arithmetic operators in Chapter 2.

120

```
// Declare loop control variable and limit
int x;
const int LIMIT = 10
// Using a while loop to display 1 through 10
x = 1;
while(x <= LIMIT)
{
    Console.WriteLine(x);
    ++x;
}

// Using a for loop to display 1 through 10
for(x = 1; x <= LIMIT; ++x)
    Console.WriteLine(x);
```

Figure 4-5 Printing integers 1 through 10 with `while` and `for` loops

After the initialization expression executes, program control passes to the middle, or test, section of the `for` statement. If the Boolean expression found there evaluates to `true`, then the body of the `for` loop is entered. In the program segment shown in Figure 4-5, x is initialized to 1, so when x <= LIMIT is tested, it evaluates to `true` and the loop body prints the value of x.

After the loop body executes, the final one-third of the `for` expression (the update section) executes, and x increases to 2. Following the third section, program control returns to the second (test) section, where x is compared to LIMIT a second time. Because the value of x is 2, it is still less than or equal to LIMIT, so the body of the `for` loop executes. The value of x is displayed. Then the third, altering portion of the `for` statement executes again. The variable x increases to 3, and the `for` loop continues.

Eventually, when x is *not* less than or equal to LIMIT (after 1 through 10 have printed), the `for` loop ends, and the program continues with any statements that follow the `for` loop.

Although the three sections of the `for` loop are most commonly used for initializing, testing, and incrementing, you can also perform other tasks:

» You can initialize more than one variable by placing commas between the separate statements, as in the following:
   ```
   for(g = 0, h = 1; g < 6; ++g)
   ```

» You can declare a new variable, as in the following:
   ```
   for(int k = 0; k < 5; ++k)
   ```

   This technique is used frequently when the variable exists only to control the loop and for no other purpose. When a variable is declared inside a loop, as k is in this example, it can be referenced only for the duration of the loop body; then it is out of scope.

LOOPING

» You can perform more than one test by evaluating compound conditions, as in the following:
```
for(g = 0; g < 3 && h > 1; ++g)
```

» You can decrement or perform some other task at the end of the loop's execution, as in:
```
for(g = 5; g >= 1; --g)
```

» You can leave one or more portions of the for expression empty, although the two semi-colons are still required as placeholders to separate the three sections.

Generally, you should use the for loop for its intended purpose, which is a shorthand way of programming a definite loop.

Just as with a decision or a while loop, statements in a for loop can be blocked. For example, the following loop displays "Hello" and "Goodbye" four times each:
```
for(var = 0; var < 4; ++var)
{
    Console.WriteLine("Hello");
    Console.WriteLine("Goodbye");
}
```

>> **NOTE**
You will learn about a similar loop, the foreach loop, when you study arrays in Chapter 5.

Without the curly braces in this code, "Hello" would be displayed four times, but "Goodbye" would be displayed only once.

USING THE do LOOP

With each of the loops you have learned about so far, the loop body might execute many times, but it is also possible that the loop will not execute at all. For example, recall the bank balance program that displays compound interest, part of which is shown in Figure 4-6. The loop begins by testing the value of response. If the user has not entered Y, the loop body never executes. The while loop checks a value at the "top" of the loop before the body has a chance to execute.

```
Console.Write("Do you want to see your balance? Y or N ...");
inputString = Console.ReadLine();
response = Convert.ToChar(inputString);
while(response == 'Y' )
{
    Console.WriteLine("Bank balance is {0}", bankBal.ToString("C"));
    bankBal = bankBal + bankBal * intRate;
    Console.Write("Do you want to see next year's balance? Y or N ...");
    inputString = Console.ReadLine();
    response = Convert.ToChar(inputString);
}
```

Figure 4-6 Part of the bank balance program using a while loop

CHAPTER FOUR

Sometimes you might need a loop body to execute at least one time. If so, you want to write a loop that checks at the "bottom" of the loop after the first iteration. The **do loop** checks the bottom of the loop after one repetition has occurred. Figure 4-7 shows a diagram of the structure of a do loop.

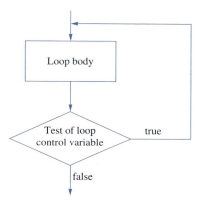

Figure 4-7 Flowchart of a do loop

Figure 4-8 shows a do loop for a bank balance program. The loop starts with the keyword do. The body of the loop follows and is contained within curly braces. Within the loop, the next balance is calculated and the user is prompted for a response. The Boolean expression that controls loop execution is written using a while statement, placed after the loop body. The bankBal variable is output the first time before the user has any option of responding. At the end of the loop, the user is prompted, "Do you want to see next year's balance? Y or N . . .". Now the user has the option of seeing more balances, but the first view of the balance was unavoidable. The user's response is checked at the bottom of the loop. If it is Y, then the loop repeats.

```
do
{
    Console.WriteLine("Bank balance is {0}", bankBal.ToString("C"));
    bankBal = bankBal + bankBal * intRate;
    Console.Write("Do you want to see next year's balance? Y or N ...");
    inputString = Console.ReadLineGetChar();
    response = Convert.ToChar(inputString);
} while(response == 'Y')
```

Figure 4-8 Part of the bank balance program using a do loop

> **NOTE** In a do loop, as a matter of style, many programmers prefer to align the while expression with the do keyword that starts the loop. Others feel that placing the while expression on its own line increases the chances that readers might misinterpret the line as the start of its own while statement instead of marking the end of a do statement.

123

LOOPING

> **NOTE**
> A while loop is a **pretest loop**—one in which the loop control variable is tested before the loop body executes. The do-while loop is a **posttest loop**—one in which the loop control variable is tested after the loop body executes.

In any situation where you want to loop, you are never required to use a do loop. Within the bank balance example, you could unconditionally display the bank balance once, prompt the user, and then start a while loop that might not be entered. However, when you know you want to perform some task at least one time, the do loop is convenient.

USING NESTED LOOPS

Just as if statements can be nested, so can loop statements. You can place a while loop within a while loop, a for loop within a for loop, a while loop within a for loop, or any other combination. When loops are nested, each pair contains an **inner loop** and an **outer loop**. The inner loop must be entirely contained within the outer loop; loops can never overlap. Figure 4-9 shows a diagram in which the shaded loop is nested within another loop; the shaded area is the inner loop as well as the body of the outer loop.

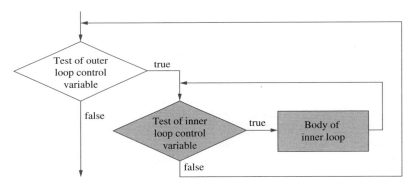

Figure 4-9 Nested loops

Suppose you want to display future bank balances for different years at a variety of interest rates. Figure 4-10 shows an application that contains an outer loop controlled by interest rates (starting with the first shaded statement in the figure) and an inner loop controlled by years (starting with the second shaded statement). The application displays annually compounded interest on $1000 at 4%, 6%, and 8% interest rates for 1 through 5 years. Figure 4-11 shows the output.

When you use a loop within a loop, you should always think of the outer loop as the all-encompassing loop. When you describe the task at hand, you often use the word "each" to refer to the inner loop. For example, if you wanted to print balances for different interest rates each year for 10 years, you could use the following nested for loops:

```
for(rate = 0.03; rate <= 0.07; rate += 0.01)
    for(year = 1; year <= 10; ++year)
```

```csharp
using System;
public class LoopingBankBal2
{
    public static void Main()
    {
        double bankBal;
        double rate;
        int year;
        const double START_BAL = 1000;
        const double START_INT = 0.04;
        const double INT_INCREASE = 0.02;
        const double LAST_INT = 0.08;
        const int END_YEAR = 5;
        for(rate = START_INT; rate <= LAST_INT; rate += INT_INCREASE)
        {
            bankBal = START_BAL;
            Console.WriteLine("Starting bank balance is {0}",
                bankBal.ToString("C"));
            Console.WriteLine("   Interest Rate: {0}",
                rate.ToString("P"));
            for(year = 1; year <= END_YEAR; ++year)
            {
                bankBal = bankBal + bankBal * rate;
                Console.WriteLine("    After year {0}, bank balance is {1}",
                    year, bankBal.ToString("C"));
            }
        }
    }
}
```

Figure 4-10 The LoopingBankBal2 program

However, if you wanted to print balances for years 1 through 10 for each possible interest rate, you would use the following:

```
for(year = 1; year <= 10; ++year)
   for(rate = 0.03; rate <= 0.07; rate += 0.01)
```

In both of these examples, the same 50 values would be displayed—five different interest rates for 10 years. However, in the first example, balances for years 1 through 10 would display "within" each interest rate, and in the second example, each balance for each interest rate would display "within" each year, 1 through 10.

LOOPING

```
C:\C#\Chapter.04>LoopingBankBal2
Starting bank balance is $1,000.00
  Interest Rate: 4.00 %
    After year 1, bank balance is $1,040.00
    After year 2, bank balance is $1,081.60
    After year 3, bank balance is $1,124.86
    After year 4, bank balance is $1,169.86
    After year 5, bank balance is $1,216.65
Starting bank balance is $1,000.00
  Interest Rate: 6.00 %
    After year 1, bank balance is $1,060.00
    After year 2, bank balance is $1,123.60
    After year 3, bank balance is $1,191.02
    After year 4, bank balance is $1,262.48
    After year 5, bank balance is $1,338.23
Starting bank balance is $1,000.00
  Interest Rate: 8.00 %
    After year 1, bank balance is $1,080.00
    After year 2, bank balance is $1,166.40
    After year 3, bank balance is $1,259.71
    After year 4, bank balance is $1,360.49
    After year 5, bank balance is $1,469.33

C:\C#\Chapter.04>
```

Figure 4-11 Output of the `LoopingBankBal2` program

ACCUMULATING TOTALS

Many computer programs display totals. When you receive a credit card or telephone service bill, you are usually provided with individual transaction details, but you are most interested in the total bill. Similarly, some programs total the number of credit hours generated by college students, the gross payroll for all employees of a company, or the total accounts receivable value for an organization. These totals are **accumulated**—that is, gathered together and added into a final sum by processing individual records one at a time in a loop.

Figure 4-12 shows an example of an interactive program that accumulates the user's total purchases. The program prompts the user to enter a purchase price or 0 to quit. While the user continues to enter nonzero values, the amounts are added to a total. With each pass through the loop, the total is calculated to be its current amount plus the new purchase amount. After the user enters the loop-terminating 0, the accumulated total can be displayed. Figure 4-13 shows a typical program execution.

In the application in Figure 4-12, it is very important that the `total` variable used for accumulation is initialized to 0. When it is not, the program will not compile. When `total` is not initialized, it might hold any value. The value could be 0 by chance, but it also could be any other value that happens to be located at the memory address of `total`. An unknown value is known as **garbage**. The C# compiler prevents you from seeing an incorrect total by requiring you to provide a starting value; C# will not use the garbage value that happens to be stored at an uninitialized memory location.

CHAPTER FOUR

```
using System;
public class TotalPurchase
{
   public static void Main()
   {
      double purchase;
      double total = 0;
      string inputString;
      Console.WriteLine("Enter purchase amount ");
      inputString = Console.ReadLine();
      purchase = Convert.ToDouble(inputString);
      while(purchase != 0)
      {
         total += purchase;
         Console.WriteLine("Enter next purchase amount, or 0 to quit ");
         inputString = Console.ReadLine();
         purchase = Convert.ToDouble(inputString);
      }
      Console.WriteLine("Your total is {0}", total.ToString("C"));
   }
}
```

Figure 4-12 An application that accumulates total purchases entered by the user

Figure 4-13 Typical execution of the `TotalPurchase` program

»NOTE In the application in Figure 4-12, the `total` variable must be initialized to 0, but the `purchase` variable is uninitialized. Many programmers would say it makes no sense to initialize this variable because no matter what starting value you provide, the value can be changed by the first input statement before the variable is ever used. As a matter of style, this book will not initialize a variable if the initialization value is never used; doing so might mislead you into thinking the starting value had some purpose.

IMPROVING LOOP PERFORMANCE

Whether you decide to use a `while`, `for`, or `do-while` loop in an application, you can improve loop performance by making sure the loop does not include unnecessary operations or statements. For example, suppose a loop should execute while x is less than the sum of two integers, a and b. The loop could be written as:

```
while (x < a + b)
    // loop body
```

If this loop executes 1000 times, then the expression a + b is calculated 1000 times. Instead, if you use the following code, the results are the same, but the arithmetic is performed only once:

```
int sum = a + b;
while(x < sum)
    // loop body
```

Of course, if a or b is altered in the loop body, then a new sum must be calculated with every loop iteration. However, if the sum of a and b is fixed prior to the start of the loop, then writing the code the second way is far more efficient. You should always be on the lookout for ways to improve program performance.

YOU DO IT

USING A while LOOP

In the next steps, you will write a program that continuously prompts the user for a valid ID number until the user enters an ID that is acceptable. For this application, assume that a valid ID number must be between 1000 and 9999 inclusive.

To create an application that verifies an ID number:

1. Open a new file in your text editor and enter the beginning of the program. It begins by declaring variables for an ID number, the user's input, and constant values for the highest and lowest acceptable ID numbers.

   ```
   using System;
   public class ValidID
   {
       public static void Main()
       {
           int idNum;
           string input;
           const int LOW = 1000;
           const int HIGH = 9999;
   ```

2. Add code to prompt the user for an ID number and to then convert it to an integer.

   ```
   Console.Write("Enter an ID number: ");
   input = Console.ReadLine();
   idNum = Convert.ToInt32(input);
   ```

CHAPTER FOUR

3. Create a loop that continues while the entered ID number is out of range. While the number is invalid, explain valid ID parameters and reprompt the user, converting the input to an integer.

    ```
    while(idNum < LOW || idNum > HIGH)
    {
        Console.WriteLine("{0} is an invalid ID number", idNum);
        Console.Write("ID numbers must be ");
        Console.WriteLine("between {0} and {1} inclusive",
            LOW, HIGH);
        Console.Write("Enter an ID number: ");
        input = Console.ReadLine();
        idNum = Convert.ToInt32(input);
    }
    ```

4. When the user eventually enters a valid ID number, the loop ends. Display a message and add closing curly braces for the `Main()` method and for the class.

    ```
            Console.WriteLine("ID number {0} is valid", idNum);
        }
    }
    ```

5. Save the file as **ValidID.cs** in the Chapter.04 folder on your Student Disk. Compile and execute the program. A typical execution during which the user makes several invalid entries is shown in Figure 4-14.

Figure 4-14 Typical execution of `ValidID` program

USING for LOOPS

In the next steps, you will write a program that creates a tipping table. Restaurant patrons can use this table to approximate the correct tip for meal prices from $10 to $100, at tipping percentage rates from 10 percent to 25 percent. The program uses several loops.

LOOPING

To create the tipping table:

1. Open a new file in your text editor and enter the beginning of the program. It begins by declaring variables to use for the price of a dinner, a tip percentage rate, and the amount of the tip.

    ```
    using System;
    public class TippingTable
    {
        public static void Main()
        {
            double dinnerPrice = 10.00;
            double tipRate = 0.10;
            double tip;
    ```

2. To create a heading for the table, display "Price". (For alignment, insert three spaces after the quotes and before the *P* in *Price*.) On the same line, use a loop that displays every tip rate from 0.10 through 0.25 in increments of 0.05. In other words, the tip rates are 0.10, 0.15, 0.20, and 0.25. Complete the heading for the table using a `WriteLine()` statement that advances the cursor to the next line of output and a `WriteLine()` statement that displays a dashed line.

    ```
    Console.Write("   Price");
    for(tipRate = 0.10; tipRate <= 0.25; tipRate += 0.05)
        Console.Write("{0, 8}",tipRate.ToString("F"));
    Console.WriteLine();
    Console.WriteLine("----------------------------------------");
    ```

    > **NOTE** Recall that within a `for` loop, the expression before the first semicolon executes once, the middle expression is tested, the loop body executes, and then the expression to the right of the second semicolon executes. In other words, 0.05 is not added to `tipRate` until after the `tipRate` displays on each cycle through the loop.

    > **NOTE** As an alternative to typing 40 dashes in the `WriteLine()` statement, you could use the following loop to display a single dash 40 times. When the 40 dashes are completed, use `WriteLine()` to advance the cursor to a new line.
    > ```
    > for(int x = 0; x < 40; ++x)
    >     Console.Write("-");
    > Console.WriteLine();
    > ```

3. Reset `tipRate` to 0.10. You must reset the rate because after the last loop, the rate will have been increased to greater than 0.25.

    ```
    tipRate = 0.10;
    ```

4. Create a nested loop that continues while the `dinnerPrice` remains 100.00 or less. Each iteration of this loop displays one row of the tip table. Within this loop, display the `dinnerPrice`, then loop to display four tips while the `tipRate` varies from 0.10 through 0.25. At the end of the loop, increase the `dinnerPrice` by 10.00, reset the `tipRate` to 0.10 so it is ready for the next row, and write a new line to advance the cursor.

CHAPTER FOUR

```
while(dinnerPrice <= 100.00)
{
    Console.Write("{0, 8}", dinnerPrice.ToString("C"));
    while(tipRate <= 0.25)
    {
        tip = dinnerPrice * tipRate;
        Console.Write("{0, 8}",tip.ToString("F"));
        tipRate += 0.05;
    }
    dinnerPrice += 10.00;
    tipRate = 0.10;
    Console.WriteLine();
}
```

» NOTE
Recall that the {0, 8} format string in the Write() statements displays the first argument in fields that are eight characters wide. You learned about format strings in Chapter 2.

5. Add two closing curly braces—one for the Main() method and one for the class.
6. Save the file as **TippingTable.cs** in the Chapter.04 folder on your Student Disk. Compile and execute the program. The output looks like Figure 4-15.

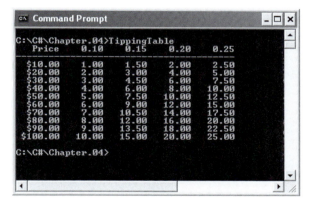

Figure 4-15 Output of TippingTable program

» NOTE In the exercises at the end of this chapter, you will be instructed to make an interactive version of the TippingTable program in which many of the values are input by the user instead of being coded into the program as unnamed constants.

CHAPTER SUMMARY

» A loop is a structure that allows repeated execution of a block of statements. Within a looping structure, a Boolean expression is evaluated. As long as it is true, a block of statements called the loop body executes and the Boolean expression is evaluated again.

LOOPING

- » You can use a `while` loop to execute a body of statements continuously while some condition continues to be `true`. A `while` loop consists of the keyword `while`, followed by a Boolean expression within parentheses, followed by the body of the loop, which can be a single statement or a block of statements surrounded by curly braces.
- » When you use a `for` statement, you can indicate the starting value for the loop control variable, the test condition that controls loop entry, and the expression that alters the loop control variable, all in one convenient place. You begin a `for` statement with the keyword `for`, followed by a set of parentheses. Within the parentheses are three sections that are separated by exactly two semicolons. The three sections are typically used to initialize, test, and update the loop control variable.
- » The `do` loop checks the bottom of the loop after one repetition has occurred.
- » You can nest any combination of loops to achieve desired results.
- » In computer programs, totals frequently are accumulated—that is, gathered together and added into a final sum by processing individual records one at a time in a loop.
- » You can improve loop performance by making sure the loop does not include unnecessary operations or statements.

KEY TERMS

A **loop** is a structure that allows repeated execution of a block of statements.

A **loop body** is the block of statements executed in a loop.

An **iteration** is one execution of any loop.

A **`while` loop** executes a body of statements continuously while some condition continues to be `true`; it uses the keyword `while`.

An **infinite loop** is one that (theoretically) never ends.

A **loop control variable** determines whether loop execution will continue.

An **empty body** has no statements in it.

Incrementing a variable means adding a value to it. (Specifically, the term often means to add 1 to a variable.)

Decrementing a variable means subtracting a value from it. (Specifically, the term often means to subtract 1 from a variable.)

In a **definite loop**, the number of iterations is predetermined.

A **counted loop** is a definite loop.

In an **indefinite loop**, the number of iterations is not predetermined.

A **sentinel value** is one that a user must supply to stop a loop.

A **`for` loop** contains the starting value for the loop control variable, the test condition that controls loop entry, and the expression that alters the loop control variable, all in one statement.

The **`do` loop** checks the bottom of the loop after one repetition has occurred.

CHAPTER FOUR

In a **pretest loop**, the loop control variable is tested before the loop body executes.

In a **posttest loop**, the loop control variable is tested after the loop body executes.

An **inner loop** is the loop in a pair of nested loops that is entirely contained within another loop.

An **outer loop** is the loop in a pair of nested loops that contains another loop.

Accumulated totals are added into a final sum by processing individual records one at a time in a loop.

An unknown memory value is known as **garbage**.

REVIEW QUESTIONS

1. A structure that allows repeated execution of a block of statements is a _____ .
   a. selection
   b. loop
   c. sequence
   d. array

2. The body of a `while` loop can consist of _____ .
   a. a single statement
   b. a block of statements within curly braces
   c. either a or b
   d. neither a nor b

3. A loop that never ends is called a(n) _____ loop.
   a. `while`
   b. `for`
   c. counted
   d. infinite

4. Which of the following is not required of a loop control variable in a correctly working loop?
   a. It is initialized before the loop starts.
   b. It is tested.
   c. It is reset to its initial value before the loop ends.
   d. It is altered in the loop body.

5. A `while` loop with an empty body contains no _____ .
   a. loop control variable
   b. statements
   c. curly braces
   d. test within the parentheses of the `while` statement

LOOPING

6. A loop for which you do not know the number of iterations is a _____ .
   a. definite loop
   b. indefinite loop
   c. counted loop
   d. `for` loop

7. What is the major advantage of using a `for` loop instead of a `while` loop?
   a. With a `for` loop, it is impossible to create an infinite loop.
   b. It is the only way to achieve an indefinite loop.
   c. Unlike with a `while` loop, the execution of multiple statements can depend on the test condition.
   d. The loop control variable is initialized, tested, and altered all in one place.

8. A `for` loop statement must contain _____ .
   a. two semicolons
   b. three commas
   c. four dots
   d. five pipes

9. In a `for` statement, the section before the first semicolon executes _____ .
   a. once
   b. once prior to each loop iteration
   c. once after each loop iteration
   d. one less time than the initial loop control variable value

10. The three sections of the `for` loop are most commonly used for _____ the loop control variable.
    a. testing, printing, and incrementing
    b. initializing, testing, and incrementing
    c. incrementing, selecting, and testing
    d. initializing, converting, and displaying

11. Which loop is most convenient to use if the loop body must always execute at least once?
    a. a `do` loop
    b. a `while` loop
    c. a `for` loop
    d. an `if` loop

12. The loop control variable is checked at the bottom of which kind of loop?
    a. a `while` loop
    b. a `do` loop
    c. a `for` loop
    d. all of the above

13. A for loop is an example of a(n) _____ loop.
    a. untested   c. posttest
    b. pretest   d. infinite

14. A while loop is an example of a(n) _____ loop.
    a. untested   c. posttest
    b. pretest   d. infinite

15. When a loop is placed within another loop, the loops are said to be _____ .
    a. infinite   c. nested
    b. bubbled   d. overlapping

16. What does the following code segment display?
    ```
    a = 1;
    while (a < 5);
    {
        Console.Write("{0} ", a);
        ++a;
    }
    ```
    a. 1 2 3 4   c. 4
    b. 1   d. nothing

17. What is the output of the following code segment?
    ```
    s = 1;
    while (s < 4)
        ++s;
        Console.Write(" {0} ", s);
    ```
    a. 1   c. 1 2 3 4
    b. 4   d. 2 3 4

18. What is the output of the following code segment?
    ```
    j = 5;
    while(j > 0)
    {
        Console.Write("{0} ", j);
        j--;
    }
    ```
    a. 0   c. 5 4 3 2 1
    b. 5   d. 5 4 3 2 1 0

19. What does the following code segment display?
    ```
    for(f = 0; f < 3; ++f);
        Console.Write("{0}  ", f);
    ```
    a. 0
    b. 0 1 2
    c. 3
    d. nothing

20. What does the following code segment display?
    ```
    for(t = 0; t < 3; ++t)
        Console.Write("{0}  ", t);
    ```
    a. 0
    b. 0 1
    c. 0 1 2
    d. 0 1 2 3

EXERCISES

As you create each exercise, save the finished program in the Chapter.04 folder of your Student Disk.

1. Write a program that allows the user to enter any number of integer values continuously (in any order) until the user enters 999. Display the sum of the values entered, not including 999. Save the file as **Sum.cs**.

2. Write a program that asks the user to type a vowel from the keyboard. If the character entered is a vowel, display "OK"; if it is not a vowel, display an error message. Be sure to allow both uppercase and lowercase vowels. The program continues until the user types '!'. Save the file as **GetVowel.cs**.

3. Write a program that prompts a user for an hourly pay rate. While the user enters values less than $5.65 or greater than $49.99, continue to prompt the user. Save the program as **EnsureValidPayRateLoop.cs**.

4. Three salespeople work at Sunshine Hot Tubs—Andrea, Brittany, and Eric. Write a program that prompts the user for a salesperson's initial ('A', 'B', or 'E'). While the user does not type 'Z', continue by prompting for the amount of a sale the salesperson made. Calculate the salesperson's commission as 10 percent of the sale amount, and add the commission to a running total for that salesperson. After the user types 'Z' for an initial, display each salesperson's total commission earned. Save the file as **TubSales.cs**.

5. Display a multiplication table that shows the product of every integer from 1 through 10 multiplied by every integer from 1 through 10. Save the file as **MultiplicationTable.cs**.

6. Write a program that prints all even numbers from 2 to 100, inclusive. Save the file as **EvenNums.cs**.

7. Write a program that prints every integer value from 1 to 20, along with its squared value. Save the file as **TableOfSquares.cs**.

8. Write a program that sums the integers from 1 to 50. Save the file as **Sum50.cs**.

9. Write a program that prints every perfect number from 1 through 1000. A number is perfect if it equals the sum of all the smaller positive integers that divide evenly into it. For example, 6 is perfect because 1, 2, and 3 divide evenly into it and their sum is 6. Save the file as **Perfect.cs**.

10. In the "You Do It" section of this chapter, you created a tipping table for patrons to use when analyzing their restaurant bills. Modify the program so that each of the following values is obtained from user input:

    » The lowest tipping percentage
    » The highest tipping percentage
    » The lowest possible restaurant bill
    » The highest restaurant bill

    Save the file as **TippingTable2.cs**.

DEBUGGING EXERCISES

Each of the following files in the Chapter.04 folder on your Student Disk has syntax and/or logical errors. In each case, determine the problem and fix the program. After you correct the errors, save each file using the same filename preceded with *Fixed*. For example, save DebugFour1.cs as **FixedDebugFour1.cs**.

a. DebugFour1.cs
b. DebugFour2.cs
c. DebugFour3.cs
d. DebugFour4.cs

UP FOR DISCUSSION

1. Suppose you wrote a program that you suspect is in an infinite loop because it keeps running for several minutes with no output and without ending. What would you add to your program to help you discover the origin of the problem?

2. Suppose that every employee in your organization has a seven-digit logon ID number for retrieving personal information, some of which might be sensitive in nature. For example, each employee has access to his own salary data and insurance claim information, but not to the information of others. Writing a loop would be useful to guess every combination of seven digits in an ID. Are there any circumstances in which you should try to guess another employee's ID number?

CHAPTER FIVE

5

USING ARRAYS

In this chapter you will:

Declare an array and assign values to array elements
Initialize an array
Use subscripts to access array elements
Use the Length property
Use foreach to control array access
Search an array to find an exact match
Search an array to find a range match
Use the BinarySearch() method
Use the Sort() and Reverse() methods
Use multidimensional arrays

USING ARRAYS

Storing values in variables provides programs with flexibility—a program that uses variables to replace constants can manipulate different values each time the program executes. When you add loops to your programs, the same variable can hold different values during successive cycles through the loop within the same program execution. This ability makes the program even more flexible. Learning to use the data structure known as an array provides you with further flexibility—you can store multiple values in adjacent memory locations and access them by varying a value that indicates which of the stored values you want to use. In this chapter, you will learn to create and manage C# arrays.

DECLARING AN ARRAY AND ASSIGNING VALUES TO ARRAY ELEMENTS

Sometimes, storing just one value in memory at a time isn't adequate. For example, a sales manager who supervises 20 employees might want to determine whether each employee has produced sales above or below the average amount. When you enter the first employee's sales figure into a program, you can't determine whether it is above or below average, because you won't know the average until you have entered all 20 figures. You might plan to assign 20 sales figures to 20 separate variables, each with a unique name, then sum and average them. That process is awkward and unwieldy, however—you need 20 prompts, 20 read statements using 20 separate storage locations, and 20 addition statements. This method might work for 20 salespeople, but what if you have 30, 40, or 10,000 salespeople?

A superior approach is to assign the sales value to the same variable in 20 successive iterations through a loop that contains one prompt, one read statement, and one addition statement. Unfortunately, when you read in the sales value for the second employee, that data item replaces the figure for the first employee, and the first employee's value is no longer available to compare to the average of all 20 values. When the data-entry loop finishes, the only sales value left in memory is the last one entered.

The best solution to this problem is to create an array. An **array** is a list of data items that all have the same data type and the same name. (As you will learn shortly, each item in the list is distinguished from the others by an index.) You declare an array variable in the same way as you declare any other variable, but you insert a pair of square brackets after the type. For example, to declare an array of `double` values to hold sales figures for salespeople, you write `double[] sales;`.

> **NOTE** In some programming languages, such as C++ and Java, you also can declare an array variable by placing the square brackets after the array name, as in `double sales[];`. This format is illegal in C#.

After you create an array variable, you still need to create the actual array. Declaring an array and actually reserving memory space for it are two distinct processes. To reserve memory locations for 20 `sales` objects, you declare the array variable with the following two statements:

```
double[] sales;
sales = new double[ 20 ];
```

CHAPTER FIVE

The keyword **new** is also known as the **new operator**; it is used to create objects. In this case, it creates 20 separate `sales`. You also can declare and create an array in one statement, such as the following:

```
double[] sales = new double[20];
```

>> **NOTE**
You will learn about creating other objects using the `new` operator in Chapter 7.

>> **NOTE** You can change the size of an array associated with an identifier, if necessary. For example, if you declare `int[] array;`, you can assign five elements later with `array = new int[5];`; later in the program, you might alter the array size to 100 with `array = new int[100];`. Still later, you could alter it again to be either larger or smaller. This feature is not allowed in most other programming languages. If you resize an array in this manner, the same identifier refers to a new array in memory and all the values are set to 0.

The statement `double[] sales = new double[20];` reserves 20 memory locations for 20 `sales` objects. Each object in an array is an **array element**. You can distinguish each element from the others in an array with a subscript. A **subscript** (also called an **index**) is an integer contained within square brackets that indicates the position of one of an array's elements. In C#, an array's elements are numbered beginning with 0, so you can legally use any subscript from 0 through 19 when working with an array that has 20 elements. In other words, the first `sales` array element is `sales[0]` and the last `sales` element is `sales[19]`. Figure 5-1 shows how the array of 20 sales figures appears in computer memory. The figure assumes that the array begins at memory address 20000. Because an `int` takes four bytes of storage, each element of the array is stored in succession at an address that is four bytes higher than the previous one.

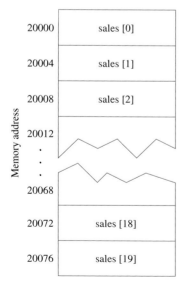

Figure 5-1 An array of 20 `sales` items in memory

>> **NOTE** In C#, an array subscript must be an integer. For example, no array contains an element with a subscript of 1.5.

>> **NOTE** The first element in an array is sometimes called the "zeroth element."

USING ARRAYS

>> **NOTE** When you instantiate an array, you cannot choose its location in memory any more than you can choose the location of any other variable. However, you do know that after the first array element, the subsequent elements will follow immediately.

>> **NOTE** Some other languages, such as COBOL, BASIC, and Visual Basic, use parentheses rather than square brackets to refer to individual array elements. By using brackets, the creators of C# made it easier for you to distinguish arrays from methods. Like C#, C++ and Java also use brackets surrounding array subscripts.

A common mistake is to forget that the first element in an array is element 0, especially if you know another programming language in which the first array element is element 1. Making this mistake means you will be "off by one" in your use of any array.

>> **NOTE** If you are "off by one" but still using a valid subscript when accessing an array element, your program will produce incorrect output. If you are "off by one" so that your subscript becomes larger than the highest value allowed, you will cause a program error.

>> **NOTE** To remember that array elements begin with element 0, it might be helpful to think of the first array element as being "zero elements away from" the beginning of the array, the second element as being "one element away from" the beginning of the array, and so on.

When you work with any individual array element, you treat it no differently than you treat a single variable of the same type. For example, to assign a value to the first sales in an array, you use a simple assignment statement, such as the following:

```
sales[ 0] = 2100.00;
```

To print the last sales in a 20-element array, you write:

```
Console.WriteLine(sales[ 19] );
```

>> **NOTE** An array subscript can be an expression, as long as the expression evaluates to an integer. For example, if x and y are integers and their sum is at least 0 but less than the size of an array named array, then it is legal to refer to array[x + y].

INITIALIZING AN ARRAY

In C#, arrays are objects. When you instantiate an array, you are creating a specific instance of a class named System.Array. When you declare objects, their numeric fields initialize to 0, character fields are set to '\0' or null, and bool fields are set to false. For example, when

CHAPTER FIVE

you initialize an array with a statement such as the following, each of the five elements of `someNums` has a value of 0 because `someNums` is a numeric array object:

```
int[] someNums = new int[ 5];
```

You already know how to assign a different value to a single element of an array, as in `someNums[ 0] = 46;`. You also can assign nondefault values to array elements upon creation. To initialize an array to nondefault values, you use a list of values that are separated by commas and enclosed within curly braces. For example, if you want to create an array named `myScores` and store five test scores within the array, you can use any of the following declarations:

```
int[] myScores = new int[ 5] {100, 76, 88, 100, 90};
int[] myScores = new int[] {100, 76, 88, 100, 90};
int[] myScores = {100, 76, 88, 100, 90};
```

The list of values provided for an array is an **initializer list**. When you initialize an array by providing a size and an initializer list, as in the first example, the stated size and number of list elements must match. However, when you initialize an array by giving it values upon creation, you are not required to give the array a size, as shown in the second example; in that case, the size is assigned based on the number of values in the initializing list. The third example shows that when you initialize an array, you do not need to use the keyword `new` and repeat the type; instead, new memory is assigned based on the stated array type and the length of the list of provided values. Use the form of array initialization that is clearest to you.

> **»NOTE** When you use curly braces at the end of a block of code, you do not follow the closing curly brace with a semicolon. Conversely, when you use curly braces to enclose a list of array values, you must complete the statement with a semicolon.

> **»NOTE** Programmers who have used other languages such as C++ and Java might expect that when an initialization list is shorter than the number of declared array elements, the "extra" elements will be set to default values. This is not the case in C#; if you declare a size, then you must list a value for each element.

USING SUBSCRIPTS TO ACCESS ARRAY ELEMENTS

If you treat each array element as an individual entity, there isn't much of an advantage to declaring an array over declaring individual variables. The power of arrays becomes apparent when you use subscripts that are variables rather than constant values.

For example, when you declare an array of five integers, such as the following, you often want to perform the same operation on each array element:

```
int[] myScores = {100, 76, 88, 100, 90};
```

USING ARRAYS

To increase each array element by 3, for example, you can write the following five statements:

```
myScores[ 0]   +=   3;
myScores[ 1]   +=   3;
myScores[ 2]   +=   3;
myScores[ 3]   +=   3;
myScores[ 4]   +=   3;
```

With five array elements, this task is manageable. However, you can shorten the task by using a variable as the subscript. Then you can use a loop to perform arithmetic on each element in the array. For example:

```
for(int sub = 0; sub < 5; ++sub)
   myScores[ sub]  += 3;
```

The variable `sub` is declared and initialized to 0, then compared to 5. Because it is less than 5, the loop executes and `myScores[ 0]` increases by 3. The variable `sub` is incremented and becomes 1, which is still less than 5, so when the loop executes again, `myScores[ 1]` increases by 3, and so on. A process that took five statements now takes only one. Additionally, if the array had 100 elements, the first method of individually increasing the array values by 3 would require 95 additional statements. The only change required using the `for` loop would be to compare `sub` to 100 instead of 5.

> **»NOTE** New array users sometimes think there is a permanent connection between a variable used as a subscript and the array with which it is used, but that is not the case. For example, if you vary `sub` from 0 to 10 to fill an array, you do not need to use `sub` later when displaying the array elements—either the same variable or a different variable can be used as a subscript elsewhere in the program.

USING THE `Length` PROPERTY

When you work with array elements, you must ensure that the subscript you use remains in the range of 0 through one less than the length. If you declare an array with five elements and use a subscript that is negative or more than 4, you will receive the error message "IndexOutOfRangeException" when you run the program. This message means the index, or subscript, does not hold a value that legally can access an array element. When you declare an array of five integers, as in the following example, you can access all five elements by coding the number 5 explicitly within the middle expression in the `for` statement. The example displays all five scores, each separated by a space:

```
int[ ] myScores = { 100, 76, 88, 100, 90};
for(int sub = 0; sub < 5; ++sub)
    Console.WriteLine("{ 0} ", myScores[ sub] );
```

If you modify your program to hold more or fewer array elements, you must remember to change every reference to the array size within the program. Many text editors have a "find and replace" feature that lets you change (for example) all of the 5s either simultaneously or one by one. However, you must be careful not to change 5s that have nothing to do with the array; for example, the program might also have a stored interest rate variable holding 5 percent. A better technique is to use a named constant that holds the array size and use it to control the loop, as in the following:

```
const int MY_ARRAYS_LENGTH = 5;
for(sub = 0; sub < MY_ARRAYS_LENGTH; ++sub)...
```

That way, if you change the size of the array, it always will use the correct maximum length.

Because every array automatically is a member of the class **System.Array**, you can use the fields and methods that are part of the System.Array class with any array you create. The **Length property** is a member of the System.Array class and automatically holds an array's length. Instead of creating your own variable or constant, it is most efficient to use this property, which always updates to reflect any changes you make to your array's size. The following segment of code displays "Array size is 5" and subsequently displays the array's contents:

```
int[] myScores = { 100, 76, 88, 100, 90};
Console.WriteLine("Array size is {0}", myScores.Length);
for(int x = 0; x < myScores.Length; ++x)
    Console.WriteLine(myScores[ x] );
```

> **NOTE**
> An array's Length is a read-only property—you cannot assign it a new value. It is capitalized, like all property identifiers. You will create property identifiers for your own classes in Chapter 7.

USING foreach TO CONTROL ARRAY ACCESS

You can easily navigate through arrays using a for or while loop that varies a subscript from 0 to Array.Length – 1. C# also supports a **foreach statement** that you can use to cycle through every array element without using a subscript. With the foreach statement, you provide a temporary **iteration variable** that automatically holds each array value in turn.

For example, the following code prints each element in the payRate array in sequence:

```
double[] payRate = { 6.00, 7.35, 8.12, 12.45, 22.22};
foreach(double money in payRate)
    Console.WriteLine("{0} ", money.ToString("C"));
```

The variable money is declared as a double within the foreach statement. During the execution of the loop, money holds each payRate value in turn—first, payRate[0] , then payRate[1] , and so on. As a simple variable, money does not require a subscript, making it easier to work with.

The foreach statement is used only under certain circumstances:

» You typically use foreach only when you want to access every array element; to access only selected array elements, you must manipulate subscripts using some other technique—for example, using a for loop or while loop.
» The foreach iteration variable is read-only—that is, you cannot assign a value to it. If you want to assign a value to array elements, you must use a different type of loop.

SEARCHING AN ARRAY FOR AN EXACT MATCH

When you want to determine whether some variable holds one of many possible valid values, one option is to use a series of `if` statements to compare the variable to a series of valid values. For example, suppose that a company manufactures 10 items. When a customer places an order for an item, you need to determine whether the item number is valid. If valid item numbers are sequential, say 101 through 110, then the following simple `if` statement that uses a logical AND operator can verify the order number and set a Boolean field to `true`:

```
if(itemOrdered >= 101 && itemOrdered <= 110)
    isValidItem = true;
```

If the valid item numbers are nonsequential, however—for example, 101, 108, 201, 213, 266, 304, and so on—you must code the following deeply nested `if` statement or a lengthy OR comparison to determine the validity of an item number:

```
if(itemOrdered == 101)
    isValidItem = true;
else if(itemOrdered == 108)
    isValidItem = true;
else if(itemOrdered == 201)
    isValidItem = true;
// and so on
```

> **NOTE**
> You might prefer to declare the `validValues` array as a constant. Presumably, the valid item numbers should not change during program execution.

USING A `for` LOOP TO SEARCH AN ARRAY

Instead of creating a long series of `if` statements, a more elegant solution is to compare the `itemOrdered` variable to a list of values in an array. You can initialize the array with the valid values by using the following statement:

```
int[] validValues = { 101, 108, 201, 213, 266, 304, 311,
    409, 411, 412};
```

Next, you can use a `for` statement to loop through the array and set a Boolean variable to `true` when a match is found:

> **NOTE**
> In place of the `for` loop, you could use a `foreach` loop.

```
for(int x = 0; x < validValues.Length; ++x)
    if(itemOrdered == validValues[ x] )
        isValidItem = true;
```

This simple `for` loop replaces the long series of `if` statements. What's more, if a company carries 1000 items instead of 10, then the list of valid items in the array must be altered, but the `for` statement does not change at all. As an added bonus, if you set up another array as a **parallel array** with the same number of elements and corresponding data, you

CHAPTER FIVE

can use the same subscript to access additional information. For example, if the 10 items your company carries have 10 different prices, then you can set up any array to hold those prices as follows:

```
double[] prices = { 0.89, 1.23, 3.50, 0.69…} ; // and so on
```

The prices must appear in the same order as their corresponding item numbers in the `validValues` array. Now the same `for` loop that finds the valid item number also finds the price, as shown in Figure 5-2. In other words, if the item number is found in the second position in the `validValues` array, then you can find the correct price in the second position in the `prices` array.

>> **NOTE**
If you initialize parallel arrays, it is convenient to use spacing so that the corresponding values visually align on the screen or printed page.

```
int[] validValues = { 101,   108,    201,   213,   266,
   304,   311,   409,   411,   412} ;
double[] prices =   { 0.89, 1.23, 3.50, 0.69, 5.79,
   3.19, 0.99, 0.89, 1.26, 8.00} ;
double itemPrice;
for(int x = 0; x < validValues.Length; ++x)
{
    if(itemOrdered == validValues[ x] )
    {
        isValidItem = true;
        itemPrice = prices[ x] ;
    }
}
```

Figure 5-2 Accessing information in parallel arrays

Within the code shown in Figure 5-2, you compare every `itemOrdered` with each of the 10 `validValues`. Even when an `itemOrdered` is equivalent to the first value in the `validValues` array (101), you always make nine additional cycles through the array. On each of these nine additional iterations, the comparison between `itemOrdered` and `validValues[ x]` is always `false`. As soon as a match for an `itemOrdered` is found, it is most efficient to break out of the `for` loop early. An easy way to accomplish this task is to set x to a high value within the block of statements executed when a match is found. Then, after a match, the `for` loop will not execute again because the limiting comparison (x < validValues.Length) will have been surpassed. Figure 5-3 shows this approach.

Instead of the statement that sets x to `validValues.Length` when a match is found, as in Figure 5-3, you could remove that statement and change the comparison in the middle section of the `for` statement to a compound statement, as follows:

```
for(int x = 0; x < validValues.Length && !isValidItem; ++x) …
```

147

USING ARRAYS

```
for(int x = 0; x < validValues.Length; ++x)
{
    if(itemOrdered == validValues[ x] )
    {
        isValidItem = true;
        itemPrice = prices[ x] ;
        x = validValues.Length;
            // break out of loop when you find a match
    }
}
```

Figure 5-3 Breaking out of a `for` loop early

As another alternative, you could remove the statement that sets x to `validValues.Length` and place a `break` statement within the loop in its place. Some programmers disapprove of breaking out of a `for` loop early, whether by setting a variable's value or by using a `break` statement. They argue that programs are easier to debug and maintain if each program segment has only one entry and one exit point. If you (or your instructor) agree with this philosophy, then select a method that uses a `while` statement, as described next.

> **NOTE** In an array with many possible matches, it is most efficient to place the most common items first, so they are matched right away. For example, if item 311 is ordered most often, place 311 first in the `validValues` array and its price ($0.99) first in the `prices` array.

USING A while LOOP TO SEARCH AN ARRAY

As an alternative to using a `for` or `foreach` loop to search an array, you can use a `while` loop to search for a match. Using this approach, you set a subscript to 0 and, while the `itemOrdered` is not equal to a value in the array, increase the subscript and keep looking. You search only while the subscript remains lower than the number of elements in the array. If the subscript increases to match `validValues.Length`, then you never found a match in the 10-element array. If the loop ends before the subscript reaches `validValues.Length`, then you found a match and the correct price can be assigned to the `itemPrice` variable. Figure 5-4 shows a complete program that contains this approach.

In the `FindItem` application in Figure 5-4, the variable used as a subscript, x, is set to 0 and the Boolean variable `isValidItem` is `false`. In the shaded portion of the figure, while the subscript remains smaller than the length of the array of valid item numbers, and while the user's requested item does not match a valid item, the subscript is increased so that subsequent array values can be tested. The `while` loop ends when a match is found or the array tests have been exhausted, whichever comes first. When the loop ends, if x is not equal to the

```
using System;
public class FindItem
{
   public static void Main()
   {
      int x;
      string inputString;
      int itemOrdered;
      double itemPrice = 0;
      bool isValidItem;
      int[] validValues = {101,  108,   201,   213,   266,
         304,   311,  409,  411,   412};
      double[] prices =   {0.89, 1.23, 3.50, 0.69, 5.79,
         3.19,  0.99, 0.89, 1.26, 8.00};
      Console.Write("Enter item number ");
      inputString = Console.ReadLine();
      itemOrdered = Convert.ToInt32(inputString);
      x = 0;
      isValidItem = false;
      while(x < validValues.Length &&
            itemOrdered != validValues[ x] )
               ++x;
      if(x != validValues.Length)
      {
         isValidItem = true;
         itemPrice = prices[ x] ;
      }
      if(isValidItem)
         Console.WriteLine("Item { 0}  sells for { 1} ",
            itemOrdered, itemPrice.ToString("C"));
      else
            Console.WriteLine("No such item as { 0} ",
               itemOrdered);
   }
}
```

Figure 5-4 The FindItem program that searches with a while loop

size of the array, then a valid item has been found and its price can be determined. Figure 5-5 shows two executions of the program. In the first execution, a match is found; in the second, an invalid item number is entered, so no match is found.

> **NOTE** In the fourth line of the Main() method in Figure 5-4, itemPrice is set to 0. Setting this variable is required, because its value is later altered only if an item number match is found in the validValues array. When C# determines that a variable's value is set depending on an if statement, C# will not allow you to display the variable, because the compiler assumes the variable might not have been set to a valid value.

USING ARRAYS

Figure 5-5 Two executions of the `FindItem` application

SEARCHING AN ARRAY FOR A RANGE MATCH

Searching an array for an exact match is not always practical. For example, suppose your mail-order company gives customer discounts based on the quantity of items ordered. Perhaps no discount is given for any order of fewer than a dozen items, but increasing discounts are available for orders of increasing quantities, as shown in Figure 5-6.

Total Quantity Ordered	Discount (%)
1 to 12	None
13 to 49	10
50 to 99	14
100 to 199	18
200 or more	20

Figure 5-6 Discount table for a mail-order company

One awkward, impractical option is to create a single array to store the discount rates. You could use a variable named `numOfItems` as a subscript to the array, but the array would need hundreds of entries, such as the following:

> **NOTE**
> Notice that 13 zeroes are listed in the discount array in this example. The first array element has a zero subscript (and a zero discount for zero items). The next 12 discounts (1 through 12 items) also have zero discounts.

```
double[] discount = { 0, 0, 0, 0, 0, 0, 0, 0, 0, 0,
    0, 0, 0, 0.10, 0.10, 0.10 ...}; // and so on
```

When `numOfItems` is 3, for example, then `discount[ numOfItems]` or `discount[ 3]` is 0. When `numOfItems` is 14, then `discount[ numOfItems]` or `discount[ 14]` is 0.10. Because a customer might order thousands of items, the array would need to be ridiculously large.

A better option is to create parallel arrays. One array will hold the five discount rates, and the other array will hold five discount range limits. Then you can perform a **range match** by determining the pair of limiting values between which a customer's order falls. The Total

150

CHAPTER FIVE

Quantity Ordered column in Figure 5-6 shows five ranges. If you use only the first figure in each range, then you can create an array that holds five low limits:

```
int[] discountRangeLimit = {1, 13, 50, 100, 200};
```

A parallel array will hold the five discount rates:

```
double[] discount = {0, 0.10, 0.14, 0.18, 0.20};
```

Then, starting at the last `discountRangeLimit` array element, for any `numOfItems` greater than or equal to `discountRangeLimit[ 4 ]`, the appropriate discount is `discount[ 4 ]`. In other words, for any `numOfItems` less than `discountRangeLimit[ 4 ]`, you should decrement the subscript and look in a lower range. Figure 5-7 shows the code.

```
// assume numOfItems is a declared integer for which a user
// has input a value
int[] discountRangeLimit = {1,    13,    50,   100,   200};
double[] discount =         {0,  0.10, 0.14,  0.18,  0.20};
double customerDiscount;
int sub = 4;
while(sub >= 0 && numOfItems < discountRangeLimit[ sub ])
    --sub;
customerDiscount = discount[ sub ];
```

Figure 5-7 Searching an array of ranges

USING THE BinarySearch() METHOD

You have already learned that because every array in C# automatically is a member of the `System.Array` class, you can use the `Length` property. Additionally, the `System.Array` class contains a variety of useful, built-in methods.

The **BinarySearch() method** finds a requested value in a sorted array. Instead of employing the logic you used to find a match in the last section, you can take advantage of this built-in method to locate a value within an array, as long as the array items are organized in ascending order.

>> **NOTE** You already have used many built-in C# methods such as `WriteLine()` and `ReadLine()`. You will learn to write your own methods in Chapter 6.

>> **NOTE** A binary search is one in which a sorted list of objects is split in half repeatedly as the search gets closer and closer to a match. Perhaps you have played a guessing game, trying to guess a number from 1 to 100. If you asked, "Is it less than 50?," then continued to narrow your guesses upon hearing each subsequent answer, then you have performed a binary search.

Figure 5-8 shows a program that declares an array of integer `idNumbers` arranged in ascending order. The program prompts a user for a value, converts it to an integer, and, rather than using a loop to examine each array element and compare it to the entered value, simply passes the array and the entered value to the `BinarySearch()` method in the shaded

USING ARRAYS

statement. The method returns –1 if the value is not found in the array; otherwise, it returns the array position of the sought value. Figure 5-9 shows two executions of this program.

```
using System;
public class BinarySearchDemo
{
    public static void Main()
    {
        int[] idNumbers = {122, 167, 204, 219, 345};
        int x;
        string entryString;
        int entryId;
        Console.Write("Enter an Employee ID ");
        entryString = Console.ReadLine();
        entryId = Convert.ToInt32(entryString);
        x = Array.BinarySearch(idNumbers, entryId);
        if(x < 0)
            Console.WriteLine("ID {0} not found", entryId);
        else
            Console.WriteLine("ID {0} found at position {1} ",
                entryId, x);
    }
}
```

Figure 5-8 `BinarySearchDemo` program

Figure 5-9 Two executions of the `BinarySearchDemo` program

When you use the following statement, you send a string to the `Write()` method:

```
Console.Write("Enter an Employee ID ");
```

When you use the following statement, you get a value back from the `ReadLine()` method:

```
entryString = Console.ReadLine();
```

In Figure 5-8, the following single statement both sends a value to a method and gets a value back:

```
x = Array.BinarySearch(idNumbers, entryId);
```

CHAPTER FIVE

The statement calls the method that performs the search, returning a –1 or the position where `entryId` was found; that value is then stored in `x`. This single line of code is easier to write, less prone to error, and easier to understand than writing a loop to cycle through the `idNumbers` array looking for a match. Still, it is worthwhile to understand how to perform the search without the `BinarySearch()` method, as you learned while studying parallel arrays. You will need to use that technique under the following conditions, when the `BinarySearch()` method proves inadequate:

» If your array items are not arranged in ascending order, the `BinarySearch()` method does not work correctly.

» If your array holds duplicate values and you want to find all of them, the `BinarySearch()` method doesn't work—it can return only one value, so it returns the position of the first matching value it finds. This matching position is the one closest to the middle of the array.

» If you want to find a range match rather than an exact match, the `BinarySearch()` method does not work.

USING THE `Sort()` AND `Reverse()` METHODS

The `System.Array` class contains other useful methods you can use to manipulate your arrays. As with the `BinarySearch()` method, you could write all of these methods yourself. C# provides them as a convenience, however.

The **`Sort()` method** arranges array items in ascending order. Ascending order is lowest to highest; it works numerically for number types and alphabetically for characters and strings. To use the method, you pass the array name to `Array.Sort()`, and the element positions within the array are rearranged appropriately. Figure 5-10 shows a program that sorts an array of strings; Figure 5-11 shows its execution.

```
using System;
public class SortArray
{
    public static void Main()
    {
        string[] names = {"Olive", "Patty",
            "Richard", "Ned", "Mindy"};
        int x;
        Array.Sort(names);
        for(x = 0; x < names.Length; ++x)
            Console.WriteLine(names[ x] );
    }
}
```

Figure 5-10 SortArray program

153

USING ARRAYS

Figure 5-11 Execution of SortArray program

> **» NOTE**
> Because the BinarySearch() method requires that array elements be sorted in order, the Sort() method is often used in conjunction with it.

> **» NOTE**
> When you Reverse() an array that contains an odd number of elements, the middle element will remain in its original location.

The **Reverse() method** reverses the order of items in an array. In other words, for any array, the element that starts in position 0 is relocated to position Length - 1, the element that starts in position 1 is relocated to position Length - 2, and so on until the element that starts in position Length - 1 is relocated to position 0. You call the Reverse() method the same way you call the Sort() method—you simply pass the array name to the method. Figure 5-12 shows a program that uses Reverse() with an array of strings, and Figure 5-13 shows its execution.

> **» NOTE**
> The Reverse() method does not sort array elements; it only rearranges their positions to the opposite order.

```
using System;
public class ReverseArray
{
    public static void Main()
    {
        string[] names = { "Zach", "Rose", "Wendy", "Marcia"};
        int x;
        Array.Reverse(names);
        for(x = 0; x < names.Length; ++x)
            Console.WriteLine(names[ x] );
    }
}
```

Figure 5-12 ReverseArray program

```
C:\C#\Chapter.05>ReverseArray
Marcia
Wendy
Rose
Zach

C:\C#\Chapter.05>
```

Figure 5-13 Execution of ReverseArray program

CHAPTER FIVE

USING MULTIDIMENSIONAL ARRAYS

When you declare an array such as `double[] sales = new double[20];`, you can envision the declared integers as a column of numbers in memory, as shown at the beginning of this chapter in Figure 5-1. In other words, you can picture the 20 declared numbers stacked one on top of the next. An array that you can picture as a column of values, and whose elements you can access using a single subscript, is a **one-dimensional** or **single-dimensional array**.

> **NOTE**
> You can think of the single dimension of a single-dimensional array as the height of the array.

C# also supports **multidimensional arrays**—those that require multiple subscripts to access the array elements. The most commonly used multidimensional arrays are two-dimensional arrays that are rectangular. **Two-dimensional arrays** have two or more columns of values for each row, as shown in Figure 5-14. In a **rectangular array**, each row has the same number of columns. You must use two subscripts when you access an element in a two-dimensional array. When mathematicians use a two-dimensional array, they often call it a **matrix** or a **table**; you might have used a two-dimensional array called a spreadsheet.

sales [0, 0]	sales [0, 1]	sales [0, 2]	sales [0, 3]
sales [1, 0]	sales [1, 1]	sales [1, 2]	sales [1, 3]
sales [2, 0]	sales [2, 1]	sales [2, 2]	sales [2, 3]

> **NOTE**
> You can think of the two dimensions of a two-dimensional array as height and width.

Figure 5-14 View of a rectangular, two-dimensional array in memory

> **NOTE** You might want to create a `sales` array with two dimensions as shown in Figure 5-14 if, for example, each row represented a category of items sold, and each column represented a salesperson who sold them.

When you declare a one-dimensional array, you type a single square bracket after the array type, and you use a single subscript in a set of square brackets when reserving memory. To declare a two-dimensional array, you type a comma in the square brackets after the array type, and you use two subscripts, separated by a comma in brackets, when reserving memory. For example, the array in Figure 5-14 can be declared as the following, creating an array named `saleFigures` that holds three rows and four columns:

```
double[ , ] sales = new double[3, 4];
```

Just as with a one-dimensional array, if you do not provide values for the elements in a two-dimensional numerical array, the values are set to the default value for the data type (zero for numeric data). You can assign other values to the array elements later. For example, the following statement assigns the value 14.00 to the element of the `sales` array that is in the first column of the first row:

```
sales[0, 0] = 14.00;
```

USING ARRAYS

Alternatively, you can initialize a two-dimensional array with values when it is created. For example, the following code assigns values to `sales` when it is created:

```
int[ , ] sales = {{ 14.00, 15.00, 16.00, 17.00},
                  { 21.99, 34.55, 67.88, 31.99},
                  { 12.03, 55.55, 32.89,  1.17}};
```

> **NOTE**
> You do not need to place each row of values that initializes a two-dimensional array on its own line. However, doing so makes the positions of values easier to understand.

The `sales` array contains three rows and four columns. You contain the entire set of values within a pair of curly braces. The first row of the array holds the four `double`s 14.00, 15.00, 16.00 and 17.00. Notice that these four values are placed within their own set of curly braces to indicate that they constitute one row, or the first row, which is row 0. Similarly, the next four values make up the second row (row 1), which you reference with the subscript 1. The value of `sales[ 0, 0]` is 14.00. The value of `sales[ 0, 1]` is 15.00. The value of `sales[ 2, 3]` is 1.17. The first value within the brackets following the array name always refers to the row; the second value, after the comma, refers to the column.

As an example of how useful two-dimensional arrays can be, assume you own an apartment building with four floors—a basement, which you refer to as floor zero, and three other floors numbered one, two, and three. In addition, each of the floors has studio (with no bedroom), one-, and two-bedroom apartments. The monthly rent for each type of apartment is different, and the rent is higher for apartments with more bedrooms. Table 5-1 shows the rental amounts.

Floor	Zero Bedrooms	One Bedroom	Two Bedrooms
0	400	450	510
1	500	560	630
2	625	676	740
3	1000	1250	1600

Table 5-1 Rents charged (in dollars)

To determine a tenant's rent, you need to know two pieces of information: the floor on which the tenant rents an apartment and the number of bedrooms in the apartment. Within a C# program, you can declare an array of rents using the following code:

```
int[ , ] rents = { { 400,  450,  510},
                   { 500,  560,  630},
                   { 625,  676,  740},
                   { 1000, 1250, 1600} };
```

Assume you declare two integers to hold the floor number and bedroom count, as in the following statement:

```
int floor, bedrooms;
```

Then any tenant's rent can be referred to as `rents[ floor, bedrooms]`.

Figure 5-15 shows a complete program that uses a rectangular, two-dimensional array to hold rent values. Figure 5-16 shows a typical execution.

```
using System;
public class Rents
{
    public static void Main()
    {
        int[ , ] rents = { { 400, 450, 510},
                           { 500, 560, 630},
                           { 625, 676, 740},
                           {1000, 1250, 1600} };
        int floor;
        int bedrooms;
        string inputString;
        Console.Write("Enter the floor on which you want to live ");
        inputString = Console.ReadLine();
        floor = Convert.ToInt32(inputString);
        Console.Write("Enter the number of bedrooms you need ");
        inputString = Console.ReadLine();
        bedrooms = Convert.ToInt32(inputString);
        Console.WriteLine("The rent is { 0} ",
            rents[ floor, bedrooms] );
    }
}
```

Figure 5-15 The Rents program

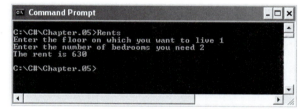

Figure 5-16 Typical execution of the Rents program

C# supports arrays with more than two dimensions. For example, if you own a multistory apartment building with different numbers of bedrooms available in apartments on each floor, you can use a two-dimensional array to store the rental fees. If you own several apartment buildings, you might want to employ a third dimension to store the building number. Figure 5-17 shows how you might define such an array.

```
int[ , , ] rents = { { { 400, 500}, { 450, 550}, { 500, 550}},
                     { { 510, 610}, { 710, 810}, { 910, 1010}},
                     { { 525, 625}, { 725, 825}, { 925, 1025}},
                     { { 850, 950}, {1050, 1150}, {1250, 1350}}};
```

Figure 5-17 A three-dimensional array definition

USING ARRAYS

Using the three-dimensional array in Figure 5-17, an expression such as `rents[ building, floor, bedrooms]` refers to a specific rent figure for a building whose number is stored in the `building` variable and whose floor and bedroom numbers are stored in the `floor` and `bedrooms` variables. Specifically, `rents[ 3, 1, 0]` refers to a studio (zero-bedroom) apartment on the first floor of building 3 ($1050 in Figure 5-17). When you are programming in C#, you can use four, five, or more dimensions in an array. As long as you can keep track of the order of the variables needed as subscripts, and as long as you don't exhaust your computer's memory, C# lets you create arrays of any size.

C# also supports jagged arrays. A **jagged array** is a one-dimensional array in which each element is another one-dimensional array. The major difference between jagged and rectangular arrays is that in jagged arrays, each row can be a different length.

For example, consider an application in which you want to store train ticket prices for each stop along five different routes. Suppose some of the routes have as many as 10 stops and others have as few as two. Each of the five routes could be represented by a row in a multidimensional array. Then you would have two logical choices for the columns:

» You could create a rectangular, two-dimensional array, allowing 10 columns for each row. In some of the rows, as many as eight of the columns would be empty, because some routes have only two stops.
» You could create a jagged two-dimensional array, allowing a different number of columns for each row. Figure 5-18 shows how you could implement this option.

```
double[][] tickets = {
   new double[] { 5.50, 6.75, 7.95, 9.00, 12.00,
      13.00, 14.50, 17.00, 19.00, 20.25},
   new double[] { 5.00, 6.00},
   new double[] { 7.50, 9.00, 9.95, 12.00, 13.00, 14.00},
   new double[] { 3.50, 6.45, 9.95, 10.00, 12.75},
   new double[] { 15.00, 16.00} };
```

Figure 5-18 A jagged, two-dimensional array

The array in Figure 5-18 contains five separate one-dimensional arrays. Two square brackets are used following the data type. Then, within the array, each row needs its own `new` operator and data type. To refer to a jagged array element, you use two sets of brackets after the array name—for example, `tickets[ route][ stop]`. In Figure 5-18, the value of `tickets[ 0][ 0]` is 5.50, the value of `tickets[ 0][ 1]` is 6.75, and the value of `tickets[ 0][ 2]` is 7.95. The value of `tickets[ 1][ 0]` is 5.00, and the value of `tickets[ 1][ 1]` is 6.00. Referring to `tickets[ 1][ 2]` is invalid because there is no column 2 in the second row (that is, there are only two stops, not three, on the second train route).

CHAPTER FIVE

YOU DO IT

CREATING AND USING AN ARRAY

In the next steps, you will create a small array to see how arrays are used. The array will hold salaries for four categories of employees.

To create a program that uses an array:

1. Open a new text file in your text editor.

2. Begin the class that will demonstrate array use by typing the following:

   ```
   using System;
   public class ArrayDemo1
   {
      public static void Main()
      {
   ```

3. Declare and create an array that can hold four `double` values by typing:

   ```
   double[] payRate;
   payRate = new double[4];
   ```

4. One by one, assign four values to the four pay rate array elements by typing:

   ```
   payRate[0] = 6.00;
   payRate[1] = 7.35;
   payRate[2] = 8.12;
   payRate[3] = 12.45;
   ```

5. To confirm that the four values have been assigned, print the pay rates, one by one, using the following code:

   ```
   Console.WriteLine("Pay rate {0} is {1}",
      0, payRate[0].ToString("C"));
   Console.WriteLine("Pay rate {0} is {1}",
      1, payRate[1].ToString("C"));
   Console.WriteLine("Pay rate {0} is {1}",
      2, payRate[2].ToString("C"));
   Console.WriteLine("Pay rate {0} is {1}",
      3, payRate[3].ToString("C"));
   ```

6. Add the two closing curly brackets that end the `Main()` method and the `ArrayDemo1` class.

7. Save the program as **ArrayDemo1.cs** in the Chapter.05 folder on your Student Disk.

USING ARRAYS

8. Compile and run the program. The program's output appears in Figure 5-19.

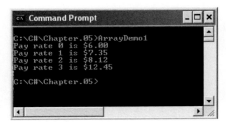

Figure 5-19 Output of `ArrayDemo1` program

INITIALIZING AN ARRAY

Next, you will alter your `ArrayDemo1` program to initialize the array of `doubles`, rather than declaring the array in one step and assigning values later.

To initialize an array of `doubles`:

1. Open the **ArrayDemo1.cs** file in your text editor and immediately save it as **ArrayDemo2.cs**. Change the class name from `ArrayDemo1` to **ArrayDemo2**.

2. Delete the first six statements within the `Main()` method; these statements declare the array, instantiate it, and assign four values. Replace them with a single statement that accomplishes the same tasks:

   ```
   double[] payRate = {6.00, 7.35, 8.12, 12.45};
   ```

3. Save, compile, and execute the program. The output looks the same as in Figure 5-19.

USING A `for` LOOP WITH AN ARRAY

Next, you will modify the `ArrayDemo2` program to use a `for` loop with the array.

To use a `for` loop with an array:

1. Open the **ArrayDemo2.cs** file in your text editor and immediately save it as **ArrayDemo3.cs**. Change the class name to **ArrayDemo3**.

2. Delete the four `WriteLine()` statements that print the four array values and replace them with the following `for` loop:

   ```
   for(int x = 0; x  < 4; ++x)
      Console.WriteLine("Pay rate {0} is {1}",
         x, payRate[x].ToString("C"));
   ```

   In this version of the statement, as x varies from 0 through 3, the value of x and the value of `payRate[ x]` are both displayed.

3. Save, compile, and run the program. Again, the output is the same as in Figure 5-19.

CHAPTER FIVE

USING THE Length PROPERTY WITH AN ARRAY

Next, you will modify the `ArrayDemo3` program to use the `Length` property. By doing so, no changes will be necessary to the `for` loop if you change the array size later—the `Length` field will automatically be updated to hold the current size of the array.

To use the Length property:

1. Open the **ArrayDemo3.cs** file in your text editor and immediately save it as **ArrayDemo4.cs**. Change the class name to **ArrayDemo4**.

2. Within the `for` statement that prints the array elements, change the 4 to **payRate.Length**.

3. Save, compile, and execute the program. The output is the same as in Figure 5-19.

4. At the end of the list of pay rates, insert a comma and a new, fifth rate of **22.22**.

5. Save the program, then compile and execute it again. The output looks like Figure 5-20. Even though you only added a new pay rate without making any other adjustments to the program, all five pay rates print correctly because C# adjusted the `Length` property.

Figure 5-20 Output of `ArrayDemo4` program

USING THE Sort() AND Reverse() METHODS

In the next steps you will create an array of integers and use the `Sort()` and `Reverse()` methods to manipulate it.

To use the Sort() and Reverse() methods:

1. Open a new file in your text editor.

2. Type the beginning of a class named `MyTestScores` that includes an array of eight integer test scores, an integer you will use as a subscript, and a string that will hold user-entered data.

```
using System;
public class MyTestScores
{
    public static void Main()
    {
        int[] scores = new int[8];
        int x;
        string inputString;
```

161

USING ARRAYS

> **NOTE**
> The program displays x + 1 with each score[x] because, although array elements are numbered starting with 0, people usually count items starting with 1.

3. Add a loop that prompts the user, accepts a test score, converts the score to an integer, and stores it as the appropriate element of the scores array.

```
for(x = 0; x < scores.Length; ++x)
{
    Console.Write("Enter your score on test {0} ", x + 1);
    inputString = Console.ReadLine();
    scores[x] = Convert.ToInt32(inputString);
}
```

> **NOTE**
> You learned to set display field sizes when you learned about format strings in Chapter 2.

4. Add a statement that creates a dashed line to visually separate the input from the output. Display "Scores in original order:", then use a loop to display each score in a field that is six characters wide.

```
Console.WriteLine("\n--------------------------------");
Console.WriteLine("Scores in original order:");
for(x = 0; x < scores.Length; ++x)
    Console.Write("{0, 6}", scores[x]);
```

5. Add another dashed line for visual separation, then pass the scores array to the Array.Sort() method. Print "Scores in sorted order:", then use a loop to display each of the newly sorted scores.

```
Console.WriteLine("\n--------------------------------");
Array.Sort(scores);
Console.WriteLine("Scores in sorted order:");
for(x = 0; x < scores.Length; ++x)
    Console.Write("{0, 6}", scores[x]);
```

6. Add one more dashed line, reverse the array elements by passing scores to the Array.Reverse() method, display "Scores in reverse order:", and show the rearranged scores.

```
Console.WriteLine("\n--------------------------------");
Array.Reverse(scores);
Console.WriteLine("Scores in reverse order:");
for(x = 0; x < scores.Length; ++x)
    Console.Write("{0, 6}", scores[x]);
```

7. Add two closing curly braces—one for the Main() method and one for the class. Save the file as **MyTestScores.cs** in the Chapter.05 folder of your Student Disk. Compile and execute the program. Figure 5-21 shows a typical execution of the program. The user-entered scores are not in order, but after the call to the Sort() method, they appear in ascending order. After the call to the Reverse() method, they appear in descending order.

C H A P T E R F I V E

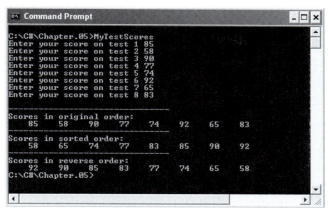

Figure 5-21 Typical execution of `MyTestScores` program

CHAPTER SUMMARY

» An array is a list of data items, all of which have the same type and the same name, but are distinguished from each other using a subscript or index. You declare an array variable by inserting a pair of square brackets after the type. You reserve memory for an array by using the keyword `new`. A subscript (also called an index) is an integer contained within square brackets that indicates one of an array's variables, or elements. Any array's elements are numbered 0 through one less than the array's length.

» In C#, arrays are objects of a class named `System.Array`. An array's fields are initialized to default values. To initialize an array to nondefault values, you use a list of values that are separated by commas and enclosed within curly braces.

» The power of arrays becomes apparent when you begin to use subscripts that are variables rather than constant values, and when you use loops to process array elements.

» When you work with array elements, you must ensure that the subscript you use remains in the range of 0 through `length` -1. You can use the `Length` property, which is a member of the `System.Array` class, to automatically hold an array's length.

» You can use the `foreach` statement to cycle through every array element without using subscripts. With the `foreach` statement, you provide a temporary variable that automatically holds each array value in turn.

» When you want to determine whether some variable holds one of many possible valid values, you can compare the variable to a list of values in an array. If you set up a parallel array with the same number of elements and corresponding data, you can use the same subscript to access additional information.

» You can create parallel arrays to more easily perform a range match.

» The `BinarySearch()` method finds a requested value in a sorted array. The method returns –1 if the value is not found in the array; otherwise, it returns the array position of the sought value. You cannot use the `BinarySearch()` method if your array items are

163

USING ARRAYS

not arranged in ascending order, if the array holds duplicate values and you want to find all of them, or if you want to find a range match rather than an exact match.
» The `Sort()` method arranges array items in ascending order. The `Reverse()` method reverses the order of items in an array.
» C# supports multidimensional arrays—those that require multiple subscripts to access the array elements. The most commonly used multidimensional arrays are two-dimensional arrays that are rectangular. Two-dimensional arrays have two or more columns of values for each row. In a rectangular array, each row has the same number of columns. C# also supports jagged arrays, which are arrays of arrays.

KEY TERMS

An **array** is a list of data items that all have the same data type and the same name, but are distinguished from each other by a subscript or index.

The keyword **new** is also known as the **new operator**; it is used to create objects.

Each object in an array is an **array element**.

A **subscript** (also called an **index**) is an integer contained within square brackets that indicates the position of one of an array's elements.

An **initializer list** is the list of values provided for an array.

The class `System.Array` defines fields and methods that belong to every array.

The **Length property** is a member of the `System.Array` class that automatically holds an array's length.

The **foreach statement** is used to cycle through every array element without using a subscript.

A temporary **iteration variable** holds each array value in turn in a `foreach` statement.

A **parallel array** has the same number of elements as another array and corresponding data.

A **range match** determines the pair of limiting values between which a value falls.

The `BinarySearch()` **method** finds a requested value in a sorted array.

The `Sort()` **method** arranges array items in ascending order.

The `Reverse()` **method** reverses the order of items in an array.

A **one-dimensional** or **single-dimensional array** is an array whose elements you can access using a single subscript.

Multidimensional arrays require multiple subscripts to access the array elements.

Two-dimensional arrays have two or more columns of values for each row.

In a **rectangular array**, each row has the same number of columns.

When mathematicians use a two-dimensional array, they often call it a **matrix** or a **table**.

A **jagged array** is a one-dimensional array in which each element is another one-dimensional array.

CHAPTER FIVE

REVIEW QUESTIONS

1. In an array, every element has the same _____ .
   - a. subscript
   - b. data type
   - c. memory location
   - d. all of the above

2. The operator used to create objects is _____ .
   - a. `=`
   - b. `+=`
   - c. `new`
   - d. `create`

3. Which of the following correctly declares an array of four integers?
   - a. `int array[ 4];`
   - b. `int[ ] array = 4;`
   - c. `int[ 4] array;`
   - d. `int[ ] array = new int[ 4];`

4. The value placed within square brackets after an array name is _____ .
   - a. a subscript
   - b. an index
   - c. always an integer
   - d. all of these

5. If you define an array to contain seven elements, then the highest array subscript you can use is _____ .
   - a. 5
   - b. 6
   - c. 7
   - d. 8

6. Initializing an array is _____ in C#.
   - a. required
   - b. optional
   - c. difficult
   - d. prohibited

7. When you declare an array of six `double` elements but provide no initialization values, the value of the first element is _____ .
   - a. 0.0
   - b. 1.0
   - c. 5.0
   - d. unknown

8. Which of the following correctly declares an array of four integers?
   - a. `int[ ] ages = new int[ 4] { 20, 30, 40, 50};`
   - b. `int[ ] ages = new int[ ] { 20, 30, 40, 50};`
   - c. `int[ ] ages = { 20, 30, 40, 50};`
   - d. all of these

USING ARRAYS

9. When an `ages` array is correctly initialized using the values { 20, 30, 40, 50}, as in Question 8, then the value of `ages[ 1]` is _____ .

   a. 0
   b. 20
   c. 30
   d. undefined

10. When an `ages` array is correctly initialized using the values { 20, 30, 40, 50}, as in Question 8, then the value of `ages[ 4]` is _____ .

    a. 0
    b. 4
    c. 50
    d. undefined

11. When you declare an array as `int[ ] temperature = { 0, 32, 50, 90, 212, 451} ;`, the value of `temperature.Length` is _____ .

    a. 5
    b. 6
    c. 7
    d. unknown

12. Which of the following doubles every value in a 10-element integer array named `amount`?

    a. `for(int x = 9; x >= 0; --x)   amount[ x] *= 2;`
    b. `foreach(int number in amount) number *= 2;`
    c. both of these
    d. neither of these

13. Which of the following adds 10 to every value in a 15-element integer array named `points`?

    a. `for(int sub = 0; sub > 15; ++sub)   points[ sub] += 10;`
    b. `foreach(int sub in points) points += 10;`
    c. both of these
    d. neither of these

14. Two arrays that store related information in corresponding element positions are _____ .

    a. analogous arrays
    b. polymorphic arrays
    c. relative arrays
    d. parallel arrays

15. Assume an array is defined as `int[] nums = {2, 3, 4, 5};`. Which of the following would display the values in the array in reverse?

    a. `for(int x = 4; x > 0; --x) Console.Write(nums[x]);`

    b. `for(int x = 3; x >= 0; --x) Console.Write(nums[x]);`

    c. `for(int x = 3; x > 0; --x) Console.Write(nums[x]);`

    d. `for(int x = 4; x >= 0; --x) Console.Write(nums[x]);`

16. Assume an array is defined as `int[] nums = {7, 15, 23, 5};`. Which of the following would place the values in the array in descending numeric order?

    a. `Array.Sort(nums);`

    b. `Array.Reverse(nums);`

    c. `Array.Sort(nums); Array.Reverse(nums);`

    d. `Array.Reverse(nums); Array.Sort(nums);`

17. Which of the following traits do the `BinarySearch()` and `Sort()` methods have in common?

    a. Both methods take a single argument that must be an array.

    b. Both methods belong to the `System.Array` class.

    c. The array that each method uses must be in ascending order.

    d. They both operate on arrays made up of simple data types but not class objects.

18. If you use the `BinarySearch()` method and the object you seek is not found in the array, _____ .

    a. an error message is displayed

    b. a zero is returned

    c. the value `false` is returned

    d. a negative value is returned

19. The `BinarySearch()` method is inadequate when _____ .

    a. array items are in ascending order

    b. the array holds duplicate values and you want to find them all

    c. you want to find an exact match for a value

    d. array items are not numeric

20. Which of the following declares an integer array that contains eight rows and five columns?

   a. `int[ 8, 5] num = new int[ , ];`
   b. `int [ 8][ 5] num = new int[ ];`
   c. `int [ ,] num = new int[ 5, 8];`
   d. `int [ ,] num = new int[ 8, 5];`

EXERCISES

As you work through each exercise, save the finished program in the Chapter.05 folder of your Student Disk.

1. Write a program containing an array that holds five integers. Assign values to the integers. Display the integers from first to last, and then display them from last to first. Save the program as **IntegerList.cs**.

2. Write a program for a package delivery service. The program contains an array that holds the 10 zip codes to which the company delivers packages. Prompt a user to enter a zip code and display a message indicating whether the zip code is one to which the company delivers. Save the program as **CheckZips.cs**.

3. Write another program for the package delivery service in Exercise 2. The program should again use an array that holds the 10 zip codes to which the company delivers packages. Create a parallel array containing 10 delivery charges that differ for each zip code. Prompt a user to enter a zip code and then display either a message indicating the price of delivery to that zip code or a message indicating that the company does not deliver to the requested zip code. Save the program as **DeliveryCharges.cs**.

4. The Chat-A-While phone company provides service to six area codes and charges the following per-minute rates for phone calls:

Area Code	Per-Minute Rate ($)
262	0.07
414	0.10
608	0.05
715	0.16
815	0.24
920	0.14

   Write a program that allows a user to enter an area code and the length of time for a call in minutes, then display the total cost of the call. Save the program as **ChatAWhile.cs**.

5. The Whippet Bus Company charges prices for tickets based on distance traveled, as follows:

Distance (miles)	Ticket Price ($)
0–99	25.00
100–299	40.00
300–499	55.00
500 and farther	70.00

   Write a program that allows a user to enter a trip distance. The output is the ticket price. Save the program as **WhippetBus.cs**.

6. Write a program that prompts the user to make a choice for a pizza size—*S*, *M*, *L*, or *X*—and then displays the price as $6.99, $8.99, $12.50, or $15.00, respectively. Save the program as **PizzaPrices.cs**.

7. Write a program that computes commissions for automobile salespeople based on the value of the car. Salespeople receive 5 percent of the sale price for any car sold for up to and including $15,000; 7 percent for any car over $15,000 up to and including $24,000; and 10 percent of the sale price of any car over $24,000. Write a program that allows a user to enter a car price. The output is the salesperson's commission. Save the program as **Commission.cs**.

8. Create an array that stores 20 prices. Prompt a user to enter 20 values, then display the sum of the values. Next, display all values of less than $5.00. Finally, calculate the average of the prices, and display all values that are higher than the calculated average. Save the program as **Prices.cs**.

9. The Tiny Tots Tee-Ball league has 12 players who have jersey numbers 0 through 11. The coach wants a program into which he can type a player's number and the number of bases the player got in a turn at bat (a number 0 through 4). Write a program that allows the coach to continually enter the values until 99 is entered. Store the statistics in a two-dimensional array. At the end of a data-entry session, display each player's number and the number of 0-base, 1-base, 2-base, 3-base, and 4-base turns the player had. The output should look similar to Figure 5-22. Save the program as **TeeBall.cs**.

USING ARRAYS

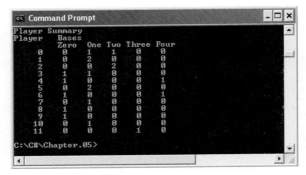

Figure 5-22 Typical execution of `TeeBall` program

DEBUGGING EXERCISES

Each of the following files in the Chapter.05 folder on your Student Disk has syntax and/or logical errors. In each case, determine the problem and fix the program. After you correct the errors, save each file using the same filename preceded with *Fixed*. For example, DebugFive01.cs will become FixedDebugFive01.cs.

a. DebugFive01.cs   c. DebugFive03.cs

b. DebugFive02.cs   d. DebugFive04.cs

UP FOR DISCUSSION

1. A train schedule is an everyday, real-life example of an array. Think of at least four more.

2. This chapter discusses sorting data. Suppose you are hired by a large hospital to write a program that displays lists of potential organ recipients. The hospital's doctors will consult this list if they have an organ that can be transplanted. You are instructed to sort potential recipients by last name and display them sequentially in alphabetical order. If more than 10 patients are waiting for a particular organ, the first 10 patients are displayed; the user can either select one of these or move on to view the next set of 10 patients. You worry that this system gives an unfair advantage to patients with last names that start with A, B, C, and D. Should you write and install the program? If you do not, many transplant opportunities will be missed while the hospital searches for another programmer to write the program.

3. This chapter discusses sorting data. Suppose your supervisor asks you to create a report that lists all employees sorted by salary. Suppose you also know that your employer will use this report to lay off the highest-paid employee in each department. Would you agree to write the program? Instead, what if the report's purpose was to list the worst performer in each department in terms of sales? What if the report grouped employees by gender? What if the report grouped employees by race? Suppose your supervisor asks you to sort employees by the dollar value of medical insurance claims they have in a year, and you fear the employer will use the report to eliminate workers who are driving up the organization's medical insurance costs. Do you agree to write the program even if you know that the purpose of the report is to eliminate workers?

CHAPTER SIX

6

USING METHODS

In this chapter you will:

Learn about methods
Write methods with no parameters and no return value
Learn about implementation hiding
Write methods that require a single argument
Write methods that require multiple arguments
Write a method that returns a value
Pass an array to a method
Use reference parameters, output parameters, and
 parameter arrays with methods
Overload methods
Learn how to avoid ambiguous methods

USING METHODS

In the first five chapters of this book, you learned to create C# programs containing `Main()` methods that declare variables, accept input, perform arithmetic, and produce output. You learned to add decisions, loops, and arrays to your programs. As your programs grow in complexity, their `Main()` methods will contain many additional statements. Rather than creating increasingly long `Main()` methods, most programmers prefer to modularize their programs, placing instructions in smaller "packages" called methods. In this chapter, you learn to create many types of C# methods. You will gain the ability to send data to these methods and to receive information back from them.

UNDERSTANDING METHODS

A **method** is an encapsulated series of statements that carry out a task. Any class can contain an unlimited number of methods. So far, you have written classes that contain a `Main()` method, but no others. Your `Main()` methods have **invoked**, or **called**, other methods; that is, your program used a method's name and the method performed a job for the class. For example, you have created many programs that call the `WriteLine()` and `ReadLine()` methods. When you used arrays in Chapter 5, you learned how to use the `BinarySearch()`, `Sort()`, and `Reverse()` methods. The methods you have used were written for you; you only had to call them to have them work.

> **NOTE**
> You first learned the term "argument" in Chapter 1.

For example, consider the simple `HelloClass` program shown in Figure 6-1. The `Main()` method contains a statement that calls the `Console.WriteLine()` method. You can identify method names because they are always followed by a set of parentheses. Depending on the method, there might be an argument within the parentheses. The call to the `WriteLine()` method within the `HelloClass` program in Figure 6-1 contains the string argument "Hello". The simplest methods you can invoke don't require any arguments.

> **NOTE**
> Methods are similar to the procedures, functions, and subroutines used in other programming languages.

```
using System;
public class HelloClass
{
    public static void Main()
    {
        Console.WriteLine("Hello");
    }
}
```

Figure 6-1 The `HelloClass` program

> **NOTE**
> In the `HelloClass` program in Figure 6-1, `Main()` is a **calling method**—one that calls another. The `WriteLine()` method is a **called method**.

When you call the `WriteLine()` method within the `HelloClass` program in Figure 6-1, you use a method that has already been created for you. Because the creators of C# knew you would often want to write a message to the output screen, they created a method you could call to accomplish that task. This method takes care of all the hardware details of producing a message on the output device; you simply call the method and pass the desired message to it. The creators of C# were able to anticipate many of the methods you would need for your programs; you will continue to use many of these methods throughout this book. However, your programs often will require custom methods that the creators of C# could not have expected. In this chapter, you will learn to write your own custom methods.

WRITING METHODS WITH NO PARAMETERS AND NO RETURN VALUE

The output of the program in Figure 6-1 is simply the word "Hello". Suppose you want to add three more lines of output to display a standard welcoming message when users execute your program. Of course, you can add three new `WriteLine()` statements to the existing program, but you also can create a method to display the three new lines.

There are two major reasons to create a method instead of adding three lines to the existing program:

» If you add a method call instead of three new lines, the `Main()` method will remain short and easy to follow. The `Main()` method will contain just one new statement that calls a method rather than three separate `WriteLine()` statements.

» More importantly, a method is easily *reusable*. After you create the welcoming method, you can use it in any program. In other words, you do the work once, and then you can use the method many times.

>> **NOTE**
When you place code in a callable method instead of repeating the same code at several points in a program, you are avoiding **code bloat**—a colorful term that describes unnecessarily long or repetitive statements.

In C#, a method must include:

» A **method declaration**, which is also known as a **method header** or **method definition**
» An opening curly brace
» A **method body**, which is a block of statements that carry out the method's work
» A closing curly brace

The method declaration defines the rules for using the method; it contains:

» Optional declared accessibility
» An optional `static` modifier
» The return type for the method
» The method name, or identifier
» An opening parenthesis
» An optional list of method parameters (you separate the parameters with commas if there is more than one)
» A closing parenthesis

The optional declared **accessibility** for a method sets limits as to how other methods can use your method; it can be any of the following:

» **Public access**, which you select by including a `public` modifier in the member declaration. This modifier allows unlimited access to a method.

USING METHODS

> **NOTE**
> You will learn about protected access and what it means to derive types in Chapter 8.

- » **Protected internal access**, which you select by including both a `protected` and an `internal` modifier in the member declaration. This modifier limits method access to the containing program or types derived from the containing class.
- » **Protected access**, which you select by including a `protected` modifier in the member declaration. This modifier limits method access to the containing class or types derived from the containing class.
- » **Internal access**, which you select by including an `internal` modifier in the member declaration. This modifier limits method access to the containing program.
- » **Private access**, which you select by including a `private` modifier in the member declaration. This modifier limits method access to the containing type.

If you do not provide an accessibility modifier for a method, it is `private` by default. As you study C#, deciding which access modifier to choose will become clearer. For example, when you begin to create your own class objects, you usually will provide them with `public` methods, but sometimes you will make methods `private`. For now, we will create methods to be `public`.

Additionally, you can declare a method to be **static** or **nonstatic**. If you use the keyword modifier `static`, you indicate that a method can be called without referring to an object. If you do not indicate that a method is `static`, it is nonstatic by default. When you begin to create your own class objects in Chapter 7, you will write many nonstatic methods and your understanding of the use of these terms will become clearer. For now, all methods you create will be `static`.

Every method has a **return type**, indicating what kind of value the method will return to any other method that calls it. If a method does not return a value, its return type is `void`. Later in this chapter, you will create methods that return values; for now, the methods will be `void` methods.

> **NOTE** When a method's return type is `void`, most C# programmers do not end the method with a `return` statement. However, you can end a `void` method with the following statement that indicates nothing is returned:
> `return;`

> **NOTE** You have used a return value from the `ReadLine()` method when you have written a statement such as `inputString = Console.ReadLine();`.

Every method has a name that must be a legal C# identifier; that is, it must not contain spaces and must begin with a letter of the alphabet or an underscore.

Every method name is followed by a set of parentheses. Sometimes these parentheses contain parameters, but in the simplest methods, the parentheses are empty.

In summary, the first methods you write will be `public`, `static`, and `void` and will have empty parameter lists. Therefore, you can write the `WelcomeMessage()` method as it is

CHAPTER SIX

shown in Figure 6-2. According to its declaration, it is `public` and `static`. It returns nothing, so its return type is `void`. Its identifier is `WelcomeMessage`, and it receives nothing, so its parentheses are empty. Its body, consisting of three `WriteLine()` statements, appears within curly braces.

```
public static void WelcomeMessage()
{
    Console.WriteLine("Welcome");
    Console.WriteLine("It's a pleasure to serve you");
    Console.WriteLine("Enjoy the program");
}
```

Figure 6-2 The `WelcomeMessage()` method

You can place any statements you want within a method body, and you can declare variables within a method. When a variable is declared within a method, it is known only from that point to the end of the method. The area in which a variable is known is its **scope**.

You can place a method in its own file, as you will learn in the next section. You also can place a method within the file of a program that will use it, but you cannot place a method within any other method. Figure 6-3 shows the two locations where you can place the `WelcomeMessage()` method within the `HelloClass` program file—before the `Main()` method header or after the `Main()` method's closing brace.

```
using System;
public class HelloClass
{
    // The WelcomeMessage() method could go here
    public static void Main()
    {
        Console.WriteLine("Hello");
    }
    // Alternatively, the WelcomeMessage() method could go here
    // But it cannot go in both places
}
```

Figure 6-3 Placement of methods

If a `Main()` method calls the `WelcomeMessage()` method, then you simply use the `WelcomeMessage()` method's name as a statement within the body of the `Main()` method. Figure 6-4 shows the complete program with the method call shaded, and Figure 6-5 shows the output.

USING METHODS

```
using System;
public class HelloClass
{
    public static void Main()
    {
        WelcomeMessage();
        Console.WriteLine("Hello");
    }
    public static void WelcomeMessage()
    {
        Console.WriteLine("Welcome");
        Console.WriteLine("It's a pleasure to serve you");
        Console.WriteLine("Enjoy the program");
    }
}
```

Figure 6-4 `HelloClass` program with `Main()` method calling the `WelcomeMessage()` method

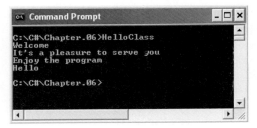

Figure 6-5 Output of `HelloClass` program

When the `Main()` method executes, it calls the `WelcomeMessage()` method, then it prints "Hello". Because the `Main()` method calls the `WelcomeMessage()` method before it prints "Hello", the three lines that make up the welcome message appear first in the output.

> **NOTE** Each of two different classes can have its own method named `WelcomeMessage()`. Such a method in the second class would be entirely distinct from the identically named method in the first class.

HIDING IMPLEMENTATION

An important principle of object-oriented programming is the notion of **implementation hiding**—keeping the details of a method's operations hidden. When you make a request to a method, you don't need to know the details of how the method is implemented. For example, when you make a dental appointment, you do not need to know how the appointment is actually recorded at the dental office—perhaps it is written in a book, marked on a large chalkboard, or entered into a computerized database. The implementation details are of no

CHAPTER SIX

concern to you as a client, and if the dental office changes its methods from one year to the next, the change does not affect your use of the appointment method. Your only concern is the way you **interface** or interact with the dental office, not how the office records appointments. Similarly, if you use a thermostat to raise the temperature in your apartment or house, you do not need to know whether the heat is generated by natural gas, electricity, solar energy, or a hamster on a wheel. As long as you receive heat, the implementation details can remain hidden.

>> **NOTE**
Hidden implementation methods often are said to exist in a black box. A **black box** is any device you can use without knowing how it works internally.

The same is true with well-written program methods; the invoking program or method must know the name of the method it is using (and what type of information to send it), but the program does not need to know how the method works. Later, you can substitute a new, improved method for the old one, and if the interface to the method does not change, you won't need to make any changes in programs that invoke the method.

>> **NOTE**
A method that uses another is called a **client** of the second method.

For example, suppose you rewrite the `WelcomeMessage()` method as shown in Figure 6-6. The method is constructed differently from the one with the identical name shown in Figure 6-2—the new method uses two statements instead of three, uses a `Write()` method for a portion of its output instead of all `WriteLine()` methods, and uses two newline escape sequences ('\n'). Nevertheless, if you substitute the new version for the old one, any program that uses the method does not need to be altered, and the output is identical.

>> **NOTE**
You first learned about escape sequences in Chapter 2. Table 2-5 provides a list of commonly used escape sequences.

```
public static void WelcomeMessage()
{
    Console.Write("Welcome\nIt's a pleasure ");
    Console.WriteLine("to serve you\nEnjoy the program");
}
```

Figure 6-6 Alternate `WelcomeMessage()` method

You should not alter the `WelcomeMessage()` method arbitrarily. However, as you learn to program, you will encounter many opportunities to substitute an improved method for an older, less efficient one. Also, you often will use methods written by others or that you "borrow" from other applications you have written. To more easily incorporate methods into a program, it is common practice to store methods (or groups of associated methods) in their own classes and files. Then you can add them into any application that uses them. The resulting compound program is called a **multifile assembly**. As you learn more about C#, you might prefer to take this approach with your own programs. For now, for simplicity, methods will be contained in the same file as any other methods that use them.

>> **NOTE**
Details on creating a multifile assembly are provided in Appendix B.

WRITING METHODS THAT REQUIRE A SINGLE ARGUMENT

Some methods require additional information. If a method could not receive arguments, then you would have to write an infinite number of methods to cover every possible situation. For example, when you make a dental appointment, you do not need to employ a different

177

USING METHODS

> **NOTE**
> In Chapter 1, you learned that arguments are passed into methods in the method call. A data item accepted by a method in its header is a parameter.

method for every date of the year at every possible time of day. Rather, you can supply the date and time as information to the method, and no matter what date and time you supply, the method is carried out in the same manner. If you design a method to triple numeric values, it makes sense that you can supply the `Triple()` method with an argument representing the value to be tripled, rather than having to develop a `Triple1()` method, a `Triple2()` method, and so on.

> **NOTE** You already have used a method to which you supplied a wide variety of parameters. At any call, the `System.WriteLine()` method can receive any one of an infinite number of strings as a parameter—"Hello", "Goodbye", and so on. No matter what message you send to the `WriteLine()` method, the message will be displayed correctly.

When you write the declaration for a method that can receive a parameter, you need to include the following items within the method declaration parentheses:

» The type of the parameter
» A local identifier (name) for the parameter

For example, consider a `public` method named `ComputeSalesTax()`, which displays the result of multiplying a value that represents a selling price by 7%. The method header for a usable `ComputeSalesTax()` method could be the following:

```
public static void ComputeSalesTax(double saleAmount)
```

You can think of the parentheses in a method declaration as a funnel into the method—data parameters listed there are "dropping in" to the method.

The argument `double saleAmount` within the parentheses indicates that the `ComputeSalesTax()` method will receive a value of type `double`. Within the method, the value will be known as `saleAmount`. Figure 6-7 shows a complete method.

```
public static void ComputeSalesTax(double saleAmount)
{
    double tax;
    const double RATE = 0.07;
    tax = saleAmount * RATE;
    Console.WriteLine("The tax on {0} is {1}",
        saleAmount, tax.ToString("f"));
}
```

Figure 6-7 The `ComputeSalesTax()` method

CHAPTER SIX

>> **NOTE** Within the `ComputeSalesTax()` method, you must use the format string and `ToString()` method if you want figures to display to exactly two decimal positions. You learned how to display values to a fixed number of decimal places in Chapter 2; recall that using the fixed format with no number defaults to two decimal places.

The `ComputeSalesTax()` method is a `void` method (has a `void` return type) because it does not return any value to any method that uses it—its only function is to receive the `saleAmount` value, multiply it by 0.07, and then display the result. It is a `static` method because you do not create an object with which to use it.

Within a program, you can call the `ComputeSalesTax()` method by using the method's name, and, within parentheses, an argument that is either a constant value or a variable. Thus, both of the following calls to the `ComputeSalesTax()` method invoke it correctly:

```
double myPurchase = 12.99;
ComputeSalesTax(12.99);
ComputeSalesTax(myPurchase);
```

You can call the `ComputeSalesTax()` method any number of times, with a different constant or variable argument each time. The value of each of these arguments becomes known as `saleAmount` within the method. The identifier `saleAmount` holds any `double` value passed into the method. Interestingly, if the argument in the method call is a variable, it might possess the same identifier as `saleAmount` or a different one, such as `myPurchase`. The identifier `saleAmount` is simply the name the value "goes by" while being used within the method, no matter what name it goes by in the calling program. That is, the variable `saleAmount` is a **local variable** to the `ComputeSalesTax()` method. The variable `saleAmount` is also an example of a **formal parameter**, a parameter within a method header that accepts a value. In contrast, arguments within a method *call* often are referred to as **actual parameters**.

>> **NOTE** A variable is local to a method when it is declared within that method.

>> **NOTE** The variable `saleAmount` is also an example of a value parameter, or a parameter that receives a copy of the value passed to it. You will learn more about value parameters as well as other types of parameters later in this chapter.

If a programmer changes the way in which the tax value is calculated—for example, by coding one of the following—programs that use the `ComputeSalesTax()` method will not be affected and will not need to be modified:

```
tax = saleAmount * 7 / 100;
tax = 0.07 * saleAmount;
tax = RATE * saleAmount;
```

Each of these statements computes `tax` as 7% of `saleAmount`. No matter how the tax is calculated, a calling program passes a value into the `ComputeSalesTax()` method, and a calculated result appears on the screen.

USING METHODS

Figure 6-8 shows a complete program called UseTaxMethod. It uses the ComputeSalesTax() method twice, first with a variable argument, and then with a constant argument. The program's output appears in Figure 6-9.

```
using System;
public class UseTaxMethod
{
    public static void Main()
    {
        double myPurchase = 12.99;
        ComputeSalesTax(myPurchase);
        ComputeSalesTax(35.67);
    }
    public static void ComputeSalesTax(double saleAmount)
    {
        double tax;
        const double RATE = 0.07;
        tax = saleAmount * RATE;
        Console.WriteLine("The tax on {0} is {1}",
            saleAmount, tax.ToString("f"));
    }
}
```

Figure 6-8 Complete program using the ComputeSalesTax() method two times

Figure 6-9 Output of the UseTaxMethod program

> **NOTE** Now that you have seen how to write methods that accept an argument, you might guess that the method header for the Console.WriteLine() method is public void WriteLine(string s). You might not know the parameter name the creators of C# have chosen, but you do know the method's return type, name, and parameter type.

WRITING METHODS THAT REQUIRE MULTIPLE ARGUMENTS

A method can require more than one argument. You can pass multiple arguments to a method by listing the arguments within the call to the method and separating them with commas. For example, rather than creating a ComputeSalesTax() method that multiplies

CHAPTER SIX

an amount by 0.07, you might prefer to create a more flexible method to which you can pass two values—the value on which the tax is calculated and the tax percentage by which it should be multiplied. Figure 6-10 shows a method that uses two such arguments.

```
public static void ComputeSalesTax(double saleAmount, double taxRate)
{
   double tax;
   tax = saleAmount * taxRate;
   Console.WriteLine("The tax on {0} at {1} is {2}",
         saleAmount.ToString("C"),
         taxRate.ToString("P"), tax.ToString("F"));
}
```

Figure 6-10 The `ComputeSalesTax()` method that takes two arguments

In Figure 6-10, two parameters (`double saleAmount` and `double taxRate`) appear within the parentheses in the method header. A comma separates the parameters, and each parameter requires its own named type (in this case, both parameters are of type `double`) and an identifier. When you pass values to the method in a statement such as `ComputeSalesTax(myPurchase, localRate);`, the first value passed will be referenced as `saleAmount` within the method, and the second value passed will be referenced as `taxRate`. Therefore, it is very important that arguments be passed to a method in the correct order. The following call results in output stating that "The tax on 200 is 20.00":

```
ComputeSalesTax(200.00, 0.10);
```

However, the following call results in output stating that "The tax on 0.10 is 20.00", which is clearly incorrect.

```
ComputeSalesTax(0.10, 200.00);
```

>> **NOTE** A declaration for a method that receives two or more arguments must list the type for each parameter separately, even if the parameters have the *same* type.

>> **NOTE** If two method parameters are of the same type—for example, two `doubles`—passing arguments to a method in the wrong order results in a logical error. If a method expects parameters of diverse types, then passing arguments in reverse order constitutes a syntax error.

Figure 6-11 shows a complete program that calls the ComputeSalesTax() method two times. Figure 6-12 shows the output.

```
using System;
public class UseSalesTax
{
    public static void Main()
    {
        double myPurchase = 239.11;
        double myRate = 0.10;
        ComputeSalesTax(myPurchase, myRate);
        ComputeSalesTax(16.55, 0.02);
    }
    public static void ComputeSalesTax(double saleAmount,
        double taxRate)
    {
        double tax;
        tax = saleAmount * taxRate;
        Console.WriteLine("The tax on {0} at {1} is {2}",
            saleAmount.ToString("C"),
            taxRate.ToString("P"), tax.ToString("F"));
    }
}
```

Figure 6-11 The UseSalesTax program

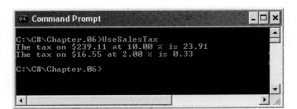

Figure 6-12 Output of the UseSalesTax program

You can write a method to take any number of parameters in any order. When you call the method, however, the arguments you send to it must match (in both number and type) the parameters listed in the method declaration. Thus, a method to compute an automobile salesperson's commission might require arguments such as an integer value of a sold car, a double percentage commission rate, and a character code for the vehicle type. The correct method will execute only when three arguments of the correct types are sent in the correct order.

CHAPTER SIX

WRITING A METHOD THAT RETURNS A VALUE

A method can return, at most, one value to a method that calls it. The return type for a method can be any type used in the C# programming language, which includes the basic built-in types `int`, `double`, `char`, and so on, as well as class types (including class types you create). Of course, a method also can return nothing, in which case the return type is `void`.

> **» NOTE** In addition to the primitive types, a method can return a class type. If a class named `BankLoan` exists, a method might return an instance of a `BankLoan` as in `public BankLoan ApprovalProcess()`. In other words, a method can return anything from a simple `int` to a complicated `BankLoan` object that contains 20 data fields. You will create classes like `BankLoan` in Chapter 7.

A method's return type is known more succinctly as a **method's type**. For example, the declaration for the `WelcomeMessage()` method shown in Figure 6-2 is:

```
public static void WelcomeMessage()
```

This method is `public` and returns no value, so it is of type `void`. A method that returns true or false depending on whether an employee worked overtime hours might be defined as:

```
public bool IsOvertimeEarned()
```

This method is `public` and returns a `bool` value, so it is of type `bool`.

Suppose you want to create a method to accept the hours an employee worked and the hourly pay rate, and to return a calculated gross pay value. The header for this method could be:

```
public static double CalcPay(double hours, double rate)
```

Figure 6-13 shows this method.

```csharp
public static double CalcPay(double hours, double rate)
{
    double gross;
    gross = hours * rate;
    return gross;
}
```

Figure 6-13 The `CalcPay()` method

Notice the return type `double` in the method header. Also notice the `return` statement, which is the last statement within the method. A **return statement** causes a value to be sent back to the calling method; in the `CalcPay()` method, the value stored in `gross` is sent

USING METHODS

back to any method that calls the `CalcPay()` method. The data type used in a method's `return` statement must be the same as the type declared in the method's header.

If a method returns a value and you call the method, you typically will want to use the returned value, although you are not required to use it. For example, when you invoke the `CalcPay()` method, you might want to assign the value to a `double` variable named `grossPay`, as in the following statement:

```
grossPay = CalcPay(myHours, myRate);
```

The `CalcPay()` method returns a `double`, so it is appropriate to assign the returned value to a `double` variable. Figure 6-14 shows a program that uses the `CalcPay()` method in the shaded statement, and Figure 6-15 shows the output.

```
using System;
public class UseCalcPay
{
   public static void Main()
   {
      double myHours = 37.5;
      double myRate = 12.75;
      double grossPay;
      grossPay = CalcPay(myHours, myRate);
      Console.WriteLine("I worked {0} hours at {1} per hour",
         myHours, myRate);
      Console.WriteLine("My gross pay is {0}",
         grossPay.ToString("C"));
   }
   public static double CalcPay(double hours, double rate)
   {
      double gross;
      gross = hours * rate;
      return gross;
   }
}
```

Figure 6-14 Program using the `CalcPay()` method

Figure 6-15 Output of `UseCalcPay` program

CHAPTER SIX

Instead of storing a method's returned value in a variable, you can use it directly, as in the following statements:

```
Console.WriteLine("My gross pay is {0}",
   CalcPay(myHours, myRate).ToString("C"));
double tax = CalcPay(myHours, myRate) * TAX_RATE;
```

In the first statement, the call to the `CalcPay()` method is made from within the `WriteLine()` method call. In the second, `CalcPay()`'s returned value is used in an arithmetic statement. Because `CalcPay()` returns a `double`, you can use the method call `CalcPay()` in the same way you would use any `double` value. The method call `CalcPay()` has a `double` value in the same way a `double` variable has a `double` value.

As an additional example, suppose you have a method named `ComputePrice()` that accepts an integer item number and returns its price. Further suppose that you want to ask the user to enter an item number from the keyboard so you can pass it to the `ComputePrice()` method. You can get the value from the user, store it in a string, convert the string to an integer, and pass the integer to the `ComputePrice()` method in three or four separate statements, or you can write the following:

```
price = ComputePrice(Convert.ToInt32(Console.ReadLine()));
```

This statement contains a method call to `ReadLine()` within a method call to `Convert.ToInt32()`, within a method call to `ComputePrice()`. When method calls are placed inside other method calls, the calls are **nested method calls**. When you write a statement with three nested method calls like the previous statement, the innermost method executes first. Its return value is then used as an argument to the intermediate method, and its return value is used as an argument to the outer method. There is no limit to how "deep" you can go with nested method calls.

> **»NOTE** Now that you have seen how to write methods that accept arguments, you might guess that the method header for the `Console.ReadLine()` method is `public static string ReadLine()`. You know the method returns a `string`, and you know it takes no parameters.

PASSING AN ARRAY TO A METHOD

In Chapter 5, you learned that you can declare an array to create a list of elements, and that you can use any individual array element in the same manner as you would use any single variable of the same type. That is, suppose you declare an integer array as follows:

```
int[] someNums = new int[ 12];
```

You can subsequently print `someNums[ 0]` or add one to `someNums[ 1]`, just as you would for any integer. Similarly, you can pass a single array element to a method in exactly the same manner as you would pass a variable.

USING METHODS

Consider the program shown in Figure 6-16. This program creates an array of four integers and prints them. Next, the program calls a method named `MethodGetsOneInt()` four times, passing each of the array elements in turn. The method prints the passed value, changes the number to 999, and then prints the number again. Finally, back in the `Main()` method, the four numbers print again. Figure 6-17 shows the output.

```
using System;
public class PassArrayElement
{
    public static void Main()
    {
        int[] someNums = {10, 12, 22, 35};
        int x;
        Console.Write("\nAt beginning of Main() method...");
        for(x = 0; x < someNums.Length; ++x)
            Console.Write("{0,6}", someNums[ x] );
        Console.WriteLine();
        for(x = 0; x < someNums.Length; ++x)
            MethodGetsOneInt(someNums[ x] );
        Console.Write("At end of Main() method..........");
        for(x = 0; x < someNums.Length; ++x)
            Console.Write("{0,6}", someNums[ x] );
    }
    public static void MethodGetsOneInt(int oneVal)
    {
        Console.Write("In MethodGetsOneInt() {0}", oneVal);
        oneVal = 999;
        Console.WriteLine("     After change {0}", oneVal);
    }
}
```

Figure 6-16 `PassArrayElement` program

Figure 6-17 Output of `PassArrayElement` program

As you can see in Figure 6-17, the program displays the four original values, then passes each to the `MethodGetsOneInt()` method, where it is displayed and then changed to 999. After the method executes four times, the `Main()` method displays the four values again, showing that they are unchanged by the assignments within `MethodGetsOneInt()`. The `oneVal` variable is local to the `MethodGetsOneInt()` method; therefore, any changes to variables passed into the method are not permanent and are not reflected in the array declared in the `Main()` program. Each `oneVal` variable in the `MethodGetsOneInt()` method holds only a copy of the array element passed into the method, and the `oneVal` variable holding the assigned value of 999 exists only while the `MethodGetsOneInt()` method is executing.

Instead of passing a single array element to a method, you can pass an entire array as a parameter. You indicate that a method parameter must be an array by placing square brackets after the data type in the method's parameter list. When you pass an array to a method, changes you make to array elements within the method are permanent; that is, they are reflected in the original array that was sent to the method. Arrays, like all objects but unlike built-in types, are **passed by reference**; that is, the method receives the actual memory address of the array and has access to the actual values in the array elements.

> **NOTE** You already have seen that methods can alter arrays passed to them. When you use the `Sort()` and `Reverse()` methods, the methods change the array contents.

> **NOTE** You can create and pass an unnamed array to a method in a single step. For example, you can write the following:
> `MethodThatAcceptsArray(new int[] {45, 67, 89});`

The program shown in Figure 6-18 creates an array of four integers. After the integers are printed, the entire array is passed to a method named `MethodGetsArray()` in the shaded statement. Within the method header, the parameter is declared as an array by using square brackets after the parameter type. Within the method, the numbers are printed, which shows that they retain their values from `Main()` upon entering the method, but then the value 888 is assigned to each number. Even though `MethodGetsArray()` is a `void` method (meaning that nothing is returned to the `Main()` method), when the program prints the array for the second time within the `Main()` method, all of the values have been changed to 888, as you can see in Figure 6-19. Because arrays are passed by reference, the `MethodGetsArray()` method "knows" the address of the array declared in `Main()` and makes its changes directly to the original array that was declared in the `Main()` method.

USING METHODS

```
using System;
public class PassEntireArray
{
   public static void Main()
   {
      int[] someNums = { 10, 12, 22, 35};
      int x;
      Console.Write("\nAt beginning of Main() method...");
      for(x = 0; x < someNums.Length; ++x)
         Console.Write("{ 0, 6}", someNums[ x]);
      Console.WriteLine();
      MethodGetsArray(someNums);
      Console.Write("At end of Main() method..........");
      for(x = 0; x < someNums.Length; ++x)
         Console.Write("{ 0, 6}", someNums[ x]);
   }
   public static void MethodGetsArray(int[] vals)
   {
      int x;
      Console.Write("In MethodGetsArray() ");
      for(x = 0; x < vals.Length; ++x)
         Console.Write(" { 0}", vals[ x]);
      Console.WriteLine();
      for(x = 0; x < vals.Length; ++x)
         vals[ x] = 888;
      Console.Write("After change");
      for(x = 0; x < vals.Length; ++x)
         Console.Write(" { 0}", vals[ x]);
      Console.WriteLine();
   }
}
```

Figure 6-18 `PassEntireArray` program

Figure 6-19 Output of the `PassEntireArray` program

You can pass a multidimensional array to a method by indicating the appropriate number of dimensions after the data type in the method header. For example, the following method headers accept two-dimensional arrays of `int`s and `double`s, respectively:

CHAPTER SIX

```
public static void displayScores(int[ ,] scoresArray)
public static boolean areAllPricesHigh(double[ ,] prices)
```

>> **NOTE**
Recall that in Chapter 5 you learned how two-dimensional arrays are stored in computer memory.

With jagged arrays, you can insert the appropriate number of square brackets after the data type in the method header. For example, the following method headers accept jagged arrays of `int`s and `double`s, respectively:

```
public static void displayIDs(int[][] idArray)
public static double computeTotal(double[][] prices)
```

In each case, notice that the brackets that define the array in the method header are empty. There is no need to insert numbers into the brackets because each passed array name is a starting memory address. The way you manipulate subscripts within the method determines how rows and columns are accessed.

>> **NOTE** The size of each dimension of a multidimensional array can be accessed using the `GetLength()` method. For example, `scoresArray.GetLength(0)` returns the value of the first dimension of `scoresArray`.

USING `ref`, `out`, AND `params` PARAMETERS WITHIN METHODS

In C#, you can write methods with four kinds of formal parameters listed within the parentheses in the method header. These four types are:

» Value parameters, which are declared without any modifiers
» Reference parameters, which are declared with the `ref` modifier
» Output parameters, which are declared with the `out` modifier
» Parameter arrays, which are declared with the `params` modifier

USING VALUE PARAMETERS

So far, all of the method parameters you have created (except arrays) have been value parameters. When you use a **value parameter** in a method header, you indicate the parameter's type and name, and the method receives a copy of the value passed to it. This copy—the formal parameter—is stored at a different memory address than the variable that was used as the parameter in the method call—the actual parameter. In other words, the actual parameter and the formal parameter refer to two separate memory locations, and any change to the formal parameter value within the method has no effect on the actual parameter value back in the calling method. Changes to value parameters never affect the original argument in the calling method.

>> **NOTE** Using a real-world analogy, you know that people with the same name living in different places are not the same person. Changes in the life of Jane Doe in Maine, such as a raise or a department transfer, have no effect on Jane Doe in Vermont. The same is true of like-named variables located in different methods.

USING METHODS

Figure 6-20 shows a program that declares a variable named `var`, assigns 4 to it, prints it, and passes it to a method that accepts a value parameter. The method assigns a new value, 777, to the formal, passed parameter and prints it. When control returns to the `Main()` method, the value of `var` remains 4. Changing the value of `var` within the `MethodWithValueParam()` method has no effect on `var` in `Main()`. Even though both methods contain a variable named `var`, they represent two separate variables, each with its own memory location. Figure 6-21 shows the output.

```
using System;
public class ParameterDemo1
{
    public static void Main()
    {
        int var = 4;
        Console.WriteLine("In Main var is {0}", var);
        MethodWithValueParam(var);
        Console.WriteLine("In Main var is {0}", var);
    }
    public static void MethodWithValueParam(int var)
    {
        var = 777;
        Console.WriteLine("In MethodWithValueParam, param is {0}",
            var);
    }
}
```

Figure 6-20 Program calling method with a value parameter

>> **NOTE**
Programmers say that a value parameter is used for "in" parameter passing—that is, values for these parameters go into a method, but modifications to them do not come "out."

Figure 6-21 Output of `ParameterDemo1` program

In the `MethodWithValueParam()` method, it makes no difference whether you use the name `var` as the `Main()` method's actual parameter or use some other name. In either case, the passed and received variables occupy separate memory locations.

CHAPTER SIX

USING REFERENCE AND OUTPUT PARAMETERS

On occasion, you might want a method to be able to alter a value you pass to it. In that case, you can use a reference parameter or an output parameter. Both **reference** and **output parameters** have memory addresses that are passed to a method, allowing it to alter the original variables. Reference and output parameters differ as follows:

» When you declare a reference parameter in a method header, the parameter must have been assigned a value; in other words, in the calling method, any argument must be a constant or a variable with an assigned value.

» When you use an output parameter, it need not contain an original value. However, an output parameter must receive a value before the method ends.

Neither reference nor output parameters occupy their own memory locations. Rather, both reference and output parameters act as **aliases**, or pseudonyms, for the same memory location occupied by the original passed variable. You use the keyword `ref` as a modifier to indicate a reference parameter and the keyword `out` as a modifier to indicate an output parameter.

Figure 6-22 shows a `Main()` program that calls a `MethodWithRefParam()` method. The `Main()` method declares a variable, displays its value, and then passes the variable to the `MethodWithRefParam()` method in the shaded statement. The modifier `ref` precedes the variable name `var` in both the method call and the method header. The method's parameter `myParam` holds the memory address of `var`, making `myParam` an alias for `var`. When the method changes the value of `myParam`, the change persists in the `var` variable within `Main()`. Figure 6-23 shows the output of the program.

>> **NOTE**
Using an alias for a variable is similar to using an alias for a person. Jane Doe might be known as "Ms. Doe" at work but "Sissy" at home. Both names refer to the same person.

```
using System;
public class ParameterDemo2
{
   public static void Main()
   {
      int var = 4;
      Console.WriteLine("In Main var is {0}", var);
      MethodWithRefParam(ref var);   // notice use of ref
      Console.WriteLine("In Main var is {0}", var);
   }
   public static void MethodWithRefParam(ref int myParam)
      // notice use of ref
   {
      myParam = 888;
      Console.WriteLine("In MethodWithRefParam, myParam is {0}",
         myParam);
   }
}
```

Figure 6-22 Program calling method with a reference parameter

191

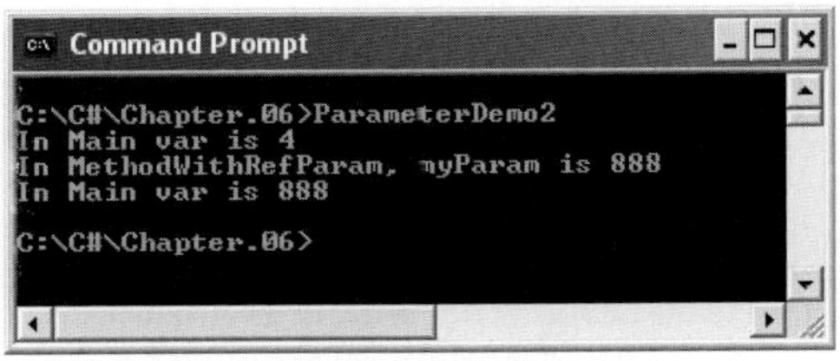

USING METHODS

Figure 6-23 Output of `ParameterDemo2` program

In the header for the `MethodWithRefParam()` method, it makes no difference whether you use the same name as the `Main()` method's passed variable (`var`) or some other name, such as `myParam`. In either case, the passed and received variables occupy the same memory location—the address of one is the address of the other.

When you use a reference parameter, the passed variable must have an assigned value. Using an output parameter is convenient when the passed variable doesn't have a value yet. For example, the program in Figure 6-24 uses `InputMethod()` to obtain values for two parameters. The parameters that are sent in the shaded statement get their values from the method, so it makes sense to provide them with no values going in. Instead, they acquire values in the method and retain the values coming out. Figure 6-25 shows a typical execution of the program.

```
using System;
public class InputMethodDemo
{
   public static void Main()
   {
      int first, second;
      InputMethod(out first, out second); // notice use of out
      Console.WriteLine("After InputMethod first is {0}", first);
      Console.WriteLine("and second is {0}", second);
   }
   public static void InputMethod(out int one, out int two)
      // notice use of out
   {
      string s1, s2;
      Console.Write("Enter first integer ");
      s1 = Console.ReadLine();
      Console.Write("Enter second integer ");
      s2 = Console.ReadLine();
      one = Convert.ToInt32(s1);
      two = Convert.ToInt32(s2);
   }
}
```

Figure 6-24 `InputMethodDemo` program

CHAPTER SIX

Figure 6-25 Output of `InputMethodDemo` program

In summary, when you need a method to alter a single value, you have two options:

» You can send a value parameter to a method, alter the local version of the variable within the method, return the altered value, and assign the return value to the original variable back in the calling method.

» You can send a reference or output parameter and alter the original value from within the method.

A major advantage to using reference or output parameters exists when you want a method to change multiple variables. A method can have only a single return type and can return at most only one value. By using reference or output parameters to a method, you can change multiple values.

> **»TIP** As with simple parameters, you can use `out` or `ref` when passing an array to a method. You do so when you want the method to create a new array by using the location of the named array in the calling method. For example, assume a `Main()` method declares an array without assigning any values or using the `new` operator to assign memory, as in:
>   `double[] payRate;`
>
> Then you can pass the array to a method with the header:
>   `AssignValues(out double[] money);`
>
> You do so by using the statement:
>   `AssignValues(out payRate);`
>
> Within the `AssignValues()` method, you can initialize the array as `money = new double[ 6] ;`, thereby creating a new array.

USING PARAMETER ARRAYS

When you don't know how many arguments you might eventually send to a method, you can declare a **parameter array**—a local array declared within the method header by using the keyword **params**. Such a method accepts any number of arguments.

For example, a method with the following header accepts an array of strings:

    public static void DisplayStrings(params string[] people)

193

USING METHODS

In the call to this method, you can use one, two, or any other number of strings as actual parameters; within the method, they will be treated as an array. Figure 6-26 shows a program that calls `DisplayStrings()` three times—once with one string argument, once with three string arguments, and once with an array of strings. In each case, the method works correctly, treating the passed strings as an array and displaying them appropriately. Figure 6-27 shows the output.

```
using System;
public class ParamsDemo
{
    public static void Main()
    {
        string[] names = { "Mark", "Paulette", "Carol", "James"};
        DisplayStrings("Ginger");
        DisplayStrings("George", "Maria", "Thomas");
        DisplayStrings(names);
    }
    public static void DisplayStrings(params string[] people)
    {
        foreach(string person in people)
            Console.Write("{0} ", person);
        Console.WriteLine("\n----------------");
    }
}
```

Figure 6-26 `ParamsDemo` program

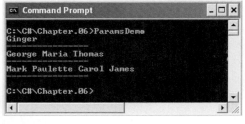

Figure 6-27 Output of `ParamsDemo` program

»NOTE
No additional parameters are permitted after the `params` keyword in a method declaration, and only one `params` keyword is permitted in a method declaration.

»NOTE You could create an even more flexible method by using a method header such as `Display(params Object[] things)`. Then the passed parameters could be any type—strings, integers, other classes, and so on. All data types are `Object`s; you will learn more about the `Object` class in Chapter 7.

CHAPTER SIX

OVERLOADING METHODS

Overloading involves using one term to indicate diverse meanings. When you use the English language, you frequently overload words. When you say "open the door," "open your eyes," and "open a computer file," you describe three very different actions that use different methods and produce different results. However, anyone who speaks English fluently has no trouble comprehending your meaning because the verb "open" is understood in the context of the noun that follows it.

>> **NOTE** Overloading a method is an example of polymorphism—the ability of a method to act appropriately depending on the context. You first learned the term *polymorphism* in Chapter 1.

>> **NOTE** Some C# operators are overloaded. For example, a + between two values indicates addition, but a single + to the left of a value means the value is positive. The + sign has different meanings based on the arguments used with it. In Chapter 7, you will learn how to overload operators to make them mean what you want with your own classes.

When you overload a C# method, you write multiple methods with a shared name. The compiler understands your meaning based on the arguments you use with the method. For example, suppose you create a method to apply a simple interest rate to a bank balance. The method receives two `double` arguments—the balance and the interest rate—and displays the multiplied result. Figure 6-28 shows the method.

>> **NOTE** A method's name and argument list constitute the method's **signature**.

```
public static void CalculateInterest(double bal, double rate)
{
    double interest;
    interest = bal * rate;
    Console.WriteLine("{0} interest on {1} earns {2}",
        rate, bal.ToString("C"), interest.ToString("C"));
}
```

Figure 6-28 The `CalculateInterest()` method with two `double` parameters

When a program calls the `CalculateInterest()` method and passes `double` values, as in `CalculateInterest(1000.00, 0.04)`, the simple interest will be calculated correctly as 4% of 1000.00. Assume, however, that the interest rate passed to the `CalculateInterest()` method comes from inconsistent user input. Some users who want to indicate an interest rate of 4% might type .04, and others might assume they are indicating a value of 4% by typing 4. When the `CalculateInterest()` method is called with arguments 1000.00 and .04, the interest is calculated correctly as 40.00. When the method is called using 1000.00 and 4, the interest is calculated incorrectly as 4000.00.

>> **NOTE** The `CalculateInterest()` method can receive integer parameters even though it is defined as needing `double` parameters, because integers will be promoted or cast automatically to `double`s, as you learned in Chapter 2.

A solution to this problem is to overload the `CalculateInterest()` method. Overloading methods involves writing multiple methods with the same name, but with different parameters.

USING METHODS

> **NOTE** In Figure 6-29, the `rateDouble` value is calculated by dividing by 100.0, not by 100. If two integers are divided, the result is a truncated integer; dividing by a `double` 100.0 causes the result to be a `double`. Alternatively, you could use a cast.

For example, in addition to the `CalculateInterest()` method shown in Figure 6-28, you could use the method shown in Figure 6-29.

```
public static void CalculateInterest(double bal, int rate)
                                                //rate is an int
{
    double interest, rateDouble;
    rateDouble = rate / 100.0;
    interest = bal * rateDouble;
    Console.WriteLine("{0} interest on {1} earns {2}",
        rateDouble, bal.ToString("C"), interest.ToString("C"));
}
```

Figure 6-29 The `CalculateInterest()` method with a `double` and an integer parameter

If both versions of `CalculateInterest()` are included in a program and you call the method using two `double` arguments, as in `CalculateInterest(1000.00, .04)`, the first version of the method shown in Figure 6-28 executes. If you use an integer as the second parameter in the call to `CalculateInterest()`, as in `CalculateInterest(1000.00, 4)`, then the method shown in Figure 6-29 executes, and the whole-number rate value will be divided by 100.0 correctly before it is used to determine the interest earned.

Of course, you could use methods with different names to solve the dilemma of producing an accurate simple interest figure—for example, `CalculateInterestRateUsingDouble()` and `CalculateInterestRateUsingIn()`. Using this approach would require that you place a decision within your program to determine which of the two methods to call. However, it is more convenient to use one method name and then let the compiler determine which method to use. Overloading the `CalculateInterest()` method also makes it more convenient for other programmers to use your method in the future. Whether their application assumes an interest rate is expressed as a `double` or as an integer, the interest will be calculated correctly. Finally, it is easier to remember one reasonable name for tasks that are functionally identical except for parameter types.

> **NOTE** In this book you have seen the `Console.WriteLine()` method used with a string parameter and with no parameter; therefore, you know it is an overloaded method.

AVOIDING AMBIGUOUS METHODS

When you overload a method, you run the risk of creating **ambiguous** methods—a situation in which the compiler cannot determine which method to use. Every time you call a method, the compiler decides whether a suitable method exists; if so, the method executes, and if not, you receive an error message.

For example, suppose you write two versions of a simple method, as in the program in Figure 6-30. The class contains two versions of a method named `SimpleMethod()`—one that takes a `double` and integer, and one that takes an integer and a `double`.

CHAPTER SIX

```
using System;
public class AmbiguousMethods
{
   public static void Main()
   {
      int iNum = 20;
      double dNum = 4.5;
      SimpleMethod(iNum, dNum);   // calls first version
      SimpleMethod(dNum, iNum);   // calls second version
      SimpleMethod(iNum, iNum);   // error! Call is ambiguous.
   }
   public static void SimpleMethod(int i, double d)
   {
       Console.WriteLine("Method receives int and double");
   }
   public static void SimpleMethod(double d, int i)
   {
       Console.WriteLine("Method receives double and int");
   }
}
```

Figure 6-30 Program containing ambiguous method call

In the Main() method in Figure 6-30, a call to SimpleMethod() with an integer argument first and a double argument second executes the first version of the method, and a call to SimpleMethod() with a double argument first and an integer argument second executes the second version of the method. With each of these calls, the compiler can find an exact match for the arguments you send. However, if you call SimpleMethod() using two integer arguments, as in the shaded statement, an ambiguous situation arises because there is no exact match for the method call. Because the first integer could be promoted to a double (matching the second version of the overloaded method), or the second integer could be promoted to a double (matching the first version), the compiler does not know which version of SimpleMethod() to use, and the program will not compile or execute. Figure 6-31 shows the error message that is generated.

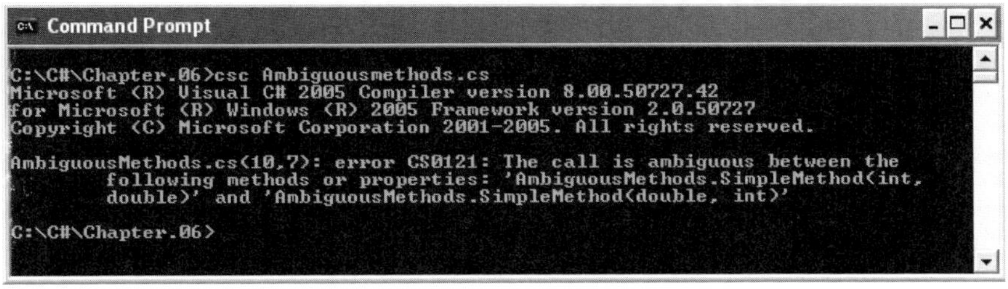

```
C:\C#\Chapter.06>csc Ambiguousmethods.cs
Microsoft (R) Visual C# 2005 Compiler version 8.00.50727.42
for Microsoft (R) Windows (R) 2005 Framework version 2.0.50727
Copyright (C) Microsoft Corporation 2001-2005. All rights reserved.

AmbiguousMethods.cs(10,7): error CS0121: The call is ambiguous between the
        following methods or properties: 'AmbiguousMethods.SimpleMethod(int,
        double)' and 'AmbiguousMethods.SimpleMethod(double, int)'

C:\C#\Chapter.06>
```

Figure 6-31 Error message generated by ambiguous method call

USING METHODS

> **NOTE** An overloaded method is not ambiguous on its own—it becomes ambiguous only if you create an ambiguous situation. A program with potentially ambiguous methods will run without problems if you make no ambiguous method calls. For example, if you remove the `SimpleMethod()` call that contains two integers from the program in Figure 6-30, the program runs as expected.

Methods can be overloaded correctly by providing different parameter lists for methods with the same name. Methods with identical names that have identical parameter lists but different return types are not overloaded—they are illegal. For example, the following two methods cannot coexist within a program.

```
public static int AMethod(int x)
public static void AMethod(int x)
```

The compiler determines which of several versions of a method to call based on parameter lists. When the method call `AMethod(17);` is made, the compiler will not know which method to execute because both possibilities take an integer argument. Similarly, the following method could not coexist with either of the previous versions:

```
public static void MethodA(int someNumber)
```

Even though this method uses a different local identifier for the passed value, its parameter list is still the same to the compiler—a single integer.

YOU DO IT

CALLING A METHOD

To write a program in which a `Main()` method calls another method that displays a company's logo:

1. Open a new file in your text editor. Enter the statement that uses the `System` namespace, then type the class header for the `DemoLogo` class and type the class-opening curly brace.

   ```
   using System;
   public class DemoLogo
   {
   ```

2. Type the `Main()` method for the `DemoLogo` class. This method prints a line, then calls the `PrintCompanyLogo()` method.

   ```
   public static void Main()
   {
       Console.Write("Our company is ");
       PrintCompanyLogo();
   }
   ```

CHAPTER SIX

3. Add a method that prints a two-line logo for a company.

   ```
   public static void PrintCompanyLogo()
   {
      Console.WriteLine("See Sharp Optical");
      Console.WriteLine("We prize your eyes");
   }
   ```

4. Add the closing curly brace for the class (**}**), then save the file as **DemoLogo.cs** in the Chapter.06 folder of your Student Disk.

5. Compile and execute the program. The output should look like Figure 6-32.

Figure 6-32 Output of `DemoLogo` program

WRITING A METHOD THAT RECEIVES PARAMETERS AND RETURNS A VALUE

Next, you will write a method named `CalcPhoneCallPrice()` that both receives parameters and returns a value. The purpose of the method is to take the length of a phone call in minutes and the rate charged per minute, and to then calculate the price of a call, assuming each call includes a 25-cent connection charge in addition to the per-minute charge. After writing the `CalcPhoneCallPrice()` method, you will write a `Main()` method that calls the `CalcPhoneCallPrice()` method using four different sets of data as arguments.

To create a class containing a method that receives two parameters and returns a value:

1. Open your text editor and type the **using System;** statement.

2. Add the class header for **public class PhoneCall** and an opening curly brace.

3. Type the following `CalcPhoneCallPrice()` method. It receives an integer and a `double` as parameters. The fee for a call is calculated as 0.25 plus the minutes times the rate per minute. The method returns the phone call fee to the calling method.

   ```
   public static double CalcPhoneCallPrice(int minutes,
      double rate)
   {
      const double BASE_FEE = 0.25;
      double callFee;
      callFee = BASE_FEE + minutes * rate;
      return callFee;
   }
   ```

199

USING METHODS

4. Add the `Main()` method header for the `PhoneCall` class. Begin the method by declaring two arrays; one contains two call lengths and the other contains two rates. You will use all the possible combinations of call lengths and rates to test the `CalcPhoneCallPrice()` method. Also, declare a `double` named `priceOfCall` that will hold the result of a calculated call price.

```
public static void Main()
{
    int[] callLength = {2, 5};
    double[] rate = { 0.03, 0.12};
    double priceOfCall;
```

5. Add a statement that prints column headings under which you can list combinations of call lengths, rates, and prices. The three column headings are right-aligned, each in a field 10 characters wide.

```
Console.WriteLine("{0, 10}{1, 10}{2, 10}",
    "Minutes", "Rate", "Price");
```

6. Add a pair of nested loops that, in turn, passes each `callLength` and each `rate` to the `CalcPhoneCallPrice()` method. As each pair is passed, the result is stored in the `priceOfCall` variable, and the details are displayed. Using the nested loops allows you to pass each combination of call time and rate so that multiple possibilities for the values can be tested conveniently.

```
for(int x = 0; x < callLength.Length; ++x)
    for(int y = 0; y < rate.Length; ++y)
    {
        priceOfCall = CalcPhoneCallPrice(callLength[x],
            rate[y]);
        Console.WriteLine("{0, 10}{1, 10}{2, 10}",
            callLength[x], rate[y], priceOfCall.ToString("C"));
    }
```

7. Add a closing curly brace for the `Main()` method and another for the `PhoneCall` class.

8. Save the file as **PhoneCall.cs**. Compile and run the program. The output looks like Figure 6-33. It shows how a single method can produce a variety of results when you use different values for the arguments.

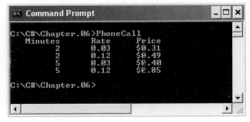

Figure 6-33 Output of the `PhoneCall` program

CHAPTER SIX

USING REFERENCE PARAMETERS

You use reference parameters when you want a method to have access to the memory address of arguments in a calling method. For example, suppose you have two values and you want to exchange them (or swap them), making each equal to the value of the other. Because you want to change two values, a method that accepts copies of arguments will not work—a method can return, at most, one value. Therefore, you can use reference parameters to provide your method with the actual addresses of the values you want to change.

To write a program that uses a method to swap two values:

1. Open your editor and begin the `SwapProgram` as follows:

   ```
   using System;
   public class SwapProgram
   {
      public static void Main()
      {
   ```

2. Declare two integers and display their values. Call the `Swap()` method and pass in the addresses of the two variables to swap. Because the parameters already have assigned values, and because you want to alter those values in `Main()`, you can use reference parameters. After the method call, display the two values again. Add the closing curly brace for the `Main()` method.

   ```
   int first = 34, second = 712;
   Console.Write("Before swap first is {0}", first);
   Console.WriteLine(" and second is {0}", second);
   Swap(ref first, ref second);
   Console.Write("After swap first is {0}", first);
   Console.WriteLine(" and second is {0}", second);
   }
   ```

3. Create the `Swap()` method as shown. You can swap two values by storing the first value in a temporary variable, then assigning the second value to the first variable. At this point, both variables hold the value originally held by the second variable. When you assign the temporary variable's value to the second variable, the two values are reversed.

   ```
   public static void Swap(ref int one, ref int two)
   {
      int temp;
      temp = one;
      one = two;
      two = temp;
   }
   ```

201

USING METHODS

4. Add the closing curly brace for the class. Save the file as **SwapProgram.cs**. Compile and execute the program. Figure 6-34 shows the output.

Figure 6-34 Output of SwapProgram program

> **NOTE** You might want to use a module like Swap() as part of a larger program in which you verify, for example, that a higher value is displayed before a lower one; you would include the call to Swap() as part of a decision whose body executes only when a first value is less than a second one.

OVERLOADING METHODS

In the next steps you will overload a method that correctly triples an integer or a string, depending on how you call the method.

1. Open a new file in your text editor. Create a method that triples and displays an integer parameter as follows:

```
public static void Triple(int num)
{
    const int THREE = 3;
    Console.WriteLine("{0} times {1} is {2}\n",
        num, THREE, num * THREE);
}
```

2. Create a second method with the same name that takes a string parameter. Assume you want to define tripling a message as printing it three times, separated by tabs.

```
public static void Triple(string message)
{
    Console.WriteLine("{0}\t{0}\t{0}\n", message);
}
```

3. Position your cursor at the top of the file and add a using statement, class header, and opening curly brace so the overloaded Triple() methods will be contained in a class named OverloadedTriples.

```
using System;
public class OverloadedTriples
{
```

4. Position your cursor at the bottom of the file and add the closing curly brace for the OverloadedTriples class.

CHAPTER SIX

5. Position your cursor after the opening curly brace for the class. On a new line, insert a `Main()` method that declares an integer and a string and, in turn, passes each to the appropriate `Triple()` method.

```
public static void Main()
{
   int num = 20;
   string message = "Go team!";
   Triple(num);
   Triple(message);
}
```

6. Save the file as **OverloadedTriples.cs** in the Chapter.06 folder on your Student Disk. Compile and execute the program. Figure 6-35 shows the output. Even though the same method name is used in the two method calls, the appropriate overloaded method executes each time.

Figure 6-35 Output of `OverloadedTriples` program

CHAPTER SUMMARY

» A method is a series of statements that carry out a task. Any class can contain an unlimited number of methods.

» You write methods to make programs easier to understand and so that you can easily reuse them. In C#, a method must include a method declaration, an opening curly brace, a method body, and a closing curly brace. The method declaration defines the rules for using the method; it contains an optional declared accessibility, an optional `static` modifier, a return type for the method, an identifier, and an optional list of method parameters between parentheses.

» Object-oriented programs hide their methods' implementation. A client method uses an interface to work with the method. To more easily incorporate methods into a program, it is common practice to store methods (or groups of associated methods) in their own classes and files, but methods can also be contained in the same file as the methods that use them.

» Some methods require passed-in information called arguments or parameters. When you write the declaration for a method that can receive a parameter, you need to include the type of parameter and a local identifier for it within the method declaration parentheses. A variable declared in a method header is a formal parameter, and an argument within a method call is an actual parameter.

USING METHODS

» You can pass multiple arguments to a method by listing the arguments within the parentheses in the call to the method and separating them with commas. You can write a method to take any number of parameters in any order. When you call the method, however, the arguments you send to it must match in both number and type with the parameters listed in the method declaration.

» The return type for a method can be any type used in the C# programming language, which includes the basic built-in types `int`, `double`, `char`, and so on, as well as class types (including class types you create). A method also can return nothing, in which case the return type is `void`. A method's return type is known more succinctly as a method's type. When a `return` statement includes a value, the value is sent back to the calling method.

» You can pass an array as a parameter to a method. You indicate that a method parameter is an array by placing square brackets after the data type in the method's parameter list. When you pass an array to a method, changes you make to array elements within the method are permanent; that is, they are reflected in the original array that was sent to the method. Arrays, like all objects but unlike built-in types, are passed by reference; that is, the method receives the actual memory address of the array and has access to the actual values in the array elements.

» In C#, you can write methods with four kinds of formal parameters listed within the parentheses in the method header: value parameters, which are declared without any modifiers; reference parameters, which are declared with the `ref` modifier; output parameters, which are declared with the `out` modifier; and parameter arrays, which are declared with the `params` modifier. A major advantage to using reference or output parameters exists when you want a method to change multiple variables. When you don't know how many arguments you might eventually send to a method, you can declare a local array within the method header by using the keyword `params`. Such a method accepts any number of arguments.

» When you overload a C# method, you write multiple methods with a shared name but different argument lists. The compiler understands your meaning based on the combination of arguments you use with the method.

» When you overload a method, you run the risk of creating an ambiguous situation—one in which the compiler cannot determine which method to use. Methods can be overloaded correctly by providing different parameter lists for methods with the same name.

KEY TERMS

A **method** is an encapsulated series of statements that carry out a task.

Methods are **invoked**, or **called**, by other methods.

A **calling method** calls another method.

A method invoked by another is a **called method**.

Code bloat is a term that describes unnecessarily long or repetitive program statements.

CHAPTER SIX

A **method declaration** is a **method header** or **method definition**.

A **method body** is a block of statements that carry out a method's work.

The optional declared **accessibility** for a method sets limits as to whether and how other methods can use your method.

Public access is a level of method accessibility that allows unlimited access to a method.

Protected internal access is a level of method accessibility that limits method access to the containing program or types derived from the containing class.

Protected access is a level of method accessibility that limits method access to the containing class or types derived from the containing class.

Internal access is a level of method accessibility that limits method access to the containing program.

Private access is a level of method accessibility that limits method access to the containing type.

A **static** method can be called without referring to an object.

A **nonstatic** method requires an object reference.

A **return type** indicates what kind of value a method will return to any other method that calls it.

A variable's **scope** is the area where it is known and can be used.

Implementation hiding means keeping the details of a method's operations hidden.

To **interface** with a system is to interact with it.

A **black box** is any device you can use without knowing how it works internally.

A **client** of a method is a method that uses it.

A **multifile assembly** is a group of files containing methods that work together to create an application.

A **local variable** is one that is declared in the current method.

A **formal parameter** is a parameter within a method header that accepts a value.

Actual parameters are arguments within a method call.

A **method's type** is its return type.

A `return statement` causes a value to be sent back from a method to its calling method.

Nested method calls are method calls placed inside other method calls.

When data is **passed by reference** to a method, the method receives the memory address of the argument passed to it.

When you use a **value parameter** in a method header, you indicate the parameter's type and name, and the method receives a copy of the value passed to it.

When you use a **reference parameter** to a method, the parameter must have been assigned a value before you use it in the method call, and the method receives the parameter's address.

When you use an **output parameter**, it need not contain an original value, and the method receives the parameter's address.

Aliases are alternate names or pseudonyms.

A **parameter array** is a local array declared within a method header.

The keyword `params` is used to declare a local array in a method so the method can receive any number of arguments.

Overloading involves using one term to indicate diverse meanings.

A method's **signature** is composed of its name and argument list.

Ambiguous methods are overloaded methods for which the compiler cannot determine which one to use.

REVIEW QUESTIONS

1. At most, a class can contain _____ method(s).

    a. 0

    b. 1

    c. 2

    d. any number of

2. What is the most important reason for creating methods within a program?

    a. Methods are easily reusable.

    b. Because all methods must be stored in the same class, they are easy to find.

    c. The `Main()` method becomes more detailed.

    d. All of these are true.

3. In C#, a method must include all of the following *except* a _____.

    a. method declaration

    b. parameter list

    c. body

    d. closing curly brace

4. A method declaration must contain _____.

    a. a statement of purpose

    b. declared accessibility

    c. the static modifier

    d. a return type

CHAPTER SIX

5. If you use the keyword modifier `static` in a method header, you indicate that the method _____.

   a. can be called without referring to an object

   b. cannot be copied

   c. cannot be overloaded

   d. can be ambiguous

6. When you write the method declaration for a method that can receive a parameter, you need to include all of the following items *except* _____.

   a. a pair of parentheses

   b. the type of the parameter

   c. a local name for the parameter

   d. an initial value for the parameter

7. Suppose you have declared a variable as `int myAge = 21;`. Which of the following is a legal call to a method with the declaration `public static void AMethod(int num)`?

   a. `AMethod(int 55);`

   b. `AMethod(myAge);`

   c. `AMethod(int myAge);`

   d. `AMethod();`

8. Suppose you have declared a method named `public static void CalculatePay(double rate)`. Which is true of a method that calls the `CalculatePay()` method?

   a. The calling method must contain a declared `double` named `rate`.

   b. The calling method might contain a declared `double` named `rate`.

   c. The calling method cannot contain a declared `double` named `rate`.

   d. The calling method can contain no declared `double` variables.

9. In the method call `PrintTheData(double salary);`, `salary` is the _____ parameter.

   a. formal

   b. actual

   c. proposed

   d. preferred

207

USING METHODS

10. A program contains the method call `PrintTheData(salary);`. In the method definition, the name of the formal parameter must be _____.

    a. `salary`
    b. any legal identifier other than `salary`
    c. any legal identifier
    d. omitted

11. What is a correct declaration for a method that receives two `double` arguments and calculates the difference between them?

    a. `public static void CalcDifference(double price1, price2)`
    b. `public static void CalcDifference(double price1, double price2)`
    c. `public static void CalcDifference(double price1, double anotherPrice)`
    d. Two of these are correct.

12. A method is declared as `double CalcPay(int hoursWorked)`. Suppose you write a `Main()` method containing `int hours = 35;` and `double pay;`. Which of the following represents a correct way to call the `CalcPay()` method from the `Main()` method?

    a. `hours = CalcPay();`
    b. `hours = CalcPay(pay);`
    c. `pay = CalcPay(hoursWorked);`
    d. `pay = CalcPay(hours);`

13. Which is *not* a type of method parameter in C#?

    a. value
    b. reference
    c. forensic
    d. output

14. Which type of method parameter receives the address of the variable passed in?

    a. a value parameter
    b. a reference parameter
    c. an output parameter
    d. two of the above

CHAPTER SIX

15. Assume you declare a variable as `int x = 100;` and correctly pass it to a method with the declaration `public static void IncreaseValue(ref int x)`. There is a single statement within the `IncreaseValue()` method: `x = x + 25;`. Back in the `Main()` method, after the method call, what is the value of x?

    a. 100
    b. 125
    c. It is impossible to tell.
    d. The program will not run.

16. Assume you declare a variable as `int x = 100;` and correctly pass it to a method with the declaration `public static void IncreaseValue(int x)`. There is a single statement within the `IncreaseValue()` method: `x = x + 25;`. Back in the `Main()` method, after the method call, what is the value of x?

    a. 100
    b. 125
    c. It is impossible to tell.
    d. The program will not run.

17. What is the difference between a reference parameter and an output parameter?

    a. A reference parameter receives a memory address; an output parameter does not.
    b. A reference parameter occupies a unique memory address; an output parameter does not.
    c. A reference parameter must have an initial value; an output parameter need not.
    d. A reference parameter need not have an initial value; an output parameter must.

18. Methods are ambiguous when they _____ .

    a. are overloaded
    b. are written in a confusing manner
    c. are indistinguishable to the compiler
    d. have the same parameter type as their return type

19. Which of the following pairs of method declarations represent correctly overloaded methods?

    a. `public static void MethodA(int a)`
       `public static void MethodA(int b, double c)`
    b. `public static void MethodB(double d)`
       `public static void MethodB()`
    c. `public static double MethodC(int e)`
       `public static double MethodD(int f)`
    d. Two of these are correctly overloaded methods.

USING METHODS

20. Which of the following pairs of method declarations represent correctly overloaded methods?

   a. `public static void Method(int a)`
      `public static void Method(int b)`

   b. `public static void Method(double d)`
      `public static int Method()`

   c. `public static double Method(int e)`
      `public static int Method(int f)`

   d. Two of these are correctly overloaded methods.

EXERCISES

As you work through each exercise, save the finished program in the Chapter.06 folder of your Student Disk.

1. a. Create a class named `Numbers` whose `Main()` method holds two integer variables. Assign values to the variables. Within the class, create two methods, `Sum()` and `Difference()`, that compute the sum of and difference between the values of the two variables, respectively. Each method should perform the computation and display the results. In turn, call each of the two methods from `Main()`, passing the values of the two integer variables. Save the program as **Numbers.cs**.

   b. Add a method named `Product()` to the `Numbers` class. This method should compute the multiplication product of two integers, but not display the answer. Instead, it should return the answer to the calling `Main()` method, which displays the answer. Save the program as **Numbers2.cs**.

2. a. Create a class named `InchesToFeet`. Its `Main()` method holds an integer variable named `inches` to which you will assign a value. Create a method to which you pass `inches`. The method displays `inches` in feet and inches. For example, 67 inches is 5 feet 7 inches. Save the program as **InchesToFeet.cs**.

   b. Add a second method to the `InchesToFeet` class. This method displays a passed argument as yards, feet, and inches. For example, 67 inches is 1 yard, 2 feet, and 7 inches. Add a statement to the `Main()` method so that after it calls the method to convert inches to feet and inches, it passes the same variable to the new method to convert the same value to yards, feet, and inches. Save the program as **InchesToYards.cs**.

3. Create a class named `Monogram`. Its `Main()` method holds six character variables that hold your first, middle, and last initials, and a friend's first, middle, and last initials, respectively. Create a method named `DisplayMonogram()` to which you pass three initials. The method displays the initials surrounded by two asterisks on each side and with periods following each initial, as shown in the following example:

   ```
   ** J. M. F. **
   ```

Within the `Main()` method, call the `DisplayMonogram()` method twice—once using your initials and once using your friend's initials. Save the program as **Monogram.cs**.

4. Create a class named `Exponent`. Its `Main()` method prompts the user for an integer value and, in turn, passes the value to a method that squares the number and to a method that cubes the number. The `Main()` method prints the results returned from each of the other methods. Save the program as **Exponent.cs**.

5. Create a class named `Square`. In the `Main()` method, declare an integer and prompt the user for a value. Display the value of the integer, then pass it to a method that accepts the value as a reference parameter and prints its square (the number times itself). In `Main()`, print the value again, proving that the original argument to the method was altered. Save the program as **Square.cs**.

6. a. Create a class named `Reverse3`. Within its `Main()` method, declare three integers named `firstInt`, `middleInt`, and `lastInt`. Assign values to the variables, display them, and then pass them to a method that places the first value in the `lastInt` variable and the last value in the `firstInt` variable. In the `Main()` method, display the three variables again, demonstrating that their positions have been reversed. Save the program as **Reverse3.cs**.

   b. Create a new class named `Reverse4`, which contains a method that reverses the positions of four variables. Write a `Main()` method that demonstrates the method works correctly. Save the program as **Reverse4.cs**.

7. Create a class named `Area`. Include three overloaded methods that compute the area of a rectangle when two dimensions are passed to it. One method takes two integers as parameters, one takes two `doubles`, and the third takes an integer and a `double`. Write a `Main()` method that demonstrates each method works correctly. Save the program as **Area.cs**.

8. Create a class named `ComputeWeeklySalary`. Include two overloaded methods—one that accepts an annual salary as an integer and one that accepts an annual salary as a `double`. Each method should calculate and display a weekly salary, assuming 52 weeks in a year. Include a `Main()` method that demonstrates both overloaded methods work correctly. Save the program as **ComputeWeeklySalary.cs**.

9. Create a class named `TaxCalculation`. Include two overloaded methods—one that accepts a price and a tax rate expressed as `doubles` (for example, 79.95 and 0.06, where 0.06 represents 6%), and one that accepts a price as a `double` and a tax rate as an integer (for example, 79.95 and 6, where 6 also represents 6%). Include a `Main()` method that demonstrates each method calculates the same tax amount appropriately. Save the program as **TaxCalculation.cs**.

10. Write an application that contains a method that calculates the conversion of any amount of money into the fewest bills; it calculates the number of 20s, 10s, 5s, and 1s needed. Create a `Main()` method that prompts the user for an integer number of dollars, uses the conversion method, and then displays the monetary breakdown. Save the program as **Dollars.cs**.

11. The `InputMethod()` in the `InputMethodDemo` program in Figure 6-24 contains repetitive code that prompts the user and retrieves integer values. Rewrite the program so the `InputMethod()` calls another method to do the work. The rewritten `InputMethod()` will need to contain only two statements:

    ```
    one = DataEntry("first");
    two = DataEntry("second");
    ```

    Save the new program as **InputMethodDemo2.cs**.

12. Create a method named `Sum()` that accepts any number of integer parameters and displays their sum. Write a `Main()` method that demonstrates the `Sum()` method works correctly when passed one, three, five, or an array of 10 integers. Save the program as **UsingSum.cs**.

DEBUGGING EXERCISES

Each of the following files in the Chapter.06 folder on your Student Disk has syntax and/or logical errors. In each case, determine the problem and fix the program. After you correct the errors, save each file using the same filename preceded with *Fixed*. For example, DebugSix1.cs will become FixedDebugSix1.cs.

a. DebugSix1.cs
b. DebugSix2.cs
c. DebugSix3.cs
d. DebugSix4.cs

UP FOR DISCUSSION

1. One of the advantages to writing a program that is subdivided into methods is that such a structure allows different programmers to write separate methods, thus dividing the work. Would you prefer to write a large program by yourself, or to work on a team in which each programmer produces one or more modules? Why?

2. In this chapter, you learned that hidden implementations are often said to exist in a black box. What are the advantages to this approach in both programming and real life? Are there any disadvantages?

CHAPTER SEVEN

7

USING CLASSES AND OBJECTS

In this chapter you will:

Learn about class concepts
Create classes from which objects can be instantiated
Declare objects
Create properties
Learn useful techniques for storing and organizing
  classes
Learn about using `public` fields and `private` methods
Learn about the `this` reference
Write constructors and use them
Pass objects to methods
Overload operators
Declare an array of objects and use the `Sort()` and
  `BinarySearch()` methods with them
Write destructors

USING CLASSES AND OBJECTS

Much of your understanding of the world comes from your ability to categorize objects and events into classes. As a young child, you learned the concept of "animal" long before you knew the word. Your first encounter with an animal might have been with the family dog, a neighbor's cat, or a goat at a petting zoo. As you developed speech, you might have used the same term for all of these creatures, gleefully shouting "Doggie!" as your parents pointed out cows, horses, and sheep in picture books or along the roadside on drives in the country. As you grew more sophisticated, you learned to distinguish dogs from cows; still later, you learned to distinguish breeds. Your understanding of the class "animal" helps you see the similarities between dogs and cows, and your understanding of the class "dog" helps you see the similarities between a Great Dane and a Chihuahua. Understanding classes gives you a framework for categorizing new experiences. You might not know the term "okapi," but when you learn it's an animal, you begin to develop a concept of what an okapi might be like.

Classes are also the basic building blocks of object-oriented programming. You already understand that differences exist among the `Double`, `Int32`, and `Float` classes, yet you also understand that items that are members of these classes possess similarities—they are all data types, you can perform arithmetic with all of them, they all can be converted to strings, and so on. Understanding classes enables you to see similarities in objects and increases your understanding of the programming process. In this chapter, you will discover how C# handles classes, learn to create your own classes, and learn to construct objects that are members of those classes.

UNDERSTANDING CLASS CONCEPTS

When you write programs in C#, you create two distinct types of classes:

» Classes that are only application programs with a `Main()` method. These classes can contain other methods that the `Main()` method calls.
» Classes from which you instantiate objects; these classes can contain a `Main()` method, but it is not required.

All of the classes you have created so far in this book have been applications with a `Main()` method that executes when you run the program in which it resides. Many classes do not contain a `Main()` method; instead, you use these classes to create objects.

When you think in an object-oriented manner, everything is an object, and every object is a member of a class. You can think of any inanimate physical item as an object—your desk, your computer, and your house are all called "objects" in everyday conversation. You can think of living things as objects, too—your houseplant, your pet fish, and your sister are objects. Events also are objects—the stock purchase you made, the mortgage closing you attended, or a graduation party in your honor are all objects.

Everything is an object, and every object is a member of a more general class. Your desk is a member of the class that includes all desks, and your pet fish is a member of the class that contains all fish. An object-oriented programmer would say that your desk is an instance of the `Desk` class and your fish is an instance of the `Fish` class. These statements represent

> **NOTE**
> In C#, an application you write to use other classes is a class itself.

is-a relationships because you can say, "My oak desk with the scratch on top *is a* `Desk` and my goldfish named Moby *is a* `Fish`." The difference between a class and an object parallels the difference between abstract and concrete. An object is an **instantiation** of a class; an object is one tangible example of a class. Your goldfish, my guppy, and the zoo's shark each constitute one instantiation of the `Fish` class.

> **» NOTE**
> Object-oriented programmers also use the term *is-a* when describing inheritance. You will learn about inheritance in Chapter 8.

The concept of a class is useful because of its reusability. Objects receive their attributes from classes. For example, if you invite me to a graduation party, I automatically know many things about the object (the party). I assume there will be a starting time, a number of guests, some quantity of food, and some nature of gifts. I understand parties because of my previous knowledge of the `Party` class, of which all parties are members. I don't know the number of guests or the date or time of this particular party, but I understand that because all parties have a date and time, then this one must as well. Similarly, even though every stock purchase is unique, each must have a dollar amount and a number of shares. All objects have predictable attributes because they are members of certain classes.

The data components of a class often are called its **instance variables**. Also, class object attributes often are called **fields** to help distinguish them from other variables you might use. The set of contents of a class object's instance variables also are known as its **state**. For example, the current state of a particular party is 8 p.m. and Friday; the state of a particular stock purchase is $10 and five shares.

In addition to their attributes, class objects have methods associated with them, and every object that is an instance of a class possesses the same methods. For example, at some point you might want to issue invitations for a party. You might name the method `IssueInvitations()`, and it might display some text, as well as the values of the party's date and time fields. Your graduation party, then, might possess the identifier `myGraduationParty`. As a member of the `Party` class, it might have data members for the date and time, like all parties, and it might have a method to issue invitations. When you use the method, you might want to be able to send an argument to `IssueInvitations()` that indicates how many copies to print. When you think of an object and its methods, it's as though you can send a message to the object to direct it to accomplish some task—you can tell the party object named `myGraduationParty` to print the number of invitations you request. Even though `yourAnniversaryParty` also is a member of the `Party` class, and even though it also has an `IssueInvitations()` method, you will send a different argument value to `yourAnniversaryParty`'s `IssueInvitations()` method than I send to `myGraduationParty`'s corresponding method. Within any object-oriented program, you continuously make requests to objects' methods, often including arguments as part of those requests.

When you program in C#, you frequently create classes from which objects will be instantiated (or other programmers create them for you). You also write applications to use the objects, along with their data and methods. Often, you will write programs that use classes created by others, as you have used the `Console` class; similarly, you might create a class that other programmers will use to instantiate objects within their own programs. A program or class that instantiates objects of another prewritten class is a **class client** or **class user**.

USING CLASSES AND OBJECTS

CREATING A CLASS FROM WHICH OBJECTS CAN BE INSTANTIATED

When you create a class, you first must assign a name to it, and then you must determine what data and methods will be part of the class. For example, suppose you decide to create a class named `Employee`. One instance variable of `Employee` might be an employee number, and one necessary method might display a welcome message to new employees. To begin, you create a **class header** or **class definition** that describes the class. It contains three parts:

1. An optional access modifier
2. The keyword `class`
3. Any legal identifier you choose for the name of your class

> **NOTE**
> You will learn other optional components you can add to a class definition as you continue to study C#.

For example, a header for an `Employee` class is `internal class Employee`. The keyword `internal` is an example of a **class access modifier**. You can declare a class to be one of the following:

- **`public`**, meaning access to the class is not limited.
- **`protected`**, meaning access to the class is limited to the class and to any classes derived from the class. (You will learn about deriving classes in Chapter 8.)
- **`internal`**, meaning access is limited to the assembly (a group of code modules compiled together) to which the class belongs.
- **`private`**, meaning access is limited to another class to which the class belongs. In other words, a class can be `private` if it is contained within another class, and only the containing class should have access to the `private` class.

Note that `private` and `protected` classes have limited uses. Furthermore, when you declare a class using a namespace, you only can declare it to be `public` or `internal`. For now, you will use either the `public` or `internal` modifier with your classes. If you do not explicitly include an access specifier, class access is `internal` by default. Because most classes you create will have `internal` access, typing an access specifier is often unnecessary.

> **NOTE**
> You first learned about namespaces in Chapter 1.

In addition to the class header, classes you create must have a class body enclosed between curly braces. Figure 7-1 shows a shell for an `Employee` class.

```
class Employee
{
    // Instance variables and methods go here
}
```

Figure 7-1 `Employee` class shell

CHAPTER SEVEN

CREATING INSTANCE VARIABLES AND METHODS

When you create a class, you define both its attributes and its methods. You declare the class's instance variables, which are the attributes or fields, within the curly braces using the same syntax you use to declare other variables—you provide a type and an identifier. When you create an instance variable, you create an attribute to hold a value that describes a feature of every object of that class. For example, within the `Employee` class, you can declare an integer ID number; when you create `Employee` objects, each will have its own `idNumber`. You can define the ID number simply as `int idNumber;`. However, programmers frequently include an access modifier for each of the class fields and declare the `idNumber` as `private int idNumber;`. Figure 7-2 shows an `Employee` class that contains the `idNumber` field.

```
class Employee
{
    private int idNumber;
}
```

Figure 7-2 `Employee` class containing `idNumber` field

>> **NOTE** If you do not provide an access specifier for a class field, its access is `private` by default.

The allowable field modifiers are `new`, `public`, `protected`, `internal`, `private`, `static`, `readonly`, and `volatile`. Most class fields are `private`, which provides the highest level of security. Identifying a field as `private` means that no other class can access the field's values, and only methods of the same class will be allowed to set, get, or otherwise use the field. Using `private` fields within classes is an example of **information hiding**, a feature found in all object-oriented languages. You see cases of information hiding in real-life objects every day. For instance, you cannot see into your automobile's gas tank to determine how full it is. Instead, you use a gauge on the dashboard to provide you with the necessary information. Similarly, data fields are frequently `private` in object-oriented programming, but their contents are accessed through `public` methods. The `private` data of a class should be changed or manipulated only by its own methods, not by methods that belong to other classes.

>> **NOTE** A benefit of information hiding is the ability to validate data. A method that sets a variable's value can ensure that the value falls within a specified range. For example, perhaps an `Employee`'s salary should not be below the federal minimum wage, or a department number should not be negative or greater than 10.

In contrast to a class's `private` data fields, most class methods are not usually `private`; they are `public`. The resulting `private` data/`public` method arrangement provides a means to control outside access to your data—only a class's non-private methods can be used to access a class's `private` data. The situation is similar to having a "public" receptionist who controls the messages passed in and out of your private office. The way in which the non-private methods are written controls how you will use the `private` data.

217

USING CLASSES AND OBJECTS

For example, one method you need for an `Employee` class that contains an `idNumber` is the method to display the company's welcoming message. A reasonable name for this method is `WelcomeMessage()`, and its declaration is `public void WelcomeMessage()`, because it will have `public` access and return nothing. Figure 7-3 shows the `Employee` class with the addition of the `WelcomeMessage()` method.

```
class Employee
{
    private int idNumber;
    public void WelcomeMessage()
    {
        Console.WriteLine("Welcome Employee #{0}", idNumber);
        Console.WriteLine("We hope you enjoy working here");
    }
}
```

Figure 7-3 `Employee` class with `idNumber` field and `WelcomeMessage()` method

Notice that the `WelcomeMessage()` method does not employ the `static` modifier, unlike many other methods you have created. The keyword `static` is used for class-wide methods, but not for instance methods that "belong" to objects. If you are creating a program with a `Main()` method that you will execute to perform some task, then many of your methods will be `static`. You can call the `static` methods from within `Main()` without creating an object. However, if you are creating a class from which objects will be instantiated, most methods will probably be nonstatic, as you will be associating the methods with individual objects. Methods used with object instantiations are called **instance methods**. Each time the `WelcomeMessage()` instance method is used in the class in Figure 7-3, it will display an `idNumber` for a specific object. In other words, the method will work appropriately for each object instance.

>> **NOTE**
You can call class (`static`) methods without creating an instance of the class. Instance methods require an instantiated object; class methods do not.

>> **NOTE** The `Employee` class in Figure 7-3 is not a program that will run; it contains no `Main()` method. Rather, it simply describes what `Employee` objects will have (an `idNumber`) and be able to do (display a greeting) when you write a program that contains one or more `Employee` objects.

>> **NOTE** A class can contain other classes as data members. For example, you might create a class named `Date` that contains a month, day, and year, and add two `Date` fields to an `Employee` class to hold the `Employee`'s birth date and hire date. Using a class object within another class object is known as **composition**. The relationship created is also called a **has-a relationship** because one class "has an" instance of another.

DECLARING OBJECTS

Declaring a class does not create any actual objects. A class is just an abstract description of what an object will be like if any objects are ever actually instantiated. Just as you might understand all the characteristics of an item you intend to manufacture long before the first item rolls off the assembly line, you can create a class with fields and methods long before you instantiate any objects that are members of that class.

A two-step process creates an object that is an instance of a class. First, you supply a type and an identifier, just as when you declare any variable. Second, you create the object, which includes allocating computer memory for it. For example, you might define an integer as `int someValue;` and you might define an `Employee` as `Employee myAssistant;`, where `myAssistant` could be any legal identifier you choose to represent an `Employee`.

>> **NOTE**
Every object name is also a reference—that is, a computer memory location where the fields for the object reside.

When you declare an integer as `int myInteger;`, you notify the compiler that an integer named `myInteger` will exist, and you reserve computer memory for it at the same time—the exact amount of computer memory depends on the declared data type. When you declare the `myAssistant` instance of the `Employee` class, you are notifying the compiler that you will use the identifier `myAssistant`. However, you are not yet setting aside computer memory in which the `Employee` named `myAssistant` can be stored—that is done only for the built-in, predefined types. To allocate the needed memory and instantiate the object, you must use the `new` operator.

>> **NOTE**
In Chapter 5, you used the `new` operator when setting aside memory for arrays.

After defining `myAssistant` with the `Employee myAssistant;` statement, you must use the statement that actually sets aside enough memory to hold `myAssistant`:

```
myAssistant = new Employee();
```

You also can define and reserve memory for `myAssistant` in one statement, as in the following:

```
Employee myAssistant = new Employee();
```

In this statement, `Employee` is the object's type (as well as its class), and `myAssistant` is the name of the object. The equal sign is the assignment operator, so a value is being assigned to `myAssistant`. The `new` operator is allocating a new, unused portion of computer memory for `myAssistant`. The value being assigned to `myAssistant` is a memory address at which it will be located. You need not be concerned with the actual memory address—when you refer to `myAssistant`, the compiler will locate it at the appropriate address for you.

>> **NOTE** Because the identifiers for class objects are references to their memory addresses, you can call any class a **reference type**—in other words, a type that refers to a specific memory location. A reference type is a type that holds an address, as opposed to the predefined types such as `int`, `double`, and `char`, which are **value types**.

You also can use the `new` operator for simple data types. For example, to declare an integer variable `x`, you can write the following:

```
int x = new int();
```

However, programmers usually use the simpler form:

```
int x;
```

With the first form, `x` is initialized to 0. With the second form, `x` holds no usable starting value.

The last portion of the statement after the `new` operator, `Employee()`, looks suspiciously like a method name with its parentheses. In fact, it is the name of a method that constructs an

USING CLASSES AND OBJECTS

`Employee` object. `Employee()` is a constructor. You will write your own constructors later in this chapter. For now, note that when you don't write a constructor for a class object, C# writes one for you, and the name of the constructor is always the same as the name of the class whose objects it constructs.

After an object has been instantiated, its public members (usually its methods) can be accessed using the object's identifier, a dot, and a method call. For example, if you declare an `Employee` named `myAssistant`, you can access `myAssistant`'s `WelcomeMessage()` method with the following statement:

```
myAssistant.WelcomeMessage();
```

> **NOTE** The statement `myAssistant.WelcomeMessage()` would be illegal if `WelcomeMessage()` was a `static` method. The method can be used with an `Employee` object only because it is nonstatic.

No class client (for example, a `Main()` method) can access `myAssistant`'s `idNumber` directly; the only way a client can access the `private` data is by sending a message through one of the object's `public` methods. Because the `WelcomeMessage()` method is part of the same class as `idNumber`, and because `WelcomeMessage()` is `public`, a `Main()` method can use the method that displays the `idNumber`. Figure 7-4 shows a class named `CreateEmployee` whose `Main()` method declares an `Employee` and displays the `Employee`'s welcome message. Figure 7-5 shows the execution of the program.

```
using System;
public class CreateEmployee
{
    public static void Main()
    {
        Employee myAssistant = new Employee();
        myAssistant.WelcomeMessage();
    }
}
```

Figure 7-4 The `CreateEmployee` program

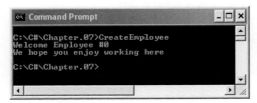

Figure 7-5 Output of the `CreateEmployee` program

CHAPTER SEVEN

In the output in Figure 7-5, the `Employee`'s ID number is 0. By default, all unassigned numeric fields in a class object are initialized to 0. When you compile the program in Figure 7-4, you receive a warning message:

```
Field 'Employee.idNumber' is never assigned to, and will always have
its default value 0.
```

Of course, usually you want to provide a different value for each `Employee`'s `idNumber` field. To accomplish this, you can create properties.

CREATING PROPERTIES

Frequently, methods you call with an object are used to alter the states of its fields. For example, you might want to set or change the date or time of a party. If the `Party` class contained a `string` field named `partyDate`, you could write a method such as `setDate()` to set a party's date, similar to the following method:

```
public void setDate(string date)
{
    partyDate = date;
}
```

Then, you could call the method with a statement like the following:

```
myGraduationParty.setDate("May 12");
```

Although this technique would work, and might be used in other programming languages, C# programmers more often create a property to perform this task. A **property** is a member of a class that provides access to a field of a class; properties define how fields will be set and retrieved. Properties have **accessors** that specify the statements that execute when a class's fields are accessed. Specifically, properties contain **set accessors** for setting an object's fields and **get accessors** for retrieving the stored values. When you create properties, the syntax in your client programs becomes more natural and easier to understand.

>> **NOTE** C# programmers refer to properties as "smart fields."

>> **NOTE** When a property has a `set` accessor, programmers say the property can be "written to." When it has a `get` accessor, programmers say the property can be "read from."

>> **NOTE** It is important to pay attention to capitalization so you can distinguish a field from a property.

Figure 7-6 shows an `Employee` class in which a property has been defined in the shaded area. The property is `IdNumber`. A property declaration resembles a variable declaration; it contains an access modifier, a data type, and an identifier. It also resembles a method in that it is followed by curly braces that contain statements. By convention, a property identifier is the same as the field it manipulates, except the first letter is capitalized. Following the property identifier, you define accessors between curly braces. The `IdNumber` property in Figure 7-6 contains both `get` and `set` accessors; a property declaration can contain a `get` accessor, a `set` accessor, or both.

>> **NOTE** When a property has only a `get` accessor (and not a `set` accessor), it is a **read-only property**.

USING CLASSES AND OBJECTS

```
class Employee
{
    private int idNumber;
    public int IdNumber
    {
        get
        {
            return idNumber;
        }
        set
        {
            idNumber = value;
        }
    }
    public void WelcomeMessage()
    {
        Console.WriteLine("Welcome Employee #{0}", IdNumber);
        Console.WriteLine("We hope you enjoy working here");
    }
}
```

Figure 7-6 `Employee` class with defined property

> **NOTE** In the altered `WelcomeMessage()` method in Figure 7-6, the `IdNumber` property is displayed. Alternately, this method could continue to use the `idNumber` field (as in Figure 7-3) because the method is a member of the same class as the field. Programmers are divided on whether a method of a class should use a field or a property to access its own methods. One popular position is that if `get` and `set` accessors are well-designed, they should be used everywhere, even from within the class. Sometimes, you want a field to be read-only, so you do not create a `set` accessor. In such a case, you can use the field (with the lowercase initial by convention) within class methods.

> **NOTE**
> Be careful with capitalization in properties. For example, within a `get` accessor for `IdNumber`, if you return `IdNumber` instead of `idNumber`, you initiate an infinite loop—the property continuously accesses itself.

Each accessor in a property looks like a method, except no parentheses are included in the identifier. A `set` accessor acts like a method that accepts a parameter and assigns it to a variable. However, it is not a method and you do not use parentheses with it. A `get` accessor returns the value of the field associated with the property, but you do not code a `return` type; the return type of a `get` accessor is implicitly the type of the property in which it is contained.

When you use `set` and `get` accessors in a method, you do not use the words "set" or "get." Instead, to set a value, you use the assignment operator (=), and to get a value, you simply use the property name. For example, if you declare an `Employee` named `myChef`, you can assign an `idNumber` as simply as you would a variable, as in the following:

```
Employee myChef = new Employee();
myChef.IdNumber = 2345;
```

In the second statement, the `IdNumber` property is set to 2345. The value to the right of the equal sign is sent to the `set` accessor as an implicit parameter named `value`. (An **implicit parameter** is one that is undeclared and that gets its value automatically.) In the statement myChef.IdNumber = 2345;, the constant 2345 is sent to the set accessor, where it becomes the value of value. Within the set accessor, value is assigned to the class field idNumber. The idNumber field could not have been set directly from Main() because it is private; however, the IdNumber property can be set through its set accessor because the property is public.

> **NOTE** The identifier value is not a C# keyword, but it acts like one within a set accessor. You can declare variables within a set accessor, but you cannot declare one named value. However, in other C# methods, you can declare a variable named value if you want. Identifiers that act like keywords in specific circumstances are **contextual keywords**. C# has six contextual keywords: get, set, value, partial, where, and yield.

Writing a get accessor allows you to use a property like you would a simple variable. For example, a declared Employee's ID number can be displayed with the following:

Console.WriteLine("ID number is {0}", myChef.IdNumber);

The expression myChef.idNumber would not be allowed in a client program because idNumber is private; however, the public get accessor of the property allows myChef.IdNumber to be displayed. Figure 7-7 shows a complete application that uses the modified class in Figure 7-6. Figure 7-8 shows the output.

```
using System;
public class CreateEmployee2
{
    public static void Main()
    {
        Employee myChef = new Employee();
        myChef.IdNumber = 2345;
        Console.WriteLine("ID number is {0}",
            myChef.IdNumber);
        myChef.WelcomeMessage();
    }
}
```

Figure 7-7 The CreateEmployee2 application that uses the Employee class containing a property

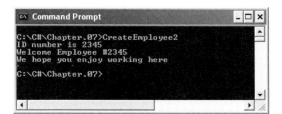

Figure 7-8 Output of the CreateEmployee2 application

At this point, declaring `get` and `set` accessors that do nothing except retrieve a value from a field or assign a value to one might seem like a lot of work for very little payoff. After all, if a class field was `public` instead of `private`, you would just use it directly and avoid the work of creating the property. However, it is conventional (and consistent with object-oriented principles) to make class fields `private` and allow accessors to manipulate them only as you deem appropriate. Keeping data hidden is an important feature of object-oriented programming, as is controlling how data values are set and used. For example, you could write a `set` accessor for the `Employee` class as follows:

```
set
{
    if(value < 500)
        idNumber = value;
    else
        idNumber = 500;
}
```

This `set` accessor would ensure that an `Employee` `idNumber` would never be greater than 500. If clients had direct access to a `private` `idNumber` field, you could not control what values could be assigned there, but when you write the `set` accessor with your class, you gain full control over the allowed data values.

> **NOTE** Because the code in `get` and `set` accessors frequently is standard as well as brief, programmers sometimes take a shorthand approach to writing properties. For example, they might write an entire `IdNumber` property on five lines, as follows:
>
> ```
> public int IdNumber
> {
>     get{ return idNumber;}
>     set{ idNumber = value;}
> }
> ```
>
> Other programmers choose an even more condensed form and write the entire property on one line as:
>
> ```
> public int IdNumber{ get{ return idNumber;} set{ idNumber = value;}}
> ```

STORING AND ORGANIZING YOUR CLASSES

When you create a class that describes objects you will instantiate, and another class that instantiates those objects, you physically can contain the two classes within a single file or place each class in its own file.

By placing both classes within the same file, you typically reduce development time and simplify the compilation process. When you first develop classes, you are likely to introduce both syntax and logical errors into each file you use. By placing your classes in the same file, you reduce the time needed to navigate through multiple files and to check issues such as consistent spelling of variable and method names and consistent use of data types. Also, when you compile only a single file, the sources of any error messages you receive are easier to locate.

There are also advantages to placing classes in separate files. One advantage is simply organization. Just as you can arrange all your nuts, bolts, and nails in the various drawers of a hardware storage cabinet and then find a quarter-inch bolt when you need it, containing each class in its own file makes the classes more manageable and easier to locate. More importantly, when a class resides within its own file, the class is easier to reuse within additional programs you create in the future.

Most classes you create will have more than a few data fields and property definitions for each field. For example, a typical `Employee` class would contain more than an `idNumber` field—a few of the many possibilities include `firstName`, `lastName`, `address`, `phoneNumber`, `salary`, `departmentNumber`, `hireDate`, `numberOfDependents`, and so on. Although there is no requirement to do so, most programmers place data fields in some logical order at the beginning of a class. For example, the `idNumber` field is most likely used as a unique identifier for each `Employee` (which database users often call a **primary key**), so it makes sense to list the employee ID number first in the class. An employee's last name and first name "go together," so it makes sense to store these two `Employee` components adjacently. Despite these common-sense rules, you have a lot of flexibility in how you position data fields within any class.

>> **NOTE** A unique identifier must have no duplicates within an application. In other words, although an organization might have many employees with the last name "Johnson" or a salary of 400.00, only one employee will have ID number 128. For that reason, if you were designing a professional `Employee` class, you might choose to make the ID number property read-only and to allow assignment only at construction using a formula that provides a unique number, or perhaps accessing a file of available numbers.

Additionally, if you define properties for each data field as well as a few methods, quite a lot of code is required. Finding your way through the list of fields, properties, and methods can become a formidable task. For ease in locating class methods and properties, many programmers prefer to store them in alphabetical order. Another logical organization scheme is to store all properties first, in the same order as their corresponding data fields, followed by other methods. Any of these organizational techniques can produce usable classes and workable programs, but your organization or instructor might have a preference for how to assemble class members.

An additional aid to keeping your classes organized is to use comments liberally. For example, comments can be used to separate functional areas within a class and to describe the purposes of methods.

>> **NOTE** Although good comments can help others to understand your programs, they are no substitute for clear, appropriate identifiers.

>> **NOTE** Although good program comments are crucial to creating understandable code, they have been left out of many examples in this book to save space. Your programs should contain many comments that identify your program components and explain the purpose and structure of your methods.

UNUSUAL USE: `public` FIELDS AND `private` METHODS

Most of the time, class data fields are `private` and class methods are `public`. This technique ensures that data will be used and changed only in the ways provided in your accessors. Novice programmers might make a data field `public` to avoid having to create a property containing `get` and `set` accessors. For example, Figure 7-9 shows a `Desk` class that contains two `public` fields. Because the fields are `public`, no `get` or `set` accessors are needed. The program that instantiates a `Desk` can set and retrieve the values in the fields without "bothering" with the accessors that would be needed if the fields were `private`. Although it is easy to work with, the `Desk` class in Figure 7-9 violates a basic principle of object-oriented programming. That is, data should be hidden when at all possible, and access to it should be controlled by well-designed accessors.

```
using System;
class Desk
{
    public string wood;    // Making these fields public
    public int drawers;    // is NOT a recommended technique
}
public class TestDesk
{
    public static void Main()
    {
        Desk myDesk = new Desk();
        myDesk.wood = "mahogany";   // notice wood and drawers
        myDesk.drawers = 4;         // are accessed directly
        Console.WriteLine("My {0} desk has {1} drawers",
            myDesk.wood, myDesk.drawers);
    }
}
```

Figure 7-9 Poorly designed `Desk` class with program that instantiates a `Desk`

Although `private` fields and `public` methods and accessors are the norm, occasionally you need to create `public` fields or `private` methods. Consider the `Carpet` class shown in Figure 7-10. Although it contains several `private` data fields, this class also contains one `public` data field (shaded). Following the three `public` property declarations, one `private` method is defined (also shaded).

```
class Carpet
{
    public const string MOTTO = "Our carpets are quality-made";
    private int length;
    private int width;
    private int area;
    public int Length
    {
        get
        {
            return length;
        }
        set
        {
            length = value;
            CalcArea();
        }
    }
    public int Width
    {
        get
        {
            return width;
        }
        set
        {
            width = value;
            CalcArea();
        }
    }
    public int Area
    {
        get
        {
            return area;
        }
    }
    private void CalcArea()
    {
        area = Length * Width;
    }
}
```

Figure 7-10 The Carpet class

>> **NOTE**
In the Carpet class, the Area property does not contain a set accessor because no outside program is allowed to set the area. Instead, it is calculated whenever width or height changes.

USING CLASSES AND OBJECTS

For example, you can create a `public` data field when you want all objects of a class to contain the same value. When you create `Carpet` objects from the class in Figure 7-10, each `Carpet` will have its own `length`, `width`, and `area`, but all `Carpet` objects will have the same `MOTTO`. The field `MOTTO` is preceded by the keyword `const`, meaning `MOTTO` is constant. That is, no program can change its value. When you define a named constant within a class, it is always `static`. That is, the field belongs to the entire class, not to any particular instance of the class. When you create a `static` field, only one copy is stored for the entire class, no matter how many objects you instantiate. On the other hand, multiple copies of nonstatic fields exist—one for each object instantiated. When you use a constant field, you use the class name rather than an object name. The class name is followed by a dot and the constant name, as in `Carpet.MOTTO`.

> **NOTE** You learned to create named constants in Chapter 2, and learned that identifiers of named constants such as `MOTTO` conventionally are capitalized. Some built-in C# classes contain useful named constants, such as `Math.PI`, which contains the value of pi. You do not create a `Math` object to use `PI`; therefore, you know it is `static`.

> **NOTE** Throughout this book, you have been using `static` to describe the `Main()` method of a class. You do not need to create an object of any class that contains a `Main()` method to be able to use `Main()`.

Figure 7-11 shows a program that instantiates and uses a `Carpet` object, and Figure 7-12 shows the results when the program executes. Notice that, although the `Console.WriteLine()` statements require an object to use `Width`, `Length`, and `Area`, `MOTTO` is referenced using the class name only.

```
using System;
public class TestCarpet
{
   public static void Main()
   {
      Carpet aRug = new Carpet();
      aRug.Width = 12;
      aRug.Length = 14;
      Console.Write("The {0} X {1} carpet ", aRug.Width,
         aRug.Length);
      Console.WriteLine("has an area of {0}", aRug.Area);
      Console.WriteLine("Our motto is: {0}", Carpet.MOTTO);
   }
}
```

Figure 7-11 The `TestCarpet` class

CHAPTER SEVEN

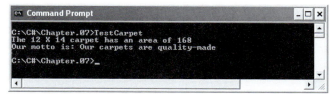

Figure 7-12 Output of the TestCarpet program

The Carpet class contains one private method named CalcArea(). As you examine the code in the TestCarpet class in Figure 7-11, notice that Width and Length are set using an assignment operator, but Area is not. The TestCarpet class can make assignments to Width and Length because these properties are public. However, you would not want a client program to assign a value to Area because the assigned value might not agree with the Width and Length values. Therefore, the Area property is a read-only property—it does not contain a set accessor, and no assignments by clients are allowed. Instead, whenever the Width or Length properties are set, the private CalcArea() method is called from the accessor. The CalcArea() method is defined as private because there is no reason for a client class like TestCarpet to call CalcArea(). The Carpet class's own accessors should call CalcArea() only after a valid value has been assigned to the Length or Width field. You create a method to be private when it should be called only by other methods or accessors within the class and not by outside classes.

>> **NOTE** Programmers probably create private methods more frequently than they create public data fields. Some programmers feel that the best style is to use public methods that are nothing but a list of method calls with descriptive names. Then, the methods that actually do the work are all private.

UNDERSTANDING THE this REFERENCE

After you create a class, you might eventually create thousands of objects from that class. When you create each object, you provide storage for each of the object's instance variables. For example, Figure 7-13 shows part of a Book class that contains only three fields, a property for the title field, and an advertising message method. When you declare several Book objects, as in the following statements, each Book object requires separate memory locations for its title, numPages, and price:

```
Book myBook = new Book();
Book yourBook = new Book();
```

USING CLASSES AND OBJECTS

> **NOTE**
> A fully developed `Book` class would most likely contain properties for the other data fields. This version excludes those properties to keep the example short.

```
class Book
{
    private string title;
    private int numPages;
    private double price;
    public string Title
    {
        get
        {
            return title;
        }
        set
        {
            title = value;
        }
    }
    public void AdvertisingMessage()
    {
        Console.WriteLine("Buy it now: {0}", Title);
    }
}
```

Figure 7-13 Partial `Book` class

> **NOTE**
> When you compile the `Book` class, you receive warnings that the `numPages` and `price` fields are never used. The omission was purposeful for this demonstration program.

> **NOTE**
> An object's nonstatic fields are "instance variables" because there is a stored version for each object instance.

> **NOTE**
> Only nonstatic methods receive a `this` reference. Nonstatic methods are instance methods—they can work differently and appropriately for each object—so it makes sense that they receive a `this` reference.

Storing a single `Book` object requires allocating storage space for three separate fields; the storage requirements for `Book` objects used by a library or retail bookstore would be far more considerable, but necessary—each `Book` must be able to "hold" its own data, including publisher, date published, author, ISBN, and so on. If each `Book` object also required its own copy of each property and method contained in the class, the storage requirements would multiply. It makes sense that each `Book` needs space to store its unique title and other data, but because every `Book` uses the same methods, storing multiple copies is wasteful and unnecessary.

Fortunately, each `Book` object does not need to store its own copy of each property and method. Whether you make the method call `myBook.AdvertisingMessage()` or `yourBook.AdvertisingMessage()`, you access the same `AdvertisingMessage()` method. However, there must be a difference between the two method calls, because each displays a different title in its message. The difference lies in an implicit, or invisible, reference that is passed to every instance method and property accessor. The implicitly passed reference is the **this reference**. When you call the method `myBook.AdvertisingMessage()`, you automatically pass the `this` reference to the method so the method knows which instance of `Book` to use.

You can explicitly refer to the `this` reference within an instance method or property, as shown in Figure 7-14. When you refer to `Title` (or `title`) within a `Book` class method or accessor, you are referring to the `title` field of "this" `Book`—the `Book` whose name you used in the method call—perhaps `myBook` or `yourBook`. Using the shaded keywords in Figure 7-14 is not required; the version of the methods shown in Figure 7-13 (where `this` was implied but not written explicitly) works just as well. Figure 7-15 shows an application that uses the Book class, and Figure 7-16 shows the output.

```
class Book
{
   private string title;
   private int numPages;
   private double price;
   public string Title
   {
      get
      {
         return this.title;
      }
      set
      {
         this.title = value;
      }
   }
   public void AdvertisingMessage()
   {
      Console.WriteLine("Buy it now: {0}", this.Title);
   }
}
```

Figure 7-14 Book class with methods explicitly using this references

```
using System;
public class CreateTwoBooks
{
   public static void Main()
   {
      Book myBook = new Book();
      Book yourBook = new Book();
      myBook.Title = "Silas Marner";
      yourBook.Title = "The Time Traveler's Wife";
      myBook.AdvertisingMessage();
      yourBook.AdvertisingMessage();
   }
}
```

Figure 7-15 Program that declares two Book objects

USING CLASSES AND OBJECTS

Figure 7-16 Output of `CreateTwoBooks` program

> **NOTE**
> On occasion, you might need to explicitly code the `this` reference. You will see some examples later in this chapter after you learn about constructors.

The `Book` class in Figure 7-14 worked without adding the references to `this`. However, you should be aware that the `this` reference is always there, working behind the scenes, even if you do not code it. Sometimes, you may want to include the `this` reference within a method for clarity, so the reader has no doubt when you are referring to a class instance variable.

UNDERSTANDING CONSTRUCTORS

> **NOTE**
> You will learn to create constructors with parameters in the next section of this chapter.

When you create a class such as `Employee` and instantiate an object with a statement such as `Employee aWorker = new Employee();`, you are actually calling a method named `Employee()` that is provided by C#. A **constructor** is a method that instantiates (creates an instance of) an object. Every class you create is automatically supplied with a `public` constructor with no parameters. The automatically supplied constructor is a class's **default constructor**. The constructor named `Employee()` establishes one `Employee` with the identifier `aWorker`, and provides the following initial values to the `Employee`'s data fields:

> **NOTE**
> The value of an object initialized with a default constructor is known as the **default value of the object**.

» Numeric fields are set to 0 (zero).
» Character fields are set to '\0', or null.
» Boolean fields are set to `false`.
» Object-type fields, such as `string` or any class object, are set to `null` (or empty).

If you do not want an `Employee`'s fields to hold these default values, or if you want to perform additional tasks when you create an `Employee`, you can write your own constructor to replace the automatically supplied version. Any constructor you write must have the same name as its class, and constructors cannot have a return type. For example, if you create an `Employee` class that contains a `Salary` property, and you want every new `Employee` object to have a salary of 300.00, you could write the constructor for the `Employee` class that appears in Figure 7-17. Any instantiated `Employee` will have a default `salary` value of 300.00.

> **NOTE**
> The constructor in Figure 7-17 assumes a `Salary` property has been defined with a `set` accessor. If there is no `set` accessor, but there is a `salary` field, then the assignment could be `salary = 300;`.

```
Employee()
{
    Salary = 300.00;
}
```

Figure 7-17 `Employee` class constructor that initializes the `Salary` property

232

CHAPTER SEVEN

You can write any statement in a constructor. Although you usually would have no reason to do so, you could print a message from within a constructor or perform any other task. The most common constructor task is to initialize fields.

PASSING PARAMETERS TO CONSTRUCTORS

You can create a constructor to ensure that all objects of a class are initialized with the same values in their data fields. After construction, you might change the value in an individual object's fields by using the appropriate set accessors. Alternatively, you might create objects that hold unique field values right from the start by writing constructors to which you pass one or more parameters. You then can use the parameter values to set properties or fields for individual object instantiations. For example, consider an Employee class with two data fields, a constructor, and a property, as shown in Figure 7-18. Its constructor assigns 999 to each potentially instantiated Employee's idNumber. Any time an Employee object is created using a statement such as Employee partTimeWorker = new Employee();, even if no other data-assigning methods are ever used, you are ensured that the Employee's idNumber holds a default value. The partTimeWorker Employee, like all Employees, will have an initial idNumber of 999.

```
public class Employee
{
    private int idNumber;
    private double salary;
    public Employee()
    {
        IdNumber = 999;
    }
    public int IdNumber
    {
        get
        {
            return idNumber;
        }
        set
        {
            idNumber = value;
        }
    }
    //  Other class members can go here
}
```

Figure 7-18 Employee class with a parameterless constructor

USING CLASSES AND OBJECTS

The constructor in Figure 7-18 is a **parameterless constructor**—one that takes no arguments. As an alternative, you might choose to create `Employee`s with initial `idNumber` fields that differ for each `Employee`. To accomplish this task within a constructor, you need to pass an employee number to the constructor. Figure 7-19 shows an `Employee` constructor that receives a parameter. With this constructor, an integer is passed in using a statement such as the following:

```
Employee partTimeWorker = new Employee(876);
```

When the constructor executes, the integer used as the actual parameter within the method call is passed to `Employee()` and assigned to the `Employee`'s `idNumber`.

```
public Employee(int empID)
{
    IdNumber = empID;
}
```

Figure 7-19 `Employee` constructor with parameter

> **TIP** Suppose you want the parameter to the `Employee` class constructor to have the identifier `idNumber`. Further, suppose you want the `Employee` class to contain a read-only property for `idNumber`; that is, there is no `set` accessor for `IdNumber`. Then you would write the constructor as follows:
>
> ```
> public Employee(int idNumber)
> {
>     this.idNumber = idNumber);
> }
> ```
>
> The `idNumber` value on the right of the assignment operator would refer to the constructor parameter, but `this.idNumber` on the left of the assignment statement refers to the current object's `idNumber` field.

OVERLOADING CONSTRUCTORS

If you create a class from which you can instantiate objects, C# automatically provides a default constructor. As soon as you create your own constructor, whether it has parameters or not, you no longer have access to the automatically created version. However, if you want a class to have both parameter and parameterless versions of a constructor, you can create them. Like any other C# methods, constructors can be overloaded. You can write as many constructors for a class as you want, as long as their argument lists do not cause ambiguity. For example, the `Employee` class in Figure 7-20 contains four constructors. The `Main()` method within the `CreateSomeEmployees` class in Figure 7-21 shows how different types of `Employee`s might be instantiated. Notice that one version of the `Employee` constructor—the one that supports a character parameter—doesn't even use the parameter; sometimes you might create a constructor with a specific parameter type simply to force that constructor to be the version that executes. The output of the `CreateSomeEmployees` program is shown in Figure 7-22.

```
public class Employee
{
    int idNumber;
    double salary;
    public int IdNumber
    {
        get
        {
            return idNumber;
        }
        set
        {
            idNumber = value;
        }
    }
    public double Salary
    {
        get
        {
            return salary;
        }
        set
        {
            salary = value;
        }
    }
    public Employee()
    {
        IdNumber = 999;
        Salary = 0;
    }
    public Employee(int empId)
    {
        IdNumber = empId;
        Salary = 0;
    }
    public Employee(int empId, double sal)
    {
        IdNumber = empId;
        Salary = sal;
    }
    public Employee(char code)
    {
        IdNumber = 111;
        Salary = 100000;
    }
}
```

Figure 7-20 Employee class with four constructors

USING CLASSES AND OBJECTS

```
using System;
public class CreateSomeEmployees
{
   public static void Main()
   {
      Employee aWorker = new Employee();
      Employee anotherWorker = new Employee(234);
      Employee theBoss = new Employee('A');
      Console.WriteLine("{0,4}{1,14}", aWorker.IdNumber,
         aWorker.Salary.ToString("C"));
      Console.WriteLine("{0,4}{1,14}", anotherWorker.IdNumber,
         anotherWorker.Salary.ToString("C"));
      Console.WriteLine("{0,4}{1,14}", theBoss.IdNumber,
         theBoss.Salary.ToString("C"));
   }
}
```

Figure 7-21 CreateSomeEmployees program

Figure 7-22 Output of CreateSomeEmployees program

Most likely, a single application would not use all four constructors of the Employee class. More likely, each application that uses the class would use only one or two constructors. You create a class with multiple constructors to provide flexibility for your clients. For example, some clients might choose to construct Employee objects with just ID numbers, and others might prefer to construct them with ID numbers and salaries.

USING CONSTRUCTOR INITIALIZERS

The Employee class in Figure 7-20 contains four constructors, and each constructor initializes the same two fields. In a fully developed class used by a company, many more fields would be initialized, creating a lot of duplicated code. Besides the original extra work of writing the repetitive statements in these constructors, even more extra work will be required when the class is modified in the future. For example, if your organization institutes a new employee ID number format that requires a specific number of digits, then each constructor will have to be modified. Besides the extra work to modify each constructor, it is possible that one or more of the constructor versions will be overlooked, introducing errors into the programs that are clients of the class.

As an alternative to repeating code in the constructors, you can use a constructor initializer. A **constructor initializer** is a clause that indicates another instance of a class constructor should be executed before any statements in the current constructor body. Figure 7-23 shows a new version of the Employee class using constructor initializers in three of the four overloaded constructor versions.

```
public class Employee
{
    int idNumber;
    double salary;
    public int IdNumber
    {
        get
        {
            return idNumber;
        }
        set
        {
            idNumber = value;
        }
    }
    public double Salary
    {
        get
        {
            return salary;
        }
        set
        {
            salary = value;
        }
    }
    public Employee() : this(999, 0)
    {
    }
    public Employee(int empId) : this(empId, 0)
    {
    }
    public Employee(int empId, double sal)
    {
        IdNumber = empId;
        Salary = sal;
    }
    public Employee(char code) : this (111, 100000)
    {
    }
}
```

Figure 7-23 Employee class with constructor initializers

USING CLASSES AND OBJECTS

In the three shaded clauses in Figure 7-23, the `this` reference is used to mean "the constructor for this object being constructed." For example, when a client calls the parameterless `Employee` constructor, 999 and 0 are passed to the two-parameter constructor. There, they become `empId` and `sal`, parameters that are assigned to the `IdNumber` and `Salary` properties. If there were statements within the parameterless constructor, they would then execute; however, in this class, there is no reason for additional statements. Similarly, if a client uses the constructor version that accepts only an ID number, that parameter and a 0 for salary are passed to the two-parameter constructor. The only time just one version of the constructor executes is when a client uses both an ID number and a salary as constructor arguments. In the future, if additional statements needed to be added to the class (for example, a decision that ensures an ID number was at least five digits at construction), the decision would be added only to the two-parameter version of the constructor, and all the other versions could use it.

PASSING OBJECTS TO METHODS

You can pass objects to methods just as you can simple data types. For example, the application in Figure 7-21 can be rewritten as shown in Figure 7-24. In this version, instead of repeating the details of the `WriteLine()` method, the statement can be placed in its own method, and each `Employee` object can be passed into it, in turn. The output of the program in Figure 7-25 is identical to the output shown in Figure 7-22.

```
using System;
public class CreateSomeEmployees2
{
    public static void Main()
    {
        Employee aWorker = new Employee();
        Employee anotherWorker = new Employee(234);
        Employee theBoss = new Employee('A');
        WriteEmployeeData(aWorker);
        WriteEmployeeData(anotherWorker);
        WriteEmployeeData(theBoss);
    }
    public static void WriteEmployeeData(Employee emp)
    {
        Console.WriteLine("{ 0,4}{ 1,14}", emp.IdNumber, emp.Salary.ToString("C"));
    }
}
```

Figure 7-24 `CreateSomeEmployees2` program

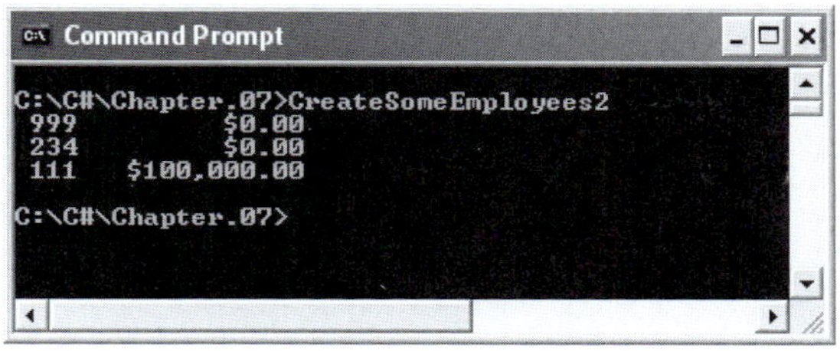

CHAPTER SEVEN

![Command Prompt output showing:
C:\C#\Chapter.07>CreateSomeEmployees2
999      $0.00
234      $0.00
111      $100,000.00

C:\C#\Chapter.07>]

Figure 7-25 Output of `CreateSomeEmployees2` program

When you pass an object to a method, you pass a reference. Therefore, any change made to an object parameter in a method also affects the object used as an argument in the calling method.

OVERLOADING OPERATORS

C# operators are the symbols you use to perform operations on objects. You have used many operators, including arithmetic operators (such as + and –) and logical operators (such as == and <). Separate actions can result from what seems to be the same operation or command. This occurs frequently in all computer programming languages, not just object-oriented languages. For example, in most programming languages and applications such as spreadsheets and databases, the + operator has a variety of meanings. A few of them include:

» Alone before a value (called unary form), + indicates a positive value, as in the expression +7.
» Between two integers (called binary form), + indicates integer addition, as in the expression 5 + 9.
» Between two floating-point numbers (also called binary form), + indicates floating-point addition, as in the expression 6.4 + 2.1.

Expressing a value as positive is a different operation from using the + operator to perform arithmetic, so + is overloaded several times in that it can take one or two arguments and have a different meaning in each case. It also can take different operand types—you use a + to add two `int`s, two `double`s, an `int` and a `double`, and a variety of other combinations. Each use results in different actions behind the scenes.

> **» NOTE** In addition to overloading, compilers often need to perform coercion, or implicit casting, when the + symbol is used with mixed arithmetic. For example, when an integer and floating-point number are added in C#, the integer is coerced into a floating-point number before the appropriate addition code executes. You learned about casting in Chapter 2.

Just as it is convenient to use a + between both integers and `double`s to add them, it also can be convenient to use a + between objects, such as `Employees` or `Books`, to add them. To be able to use arithmetic symbols with your own objects, you must overload the symbols.

C# operators are classified as unary or binary, depending on whether they take one or two arguments, respectively. The rules for overloading are shown in the following list.

USING CLASSES AND OBJECTS

> **» NOTE**
> Although `true` and `false` are not used explicitly as operators in expressions, they are considered operators in Boolean expressions and in expressions involving the conditional operator and conditional logical operators.

» The overloadable unary operators are:

`+ - ! ~ ++ -- true false`

» The overloadable binary operators are:

`+ - * / % & | ^ == != > < >= <=`

» You cannot overload the following operators:

`= && || ?? ?: checked unchecked new typeof as is`

» You cannot overload an operator for a built-in data type. For example, you cannot change the meaning of + between two `int`s.

» When a binary operator is overloaded and it has a corresponding assignment operator, it is also overloaded. For example, if you overload +, then += is automatically overloaded too.

» Some operators must be overloaded in pairs. For example, when you overload ==, you also must overload !=, and when you overload >, you also must overload <.

> **» NOTE**
> When you overload ==, you also receive warnings about methods in the `Object` class. You will learn about this class in Chapter 8; you should not attempt to overload == until you have studied that chapter.

You have used many of the operators listed above. If you want to include these operators in your own classes, you must decide what the operator will mean in your class. When you do, you write statements in a method to carry out your meaning. The method has a return type and arguments just like other methods, but its identifier is required to be followed by the operator being overloaded; for example, `operator+()` or `operator*()`.

> **» NOTE** For an overloaded unary operator, the method has the following format:
> *type* `operator` *overloadable-operator* (*type identifier*)
> For an overloaded binary operator, the method has the following format:
> *type* `operator` *overloadable-operator* (*type identifier, type operand*)

For example, suppose you create a `Book` class in which each object has a title, number of pages, and a price. Further assume that, as a publisher, you have decided to "add" `Book`s together. That is, you want to take two existing `Book`s and combine them into one. Assume you want the new book to have the following characteristics:

» The new title is a combination of the old titles, joined by the word "and."

» The number of pages in the new book is equal to the sum of the pages in the original `Book`s.

» Instead of charging twice as much for a new `Book`, you have decided to charge the price of the more expensive of the two original `Book`s, plus $10.

A different publisher might have decided that "adding `Book`s" means something different—for example, an added `Book` might have a fixed new price of $29.99. The statements you write in your `operator+()` method depend on how you define adding for your class. You could write an ordinary method to perform these tasks, but you could also overload the + operator to mean "add two `Book`s." Figure 7-26 shows an expanded version of the `Book` class in Figure 7-13. This class has properties for each field and a shaded `operator+()` method.

```
class Book
{
   private string title;
   private int numPages;
   private double price;
   public Book(string title, int pages, double price)
   {
      Title = title;
      NumPages = pages;
      Price = price;
   }
   public static Book operator+(Book first, Book second)
   {
      const double EXTRA = 10.00;
      string newTitle = first.Title + " and " +
         second.Title;
      int newPages = first.NumPages + second.NumPages;
      double newPrice;
      if(first.Price > second.Price)
         newPrice = first.Price + EXTRA;
      else
         newPrice = second.Price + EXTRA;
      return(new Book(newTitle, newPages, newPrice));
   }
   public string Title
   {
     get
     {
        return title;
     }
     set
     {
        title = value;
     }
   }
   public int NumPages
   {
     get
     {
        return numPages;
     }
     set
     {
        numPages = value;
     }
   }
```

Figure 7-26 Book class with overloaded + operator (*continued*)

USING CLASSES AND OBJECTS

```
    public double Price
    {
       get
       {
           return price;
       }
       set
       {
           price = value;
       }
    }
}
```

Figure 7-26 (*continued*)

The `operator+()` method in Figure 7-26 is declared to be `public` (so that class clients can use it) and `static`, which is required. The return type is `Book` because the addition of two `Book`s is defined to be a new `Book` with different values from either of the originals. You could overload the + operator so that when two `Book`s are added they return some other type, but it is most common to make the addition of two objects result in an "answer" of the same type.

The two parameters in the `operator+()` method in the `Book` class are both `Book`s. Therefore, when you eventually call this method, the data types on both sides of the + sign will be `Book`s. For example, you could write other methods that add a `Book` and an `Employee`, or a `Book` and a `double`.

Within the `operator+()` method, the statements perform the following tasks:

» A constant is declared to hold the extra price used in creating a new `Book` from two existing ones.

» A new string is created and assigned the first parameter `Book`'s title, plus the `string` " and ", plus the second parameter `Book`'s title.

» A new integer is declared and assigned the sum of the number of pages in each of the parameter `Book`s.

» A new `double` is declared and assigned the value of the more expensive original `Book` plus $10.00.

» Within the `return` statement, a new anonymous `Book` is created (an anonymous object is one without an identifier) using the new title, page number, and price, and returned to the calling method. (Instead of an anonymous `Book`, it would have been perfectly acceptable to use two statements—the first one creating a named `Book` with the same arguments, and the second one returning the named `Book`.)

>> **NOTE**
Notice that the + between the `string`s in creating the new `Book` title is itself an overloaded operator; concatenating strings is a different operation from adding `int`s or `double`s.

> **NOTE** It is possible to rewrite the operator+() method in the Book class in Figure 7-26 so that all the work is done in the return statement. For example:
>
> ```
> public static Book operator+(Book first, Book second)
> {
>    const double EXTRA = 10.00;
>    return(new Book(first.Title + " and " + second.Title,
>       first.NumPages + second.NumPages,
>       first.Price > second.Price ? first.Price + EXTRA :
>          second.Price + EXTRA));
> }
> ```

Figure 7-27 shows a client program that can use the + operator in the Book class. It first declares three Books; then, in the shaded statement, it adds two Books together and assigns the result to the third. When book1 and book2 are added, the operator+() method is called. The returned Book is assigned to book3, which is then displayed. Figure 7-28 shows the results.

```
using System;
public class AddBooks
{
   public static void Main()
   {
      Book book1 = new Book("Silas Marner", 350, 15.95);
      Book book2 = new Book("Moby Dick", 250, 16.00);
      Book book3;
      book3 = book1 + book2;
      Console.WriteLine("The new book is \"{0}\"", book3.Title);
      Console.WriteLine("It has {0} pages and costs {1}",
         book3.NumPages, book3.Price.ToString("C"));
   }
}
```

Figure 7-27 The AddBooks program

Figure 7-28 Output of the AddBooks program

> **NOTE** Because each addition operation returns a Book, it is possible to chain addition in a statement such as collection = book1 + book2 + book3; (assuming all the variables have been declared to be Book objects). In this example, book1 and book2 would be added, returning a temporary Book. Then the temporary Book and book3 would be added, returning a different temporary Book that would be assigned to collection.

In the `Book` class, it took many statements to overload the operator; however, in the client class, just typing a + between objects allows a programmer to use the objects and operator intuitively. You could write any statements you wanted within the operator method. However, for clarity, you should write statements that intuitively have the same meaning as the common use of the operator. For example, although you could overload the `operator*()` method to display a `Book`'s title and price, it would be a bad programming technique.

> **NOTE** When you overload an operator in a class, at least one argument to the method must be a member of the class. In other words, within the `Book` class, you can overload `operator*()` to multiply a `Book` by an integer, but you cannot overload `operator*()` to multiply a `double` by an integer.

DECLARING AN ARRAY OF OBJECTS

Just as you can declare arrays of integers or `doubles`, you can declare arrays that hold elements of any type, including objects. For example, Figure 7-29 shows an abbreviated `Employee` class that contains just one data field and a property to get and set it.

```
class Employee
{
    private int idNumber;
    public int IdNumber
    {
        get
        {
            return idNumber;
        }
        set
        {
            idNumber = value;
        }
    }
}
```

Figure 7-29 A simple `Employee` class

Of course, you also can create separate `Employee` objects with unique names, such as in the following statement:

```
Employee painter, electrician, plumber;
```

For many programs, however, it is far more convenient to create an array of `Employee` objects. An array named `empArray` that holds seven `Employee` objects is defined by the following:

```
Employee[] empArray = new Employee[7];
```

This statement reserves enough computer memory for seven `Employee` objects named `empArray[0]` through `empArray[6]`. It does not actually construct those `Employees`;

CHAPTER SEVEN

instead, you must call the seven individual constructors to do so. Because the `Employee` class in Figure 7-29 contains a default constructor that requires no arguments, the following loop calls the constructor seven times:

```
for(int x = 0; x < empArray.Length; ++x)
    empArray[ x] = new Employee();
```

As x varies from 0 through 6, each of the seven `empArray` objects is constructed.

>> **NOTE** When you create an array from a value type, such as `int` or `char`, the array holds the actual values. When you create an array from a reference type, such as a class you create, then the array holds the memory addresses of the objects. In other words, the array "refers to" the objects instead of containing the objects.

>> **NOTE** You can create an array of objects and provide default values to the elements' constructors in one step. For example, if an `Inventory` class contains a constructor that requires an integer argument, you can declare an array of `Inventory` objects by writing the following:

```
Inventory[ ] items = { new Inventory(123), new
    Inventory(345), new Inventory(678)};
```

To use a method that belongs to an object that is part of an array, you insert the appropriate subscript notation after the array name and before the dot-method. For example, to set all seven `Employee IdNumber` properties to 999, you can write the following:

```
for(int x = 0; x < empArray.Length; ++x)
{
    empArray[ x] .IdNum = 999;
}
```

USING THE Sort() AND BinarySearch() METHODS WITH ARRAYS OF OBJECTS

In Chapter 6, you learned about using the `System.Array` class's built-in `BinarySearch()` and `Sort()` methods with simple data types such as `int`, `double`, and `string`. The `Sort()` method accepts an array parameter and arranges its elements in descending order. The `BinarySearch()` method accepts a sorted array and a value that it attempts to match in the array.

>> **NOTE** You learned about the built-in data type class names in Chapter 2; they are summarized in Table 2-1.

A complication arises when you consider searching or sorting arrays of objects you create. When you create and sort an array of simple data items, there is only one type of value to consider, and the order is based on the Unicode value of that item. The classes that support simple data items each contain a method named **CompareTo()**, which provides the details of how the basic data types compare to each other. In other words, they define comparisons such as "2 is more than 1" and "B is more than A." The `Sort()` and `BinarySearch()` methods use the `CompareTo()` method for the current type of data being sorted. In other words, `Sort()` uses the `Int32` version of `CompareTo()` when sorting integers and the `Char` version of `CompareTo()` when sorting characters.

>> **NOTE** You have been using the `String` class (and its `string` alias) throughout this book. The class also contains a `CompareTo()` method that you first used in Chapter 2.

When you create a class that contains many fields, however, you must tell the compiler which field to use when making comparisons. For example, you logically might sort an organization's

Employee class objects by ID number, salary, department number, last name, hire date, or any field contained in the class. To tell C# which field to use for placing Employee objects in order, you must create an interface. An **interface** is a collection of methods (and perhaps other members) that can be used by any class, as long as the class provides a definition to override the interface's do-nothing, or abstract, method definitions. When a method **overrides** another, it takes precedence over the method, hiding the original version. In other words, the methods in an interface are empty, and any class that uses them must contain a new version that provides the details. Interfaces define named behaviors that classes can implement, so that all classes can use the same method names but use them appropriately for the class. In this way, interfaces provide for polymorphism—the ability of different objects to use the same method names but act appropriately based on the context.

>> **NOTE** You first learned about polymorphism in Chapter 1.

>> **NOTE** When a method overrides another, it has the same signature as the method it overrides. When methods are overloaded, they have different signatures. You learned about method signatures in Chapter 6. You will learn more about overriding methods and abstract methods and classes in Chapter 8.

>> **NOTE** C# supports many interfaces. You can identify an interface name by its initial letter I.

C# contains an **IComparable interface**, which contains the definition for the CompareTo() method that compares one object to another and returns an integer. Figure 7-30 shows the definition of IComparable. The CompareTo() method accepts an Object, but does not contain any statements; you must override this definition in classes you create if you want the objects to be comparable.

```
interface IComparable
{
    int CompareTo(Object o);
}
```

Figure 7-30 The IComparable interface

When you create a class whose members you predict clients will want to compare:

» You must include a single colon and the interface name IComparable after the class name.
» You must write a method that contains the following header:
   int IComparable.CompareTo(Object o)

>> **NOTE** Object is a class—the most generic of all classes. Every Employee object you create is not only an Employee, but also an Object. (This concept is similar to "every banana is a fruit" or "every collie is a dog.") By using the type Object as a parameter, the CompareTo() method can accept anything. You will learn more about the Object class in Chapter 8.

To work correctly in methods such as BinarySearch() and Sort(), the CompareTo() method you create for your class must return an integer value. Table 7-1 shows the return values that every version of CompareTo() should provide.

Return Value	Meaning
Negative	This instance is less than the compared object.
Zero	This instance is equal to the compared object.
Positive	This instance is greater than the compared object.

Table 7-1 Return values of `IComparable.CompareTo()` method

When you create a class that contains an `IComparable.CompareTo()` method, the method is an instance method and receives a `this` reference to the object used to call it. A second object is passed to the method; within the method, you first must convert, or cast, the passed object to the same type as the calling object's class, and then compare the corresponding fields you want from the `this` object and the passed object. For example, Figure 7-31 shows an `Employee` class that contains a shaded `CompareTo()` method and compares `Employee` objects based on the contents of their `idNumber` fields.

>> **NOTE**
You first learned about casting in Chapter 2.

```
class Employee : IComparable
{
    private int idNumber;
    private double salary;
    public int IdNumber
    {
        get
        {
            return idNumber;
        }
        set
        {
            idNumber = value;
        }
    }
    public double Salary
    {
        get
        {
            return salary;
        }
        set
        {
            salary = value;
        }
    }
```

Figure 7-31 `Employee` class using `IComparable` interface (*continued*)

USING CLASSES AND OBJECTS

```
int IComparable.CompareTo(Object o)
{
    int returnVal;
    Employee temp = (Employee)o;
    if(this.IdNumber > temp.IdNumber)
        returnVal = 1;
    else
        if(this.IdNumber < temp.IdNumber)
            returnVal = -1;
        else
            returnVal = 0;
    return returnVal;
}
```

Figure 7-31 (*continued*)

The `Employee` class in Figure 7-31 uses a colon and `IComparable` in its class header to indicate an interface. The shaded method is an instance method; that is, it "belongs" to an `Employee` object. When another `Employee` is passed in as `Object O`, it is cast as an `Employee` and stored in the `temp` variable. The `idNumber` values of the `this` `Employee` and the passed `Employee` are compared, and one of three integer values is returned.

For example, if you declare two `Employee` objects named `worker1` and `worker2`, you can use the following statement:

```
int answer = worker1.CompareTo(worker2);
```

Within the `CompareTo()` method in the `Employee` class, `worker1` would be "`this`" `Employee`—the controlling `Employee` in the method. The `temp Employee` would be `worker2`. If, for example, `worker1` had a higher ID number than `worker2`, the value of `answer` would be 1.

> **NOTE** The controlling "`this`" object in an instance method is the **invoking object**.

Figure 7-32 shows a program that uses the `Employee` class. The program declares an array of five `Employee` objects with different ID numbers and salaries; the ID numbers are purposely out of order to demonstrate that the `Sort()` method works correctly. The program also declares a `seekEmp` object with an ID number of 222. The program sorts the array, displays the sorted elements, then finds the array element that matches the `seekEmp` object. Figure 7-33 shows the program execution.

CHAPTER SEVEN

```
using System;
public class ComparableEmployeeArray
{
   public static void Main()
   {
      Employee[] empArray = new Employee[5];
      int x;
      for(x = 0; x < empArray.Length; ++x)
         empArray[x] = new Employee();
      empArray[0].IdNumber = 333;
      empArray[0].Salary = 200;
      empArray[1].IdNumber = 444;
      empArray[1].Salary = 100;
      empArray[2].IdNumber = 555;
      empArray[2].Salary = 600;
      empArray[3].IdNumber = 111;
      empArray[3].Salary = 300;
      empArray[4].IdNumber = 222;
      empArray[4].Salary = 500;
      Employee seekEmp = new Employee();
      seekEmp.IdNumber = 222;
      Array.Sort(empArray);
      Console.WriteLine("Sorted employees:");
      for(x = 0; x < empArray.Length; ++x)
         Console.WriteLine("Employee #{0} : {1} {2}",
            x, empArray[x].IdNumber,
            empArray[x].Salary.ToString("C"));
      x = Array.BinarySearch(empArray, seekEmp);
      Console.WriteLine("Employee #{0} was found at position {1}",
         seekEmp.IdNumber, x + 1);
   }
}
```

Figure 7-32 ComparableEmployeeArray program

Figure 7-33 Output of ComparableEmployeeArray program

249

USING CLASSES AND OBJECTS

Notice that the `seekEmp` object matches the `Employee` in the second array position based on the `idNumber` only—not the salary—because the `CompareTo()` method in the `Employee` class uses only `idNumber` values and not salaries to make comparisons. You *could* have written code that requires both the `idNumber` and `salary` values to match before returning a positive number.

UNDERSTANDING DESTRUCTORS

> **» NOTE**
> You learned about an object's scope in Chapter 6.

A **destructor** contains the actions you require when an instance of a class is destroyed. Most often, an instance of a class is destroyed when it goes out of scope. As with constructors, if you do not explicitly create a destructor for a class, C# automatically provides one.

To explicitly declare a destructor, you use an identifier that consists of a tilde (~) followed by the class name. You cannot provide any parameters to a destructor; it must have an empty argument list. As a consequence, destructors cannot be overloaded; a class can have at most one destructor. Like a constructor, a destructor has no return type.

Figure 7-34 shows an `Employee` class that contains only one field (`idNumber`), a property, a constructor, and a (shaded) destructor. When you execute the `Main()` method in the `DemoEmployeeDestructor` class in Figure 7-35, you instantiate two `Employee` objects, each with its own `idNumber` value. When the `Main()` method ends, the two `Employee` objects go out of scope, and the destructor for each object is called. Figure 7-36 shows the output.

```
class Employee
{
    int idNumber;
    public int IdNumber
    {
        get
        {
            return idNumber;
        }
        set
        {
            idNumber = value;
        }
    }
    public Employee(int empID)
    {
        IdNumber = empID;
        Console.WriteLine("Employee object {0} created", IdNumber);
    }
    ~Employee()
    {
        Console.WriteLine("Employee object {0} destroyed!", IdNumber);
    }
}
```

Figure 7-34 `Employee` class with destructor

CHAPTER SEVEN

```
using System;
public class DemoEmployeeDestructor
{
   public static void Main()
   {
      Employee aWorker = new Employee(101);
      Employee anotherWorker = new Employee(202);
   }
}
```

Figure 7-35 `DemoEmployeeDestructor` program

Figure 7-36 Output of `DemoEmployeeDestructor` program

The program in Figure 7-35 never explicitly calls the `Employee` class destructor, yet you can see from the output that the destructor executes twice. Destructors are invoked automatically; you cannot explicitly call one. Interestingly, the last object created is the first object destroyed; the same relationship would hold true no matter how many objects the program instantiated.

>> **NOTE** An instance of a class becomes eligible for destruction when it is no longer possible for any code to use it—that is, when it goes out of scope. The actual execution of an object's destructor might occur at any time after the object becomes eligible for destruction.

For now, you have little reason to create a destructor except to demonstrate how it is called automatically. Later, when you write more sophisticated C# programs that work with files, databases, or large quantities of computer memory, you might want to perform specific clean-up or close-down tasks when an object goes out of scope. Then you will place appropriate instructions within a destructor.

YOU DO IT
CREATING A CLASS AND OBJECTS
In this section, you will create a `Student` class and instantiate objects from it. This class contains an ID number, last name, and grade point average for the `Student`. It also contains properties that get and set each of these fields. You will also pass each `Student` object to a method.

251

USING CLASSES AND OBJECTS

To create a Student class:

1. Open a new file in your text editor. Begin the Student class by declaring the class name, inserting an opening curly brace, and declaring three private fields that will hold an ID number, last name, and grade point average, as follows:

   ```
   class Student
   {
       private int idNumber;
       private string lastName;
       private double gradePointAverage;
   ```

2. Add two constants that represent the highest and lowest possible values for a grade point average.

   ```
   public const double HIGHEST_GPA = 4.0;
   public const double LOWEST_GPA = 0.0;
   ```

3. Add two properties that get and set idNumber and lastName. By convention, properties have an identifier that is the same as the field they service, except they start with a capital letter.

   ```
   public int IdNumber
   {
       get
       {
           return idNumber;
       }
       set
       {
           idNumber = value;
       }
   }
   public string LastName
   {
       get
       {
           return lastName;
       }
       set
       {
           lastName = value;
       }
   }
   ```

4. Add the following set accessor in the property for the gradePointAverage field. It sets limits on the value assigned, assigning 0 if the value is out of range.

```
public double GradePointAverage
{
   get
   {
      return gradePointAverage;
   }
   set
   {
      if(value >= LOWEST_GPA && value <= HIGHEST_GPA)
         gradePointAverage = value;
      else
         gradePointAverage = LOWEST_GPA;
   }
}
```

5. Add a closing curly brace for the class. Save the file as **Student.cs** in the Chapter.07 folder of your Student Disk.

6. Open a new file in your text editor and begin a program that creates two Student objects, assigns some values, and displays the Students.

```
using System;
public class CreateStudents
{
```

7. Add a Main() method that declares two Students. Assign field values, including one "illegal" value—a grade point average that is too high.

```
public static void Main()
{
   Student first = new Student();
   Student second = new Student();
   first.IdNumber = 123;
   first.LastName = "Anderson";
   first.GradePointAverage = 3.5;
   second.IdNumber = 789;
   second.LastName = "Daniels";
   second.GradePointAverage = 4.1;
```

8. Instead of creating similar WriteLine() statements to display the two Students, call a method with each Student. You will create the method to accept a Student argument in the next step. Add a closing curly brace for the Main() method.

```
   Display(first);
   Display(second);
}
```

USING CLASSES AND OBJECTS

>> **NOTE**
Recall from Chapter 2 that field contents are left aligned when you use a minus sign before the field size. Also recall that the "F1" argument to the `ToString()` method causes the value to be displayed to one decimal place.

9. Write the `Display()` method so that the passed-in `Student`'s `IdNumber`, `LastName`, and `GradePointAverage` are displayed and aligned. Add a closing curly brace for the class.

   ```
   public static void Display(Student stu)
   {
       Console.WriteLine("{0,5}    {1,-10}{2,6}",
           stu.IdNumber, stu.LastName,
           stu.GradePointAverage.ToString("F1"));
   }
   }
   ```

10. Save the file as **CreateStudents.cs** in the Chapter.07 folder on your Student Disk.

11. You can choose to create a multifile assembly, as described in Appendix B; or, for convenience, you can combine the two files into one. Either way, compile the files and execute the program. Figure 7-37 shows the output. Each `Student` has unique data values and uses the same `Display()` method. Notice how the second `Student`'s grade point average was forced to 0 by the `set` accessor in the property for the field.

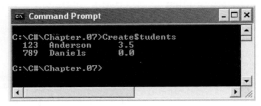

Figure 7-37 Output of `CreateStudents` program

ADDING OVERLOADED CONSTRUCTORS TO A CLASS

Frequently, you create constructors for a class so that fields will hold initial values when objects are instantiated. You can overload constructors by writing multiple versions with different parameter lists; you often want to do this so that different clients can use your class in the way that suits them best.

To add overloaded constructors to a class:

1. Open the **Student.cs** file if it is not still open on your screen. Just before the closing curly brace for the `Student` class, add the following constructor. It takes three parameters and assigns them to the appropriate fields:

   ```
   public Student(int id, string name, double gpa)
   {
       IdNumber = id;
       LastName = name;
       GradePointAverage = gpa;
   }
   ```

2. Add a second parameterless constructor. It calls the first constructor, passing 0 for the ID number, "XXX" for the name, and 0.0 for the grade point average. Its body is empty.

   ```
   public Student() : this(0, "XXX", 0.0)
   {
   }
   ```

3. Save the file.

4. Open the **CreateStudents.cs** file and immediately save it as **CreateStudents2.cs**. Change the class name to CreateStudents2. If you previously included a copy of the Student class within this file, replace the Student class with the new version to which you just added constructors.

5. After the existing declarations of the Student objects, add two more declarations. With one, use three arguments, but with the other, do not use any.

   ```
   Student third = new Student(456, "Marco", 2.4);
   Student fourth = new Student();
   ```

6. At the end of the Main() method, just after the two existing calls to the Display() method, add two more calls using the new objects:

   ```
   Display(third);
   Display(fourth);
   ```

7. Save the file, then compile and execute it. The output looks like Figure 7-38. All four objects are displayed. The first two have had values assigned to them after declaration, but the third and fourth ones obtained their values from their constructors.

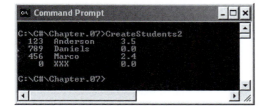

Figure 7-38 Output of CreateStudents2 program

CREATING AN ARRAY OF OBJECTS

Just like variables of the built-in, primitive data types, objects you create can be stored in arrays. In the next steps, you will create an array of Student objects. You will prompt the user for data to fill the array, and you will sort the array by student ID number before displaying all the data.

USING CLASSES AND OBJECTS

To create and use an array of objects:

1. Open the **CreateStudents2.cs** file and immediately save it as **CreateStudents3.cs**. Change the class name to **CreateStudents3**.

2. Delete all the existing statements in the `Main()` method, leaving the opening and closing curly braces. Between the braces, declare an array of eight `Student` objects. Also declare a variable to use as an array subscript and declare three variables that will temporarily hold a user's input data before `Student` objects are constructed.

   ```
   Student[] student = new Student[8];
   int x;
   int id;
   string name;
   double gpa;
   ```

3. In a loop, call a `GetData()` method (which you will write shortly); send it `out` arguments so that you can retrieve values for variables that will hold an ID number, name, and grade point average. Then, in turn, send these three values to the `Student` constructor for each of the eight `Student` objects.

   ```
   for(x = 0; x < student.Length; ++x)
   {
      GetData(out id, out name, out gpa);
      student[x] = new Student(id, name, gpa);
   }
   ```

4. Call the `Array.Sort()` method, sending it the student array. Then, one object at a time in a loop, call the `Display()` method that you wrote in the last set of steps.

   ```
   Array.Sort(student);
   Console.WriteLine("Sorted List:");
   for(x = 0; x < student.Length; ++x)
      Display(student[x]);
   ```

5. Write the `GetData()` method. Its parameters are `out` parameters so that their values will be known to the calling method. The method simply prompts the user for each data item, reads it, and converts it to the appropriate type, if necessary.

   ```
   public static void GetData(out int id, out string name,
      out double gpa)
   {
      string inString;
      Console.Write("Please enter student ID number ");
      inString = Console.ReadLine();
      id = Convert.ToInt32(inString);
   ```

```
        Console.Write("Please enter last name for " +
            "student {0} ", id);
        name = Console.ReadLine();
        Console.Write("Please enter grade point average ");
        inString = Console.ReadLine();
        gpa = Convert.ToDouble(inString);
    }
```

6. Copy the existing Student class to the bottom of the current file, if necessary. After the class header, add a colon and **IComparable** so that objects of the class can be sorted:

```
public class Student : IComparable
```

7. Just before the closing curly brace for the Student class, add the IComparable.CompareTo() method that is required for class objects to be sortable. The method will sort Student objects based on their ID numbers, so it returns 1, –1, or 0 based on IdNumber property comparisons. The method accepts an object that is cast to a Student object. If the IdNumber of the controlling Student object is greater than the argument's IdNumber, then the return value is set to 1. If the IdNumber of the controlling Student object is less than the argument's IdNumber, then the return value is –1. Otherwise, the return value is 0.

```
int IComparable.CompareTo(Object o)
{
    int returnVal;
    Student temp = (Student)o;
    if(this.IdNumber > temp.IdNumber)
        returnVal = 1;
    else
        if(this.IdNumber < temp.IdNumber)
            returnVal = -1;
        else
            returnVal = 0;
    return returnVal;
}
```

8. Save the file (as CreateStudents3.cs) and compile and execute it. When prompted, enter any student IDs, names, and grade point averages you choose. The objects will be sorted and displayed. Figure 7-39 shows a typical execution. After the Student array is sorted, the Student objects appear in idNumber order.

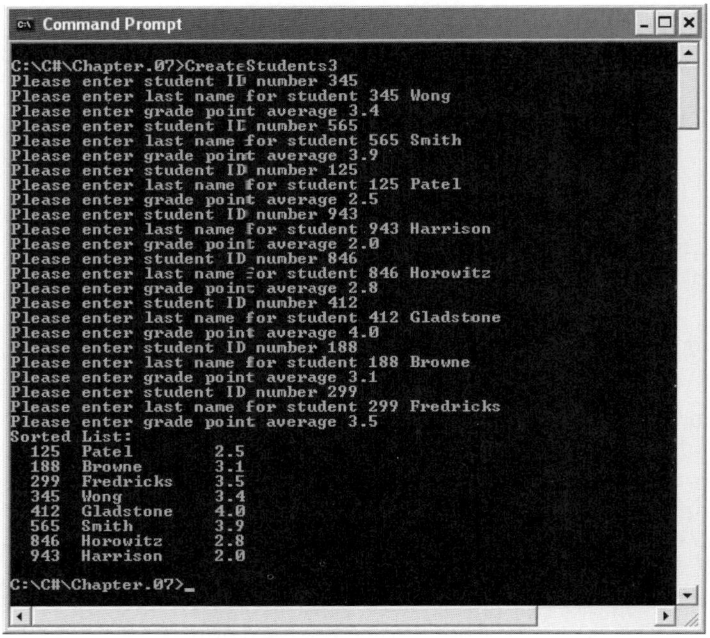

USING CLASSES AND OBJECTS

Figure 7-39 Typical execution of `CreateStudents3` program

CHAPTER SUMMARY

» When you write programs in C#, you create classes that are only programs with a `Main()` method and classes from which you instantiate objects. The data components of a class are its instance variables. Class object attributes often are called fields to help distinguish them from other variables you might use. In addition to their attributes, class objects have methods associated with them, and every object that is an instance of a class is assumed to possess the same methods. A program or class that instantiates objects of another prewritten class is a class client or class user.

» When you create a class, you must assign a name to it and determine what data and methods will be part of the class. A class header or class definition contains an optional access modifier, the keyword `class`, and any legal identifier you choose for the name of your class. In addition to the class header, classes you create must have a class body enclosed between curly braces.

» When you create a class, you define both its attributes and its methods. You usually declare instance variables to be `private` and instance methods to be `public`.

» When you create an object that is an instance of a class, you supply a type and an identifier, and you allocate computer memory for that object using the `new` operator. After an

CHAPTER SEVEN

object has been instantiated, its `public` methods can be accessed using the object's identifier, a dot, and a method call.

» A property is a member of a class that provides access to a field of a class; properties define how fields will be set and retrieved. Properties have `set` accessors for setting an object's fields and `get` accessors for retrieving the stored values. When you create properties, the syntax in your client programs becomes more natural and easier to understand.

» When you create a class that describes objects you will instantiate and another class that instantiates those objects, you can contain the two classes within a single file or place each class in its own file. A class can contain many fields and methods. Although there is no requirement to do so, most programmers place data fields in some logical order at the beginning of a class. For ease in locating class methods and properties, many programmers prefer to store them in alphabetical order. Another logical organization scheme is to store all properties first, in the same order as their corresponding data fields, followed by other methods. An additional aid to keeping your classes organized is to use comments liberally.

» Most of the time, class data fields are `private` and class methods are `public`. This technique ensures that data will be used and changed only in the ways provided in your accessors. Occasionally, however, you need to create `public` fields or `private` methods. For example, you can create a `public` data field when you want all objects of a class to contain the same value. You create a method to be `private` when it should be called only by other methods or accessors within the class and not by outside classes.

» Each instantiation of a class accesses the same copy of its methods. This is possible because an implicit reference, the `this` reference, is passed to every instance method and property accessor. You can explicitly refer to the `this` reference within an instance method or property, but usually you are not required to do so.

» A constructor is a method that instantiates (creates an instance of) an object. Every class you create is automatically supplied with a `public` constructor with no parameters. You can write your own constructor to replace the automatically supplied version. Any constructor you write must have the same name as its class, and constructors cannot have a return type.

» You can pass one or more arguments to a constructor. Frequently you do so to initialize fields.

» Like any other C# methods, constructors can be overloaded. You can write as many constructors for a class as you want, as long as their argument lists do not cause ambiguity.

» A constructor initializer is a clause that indicates another instance of a class constructor should be executed before any statements in the current constructor body.

» You can pass objects to methods just as you can simple data types.

» You can overload operators to use with objects by writing a method to carry out your meaning. The method has a return type and arguments just like other methods, but its identifier is required to be followed by the operator being overloaded—for example, `operator+()` or `operator*()`. When you overload an operator, you should write statements that intuitively have the same meaning as the common use of the operator.

- » Just as you can declare arrays of integers or `double`s, you can declare arrays that hold elements of any type, including objects. After you declare an array of objects, you must call a constructor for each object. To use a method that belongs to an object that is part of an array, you insert the appropriate subscript notation after the array name and before the dot-method.
- » When you create a class that contains many fields, you must tell the compiler which field to use when making comparisons by using an interface—a collection of methods (and perhaps other members) that can be used by any class, as long as the class provides a definition to override the interface's do-nothing, or abstract, method definitions. C# contains an interface named `IComparable`, which in turn contains the definition for the `CompareTo()` method that compares one object to another and returns an integer. You must override this definition in classes you create if you want the objects to be comparable.
- » A destructor contains the actions you require when an instance of a class is destroyed. If you do not explicitly create a destructor for a class, C# automatically provides one. To explicitly declare a destructor, you use an identifier that consists of a tilde (~) followed by the class name. You cannot provide any parameters to a destructor; a class can have at most one destructor.

KEY TERMS

Is-a relationships describe object-class relationships.

An **instantiation** of a class is a created object.

The **instance variables** of a class are the data components that exist separately for each instantiation.

Fields are instance variables within a class.

An object's **state** is the set of contents of its fields.

A **class client** or **class user** is a program or class that instantiates objects of another prewritten class.

A **class header** or **class definition** describes a class; it contains an optional access modifier, the keyword `class`, and any legal identifier for the name of the class.

A **class access modifier** describes access to a class.

The `public` class access modifier means access to the class is not limited.

The `protected` class access modifier means access to the class is limited to the class and to any classes derived from the class.

The `internal` class access modifier means access is limited to the assembly to which the class belongs.

The `private` class access modifier means access is limited to another class to which the class belongs. In other words, a class can be `private` if it is contained within another class, and only the containing class should have access to the `private` class.

CHAPTER SEVEN

Information hiding is a feature found in all object-oriented languages, in which a class's data is private and changed or manipulated only by its own methods.

Instance methods are methods that are used with object instantiations.

Composition is the technique of using a class object within another class object.

The relationship created using composition is called a **has-a relationship** because one class "has an" instance of another.

A **reference type** is a type that holds a memory address.

Value types hold a value; they are predefined types such as `int`, `double`, and `char`.

A **property** is a member of a class that provides access to a field of a class; properties define how fields will be set and retrieved.

Accessors in properties specify how a class's fields are accessed.

An object's fields are assigned by **set accessors** that allow use of the assignment operator with a property name.

An object's fields are accessed by **get accessors** that allow retrieval of a field value by using a property name.

A **read-only property** has only a `get` accessor, and not a `set` accessor.

An **implicit parameter** is undeclared and gets its value automatically.

Contextual keywords are identifiers that act like keywords in specific circumstances.

A **primary key** is a field that uniquely identifies a record; the term is often used in databases.

The **`this` reference** is the reference to an object that is implicitly passed to an instance method of its class.

A **constructor** is a method that instantiates (creates an instance of) an object.

A **default constructor** is an automatically supplied parameterless constructor.

The **default value of an object** is the value initialized with a default constructor.

A **parameterless constructor** is one that takes no arguments.

A **constructor initializer** is a clause that indicates another instance of a class constructor should be executed before any statements in the current constructor body.

The **`CompareTo()` method** of the `IComparable` interface compares one object to another and returns an integer.

An **interface** is a collection of methods (and perhaps other members) that can be used by any class, as long as the class provides a definition to override the interface's do-nothing, or abstract, method definitions.

When a method **overrides** another, it takes precedence over the method, hiding the original version.

The **`IComparable` interface** contains the definition for the `CompareTo()` method.

An instance method's **invoking object** is the object referenced by `this`.

A **destructor** contains the actions you require when an instance of a class is destroyed.

USING CLASSES AND OBJECTS

REVIEW QUESTIONS

1. An object is a(n) _____ of a class.
   a. child
   b. institution
   c. instantiation
   d. relative

2. A class header or class definition can contain all of the following *except* _____.
   a. an optional access modifier
   b. the keyword `class`
   c. an identifier
   d. initial field values

3. Most class fields are created with the _____ modifier.
   a. `public`
   b. `protected`
   c. `new`
   d. `private`

4. Most class methods are created with the _____ modifier.
   a. `public`
   b. `protected`
   c. `new`
   d. `private`

5. Instance methods that belong to individual class objects are _____ `static` methods.
   a. always
   b. usually
   c. occasionally
   d. never

6. To allocate memory for an object instantiation, you must use the _____ operator.
   a. `mem`
   b. `alloc`
   c. `new`
   d. `instant`

7. Assume you have created a class named `MyClass`. The header of the `MyClass` constructor can be _____.
   a. `public void MyClass()`
   b. `public MyClassConstructor()`
   c. Either of these can be the constructor header.
   d. Neither of these can be the constructor header.

8. Assume you have created a class named MyClass. The header of the MyClass constructor can be _____.

   a. public MyClass()
   b. public MyClass (double d)
   c. Either of these can be the constructor header.
   d. Neither of these can be the constructor header.

9. Assume you have created a class named DemoCar. Within the Main() method of this class, you instantiate a Car object named myCar and the following statement executes correctly:

   ```
   Console.WriteLine("The Car gets {0} miles per gallon",
       myCar.ComputeMpg());
   ```

   Within the Car class, the ComputeMpg() method must be _____.

   a. public and static
   b. public and nonstatic
   c. private and static
   d. private and nonstatic

10. Assume you have created a class named TermPaper that contains a character field named letterGrade. You also have created a property for the field. Which of the following cannot be true?

    a. The property name is letterGrade.
    b. The property is read-only.
    c. The property contains a set accessor that does not allow a grade lower than 'C'.
    d. The property does not contain a get accessor.

11. A this reference is _____.

    a. implicitly passed to nonstatic methods
    b. implicitly passed to static methods
    c. explicitly passed to nonstatic methods
    d. explicitly passed to static methods

12. When you use an instance variable within a class's nonstatic methods, you _____ explicitly refer to the method's this reference.

    a. must
    b. can
    c. cannot
    d. should (even though it is not required)

13. A class's default constructor _____.
    a. sets numeric fields to 0
    b. is parameterless
    c. both of these
    d. none of these

14. Assume you have created a class named `Chair` with a constructor defined as `Chair(int height)`. Which of the following overloaded constructors could coexist with the `Chair` constructor without ambiguity?
    a. `Chair(int legs)`
    b. `Chair(int height, int legs)`
    c. both of these
    d. none of these

15. Which of the following statements correctly instantiates a `House` object if the `House` class contains a single constructor with the declaration `House(int bedrooms, double price)`?
    a. `House myHouse = new House();`
    b. `House myHouse = new House(3, 125000.00);`
    c. `House myHouse = House(4, 200,000.00);`
    d. two of these

16. You explicitly call a destructor _____.
    a. when you are finished using an object
    b. when an object goes out of scope
    c. when a class is destroyed
    d. You cannot explicitly call a destructor.

17. In a program that creates five object instances of a class, the constructor executes _____ time(s) and the destructor executes _____ time(s).
    a. one; one
    b. one; five
    c. five; one
    d. five; five

18. Suppose you declare a class named `Furniture` that contains a `string` field named `woodType` and a conventionally named property with a `get` accessor. When you declare an array of 200 `Furniture` objects named `myChairs`, which of the following accesses the last `Furniture` object's wood type?

   a. `Furniture.Get(woodType[199])`

   b. `myChairs[199].WoodType()`

   c. `myChairs.WoodType[199]`

   d. `myChairs[199].WoodType`

19. What is a collection of methods (and perhaps other members) that can be used by any class, as long as the class provides a definition to override the collection's do-nothing, or abstract, definitions?

   a. a superclass   c. a perimeter

   b. a polymorph   d. an interface

20. When you create a class whose members clients are likely to want to compare using the `Array.Sort()` or `Array.BinarySearch()` method, you must _____.

   a. include at least one numeric field within the class

   b. write a `CompareTo()` method for the class

   c. be careful not to override the existing `IComparable.CompareTo()` method

   d. Two of these are true.

EXERCISES

As you work through each exercise, save the finished program in the Chapter.07 folder of your Student Disk.

1. Create a class named `Pizza`. Data fields include a string for toppings (such as pepperoni), an integer for diameter in inches (such as 12), and a `double` for price (such as 13.99). Include properties to get and set values for each of these fields. Create a class named `TestPizza` that instantiates one `Pizza` object and demonstrates the use of the `Pizza` set and get accessors. Save this class as **TestPizza.cs**.

2. Create a class named `HousePlant`. A `HousePlant` has fields for a name (for example, "Philodendron"), a price (for example, 29.99), and a value indicating whether the plant has been fed in the last month (for example, `true`). Include properties that contain `get` and `set` accessors for each field. Create a class named `DisplayHousePlants` that instantiates three `HousePlant` objects. Demonstrate the use of each property for each object. Save the file as **DisplayHousePlants.cs**.

USING CLASSES AND OBJECTS

3. Create a class named `Circle` with fields named `radius`, `area`, and `diameter`. Include a constructor that sets the radius to 1. Also include `public` properties for each field. The `Radius` property should have `get` and `set` accessors, but `Area` and `Diameter` should be read-only. The `set` accessor for the radius should also provide values for the `diameter` and `area`. (The diameter of a circle is twice its radius; the area is pi multiplied by the square of the radius. You can use the public `Math` class property `Math.PI` for the value of pi.) Create a class named `TestCircles` whose `Main()` method declares three `Circle` objects. Assign a small radius value to one `Circle` and assign a larger radius value to another `Circle`. Do not assign a value to the radius of the third circle; instead, retain the value assigned at construction. Display all the statistics for each `Circle`. (Display the area to two decimal places.) Save the program as **TestCircles.cs**.

4. Create a class named `Square` that contains fields for area and the length of a side and whose constructor requires a parameter for the length of one side of a `Square`. The constructor assigns its parameter to the length of the `Square`'s side field and calls a `private` method that computes the area field. Also include read-only properties to get a `Square`'s side and area. Create a class named `DemoSquares` that instantiates an array of 10 `Square` objects with sides that have values of 1 through 10. Display the values for each `Square`. Save the class as **DemoSquares.cs**.

5. Create a class named `GirlScout` that contains fields for a `GirlScout`'s name, troop number, and dues owed. Include a constant `static` field that contains the last words of the `GirlScout` motto ("to obey the Girl Scout law"). Include overloaded constructors that allow you to set all three nonstatic `GirlScout` fields to default values or to parameter values. Also include properties for each field. Create a class named `DemoScouts` that instantiates two `GirlScout` objects and displays their values. Create one object to use the default constructor and the other to use the constructor that requires arguments. Also display the `GirlScout` motto. Save the class as **DemoScouts.cs**.

6. a. Create a class named `Taxpayer`. Data fields for `Taxpayer` objects include the Social Security number (use a `string` for the type, but do not use dashes within the Social Security number), the yearly gross income, and the tax owed. Include a property with `get` and `set` accessors for the first two data fields, but make the tax owed a read-only property. The tax should be calculated whenever the income is set. Assume the tax is 15% of income for incomes under $30,000 and 28% for incomes that are $30,000 or higher. Write a program that declares an array of 10 `Taxpayer` objects. Prompt the user for data for each object and display the 10 objects. Save the program as **TaxPayerDemo.cs**.

   b. Modify the `Taxpayer` class so its objects are comparable to each other based on tax owed. Modify the `TaxPayerDemo` application so that after the 10 objects are displayed, they are sorted in order by the amount of tax owed; then display the objects again. Save the program as **TaxPayerDemo2.cs**.

7. Create a class named `Car` with fields that hold a vehicle ID number, make, model, color, and value for a `Car` object. Include appropriate properties for each field. Write a `DisplayFleet()` method that accepts any number of `Car` objects, displays their values, and displays the total value of all `Car` objects passed to the method. Write a `Main()` method that declares five `Car` objects and assigns values to each, then calls `DisplayFleet()` three times—passing three, four, and five `Car` objects in successive calls. Save the program as **CarsDemo.cs**.

8. a. Create a class named `School` that contains fields for the `School` name and number of students enrolled and properties for each field. Also, include an `IComparable.CompareTo()` method so that `School` objects can be sorted by enrollment. Write a program that allows a user to enter information about five `School` objects. Display the `School` objects in order of enrollment size from smallest to largest `School`. Save the program as **SchoolsDemo.cs**.

   b. Modify the program created in Exercise 8a so that after the `School` objects are displayed in order, the program prompts the user to enter a minimum enrollment figure. Display all `School` objects that have an enrollment at least as large as the entered value. Save the program as **SchoolMinEnroll.cs**.

9. a. Create a class named `Friend`. Its fields include a `Friend`'s name, phone number, and three integer fields that together represent the `Friend`'s birthday—month, day, and year. Write a program that declares an array of eight `Friend` objects and prompts the user to enter data about eight friends. Display the `Friend` objects in alphabetical order by first name. Save the program as **FriendList.cs**.

   b. Modify the program created in Exercise 9a so that after the list of `Friend` objects is displayed, the program prompts the user for a specific `Friend`'s name and the program returns the `Friend`'s phone number and birthday. Display an appropriate message if the friend the user requests is not found. Save the program as **FriendBirthday.cs**.

   c. Modify the program in Exercise 9b so that after the requested `Friend`'s birthday displays, the program also displays a list of every `Friend` who has a birthday in the same month. Save the program as **AllFriendsInSameMonth.cs**.

10. a. Design a `Job` class for Harold's Home Services. The class contains four data fields—`Job` description (for example, "wash windows"), time in hours to complete the `Job` (for example, 3.5), per-hour rate charged for the `Job` (for example, $25.00), and total fee for the `Job` (hourly rate times hours). Include properties to get and set each field except the total fee—that field will be read-only, and its value is calculated each time either the hourly fee or the number of hours is set. Overload the + operator so that two `Jobs` can be added. The sum of two `Jobs` is a new `Job` containing the descriptions of both original `Jobs` (joined by "and"), the sum of the time in hours for the original `Jobs`, and the average of the hourly rate for the original `Jobs`. Write a `Main()` function that demonstrates all the methods work correctly. Save the file as **DemoJobs.cs**.

267

USING CLASSES AND OBJECTS

b. Harold has realized that his method for computing the fee for combined jobs is not fair. For example, consider the following:

» His fee for painting a house is $100 per hour. If a job takes 10 hours, he earns $1000.

» His fee for dog walking is $10 per hour. If a job takes 1 hour, he earns $10.

» If he combines the two jobs and works a total of 11 hours, he earns only the average rate of $55 per hour or $605.

Devise an improved, weighted method for calculating Harold's fees for combined Jobs and include it in the overloaded operator+() method. Write a Main() function that demonstrates all the methods in the class work correctly. Save the file as **DemoJobs2.cs**.

11. a. Create a Fraction class with fields that hold a whole number, a numerator, and a denominator. In addition:

» Create properties for each field. The set accessor for the denominator should not allow a 0 value; the value defaults to 1.

» Add three constructors. One takes three parameters for a whole number, numerator, and denominator. Another accepts two parameters for the numerator and denominator; when this constructor is used, the whole number value is 0. The last constructor is parameterless; it sets the whole number and numerator to 0 and the denominator to 1. (After construction, Fractions do not have to be reduced to proper form. For example, even though 3/9 could be reduced to 1/3, your constructors do not have to perform this task.)

» Add a Reduce() method that reduces a Fraction if it is in improper form. For example, 2/4 should be reduced to 1/2.

» Add an operator+() method that adds two Fractions. To add two fractions, first eliminate any whole number part of the value. For example, 2 1/4 becomes 9/4 and 1 3/5 becomes 8/5. Find a common denominator and convert the fractions to it. For example, when adding 9/4 and 8/5, you can convert them to 45/20 and 32/20. Then you can add the numerators, giving 77/20. Finally, call the Reduce() method to reduce the result, restoring any whole number value so the fractional part of the number is less than 1. For example, 77/20 becomes 3 17/20.

» Include a function that returns a string that contains a Fraction in the usual display format—the whole number, a space, the numerator, a slash (/), and a denominator. When the whole number is 0, just the Fraction part of the value should be displayed (for example, 1/2 instead of 0 1/2). If the numerator is 0, just the whole number should display (for example, 2 instead of 2 0/3).

Write a Main() method that instantiates several Fractions and demonstrate that all the methods work correctly. Save the program as **FractionDemo.cs**.

b. Add an operator*() method to the Fraction class created in Exercise 11a so that it correctly multiplies two Fractions. The result should be in proper, reduced format. Demonstrate that the method works correctly. Save the program as **FractionDemo2.cs**.

c. Create an array of four Fractions. Prompt the user for values for each. Display every possible combination of addition results and every possible combination of multiplication results for each Fraction pair (that is, each type will have 16 results). Figure 7-40 shows a sample execution. Save the program as **FractionDemo3.cs**.

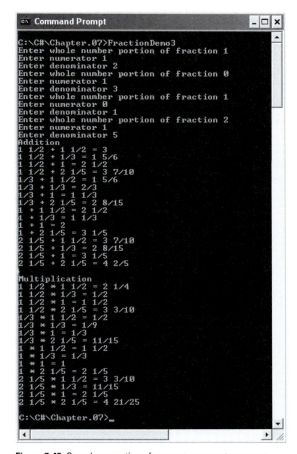

Figure 7-40 Sample execution of FractionDemo3 program

DEBUGGING EXERCISES

Each of the following files saved in the Chapter.07 folder on your Student Disk has syntax and/or logical errors. In each case, determine the problem and fix the program. After you correct the errors, save each file using the same filename preceded with *Fixed*. For example, DebugSeven1.cs will become FixedDebugSeven1.cs.

a. DebugSeven1.cs

b. DebugSeven2.cs

c. DebugSeven3.cs

d. DebugSeven4.cs

UP FOR DISCUSSION

1. In this chapter, you learned that instance data and methods belong to objects (which are class members), but that static data and methods belong to a class as a whole. Consider the real-life class named `StateInTheUnitedStates`. Name some real-life attributes of this class that are static attributes and instance attributes. Create another example of a real-life class and discuss what its static and instance members might be.

2. Some programmers use a system called Hungarian notation when naming their variables and class fields. What is Hungarian notation and why do many object-oriented programmers feel it is not a valuable style to use?

3. If you are completing all the programming exercises at the ends of the chapters in this book, you can see how much work goes into a full-blown professional program. How would you feel if someone copied your work without compensating you? Investigate the magnitude of software piracy in our society. What are the penalties for illegally copying software? Are there circumstances under which it is acceptable to copy a program? If a friend asked you to make a copy of a program for him, would you? What do you suggest we do about this problem, if anything?

CHAPTER EIGHT

INTRODUCTION TO INHERITANCE

In this chapter you will:

Learn about the concept of inheritance
Learn inheritance terminology
Extend classes
Use the `protected` access specifier
Override base class methods
Access base class methods from a derived class
Understand how a derived class object "is an" instance
  of the base class
Learn about the `Object` class
Work with base classes that have constructors
Create and use abstract classes
Create and use interfaces
Understand the benefits of inheritance

INTRODUCTION TO INHERITANCE

Understanding classes helps you organize objects in real life. Understanding inheritance helps you organize them more precisely. If you have never heard of a Braford, for example, you would have a hard time forming a picture of one in your mind. When you learn that a Braford is an animal, you gain some understanding of what it must be like. That understanding grows when you learn it is a mammal, and the understanding is almost complete when you learn it is a cow. When you learn that a Braford is a cow, you understand it has many characteristics that are common to all cows. To identify a Braford, you must learn only relatively minor details—its color or markings, for example. Most of a Braford's characteristics, however, derive from its membership in a particular hierarchy of classes: animal, mammal, and cow.

All object-oriented programming languages make use of inheritance for the same reasons—to organize the objects programs use, and to make new objects easier to understand based on your knowledge of their inherited traits. In this chapter, you will learn to make use of inheritance with your C# objects.

UNDERSTANDING THE CONCEPT OF INHERITANCE

Inheritance is the principle that you can apply your knowledge of a general category to more specific objects. You are familiar with the concept of inheritance from all sorts of situations. When you use the term *inheritance*, you might think of genetic inheritance. You know from biology that your blood type and eye color are the products of inherited genes. You can say that many other facts about you (your attributes) are inherited. Similarly, you often can attribute your behaviors to inheritance; for example, the way you handle money might be similar to the way your grandmother handles it, and your gait might be the same as your father's—so your methods are inherited, too.

> **NOTE**
> You first learned about inheritance in Chapter 1.

You also might choose to have plants and animals based on their inherited attributes. You plant impatiens next to your house because they thrive in the shade; you adopt a poodle because you know poodles don't shed. Every plant and pet has slightly different characteristics, but within a species, you can count on many consistent inherited attributes and behaviors. In other words, you can reuse the knowledge you gain about general categories and apply it to more specific categories. Similarly, the classes you create in object-oriented programming languages can inherit data and methods from existing classes. When you create a class by making it inherit from another class, you are provided with data fields and methods automatically; you can reuse fields and methods that are already written and tested.

You already know how to create classes and how to instantiate objects that are members of those classes. For example, consider the `Employee` class in Figure 8-1. The class contains two data fields, `empNum` and `empSal`, as well as properties that contain accessors for each field and a method that creates an `Employee` greeting.

```
public class Employee
{
    private int empNum;
    private double empSal;
    public int EmpNum
    {
        get
        {
            return empNum;
        }
        set
        {
            empNum = value;
        }
    }
    public double EmpSal
    {
        get
        {
            return empSal;
        }
        set
        {
            empSal = value;
        }
    }
    public string GetGreeting()
    {
        string greeting = "Hello employee #" + EmpNum;
        return greeting;
    }
}
```

Figure 8-1 An Employee class

After you create the Employee class, you can create specific Employee objects, as in the following:

```
Employee receptionist = new Employee();
Employee deliveryPerson = new Employee();
```

These Employee objects can eventually possess different numbers and salaries, but because they are Employee objects, you know that each possesses *some* number and salary.

Suppose you hire a new type of Employee who earns a commission as well as a salary. You can create a class with a name such as CommissionEmployee, and provide this class with

INTRODUCTION TO INHERITANCE

three fields (`empNum`, `empSal`, and `commissionRate`), three properties (with accessors to get and set each of the three fields), and a greeting method. However, this work would duplicate much of the work that you already have done for the `Employee` class. The wise and efficient alternative is to create the class `CommissionEmployee` so it inherits all the attributes and methods of `Employee`. Then, you can add just the single field and property with two accessors that are additions within `CommissionEmployee` objects. Figure 8-2 depicts these relationships.

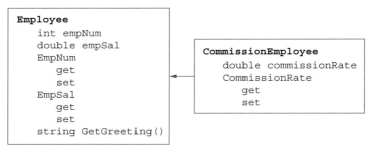

Figure 8-2 `CommissionEmployee` inherits from `Employee`

When you use inheritance to create the `CommissionEmployee` class, you acquire the following benefits:

» You save time, because you need not recreate the `Employee` fields, properties, and methods.
» You reduce the chance of errors, because the `Employee` properties and methods have already been used and tested.
» You make it easier for anyone who has used the `Employee` class to understand the `CommissionEmployee` class because such users can concentrate on the new features only.

The ability to use inheritance makes programs easier to write, easier to understand, and less prone to errors. Imagine that besides `CommissionEmployee`, you want to create several other specific `Employee` classes (perhaps `PartTimeEmployee`, including a field for hours worked, or `DismissedEmployee`, including a reason for dismissal). By using inheritance, you can develop each new class correctly and more quickly.

>> **NOTE**
In part, the concept of class inheritance is useful because it makes class code reusable. However, you do not use inheritance simply to save work. When properly used, inheritance always involves a general-to-specific relationship.

UNDERSTANDING INHERITANCE TERMINOLOGY

A class that is used as a basis for inheritance, like `Employee`, is called a **base class**. When you create a class that inherits from a base class (such as `CommissionEmployee`), it is a **derived class** or **extended class**. When presented with two classes that have a parent-child relationship, you can tell which class is the base class and which is the derived class by using the two classes in a sentence with the phrase "is a." A derived class always "is a" case or instance of the more general base class. For example, a `Tree` class may be a base class to an `Evergreen` class. Every `Evergreen` "is a" `Tree`; however, it is not true that every `Tree` is an `Evergreen`. Thus, `Tree` is the base class and `Evergreen` is the derived class. Similarly, a `CommissionEmployee` "is an" `Employee`—not always the other way around—so `Employee` is the base class and `CommissionEmployee` is derived.

You can use the terms **superclass** and **subclass** as synonyms for base class and derived class. Thus, `Evergreen` can be called a subclass of the `Tree` superclass. You also can use the terms **parent class** and **child class**. A `CommissionEmployee` is a child to the `Employee` parent. Use the pair of terms with which you are most comfortable; all of these terms will be used interchangeably in this book.

As an alternative way to discover which of two classes is the base class and which is the derived class, you can try saying the two class names together (although this technique might not work with every base-subclass pair). When people say their names together in the English language, they state the more specific name before the all-encompassing family name, such as "Ginny Kroening." Similarly, with classes, the order that "makes more sense" is the child-parent order. Thus, because "Evergreen Tree" makes more sense than "Tree Evergreen," you can deduce that `Evergreen` is the child class.

>> **NOTE** It also is convenient to think of a derived class as building upon its base class by providing the "adjectives" or additional descriptive terms for the "noun." Frequently, the names of derived classes are formed in this way, as in `CommissionEmployee`.

>> **NOTE** Do not think of a subclass as a "subset" of another class—in other words, possessing only parts of its base class. In fact, a derived class usually contains more than its parent.

Finally, you usually can distinguish base classes from their derived classes by size. Although it is not required, a derived class is generally larger than a base class, in the sense that it usually has additional fields and methods. A subclass description may look small, but any subclass contains all of its base class's fields and methods as well as its own more specific fields and methods.

A derived class can be further extended. In other words, a subclass can have a child of its own. For example, after you create a `Tree` class and derive `Evergreen`, you might derive a `Spruce` class from `Evergreen`. Similarly, a `Poodle` class might derive from `Dog`, `Dog` from `DomesticPet`, and `DomesticPet` from `Animal`. The entire list of parent classes from which a child class is derived constitutes the **ancestors** of the subclass.

>> **NOTE** After you create the `Spruce` class, you might be ready to create `Spruce` objects. For example, you might create `theTreeInMyBackYard`, or you might create an array of 1000 `Spruce` objects for a tree farm.

Inheritance is **transitive**, which means a child inherits all the members of all its ancestors. In other words, when you declare a `Spruce` object, it contains all the attributes and methods of both an `Evergreen` and a `Tree`. As you work with C#, you will encounter many examples of such transitive chains of inheritance.

>> **NOTE** In math, a transitive relationship occurs when something that is true for a and b and for b and c is also true for a and c. For example, equality is transitive. If a = b and b = c, then a = c.

>> **NOTE** When you create your own transitive inheritance chains, you want to place fields and methods at their most general level. In other words, a method named `Grow()` rightfully belongs in a `Tree` class, whereas `LeavesTurnColor()` does not, because the method applies to only some of the `Tree` child classes. Similarly, a `LeavesTurnColor()` method would be better located in a `Deciduous` class than separately within the `Oak` or `Maple` child class.

INTRODUCTION TO INHERITANCE

EXTENDING CLASSES

When you create a class that is an extension or child of another class, you use a single colon between the derived class name and its base class name. For example, the following class header creates a subclass-superclass relationship between `CommissionEmployee` and `Employee`.

```
public class CommissionEmployee : Employee
```

Each `CommissionEmployee` object automatically contains the data fields and methods of the base class; you then can add new fields and methods to the new derived class. Figure 8-3 shows a `CommissionEmployee` class.

```
public class CommissionEmployee : Employee
{
    private double commissionRate;
    public double CommissionRate
    {
        get
        {
            return commissionRate;
        }
        set
        {
            commissionRate = value;
        }
    }
}
```

Figure 8-3 `CommissionEmployee` class

The `CommissionEmployee` class in Figure 8-3 contains three fields: `empNum` and `empSal`, inherited from `Employee`, and `commissionRate`, which is defined within the `CommissionEmployee` class. Similarly, the `CommissionEmployee` class contains three properties and a method—two properties and the method are inherited from `Employee`, and one property is defined within `CommissionEmployee` itself. When you write a program that instantiates an object using the following statement, then you can use any of the next statements to set field values for the salesperson:

```
CommissionEmployee salesperson = new CommissionEmployee();
salesperson.EmpNum = 234;
salesperson.EmpSal = Convert.ToDouble(Console.ReadLine());
salesperson.CommissionRate = 0.07;
```

The `salesperson` object has access to all three `set` accessors (two from its parent and one from its own class) because it is both a `CommissionEmployee` and an `Employee`. Similarly, the object has access to three `get` accessors and the `GetGreeting()` method. Figure 8-4 shows a `Main()` method that declares `Employee` and `CommissionEmployee` objects and shows all the properties and methods that can be used with each. Figure 8-5 shows the program output.

```
using System;
public class DemoEmployees
{
    public static void Main()
    {
        Employee clerk = new Employee();
        CommissionEmployee salesperson = new CommissionEmployee();
        clerk.EmpNum = 123;
        clerk.EmpSal = 30000.00;
        salesperson.EmpNum = 234;
        salesperson.EmpSal = 20000;
        salesperson.CommissionRate = 0.07;
        Console.WriteLine("\n" + clerk.GetGreeting());
        Console.WriteLine("Clerk #{0} makes {1} per year",
            clerk.EmpNum,
            clerk.EmpSal.ToString("C"));
        Console.WriteLine("\n" + salesperson.GetGreeting());
        Console.WriteLine("Salesperson #{0} makes {1} per year",
            salesperson.EmpNum,
            salesperson.EmpSal.ToString("C"));
        Console.WriteLine("...plus {0} commission on all sales",
            salesperson.CommissionRate.ToString("P"));
    }
}
```

Figure 8-4 DemoEmployees class that declares Employee and CommissionEmployee objects

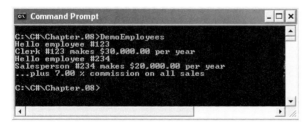

Figure 8-5 Output of the DemoEmployees program

Inheritance works only in one direction: A child inherits from a parent—not the other way around. If a program instantiates an Employee object as in the following statement, the Employee object does *not* have access to the CommissionEmployee fields or methods.

```
Employee clerk = new Employee();
```

INTRODUCTION TO INHERITANCE

> **NOTE** As with doctors, it is convenient to think of derived classes as *specialists*. That is, their fields and methods are more specialized than those of the parent class.

`Employee` is the parent class, and `clerk` is an object of the parent class. It makes sense that a parent class object does not have access to its child's data and methods. When you create the parent class, you do not know how many future child classes might be created, or what their data or methods might look like. In addition, derived classes are more specific. A `HeartSurgeon` class and an `Obstetrician` class are children of a `Doctor` class. You do not expect all members of the general parent class `Doctor` to have the `HeartSurgeon`'s `RepairValve()` method or the `Obstetrician`'s `DeliverBaby()` method. However, `HeartSurgeon` and `Obstetrician` objects have access to the more general `Doctor` methods `TakeBloodPressure()` and `BillPatients()`.

USING THE protected ACCESS SPECIFIER

The `Employee` class in Figure 8-1 is a typical C# class in that its data fields are `private` and its properties and methods are `public`. In Chapter 7, you learned that this scheme provides for information hiding—protecting your `private` data from alteration by methods outside the data's own class. When a program is a client of the `Employee` class (that is, it instantiates an `Employee` object), the client cannot alter the data in any `private` field directly. For example, when you write a `Main()` method that creates an `Employee` named `clerk`, you cannot change the `Employee`'s `empNum` or `empSal` directly using a statement such as `clerk.empNum = 2222;`. Instead, you must use the `EmpNum` property to set the `idNum` field of the `clerk` object.

When you use information hiding, you are assured that your data will be altered only by the properties and methods you choose and only in ways that you can control. If outside classes could alter an `Employee`'s `private` fields, then the fields could be assigned values that the `Employee` class couldn't control. In such a case, the principle of information hiding would be destroyed, causing the behavior of the object to be unpredictable.

Any derived class you create, such as `CommissionEmployee`, inherits all the data and methods of its base class. However, even though a child of `Employee` has `empNum` and `empSal` fields, the `CommissionEmployee` methods cannot alter or use those `private` fields directly. If you could use `private` data outside of its class, the principle of information hiding would be destroyed. If you intend the `Employee` class data field `empNum` to be `private`, then you don't want any outside classes using the field. If a new class could simply extend your `Employee` class and "get to" its data fields without "going through the proper channels," then information hiding would not be operating.

On some occasions, you do want to access parent class data from within a child class. For example, suppose that the `Employee` class `EmpSal` property `set` accessor has been written so that no `Employee`'s salary is ever set to less than 15000, as follows:

```
set
{
   if(value < 15000)
      empSal = 15000;
   else
      empSal = value;
}
```

> **NOTE** In this example, you probably would prefer to use a named constant for the value 15000.

Also assume that a `CommissionEmployee` draws commission only and no regular salary; that is, when you set a `CommissionEmployee`'s `commissionRate` field, the `empSal` should become 0. You would write the `CommissionEmployee` class `CommissionRate` property set accessor as follows:

```
set
{
    commissionRate = value;
    EmpSal = 0;
}
```

Using this implementation, when you create a `CommissionEmployee` object and set its `CommissionRate`, 0 is sent to the `set` accessor for the `Employee` class `EmpSal` property. There, because the value of the salary is less than 15000, the salary is forced to 15000 even though you want it to be 0.

An alternative is to rewrite the `set` accessor for the `CommissionRate` property in the `CommissionEmployee` class as follows:

```
set
{
    commissionRate = value;
    empSal = 0;
}
```

In this `set` accessor, you bypass the parent class's `EmpSal` set accessor and directly use the `empSal` field. However, when you include this accessor in a program and compile it, you receive an error message: "Employee.empSal is inaccessible due to its protection level". In other words, `Employee.empSal` is `private`, and no other class can access it. So, in summary:

» Using the `public set` accessor in the parent class does not work because of the minimum salary requirement.

» Using the `private` field in the parent class does not work because it is inaccessible.

» Making the parent class field `public` would work, but doing so would violate the principle of information hiding.

Fortunately, there is a fourth option. If you want a derived class property or method to be able to access `empSal`, then it cannot be `private`. However, if you don't want other, nonchild classes to access the field, then it cannot be `public`. The solution is to create the `empSal` field using the modifier `protected`, which provides you with an intermediate level of security between `public` and `private` access. A **protected** data field or method can be used within its own class or in any classes extended from that class, but it cannot be used by "outside" classes. In other words, `protected` members can be used "within the family"—by a class and its descendants.

Figure 8-6 shows how you can declare `empSal` as `protected` within the `Employee` class so that it becomes legal to access it directly within the `CommissionRate set` accessor of the `CommissionEmployee` derived class. Figure 8-7 shows a program that instantiates a `CommissionEmployee` object, and Figure 8-8 shows the output. Notice that the `CommissionEmployee`'s salary initially is set to 20000 in the program, but the salary becomes 0 when the `CommissionRate` is set later.

INTRODUCTION TO INHERITANCE

```
public class Employee
{
    private int empNum;
    protected double empSal;
    public int EmpNum
    {
        get
        {
            return empNum;
        }
        set
        {
            empNum = value;
        }
    }
    public double EmpSal
    {
        get
        {
            return empSal;
        }
        set
        {
            if(value < 15000)
                empSal = 15000;
            else
                empSal = value;
        }
    }
    public string GetGreeting()
    {
        string greeting = "Hello employee #" + EmpNum;
        return greeting;
    }
}
public class CommissionEmployee : Employee
{
    private double commissionRate;
    public double CommissionRate
    {
        get
        {
            return commissionRate;
        }
        set
        {
            commissionRate = value;
            empSal = 0;
        }
    }
}
```

Figure 8-6 `Employee` with a `protected` field and `CommissionEmployee` class

CHAPTER EIGHT

```
using System;
public class DemoSalesperson
{
   public static void Main()
   {
      CommissionEmployee salesperson = new CommissionEmployee();
      salesperson.EmpNum = 345;
      salesperson.EmpSal = 20000;
      salesperson.CommissionRate = 0.07;
      Console.WriteLine("Salesperson #{0} makes {1} per year",
         salesperson.EmpNum,
         salesperson.EmpSal.ToString("C"));
      Console.WriteLine("...plus {0} commission on all sales",
         salesperson.CommissionRate.ToString("P"));
   }
}
```

Figure 8-7 The `DemoSalesperson` program

Figure 8-8 Output of the `DemoSalesperson` program

>> **NOTE** If you set the salesperson's `CommissionRate` first in the `DemoSalesperson` program, then set `EmpSal` to a nonzero value, `empSal` will not be reduced to 0. If your intention is to always create `CommissionEmployee`s with salaries of 0, then the `EmpSal` property should also be overridden in the derived class.

Using the `protected` access modifier for a field can be convenient, and it also improves program performance a little by using a field directly instead of "going through" property accessors. Also, using the `protected` access modifier is occasionally necessary. However, `protected` data members should be used sparingly. Whenever possible, the principle of information hiding should be observed, and even child classes should have to go through accessors to "get to" their parent's private data. When child classes are allowed direct access to a parent's fields, the likelihood of future errors increases. For example, if a programmer changes the field name in the `Employee` class from `empSal` to `annualSalary` in the future, then the programmer will have to remember to change the field reference in the child class too. Worse, the programmer might not be aware of all the child classes that others have derived from the original class.

>> **NOTE**
Classes that depend on field names from parent classes are said to be **fragile** because they are prone to errors—that is, they are easy to "break."

INTRODUCTION TO INHERITANCE

OVERRIDING BASE CLASS METHODS

When you create a derived class by extending an existing class, the new derived class contains data and methods that were defined in the original base class. Sometimes, the superclass fields, properties, and methods are not entirely appropriate for the subclass objects.

>> **NOTE**
In Figure 8-9, the Student fields that hold credits and tuition are declared as protected because a child class will use them.

For example, suppose you have created a Student class as shown in Figure 8-9. Students have names, credits for which they are enrolled, and tuition amounts. You can set a Student's name and credits by using the set accessors in the Name and Credits properties, but you cannot set a Student's tuition directly because there is no set accessor for the Tuition property. Instead, tuition is calculated based on a standard RATE (of $55.75) for each credit that the Student takes.

```
class Student
{
    private const double RATE = 55.75;
    private string name;
    protected int credits;
    protected double tuition;
    public string Name
    {
        get
        {
            return name;
        }
        set
        {
            name = value;
        }
    }
    public int Credits
    {
        get
        {
            return credits;
        }
        set
        {
            credits = value;
            tuition = credits * RATE;
        }
    }
    public double Tuition
    {
        get
        {
            return tuition;
        }
    }
}
```

Figure 8-9 The Student class

Suppose you derive a subclass from Student called ScholarshipStudent. A ScholarshipStudent has a name, credits, and tuition, but the tuition is not calculated in the same way as it is for a Student; instead, tuition for a ScholarshipStudent should be set to 0. You want to use the Credits property to set a ScholarshipStudent's credits, but you want the property to behave differently than the parent class Student's Credits property. Using the same method or property name to indicate different implementations is called polymorphism. The word *polymorphism* means "many forms"; it means that many forms of action take place, even though you use the same name to describe the action. In other words, there are many forms of the same method depending on the object associated with the word.

>> **NOTE**
You first learned about polymorphism in Chapter 1.

The English language provides many examples of polymorphism:

» You *run* a race differently than you *run* a business.
» You *play* chess differently than you *play* a guitar.
» You *open* a door differently than you *open* a bank account.

You understand each use of these English verbs based on its context. In a similar way, C# understands your use of the same method name based on the type of object associated with it. Figure 8-10 shows a ScholarshipStudent class. As a child of Student, a ScholarshipStudent possesses all the attributes, properties, and methods of a Student, but its Credits property behaves differently.

```
class ScholarshipStudent : Student
{
    new public int Credits
    {
       set
       {
           credits = value;
           tuition = 0;
       }
    }
}
```

Figure 8-10 The ScholarshipStudent class

In the child ScholarshipStudent class in Figure 8-10, the Credits property is declared as new (see shading) because it has the same header as a property in its parent class—it overrides and **hides** its counterpart in the parent class. (You could do the same thing with methods.) If you omit new, the program will still operate correctly, but you will receive a warning that you are hiding an inherited member with the same name in the base class. Using the keyword new eliminates the warning and makes your intentions clear. When you use the Name property with a ScholarshipStudent object, a program uses the parent class property Name; it is not hidden. However, when you use Credits to set a

INTRODUCTION TO INHERITANCE

value for a ScholarshipStudent object, the program uses the new, overriding property from its own class.

> **NOTE** If credits and tuition had been declared as private within the Student class, then ScholarshipStudent would not be able to use them.

> **NOTE** If a base class and its derived class have methods with the same name but different argument lists, you are overloading methods, and not overriding them. You learned about overloading methods in Chapter 3.

> **NOTE** A superclass member that is not hidden by the derived class is **visible** in the derived class.

Figure 8-11 shows a program that uses Student and ScholarshipStudent objects. Even though each object assigns the Credits property with the same number of credit hours (in the two shaded statements), the calculated tuition values are different because each object uses a different version of the Credits property. Figure 8-12 shows the execution of the program.

```
using System;
class DemoStudents
{
    public static void Main()
    {
        Student payingStudent = new Student();
        ScholarshipStudent freeStudent = new ScholarshipStudent();
        payingStudent.Name = "Megan";
        payingStudent.Credits = 15;
        freeStudent.Name = "Luke";
        freeStudent.Credits = 15;
        Console.WriteLine("{0}'s tuition is {1}",
            payingStudent.Name,
            payingStudent.Tuition.ToString("C"));
        Console.WriteLine("{0}'s tuition is {1}",
            freeStudent.Name,
            freeStudent.Tuition.ToString("C"));
    }
}
```

Figure 8-11 The DemoStudents program

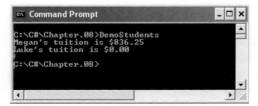

Figure 8-12 Output of the DemoStudents program

284

CHAPTER EIGHT

ACCESSING BASE CLASS METHODS FROM A DERIVED CLASS

A derived class can contain a method with the same name and arguments as a method in its parent class; when this happens, using the derived class method overrides the parent class method. In some situations, you might want to use the parent class method within a subclass. If so, you can use the keyword base to access the parent class method. For example, recall the GetGreeting() method that appears in the Employee class in Figure 8-6. If its child, CommissionEmployee, also contains a GetGreeting() method, as shown in Figure 8-13, then within the CommissionEmployee class you can call base.GetGreeting() to access the base class version of the method. Figure 8-14 shows an application that uses the method with a CommissionEmployee object. Figure 8-15 shows the output.

```
public class CommissionEmployee : Employee
{
    private double commissionRate;
    public double CommissionRate
    {
        get
        {
            return commissionRate;
        }
        set
        {
            commissionRate = value;
            empSal = 0;
        }
    }
    new public string GetGreeting()
    {
        string greeting = base.GetGreeting();
        greeting += "\nGood luck with sales!";
        return greeting;
    }
}
```

Figure 8-13 The CommissionEmployee class with a GetGreeting() method

285

INTRODUCTION TO INHERITANCE

```
using System;
public class DemoSalesperson2
{
    public static void Main()
    {
        CommissionEmployee salesperson = new CommissionEmployee();
        salesperson.EmpNum = 345;
        Console.WriteLine(salesperson.GetGreeting());
    }
}
```

Figure 8-14 The `DemoSalesperson2` program

Figure 8-15 Output of the `DemoSalesperson2` program

In Figure 8-13, the child class method uses the keyword `new` to eliminate a compiler warning. Then, within the `GetGreeting()` method, the parent's version is called. The returned string is stored in the `greeting` variable, and then a "Good luck with sales!" message is added to it before the complete message is returned to the calling program. By overriding the base class method in the child class, the duplicate typing to create the first part of the message was eliminated. Additionally, if the first part of the message is altered in the future, it will be altered in only one place—in the base class.

UNDERSTANDING HOW A DERIVED CLASS OBJECT "IS AN" INSTANCE OF THE BASE CLASS

Every derived class object "is a" specific instance of both the derived class and the base class. In other words, `myCar` "is a" `Car` as well as a `Vehicle`, and `myDog` "is a" `Dog` as well as a `Mammal`. You can assign a derived class object to an object of any of its superclass types. When you do, C# makes an **implicit conversion** from derived class to base class.

> **NOTE** C# also makes implicit conversions when casting one data type to another. For example, in the statement `double money = 10;`, the value 10 is implicitly converted (or cast) to a double.

> **NOTE** When a derived class object is assigned to its ancestor's data type, the conversion can more specifically be called an **implicit reference conversion**. This term is more accurate because it emphasizes the difference between numerical conversions and reference objects. When you assign a derived class object to a base class type, the object is treated as though it had only the characteristics defined in the base class.

For example, when a `CommissionEmployee` class inherits from `Employee`, an object of either type can be passed to a method that accepts an `Employee` parameter. In Figure 8-16, an `Employee` is passed to `DisplayGreeting()` in the first shaded statement, and a `CommissionEmployee` is passed in the second shaded statement. Each is referred to as `emp` within the method, and each is used correctly, as shown in Figure 8-17.

```
using System;
public class DemoSalesperson3
{
    public static void Main()
    {
        Employee clerk = new Employee();
        CommissionEmployee salesperson = new CommissionEmployee();
        clerk.EmpNum = 234;
        salesperson.EmpNum = 345;
        DisplayGreeting(clerk);
        DisplayGreeting(salesperson);
    }
    public static void DisplayGreeting(Employee emp)
    {
        Console.WriteLine("Hi there #" + emp.EmpNum);
        Console.WriteLine(emp.GetGreeting());
    }
}
```

Figure 8-16 The `DemoSalesperson3` program

Figure 8-17 Output of the `DemoSalesperson3` program

> **NOTE** In C#, you can use either `new` or `override` when defining a derived class member that has the same name as a base class member. When you write a statement such as `ScholarshipStudent s1 = new ScholarshipStudent();`, you won't notice the difference. However, if you use `new` when defining the derived class `Credits` property and write a statement such as `Student s2 = new ScholarshipStudent();`, then `s.Credits` accesses the base class property. On the other hand, if you use `override` when defining `Credits` in the derived class, then `s2.Credits` uses the derived class property.

INTRODUCTION TO INHERITANCE

USING THE Object CLASS

Every class you create in C# derives from a single class named `System.Object`. In other words, the **object** (or `Object`) class type in the `System` namespace is the ultimate base class for all other types. The keyword `object` is an alias for the `System.Object` class. You can use the lowercase and uppercase versions of the class interchangeably.

> **»NOTE** When you create a class such as `Employee`, you usually use the header `class Employee`, which implicitly, or automatically, descends from the `Object` class. Alternatively, you could use the header `class Employee : Object` to explicitly show the name of the base class, but you have not seen this format in this book, and it would be extremely unusual to see such a format in a C# program.

Because every class descends from `Object`, every object "is an" `Object`. As proof, you can write a method that accepts an argument of type `Object`; it will accept arguments of any type. Figure 8-18 shows a program that declares three objects—a `Student`, a `ScholarshipStudent`, and an `Employee`. Even though these types possess different attributes and methods (and one type, `Employee`, has nothing in common with the other two), each type can serve as an argument to the `DisplayObjectMessage()` because each type "is an" `Object`. Figure 8-19 shows the execution of the program.

```
using System;
class DiverseObjects
{
    public static void Main()
    {
        Student payingStudent = new Student();
        ScholarshipStudent freeStudent = new ScholarshipStudent();
        Employee clerk = new Employee();
        Console.Write("Using Student: ");
        DisplayObjectMessage(payingStudent);
        Console.Write("Using ScholarshipStudent: ");
        DisplayObjectMessage(freeStudent);
        Console.Write("Using Employee: ");
        DisplayObjectMessage(clerk);
    }
    public static void DisplayObjectMessage(Object o)
    {
        Console.WriteLine("Method successfully called");
    }
}
```

Figure 8-18 `DiverseObjects` program

CHAPTER EIGHT

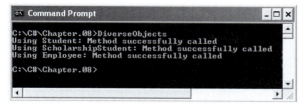

Figure 8-19 Output of the `DiverseObjects` program

When you create any child class, it inherits all the methods of its parent. Because all classes inherit from the `Object` class, all classes inherit the `Object` class methods. The `Object` class contains a constructor, a destructor, and four `public` instance methods, as summarized in Table 8-1.

Method	Explanation
Equals()	Determines whether two `Object` instances are equal
GetHashCode()	Gets a unique code for each object; useful in certain sorting and data management tasks
GetType()	Returns the `type`, or class, of an object
ToString()	Returns a `String` that represents the object

Table 8-1 The four `public` instance methods of the `Object` class

>> **NOTE**
The `Object` class contains other non-public and non-instance (static) methods in addition to the four methods listed in Table 8-1. The C# documentation provides more details on these methods.

USING THE `Object` CLASS'S `GetType()` METHOD
The `GetType()` method returns an object's type, or class. For example, if you have created an `Employee` object named `someWorker`, then the following statement displays `Employee`:

    Console.WriteLine(someWorker.GetType());

USING THE `Object` CLASS'S `ToString()` METHOD
The `Object` class methods are not very useful as they stand. For example, when you use the `Object` class's `ToString()` method with an object you create, it simply returns a string that holds the name of the class, just as `GetType()` does. That is, if `someWorker` is an `Employee`, then `Console.WriteLine(someWorker.ToString());` displays `Employee`. When you create a class such as `Employee`, you should override the `Object` class's `ToString()` method with your own, more useful version—perhaps one that returns an `Employee`'s ID number, name, or combination of the two. Of course, you could create a differently named method to do the same thing—perhaps `GetEmployeeIdentification()` or `ConvertEmployeeToString()`. However, by naming your class method `ToString()`, you make the class easier for others to understand and use. Programmers know the `ToString()` method works with every object; when they use it with your objects, you can provide a useful set of information.

INTRODUCTION TO INHERITANCE

> **» NOTE**
> A class's `ToString()` method is often a useful debugging aid.

Additionally, many C# built-in classes use the `ToString()` method; if you have named your method conventionally, those classes will use your version because it is more helpful than the generic one.

For example, you might create an `Employee` class `ToString()` method, as shown in Figure 8-20. This method assumes that `EmpNum` and `Name` are `Employee` properties with `get` accessors. The returned `string` will have a value such as "Employee: 234 Johnson".

> **» NOTE**
> You have been using overloaded versions of the `ToString()` method to format numeric output since Chapter 2.

```
public override string ToString()
{
    return(getType() + ": " + EmpNum + " " + Name);
}
```

Figure 8-20 An `Employee` class `ToString()` method

USING THE `Object` CLASS'S `Equals()` METHOD

> **» NOTE**
> The `Equals()` method compares objects for reference equality. **Reference equality** occurs when two reference type objects refer to the same object.

The `Object` class's `Equals()` method returns `true` if two `Object`s have the same memory address—that is, if one object is a reference to the other and both are literally the same object. For example, you might write the following:

```
if oneObject.Equals(anotherObject) ...
```

Like the `ToString()` method, this method might not be useful to you in its original form. For example, you might prefer to think of two `Employee` objects as equal if their ID numbers or names are equal. You might want to override the `Equals()` method for any class you create if you anticipate that class clients will want to compare objects based on any of their field values.

If you overload the `Equals()` method, it should meet the following requirements by convention:

» Its header should be as follows (you can use any identifier for the `Object` parameter):
  ```
  public override bool Equals(Object o)
  ```

» It should return `false` if the argument is `null`.
» It should return `true` if an object is compared to itself.
» It should return `true` only if both of the following are true:
  ```
  oneObject.Equals(anotherObject)
  anotherObject.Equals(oneObject)
  ```

» If `oneObject.Equals(anotherObject)` returns `true` and `oneObject.Equals(aThirdObject)` returns `true`, then `anotherObject.Equals(aThirdObject)` should also be `true`.

USING THE `Object` CLASS'S `GetHashCode()` METHOD

When you override the `Equals()` method, you should also override the `GetHashCode()` method, because `Equals()` uses `GetHashCode()`. A **hash code** is a number that uniquely identifies an object; you might use hash codes in some advanced C# applications. For example,

Figure 8-21 shows an application that declares two Employees from a class in which the GetHashCode() method has not been overridden. The output in Figure 8-22 shows a unique number for each object. (The number, however, is meaningless to you.) If you choose to override the GetHashCode() method, you should write this method so it returns a unique integer for every object—an Employee number, for example.

>> **NOTE** In cooking, hash is a dish that is created by combining ingredients. The term *hash code* derives from the fact that the code is sometimes created by mixing some of an object's data.

>> **NOTE** A hash code is sometimes called a "fingerprint" for an object because it uniquely identifies the object. In C#, the default implementation of the GetHashCode() method does not guarantee unique return values for different objects. However, derived classes must override GetHashCode() with an implementation that returns a unique hash code.

```
using System;
public class TestHashCode
{
    public static void Main()
    {
        Employee first = new Employee();
        Employee second = new Employee();
        Console.WriteLine(first.GetHashCode());
        Console.WriteLine(second.GetHashCode());
    }
}
```

Figure 8-21 TestHashCode program

Figure 8-22 Output of the TestHashCode program

>> **NOTE** You first used the Equals() method to compare String objects in Chapter 2. When you use Equals() with Strings, you use the String class's Equals() method that compares String contents as opposed to String addresses. In other words, the Object class's Equals() method has already been overridden in the String class.

>> **NOTE** Although you can write an Equals() method for a class without overriding GetHashCode(), you receive a warning message. See the C# documentation for information on the HashTable class.

>> **NOTE** In Chapter 7, you learned to overload operators. If you overload == or != for a class, you will receive warning messages if you do not also override both the Equals() and GetHashCode() methods.

INTRODUCTION TO INHERITANCE

When you create an `Equals()` method to override the one in the `Object` class, the parameter must be an `Object`. For example, if you consider `Employee` objects equal when the `EmpNum` properties are equal, then an `Employee` class `Equals()` method might be created as follows:

```
public override bool Equals(Object e)
{
   bool equal;
   Employee temp = (Employee)e;
   if(EmpNum == temp.EmpNum)
      equal = true;
   else
      equal = false;
   return equal;
}
```

In the shaded second statement in the method, the `Object` argument is cast to an `Employee` so the `Employee`'s `EmpNum` can be compared. If you did not perform the cast, and tried to make the comparison with `o.EmpNum`, the method would not compile because an `Object` does not have an `EmpNum`.

An even better alternative is to ensure that compared objects are the same type before making any other decisions. For example, the `Equals()` method in Figure 8-23 uses the `GetType()` method with both the `this` object and the parameter before proceeding. If compared objects are not the same type, then the `Equals()` method should return `false`.

```
public override bool Equals(Object e)
{
   bool equal;
   if(this.GetType() != e.GetType())
      equal = false;
   else
   {
      Employee temp = (Employee)e;
      if(EmpNum == temp.EmpNum)
         equal = true;
      else
         equal = false;
   }
   return equal;
}
```

Figure 8-23 An `Equals()` method for the `Employee` class

CHAPTER EIGHT

WORKING WITH BASE CLASSES THAT HAVE CONSTRUCTORS

When you create any object, you are calling a class constructor method that has the same name as the class itself. For example:

```
SomeClass anObject = new SomeClass();
```

When you instantiate an object that is a member of a derived class, you call both the constructor for the base class and the constructor for the extended, derived class. When you create any derived class object, the base class constructor must execute first; only then does the derived class constructor execute.

> **» NOTE** When you create any object, you call its constructor and the `Object` constructor because all classes are derived from `Object`. So, when you create a derived class, you call three constructors: one from the `Object` class, one from the base class, and one from the derived class.

In the examples of inheritance you have seen so far in this chapter, each class contained default constructors, so their execution was transparent. However, you should realize that when you create a subclass, both the base and derived constructors execute. For example, consider the abbreviated `Employee` and `CommissionEmployee` classes in Figure 8-24. `Employee` contains just two fields and a constructor; `CommissionEmployee` descends from `Employee` and contains a constructor as well. The `DemoSalesperson4` program in Figure 8-25 contains just one statement; it instantiates a `CommissionEmployee`. The output in Figure 8-26 shows that this one statement causes both constructors to execute.

```
public class Employee
{
    private int empNum;
    protected double empSal;
    public Employee()
    {
        Console.WriteLine("Employee constructed");
    }
}
public class CommissionEmployee : Employee
{
    private double commissionRate;
    public CommissionEmployee()
    {
        Console.WriteLine("CommissionEmployee constructed");
    }
}
```

Figure 8-24 `Employee` and `CommissionEmployee` classes with parameterless constructors

INTRODUCTION TO INHERITANCE

```
using System;
public class DemoSalesperson4
{
    public static void Main()
    {
        CommissionEmployee salesperson = new CommissionEmployee();
    }
}
```

Figure 8-25 The `DemoSalesperson4` program

Figure 8-26 Output of the `DemoSalesperson4` program

Of course, most constructors perform many more tasks than printing a message to inform you that they exist. When constructors initialize variables, you usually want the base class constructor to initialize the data fields that originate in the base class. The derived class constructor needs to initialize only the data fields that are specific to the derived class.

USING BASE CLASS CONSTRUCTORS THAT REQUIRE ARGUMENTS

>> **NOTE**
Don't forget that a class can have many overloaded constructors. As soon as you create at least one constructor for a class, you can no longer use the automatic version.

When you create a class and do not provide a constructor, C# automatically supplies one that never requires arguments. When you write your own constructor for a class, you replace the automatically supplied version. Depending on your needs, the constructor you create for a class might require arguments. When you use a class as a base class and it has a constructor that requires arguments, you must make sure that any derived classes provide the base class constructor with what it needs.

When a base class constructor requires arguments, you must include a constructor for each derived class you create. Your derived class constructor can contain any number of statements; however, within the header of the constructor, you must provide values for any arguments required by the base class constructor. Even if you have no other reason for creating a derived class constructor, you must write the derived class constructor so it can call its parent's constructor.

The format of the portion of the constructor header that calls a base class constructor is `base(list of arguments)`. The keyword **base** always refers to the superclass of the class in which you use it. For example, if you create an `Employee` class with a constructor that requires two arguments—an integer and a string—and you create a `CommissionEmployee` class that is a subclass of `Employee`, then the following code shows a valid constructor for `CommissionEmployee`:

```
public CommissionEmployee() : base(1234, "XXXX")
{
    // Other statements can go here
}
```

In this example, the `CommissionEmployee` constructor requires no arguments, but it passes two arguments to its base class constructor. Every `CommissionEmployee` passes 1234 and "XXXX" to the `Employee` constructor. A different `CommissionEmployee` constructor might require arguments; then it could pass the appropriate arguments on to the base class constructor, as in the following example:

```
public CommissionEmployee(int id, string name) : base(id, name)
{
   // Other statements can go here
}
```

>> **NOTE**
Although it seems as though you should be able to use the base class constructor name to call the base class constructor, C# does not allow you to do so. You must use the keyword `base`.

Yet another `CommissionEmployee` constructor might require three or more arguments. Some arguments might be passed to the base class constructor, and some might be used within `CommissionEmployee`. Consider the following example:

```
public CommissionEmployee(int id, string name, double rate) :
   base(id, name) // two parameters passed to base constructor
{
    CommissionRate = rate;
    // rate is used within child constructor
    // Other statements can go here
}
```

CREATING AND USING ABSTRACT CLASSES

Creating classes is easier after you understand the concept of inheritance. When you create a child class, it inherits all the general attributes you need; you must create only the new, more specific attributes required by the child class. For example, a `Painter` and a `Sculptor` are more specific than an `Artist`. They inherit all the general attributes of `Artists`, but you must add the attributes and methods that are specific to `Painter` and `Sculptor`.

Another way to think about a superclass is to notice that it contains the features shared by its subclasses. The derived classes are more specific examples of the base class type; they add features to the shared, general features. Conversely, when you examine a derived class, you notice that its parent is more general. Sometimes you create a parent class to be so general that you never intend to create any specific instances of the class. For example, you might never create "just" an `Artist`; each `Artist` is more specifically a `Painter`, `Sculptor`, `Illustrator`, and so on. A class that you create only to extend from, but not to instantiate from, is an abstract class. An **abstract class** is one from which you cannot create concrete

>> **NOTE**
Nonabstract classes from which objects *can* be instantiated are called **concrete** classes.

INTRODUCTION TO INHERITANCE

objects, but from which you can inherit. You use the keyword `abstract` when you declare an abstract class.

Abstract classes are like regular classes in that they can contain data fields and methods. The difference is that you cannot create instances of abstract classes by using the `new` operator. Rather, you create abstract classes simply to provide a base class from which other objects may be derived. Abstract classes usually contain abstract methods, although methods are not required. An **abstract method** has no method statements; any class derived from a class that contains an abstract method must override the abstract method by providing a body (that is, an implementation) for it. (Alternatively, the derived class can declare the method to be abstract; in that case, the derived class's children must implement the method.)

> **» NOTE**
> If you attempt to instantiate an object from an abstract class, you will receive a compiler error message.

When you create an abstract method, you provide the keyword `abstract` and the intended method type, name, and arguments, but you do not provide statements within the method; you do not even supply curly braces. When you create a derived class that inherits an abstract method from a parent, you must use the keyword **override** in the method header and provide the actions, or implementation, for the inherited method within the derived class. In other words, you are required to code a derived class method to override the empty base class method that is inherited.

> **» NOTE**
> An abstract method also is known as a **virtual method**.

For example, suppose you want to create classes to represent different animals. You can create a generic, abstract class named `Animal` so you can provide generic data fields, such as the animal's name, only once. An `Animal` is generic, but each specific `Animal`, such as `Dog` or `Cat`, makes a unique sound. If you code an abstract `Speak()` method in the abstract `Animal` class, then you require all future `Animal` derived classes to override the `Speak()` method and provide an implementation that is specific to the derived class. Figure 8-27 shows an abstract `Animal` class that contains a data field for the name, a constructor that assigns a name, a `Name` property, and an abstract `Speak()` method.

```
abstract class Animal
{
    protected string name;
    public Animal(string name)
    {
        this.name = name;
    }

    public string Name
    {
        get
        {
            return name;
        }
    }
    public abstract string Speak();
}
```

Figure 8-27 `Animal` class

The Animal class in Figure 8-27 is declared to be abstract. (The keyword is shaded.) You cannot place a statement such as Animal myPet = new Animal("Murphy"); within a program, because the program will not compile. Because Animal is an abstract class, no Animal objects can exist.

You create an abstract class like Animal so that you can extend it. For example, you can create Dog and Cat classes as shown in Figure 8-28. Because the Animal class contains a constructor that requires a string argument, both Dog and Cat must contain constructors that provide string arguments for their base class.

```
class Dog : Animal
{
   public Dog(string name) : base(name)
   {
   }
   public override string Speak()
   {
       return "woof";
   }
}
class Cat : Animal
{
    public Cat(string name) : base(name)
    {
    }
    public override string Speak()
    {
        return "meow";
    }
}
```

Figure 8-28 Dog and Cat classes

»NOTE
You can create an abstract class with no abstract methods, but you cannot create an abstract method outside of an abstract class.

The Dog and Cat constructors perform no tasks other than passing out the name to the Animal constructor. The overriding Speak() methods within Dog and Cat are required because the abstract parent Animal class contains an abstract Speak() method. The keyword override (shaded) is required in the method header. You can code any statements you want within the Dog and Cat class Speak() methods, but the Speak() methods must exist.

Figure 8-29 shows a program that implements Dog and Cat objects, and Figure 8-30 shows the output. Speak() operates polymorphically; that is, each object acts appropriately using the correct Speak() method.

INTRODUCTION TO INHERITANCE

```
using System;
class DemoAnimals
{
   public static void Main()
   {
      Dog spot = new Dog("Spot");
      Cat puff = new Cat("Puff");
      Console.WriteLine(spot.Name + " says " + spot.Speak());
      Console.WriteLine(puff.Name + " says " + puff.Speak());
   }
}
```

Figure 8-29 `DemoAnimals` program

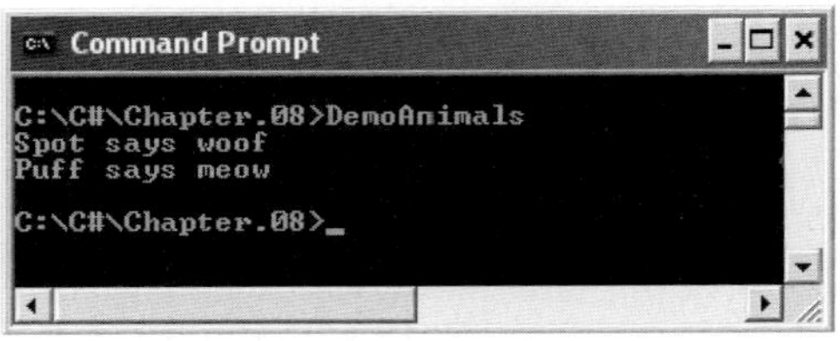

```
C:\C#\Chapter.08>DemoAnimals
Spot says woof
Puff says meow
C:\C#\Chapter.08>
```

Figure 8-30 Output of the `DemoAnimals` program

CREATING AND USING INTERFACES

Some object-oriented programming languages, notably C++, allow a subclass to inherit from more than one parent class. For example, you might create an `Employee` class that contains data fields pertaining to each employee in your organization. You also might create a `Product` class that holds information about each product your organization manufactures. When you create a `Patent` class for each product for which your company holds a patent, you might want to include product information as well as information about the employee who was responsible for the invention. In this situation, it would be convenient to inherit fields and methods from both the `Product` and `Employee` classes. The ability to inherit from more than one class is called **multiple inheritance**.

Multiple inheritance is a difficult concept, and programmers encounter many problems when they use it. For example, variables and methods in the parent classes may have identical names, creating a conflict when the child class uses one of the names. Additionally, as you already have learned, a child class constructor must call its parent class constructor. When two or more parents exist, this becomes a more complicated task: To which class should `base` refer when a child class has multiple parents?

For all of these reasons, multiple inheritance is prohibited in C#. However, C# does provide an alternative to multiple inheritance, known as an interface. Much like an abstract class, an interface is a collection of methods (and perhaps other members) that can be used by any

CHAPTER EIGHT

class as long as the class provides a definition to override the interface's abstract definitions. Within an abstract class, some methods can be abstract, while others need not be. Within an interface, all methods are abstract.

You create an interface much as you create an abstract class definition, except that you use the keyword `interface` instead of `abstract class`. For example, suppose you create an `IWork` interface as shown in Figure 8-31. For simplicity, the `IWork` interface contains a single method named `Work()`.

>> **NOTE**
You first learned about interfaces in Chapter 7 when you used the `IComparable` interface.

```
public interface IWork
{
    string Work();
}
```

Figure 8-31 The `IWork` interface

>> **NOTE**
Although not required, in C# it is customary to start interface names with an uppercase "I". Other languages follow different conventions. Interface names frequently end with "able".

When any class implements `IWork`, it must also include a `Work()` method that returns a string. Figure 8-32 shows two classes that implement `IWork`: the `Employee` class and the `Animal` class. Because each implements `IWork`, each must declare a `Work()` method. The `Employee` class implements `Work()` to return the "I do my job" string. The abstract `Animal` class defines `Work()` as an abstract method, meaning that descendants of `Animal` must implement `Work()`. Figure 8-32 also shows two child classes of `Animal`: `Dog` and `Cat`. Note how `Work()` is defined differently for each.

```
class Employee : IWork
{
    private string name;
    public Employee(string name)
    {
        Name = name;
    }
    public string Name
    {
        get
        {
            return name;
        }
        set
        {
            name = value;
        }
    }
```

Figure 8-32 `Employee`, `Animal`, `Cat`, and `Dog` classes with the `IWork` interface (*continued*)

INTRODUCTION TO INHERITANCE

```csharp
    public string Work()
    {
        return "I do my job";
    }
}
abstract class Animal : IWork
{
    protected string name;
    public Animal(string name)
    {
        Name = name;
    }
    public string Name
    {
        get
        {
            return name;
        }
        set
        {
            name = value;
        }
    }
    public abstract string Work();
}
class Dog : Animal
{
    public Dog(string name) : base(name)
    {
    }
    public override string Work()
    {
        return "I watch the house";
    }
}
class Cat : Animal
{
    public Cat(string name) : base(name)
    {
    }
    public override string Work()
    {
        return "I catch mice";
    }
}
```

Figure 8-32 (*continued*)

When you create a program that instantiates an `Employee`, a `Dog`, or a `Cat`, as in the `DemoWorking` program in Figure 8-33, each object type knows how to "`Work()`" appropriately. Figure 8-34 shows the output.

```
using    System;
class    DemoWorking
{
   public static void   Main()
   {
       Employee bob = new   Employee("Bob");
       Dog spot = new   Dog("Spot");
       Cat puff = new   Cat("Puff");
       Console.WriteLine(bob.Name + " says " + bob.Work());
       Console.WriteLine(spot.Name + " says " + spot.Work());
       Console.WriteLine(puff.Name + " says " + puff.Work());
   }
}
```

Figure 8-33 `DemoWorking` program

Figure 8-34 Output of the `DemoWorking` program

Abstract classes and interfaces are similar in that you cannot instantiate concrete objects from either one. Abstract classes differ from interfaces in that abstract classes can contain nonabstract methods, but all methods within an interface must be abstract. A class can inherit from only one base class (whether abstract or not), but it can implement any number of interfaces. For example, if you want to create a `Child` that inherits from a `Parent` class and implements two interfaces, `IWork` and `IPlay`, you would define the class name and list the base class and interfaces separated by commas:

```
class Child : Parent, IWork, IPlay
```

You implement an existing interface because you want a class to be able to use a method that already exists in other applications. For example, suppose you have created a `Payroll` application that uses the `Work()` method in the interface class. Also suppose you create a new class named `BusDriver`. If `BusDriver` implements the `IWork` interface, then `BusDriver` objects can be used by the existing `Payroll` program. As another example, suppose you have written a game program that uses an `IAttack` interface with methods that determine how and when an object can attack. When you create new classes such as `MarsAlien`, `Vampire`,

NOTE
You can think of an interface as a contract. A class that implements an interface must abide by the rules of the contract.

INTRODUCTION TO INHERITANCE

and `CivilWarSoldier`, and each implements the interface, you can define how each one attacks and how each type of object can be added to the game.

Beginning programmers sometimes find it difficult to decide when to create an abstract base class and when to create an interface. Typically, you create an abstract class when you want to provide some data or methods that derived classes can inherit, but you want the subclasses to override some specific methods that you declare to be `abstract`. You create an interface when you want derived classes to override every method. Use a base class when the class you want to create "is a" subtype of another class; use an interface when the class you want to create will act like the interface.

> **NOTE**
> Now that you understand how to construct your own interfaces, you will benefit from rereading the section describing the `IComparable` interface in Chapter 7.

Interfaces provide you with a way to exhibit polymorphic behavior. If diverse classes implement the same interface in unique ways, then you can treat each class type in the same way using the same language. When various classes use the same interface, you know the names of the methods that are available with those classes, and C# classes adopt a more uniform functionality; this consistency helps you to understand new classes you encounter more easily. If you know, for example, the method names contained in the `IWork` interface, and you see that a class implements `IWork`, you have a head start in understanding how the class functions.

RECAPPING THE BENEFITS OF USING INHERITANCE

When an automobile company designs a new car model, it does not build every component from scratch. The car might include a new feature—for example, some model contained the first air bag—but many of a new car's features are simply modifications of existing features. The manufacturer might create a larger gas tank or a more comfortable seat, but these new features still possess many of the properties of their predecessors from older models. Most features of new car models are not even modified; instead, existing components, such as air filters and windshield wipers, are included on the new model without any changes.

Similarly, you can create powerful computer programs more easily if many of their components are used either "as is" or with slight modifications. Inheritance does not enable you to write any programs that you could not write if inheritance did not exist; you *could* create every part of a program from scratch, but reusing existing classes and interfaces makes your job easier.

You already have used many "as is" classes, such as `Console`, `Int32`, and `String`. Using these classes made it easier to write programs than if you had to invent the classes yourself. Now that you have learned about inheritance, you can extend existing classes as well as just use them. When you create a useful, extendable base class, you and other future programmers gain several advantages:

» Derived class creators save development time because much of the code that is needed for the class already has been written.

» Derived class creators save testing time because the base class code already has been tested and probably used in a variety of situations. In other words, the base class code is reliable.

CHAPTER EIGHT

» Programmers who create or use new derived classes already understand how the base class works, so the time it takes to learn the new class features is reduced.

» When you create a derived class in C#, the base class source code is not changed. Thus, the base class maintains its integrity.

When you think about classes, you need to think about the commonalities between them, and then you can create base classes from which to inherit. You might even be rewarded professionally when you see your own superclasses extended by others in the future.

YOU DO IT

In this section, you will create a working example of inheritance. You will create this example in four parts:

1. You will create a general `BankLoan` class that holds data pertaining to a bank loan—a loan number, a customer name, and the amount borrowed.
2. After you create the general `BankLoan` class, you will write a program to instantiate and use a `BankLoan` object.
3. You will create a more specific `CarLoan` derived class that inherits the attributes of the `BankLoan` class but adds information about the automobile that serves as collateral for the loan.
4. You will modify the `BankLoan` demonstration program to add a `CarLoan` object and demonstrate its use.

> **»NOTE**
> Classes that are not intended to be instantiated and that contain only `static` members are declared as `static` classes. You cannot extend `static` classes. For example, `System.Console` is a static class.

To create the `BankLoan` class:

1. Open a new file in your text editor, then enter the following first few lines for a `BankLoan` class. The class will host three data fields—the loan number, the last name of the customer, and the value of the loan.

    ```
    public class BankLoan
    {
        private int loanNumber;
        private string lastName;
        private double loanAmount;
    ```

2. Add a property with `get` and `set` accessors for each of the three data fields.

    ```
        public int LoanNumber
        {
           get
           {
              return loanNumber;
           }
           set
           {
              loanNumber = value;
           }
        }
    ```

INTRODUCTION TO INHERITANCE

```csharp
        public string LastName
        {
            get
            {
                return lastName;
            }
            set
            {
                lastName = value;
            }
        }
        public double LoanAmount
        {
            get
            {
                return loanAmount;
            }
            set
            {
                loanAmount = value;
            }
        }
```

3. Add a closing curly brace for the class. Save the file as **DemoBankLoan.cs** in the Chapter.08 folder of your Student Disk. Compile the file and correct any errors other than the one error you expect, which tells you that the program does not define an entry point. The message means that you cannot execute the file because it doesn't contain a class with a `Main()` method yet.

4. At the top of the file, enter the following code to add a `DemoBankLoan` class that contains a `Main()` method. The class declares a `BankLoan` object and shows how to set each field and display the results.

```csharp
using System;
public class DemoBankLoan
{
    public static void Main()
    {
        BankLoan aLoan = new BankLoan();
        aLoan.LoanNumber = 2239;
        aLoan.LastName = "Mitchell";
        aLoan.LoanAmount = 1000.00;
        Console.WriteLine("Loan #{0} for {1} is for {2}",
            aLoan.LoanNumber, aLoan.LastName,
            aLoan.LoanAmount.ToString("C2"));
    }
}
```

5. Save the file, then compile and execute the program. The output looks like Figure 8-35. There is nothing unusual about this class or how it operates; it is similar to many you saw in Chapter 7.

CHAPTER EIGHT

Figure 8-35 Output of the `DemoBankLoan` program

EXTENDING A CLASS

Next, you will create a class named `CarLoan`. A `CarLoan` "is a" type of `BankLoan`. As such, it has all the attributes of a `BankLoan`, but it also has the year and make of the car that the customer is using as collateral for the loan. Therefore, `CarLoan` is a subclass of `BankLoan`.

To create the `CarLoan` class that extends the `BankLoan` class:

1. Save the DemoBankLoan.cs file as **DemoCarLoan.cs** in the Chapter.08 folder of your Student Disk. Position your cursor after the closing brace for the `BankLoan` class, press **Enter** to start a new line, and begin the definition of the `CarLoan` class. It extends `BankLoan` and contains two fields: `year` and `make`.

   ```
   class CarLoan : BankLoan
   {
      private int year;
      private string make;
   ```

2. Include properties for the fields you created in Step 1:

   ```
      public int Year
      {
         get
         {
            return year;
         }
         set
         {
            year = value;
         }
      }
      public string Make
      {
         get
         {
            return make;
         }
         set
         {
            make = value;
         }
      }
   ```

305

INTRODUCTION TO INHERITANCE

3. Add a closing curly brace for the class. Save the program, compile it, and correct any errors.
4. Modify the DemoBankLoan class to include a CarLoan object. First, change the name of the class from DemoBankLoan to **DemoCarLoan**.
5. Within the Main() method, just after the declaration of the BankLoan object, declare a CarLoan as follows:

```
CarLoan aCarLoan = new CarLoan();
```

6. After the three property assignments for the BankLoan object, insert five assignment statements for the CarLoan object.

```
aCarLoan.LoanNumber = 3358;
aCarLoan.LastName = "Jansen";
aCarLoan.LoanAmount = 20000.00;
aCarLoan.Make = "Ford";
aCarLoan.Year = 1999;
```

7. Following the WriteLine() statement that displays the BankLoan object data, insert two WriteLine() statements that display the CarLoan object's data.

```
Console.WriteLine("Loan #{0} for {1} is for {2}",
    aCarLoan.LoanNumber, aCarLoan.LastName,
    aCarLoan.LoanAmount.ToString("C2"));
Console.WriteLine("Loan #{0} is for a {1} {2}",
    aCarLoan.LoanNumber, aCarLoan.Year,
    aCarLoan.Make);
```

8. Save the program, then compile and execute it. The output looks like Figure 8-36. The CarLoan object correctly uses its own fields and properties as well as those of the parent BankLoan class.

Figure 8-36 Output of the DemoCarLoan program

USING BASE CLASS MEMBERS IN A DERIVED CLASS

In the previous sections, you created BankLoan() and CarLoan() classes and objects. Suppose the bank adopts new rules as follows:

» No regular loan will be made for less than $5000.
» No car loan will be made for any car older than model year 2000.

CHAPTER EIGHT

» Although `BankLoans` might have larger loan numbers, `CarLoans` will have loan numbers that are no more than three digits. If a larger loan number is provided, the program will use only the last three digits for the loan number.

To implement the new `CarLoan` rules:

1. Open the DemoCarLoan.cs file and immediately save it as **DemoCarLoan2.cs**. Also change the class name from `DemoCarLoan` to **DemoCarLoan2**.

2. Within the `BankLoan` class, add a new constant that represents the minimum loan value:

   ```
   public const double MINIMUM_LOAN = 5000;
   ```

3. Change the `set` accessor of the `LoanAmount` property of the `BankLoan` class, as follows. This change ensures that no loan is made for less than the minimum allowed value.

   ```
   set
   {
      if(value < MINIMUM_LOAN)
         loanAmount = MINIMUM_LOAN;
      else
         loanAmount = value;
   }
   ```

4. Within the `BankLoan` class, change the access modifier of `loanAmount` from `private` to **protected**. You do so to enable the `CarLoan` child class to change the `loanAmount` to 0 if a car year is older than 2000. If the child class had to use the `public` property to change the loan value, the value would become equal to `MINIMUM_LOAN` instead of 0.

5. Within the `CarLoan` class, add two new constants to hold the earliest year for which car loans will be given and the lowest allowed loan number:

   ```
   private const int EARLIEST_YEAR = 2000;
   private const int LOWEST_INVALID_NUM = 1000;
   ```

6. Also within the `CarLoan` class, replace the existing `set` accessor in the `Year` property so that it not only sets the `carYear` field, it sets `loanAmount` to 0 when a car's year is less than 2000.

   ```
   set
   {
      if(value < EARLIEST_YEAR)
      {
         year = value;
         loanAmount = 0;
      }
      else
         year = value;
   }
   ```

   If `loanAmount` was `private` in the parent `BankLoan` class, you would not be able to set its value in the child `CarLoan` class, as you do here. You could use the `public` property `LoanAmount` to set the value, but the parent class `set` accessor would force the value to 5000.

INTRODUCTION TO INHERITANCE

7. Also within the `CarLoan` class, just before the closing curly brace, change the inherited `LoanNumber` property to accommodate the new rules. If a car loan number is three digits or fewer, pass it on to the base class property. If not, obtain the last three digits by calculating the remainder when the loan number is divided by 1000 and pass the new number to the base class property. Add the following property after the closing curly brace for the `Make` property.

```
public new int LoanNumber
{
    get
    {
        return loanNumber;
    }
    set
    {
        if(value < LOWEST_INVALID_NUM)
            base.LoanNumber = value;
        else
            base.LoanNumber = value % LOWEST_INVALID_NUM;
    }
}
```

> **NOTE**
> A method that calls itself is a **recursive** method. Recursive methods are sometimes useful, but not in this case.

If you did not use the keyword `base` to access the `LoanNumber` property within the `CarLoan` class, you would be telling this version of the `LoanNumber` property to call itself. Although the program would compile, it would run continuously in an infinite loop until it ran out of memory and issued an error message.

8. Save the file. Compile it and correct any errors. When you execute the program, the output looks like Figure 8-37. Compare the output to Figure 8-36. Notice that the $1000 bank loan has been forced to $5000. Also notice that the car loan number has been shortened to three digits and the value of the loan is $0 because of the age of the car.

Figure 8-37 Output of the `DemoCarLoan2` program

9. Change the assigned values within the `DemoCarLoan2` class to combinations of early and late years and valid and invalid loan numbers. After each change, save the program, compile and execute it, and confirm that the program operates as expected.

CHAPTER EIGHT

ADDING CONSTRUCTORS TO BASE AND DERIVED CLASSES

When a base class contains only constructors that require parameters, then any derived classes must provide for the base class constructor. In the next steps, you will add constructors to the `BankLoan` and `CarLoan` classes and demonstrate that they work as expected.

To add constructors to the classes:

1. Open the `DemoCarLoan2` program and change the class name to `DemoCarLoan3`. Save the file as **DemoCarLoan3.cs**.

2. In the `BankLoan` class, just after the declaration of the fields and constants, add a constructor that requires values for all the `BankLoan`'s fields and assigns them to the properties:

   ```
   public BankLoan(int num, string name, double amount)
   {
      LoanNumber = num;
      LastName = name;
      LoanAmount = amount;
   }
   ```

3. In the `CarLoan` class, just after the declaration of the fields and constants, add a constructor that takes five parameters. It passes three of the parameters to the base class constructor and uses the other two to assign values to the properties that are unique to the child class.

   ```
   public CarLoan(int num, string name, double amount,
      int year, string make) : base(num, name, amount)
   {
      Year = year;
      Make = make;
   }
   ```

4. In the `Main()` method of the `DemoCarLoan3` class, remove the existing declarations for `aLoan` and `aCarLoan` and replace them with two declarations that use the arguments passed to the constructors.

   ```
   BankLoan aLoan = new BankLoan(333, "Hanson", 7000.00);
   CarLoan aCarLoan = new CarLoan(444, "Carlisle", 30000.00,
      2007, "BMW");
   ```

5. Remove the seven statements that assigned values to the `BankLoan` and `CarLoan`, but retain the `Console.WriteLine()` statements that display the values.

6. Save the program, then compile and execute it. The output looks like Figure 8-38. Both constructors work as expected. The `CarLoan` constructor has called its parent's constructor to set the necessary fields before executing its own unique statements.

309

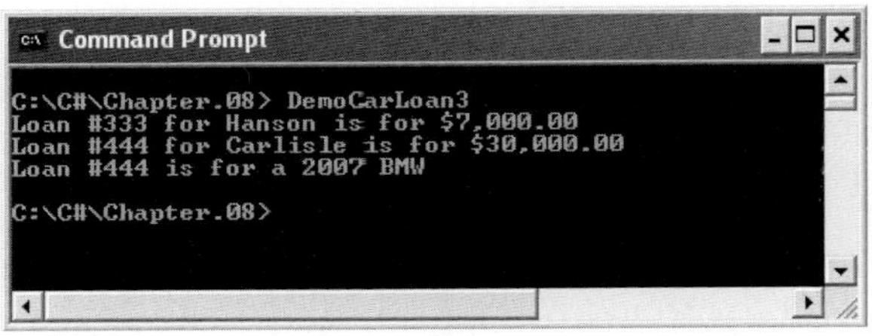

Figure 8-38 Output of the `DemoCarLoan3` program

CHAPTER SUMMARY

» Inheritance is the principle that you can apply your knowledge of a general category to more specific objects. The classes you create in object-oriented programming languages can inherit data and methods from existing classes. The ability to use inheritance makes programs easier to write, easier to understand, and less prone to errors.

» A class that is used as a basis for inheritance is called a base class. When you create a class that inherits from a base class, it is called a derived class or extended class. A derived class always "is a" case or instance of the more general base class. You can use the terms *superclass* and *parent class* as synonyms for base class, and the terms *subclass* and *child class* as synonyms for derived class.

» When you create a class that is an extension or child of another class, you use a single colon between the derived class name and its base class name. The child class inherits all the methods and fields of its parent. Inheritance works only in one direction—a child inherits from a parent, but not the other way around.

» If you could use private data outside of its class, the principle of information hiding would be destroyed. On some occasions, however, you want to access parent class data from within a derived class. For those occasions, you declare parent class fields using the keyword `protected`, which provides you with an intermediate level of security between `public` and `private` access.

» You can declare a child class method with the same name and argument list as a method within its parent class. When you do so, you override the parent class method and allow your class objects to exhibit polymorphic behavior. You can use the keyword `new` or `override` with the derived class method.

» When a derived class overrides a parent class method but you want to access the parent class version of the method, you can use the keyword `base`.

» Every derived class object "is a" specific instance of both the derived class and the base class. Therefore, you can assign a derived class object to an object of any of its base class types. When you do so, C# makes an implicit conversion from derived class to base class.

» Every class you create in C# derives from a single class named `System.Object`. Because all classes inherit from the `Object` class, all classes inherit the `Object` class methods. The `Object` class contains four `public` instance methods: `Equals()`, `GetHashCode()`, `GetType()`, and `ToString()`.

CHAPTER EIGHT

» When you instantiate an object that is a member of a subclass, you actually call two constructors: the constructor for the base class and the constructor for the extended, derived class. When you create any derived class object, the base class constructor must execute first; only then does the derived class constructor execute.

» When you use a class as a base class and the class has a constructor that requires arguments, then within the header of the derived class constructor you must provide values for any arguments required by the base class constructor. Even if you have no other reason for creating a derived class constructor, you must write the subclass constructor so it can call its parent's constructor.

» An abstract class is one from which you cannot create concrete objects, but from which you can inherit. Usually, abstract classes contain abstract methods; an abstract method has no method statements. Any class derived from a class that contains an abstract method must override the abstract method by providing a body (that is, an implementation) for it.

» C# provides an alternative to multiple inheritance, known as an interface. Much like an abstract class, an interface is a collection of methods (and perhaps other members) that can be used by any class as long as the class provides a definition to override the interface's abstract definitions. Within an abstract class, some methods can be abstract, while others need not be. Within an interface, all methods are abstract. A class can inherit from only one abstract base class, but it can implement any number of interfaces.

KEY TERMS

Inheritance is the application of your knowledge of a general category to more specific objects.

A **base class** is a class that is used as a basis for inheritance.

A **derived class** or **extended class** is one that has inherited from a base class.

A **superclass** is a base class.

A **subclass** is a derived class.

A **parent class** is a base class.

A **child class** is a derived class.

The **ancestors** of a derived class are all the superclasses from which the subclass is derived.

Inheritance is **transitive**, which means that a child inherits all the members of all its ancestors.

Using the keyword **protected** provides you with an intermediate level of security between public and private access. A protected data field or method can be used within its own class or in any classes extended from that class, but it cannot be used by "outside" classes.

Classes that depend on field names from parent classes are said to be **fragile** because they are prone to errors—that is, they are easy to "break."

A derived class member that overrides a parent class member **hides** it.

311

A base class member that is not hidden by the derived class is **visible** in the derived class.

An **implicit conversion** occurs when a type is automatically converted to another upon assignment.

An **implicit reference conversion** occurs when a derived class object is assigned to its ancestor's data type.

The `object` (or `Object`) class type in the `System` namespace is the ultimate base class for all other types.

Reference equality occurs when two reference type objects refer to the same object.

A **hash code** is a number that uniquely identifies an object.

The keyword `base` always refers to the superclass of the class in which you use it.

An **abstract class** is one from which you cannot create concrete objects, but from which you can inherit.

Concrete classes are nonabstract classes from which objects can be instantiated.

An **abstract method** has no method statements; any class derived from a class that contains an abstract method must override the abstract method by providing a body (that is, an implementation) for it.

The keyword `override` is used in method headers when you create a derived class that inherits an abstract method from a parent.

A **virtual method** is an abstract method.

Multiple inheritance is the ability to inherit from more than one class.

A method that calls itself is a **recursive** method.

REVIEW QUESTIONS

1. The principle that you can apply your knowledge of a general category to more specific objects is _____ .

   a. polymorphism
   b. encapsulation
   c. inheritance
   d. structure

2. Which of the following is *not* a benefit of using inheritance when creating a new class?

   a. You save time, because you need not create fields and methods that already exist in a parent class.

   b. You reduce the chance of errors, because the parent class methods have already been used and tested.

   c. You make it easier for anyone who has used the parent class to understand the new class because the programmer can concentrate on the new features.

   d. You save computer memory because when you create objects of the new class, storage is not required for parent class fields.

3. A child class is also called a(n) _____ .
   a. extended class
   b. base class
   c. superclass
   d. delineated class

4. Assuming that the following classes are well named, which of the following is a parent class of `House`?
   a. `Apartment`
   b. `Building`
   c. `Victorian`
   d. `myHouse`

5. A derived class usually contains _____ than its parent.
   a. more fields and methods
   b. the same number of fields but fewer methods
   c. fewer fields but more methods
   d. fewer fields and methods

6. When you create a class that is an extension or child of another class, you use a(n) _____ between the derived class name and its base class name.
   a. ampersand
   b. colon
   c. dot
   d. hyphen

7. A base class named `Garden` contains a private field `width` and a property `public int Width` that contains `get` and `set` accessors. A child class named `VegetableGarden` does not contain a `Width` property. When you write a class in which you declare an object as follows, what statement can you use to access the `VegetableGarden`'s width?

   `VegetableGarden myGarden = new VegetableGarden();`

   a. `myGarden.Width`
   b. `myGarden.base.Width`
   c. `VegetableGarden.Width`
   d. You cannot use `Width` with a `VegetableGarden` object.

8. When a parent class contains a `private` data field, the field is _____ the child class.
   a. hidden in
   b. not a member of
   c. directly accessible in
   d. `public` in

9. When a base class and a derived class contain a method with the same name and argument list, and you call the method using a derived class object, _____.
    a. you receive an error message
    b. the base class version overrides the derived class version
    c. the derived class version overrides the base class version
    d. both method versions execute

10. Which of the following is an English-language form of polymorphism?
    a. seeing a therapist and seeing the point
    b. moving friends with a compelling story and moving friends to a new apartment
    c. both of these
    d. neither of these

11. When base and derived classes contain a method with the same name and argument list, you can use the base class method within the derived class by using the keyword _____ before the method name.
    a. `new`   c. `base`
    b. `override`   d. `super`

12. In a program that declares a derived class object, you _____ assign it to an object of its base class type.
    a. can   c. must
    b. cannot   d. should not

13. The ultimate base class for all other class types is _____.
    a. `Base`   c. `Parent`
    b. `Super`   d. `Object`

14. All of the following are `Object` class methods *except* _____.
    a. `ToString()`   c. `Print()`
    b. `Equals()`   d. `GetHashCode()`

15. When you create any derived class object, _____.
    a. the base class and derived class constructors execute simultaneously
    b. the base class constructor must execute first; then the derived class constructor executes
    c. the derived class constructor must execute first; then the base class constructor executes
    d. neither the base class nor the derived class constructor executes

16. When a base class constructor requires arguments, then each derived class _____.
    a. must include a constructor
    b. must include a constructor that requires arguments
    c. must include two or more constructors
    d. must not include a constructor

17. When you create an abstract class, _____.
    a. you can inherit from it
    b. you can create concrete objects from it
    c. both of these are true
    d. neither of these is true

18. When you create an abstract method, you provide _____.
    a. the keyword `abstract`
    b. curly braces
    c. method statements
    d. all of these

19. Within an interface, _____.
    a. no methods can be `abstract`
    b. some methods might be `abstract`
    c. some, but not all, methods must be `abstract`
    d. all methods must be `abstract`

20. Abstract classes and interfaces are similar in that _____.
    a. you can instantiate concrete objects from both
    b. you cannot instantiate concrete objects from either one
    c. all methods in both must be `abstract`
    d. neither can contain nonabstract methods

INTRODUCTION TO INHERITANCE

EXERCISES

As you create the solution to each exercise, save the finished file in the Chapter.08 folder of your Student Disk.

1. Create a class named Game that contains a string with the name of the Game and an integer that holds the maximum number of players. Include properties with get and set accessors for each field. Also, include a ToString() Game method that overrides the Object class's ToString() method and returns a string that contains the name of the class (using GetType()), the name of the Game, and the number of players. Create a child class named GameWithTimeLimit that includes an integer time limit in minutes and a property that contains get and set accessors for the field. Write a program that instantiates an object of each class and demonstrates all the methods. Save the file as **GameDemo.cs**.

2. Create a class named Tape that includes fields for length and width in inches and properties for each field. Also include a ToString() method that returns a string constructed from the return value of the object's GetType() method and the values of the length and width fields. Derive two subclasses—VideoCassetteTape and AdhesiveTape. The VideoCassetteTape class includes an integer field to hold playing time in minutes and a property for the field. The AdhesiveTape class includes an integer field that holds a stickiness factor—a value from 1 to 10—and a property for the field. Write a program that instantiates one object of each of the three classes, and demonstrate that all of each class's methods work correctly. Be sure to use valid and invalid values when testing the numbers you can use to set the AdhesiveTape class stickiness factor. Save the file as **TapeDemo.cs**.

3. a. Create a class named Order that performs order processing of a single item that sells for $19.95 each. The class has four variable fields: order number, customer name, quantity ordered, and total price. Create a constructor that requires parameters for all the fields except total price. Include public get and set accessors for each field except the total price field; that field is calculated as quantity ordered times unit price (19.95) whenever the quantity is set, so it needs only a get accessor. Also create the following for the class:

    » An Equals() method that determines two Orders are equal if they have the same order number
    » A GetHashCode() method that returns the order number
    » A ToString() method that returns a string containing all order information

    Write an application that declares a few Order objects and sets their values, making sure to create at least two with the same order number. Display the string from the ToString() method for each order. Write a method that compares two orders at a time and displays a message if they are equal. Send the Orders you created to the method two at a time and display the results. Save the file as **OrderDemo.cs**.

b. Using the `Order` class you created in Exercise 3a, write a new application that creates an array of five `Order`s. Prompt the user for values for each `Order`. Do not allow duplicate order numbers; force the user to reenter the order when a duplicate order number is entered. When five valid orders have been entered, display them all, plus a total of all orders. Save the program as **OrderDemo2.cs**.

c. Create a `ShippedOrder` class that derives from `Order`. A `ShippedOrder` has a $4.00 shipping fee (no matter how many items are ordered). Override any methods in the parent class as necessary. Write a new application that creates an array of five `ShippedOrder`s. Prompt the user for values for each, and do not allow duplicate order numbers; force the user to reenter the order when a duplicate order number is entered. When five valid orders have been entered, display them all, plus a total of all orders. Save the program as **OrderDemo3.cs**.

d. Make any necessary modifications to the `ShippedOrder` class so that it can be sorted by order number. Modify the `OrderDemo3` application so the displayed orders have been sorted. Save the application as **OrderDemo4.cs**.

4. a. Create a class named `Book` that includes fields for the International Standard Book Number (ISBN), title, author, and price. Include properties for each field. (An ISBN is a unique number assigned to each published book.) Create a child class named `TextBook` that includes a grade level and a `CoffeeTableBook` child class that contains no additional fields. In the child classes, override the accessor that sets a `Book`'s price so that `TextBook`s must be priced between $20.00 and $80.00, inclusive, and `CoffeeTableBook`s must be priced between $35.00 and $100.00, inclusive. Write a program that creates a few objects of each type and demonstrate that all of the methods and properties work correctly. Be sure to use valid and invalid values when testing the child class properties. Save the file as **BookDemo.cs**.

b. In the `Book` class you created in Exercise 4a, overload the `Object` class `Equals()` method to consider two `Book`s equal if they have the same ISBN. Create a program that declares three `Book`s; two should have the same ISBN and one should have a different one. Demonstrate that the `Equals()` method works correctly to compare the `Book`s. Save the program as **BookDemo2.cs**.

5. a. Create a `Patient` class for the Wrightstown Hospital Billing Department. Include a patient ID number, name, age, and amount due to the hospital. Include properties and any other methods you need. Override the `ToString()` method to return all the details for a patient. Write an application that prompts the user for data for five `Patient`s. Sort them in patient ID number order and display them all, including a total amount owed. Save the program as **PatientDemo.cs**.

INTRODUCTION TO INHERITANCE

b. Using the `Patient` class as a base, derive an `InsuredPatient` class. An `InsuredPatient` contains all the data of a `Patient`, plus fields to hold an insurance company name and the percentage of the hospital bill the insurance company will pay. Insurance payments are based on the following table:

Insurance Company	Portion of bill paid by insurance (%)
Wrightstown Mutual	80
Red Umbrella	60
All other companies	25

Create an array of five `InsuredPatient` objects. Prompt the user for all the patient data, plus the name of the insurance company; the insurance company `set` accessor determines the percentage paid. Override the parent class `ToString()` method to include the name of the insurance company, the percent paid, and the amount due after the insurance has been applied to the bill. Sort all the records in ID number order and display them with a total amount due from all insured patients. Save the program as **PatientDemo2.cs**.

6. Create an abstract class called `GeometricFigure`. Each figure includes a height, a width, and an area. Provide `get` and `set` accessors for each field except for area; the area is computed and is read-only. Include an abstract method called `ComputeArea()` that computes the area of the `GeometricFigure`. Create three additional classes:

    » A `Rectangle` is a `GeometricFigure` whose area is determined by multiplying width by height.

    » A `Square` is a `Rectangle` in which the width and height are the same. Provide a constructor that accepts both height and width, forcing them to be equal if they are not. Provide a second constructor that accepts just one dimension and uses it for both height and width. The `Square` class uses the `Rectangle`'s `ComputeArea()` method.

    » A `Triangle` is a `GeometricFigure` whose area is determined by multiplying the width by half the height.

    Create an application that demonstrates creating objects of each class. After each is created, pass it to a method that accepts a `GeometricFigure` argument in which the figure's data is displayed. Change some dimensions of some of the figures and pass each to the display method again. Save the program as **ShapesDemo.cs**.

7. Create an interface named `IRecoverable`. It contains a single method named `Recover()`. Create classes named `Patient`, `Furniture`, and `Football`; each of these classes implements `IRecoverable`. Create each class's `Recover()` method to display an appropriate message. For example, the `Patient`'s `Recover()` method might display "I am getting better." Write a program that declares an object of each of the three types and uses its `Recover()` method. Save the file as **RecoveringDemo.cs**.

CHAPTER EIGHT

8. Create an interface named `ITurnable`. It contains a single method named `Turn()`. Create classes named `Page`, `Corner`, `Pancake`, and `Leaf`; each of these classes implements `ITurnable`. Create each class's `Turn()` method to display an appropriate message. For example, the `Page`'s `Turn()` method might display "You turn a page in a book." Write a program that declares an object of each of the four types and uses its `Turn()` method. Save the file as **TurningDemo.cs**.

9. Create an abstract class named `Salesperson`. Fields include first and last names; the `Salesperson` constructor requires both these values. Include properties for the fields. Include a method that returns a string that holds the `Salesperson`'s full name—the first and last names separated by a space. Then perform the following tasks:

    » Create two child classes of `Salesperson`: `RealEstateSalesperson` and `GirlScout`. The `RealEstateSalesperson` class contains fields for total value sold in dollars and total commission earned (both of which are initialized to 0), and a commission rate field required by the class constructor. The `GirlScout` class includes a field to hold the number of boxes of cookies sold, which is initialized to 0. Include properties for every field.

    » Create an interface named `ISell` that contains two methods: `SalesSpeech()` and `MakeSale()`. In each `RealEstateSalesperson` and `GirlScout` class, implement `SalesSpeech()` to display an appropriate one- or two-sentence sales speech that the objects of the class could use. In the `RealEstateSalesperson` class, implement the `MakeSale()` method to accept an integer dollar value for a house, add the value to the `RealEstateSalesperson`'s total value sold, and compute the total commission earned. In the `GirlScout` class, implement the `MakeSale()` method to accept an integer representing the number of boxes of cookies sold and add it to the total field.

    » Write a program that instantiates a `RealEstateSalesperson` object and a `GirlScout` object. Demonstrate the `SalesSpeech()` method with each object, then use the `MakeSale()` method two or three times with each object. Display the final contents of each object's data fields. Save the file as **SalespersonDemo.cs**.

DEBUGGING EXERCISES

Each of the following files in the Chapter.08 folder on your Student Disk has syntax and/or logical errors. In each case, determine the problem and fix the program. After you correct the errors, save each file using the same filename preceded with *Fixed*. For example, DebugEight01.cs will become FixedDebugEight01.cs.

   a. DebugEight01.cs
   b. DebugEight02.cs
   c. DebugEight03.cs
   d. DebugEight04.cs

INTRODUCTION TO INHERITANCE

UP FOR DISCUSSION

1. In this chapter, you learned the difference between `public`, `private`, and `protected` class members. Why are some programmers opposed to classifying class members as `protected`? Do you agree with them?

2. Playing computer games has been shown to increase the level of dopamine in the human brain. High levels of this substance are associated with addiction to drugs. Suppose you work for a company that manufactures games and it decides to research how its games can produce more dopamine in the brains of players. Would you support the company's decision?

3. If you are completing all the programming exercises at the ends of the chapters in this book, you know that it takes a lot of time to write and test programs that work. Professional programs require even more hours of work. In the workplace, programs frequently must be completed by strict deadlines—for example, a tax-calculating program must be completed by year's end, or an advertising Web site must be completed by the launch of the product. Programmers often find themselves working into the evenings or weekends to complete rush projects at work. How would you feel about having to do this? What types of compensation would make the extra hours worthwhile for you?

4. Suppose your organization asks you to develop a code of ethics for the Information Technology Department. What would you include?

CHAPTER NINE

9

EXCEPTION HANDLING

In this chapter you will:

Learn about exceptions and the Exception class
Purposely generate a SystemException
Learn about traditional error-handling methods
Learn about object-oriented exception-handling methods
Use the Exception class's ToString() method and Message property
Catch multiple Exceptions
Use the finally block
Handle an Exception with a loop
Throw an Exception
Trace Exceptions through the call stack
Create your own Exception classes
Rethrow Exceptions

EXCEPTION HANDLING

While visiting Web sites, you have probably seen an unexpected and cryptic message that announces an error and then shuts down your browser immediately. Perhaps something similar has happened to you while using a piece of application software. Certainly, if you have worked your way through all of the programming exercises in this book, you have encountered such errors while running your own programs. When a program just stops, it is aggravating, especially when you lose data you have typed and the program error message seems to indicate the program "knows" exactly what is wrong. You might grumble, "If it knows what is wrong, why doesn't it just fix it?" In this chapter, you will learn how to handle these unexpected error conditions so your programs can be more user-friendly than those that simply shut down in the face of errors.

UNDERSTANDING EXCEPTIONS

An **exception** is any error condition or unexpected behavior in an executing program. The programs you write can generate many types of potential exceptions, including when:

» Your program asks for user input, but the user enters invalid data.
» The program attempts to divide a value by zero.
» You attempt to access an array with a subscript that is too large or too small.
» You calculate a value that is too large for the answer's variable type.

These errors are called exceptions because presumably, they are not usual occurrences; they are "exceptional." The object-oriented techniques used to manage such errors make up the group of methods known as **exception handling**.

In C#, all exceptions are objects that are members of the Exception class or one of its derived classes. Like all other classes in the C# programming language, the Exception class is a descendant of the Object class. The Exception class has several descendant classes of its own, many with unusual names such as CodeDomSerializerException, SUDSParserException, and SoapException. Others have names that are more easily understood, such as IOException (for input and output errors), InvalidPrinterException (for when a user requests an invalid printer), and PathTooLongException (used when the path to a file contains more characters than a system allows). C# has more than 100 defined Exceptions; Table 9-1 lists just a few to give you an idea of the wide variety of circumstances they cover.

Most exceptions you will use derive from three classes:

» The predefined Common Language Runtime exception classes derived from SystemException
» The user-defined application exception classes you derive from ApplicationException
» The Exception class, which is the parent of SystemException and ApplicationException

> **» NOTE** Managing exceptions involves an oxymoron; you must expect the unexpected.

> **» NOTE** Errors you discover when compiling a program are not exceptions; only execution-time errors are called exceptions.

> **» NOTE** Table 9-1 uses the term "thrown," which is explained later in this chapter.

> **» NOTE** Microsoft previously advised that you should create your own custom exceptions from the ApplicationException class. They have revised their thinking because in practice, they have not found the approach to be of significant value. For updates, visit http://msdn2.microsoft.com.

CHAPTER NINE

Class	Description
System.ArgumentException	Thrown when one of the arguments provided to a method is not valid
System.ArithmeticException	Thrown for errors in an arithmetic, casting, or conversion operation
System.ArrayTypeMismatchException	Thrown when an attempt is made to store an element of the wrong type within an array
System.Data.OperationAbortedException	Thrown when an ongoing operation is aborted by the user
System.Drawing.Printing.InvalidPrinterException	Thrown when you try to access a printer using printer settings that are not valid
System.FormatException	Thrown when the format of an argument does not meet the parameter specifications of the invoked method
System.IndexOutOfRangeException	Thrown when an attempt is made to access an element of an array with an index that is outside the bounds of the array; this class cannot be inherited
System.InvalidCastException	Thrown for an invalid casting or explicit conversion
System.InvalidOperationException	Thrown when a method call is invalid for the object's current state
System.IO.InvalidDataException	Thrown when a data stream is in an invalid format
System.IO.IOException	Thrown when an I/O error occurs
System.MemberAccessException	Thrown when an attempt to access a class member fails
System.NotImplementedException	Thrown when a requested method or operation is not implemented
System.NullReferenceException	Thrown when there is an attempt to dereference a null object reference
System.OperationCanceledException	Thrown in a thread upon cancellation of an operation that the thread was executing
System.OutOfMemoryException	Thrown when there is not enough memory to continue the execution of a program
System.RankException	Thrown when an array with the wrong number of dimensions is passed to a method
System.StackOverflowException	Thrown when the execution stack overflows because it contains too many nested method calls; this class cannot be inherited

Table 9-1 Selected C# Exceptions

EXCEPTION HANDLING

PURPOSELY GENERATING A SystemException

You can deliberately generate a `SystemException` by forcing a program to contain an error. As an example, in every programming language, it is illegal to divide a value by zero because the operation is mathematically undefined. Consider the `MilesPerGallon` program in Figure 9-1. It is a simple program that prompts a user for two values and divides them. If the user enters nonzero integers, the program runs correctly and without incident. However, if the user enters 0 when prompted to enter gallons, division by 0 takes place and an error is generated. Figure 9-2 shows two executions of the program.

```
using System;
public class MilesPerGallon
{
    public static void Main()
    {
        int milesDriven;
        int gallonsOfGas;
        int mpg;
        Console.Write("Enter miles driven ");
        milesDriven = Convert.ToInt32(Console.ReadLine());
        Console.Write("Enter gallons of gas purchased ");
        gallonsOfGas = Convert.ToInt32(Console.ReadLine());
        mpg = milesDriven / gallonsOfGas;
        Console.WriteLine("You got {0} miles per gallon", mpg);
    }
}
```

Figure 9-1 `MilesPerGallon` program

```
C:\C#\Chapter.09>MilesPerGallon
Enter miles driven 100
Enter gallons of gas purchased 4
You got 25 miles per gallon

C:\C#\Chapter.09>MilesPerGallon
Enter miles driven 100
Enter gallons of gas purchased 0

Unhandled Exception: System.DivideByZeroException: Attempted to divide by zero.
   at MilesPerGallon.Main()

C:\C#\Chapter.09>
```

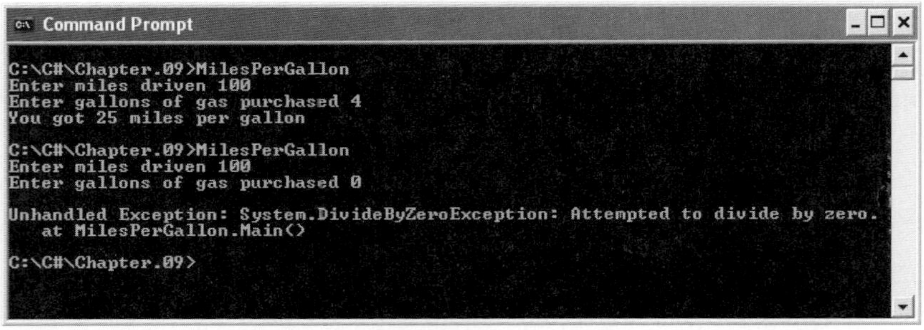

Figure 9-2 Two executions of the `MilesPerGallon` program

CHAPTER NINE

> **NOTE** When the user enters a 0 for gallons in the `MilesPerGallon` program, a dialog box reports that the application has encountered a problem and needs to close. The dialog asks whether the user would like to send information about the error to Microsoft. Because this error is intentional for demonstration purposes, the user should click "Don't Send."

In the first execution of the `MilesPerGallon` program in Figure 9-1, the user entered two usable integers, and division was carried out successfully. However, in the second execution, the user entered 0, and the error message indicates that an unhandled exception named `System.DivideByZeroException` was created. The message gives further information ("Attempted to divide by zero."), and shows the method where the exception occurred—in `MilesPerGallon.Main()`.

> **NOTE** The `DivideByZeroException` object was generated automatically by C#. It is an instance of the `DivideByZeroException` class that has four ancestors. It is a child of the `ArithmeticException` class, which descends from the `SystemException` class. The `SystemException` class derives from the `Exception` class, which is a child of the `Object` class.

Just because an exception occurs and an `Exception` object is created, you don't necessarily have to deal with it. In the `MilesPerGallon` class, you simply let the offending program terminate; that's why the error message in Figure 9-2 indicates that the `Exception` is "Unhandled." However, the termination of the program is abrupt and unforgiving. When a program divides two numbers, or even performs a more trivial task like playing a game, the user might be annoyed if the program ends abruptly. If the program is used for air-traffic control or to monitor a patient's vital statistics during surgery, an abrupt conclusion could be disastrous. Object-oriented error-handling techniques provide more elegant solutions than simply shutting down.

> **NOTE** With exception handling, a program can continue after dealing with a problem. This is especially important in mission-critical applications. The term **mission critical** refers to any process that is crucial to an organization.

> **NOTE** Programs that can handle exceptions appropriately are said to be more fault tolerant and robust than those that do not. **Fault-tolerant** applications are designed so that they continue to operate, possibly at a reduced level, when some part of the system fails. **Robustness** represents the degree to which a system is resilient to stress, maintaining correct functioning.

UNDERSTANDING TRADITIONAL ERROR-HANDLING METHODS

Programmers had to deal with error conditions long before object-oriented methods were conceived. For example, dividing by zero is an avoidable error for which programmers always have had to plan. If you simply check a variable's value with an `if` statement before attempting to divide it into another number, you can prevent the creation of an `Exception` object.

For example, the following code uses a traditional, non-object-oriented method to check a variable to prevent division by zero.

```
if(gallonsOfGas != 0)
    mpg = milesDriven / gallonsOfGas;
else
    mpg = 0;
```

This code successfully prevents division by zero, but it does not really "handle an exception" because no `Exception` class object is created. The example code illustrates a perfectly legal and reasonable method of preventing division by zero, and it represents the most efficient method of handling the error if you think it will be a frequent problem. Because a program that contains this code does not have to instantiate an `Exception` object every time the user enters a 0 for the value of `gallonsOfGas`, the program saves time and computer memory. (Programmers say this program has little "overhead.") On the other hand, if you think dividing by zero will be infrequent—that is, the *exception* to the rule—then the decision will execute many times when it is not needed. In other words, if a user enters 0 for `gallonsOfGas` in only one case out of 1000, then the `if` statement is executed unnecessarily 999 times. In that case, it is more efficient to eliminate the `if` test and instantiate an `Exception` object when needed.

> **NOTE** The creators of C# define "infrequent" as an event that happens less than 30 percent of the time. That is, if you think an error will occur in less than 30 percent of all program executions, create an `Exception`; if you think the error will occur more often, use traditional error checking.

UNDERSTANDING OBJECT-ORIENTED EXCEPTION-HANDLING METHODS

In object-oriented terminology, you "try" a procedure that may not complete correctly. A method that detects an error condition or `Exception` "throws" an `Exception`, and the block of code that processes the error "catches" the `Exception`.

When you write a block of code in which something can go wrong, you can place the code in a **try block**, which consists of the following elements:

» The keyword `try`
» A pair of curly braces containing statements that might cause `Exceptions`

You must code at least one `catch` block or `finally` block immediately following a `try` block. (You will learn about `finally` blocks later in this chapter.) Each **catch block** can "catch" one type of `Exception`. You create a `catch` block by typing the following elements:

CHAPTER NINE

- » The keyword `catch`
- » Parentheses containing an `Exception` type, and optionally, a name for an instance of the `Exception` type
- » A pair of curly braces containing statements that deal with the error condition

Figure 9-3 shows the general format of a `try...catch` pair. The placeholder `XxxException` represents the `Exception` class or any of its more specific subclasses. If an `Exception` occurs during the execution of the `try` block, then the statements in the `catch` block will execute. If no `Exception` occurs within the `try` block, then the `catch` block will not execute. Either way, the statements following the `catch` block execute normally.

> » **NOTE** As `XxxException` implies, `Exception` classes typically are created using `Exception` as the second half of the name, as in `SystemException` and `ApplicationException`. The compiler does not require this naming convention, but the convention does make `Exception` descendants easier to identify.

```
try
{
    // Statements that might cause an Exception
}
catch(XxxException anExceptionInstance)
{
    // Do something about it
}
// Statements here execute whether there was an Exception or not
```

Figure 9-3 General form of a `try...catch` pair

Any one of the statements you place within the `try` block in Figure 9-3 might throw an `Exception`. If one is thrown, it goes to the `catch` block, in which its local identifier is `anExceptionInstance`. A `catch` block looks a lot like a method named `catch()`, which takes an argument that is an instance of `XxxException`. However, it is not a method; it has no return type and you can't call it directly.

> » **NOTE** Some programmers refer to a `catch` block as a `catch` clause.

For example, Figure 9-4 contains a program in which the statements that prompt for, accept, and use `gallonsOfGas` are encased in a `try` block. Figure 9-5 shows two executions of the program. In the first execution, a usable value is entered for `gallonsOfGas` and the program operates normally, bypassing the `catch` block. In the second execution, however, the user enters 0 for `gallonsOfGas`. When division is attempted, an `Exception` object is automatically created and thrown. The `catch` block catches it, where it becomes known as `e`. The statements in the `catch` block set `mpg` to 0 and display a message. Whether the `catch` block executes or not, the final `WriteLine()` statement that follows the `catch` block's closing curly brace executes.

EXCEPTION HANDLING

```
using System;
public class MilesPerGallon2
{
    public static void Main()
    {
        int milesDriven;
        int gallonsOfGas;
        int mpg;
        try
        {
            Console.Write("Enter miles driven ");
            milesDriven = Convert.ToInt32(Console.ReadLine());
            Console.Write("Enter gallons of gas purchased ");
            gallonsOfGas = Convert.ToInt32(Console.ReadLine());
            mpg = milesDriven / gallonsOfGas;
        }
        catch(Exception e)
        {
            mpg = 0;
            Console.WriteLine("You attempted to divide by zero!");
        }
        Console.WriteLine("You got {0} miles per gallon", mpg);
    }
}
```

>> **NOTE**
In the application in Figure 9-4, the throw and catch operations reside in the same method. Later in this chapter, you will learn that throws and their corresponding catches frequently reside in separate methods.

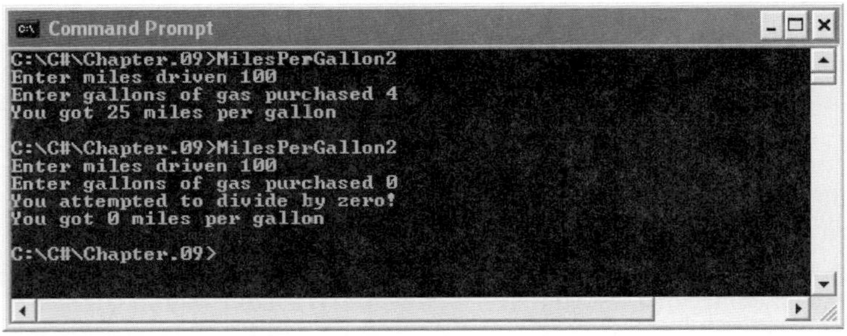

Figure 9-4 MilesPerGallon2 program

```
C:\C#\Chapter.09>MilesPerGallon2
Enter miles driven 100
Enter gallons of gas purchased 4
You got 25 miles per gallon

C:\C#\Chapter.09>MilesPerGallon2
Enter miles driven 100
Enter gallons of gas purchased 0
You attempted to divide by zero!
You got 0 miles per gallon

C:\C#\Chapter.09>
```

Figure 9-5 Two executions of MilesPerGallon2 program

>> **NOTE** When you compile the program in Figure 9-4, you receive a warning that e is declared but never used. You can declare a variable to hold the thrown Exception, but you do not want to use it in this example, so you can safely ignore the warning. If you do not want to use the caught Exception object within a catch block, then you do not have to provide an instance name for it. For example, in Figure 9-4, the catch clause could begin as follows:
>
>   catch(Exception)
>
> In later examples in this chapter, the Exception object will be used to provide information. In those cases, it is required to have an identifier.

CHAPTER NINE

In the `MilesPerGallon2` program, you could catch a more specific `DivideByZeroException` object instead of catching an `Exception` object. You will employ this technique later in the chapter. If you are working on a professional project, Microsoft recommends that you never use the general `Exception` class in a `catch` block.

USING THE `Exception` CLASS'S `ToString()` METHOD AND `Message` PROPERTY

When the `MilesPerGallon2` program prints the error message ("You attempted to divide by zero!"), you actually cannot confirm from the message that division by zero was the source of the error. In reality, any `Exception` generated from within the `try` block in the program would be caught by the `catch` block in the method because the argument in the `catch` block is an `Exception`.

Instead of writing your own message, you can use the `ToString()` method that every `Exception` inherits from the `Object` class. The `Exception` class overrides `ToString()` to provide a descriptive error message so a user can receive precise information about the nature of any `Exception` that is thrown. For example, Figure 9-6 shows a `MilesPerGallon3` program. The only changes from the `MilesPerGallon2` program are shaded: the name of the class and the message that is displayed when an `Exception` is thrown. In this example, the `ToString()` method is used with the caught `Exception` e. Figure 9-7 shows an execution of the program in which the user enters 0 for `gallonsOfGas`.

>> **NOTE**
You learned about overriding the `Object` class `ToString()` method in Chapter 8.

```
using System;
public class MilesPerGallon3
{
    public static void Main()
    {
        int milesDriven;
        int gallonsOfGas;
        int mpg;
        try
        {
            Console.Write("Enter miles driven ");
            milesDriven = Convert.ToInt32(Console.ReadLine());
            Console.Write("Enter gallons of gas purchased ");
            gallonsOfGas = Convert.ToInt32(Console.ReadLine());
            mpg = milesDriven / gallonsOfGas;
        }
```

Figure 9-6 `MilesPerGallon3` program (*continued*)

EXCEPTION HANDLING

```
        catch(Exception e)
        {
            mpg = 0;
            Console.WriteLine(e.ToString());
        }
        Console.WriteLine("You got {0} miles per gallon", mpg);
    }
}
```

Figure 9-6 (*continued*)

```
C:\C#\Chapter.09>MilesPerGallon3
Enter miles driven 77
Enter gallons of gas purchased 0
System.DivideByZeroException: Attempted to divide by zero.
   at MilesPerGallon3.Main()
You got 0 miles per gallon

C:\C#\Chapter.09>_
```

Figure 9-7 Execution of `MilesPerGallon3` program

The error message displayed in Figure 9-7 ("System.DivideByZeroException: Attempted to divide by zero.") is the same message that appeared in Figure 9-2 when you provided no exception handling. Therefore, you can assume that the operating system uses the same `ToString()` method you can use when displaying information about an `Exception`. In the program in which you provided no exception handling, execution simply stopped; in this one, execution continues and the final output statement is displayed whether the user's input was usable or not. Programmers would say this second version ended more "elegantly."

The `Exception` class also contains a property named `Message` that contains useful information about an `Exception`. For example, the program in Figure 9-8 contains just two shaded changes from the `MilesPerGallon3` program: the class name and the use of the `Message` property in the statement that displays the error message in the `catch` block. The program produces the output shown in Figure 9-9. The value of `e.Message` is a `string` that is identical to the second part of the value returned by the `ToString()` method. You can guess that the `DivideByZeroException` class's `ToString()` method used in `MilesPerGallon3` constructs its string from two parts: the return value of the `getType()` method (that indicates the name of the class) and the return value from the `Message` property.

```
using System;
public class MilesPerGallon4
{
    public static void Main()
    {
        int milesDriven;
        int gallonsOfGas;
        int mpg;
        try
        {
            Console.Write("Enter miles driven ");
            milesDriven = Convert.ToInt32(Console.ReadLine());
            Console.Write("Enter gallons of gas purchased ");
            gallonsOfGas = Convert.ToInt32(Console.ReadLine());
            mpg = milesDriven / gallonsOfGas;
        }
        catch(Exception e)
        {
            mpg = 0;
            Console.WriteLine(e.Message);
        }
        Console.WriteLine("You got {0} miles per gallon", mpg);
    }
}
```

Figure 9-8 The MilesPerGallon4 program

Figure 9-9 Execution of MilesPerGallon4 program

CATCHING MULTIPLE ExceptionS

You can place as many statements as you need within a try block, and you can catch as many different Exceptions as you want. If you try more than one statement, only the first error-generating statement throws an Exception. As soon as the Exception occurs, the logic transfers to the catch block, which leaves the rest of the statements in the try block unexecuted.

EXCEPTION HANDLING

When multiple `catch` blocks are present, they are examined in sequence until a match is found for the `Exception` that has occurred. The matching `catch` block then executes, and each remaining `catch` block is bypassed.

For example, consider the program in Figure 9-10. The `Main()` method in the `TwoErrors` class potentially throws two types of `Exceptions`—a `DivideByZeroException` and an `IndexOutOfRangeException`. (An `IndexOutOfRangeException` occurs when an array subscript is not within the allowed range. In the `TwoErrors` program, the array has only three elements, but 13 is used as a subscript.)

The `TwoErrors` class declares three integers and an integer array with three elements. In the `Main()` method, the `try` block executes, and at the first statement within the `try` block, an `Exception` occurs because the `denom` in the division problem is zero. The `try` block is abandoned, and the logic transfers to the first `catch` block. Division by zero causes a `DivideByZeroException`, and because the first `catch` block receives that type of `Exception`, the message "In first catch block" appears along with the `Message` value of the `Exception`. In this example, the second `try` statement is never attempted, and the second `catch` block is skipped. Figure 9-11 shows the output.

```
using System;
public class TwoErrors
{
    public static void Main()
    {
        int num = 13, denom = 0, result;
        int[] array = { 22, 33, 44 };
        try
        {
            result = num / denom; // First try
            result = array[ num]; // Second try
        }
        catch(DivideByZeroException error)
        {
            Console.WriteLine("In first catch block: ");
            Console.WriteLine(error.Message);
        }
        catch(IndexOutOfRangeException error)
        {
            Console.WriteLine("In second catch block: ");
            Console.WriteLine(error.Message);
        }
    }
}
```

Figure 9-10 `TwoErrors` program with two `catch` blocks

Figure 9-11 Output of `TwoErrors` program

If you reverse the two statements within the `try` block in the `TwoErrors` program, the process changes. If you use the following `try` block, the division by zero does not take place because the invalid array access throws an `Exception` first:

```
try
{
    result = array[ num] ;  // New first try
    result = num / denom;  // Old first try
}
```

The new first statement within the `try` block attempts to access element 13 of a three-element array, so it throws an `IndexOutOfRangeException`. The `try` block is abandoned, and the first `catch` block is examined and found unsuitable because the `Exception` is of the wrong type—it is not a `DivideByZeroException` object. The program logic proceeds to the second `catch` block, whose `IndexOutOfRangeException` argument type is a match for the thrown `Exception`. The message "In second catch block" and the `Exception`'s `Message` value are therefore displayed. Figure 9-12 shows the output.

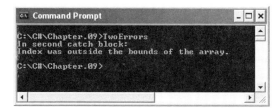

Figure 9-12 Output of `TwoErrors` program when the positions of the statements in the `try` block are reversed

Sometimes you want to execute the same code, no matter which `Exception` type occurs. For example, in the `TwoErrors` program in Figure 9-10, each of the two `catch` blocks prints a unique message. Instead, you might want both the `DivideByZeroException` catch block and the `IndexOutOfRangeException` catch block to simply use the thrown `Exception`'s `Message` field. Because both `DivideByZeroExceptions` and `IndexOutOfRangeExceptions` are subclasses of `Exception`, you can rewrite the

EXCEPTION HANDLING

TwoErrors class as shown in Figure 9-13 and include only one Exception catch block that catches any type of Exception.

```
using System;
public class TwoErrors2
{
    public static void Main()
    {
        int num = 13, denom = 0, result;
        int[] array = { 22, 33, 44 };
        try
        {
            result = num / denom; // First try
            result = array[ num]; // Second try
        }
        catch(Exception error)
        {
            Console.WriteLine(error.Message);
        }
    }
}
```

Figure 9-13 TwoErrors2 class with one catch block

>> **NOTE** As an alternative to using a single catch block for multiple Exception types that require the same action, as in Figure 9-13, you could create the class to have separate catch blocks, each of which calls the same method that contains the action.

The catch block in Figure 9-13 accepts a more generic Exception argument type than either of the potentially error-causing try statements throw, so the generic catch block can act as a "catch-all" block. That is, when either a division arithmetic error or an array error occurs, the thrown error is "promoted" to an Exception error in the catch block. Through inheritance, DivideByZeroExceptions and IndexOutOfRangeExceptions are Exceptions.

>> **NOTE** As stated earlier, Microsoft recommends that a catch block should not handle general Exceptions. They say that if you cannot predict all possible causes of an exception and ensure that malicious code cannot exploit the resulting application state, you should allow the application to terminate instead of handling the exception.

Although a method can throw any number of Exception types, many developers believe that it is poor style for a method to throw more than three or four types. If it does, one of the following conditions might be true:

CHAPTER NINE

» Perhaps the method is trying to accomplish too many diverse tasks and should be broken up into smaller methods.
» Perhaps the Exception types thrown are too specific and should be generalized, as they are in the TwoErrors2 program in Figure 9-13. As another example, both DivideByZeroExceptions and OverflowExceptions (which occur in some situations when an arithmetic answer is too large) are children of the ArithmeticException class (which, in turn, is a child of the Exception class). If a method throws both subclass Exception types, and you want (for example) to set a result to 0 in either case, then catching one superclass Exception type is sufficient and clearer.

When you list multiple catch blocks following a try block, you must be careful that some catch blocks don't become unreachable. **Unreachable** blocks contain statements that can never execute under any circumstances because the program logic "can't get there." For example, if successive catch blocks catch a DivideByZeroException and an "ordinary" Exception, then DivideByZeroException errors will cause the first catch to execute and other Exceptions will "fall through" to the more general Exception catch. However, if you reverse the sequence of the catch blocks (so the catch block that catches the more general Exception objects comes first), then you indicate that even DivideByZeroExceptions should be caught by the Exception catch. The DivideByZeroException catch block is unreachable because the more general Exception catch block is in its way, and therefore the class will not compile. Figure 9-14 shows a program in which the second catch block is not reachable, and Figure 9-15 shows the error message generated when you try to compile this program.

»NOTE
Programmers also call unreachable code **dead code**.

```
using System;
public class UnreachableCatch
{
    public static void Main()
    {
        int num = 13, denom = 0, result;
        try
        {
            result = num / denom;
        }
        catch(Exception error)
        {
            Console.WriteLine(error.Message);
        }
        catch(DivideByZeroException error)
        {
            Console.WriteLine(error.Message);
        }
    }
}
```

Figure 9-14 Program with unreachable catch block

EXCEPTION HANDLING

Figure 9-15 Compiler message generated by `UnreachableCatch` program

USING THE `finally` BLOCK

When you have actions to perform at the end of a `try...catch` sequence, you can use a **finally block**, which executes whether the `try` block identifies any `Exception`s or not. Typically, you use the `finally` block to perform clean-up tasks that must occur, regardless of whether any errors occurred or were caught. Figure 9-16 shows the format of a `try...catch` sequence that uses a `finally` block.

```
try
{
    // Statements that might cause an Exception
}
catch(SomeException anExceptionInstance)
{
    // What to do about it
}
finally
{
    // Statements here execute
    // whether an Exception occurred or not
}
```

Figure 9-16 General form of a `try...catch` block with a `finally` block

At first glance, it seems as though the `finally` block serves no purpose. When a `try` block works without error, control passes to the statements that come after the `catch` block. Additionally, if the `try` code fails and throws an `Exception` that is caught, then the `catch` block executes, and control again passes to any statements that are coded after the `catch` block. Therefore, it seems as though the statements after the `catch` block always execute, so there is no need to place any statement within a special `finally` block. However, the last set of statements after the `catch` might never execute for at least two reasons:

» An `Exception` for which you did not plan might occur.
» The `try` or `catch` block might contain a statement that quits the application.

CHAPTER NINE

> **NOTE** You can quit an application with a statement such as Environment.Exit(0);. The Environment.Exit() method is part of the System namespace. It terminates a program and passes the argument (which can be any integer) to the operating system. You also might exit a catch block with a break statement or a return statement. You encountered break statements when you learned about the switch statement in Chapter 3. You learned about return statements and how they return values from methods in Chapter 6.

The possibility exists that your try block might throw an Exception for which you did not provide a catch. After all, Exceptions occur all the time without your handling them, as you saw in the first MilesPerGallon program at the beginning of this chapter. In case of an unhandled Exception, program execution stops immediately, sending the error to the operating system for handling and abandoning the current method. Likewise, if the try block contains an exit statement, execution stops immediately. When you include a finally block, you are assured that its enclosed statements will execute before the program is abandoned, even if the method concludes prematurely.

For example, the finally block is used frequently with file input and output to ensure that open files are closed. You will learn more about writing to and reading from data files in Chapter 13. For now, however, consider the format shown in Figure 9-17, which represents part of the logic for a typical file-handling program. The catch block was written to catch an IOException, which is the type of exception automatically generated if there is a problem opening a file, reading data from a file, or writing to a file.

```
try
{
    // Open the file
    // Read the file
    // Place the file data in an array
    // Calculate an average from the data
    // Display the average
}
catch(IOException e)
{
    // Issue an error message
    // Exit
}
finally
{
    // If the file is open, close it
}
```

Figure 9-17 Pseudocode that tries reading a file and handles an Exception

The pseudocode in Figure 9-17 handles any file problems. However, because the application uses an array (see the statement "Place the file data in an array"), an uncaught Exception could occur when using the array or performing the division, even though the file opened successfully. In such an event, you would want to close the file before proceeding. By using the `finally` block, you ensure that the file is closed, because the code in the `finally` block executes before the uncaught exception returns control to the operating system. The code in the `finally` block executes no matter which of the following outcomes of the `try` block occurs:

- The `try` ends normally.
- The `catch` executes.
- An `Exception` causes the method to abandon prematurely—perhaps the array is not large enough to hold the data, or calculating the average results in division by 0. These `Exceptions` do not allow the `try` block to finish, nor do they cause the `catch` block to execute.

>> **NOTE** If an application might throw several types of exceptions, you can try some code, catch the possible exception, try some more code, catch the possible exception, and so on. Usually, however, the superior approach is to try all the statements that might throw exceptions, then include all the needed `catch` blocks and an optional `finally` block. This is the approach shown in Figure 9-17, and it usually results in logic that is easier to follow.

>> **NOTE** Many well-designed programs that try code do not include any `catch` blocks; instead, they contain only `try-finally` pairs. The `finally` block is used to release resources that other applications might be waiting for, such as database connections.

>> **NOTE** Java and C++ provide `try` and `catch` blocks. Java also provides a `finally` block, but C++ does not.

You often can avoid using a `finally` block, but you would need repetitious code. For example, instead of using the `finally` block in the pseudocode in Figure 9-17, you could insert the statement "If the file is open, close it" as both the last statement in the `try` block and the second-to-last statement in the `catch` block, just before the program exits. However, writing code just once in a `finally` block is clearer and less prone to error.

HANDLING AN `Exception` WITH A LOOP

Different programs require different ways of handling `Exceptions`. In some programs you write, you simply want to display an error message when an `Exception` occurs. In others, you want to remedy the situation the same way every time, such as setting a result to 0. In yet others, you want to keep trying the offending code until it is correct. In these cases, you can place a `try...catch` block within a loop that continues to execute until the code is successful.

As an example, consider the `HandlingAFormatException` program in Figure 9-18. This program asks a user to input an integer value that will be used as a sports team player's number. A Boolean variable named `isGoodNumber` is initialized to `false`; this variable controls the data entry loop that will continue to execute until the variable's value becomes `true`.

```
using System;
public class HandlingAFormatException
{
    public static void Main()
    {
        int playerNumber = 0;
        string strNumber;
        bool isGoodNumber = false;
        while(!isGoodNumber)
        {
            try
            {
                Console.Write("Enter player's number ");
                strNumber = Console.ReadLine();
                playerNumber = Convert.ToInt32(strNumber);
                isGoodNumber = true;
            }
            catch(FormatException fe)
            {
                Console.WriteLine(fe.Message +
                    " Player's number should be an integer.");
            }
        }
        Console.WriteLine("Player's number is " + playerNumber);
    }
}
```

Figure 9-18 HandlingAFormatException program

Within the `try` block in Figure 9-18, a `string` value is read from the keyboard and then converted to an integer. However, when users enter values from the keyboard, they don't always enter the correct value types. For example, instead of an integer, a user might enter a floating-point number or a non-numeric character. Any keyboard data will successfully be accepted into a string, but only strings containing all digits (or a + or – sign) will successfully be converted to integers. If the user enters a noninteger, the `Convert.ToInt32()` method throws a `FormatException` and execution continues with the `catch` block at the bottom of the loop. The program "gets past" the `Convert.ToInt32()` method only when the user enters an integer and the `ToInt32()` method is successful. Only then will `isGoodNumber` change to `true`, ending the loop when the `while` statement executes. Figure 9-19 shows a typical execution of the program in which the user enters invalid data twice before "getting it right." Trying and catching the `Exception` in a loop ensures that the input data will be the correct type before the program proceeds.

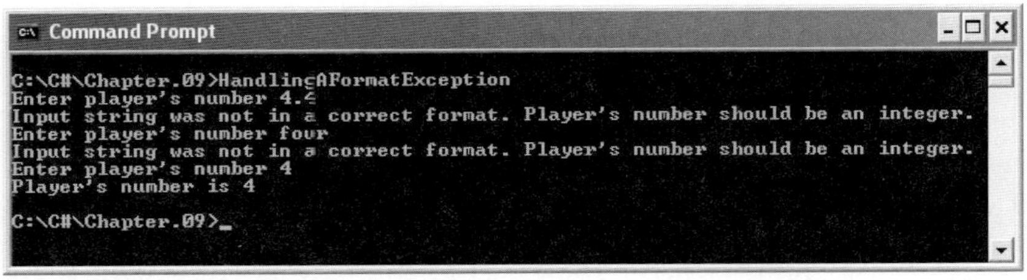

EXCEPTION HANDLING

Figure 9-19 Typical execution of `HandlingAFormatException` program

> **NOTE** In the `HandlingAFormatException` program, the `Convert.ToInt32()` method fails when a floating-point value is entered. If you use the `Convert.ToDouble()` method, it would not throw an `Exception` if you attempted to convert an integer, because an integer can be automatically promoted to a `double`.

THROWING `Exception`S BETWEEN METHODS

An advantage of using object-oriented exception-handling techniques is the ability to deal with `Exception`s appropriately as you decide how to handle them. When methods from other classes throw `Exception`s, they don't have to catch them; instead, your calling program can catch them, and you can decide what to do. For example, in the `HandlingAFormatException` program in Figure 9-18, the `Convert.ToInt32()` method threw an `Exception` when the user entered a noninteger value, but the `Convert.ToInt32()` method did not catch the `Exception`. Instead, the `HandlingAFormatException` program caught it and handled it by placing the `catch` in a loop, forcing the user to reenter a value. A different program might force the `playerNumber` to a default value, or it might display an error message and quit the program. This flexibility is an advantage when you need to create specific reactions to thrown `Exception`s.

When a method you write throws an `Exception`, the same method can catch the `Exception`, although it is not required, and in most object-oriented programs, it does not. Often, you don't want a method to handle its own `Exception`. In many cases, you want the method to check for errors, but you do not want to require a method to handle an error if it finds one. An advantage to object-oriented exception handling is that you gain the ability to appropriately deal with `Exception`s in each client program. Just as a police officer can deal with a speeding driver differently depending on circumstances, you can react to `Exception`s specifically for your current purposes.

When you design classes containing methods that have statements that might throw `Exception`s, most of the time you should create the methods so they throw the `Exception`, but not handle it. Handling an `Exception` should be left to the client—the program that uses your class—so the `Exception` can be handled in an appropriate way for the application.

For example, consider the very brief `PriceList` class in Figure 9-20. The class contains a list of prices and a single method that displays one price based on a parameter subscript value. Because the `DisplayPrice()` method uses an array, an `IndexOutOfRangeException` might be thrown. However, the `DisplayPrice()` method does not handle the potential Exception.

```
public class PriceList
{
   private static double[] price = {15.99, 27.88, 34.56, 45.89};
   public static void DisplayPrice(int item)
   {
      Console.WriteLine("The price is " +
         price[ item] .ToString("C"));
   }
}
```

Figure 9-20 The `PriceList` class

Figure 9-21 shows an application that uses the `DisplayPrice()` method. It calls the method in a `try` block and handles an `IndexOutOfRangeException` by displaying a price of $0. Figure 9-22 shows the output when a user enters an invalid item number.

```
using System;
public class PriceListApplication1
{
   public static void Main()
   {
      int item;
      try
      {
         Console.Write("Enter an item number from 0 through 3 ");
         item = Convert.ToInt32(Console.ReadLine());
         PriceList.DisplayPrice(item);
      }
      catch(IndexOutOfRangeException e)
      {
         Console.WriteLine(e.Message + " Price is $0");
      }
   }
}
```

Figure 9-21 The `PriceListApplication1` program

Figure 9-22 Output of `PriceListApplication1` program when user enters invalid item number

Figure 9-23 shows a different application that uses the same `PriceList` class, but handles the exception differently. In this case, the program author wanted the user to keep responding until a correct entry was made. Because the `DisplayPrice()` method in the `PriceList` class was written to throw an `Exception` but not handle it, the programmer of `PriceListApplication2` could handle the `Exception` in a totally different manner from the way it was handled in `PriceListApplication1`. Figure 9-24 shows a typical execution of this program.

```
using System;
public class PriceListApplication2
{
   public static void Main()
   {
      int item = 0;
      bool isGoodItem = false;
      while(!isGoodItem)
      {
         try
         {
            Console.Write("Enter an item number from " +
               "0 through 3 ");
            item = Convert.ToInt32(Console.ReadLine());
            PriceList.DisplayPrice(item);
            isGoodItem = true;
         }
         catch(IndexOutOfRangeException e)
         {
            Console.WriteLine("You must enter a number less " +
               "than 4");
            Console.WriteLine("Please reenter item number ");
         }
      }
      Console.WriteLine("Thank you");
   }
}
```

Figure 9-23 The `PriceListApplication2` program

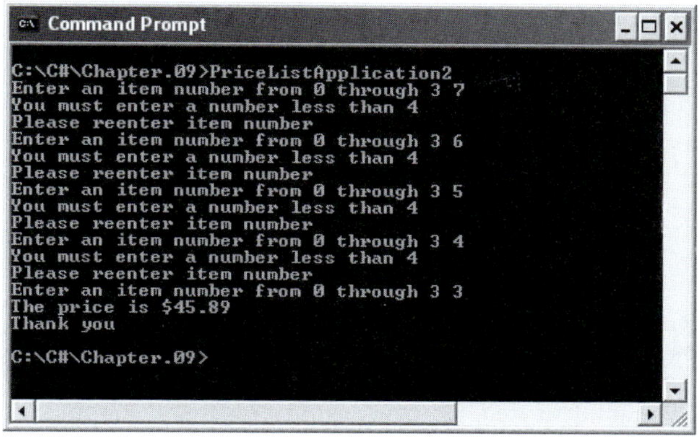

CHAPTER NINE

Figure 9-24 Output of `PriceListApplication2` program when user enters invalid item number several times

TRACING `Exception`S THROUGH THE CALL STACK

When one method calls another, the computer's operating system must keep track of where the method call came from, and program control must return to the calling method when the called method is complete. For example, if `MethodA()` calls `MethodB()`, the operating system has to "remember" to return to `MethodA()` when `MethodB()` ends. Similarly, if `MethodB()` calls `MethodC()`, then while `MethodC()` is executing, the computer needs to "remember" that it will return to `MethodB()` and, eventually, to `MethodA()`. The memory location where the computer stores the list of locations to which the system must return is known as the **call stack**.

If a method throws an `Exception` and the same method does not catch it, then the `Exception` is thrown to the next method "up" the call stack; in other words, it is thrown to the method that called the offending method. Consider this sequence of events:

1. `MethodA()` calls `MethodB()`.
2. `MethodB()` calls `MethodC()`.
3. `MethodC()` throws an `Exception`.
4. C# looks first for a `catch` block in `MethodC()`.
5. If none exists, then C# looks for the same thing in `MethodB()`.
6. If `MethodB()` does not have a `catch` block for the `Exception`, then C# looks to `MethodA()`.
7. If `MethodA()` doesn't catch the `Exception`, then the program terminates and the operating system displays an error message.

EXCEPTION HANDLING

This system of passing `Exception`s through the chain of calling methods has great advantages because it allows your methods to handle `Exception`s more appropriately. However, a program that uses several classes has the disadvantage of making it very difficult for the programmer to locate the original source of an `Exception`.

You already have used the `Message` property to obtain information about an `Exception`. Another useful `Exception` property is the `StackTrace` property. When you catch an `Exception`, you can print the value of `StackTrace` to display a list of methods in the call stack so you can determine the location of the `Exception`.

The `StackTrace` property can be a useful debugging tool. When your program stops abruptly, it is helpful to discover in which method the `Exception` occurred. Often, you do not want to display a `StackTrace` property in a finished program; the typical end user has no interest in the cryptic messages that would be printed. However, while you are developing a program, using `StackTrace` can help you diagnose your program's problems.

A CASE STUDY: USING `StackTrace`

As an example of when `StackTrace` can be useful, consider the `Tax` class in Figure 9-25. Suppose your company has created or purchased this class to make it easy to calculate tax rates on products sold. For simplicity, assume that only two tax rates are in effect—6% for sales of $20 or less and 7% for sales over $20. The `Tax` class would be useful for any programmer who wrote a program involving product sales, except for one flaw: in the shaded statement, the subscript is erroneously set to 2 instead of 1 for the higher tax rate. If this subscript is used with the `taxRate` array in the next statement, it will be out of bounds.

```
public class Tax
{
    private static double[ ] taxRate = { 0.06, 0.07};
    private static double CUTOFF = 20.00;
    public static double DetermineTaxRate(double price)
    {
        int subscript;
        double rate;
        if(price <= CUTOFF)
            subscript = 0;
        else
            subscript = 2;
        rate = taxRate[ subscript] ;
        return rate;
    }
}
```

Figure 9-25 The `Tax` class

Assume your company has also created a revised `PriceList` class, as shown in Figure 9-26. This class is similar to the one in Figure 9-20, except that it includes a tax calculation in the shaded statement.

CHAPTER NINE

```
public class PriceList
{
    private static double[] price = {15.99, 27.88, 34.56, 45.89};
    public static void DisplayPrice(int item)
    {
        double tax;
        double total;
        double pr;
        pr = price[ item] ;
        tax = pr * Tax.DetermineTaxRate(pr);
        total =  pr + tax;
        Console.WriteLine("The total price is " +
            total.ToString("C"));
    }
}
```

Figure 9-26 `PriceList` class that includes call to the `Tax` class method `DetermineTaxRate()`

Suppose you write the application shown in Figure 9-27. Your application is similar to the price list applications earlier in this chapter, including a call to `PriceList.DisplayPrice()`. As in `PriceListApplication1` and `PriceListApplication2`, your new program tries the data entry and display statement and then catches an exception. When you run the program using what you know to be a good item number, as in Figure 9-28, you are surprised to see the shaded "Error!" message you have coded in the `catch` block. In the earlier examples that used `PriceList.DisplayPrice()`, using an item number 1 would have resulted in a successful program execution.

```
using System;
public class PriceListApplication3
{
    public static void Main()
    {
        int item;
        try
        {
            Console.Write("Enter an item number from 0 through 3 ");
            item = Convert.ToInt32(Console.ReadLine());
            PriceList.DisplayPrice(item);
        }
        catch(Exception e)
        {
            Console.WriteLine("Error!");
        }
    }
}
```

Figure 9-27 `PriceListApplication3` class

345

EXCEPTION HANDLING

Figure 9-28 Execution of `PriceListApplication3` program when user enters 1 for item number

To attempt to discover what caused the "Error!" message, you can replace the statement that writes it as follows:

```
Console.WriteLine(e.Message);
```

However, when you execute the program with this modification, you receive the output in Figure 9-29, indicating that the index is out of the bounds of the array. You are puzzled because you know 1 is a valid item number for the price array, and it should not be considered out of bounds.

Figure 9-29 Execution of `PriceListApplication4` program in which `e.Message` is displayed in the `catch` block

Finally, you decide to replace the `catch` block statement with a `StackTrace` call, as follows:

```
Console.WriteLine(e.StackTrace);
```

The output is shown in Figure 9-30. You can see from the list of methods that the error in your application came from `PriceList.DisplayPrice()`, which in turn came from `Tax.DetermineTaxRate()`. You had not even considered that the `Tax` class could have been the source of the problem. If you work in a small organization, you can look at the code yourself and fix it. If you work in a larger organization or you purchased the class from an outside vendor, you can contact the programmer who created the class for assistance.

CHAPTER NINE

```
C:\C#\Chapter.09>PriceListApplication5
Enter an item number from 0 through 3 1
   at Tax.DetermineTaxRate(Double price)
   at PriceList.DisplayPrice(Int32 item)
   at PriceListApplication5.Main()

C:\C#\Chapter.09>
```

Figure 9-30 Execution of `PriceListApplication5` program in which `e.StackTrace` is displayed in the `catch` block

The classes in this example were small to help you easily follow the discussion. However, a full-blown application might have many more classes that contain many more methods, and so using `StackTrace` would become increasingly beneficial.

> **NOTE** You might find it useful to locate `StackTrace` calls strategically throughout a program while testing it and then remove them or comment them out when the program is complete.

CREATING YOUR OWN Exception CLASSES

C# provides more than 100 categories of `Exceptions` that you can throw in your programs. However, C#'s creators could not predict every condition that might be an `Exception` in the programs you write. For example, you might want to declare an `Exception` when your bank balance is negative or when an outside party attempts to access your e-mail account. Most organizations have specific rules for exceptional data, such as "an employee number must not exceed three digits" or "an hourly salary must not be less than the legal minimum wage." Of course, you can handle these potential error situations with `if` statements, but you also can create your own `Exceptions`.

To create your own `Exception` that you can throw, you can extend the `ApplicationException` class, which is a subclass of `Exception`, or you can extend `Exception`. As you saw earlier in the chapter, Microsoft's advice on this matter has changed over time. Although you might see extensions of `ApplicationException` in classes written by others, the current advice is to simply derive your own classes from `Exception`. Either approach will produce workable programs.

Figure 9-31 shows a `NegativeBalanceException` class that extends `Exception`. This class passes an appropriate `string` message to its parent's constructor. If you create an `Exception` and display its `Message` property, you will see the message "Error in the application." When the `NegativeBalanceException` constructor passes the string "Bank balance is negative." to its parent's constructor, the `Message` property will hold this more descriptive message.

EXCEPTION HANDLING

> **NOTE** The C# documentation recommends that you create all Exception messages to be grammatically correct, complete sentences ending in a period.

```
public class NegativeBalanceException : Exception
{
    private static string msg = "Bank balance is negative.";
    public NegativeBalanceException() : base(msg)
    {
    }
}
```

Figure 9-31 The NegativeBalanceException class

When you create a BankAccount class like the one shown in Figure 9-32, you can create the Balance property set accessor to throw a NegativeBalanceException when a client attempts to set the balance to be negative.

```
public class BankAccount
{
    private int accountNum;
    private double balance;
    public int AccountNum
    {
        get
        {
            return accountNum;
        }
        set
        {
            accountNum = value;
        }
    }
    public double Balance
    {
        get
        {
            return balance;
        }
```

Figure 9-32 The BankAccount class (*continued*)

CHAPTER NINE

```
        set
        {
            if(value < 0)
            {
                NegativeBalanceException nbe =
                    new NegativeBalanceException();
                throw(nbe);
            }
            balance = value;
        }
    }
}
```

Figure 9-32 (*continued*)

> **NOTE** Instead of creating the nbe object in the SetBalance() method in Figure 9-32, you could code the following statement, which creates and throws an anonymous NegativeBalanceException in a single step:
>
> throw(new NegativeBalanceException());

Figure 9-33 shows a program that attempts to set a BankAccount balance to a negative value in the shaded statement. When the BankAccount class's SetBalance() method throws the NegativeBalanceException, the catch block in the TryBankAccount program executes, displaying both the NegativeBalanceException Message and the value of StackTrace. Figure 9-34 shows the output.

```
using System;
public class TryBankAccount
{
    public static void Main()
    {
        BankAccount acct = new BankAccount();
        try
        {
            acct.AccountNum = 1234;
            acct.Balance = -1000;
        }
        catch(NegativeBalanceException e)
        {
            Console.WriteLine(e.Message);
            Console.WriteLine(e.StackTrace);
        }
    }
}
```

Figure 9-33 The TryBankAccount program

EXCEPTION HANDLING

Figure 9-34 Output of `TryBankAccount` program

>> **NOTE** In Figure 9-34, notice that the `set` accessor for the `Balance` property is known internally as `set_Balance`. You can guess that the `set` accessor for the `AccountNum` property is known as `set_AccountNum`.

>> **NOTE**
The `StackTrace` begins at the point where an `Exception` is thrown, not where it is created. This consideration makes a difference when you create an `Exception` and throw it from two different methods.

In C#, you can't throw an object unless it is an `Exception` or a descendant of the `Exception` class. In other words, you cannot throw a `double` or a `BankAccount`. However, you can throw any type of `Exception` at any time, not just `Exceptions` of your own creation. For example, within any program you can code any of the following:

```
throw(new ApplicationException());
throw(new IndexOutOfRangeException());
throw(new Exception());
```

>> **NOTE**
`Exceptions` can be particularly useful when you throw them from constructors. Constructors do not have a return type, so they have no other way to send information back to the calling method.

Of course, you should not throw an `IndexOutOfRangeException` when you encounter division by 0 or data of an incorrect type; you should use it only when an index (subscript) is too high or too low. However, if a built-in `Exception` type is appropriate and suits your needs, you should use it. You should not create an excessive number of special `Exception` types for your classes, especially if the C# development environment already contains an `Exception` that accurately describes the error. Extra `Exception` types add a level of complexity for other programmers who will use your classes. Nevertheless, when appropriate, creating a specialized `Exception` class is an elegant way for you to take care of error situations. They provide you with the capability of separating your error code from the usual, nonexceptional sequence of events. They also allow for errors to be passed up the stack and traced.

RETHROWING AN Exception

When you write a method that catches an `Exception`, your method does not have to handle the `Exception`. Instead, you might choose to **rethrow the Exception** to the method that called your method. Then you can let the calling method handle the problem. Within a `catch` block, you can rethrow the `Exception` that was caught by using the keyword `throw` with no object after it. For example, Figure 9-35 shows a class that contains four methods. In this program, the following sequence of events takes place:

1. The `Main()` method calls `MethodA()`.
2. `MethodA()` calls `MethodB()`.

CHAPTER NINE

3. `MethodB()` calls `MethodC()`.
4. `MethodC()` throws an `Exception`.
5. When `MethodB()` catches the `Exception`, it does not handle the `Exception`; instead, it throws the `Exception` back to `MethodA()`.
6. `MethodA()` catches the `Exception`, but does not handle it either. Instead, `MethodA()` throws the `Exception` back to the `Main()` method.
7. The `Exception` is caught in the `Main()` method, where the message that was created in `MethodC()` is finally displayed.

Figure 9-36 shows the execution of the program.

```
using System;
public class ReThrow
{
   public static void Main()
   {
      try
      {
         Console.WriteLine("Trying in Main() method");
         MethodA();
      }
      catch(Exception ae)
      {
         Console.Write("Caught in Main() method – ");
         Console.WriteLine(ae.Message);
      }
      Console.WriteLine("Main() method is done");
   }
   public static void MethodA()
   {
      try
      {
         Console.WriteLine("Trying in method A");
         MethodB();
      }
      catch(Exception)
      {
         Console.WriteLine("Caught in method A");
         throw;
      }
   }
```

Figure 9-35 The `ReThrow` program (*continued*)

EXCEPTION HANDLING

```
    public static void MethodB()
    {
        try
        {
            Console.WriteLine("Trying in method B");
            MethodC();
        }
        catch(Exception)
        {
            Console.WriteLine("Caught in method B");
            throw;
        }
    }
    public static void MethodC()
    {
        Console.WriteLine("In method C");
        throw(new Exception("This came from method C"));
    }
}
```

Figure 9-35 (*continued*)

> **NOTE** If you name the `Exception` argument to the `catch` block in the preceding figure (for example, `catch (Exception e)`), then you should use that identifier in the `throw` statement at the end of the block (for example, `throw e;`).

Figure 9-36 Execution of the `ReThrow` program

YOU DO IT

PURPOSELY CAUSING ExceptionS

C# generates `SystemExceptions` automatically under many circumstances. In the next steps, you will purposely generate a `SystemException` by executing a program that provides multiple opportunities for `Exceptions`.

CHAPTER NINE

To create a program that purposely generates Exceptions:

1. Open a new file in your text editor and type the following program, which allows you to generate several different Exceptions.

```
using System;
public class ExceptionsOnPurpose
{
    public static void Main()
    {
        int answer;
        int result;
        int zero = 0;
        Console.Write("Enter an integer ");
        answer = Convert.ToInt32(Console.ReadLine());
        result = answer / zero;
        Console.WriteLine("The answer is " + answer);
    }
}
```

>> **NOTE**
You would never write a program that purposely divides by zero; you do so here to demonstrate C#'s Exception-generating capabilities.

2. Save the program as **ExceptionsOnPurpose.cs** in the Chapter.09 folder on your Student Disk. Compile the program.

3. Execute the program several times using different values and observe the results. Figure 9-37 shows the window that appears with each execution. The window indicates that ExceptionsOnPurpose.exe has encountered a problem. If you were executing a professional application, the developers would want to know what caused this occurrence so they could repair the program flaw. However, because you generated the error on purpose, click the **Don't Send** button.

>> **NOTE**
The variable zero cannot be defined as a constant; if it is, the program will not compile. As a variable, the compiler "trusts" that a legitimate value will be provided for it before division occurs (although in this case, the trust was not warranted).

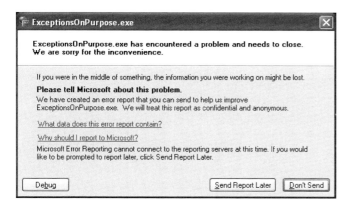

Figure 9-37 Error report window generated by an unhandled Exception

EXCEPTION HANDLING

Figure 9-38 shows three executions of the program during which the user typed the following:

» **seven**—This generates a `System.FormatException`, which occurs when the program tries to convert the input value to an integer, because letters are not allowed in integers.

» **7.7**—This also generates a `System.FormatException` because the decimal point is not allowed in an integer.

» **7**—This does not generate a `System.FormatException`, but instead causes a `System.DivideByZero` exception when the result is calculated.

Figure 9-38 Error messages generated by successive executions of `ExceptionsOnPurpose` program

HANDLING ExceptionS

You can handle `Exceptions` by placing them in a `try` block and then catching any `Exceptions` that are thrown from it.

To add a `try...catch` block to your application:

1. Open the ExceptionsOnPurpose.cs file if it is not still open. Change the class name to **ExceptionsOnPurpose2** and immediately save the file as **ExceptionsOnPurpose2.cs**.

2. In the `Main()` method, after the three variable declarations, enclose the next three statements in a `try` block as follows:

    ```
    try
    {
        Console.Write("Enter an integer ");
        answer = Convert.ToInt32(Console.ReadLine());
        result = answer / zero;
    }
    ```

CHAPTER NINE

3. Following the `try` block, add a `catch` block that catches any thrown `Exception` and displays its `Message` property:

   ```
   catch(Exception e)
   {
       Console.WriteLine(e.Message);
   }
   ```

4. Save the program and compile it. You should receive a compiler error that indicates that `answer` is an unassigned local variable. This error occurs at the last line of the program where `answer` is displayed. In the first version of this program, no such message appeared. However, now that the assignment to `answer` is within the `try` block, the compiler understands that an `Exception` might be thrown before a valid value is assigned to `answer`. To eliminate this problem, initialize `answer` at its declaration:

   ```
   int answer = 0;
   ```

5. Compile and execute the program again. Figure 9-39 shows three executions. The values typed by the user are the same as in Figure 9-38. However, the results are different in several significant ways:

   » No error message window appears (as in Figure 9-37) and asks you to inform Microsoft of the problem.
   » The error messages displayed are cleaner and "friendlier" than the automatically generated versions in Figure 9-38.
   » The program ends normally in each case, with the `answer` value displayed in a user-friendly manner.

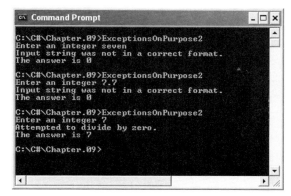

Figure 9-39 Error messages generated by successive executions of `ExceptionsOnPurpose2` program

CATCHING VARIOUS `Exception` TYPES

When you want appropriate actions to occur for various `Exceptions`, you can provide multiple `catch` blocks.

EXCEPTION HANDLING

To provide multiple `catch` blocks for the `ExceptionsOnPurpose` program:

1. Open the ExceptionsOnPurpose2.cs file if it is not still open. Change the class name to **ExceptionsOnPurpose3** and immediately save the file as **ExceptionsOnPurpose3.cs**.

2. Replace the existing generic `catch` block with two `catch` blocks. The first catches any `FormatException` and displays a short message. The second catches a `DivideByZeroException` and displays a much longer message.

   ```
   catch(FormatException e)
   {
       Console.WriteLine("You did not enter an integer");
   }
   catch(DivideByZeroException e)
   {
       Console.WriteLine("This is not your fault.");
       Console.WriteLine("You entered the integer correctly.");
       Console.WriteLine("The program divides by zero.");
   }
   ```

3. Save the program and compile it. When you execute the program and enter an invalid integer, the first `catch` block executes. When you enter an integer so that the program can proceed to the statement that divides by 0, the second `catch` block executes. Figure 9-40 shows two typical executions of the program.

Figure 9-40 Error messages generated by successive executions of ExceptionsOnPurpose3 program

CHAPTER SUMMARY

» An exception is any error condition or unexpected behavior in an executing program; the object-oriented techniques used to manage such errors make up the group of methods known as exception handling. In C#, all exceptions are objects that are members of the `Exception` class or one of its derived classes. Most exceptions you will use are derived from three classes: `SystemException`, `ApplicationException`, and their parent, `Exception`.

CHAPTER NINE

» You can purposely generate a `SystemException` by forcing a program to contain an error. Although you are not required to handle `Exceptions`, you can use object-oriented techniques to provide elegant error-handling solutions.

» When you think an error will occur frequently, it is most efficient to handle it in the traditional way, with `if` statements. If an error will occur infrequently, it is more efficient to instantiate an `Exception` object when needed.

» In object-oriented terminology, you "try" a procedure that may not complete correctly. A method that detects an error condition or `Exception` "throws" an `Exception`, and the block of code that processes the error "catches" the `Exception`. You must include at least one `catch` block or `finally` block immediately following a `try` block.

» Every `Exception` object contains a `ToString()` method and a `Message` property that contains useful information about the `Exception`.

» You can place as many statements as you need within a `try` block, and you can `catch` as many different `Exceptions` as you want. If you `try` more than one statement, only the first error-generating statement will throw an `Exception`. When multiple `catch` blocks are present, they are examined in sequence until a match is found for the `Exception` that occurred. When you list multiple `catch` blocks after a `try` block, you must be careful about their order, or some `catch` blocks might become unreachable.

» When you have actions to perform at the end of a `try...catch` sequence, you can use a `finally` block.

» When you want to keep trying a block of code until some value or state within a program is correct, you can place a `try...catch` block within a loop.

» When methods throw `Exceptions`, they don't have to catch them; instead, the program that calls a method that throws an `Exception` can catch it and determine what to do. For the best software design, you should create your classes to throw any `Exceptions` so that various application programs can catch them and handle them appropriately.

» If a method throws an `Exception` and does not catch it, then the `Exception` is thrown to the method that called the offending method. When you catch an `Exception`, you can print the value of the `StackTrace` property to display a list of methods in the call stack, allowing you to determine the location of the `Exception`.

» To create your own `Exception` that you can throw, you can extend the `ApplicationException` class or the `Exception` class. The current advice is to extend `Exception`.

» When you write a method that catches an `Exception`, your method does not have to handle the `Exception`. Instead, you might choose to rethrow the `Exception` to the method that called your method and let that method handle it.

EXCEPTION HANDLING

KEY TERMS

An **exception** is any error condition or unexpected behavior in an executing program.

Exception handling is the set of object-oriented techniques used to manage unexpected errors.

Fault-tolerant applications are designed so that they continue to operate, possibly at a reduced level, when some part of the system fails.

Robustness represents the degree to which a system is resilient to stress, maintaining correct functioning even in the presence of errors.

The term **mission critical** refers to any process that is crucial to an organization.

A `try` **block** contains code that might create exceptions you want to handle.

A `catch` **block** can catch one type of `Exception`.

Unreachable blocks contain statements that can never execute under any circumstances because the program logic "can't get there."

Dead code is unreachable code.

A `finally` **block** can follow a `try` block; code within one executes whether the `try` block identifies any `Exception`s or not.

The **call stack** is the memory location where the computer stores the list of locations to which the system must return after method calls.

A method can catch an `Exception` and **rethrow the** `Exception` instead of handling it.

REVIEW QUESTIONS

1. Any error condition or unexpected behavior in an executing program is known as an _____.

    a. exception
    b. anomaly
    c. exclusion
    d. omission

2. Which of the following is *not* treated as a C# `Exception`?

    a. Your program asks the user to input a number, but the user enters a character.
    b. You attempt to execute a C# program, but the C# compiler has not been installed.
    c. You attempt to access an array with a subscript that is too large.
    d. You calculate a value that is too large for the answer's variable type.

3. Most exceptions you will use derive from three classes: _____ .
   a. `Object`, `ObjectException`, and `ObjectApplicationException`
   b. `Exception`, `SystemException`, and `ApplicationException`
   c. `FormatException`, `ApplicationException`, and `IOException`
   d. `SystemException`, `IOException`, and `FormatException`

4. `Exception`s can be _____ .
   a. generated automatically by C#
   b. created by a program
   c. both of these
   d. neither of these

5. When a program creates an `Exception`, you _____ .
   a. must handle it
   b. can handle it
   c. must not handle it
   d. none of these; programs cannot create `Exception`s

6. Without using object-oriented techniques, _____ .
   a. there are no error situations
   b. you cannot manage error situations
   c. you can manage error situations, but with great difficulty
   d. you can manage error situations

7. In object-oriented terminology, you _____ a procedure that may not complete correctly.
   a. circumvent
   b. attempt
   c. catch
   d. try

8. In object-oriented terminology, a method that detects an error condition _____ an `Exception`.
   a. throws
   b. catches
   c. tries
   d. unearths

9. When you write a block of code in which something can go wrong, you can place the code in a _____ block.
   a. `catch`
   b. `blind`
   c. `system`
   d. `try`

EXCEPTION HANDLING

10. A `catch` block executes when its `try` block _____.
    a. completes
    b. throws any `Exception`
    c. throws an `Exception` of an acceptable type
    d. completes without throwing anything

11. Which of the following `catch` blocks will catch any `Exception`?
    a. `catch(Any e) {}`
    b. `catch(Exception e) {}`
    c. `catch(e)`
    d. All of the above will catch any `Exception`.

12. Which of the following is valid within a `catch` block with the header `catch(Exception error)`?
    a. `Console.WriteLine(error.ToString());`
    b. `Console.WriteLine(error.Message);`
    c. `return(error.ToString());`
    d. two of these

13. You can place _____ statement(s) within a `try` block.
    a. zero
    b. one
    c. two
    d. any number of

14. How many `catch` blocks can follow a `try` block?
    a. only one
    b. any number as long as it is greater than zero
    c. any number as long as it is greater than one
    d. any number, including zero or one

15. Consider the following `try` block. If x is 15, what is the value of a when this code completes?
    ```
    try
    {
        a = 99;
        if(x > 10)
            throw(new Exception());
        a = 0;
        ++a;
    }
    ```
    a. 0
    b. 1
    c. 99
    d. undefined

16. Consider the following catch blocks. The variable b has been initialized to 0. If a DivideByZeroException occurs in a try block just before this catch block, what is the value of b when this code completes?

```
catch(DivideByZeroException e)
{
    ++b;
}
catch(Exception e)
{
    ++b;
}
```

a. 0
b. 1
c. 2
d. 3

17. Consider the following catch blocks. The variable c has been initialized to 0. If an IndexOutOfRangeException occurs in a try block just before this catch block, what is the value of c when this code completes?

```
catch(IndexOutOfRangeException e)
{
    ++c;
}
catch(Exception e)
{
    ++c;
}
finally
{
    ++c;
}
```

a. 0
b. 1
c. 2
d. 3

18. If your program throws an IndexOutOfRangeException and the only available catch block catches an Exception, _____.

   a. an IndexOutOfRangeException catch block is generated automatically

   b. the Exception catch block executes

   c. the catch block is bypassed

   d. an Exception is thrown to the operating system

EXCEPTION HANDLING

19. When you design your own classes that might cause `Exceptions`, and other classes will use your classes as clients, you should usually create your methods to _____ .

    a. neither throw nor handle `Exceptions`

    b. throw `Exceptions` but not handle them

    c. handle `Exceptions` but not throw them

    d. both throw and handle `Exceptions`

20. When you create an `Exception` of your own, you should extend the _____ class.

    a. `SystemException`   c. `OverloadedException`

    b. `PersonalException`   d. `Exception`

EXERCISES

Save the programs that you create for these exercises in the Chapter.09 folder on your Student Disk.

1. Write a program in which you declare an array of five integers and store five values in the array. Write a `try` block in which you place a loop that attempts to access each element of the array, incrementing a subscript from 0 to 10. Create a `catch` block that catches the eventual `ArrayIndexOutOfRangeException`; within the block, display "Now you've gone too far." on the screen. Save the file as **GoTooFar.cs**.

2. a. The `Convert.ToInt32()` method requires a string argument that can be converted to an `int`. Write a program in which you prompt the user for a stock number and quantity ordered. Accept the strings the user enters and convert them to integers. Catch the `Exception` that is thrown when the user enters noninteger data for either field. Within the `catch` block, display an error message and set both the stock number and quantity values to 0. Save the file as **PlacingOrder.cs**.

   b. Modify the `PlacingOrder` application so that data entry is performed in a `DataEntry()` function that accepts a string parameter to use as a prompt. The function prompts the user, reads a value from the keyboard, attempts to convert it to an integer, and then returns the integer. If an `Exception` is encountered, the function should return 0. Save the file as **PlacingOrder2.cs**.

3. `ArgumentException` is an existing class that derives from `Exception`; you use it when one or more of a method's arguments do not fall within an expected range. Create a class named `CarInsurance` containing variables that can hold a driver's age and state of residence. Within the class, create a method that accepts the two input values and calculates a premium. The premium base price is $100 for residents of Illinois (IL) and $50 for residents of Wisconsin (WI). Additionally, each driver pays $3 times the value of 100 minus his or her age. If the driver is younger than 16, older than 80, or not a resident of IL or

WI, throw an `ArgumentException` from the method. In the `Main()` method of the `CarInsurance` class, try code that prompts the user for each value. If the user does not enter a numeric value for age, catch a `FormatException` and display an error message. Call the method that calculates the premium and `catch` the potential `ArgumentException` object. Save the file as **CarInsurance.cs**.

4. The `Math` class contains a static method named `Sqrt()` that accepts a `double` and returns the parameter's square root. Write a program that declares two `doubles`: `number` and `sqrt`. Accept an input value for `number` from the user. Handle the `FormatException` that is thrown if the input value cannot be converted to a `double` by displaying the message "The input should be a number." and setting the `sqrt` variable to 0. If no `FormatException` is thrown, test the input number's value. If it is negative, throw a `new ApplicationException` to which you pass the message "Number can't be negative." and again set `sqrt` to 0. If `number` is not negative, pass it to the `Math.Sqrt()` method, returning the square root to the `sqrt` variable. As the last program statement, display the value of `sqrt`. Save the file as **FindSquareRoot.cs**.

5. a. Create an `Employee` class with two fields: `IDNum` and `hourlyWage`. The `Employee` constructor requires values for both fields. Upon construction, throw an `ArgumentException` if the `hourlyWage` is less than 6.00 or more than 50.00.

   Write a program that establishes, one at a time, at least three `Employees` with `hourlyWages` that are above, below, and within the allowed range. Immediately after each instantiation attempt, handle any thrown `Exceptions` by displaying an error message. Save the file as **EmployeeExceptionDemo.cs**.

   b. Using the `Employee` class created in Exercise 5a, write an application that creates an array of five `Employees`. Prompt the user for values for each field for each `Employee`. If the user enters improper or invalid data, handle any exceptions that are thrown by setting the `Employee`'s ID number to 999 and the `Employee`'s pay rate to the $6.00 minimum. At the end of the program, display all the entered, and possibly corrected, records. Save the file as **EmployeeExceptionDemo2.cs**.

6. a. The Peterman Publishing Company has decided that no published book should cost more than 10 cents per page. Create a `BookException` class whose constructor requires three arguments: a `string` Book title, a `double` price, and an `int` number of pages. Create an error message that is passed to the `Exception` class constructor for the `Message` property when a `Book` does not meet the price-to-pages ratio. For example, an error message might be:

   ```
   For Goodnight Moon, ratio is invalid.
   ...Price is $12.99 for 25 pages.
   ```

   Create a `Book` class that contains fields for title, author, price, and number of pages. Include properties for each field. Throw a `BookException` if a client program tries to construct a `Book` object for which the price is more than 10 cents per page. Create a program that creates at least four `Book` objects—some where the ratio is acceptable and others where it is not. Catch any thrown exceptions and display the `BookException Message`. Save the file as **BookExceptionDemo.cs**.

b. Using the `Book` class created in Exercise 6a, write an application that creates an array of five `Books`. Prompt the user for values for each `Book`. To handle any exceptions that are thrown because of improper or invalid data entered by the user, set the `Book`'s price to the maximum 10 cents per page. At the end of the program, display all the entered, and possibly corrected, records. Save the file as **BookExceptionDemo2.cs**.

DEBUGGING EXERCISES

Each of the following files in the Chapter.09 folder on your Student Disk has syntax and/or logical errors. In each case, determine the problem and fix the program. After you correct the errors, save each file using the same filename preceded with *Fixed*. For example, DebugNine1.cs will become FixedDebugNine1.cs.

a. DebugNine1.cs   c. DebugNine3.cs

b. DebugNine2.cs   d. DebugNine4.cs

UP FOR DISCUSSION

1. What do the terms *syntactic sugar* and *syntactic salt* mean? From your knowledge of the C# programming language, list as many syntactic sugar and salt features as you can.

2. Have you ever been victimized by a computer error? For example, were you ever incorrectly denied credit, billed for something you did not purchase, or assigned an incorrect grade in a course? How did you resolve the problem? On the Web, find the most outrageous story you can involving a computer error.

3. Search the Web for information about educational video games in which historical simulations are presented in an effort to teach students about history. For example, Civilization III is a game in which players control a society as it progresses through time. Do you believe such games are useful to history students? Does the knowledge gained warrant the hours it takes to master the games? Do the makers of the games have any obligations to present history factually? Do they have a right to penalize players who choose options of which the game writers disapprove (such as using nuclear weapons or allowing slavery)? Do game creators have the right to create characters who possess negative stereotypical traits—for example, a person of a specific nationality portrayed as being stupid, weak, or evil? Would you like to take a history course that uses such games?

CHAPTER TEN

10

USING GUI OBJECTS AND THE VISUAL STUDIO IDE

In this chapter you will:

Create a `MessageBox`
Add functionality to `MessageBox` buttons
Create a `Form`
Create a `Form` that is a program's main window
Place a `Button` on a window
Use the Visual Studio IDE to design a `Form`
Learn about the code created by the IDE
Add functionality to a `Button` on a `Form`
Use Visual Studio Help

USING GUI OBJECTS AND THE VISUAL STUDIO IDE

Using the knowledge you have gained so far in this book, you can write many useful C# applications that can accept input, produce output, perform arithmetic, make decisions, handle exceptions, and so on. You also can create classes and instantiate objects from those classes by using the fundamental object-oriented principles of encapsulation, polymorphism, and inheritance. You can create a virtually infinite number of applications that will solve users' problems and provide services for them.

Unfortunately, your applications look dull. When you execute the programs you have written so far, input is accepted from a lackluster command prompt, and output is displayed in the same way. Most modern applications, and certainly most programs you have used on the Internet, use visually pleasing graphic objects to interact with users. These **graphical user interface (GUI)** objects include the buttons, check boxes, and toolbars you are used to controlling with a mouse when you interact with Windows-type programs. You can apply everything you have learned about C# classes and methods to the GUI objects that are built into the .NET environment so you can use Visual Studio to create your own interactive GUI applications.

> **»NOTE**
> GUI is pronounced "gooey."

The programs you have written have also been relatively small. When you start to use graphical objects in your programs, the program size quickly can become daunting. So far, you may have been using a simple text editor, such as Notepad, to write your C# programs. If so, it is time to explore the tools in the Visual Studio integrated development environment (IDE). These tools automatically create much of the code you need to develop appealing and attention-grabbing GUI programs. Of course, if you do not understand the C# code that the tools create, you cannot say you have mastered the C# programming language. In this chapter, you will build some graphical objects "by hand." Then, after you understand the details, you will create the same objects by using the IDE.

CREATING A `MessageBox`

A **MessageBox** is a GUI object that can contain text, buttons, and symbols that inform and instruct a user. You cannot create a new instance of the `MessageBox` class because its constructor is not `public`. Instead, you use the `static` class method `Show()` to display a `MessageBox`. The `MessageBox` class contains 12 overloaded versions of the `Show()` method; the simplest version accepts a string argument that is displayed within the `MessageBox`. Figure 10-1 shows a program that uses the `MessageBox.Show()` method with the string argument "Hello!". The program must contain the statement `using System.Windows.Forms;` to include the `MessageBox` class. Figure 10-2 shows the output.

> **»NOTE** You could remove the statement `using System.Windows.Forms;` from the program in Figure 10-1 and change the `Show()` statement to its full version: `System.Windows.Forms.MessageBox.Show("Hello!");`. You first learned about the `using` statement in Chapter 1 when you shortened `System.Console.Out.WriteLine()` to `Console.WriteLine();`. Including the statement that uses the `System.Windows.Forms` namespace provides you with access to many `Form` features in addition to the `MessageBox`. You will use many of these features as you work through the exercises in the next few chapters.

CHAPTER TEN

```
using System;
using System.Windows.Forms;
public class MessageBox1
{
    public static void Main()
    {
        MessageBox.Show("Hello!");
    }
}
```

Figure 10-1 Program that displays a `MessageBox`

Figure 10-2 Output of `MessageBox1` program

The `MessageBox` in Figure 10-2 is similar to those you have used in many Windows programs. It contains a title bar at the top, a Close button in the upper-right corner, the message "Hello!", and an OK button. When the user clicks either the Close button or the OK button, the `MessageBox` disappears. Because the .NET framework contains the `MessageBox` class, you do not have to design these standard `MessageBox` features and capabilities yourself when you write a program. Instead, you can simply use the `MessageBox` class and concentrate on the message you want to convey within the `MessageBox`. Besides saving development time, the built-in `MessageBox` makes your programs look and feel like others your users usually see.

Besides a `string`, you can pass additional arguments to the `MessageBox.Show()` method. You pass these arguments when you want to display a caption in a `MessageBox`'s title bar or add buttons and an icon. Table 10-1 summarizes the features of six of the 12 versions of the `MessageBox.Show()` method. (The other six versions correspond to the table entries, with the addition of naming a component in front of which you want the `MessageBox` to display.) When you use any version of the `Show()` method, you must provide values in the correct order for each argument listed in the table.

USING GUI OBJECTS AND THE VISUAL STUDIO IDE

Argument to `MessageBox.Show()`	Explanation
`string`	Displays a message box with the specified text
`string, string`	Displays a message box with the specified text and caption
`string, string, MessageBoxButtons`	Displays a message box with specified text, caption, and buttons
`string, string, MessageBoxButtons, MessageBoxIcon`	Displays a message box with specified text, caption, buttons, and icon
`string, string, MessageBoxButtons, MessageBoxIcon, MessageBoxDefaultButton`	Displays a message box with the specified text, caption, buttons, icon, and default button
`string, string, MessageBoxButtons, MessageBoxIcon, MessageBoxDefaultButton, MessageBoxOptions`	Displays a message box with the specified text, caption, buttons, icon, default button, and options

Table 10-1 Arguments used with the `MessageBox.Show()` method

```
using System;
using System.Windows.Forms;
public class MessageBox2
{
    public static void Main()
    {
        MessageBox.Show("Hello!", "MessageBox2 program");
    }
}
```

Figure 10-3 Using two `string` parameters with `MessageBox.Show()`

For example, the program in Figure 10-3 uses two `string` arguments with the `MessageBox.Show()` method. Figure 10-4 shows the execution; notice that the second `string` argument passed to the `Show()` method in the program appears in the title bar of the `MessageBox`.

Figure 10-4 Output of `MessageBox2` program

CHAPTER TEN

Besides `string` parameters, the `MessageBox.Show()` method can also accept `MessageBoxButtons`, `MessageBoxIcon`, `MessageBoxDefaultButton`, and `MessageBoxOptions` parameters. Tables 10-2 through 10-5 describe all of the possible values for each of the arguments you can send to `MessageBox.Show()`. Using different combinations of these arguments provides you with a wide variety of appearances for your `MessageBox` objects.

Member Name	Description
`AbortRetryIgnore`	The message box contains Abort, Retry, and Ignore buttons
`OK`	The message box contains an OK button
`OKCancel`	The message box contains OK and Cancel buttons
`RetryCancel`	The message box contains Retry and Cancel buttons
`YesNo`	The message box contains Yes and No buttons
`YesNoCancel`	The message box contains Yes, No, and Cancel buttons

Table 10-2 `MessageBoxButtons` values

Member Name	Description
`Asterisk`	The message box contains a lowercase letter *i* in a circle (the result is the same as `Information`)
`Error`	The message box contains a white *X* in a circle with a red background
`Exclamation`	The message box contains an exclamation point in a triangle with a yellow background (the result is the same as `Warning`)
`Hand`	The message box contains a white *X* in a circle with a red background (the result is the same as `Stop`)
`Information`	The message box contains a lowercase letter *i* in a circle
`None`	The message box contains no symbols
`Question`	The message box contains a question mark in a circle
`Stop`	The message box contains a white *X* in a circle with a red background
`Warning`	The message box contains an exclamation point in a triangle with a yellow background

Table 10-3 `MessageBoxIcon` values

USING GUI OBJECTS AND THE VISUAL STUDIO IDE

> **NOTE** The description of each `MessageBoxIcon` value contains a typical representation of the symbol. The actual graphic displayed is a function of the operating system in which the program is running.

Member Name	Description
Button1	The first button on the message box is the default button
Button2	The second button on the message box is the default button
Button3	The third button on the message box is the default button

Table 10-4 `MessageBox` default `Button` values

Member Name	Description
DefaultDesktopOnly	The message box appears on the active desktop
RightAlign	The message box text is right-aligned
RtlReading	The message box text is displayed with right-to-left reading order
ServiceNotification	The message box appears on the active desktop even if no user is logged on to the computer

Table 10-5 `MessageBoxOptions` values

> **NOTE** The `MessageBoxOptions` values are not used frequently. They are listed in Table 10-5 but are not used in this chapter.

> **NOTE** You can combine `MessageBoxOptions` values by placing an ampersand (`&`) between them. In Chapter 3, you learned that the single ampersand is the logical AND operator.

Figure 10-5 shows an application that uses a variety of `MessageBox.Show()` options. Figure 10-6 shows how the `MessageBox`es display in sequence:

```
using System;
using System.Windows.Forms;
public class MessageBoxDemo
{
    public static void Main()
    {
        string message = "This is message ";
        string caption = "Message box experiment ";
        int count = 1;
        MessageBox.Show(message + count);
        ++count;
        MessageBox.Show(message + count, caption + count);
        ++count;
        MessageBox.Show(message + count, caption + count,
            MessageBoxButtons.OKCancel);
        ++count;
        MessageBox.Show(message + count, caption + count,
            MessageBoxButtons.RetryCancel, MessageBoxIcon.Warning);
        ++count;
        MessageBox.Show(message + count, caption + count,
            MessageBoxButtons.YesNoCancel,
            MessageBoxIcon.Information,
            MessageBoxDefaultButton.Button3);
    }
}
```

Figure 10-5 MessageBoxDemo program

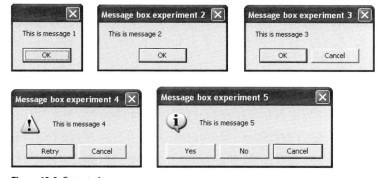

Figure 10-6 Output of MessageBoxDemo program

When the first shaded statement in Figure 10-5 executes, the first `MessageBox` in Figure 10-6 appears and a sound is played. The user hears the sound only if the user's system has speakers and they are turned on. This sound calls the user's attention to the `MessageBox`. No caption appears in the first `MessageBox`—just the message "This is message 1". A Close button is available in the upper-right corner. A `MessageBox` is a **modal dialog box**, which means that the program cannot progress until the user dismisses the box. (When you **dismiss** a component, you get rid of it, frequently by pressing its Close button, but in some cases by making some other selection.) When the user clicks OK or Close, the program proceeds; in this case, the second `MessageBox` appears.

The second shaded statement in Figure 10-5 creates a `MessageBox` to which a caption is added. In the second box in Figure 10-6, the message is updated with the new value of `count`, and the `count` is displayed in the caption. This `MessageBox` is automatically wider than the first one to accommodate the title bar caption.

OK and Cancel buttons are added in the third `MessageBox`. The OK button has a darker outline than the Cancel button, which means that the OK button has focus. When a button has **focus**, not only is the user's attention drawn to it visually, but if the user presses the Enter key, the action associated with the button executes, just as it would if the user clicked the button. If you press the Tab key or use the right and left arrow keys on your keyboard, you can change the focus from one button to the other. In this example, whether a user dismisses the third `MessageBox` by pressing the Enter key, closing the box, or clicking one of the two buttons, the fourth `MessageBox` appears.

The fourth `MessageBox` contains Retry and Cancel buttons and the Warning icon—an exclamation point in a triangle. The Warning icon might come with a different sound than a box without a warning. Because you normally would use the Warning icon in a "dangerous" situation, the sound is intended to get the user's attention. For example, you might use the Warning icon if a user leaves a required field blank on an order form or enters a phone number with too few or too many digits.

The last `MessageBox` includes an Information icon and three buttons. When this box appears, the button on the far right has focus because `MessageBoxDefaultButton.Button3` was used as an argument to the `MessageBox.Show()` method.

ADDING FUNCTIONALITY TO `MessageBox` BUTTONS

`MessageBox` objects provide an easy way to display information to a user in a GUI format. When you use a `MessageBox` to display some text you want the user to read, it makes sense to include only an OK button that the user can click after reading the text. Including multiple

`MessageBoxButtons`, all of which dismiss the `MessageBox`, doesn't make sense. Usually you want to determine users' interactions with a `MessageBox`'s buttons and take appropriate action based on the users' choices. **`DialogResult`** is an **enumeration**, or list of values in which names are substituted for numeric values. Each value corresponds to a user's potential `MessageBox` button selection. Table 10-6 contains `DialogResult` values you can compare to the return value of `MessageBox.Show()`. The `DialogResult` member names correspond to the button labels available within a `MessageBox`.

Member Name	Description
Abort	The dialog box return value is Abort
Cancel	The dialog box return value is Cancel
Ignore	The dialog box return value is Ignore
No	The dialog box return value is No
None	Nothing is returned from the dialog box, which means that the modal dialog box stays open
OK	The dialog box return value is OK
Retry	The dialog box return value is Retry
Yes	The dialog box return value is Yes

Table 10-6 `DialogResult` values

Figure 10-7 shows a program written for a fast-food restaurant. Its `MessageBox` asks the user to click Yes or No in response to a standard fast-food question. If the user clicks the Yes button, then the return value of `MessageBox.Show()` is equivalent to `DialogResult.Yes`, and the price increases by 0.75; otherwise, the price remains at $3.00. Whatever button the user chooses, a new `MessageBox` displays the final meal price. Figure 10-8 shows the `MessageBox` that contains the question and two results: the first occurs when the user clicks Yes, and the second occurs when the user clicks No.

USING GUI OBJECTS AND THE VISUAL STUDIO IDE

```
using System;
using System.Windows.Forms;
public class HamburgerAddition
{
    public static void Main()
    {
        string question = "Do you want fries with that?";
        string caption = "Hamburger addition";
        double price = 3.00;
        const double FRIES_PRICE = 0.75;
        if(MessageBox.Show(question, caption,
            MessageBoxButtons.YesNo, MessageBoxIcon.Question) ==
            DialogResult.Yes)
                price += FRIES_PRICE;
        MessageBox.Show("Total is " + price.ToString("C"));
    }
}
```

Figure 10-7 `HamburgerAddition` program

Figure 10-8 `MessageBox` in `HamburgerAddition` program, and results when user clicks Yes and No

> **»TIP** Instead of the long, shaded `if` statement in Figure 10-7, you could create a `DialogResult` object and assign the result of the `MessageBox.Show()` method to it, as in the following code:
> ```
> DialogResult dResult = MessageBox.Show(question, caption,
>     MessageBoxButtons.YesNo, MessageBoxIcon.Question);
> ```
>
> Then the `if` statement becomes simpler:
> ```
> if(dResult = DialogResult.Yes)
>    price += FRIES_PRICE;
> ```
>
> Also, when you use this technique, you can reuse `dResult`, comparing it to different values one at a time.

CREATING A Form

`MessageBox`es offer a large, but not infinite, number of ways to interact with users. They provide information and can allow a user to select one of two or three button options. However, some applications require more components than a few buttons; for example, they

CHAPTER TEN

might require an entire grid of buttons, lists of available options from which to select, or text fields in which to type. **Form**s provide an interface for collecting, displaying, and delivering such information; they are key components of GUI programs. You can use a Form to represent any window you want to display within your application. Although they are not required, you can include **controls** such as text fields, buttons, and check boxes that users can manipulate to interact with a program.

The Form class descends from the Object class like all other C# classes, but not directly. It is six generations removed from the Object class in the following line of descent:

» Object
» MarshalByRefObject
» Component
» Control
» ScrollableControl
» ContainerControl
» Form

You can create an instance of the Form class. (This is different from the MessageBox class, in which you cannot create an instance but must use the Show() method.) Figure 10-9 shows a program that creates the simplest Form possible, and Figure 10-10 shows the output.

> **NOTE** To use a Form, you must include the using statement at the top of the program file, as shown in Figure 10-9.

```
using System.Windows.Forms;
public class CreateForm1
{
    public static void Main()
    {
        Form form1 = new Form();
        form1.ShowDialog();
    }
}
```

Figure 10-9 CreateForm1 program

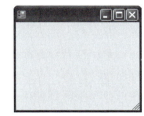

Figure 10-10 Output of CreateForm1 program

> **NOTE** If you use a Microsoft product such as Word and open a new, unnamed document, it is called Document1. When you open Excel, the first unnamed spreadsheet is called Sheet1. Microsoft uses the same naming convention for Forms, WindowsApplications, and other components in the IDE.

USING GUI OBJECTS AND THE VISUAL STUDIO IDE

In Figure 10-9, the object form1 is an instance of the Form class. The ShowDialog() method displays the Form as a modal dialog box, so the user must dismiss the box before the program proceeds. The Form contains neither a caption nor components, but it does possess a title bar with an icon. You can use your mouse to minimize, restore, resize (by dragging on the Form's borders), and close the Form, just as you can with most of the Forms you have encountered when you have used programs written by others.

You can change the appearance, size, color, and window management features of a Form by setting its properties. The Form class contains approximately 100 properties, many of which it inherits from the Control class. Table 10-7 lists just some of them. For example, setting the Text property allows you to specify the caption of the Form in the title bar. The Size and DesktopLocation properties allow you to define the size and position of the window when it is displayed.

> **»NOTE** If you use the Visual Studio .NET Search option, you can find descriptions for all the Form class properties. Additionally, if you highlight a property name and press F1 or click a property name, you will see a description of the property at the bottom of the Properties window. Not every property you can use with a Form appears in the Properties window in the Visual Studio IDE—only the most frequently used are listed.

Member Name	Description
AcceptButton	Gets or sets the button on the form that is clicked when the user presses the Enter key
AllowDrop	Gets or sets a value indicating whether the control can accept data that the user drags and drops into it
BackColor	Gets or sets the background color for this control
BackgroundImage	Gets or sets the background image displayed in the control
Bottom	Gets the distance between the bottom edge of the control and the top edge of its container's client area
CancelButton	Gets or sets the button control that is clicked when the user presses the Esc key
CanFocus	Gets a value indicating whether the control can receive focus
CanSelect	Gets a value indicating whether the control can be selected
ContainsFocus	Gets a value indicating whether the control or one of its child controls currently has the input focus
ControlBox	Gets or sets a value indicating whether a control box is displayed in the title bar of the form
Cursor	Gets or sets the cursor that is displayed when the user moves the mouse pointer over this control
DesktopBounds	Gets or sets the size and location of the form on the Windows desktop
DesktopLocation	Gets or sets the location of the form on the Windows desktop

Table 10-7 Properties of Forms (*continued*)

Member Name	Description
DialogResult	Gets or sets the dialog result for the form
Focused	Gets a value indicating whether the control has input focus
Font	Gets or sets the current font for the control
ForeColor	Gets or sets the foreground color of the control
FormBorderStyle	Gets or sets the border style of the form
Height	Gets or sets the height of the control
HelpButton	Gets or sets a value indicating whether a Help button should be displayed in the title bar of the form
Icon	Gets or sets the icon for the form
Left	Gets or sets the x-coordinate of a control's left edge in pixels
Location	Gets or sets the coordinates of the upper-left corner of the control relative to the upper-left corner of its container
MaximizeBox	Gets or sets a value indicating whether the Maximize button is displayed in the title bar of the form
MaximumSize	Gets the maximum size to which the form can be resized
Menu	Gets or sets the main menu that is displayed in the form
MinimizeBox	Gets or sets a value indicating whether the Minimize button is displayed in the title bar of the form
MinimumSize	Gets the minimum size to which the form can be resized
Modal	Gets a value indicating whether this form is displayed modally
Name	Gets or sets the name of the control
Opacity	Gets or sets the opacity level of the form
Right	Gets the distance between the right edge of the control and the left edge of its container
RightToLeft	Gets or sets whether the alignment of the control's elements is reversed to support locales using right-to-left fonts
ShowInTaskbar	Gets or sets a value indicating whether the form is displayed in the Windows taskbar
Size	Gets or sets the size of the form
StartPosition	Gets or sets the starting position of the form at run time
TabStop	Gets or sets a value indicating whether the user can give the focus to this control using the Tab key
Text	Gets or sets the text associated with this control
Top	Gets or sets the top coordinate of the control
Visible	Gets or sets a value indicating whether the control is visible
Width	Gets or sets the width of the control

Table 10-7 (*continued*)

USING GUI OBJECTS AND THE VISUAL STUDIO IDE

Figure 10-11 shows a `CreateForm2` class that instantiates a `Form` object and sets several of its properties: a caption and a Help button with a question mark are set in the title bar, and the Minimize and Maximize buttons that usually appear on a `Form` are removed. Figure 10-12 shows the output.

```
using System.Windows.Forms;
public class CreateForm2
{
    public static void Main()
    {
        Form form2 = new Form();
        form2.Text = "This is a Form2 Form";
        form2.HelpButton = true;
        form2.MaximizeBox = false;
        form2.MinimizeBox = false;
        form2.ShowDialog();
    }
}
```

Figure 10-11 `CreateForm2` class

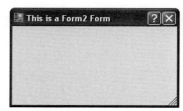

Figure 10-12 Output of `CreateForm2` program

CREATING A Form THAT IS A PROGRAM'S MAIN WINDOW

You can instantiate a `Form` within an application and use the `ShowDialog()` method to display it, as in Figure 10-11. More frequently, you create a child class from `Form` that becomes the main window of an application. When you create a new main window, you must complete two steps:

» You must derive a new custom class from the base class `System.Windows.Forms.Form`.

» You must write a `Main()` method that calls the `Application.Run()` method, and you must pass an instance of your newly created `Form` class as an argument. This activity starts the program and makes the form visible.

> **NOTE** Later in this chapter, you will learn to create a `Form` using the Visual Studio IDE. Here, you learn to create one "by hand" so you better understand what the IDE does automatically.

Figure 10-13 shows the simplest program you can write that creates a new main window for a program. The class name is `Window1`; it extends the `Form` class, as you can see by the shaded colon and base class name in the class header.

CHAPTER TEN

```
using System.Windows.Forms;
public class Window1 : Form
{
    public static void Main()
    {
        Application.Run(new Window1());
    }
}
```

Figure 10-13 The `Window1` class

>> **NOTE**
You learned about inheritance and the syntax of using the colon and the base class name in Chapter 8.

>> **NOTE** The statement `Application.Run(new Window1());` creates an unnamed instance of the `Window1` class. Alternatively, you could instantiate a named `Window` object using `Window1 aWindow = new Window();` and then call `Application.Run(aWindow);`. However, because this application never needs to use the name `aWindow`, there is no need to provide the new `Window1` object with a unique identifier.

The `Window1` class in Figure 10-13 contains a single method: a `Main()` method that calls the `Application.Run()` method, passing a new instance of the `Window1` class. Figure 10-14 shows the output. The `Form` created has no title and contains no components, but it has a title bar that displays an icon and Minimize, Restore, and Close buttons in the expected locations.

Figure 10-14 Output of `Window1` program

The `Application.Run()` method processes messages from the operating system to the application. Without the call to `Application.Run()`, the program would compile and execute, but the program would end without displaying the window.

When you want to add property settings to a program's main window, you can do so within the class constructor. Figure 10-15 shows a `Window2` class in which the `Size` and `Text` attributes of a `Window` are set. The keyword `this` in the constructor method refers to "this `Form` being constructed"; you could eliminate `this`, and the constructor would work in the same way. The `Size` property uses the `System.Drawing.Size()` method, which takes two parameters. The first indicates the horizontal size, or width, of a component; the second indicates the vertical size (or height) of a component. Setting the `Size` to `System.Drawing.Size(500, 100)` creates a window that is five times wider than it is tall. The `Text` property supplies the caption that appears in the window's title bar. Figure 10-16 shows the created `Window2` object.

USING GUI OBJECTS AND THE VISUAL STUDIO IDE

```
using System.Windows.Forms;
public class Window2 : Form
{
    public Window2()
    {
        this.Size = new System.Drawing.Size(500, 100);
        this.Text = "This is a Window2 Object";
    }
    public static void Main()
    {
        Application.Run(new Window2());
    }
}
```

Figure 10-15 `Window2` class

Figure 10-16 Output of `Window2` program

PLACING A Button ON A Window

Although it has interesting dimensions, the window in Figure 10-16 is not yet as useful as a `MessageBox`. However, a window is more flexible than a `MessageBox` because you can place manipulatable `Window` controls wherever you like on the surface of the `Window`.

One type of control the user can manipulate is a `Button`. A **Button** is a GUI object you can click to cause some action. (Alternatively, you can press the Enter key if the `Button` has focus.) You can create your own `Button` objects by using the `Button` class. This class contains more than 60 properties; two of the most useful are its `Text` and `Location` properties. You use the `Text` property to set a `Button`'s label. You can use the `Location` property to position a `Button` relative to the upper-left corner of the `Form` (or any other `ContainerControl` object) that contains it.

>>**NOTE** The properties in classes like `Button` are just like properties you have created for your own classes starting in Chapter 7. The creators of C# developed properties that contain `get` and `set` accessors for many of the fields in the classes you want to use so that you can easily work with objects of those classes.

When you use the `Location` property, you must supply two integer arguments to the `System.Drawing.Point()` method. The first argument represents a number of horizontal pixels to the right of the upper-left corner of a `Form` (or other container). The second argument represents the vertical position down from the top. For example, 0, 0 is the upper-left corner, and 10, 200 is a little to the right but much further down.

CHAPTER TEN

For a `Button` to be clickable, you need to use the `System.Windows.Forms.Control` class, which implements very basic functionality required by any classes that display GUI objects to the user. This class handles user input through the keyboard and pointing device. To use the `Control` class, you can create an array of GUI components (such as `Button`s) and add them to a `Form`'s `Controls` property with the `AddRange()` method. The `Controls.AddRange()` method makes any argument, such as a `Button`, become one of the `Form`'s usable controls. The statement that adds components to the list of a `Form`'s controls is structured like the following, in which *identifier* represents the name of a control object you have instantiated:

```
this.Controls.AddRange(new System.Windows.Forms.Control[]
   {this.identifier});
```

Figure 10-17 shows a `WindowWithButton` class that descends from `Form`. The class declares a `Button` named `button1`. The class constructor sets the form size to 300 by 150—a size that is twice as wide as it is tall. The `Form`'s `Text` property is set, as is the `Button`'s `Text` property. Then the `Button` is added to the `Form`'s `Controls` property using the `AddRange()` method. The `Button` is located at `Point(25, 50)`, not very far from the `Form`'s left side. Figure 10-18 shows the resulting `Form`—a `Window` with `Text` in the title bar and a clickable `Button` with text.

```
using System.Windows.Forms;
public class WindowWithButton : Form
{
    Button button1 = new Button();
    public WindowWithButton()
    {
        this.Size = new System.Drawing.Size(300, 150);
        this.Text = "Window Object With Button";
        button1.Text = "Press";
        this.Controls.AddRange(new System.Windows.Forms.Control[]
            {this.button1});
        this.button1.Location = new System.Drawing.Point(25, 50);
    }
    public static void Main()
    {
        Application.Run(new WindowWithButton());
    }
}
```

Figure 10-17 `WindowWithButton` class

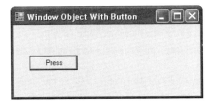

Figure 10-18 Output of `WindowWithButton` program

USING GUI OBJECTS AND THE VISUAL STUDIO IDE

>> **NOTE** In the `WindowWithButton` class, you could leave out the four instances of `this`. For example, the statement `Text = "Window Object With Button";` would work exactly like the one that uses the `this` reference. Figure 10-17 includes the `this` reference for two reasons. First, it helps you understand that "this" object, the `WindowWithButtonForm`, has `Text` that is being altered, and not some other component on the `Form`. Second, when you create programs visually using the IDE, as you will do later in this chapter, you will see liberal uses of `this` in the automatically generated code. That's because the IDE cannot predict what identifiers you will use for your components, so it fully qualifies its statements to avoid conflicts.

USING THE VISUAL STUDIO IDE TO DESIGN A Form

The window in Figure 10-18 consists of only a `Form` and a `Button`, and even though the `Button` doesn't do anything yet, scores of additional options are available to you. The program in Figure 10-17 sets only two attributes for the `Form` (`Size` and `Text`), yet Table 10-7 shows dozens of additional properties you can set—and that table lists only half the available properties. Likewise, the program in Figure 10-17 sets only two `Button` properties (`Text` and `Location`); by the time you create a full-blown Windows application, you might want to set several more properties for the existing `Button`, add more `Button`s, and set all their properties. You might want to add other components to the window, supplying locations and appropriate actions for each of them as well. Just determining an attractive and useful layout in which to position all the components on your `Form` would take many lines of code and a lot of trial and error. A simple but fully functional GUI program might require several hundred statements. Therefore, coding such a program can be tedious.

The Visual Studio IDE provides a wealth of tools to help you design `Form`s. Rather than having to write multiple assignment statements and guess at appropriate component locations, it allows you to use a visual environment for designing your `Form`s.

>> **NOTE** Designing aesthetically pleasing, functional, and user-friendly `Form`s is an art; entire books are devoted to the topic.

>> **NOTE** Chapter 1 contains instructions for creating and running a console application using the IDE. If you have been using the IDE throughout this book to create programs, you are already familiar with many of the menu options. If you have been using a simple text editor instead of the IDE, you might want to return to the "You Do It" section in Chapter 1 and create, compile, and execute a simple console application, just to get used to the IDE. In the "You Do It" section at the end of this chapter, you will create your own Windows application. Note that when you use the IDE to create Windows applications, you choose the Windows Application option instead of Console Application when starting the new project.

Figure 10-19 shows the environment in which you can create Windows applications. Some key features in Visual C# include:

>> **NOTE** Your title bar or other features might be slightly different if you are using a different edition of Microsoft Visual Studio.

- » The **main menu**, which includes a File menu from which you open, close, and save projects. It also contains submenus for editing, debugging, and help tasks, among others.
- » The **Toolbox**, which provides a list of controls you can drag onto a `Form` so that you can develop programs visually, using a mouse.
- » The **Form Designer** and **Code Editor**, which appear in the center of the screen. You can switch back and forth between these two when you want to design an application by dragging components onto the screen or when you want to write or view code statements.

CHAPTER TEN

» The **Solution Explorer**, for viewing and managing project files and settings.
» The **Properties window**, for configuring properties and events on controls in your user interface. For example, you can use this window to set the Size property of a Button or the Text property of a Form without writing the necessary C# statements; the IDE will create the statements for you.
» The **error list**, which displays any compiler errors in your code.

NOTE
If some of these features are not immediately visible after you start a project in the IDE, you can select them from the View menu.

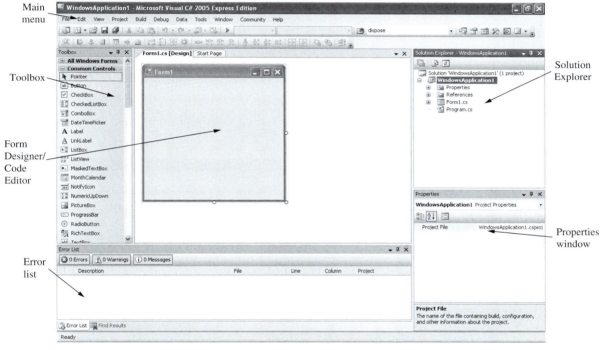

Figure 10-19 Features of the Visual Studio IDE

When you create a Windows Forms project, Visual C# names the project WindowsApplication1 by default. In Figure 10-19, you see this name in the following locations:

» In the title bar above the main menu
» In the title bar of the Solution Explorer
» In the Solution Explorer file list
» In two locations in the Properties window

383

USING GUI OBJECTS AND THE VISUAL STUDIO IDE

When you create a Windows Forms project, Visual C# adds a form to the project and calls it `Form1`. You can see `Form1` in the following locations in Figure 10-19:

» On the folder tab at the top of the Form Designer area
» In the title bar of the form in the Form Designer area
» In the Solution Explorer file list

The Solution Explorer file list shows the files that are part of the current project. The two files that represent the form are called Form1.cs and Form1.designer.cs. As you develop an application, you write your code in the Form1.cs file. The Windows Forms Designer automatically writes code in the designer.cs file; the code created there implements all the actions that are performed when you drag and drop controls from the Toolbox.

»NOTE
You learn more about controls in Chapter 11.

In Figure 10-19, the Toolbox contains a list of controls—the GUI objects a user can click or manipulate. The list includes controls you probably have seen when using Windows applications—for example, `Button`, `CheckBox`, and `Label`. You can drag these controls onto the `Form`. For example, Figure 10-20 contains a `Form` onto which a `Button` has been dragged.

»NOTE All of the windows in Visual C# can be made dockable or floating, hidden or visible, or can be moved to new locations. To change the behavior of a window, click the down arrow or push-pin icons on the title bar and select from among the available options. You can customize many aspects of the IDE by clicking the Tools menu, then clicking Options.

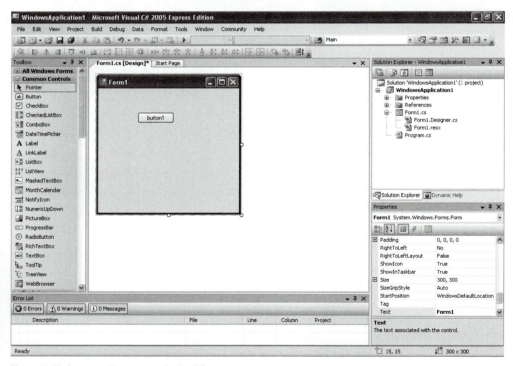

»NOTE
In Figure 10-20, notice that the file folder tab for `Form1` now contains an asterisk, which means the file contents have changed since the last time the file was saved.

Figure 10-20 A `Form` with a `Button` in the IDE

CHAPTER TEN

When you select View from the main menu bar and then select Code, the IDE appears as in Figure 10-21. This code (and more that is currently hidden) was automatically generated for you.

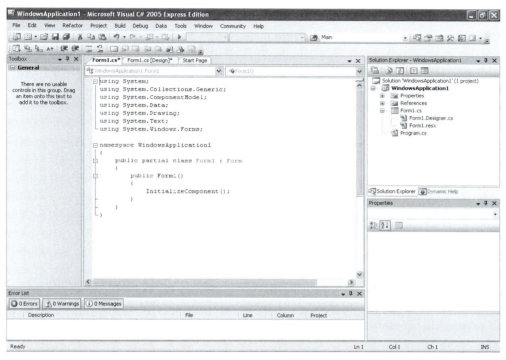

Figure 10-21 Sample code generated by C#

UNDERSTANDING THE CODE CREATED BY THE IDE

Using the Visual Studio IDE, it is easy to create elaborate forms with a few keystrokes. However, if you don't understand the code behind the forms you create, you cannot say you have truly mastered the C# language, and you won't be able to troubleshoot problems as easily. Everything you have learned to this point has prepared you to understand the code that underlies a visually designed form. The generated code is simply a collection of C# statements and method calls similar to those you have used throughout this book. When you use the Designer in the IDE to design your forms, you save a lot of typing, which reduces the errors you create. As shown in Figure 10-21, it takes quite a bit of code to create even a simple form with a single button. Examine the code piece by piece.

>> **NOTE**
Because the IDE generates so much code automatically, it is often more difficult to find and correct errors in programs created using the IDE than in programs you code by hand.

USING GUI OBJECTS AND THE VISUAL STUDIO IDE

The code in Figure 10-21 contains a list of `using` statements as follows:

```
using System.Data;
using System.Drawing;
using System.Text;
using System.Windows.Forms;
```

You have placed many statements like these within your earlier programs. These statements simply list the namespaces for the classes the program will use.

The next code segment in Figure 10-21 creates a namespace using the name the programmer supplied when this C# Windows project was started: `namespace WindowsApplication1`. You have been using the `System` namespace since Chapter 1. Using the IDE, C# creates a namespace for you. The namespace declaration is followed by an opening curly brace and, several statements later, a closing curly brace.

In Figure 10-21, you can see the declaration of the `Form1` class as follows:

```
public partial class Form1 : Form
{
    public Form1()
    {
        InitializeComponent();
    }
}
```

The name `Form1` was supplied by default; you can change this name using the form's `Name` property if you want. The `Form1` class header shows that the class descends from the `Form` class. The class header is followed by an opening curly brace, and several lines later, the matching closing brace.

>> **NOTE** You should change the IDE's automatically supplied identifiers, such as `Form1`, to more meaningful names. However, many examples in this book show components with their original names so changes are kept to a minimum and you can concentrate on the topic at hand.

>> **NOTE**
In Chapter 7, you learned that `partial` is a contextual keyword, like `get` and `set`.

The `Form1` class is declared as a `partial` class. As you might imagine, a `partial` class contains only part of the class; the rest is spread among multiple files. (The rest of the class will be discussed shortly.)

The `Form1` class contains one method—a constructor. It looks like many other constructors you have created: it is `public`, has no `return` type, and has the same name as the class. The `Form1()` constructor is parameterless and contains one statement—a call to a method named `InitializeComponent()`.

In Figure 10-21, notice that three folder tabs are available at the top of the code window. Figure 10-22 shows the IDE after the Form1.Designer.cs tab is selected to reveal more of the partial `Form1()` class. All the generated code in this view does not fit on the screen; scroll down to see more.

CHAPTER TEN

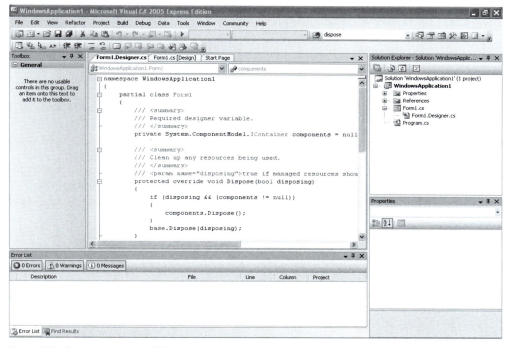

Figure 10-22 Code revealed in the IDE after user clicks the Form1.Designer tab

The significant parts of the automatically generated code include:

- » Comments
- » The `Dispose()` method
- » Object declarations
- » The `InitializeComponent()` method
- » Preprocessor directives
- » A `Main()` method

The following sections describe each part of the generated code. Again, you might need to scroll down to see it.

COMMENTS

The code in Figure 10-22 contains many comments, such as the following:

```
/// <summary>
/// Clean up any resources being used.
/// </summary>
```

USING GUI OBJECTS AND THE VISUAL STUDIO IDE

In other C# programs, you have seen many line comments that begin with two slashes. C# uses three slashes (///) to begin an XML comment. When C# inserts the tag pairs `<summary>` and `</summary>` within the code, it allows the IntelliSense feature in Visual Studio to display additional information about the members contained between the tags. The IntelliSense feature automatically completes statements for you within the Visual Studio IDE.

> **»NOTE** You first learned about XML comments when you learned about block and line comments in Chapter 1. Recall that XML stands for eXtensible Markup Language. To obtain more information, search for XML in the Visual Studio Help facility; it will direct you to several articles that discuss XML.

THE `Dispose()` METHOD

The code created by C# in Figure 10-22 and visible in the IDE includes a method named `Dispose()`, as follows:

```
protected override void Dispose(bool disposing)
{
    if (disposing && (components != null))
    {
        components.Dispose();
    }
    base.Dispose(disposing);
}
```

By now, you should be familiar and comfortable with most of the elements in the method:

- » This method is `protected`, meaning any descendants can access it.
- » The method header uses the term `override`, meaning it overrides a method with the same name in an interface named `IDisposable`. That interface provides a mechanism for releasing program resources, such as files, that can be used by only one program at a time. This method contains any cleanup activities you need when a `Form` is dismissed. When you write an application that leaves open files or other unfinished business, you might want to add statements to this method. You do not need to understand all the details of the `Dispose()` method in order to create a workable program. C# has created the method for you, and for now, you can let C# take care of the cleanup tasks that are invisible to you.
- » The method's return type is `void`, so the method returns nothing to any method that calls it.
- » The method accepts a `bool` parameter.
- » The method includes an `if` statement and a call to another method that resides in its base class.

OBJECT DECLARATIONS

In the preceding example, the statement that defines the reference to a `Button` object named `button1` is included in the following code:

```
private System.Windows.Forms.Button button1;
```

CHAPTER TEN

This object declaration was added to the code when the programmer dragged the Button onto the Form's surface. You could change the Button's access from private to public if you liked, but it is defined as private because it will be used only within this class. You also could eliminate the fully qualified System.Windows.Forms.Button class name and replace it with Button because the using statement at the top of the file includes System.Windows.Forms. You also can change the name of button1 to any other legal identifier you choose. However, if you delete button1 in the declaration and replace it with a new name, then you must be sure to change every instance of button1 in the program. The safer, and recommended, alternative is to change button1's Name property in the IDE. (You change it in the Settings box for the Name property, which you can locate in the Properties window of the Designer view. You can see the Properties window in the lower-right corner of Figure 10-19. You will get the opportunity to perform similar steps in the "You Do It" section later in this chapter.) When you change a control's Name property in the Properties window, every reference to the control will be replaced with its new identifier.

> **» NOTE** If you change button1's Name property within the code, switch to Designer view and then double-click the button to switch back to Code view. You will find that every instance of button1 has been changed to the new name you assigned.

When you create more complicated forms that contain additional objects such as Checkboxes, Labels, or more Buttons, more objects will be declared in the code.

THE InitializeComponent() METHOD

The Form1 constructor contains a single method call to a method named InitializeComponent(). The tasks performed by this method could be performed directly within the constructor; InitializeComponent() is simply used as a helper method to organize all of the component initialization tasks in one location.

Many of the statements within the InitializeComponent() method should look familiar to you. These statements reflect the code generated by the properties that have been selected for the Form. For example, the button1.Text and Form this.Text properties contain values like those you would have typed into the code when creating a GUI application "by hand," without using the Visual Studio design environment. Similarly, the following statement sets a drawing size:

```
this.button1.Size = new System.Drawing.Size(107, 44);
```

PREPROCESSOR DIRECTIVES

The statements in the code that do not look familiar begin with a pound sign (#). The statements #region and #endregion are preprocessor directives. Any code placed between #region and #endregion statements constitutes a group that can be used by some of the IDE's automated tools.

For example, the Code Editor treats namespaces, classes, and methods as regions that you can collapse. Collapsing regions provides an outline of your code, hiding the details. Using this feature can make parts of your code easier to find. On the vertical line to the left of the code in the Code Editor, you can click a + to expand code and a – to collapse it. You can make your

389

USING GUI OBJECTS AND THE VISUAL STUDIO IDE

own collapsible code regions by surrounding sections with #region and #endregion. The #region and #endregion statements do not affect the way the code operates; they help you navigate the editor.

THE PROJECT'S Main() METHOD

At the right side of Figure 10-22, the Solution Explorer screen contains a file named Program.cs. This file contains the Main() program for the FormAndAButton application, as shown in Figure 10-23. You can see that the last line of code calls Application.Run() for this Form, just as you did manually for the Windows in Figures 10-13, 10-15, and 10-17 earlier in this chapter.

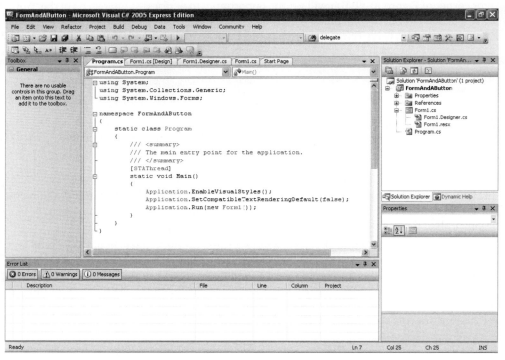

Figure 10-23 Program.cs file

ADDING FUNCTIONALITY TO A Button ON A Form

In most cases, it is easier to design a Form using the IDE than it is to write by hand all the code a Form requires. Adding functionality to a Button is particularly easy when you use the IDE. After you have dragged a Button onto a Form, you can double-click it. Figure 10-24 shows the generated code. The code contains a new part of the `partial` class `Form1`. Following the constructor, a shell of a method named `button1_Click()` is created. In Figure 10-24, you can see that the method is `private` and `void`. When a user interacts with a GUI object, an **event** is generated that causes the program to perform a task. When a user clicks a `Button`, the action fires a **click event**. This event causes the `Button`'s `Click()` method to execute. You might guess that if you placed a second button on the form, its method would be named `button2_Click()`. You might also guess that if you changed the `Name` property of the `button1` object in the IDE, the name of this method should also change. For example, if you renamed the `Button` `acceptLicenseAgreement`, the name of the method should become:

```
acceptLicenseAgreement_Click()
```

>>> **NOTE** Using a process called refactoring, C# can automatically change a method name when its associated object's name changes. See Appendix C.

>>> **NOTE** Chapter 12 describes event handling in detail.

>>> **NOTE** You are not required to create a `Click()` method for a `Button`. If, for some reason, you did not want to take any action when a user clicked a button, you simply would not include the method in your program. Alternatively, you could create an empty method that contains no statements between its curly braces and thus does nothing. However, these choices would be unusual—you usually place a `Button` on a `Form` because you expect it to be clicked at some point. You will frustrate users if you do not allow your `Control`s to act in expected ways.

```
namespace FormAndAButton
{
    public partial class Form1 : Form
    {
        public Form1()
        {
            InitializeComponent();
        }

        private void button1_Click(object sender, EventArgs e)
        {

        }
    }
}
```

Figure 10-24 Partial `Form1` class that contains a constructor and `Click()` method

You can write any statements you want between the curly braces of the `button1_Click()` method. For example, if you write the following statement, a `MessageBox` will be displayed when the user clicks the `Button`:

```
MessageBox.Show("You clicked the button");
```

Alternatively, you could declare a string that contains a message and use it within the class (see Figure 10-25).

USING GUI OBJECTS AND THE VISUAL STUDIO IDE

> **» NOTE**
> In Chapter 11, you will learn to place additional statements within your application's `Click()` methods.

> **» NOTE**
> If you see a code screen in the IDE, you can return to the visual view of the `Form` by double-clicking Form1.cs in the Solution Explorer panel at the right side of the screen.

```
namespace FormAndAButton
{
    public partial class Form1 : Form
    {
        const string MESSAGE = "You clicked the button";
        public Form1()
        {
            InitializeComponent();
        }

        private void button1_Click(object sender, EventArgs e)
        {
            MessageBox.Show(MESSAGE);
        }
    }
}
```

Figure 10-25 `Form1` class that contains a declaration

USING VISUAL STUDIO HELP

When you are working with a class that is new to you, such as `Button` or `Form`, no book can answer all of your questions. The ultimate authority on C# classes is the Visual Studio Help documentation. You should use this tool often as you continue to learn about C# in particular, and the Visual Studio products in general.

The Help documentation for Visual Studio is in the MSDN Library, which you can install locally on your own computer. It is also available at *http://msdn.microsoft.com/library*. You can install all or part of the library on your machine; the complete MSDN installation is close to 2 GB in size, and includes documentation for many Microsoft technologies besides C#.

There are multiple ways to access Help while working in Visual C#:

- » *F1 Search*—In the Code Editor, you can position the cursor on or just after a keyword or class member and press F1. The Help provided is context-sensitive, which means the screen you see depends on where your cursor is located.
- » *Search*—On the main menu, you can click Help, click Search, and type in a topic.
- » *Index*—You can select Help from the main menu and click Index. The index provides a quick way to locate documents in your local MSDN library. It searches only the index keywords that have been assigned to each document.
- » *Table of Contents*—The MSDN library table of contents shows all the topics in the library in a hierarchical tree structure. It is a useful tool for browsing through the documentation to see what is in the library, and for exploring documents that you might not find through the Index or Search tools. Often, when you find a document using F1, Index,

CHAPTER TEN

or Search, it is useful to know where the document is located in the table of contents so you can see other related documentation.

» *How Do I*—How Do I provides a view of MSDN documents called How-to's or Walkthroughs. These documents show you how to perform a specific task.

» *Dynamic Help*—Dynamic Help provides a way to get information about the IDE. To open the Dynamic Help window, select Help from the main menu, and then click Dynamic Help. Then, when you click a word in the code, help topics are displayed accordingly. For example, Figure 10-26 shows the Help window on the right side of the screen after the user selects Dynamic Help and then clicks the keyword `public` in the code. Figure 10-27 shows the screen displayed when the user follows the `public` link.

Figure 10-26 Dynamic help when user places cursor on `public` in the code window

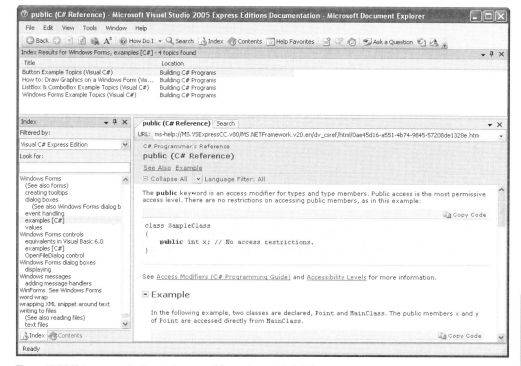

Figure 10-27 Help screen displayed when user follows dynamic help link

>> **NOTE**
You will learn much more about creating Windows applications using the IDE in the next two chapters.

393

USING GUI OBJECTS AND THE VISUAL STUDIO IDE

YOU DO IT

CREATING MessageBoxES
In the following steps, you will create GUI objects using the MessageBox class, and you will experiment with MessageBox.Show() method arguments.

> **NOTE**
> Appendix C contains details about using and getting the most benefit from the Visual C# editor, including why words appear in different colors as you type.

To create MessageBoxes:

1. Open a new file in your text editor. Enter the first few lines of a program that will instantiate several MessageBox objects.

   ```
   using System;
   using System.Windows.Forms;
   public class MessageBoxExperiment
   {
   ```

2. Add a Main() method that declares two constant strings to serve as the MessageBox messages and captions.

   ```
   public static void Main()
   {
       const string MESSAGE = "Hello";
       const string CAPTION = "Message box experiment";
   ```

3. Create three MessageBox objects. The first has a single string argument that is the MessageBox's message. The second MessageBox adds a caption, and the third adds two buttons.

   ```
       MessageBox.Show(MESSAGE);
       MessageBox.Show(MESSAGE, CAPTION);
       MessageBox.Show(MESSAGE, CAPTION,
           MessageBoxButtons.OKCancel);
   ```

4. Add two closing curly braces—one for the Main() method and one for the class.

5. Save the file as **MessageBoxExperiment.cs**. Compile and execute the program. The first MessageBox appears on the left in Figure 10-28. Notice that the string "Hello" appears as the message, but no caption appears in the MessageBox title bar. A Close button is available in the upper-right corner of the MessageBox. Whether you click **OK** or **Close**, the second MessageBox appears, including the caption. Notice that this MessageBox is slightly wider than the first one to accommodate the title bar caption.

  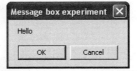

Figure 10-28 The three MessageBox objects created by MessageBoxExperiment

> **NOTE** After you save the project, use My Computer or Windows Explorer to examine the MessageBoxExperiment folder in the directory where you saved the project. You will find multiple files and folders that require much more disk storage space than the simple .exe files for the applications you created without the IDE.

6. Whether you click **OK** or **Close** in the second MessageBox, the third MessageBox appears; it contains OK and Cancel buttons (see Figure 10-28). The OK button has a darker outline than the Cancel button, which means that the OK button has focus. If you press the Tab key or use the right and left arrow keys on your keyboard, you can change the focus from one button to the other. Whether you dismiss this MessageBox by pressing the Enter key, closing the box, or clicking one of the two buttons, the program ends.

7. Run the program several times and experiment by dismissing the MessageBoxes using the various options (the Enter key, the Buttons, or the Close button.).

> **NOTE** After you run a program, you must remember to end it by clicking the Close button on the Form. If you return to the editor and make changes without closing the Form, the next time you attempt to run the program, you will receive an error message indicating that it cannot execute because it is being used by another process.

8. Resave the program as **MessageBoxExperiment2.cs**, then experiment by using different values for the message, caption, MessageBoxButtons, MessageBoxIcon, MessageBoxDefaultButton, and MessageBoxOptions for the individual MessageBoxes.

WORKING WITH THE VISUAL STUDIO IDE

You can most easily understand the Visual Studio environment by using it. In the next steps, you will use the IDE to create a Form with a Button.

To use the IDE:

1. Open Microsoft Visual C# 2005 Express Edition. You might have a desktop shortcut you can double-click, or you might click **Start** on the taskbar, point to **All Programs**, and then click **Microsoft Visual C# 2005 Express Edition**. If you are using a school network, you might be able to select Visual Studio from the school's computing menu. Figure 10-29 shows the Visual C# Start Page.

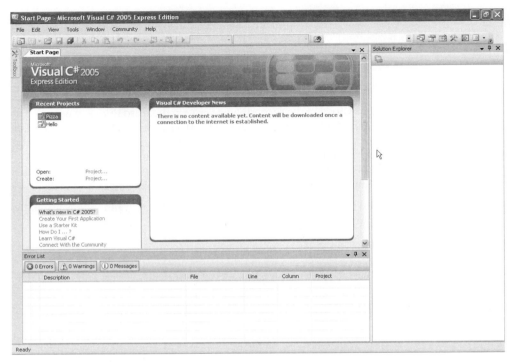

Figure 10-29 Visual C# Start Page

2. Click **File** on the menu bar and click **New Project**, as shown in Figure 10-30.

Figure 10-30 Opening a new project

3. A New Project window (see Figure 10-31) appears. Click **Windows Application**. Near the bottom of the New Project window, click in the **Name** text box and replace the default name there (WindowsApplication1) with **WindowCreatedWithIDE** as the name for your application. Figure 10-32 shows the design screen that appears.

CHAPTER TEN

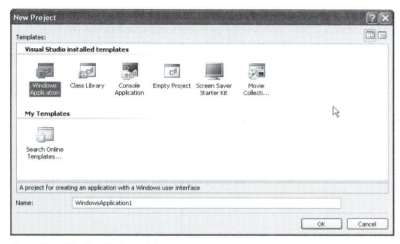

Figure 10-31 The New Project window

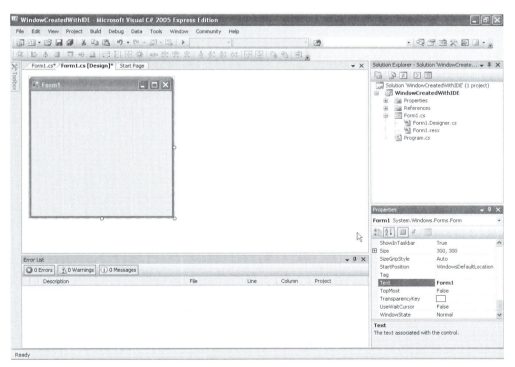

Figure 10-32 The `WindowCreatedWithIDE` project environment

USING GUI OBJECTS AND THE VISUAL STUDIO IDE

> **NOTE**
> If you do not see the Properties window in the lower-right corner of your screen, click the title bar on the Form. Alternatively, click **View** in the main menu and click **Properties Window**.

4. The text in the title bar of the blank Form contains the default name Form1. In the Properties window in the lower-right portion of the screen, you can see that the Text property is set to Form1. Take a moment to scroll through the list in the Properties window, examining the values of other properties of the Form. For example, the value of the Size property is 300, 300.

5. In the Properties window, click the description **Form1** in the Settings box for the Text property. Delete Form1 and type **My First Form**. Press **Enter**; the title of the Form in the center of the screen changes to "My First Form". See Figure 10-33.

Figure 10-33 My First Form window

Figure 10-34 The Toolbox

> **NOTE**
> If you do not see the Toolbox, you can select **View** from the main menu bar at the top of the screen and then click **Toolbox**.

6. At the left side of the design screen, you see the Toolbox. As shown in Figure 10-34, the Toolbox contains a list of common components that can be added to a Form, including Pointer, Button, CheckBox, and many others.

CHAPTER TEN

7. In the Toolbox, click **Button**. As you move your mouse off the Toolbox and onto the form, the mouse pointer changes so that it appears to carry a Button. Position your mouse anywhere on the form, then click and drag down and to the right. When you release the mouse button, the Button appears on the Form and contains the text "button1" (see Figure 10-35). When you click the Button, it displays handles that you can drag to resize the Button. When you click off the Button on the Form, the handles disappear.

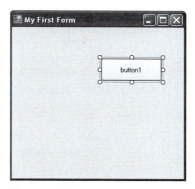

Figure 10-35 A Button on a Form

8. If you click the Form on the right side of the screen under Properties, the list box shows that you are viewing the properties for Form1. If you click the Button, the list displays the properties for button1. Change the Text property of button1 to **Press**, then press **Enter**. The text of the Button on the Form changes to "Press". See Figure 10-36.

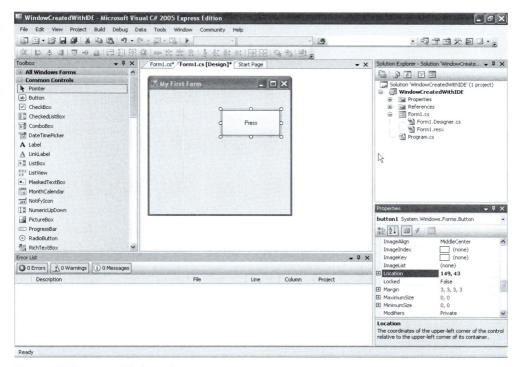

Figure 10-36 A Button with changed Text

399

9. Scroll through the other `button1` properties. In Figure 10-36, notice that the value in the Settings box for the `Location` property is 149, 43. Your `Location` property might be different, depending on where you released the `Button` when you dragged it onto the `Form`. Drag the `Button` across the `Form` to a new position. Each time you release your mouse button, the value of the `Form Button`'s `Location` property is updated to reflect the new location. Try to drag the `Button` to Location 80, 64. Alternatively, delete the contents of the Location property field and type **80, 64**. The `Button` moves to the requested location on the `Form`.

10. Save your form by clicking **File** on the menu bar, then clicking **Save All**. Alternatively, you can click the **Save All** button on the toolbar; its icon is a stack of diskettes. A Save Project dialog box appears, as in Figure 10-37. Confirm that the program name and disk location are correct. (You can click the **Browse** button to choose another storage location, or you can just type in the location.)

Figure 10-37 The Save Project dialog box

11. Although the `Form` you have designed doesn't do much yet, you can execute the program anyway. Click **Debug** on the menu bar and then click **Start Without Debugging**, or press **Ctrl+F5**. The `Form` appears. (See Figure 10-38.) You can drag, minimize, and restore it, and you can click its `Button`. The `Button` has not yet been programmed to do anything, but it appears to be pressed when you click it. Click the `Form`'s **Close** button to dismiss the `Form`.

Figure 10-38 My First Form with a Press button

CHAPTER TEN

12. Click **View** on the menu bar, then click **Code**. A list box of project members appears at the top of the code window (see Figure 10-39). You can select other components to view the code generated for them. (You also can drag the window borders to get a larger viewing area.) Based on the description of the code presented in this chapter, how many components of the code do you recognize? For example, you should be able to identify comments, method calls, and the Form1 constructor.

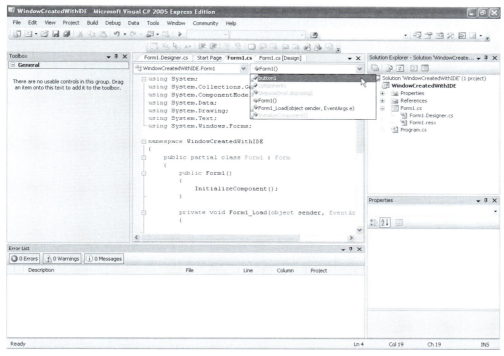

Figure 10-39 The list of project members

13. Make some modifications to the properties. For example, if you want to change the location of the Button on the Form, return to Designer View by choosing **View** on the menu bar and then **Designer**. (You can also click the **Form1.cs [Design]** page tab at the top of the code area.) Next, change the values in the Properties window.

> **» NOTE** Recall that after any changes, an asterisk appears on the tab for Form1.Designer.cs. The asterisk means that changes have been made but not yet saved. When you save the project, the asterisk disappears.

Also experiment by changing the Font, Forecolor, and Text of the Button. You can preview any changes by clicking the **Form1.Design** tab, or you can save the program and execute it again; the Button's appearance will be modified.

401

USING GUI OBJECTS AND THE VISUAL STUDIO IDE

14. Exit Visual Studio by clicking the **Close** button in the upper-right corner of the screen, or by clicking **File** on the menu bar and then clicking **Exit**. If you have made more changes since the last time you saved, you will be prompted to save again. When you choose **Yes**, the program closes.

PROVIDING FUNCTIONALITY FOR A Button

In the next steps, you will make the Button on the WindowCreatedWithIDE Form functional; it will display a MessageBox when the user clicks it.

To make a Button functional:

1. Start Visual Studio. Click **File** on the menu bar and then click **Open Project**. In the Open Project window, make sure the **Look in** box indicates that you are looking in the Chapter.10 folder on your Student Disk (or wherever you stored the WindowCreatedWithIDE project). If the Look in box contains an incorrect location, you can use the list box to browse for the correct location.

2. Double-click the **WindowCreatedWithIDE** folder. Double-click the **WindowCreatedWithIDE** C# source code file. See Figure 10-40.

Figure 10-40 Opening the WindowCreatedWithIDE file

3. The code for the Form you created should appear. To see the Form in Designer View, double-click **Form1.cs** in the Solution Explorer at the right side of the screen.

4. Double-click the **Press** Button on the Form. A new window that contains program code appears, revealing a newly created method with no statements:

```
private void button1_Click(object sender, EventArgs e)
{
}
```

CHAPTER TEN

5. The method named `button1_Click()` will contain the code that identifies the actions you want to perform when a user clicks `button1`. The method receives two arguments—an `object` named `sender` and an `EventArgs` object named `e`. You will examine these objects more thoroughly in Chapter 11. For now, add some code that will display a `MessageBox` when the user clicks `button1`. Place your insertion point between the curly braces of the `button1_Click()` method, if necessary, and add the following:

   `MessageBox.Show("Thank you");`

6. Save the file, then run the program by clicking **Debug** on the menu bar and clicking **Start Without Debugging**, or press **Ctrl+F5**. When `My First Form` appears, click the **Press** button. The `MessageBox` that contains "Thank you" is displayed, as shown in Figure 10-41.

Figure 10-41 The `MessageBox` displayed after the user clicks the `Button` on My First Form

7. Dismiss the `MessageBox`, then close the `Form`.

8. Examine the code for the Form1.Designer.cs file. In the twelfth line of the `InitializeComponent()` method, a new statement has been added:

   `this.button1.Click += new System.EventHandler(this.button1_Click);`

   This statement associates the `button1_Click()` method with the `button1.Click` event that is generated when a user clicks the `button1` Button. In Chapter 12, you will learn more about events. Fortunately, the IDE allows you to use an event without understanding all the details of how one operates.

9. Select **Save All**, then close the IDE.

ADDING A SECOND Button TO A Form

`Form`s often contain multiple `Button` objects; a `Form` can contain as many `Button`s as you need. Because each `Button` has a unique identifier, you can provide unique methods that execute when a user clicks each `Button`.

When you first use the IDE, the generated code appears intimidating. However, it is just C# code. You are already familiar with many of the statements you need to create useful and interesting programs. In the next steps, you will create a form that allows a customer to select one of two `Button`s that identify two types of pizza—Cheese or Sausage. The form will then display one of two pizza prices—$10 or $12, depending on the user's selection. You will use your knowledge of the `if` statement, which you have used since Chapter 3, to create this application.

To add a second `Button` to a `Form`:

1. Start Visual Studio. Click **File** on the menu bar, click **New Project**, and then click **Visual C# Projects** and **Windows Application**. Change the name of the project to `WindowWithTwoButtons`, as shown in Figure 10-42. Click **OK**.

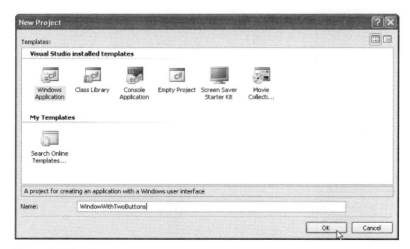

Figure 10-42 Opening a project

2. Click the title bar of the Form Designer that appears. In the `Form`'s Properties window, change the `Text` property of the form to **Make a Choice**. When you press **Enter**, "Make a Choice" appears in the `Form`'s title bar. Drag a `Button` onto the `Form`. Release your mouse button to place the `Button` on the `Form`, then drag a second `Button` onto the `Form`. The `Button`s automatically contain text labels `button1` and `button2`, as shown in Figure 10-43.

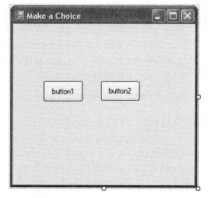

Figure 10-43 Two `Button`s on a `Form`

3. In the Properties window, click the list box and click **button1**. Alternatively, click button1 on the Form. Either way, the Properties window for button1 appears. Change its Text property setting to **Cheese**. In the Properties window, click **button2**. Change its Text property to **Sausage**.

4. Double-click the **Cheese** button to view the code for the button1_Click() method. Between the curly braces, type the following:

   `MessageBox.Show("Price is $10");`

5. Return to Designer View. Double-click the **Sausage** button. Between the curly braces of the method, add the following:

   `MessageBox.Show("Price is $12");`

6. Save the file, and then run the program by pressing **Ctrl+F5** or by clicking **Debug** on the menu bar and clicking **Start Without Debugging**. When the Form appears, notice that the Cheese button has a darker outline than the Sausage button; this means the Cheese button has focus. When a Button has focus, it appears darker than other Buttons, and you can activate it by clicking it or pressing the Enter key. By default, the first Button you place on a Form has focus. The user can press the Tab key to change the focus from one Button to the next. Experiment with the **Tab** key, then click either Button and confirm that the correct price message is displayed.

7. Dismiss the MessageBox and click the other Button. Again, the correct price is displayed. Figure 10-44 shows the result when the user clicks **Sausage**.

Figure 10-44 A MessageBox displayed by the WindowWithTwoButtons project

8. Dismiss the MessageBox and close the Form.

9. If you want, you can experiment with the Size and Location properties of the Buttons. For example, when you dragged them onto the Form, you might not have created the Button objects to be exactly the same size or distance from the top of the Form. Correct this in the Properties window if necessary.

10. Close Visual Studio.

CHAPTER SUMMARY

» A `MessageBox` is a GUI object that can contain text, buttons, and icons that inform and instruct a user. You use the `static` class method `Show()` to display a `MessageBox`; the method can accept strings as text or as a title for the `MessageBox`, and it can also accept arguments for buttons, icons, and other options.

» Usually you want to determine users' interactions with a `MessageBox`'s buttons and take appropriate action based on the users' choices. `DialogResult` is an enumeration, or list of values, that correspond to a user's potential `MessageBox` button selections.

» `Forms` provide an interface for collecting, displaying, and delivering information; they are key components of GUI programs. `Forms` often contain controls such as text fields, buttons, and check boxes that users can manipulate to interact with a program. You can change the appearance, size, color, and window management features of a `Form` by setting its properties.

» You can create a child class from `Form` that becomes the main window of an application. You must derive a new custom class from the base class `System.Windows.Forms.Form` and write a `Main()` method that calls the `Application.Run()` method, passing an instance of your newly created `Form` class as an argument. This activity starts the program and makes the form visible.

» A window is more flexible than a `MessageBox` because you can place manipulatable `Window` controls wherever you like on the surface of the window. For example, you can create `Button` objects.

» The Visual Studio IDE provides a wealth of tools to help you design `Forms`. It allows you to use a visual environment rather than having to write multiple assignment statements and guess at appropriate component locations.

» Using the Visual Studio IDE, it is easy to create elaborate forms with a few keystrokes. The generated code is simply a collection of C# statements. When you use the Designer in the IDE to design your forms, you save a lot of typing, which reduces the errors you create. The IDE creates a `Form` onto which you can drag controls. The generated code contains familiar components such as comments, object declarations, and methods.

» Adding functionality to a `Button` is particularly easy using the IDE. After you have dragged a `Button` onto a `Form`, you can double-click it to generate a shell method into which you can place statements.

» The ultimate authority on C# classes is the Visual Studio Help documentation. You should use this tool often as you continue to learn about C# in particular and the Visual Studio products in general. The Help documentation for Visual Studio is in the MSDN Library, which you can install locally on your own computer or view online.

CHAPTER TEN

KEY TERMS

A **graphical user interface (GUI)** employs graphical images that the user manipulates. GUI objects include the buttons, check boxes, and toolbars you are used to controlling with a mouse when you interact with Windows-type programs.

A `MessageBox` is a GUI object that can contain text, buttons, and icons that inform and instruct a user.

A **modal dialog box** prevents a program from further progress until the user dismisses the box.

When you **dismiss** a component, you get rid of it, frequently by pressing its Close button, but in some cases by making some other selection.

When a button has **focus**, not only is the user's attention drawn to it visually, but if the user presses the Enter key, the action associated with the button executes, just as it would if the user clicked the button.

`DialogResult` is an enumeration that contains a user's potential `MessageBox` button selections.

An **enumeration** is a list of values in which names are substituted for numeric values.

`Forms` provide an interface for collecting, displaying, and delivering information; they are key components of GUI programs.

Controls are GUI components such as text fields, buttons, and check boxes that users can manipulate to interact with a program.

A `Button` is a GUI object you can click to cause some action.

The **main menu** of the IDE runs horizontally across the top of the screen; it includes a File menu from which you open, close, and save projects.

The **Toolbox** of the IDE contains controls you can drag onto a `Form` so that you can develop programs visually, using a mouse.

The **Form Designer** and **Code Editor** of the IDE appear in the center of the Visual Studio screen. You can switch back and forth between these two when you want to design an application by dragging components onto the screen or you want to write or view code statements.

The **Solution Explorer** of the IDE allows you to view and manage project files and settings.

The **Properties Window** of the IDE allows you to configure properties and events on controls in your user interface.

The **error list** of the IDE displays any compiler errors.

When a user interacts with a GUI object, an **event** is generated that causes the program to perform a task.

When a user clicks a button, the action fires a **click event**.

REVIEW QUESTIONS

1. Which is true of the `MessageBox` class?
   a. You cannot create a new instance of this class.
   b. Its constructor is `public`.
   c. Its methods cannot be overloaded.
   d. Its `Show()` method is not overloaded.

2. A programmer who uses a `MessageBox` must _____.
   a. determine the message that will appear on the OK button
   b. write the message that will appear in the `MessageBox`
   c. write an overloaded version of the `Show()` method
   d. select an icon to be displayed within the `MessageBox`

3. A programmer can select all of the following for a `MessageBox` except _____.
   a. a message within it
   b. a caption in its title bar
   c. its default button
   d. its modality

4. A `MessageBox` is modal, meaning _____.
   a. it can appear in several different styles
   b. the program will not progress until a user dismisses the `MessageBox`
   c. it is always rectangular with a title bar
   d. it appears in the Windows style so that all components have the same look and feel

5. An enumeration is a _____ in a program.
   a. list of values you can use
   b. sum or total of values used
   c. count of the number of values used
   d. list of values that cannot be used

6. Which of the following is not a possible `DialogResult`?
   a. Cancel   c. End
   b. OK   d. Retry

7. The Form class descends from the _____ class.
   a. Object
   b. Component
   c. Control
   d. all of these

8. The Form class differs from the MessageBox class in that _____.
   a. you can create an instance of the Form class, but not the MessageBox class
   b. you can create an instance of the MessageBox class, but not the Form class
   c. Forms can contain Buttons, but MessageBoxes cannot
   d. MessageBoxes can contain Buttons, but Forms cannot

9. The Form class contains _____ properties.
   a. 2
   b. 5
   c. about 100
   d. more than 4000

10. Which of the following is not a Form property?
    a. BackColor
    b. DesktopLocation
    c. Invisible
    d. Size

11. When you create a new main window, you must _____.
    a. derive a new custom class from the base class System.Windows.Forms.Form
    b. write a Main() method that calls the Application.Run() method
    c. either a or b, but not both
    d. both a and b

12. When used with a component, the System.Drawing.Size() method takes two parameters representing _____.
    a. width and height
    b. line thickness and horizontal position
    c. height and degrees of rotation
    d. horizontal position and width

13. A Form's Controls are its _____.
    a. static methods
    b. nonstatic methods
    c. manipulatable components
    d. parents

USING GUI OBJECTS AND THE VISUAL STUDIO IDE

14. For a `Button` to appear to be pressed when a user clicks it, you _____.
    a. need only to add the `Button` to a `Form`
    b. use the `System.Windows.Forms.Control` class
    c. include a `GUIImplement()` method within your program
    d. write a method named `ClickButton()`

15. The main reason to use the Visual Studio integrated development environment is to _____.
    a. use methods that are not available when you write code by hand
    b. have access to the Studio's private data types
    c. make programs easier to design
    d. all of these

16. When you begin to create a `Form` using the Visual Studio IDE, the default `Form` name is _____.
    a. `MyForm`
    b. `IDEForm`
    c. `Form1`
    d. `null`

17. When you design a `Form` using the IDE, _____.
    a. much less code is generated than when you design a `Form` by hand
    b. the generated code is written in machine language so you cannot read it
    c. you cannot alter the generated code
    d. none of these

18. If you do not like the default name the IDE gives to a `Button`, you should _____.
    a. change the `Name` property in the code
    b. change the `Name` property in the Properties window in the IDE
    c. either of these
    d. none of these

19. A partial class _____.
    a. exists as an outline into which you must add statements
    b. is still being written
    c. has been saved, but not yet compiled
    d. is spread among multiple files

CHAPTER TEN

20. If a Form contains a Button named agreeButton, then you should code the actions to be performed when the user clicks the Button in a method named _____.

    a. ButtonClick()

    b. Button_Click()

    c. agreeButtonClick()

    d. agreeButton_Click()

EXERCISES

Save the programs that you create in these exercises in the Chapter.10 folder on your Student Disk.

1. Write a program that displays a MessageBox that contains contact information for your company. Save the program as **Contact.cs**.

2. Write a program for an Internet provider that displays a MessageBox asking users whether they want Internet access. If they do not, their total price is $0. If they do, display a second MessageBox asking whether they want limited access (at $10.95 per month) or unlimited access (at $19.95 per month). Display the total price in a third MessageBox. Save the program as **InternetAccess.cs**.

3. Write a program for an Internet provider that displays a MessageBox asking users whether they want to read the company's usage policy. Include a question icon. If the user chooses Yes, display a MessageBox that contains a short usage policy. If the user chooses No, display a MessageBox reminding the user to read the policy later. If the user chooses Cancel, end the program. Save the program as **Policy.cs**.

4. Write a program that simulates an Internet connection error. Display a MessageBox that notifies the user of the error and provide three buttons: Abort, Retry, and Ignore. If the user chooses Retry, display a message indicating that the connection succeeded. If the user chooses Ignore, display a message indicating that the user will work off-line. If the user chooses Abort, end the program. Save the program as **Connection.cs**.

5. Using the Visual Studio IDE, create a Form that contains a button labeled "About". When a user clicks the button, display a MessageBox that contains your personal copyright statement for the program. Save the project as **About**.

6. Create a Form that contains two buttons for a book publisher. If a user clicks the Paperback button, display a MessageBox that contains a book price of $6.99. If the user clicks the Hardback button, display $24.99. Save the project as **Book**.

7. Create a game Form that contains six buttons. Display different prizes depending on the button the user selects. Save the project as **Game**.

411

DEBUGGING EXERCISES

Each of the following files or projects in the Chapter.10 folder on your Student Disk has syntax and/or logical errors. In each case, determine the problem and fix the program. After you correct the errors, save each file or project using the same filename preceded with *Fixed*. For example, the file DebugTen1.cs will become FixedDebugTen1.cs and the project folder for DebugTen3 will become FixedDebugTen3.

  a. DebugTen1.cs   c. DebugTen3
  b. DebugTen2.cs   d. DebugTen4

UP FOR DISCUSSION

1. Think of some practice or position to which you are opposed. For example, you might have objections to organizations on the far right or left politically. Now suppose that such an organization offered you twice your annual salary to create Web sites for them. Would you do it? Is there a price at which you would do it? What if the organization was not so extreme, but featured products you found distasteful? What if the Web site you designed was not objectionable, but the parent company's policies were objectionable? For example, if you are opposed to smoking, would you design a Web site for a tobacco company? At what price? What if the site just displayed sports scores without promoting smoking directly?

2. Suppose you have learned a lot about programming from your employer. Is it ethical for you to use this knowledge to start your own home-based programming business on the side? Does it matter whether you are in competition for the same clients as your employer? Does it matter whether you use just your programming expertise or whether you also use information about clients' preferences and needs gathered from your regular job?

CHAPTER ELEVEN

USING CONTROLS

In this chapter you will:

Learn about Controls
Create a Form that contains Labels
Set a Label's Font
Create a Form that contains LinkLabels
Add color to a Form
Add CheckBox and RadioButton objects to a Form
Add a PictureBox to a Form
Add ListBox, ComboBox, and CheckedListBox items
   to a Form
Add a MonthCalendar and DateTimePicker to a Form
Work with a Form's layout
Learn about GroupBoxes and Panels
Add a MenuStrip to a Form
Learn to use other controls

USING CONTROLS

In the last chapter, you learned to create Forms by hand using an ordinary text editor and by using the Visual Studio IDE. Both approaches yield the same results, but the IDE provides you with an easy-to-use design environment. Additionally, by examining the IDE-generated program code, you can learn more about code you want to write by hand.

The Form and Button objects you created in Chapter 10 represent only a tiny fraction of the types of objects that are available to you in C#. When using programs or visiting Internet sites, you have encountered and used many other interactive **widgets**—short for "windows gadgets"—such as labels, scroll bars, check boxes, and radio buttons. C# has many classes that represent these GUI objects, and the Visual Studio IDE makes it easy to add them to your programs. In this chapter, you will learn to incorporate some of the most common and useful widgets into your programs. Additionally, you will see how these components work in general so you can use other widgets that are not covered in this book or that become available to programmers in future releases of C#.

UNDERSTANDING Controls

When you design a Form, you can place Buttons and other controls on the Form surface. The **Control** class provides the definitions for these GUI objects. Control objects such as Forms and Buttons, like all other objects in C#, ultimately derive from the Object class. Figure 11-1 shows where the Control class fits into the inheritance hierarchy.

```
System.Object
    System.MarshalByRefObject
        System.ComponentModel.Compcnent
            System.Windows.Forms.Control
                26 Derived classes
```

Figure 11-1 Control class inheritance hierarchy

Figure 11-1 shows that all Controls are Objects, of course. They are also all MarshalByRefObjects. (A MarshalByRefCbject is one you can instantiate on a remote computer so that you can manipulate a reference to the object rather than a local copy of the object.) Controls also descend from Component. (The **Component** class provides containment and cleanup for other objects. The Control class adds visual representation to Components.) The Control class implements very basic functionality required by classes that appear to the user—in other words, the GUI objects the user sees on the screen. This class handles user input through the keyboard and pointing devices as well as message routing and security. It defines the bounds of a Control by determining its position and size.

Table 11-1 shows the 26 direct descendants of Control and some commonly used descendants of those classes. It does not show all the descendants that exist; rather, it shows only the descendants covered in this chapter. For example, the ButtonBase class is the parent of Button, a class you used in Chapter 10. In this chapter, you will use two other ButtonBase children—CheckBox and RadioButton. This chapter cannot cover every Control that has been invented; however, after you learn to use some `Control`s, you will find that others work in much the same way. You also can read more about them in the Visual Studio Help documentation.

Class	Commonly used descendants
`Microsoft.WindowsCE.Forms.DocumentList`	
`System.Windows.Forms.AxHost`	
`System.Windows.Forms.ButtonBase`	`Button`, `CheckBox`, `RadioButton`
`System.Windows.Forms.DataGrid`	
`System.Windows.Forms.DataGridView`	
`System.Windows.Forms.DateTimePicker`	
`System.Windows.Forms.GroupBox`	
`System.Windows.Forms.Integration.ElementHost`	
`System.Windows.Forms.Label`	`LinkLabel`
`System.Windows.Forms.ListControl`	`ListBox`, `ComboBox`, `CheckedListBox`
`System.Windows.Forms.ListView`	
`System.Windows.Forms.MdiClient`	
`System.Windows.Forms.MonthCalendar`	
`System.Windows.Forms.PictureBox`	
`System.Windows.Forms.PrintPreviewControl`	
`System.Windows.Forms.ProgressBar`	
`System.Windows.Forms.ScrollableControl`	
`System.Windows.Forms.ScrollBar`	
`System.Windows.Forms.Splitter`	
`System.Windows.Forms.StatusBar`	
`System.Windows.Forms.TabControl`	
`System.Windows.Forms.TextBoxBase`	
`System.Windows.Forms.ToolBar`	
`System.Windows.Forms.TrackBar`	
`System.Windows.Forms.TreeView`	
`System.Windows.Forms.WebBrowserBase`	

Table 11-1 Classes derived from `System.Windows.Forms.Control`

Because `Control`s are all relatives, they share many of the same attributes. Each `Control` has more than 80 `public` properties and 20 `protected` ones. For example, each `Control` has a `Font` and a `ForeColor` that dictate how its text is displayed, and each `Control` has a `Width` and `Height`. Table 11-2 shows just some of the `public` properties associated with `Control`s in general; reading through them will give you an idea of the `Control` attributes that you can change.

USING CONTROLS

Property	Description
AllowDrop	Gets or sets a value indicating whether the control can accept data that the user drags onto it
Anchor	Gets or sets the edges of the container to which a control is bound and determines how a control is resized with its parent
BackColor	Gets or sets the background color for the control
BackgroundImage	Gets or sets the background image displayed in the control
Bottom	Gets the distance, in pixels, between the bottom edge of the control and the top edge of its container's client area
Bounds	Gets or sets the size and location of the control, including its nonclient elements, in pixels, relative to the parent control
CanFocus	Gets a value indicating whether the control can receive focus
CanSelect	Gets a value indicating whether the control can be selected
Capture	Gets or sets a value indicating whether the control has captured the mouse
Container	Gets the IContainer that contains the Component (inherited from Component)
ContainsFocus	Gets a value indicating whether the control or one of its child controls currently has the input focus
Cursor	Gets or sets the cursor that is displayed when the mouse pointer is over the control
Disposing	Gets a value indicating whether the base Control class is in the process of disposing
Dock	Gets or sets which control borders are docked to its parent control and determines how a control is resized with its parent
Enabled	Gets or sets a value indicating whether the control can respond to user interaction
Focused	Gets a value indicating whether the control has input focus
Font	Gets or sets the font of the text displayed by the control
ForeColor	Gets or sets the foreground color of the control
HasChildren	Gets a value indicating whether the control contains one or more child controls
Height	Gets or sets the height of the control
IsDisposed	Gets a value indicating whether the control has been disposed of
Left	Gets or sets the distance, in pixels, between the left edge of the control and the left edge of its container's client area
Location	Gets or sets the coordinates of the upper-left corner of the control relative to the upper-left corner of its container

Table 11-2 Selected public Control properties (*continued*)

CHAPTER ELEVEN

Property	Description
`Margin`	Gets or sets the space between controls
`ModifierKeys`	Gets a value indicating which of the modifier keys (Shift, Ctrl, and Alt) is in a pressed state
`MouseButtons`	Gets a value indicating which of the mouse buttons is in a pressed state
`MousePosition`	Gets the position of the mouse cursor in screen coordinates
`Name`	Gets or sets the name of the control
`Parent`	Gets or sets the parent container of the control
`Right`	Gets the distance, in pixels, between the right edge of the control and the left edge of its container's client area
`Size`	Gets or sets the height and width of the control
`TabIndex`	Gets or sets the tab order of the control within its container
`TabStop`	Gets or sets a value indicating whether the user can give focus to the control using the Tab key
`Text`	Gets or sets the text associated with this control
`Top`	Gets or sets the distance, in pixels, between the top edge of the control and the top edge of its container's client area
`TopLevelControl`	Gets the parent control that is not parented by another Windows `Forms` control; typically, this is the outermost `Form` in which the control is contained
`Visible`	Gets or sets a value indicating whether the control and all its parent controls are displayed
`Width`	Gets or sets the width of the control

Table 11-2 (*continued*)

>> **NOTE** The description of each property in Table 11-2 indicates whether the property is read-only; such properties only get values and do not set them.

>> **NOTE** In Chapter 10, you learned about the `Button Control` and how to declare a `Button`. You learned that you could change `Button` properties such as its `Text`, either by typing statements or using the Properties window in Visual Studio. All the other `Controls` you learn about in this chapter can be manipulated in the same ways.

CREATING A Form WITH LabelS

A **Label** is one of the simplest GUI `Control` objects you can place on a `Form`. The `Label` class descends directly from `Control`. Typically, you use a `Label` to provide descriptive text for another `Control` object (for example, to tell the user what pressing a `Button` will accomplish). You can also use a `Label` to display other text information on a `Form`.

USING CONTROLS

Creating a `Label` is very similar to creating a `Button`. You can manually create a `Label` by using the class name and an identifier and then calling the class constructor. For example:

```
private Label label1;
label1 = new Label();
```

Alternatively, you could use the fully qualified class name and the `this` reference with the `label1` object, as in the following:

```
private System.Windows.Forms.Label label1;
this.label1 = new System.Windows.Forms.Label();
```

As when you created `Button` objects in Chapter 10, it is almost always more convenient to use the Visual Studio IDE to design `Form`s than it is to write the code statements. Figure 11-2 shows a `Form` created in the IDE. Three `Label`s have been dragged onto a `Form`. The `Text` property of the `Form` has been set to "FormWithThreeLabels", and the `Text` property of each `Label` has been set. Additionally, a different `Font` has been selected for each `Label`.

Figure 11-2 `Form` generated by `FormWithThreeLabels` program

Within the Form1.Designer.cs file in Visual Studio, three lines of code are generated as follows:

```
private System.Windows.Forms.Label label1;
private System.Windows.Forms.Label label2;
private System.Windows.Forms.Label label3;
```

These lines declare the three `Label`s just as you could have by typing the statements yourself.

To create this `Form`, the programmer only had to drag three objects and type four `string`s—one for the `Form` caption and three for the contents of the `Label`s. These actions generate all the code in Figure 11-3. (You must expand the `InitializeComponent()` method node to see it.) More than 30 statements are generated. By using the Visual Studio Designer, you save lots of time and eliminate many chances for error.

> **NOTE** In Visual Studio, a **method node** is a box that appears to the left of the code you are viewing. When the node contains a plus (+), you see only the method header; clicking the node reveals hidden code. When the node contains a minus (–), you see all the code in the method; clicking the node collapses the code so you can work with a condensed view.

```
private void InitializeComponent()
{
    this.label1 = new System.Windows.Forms.Label();
    this.label2 = new System.Windows.Forms.Label();
    this.label3 = new System.Windows.Forms.Label();
    this.SuspendLayout();
    //
    // label1
    //
    this.label1.AutoSize = true;
    this.label1.Font = new System.Drawing.Font
        ("Microsoft Sans Serif", 24F,
        System.Drawing.FontStyle.Regular,
        System.Drawing.GraphicsUnit.Point, ((byte)(0)));
    this.label1.Location = new
        System.Drawing.Point(23, 19);
    this.label1.Name = "label1";
    this.label1.Size = new System.Drawing.Size(244, 37);
    this.label1.TabIndex = 0;
    this.label1.Text = "C Sharp Optical";
    //
    // label2
    //
    this.label2.AutoSize = true;
    this.label2.Font = new System.Drawing.Font
        ("Microsoft Sans Serif", 12F,
        System.Drawing.FontStyle.Regular,
        System.Drawing.GraphicsUnit.Point, ((byte)(0)));
    this.label2.Location = new
        System.Drawing.Point(12, 91);
    this.label2.Name = "label2";
    this.label2.Size = new System.Drawing.Size(262, 20);
    this.label2.TabIndex = 1;
    this.label2.Text =
        "Providing you with designer eyeware";
    //
    // label3
    //
    this.label3.AutoSize = true;
    this.label3.Font = new System.Drawing.Font
        ("Microsoft Sans Serif", 9.75F,
        System.Drawing.FontStyle.Bold,
        System.Drawing.GraphicsUnit.Point, ((byte)(0)));
    this.label3.Location = new
        System.Drawing.Point(72, 130);
    this.label3.Name = "label3";
    this.label3.Size = new System.Drawing.Size(143, 16);
```

Figure 11-3 InitializeComponent() method for FormWithThreeLabels (*continued*)

USING CONTROLS

```
            this.label3.TabIndex = 2;
            this.label3.Text = "at affordable prices";
            //
            // Form1
            //
            this.AutoScaleDimensions = new
                System.Drawing.SizeF(6F, 13F);
            this.AutoScaleMode =
                System.Windows.Forms.AutoScaleMode.Font;
            this.ClientSize = new
                System.Drawing.Size(292, 266);
            this.Controls.Add(this.label3);
            this.Controls.Add(this.label2);
            this.Controls.Add(this.label1);
            this.Name = "Form1";
            this.Text = "FormWithThreeLabels";
            this.ResumeLayout(false);
            this.PerformLayout();

        }
```

Figure 11-3 (*continued*)

> **NOTE** In Figure 11-3, every instance of `this` means "this Form."

> **NOTE** When you view code in the IDE, some lines will be longer than those in Figure 11-3. Many code statements in this book have been split into multiple lines to fit the size of the page.

> **NOTE** So much code is automatically generated by Visual Studio that it can be hard to find what you want. To locate a line of code, click **Edit** on the main menu in the IDE, point to **Find and Replace**, click **Quick Find**, type a key phrase to search for, and click the **Find Next** button.

Do not be intimidated by the amount of code generated in Figure 11-3. You can easily understand most of it.

- » After the `InitializeComponent()` method header and opening brace, the next three statements call the `Label` constructor for each `Label`.
- » `SuspendLayout()` is a method that prevents conflicts when you are placing `Controls` on a form. Its counterparts are `ResumeLayout()` and `PerformLayout()`, which appear at the bottom of the method. If you remove these method calls from small applications, you won't notice the difference. However, in large applications, suspending the layout logic while you adjust the appearance of components improves performance.
- » Comments serve to separate the `label1` code from other code in the method. Following the `label1` comment lines, seven statements set properties of the `Label`. For example, you can see that the `Font`, `Location`, `Size`, and `Text` have been assigned values based on the programmer's choices in the IDE.
- » The property statements for `label2` and `label3` are similar to those for `label1`. Notice that the `Font` statement for `label3` is much longer than the corresponding statements for `label1` and `label2`. The programmer has chosen `label3` to be bold, which generates extra code. The `TabIndex` for `label1` is 0 by default, the `TabIndex` for `label2` is 1, and so on. The `TabIndex` values determine the order in which `Controls` receive focus

CHAPTER ELEVEN

when the user presses the Tab key. This property is typically more useful for selectable items like `Buttons`.

» The `InitializeComponent()` method ends with statements that set the properties of the `Form`, such as its drawing size and text. You can also see the statements that add the three `Label`s to the `Form` using the `Add()` method.

>> **NOTE** Although the property settings for the `Label`s refer to the label identifiers (for example, `this.label1.Name` or `this.label2.Font`), the property settings for the `Form` itself use only the reference `this`.

If you wanted to add a fourth label to the form while designing it, you *could* code a statement to declare it, code another statement to call its constructor, write all the statements to set all the properties, and insert a new `Add()` method call into the code for the `Form`. However, you should not design programs in this way. Instead, you should return to the Design view of the `Form` in the IDE, drag a new `Label` onto the form, and make changes in the Properties window. It is far easier this way, and you are less likely to generate errors.

>> **NOTE** In this chapter, you will learn about several additional `Control`s. When designing a `Form`, you usually will use the drag-and-drop design features in the IDE instead of typing code statements. However, this chapter also teaches you about the code behind these actions so you can troubleshoot problems in projects and write usable statements when necessary.

SETTING A Label'S Font

You use the **Font** class to change the appearance of printed text on your `Form`s. When designing a `Label` or other `Control` on a `Form`, it is easiest to select a `Font` from the Properties list. After you place a `Control` on a `Form` in the IDE, you can select the ellipsis (three dots) that follows the current `Font` property name in the Properties list. (See Figure 11-4.) This selection displays a `Font` window in which you can choose a `Font` name, size, style, and other effects. (See Figure 11-5.)

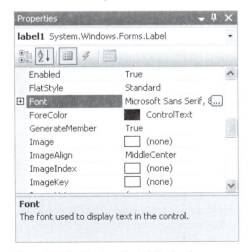

Figure 11-4 Clicking the ellipsis following the `Font` property

USING CONTROLS

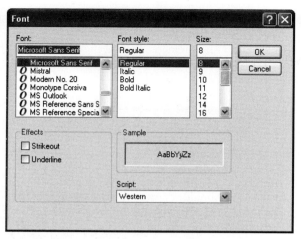

Figure 11-5 The Font window

However, if you wanted to change a Font later in a program—for example, after a user clicks a button—you might want to create your own instance of the Font class. As another example, suppose you want to create multiple controls that use the same Font. In that case, it makes sense to declare a named instance. For example, you can declare the following Font:

```
System.Drawing.Font myFont = new
    System.Drawing.Font("Courier New", 16f);
```

Then, in the three statements that set the Font in the InitializeComponent() method in Figure 11-3, you can code the following:

```
this.label1.Font = myFont;
this.label2.Font = myFont;
this.label3.Font = myFont;
```

All three labels will display the same font: size 16 Courier New. If you want to change the font size or style later, you change it only in the one location where it is defined.

The Font class includes a number of overloaded constructors. For example, you can create a Font using two arguments (a type and a size) as follows:

```
System.Drawing.Font myFavoriteFont = new
    System.Drawing.Font("Courier New", 12.5F);
```

The string you pass to the Font constructor is the name of the font. If you use a font name that does not exist in your system, the Font defaults to Microsoft Sans Serif. The second value is a float that represents the font size. Notice that you must use an *F* (or an *f*) following the Font size value constant when it contains a decimal point to ensure that the constant will be recognized as a float and not a double. The Font constructor parameter list contains a float for size; using a double will generate a compiler error indicating that the double cannot be converted to a float. (If you use an int as the font size, you do not need

>>> **NOTE**
If you want to change the properties of several objects at once in the IDE, you can drag your mouse around them to create a temporary group, and then change the property for all of them with one entry in the Properties list.

the *f*, because the `int` will automatically be cast to a `float`, but a numeric constant such as 12.5 is a `double` by default.) An alternative would be to instantiate a `float` constant or variable, as in the following example, and use its name in the argument to the `Font` constructor:

```
const float PREFERRED_SIZE = 12.5f;
```

You also can create a `Font` using three arguments, adding a `FontStyle`, as in the following example:

```
Font aFancyFont = new Font("Arial", 24, FontStyle.Italic);
```

Table 11-3 lists the available `FontStyle`s. You can combine multiple styles using the pipe (|), which is also called the logical OR. For example, the following code creates a `Font` that is bold and underlined:

```
Font boldAndUnderlined = new Font("Helvetica",
    10, FontStyle.Bold | FontStyle.Underline);
```

Member Name	Description
Bold	Bold text
Italic	Italic text
Regular	Normal text
Strikeout	Text with a line through the middle
Underline	Underlined text

Table 11-3 `FontStyle` enumeration

Once you have defined a `Font`, you can set a `Label`'s `Font` with a statement like the following:

```
this.label1.Font = myFavoriteFont;
```

Alternatively, you can create and assign an anonymous `Font` in one step. In other words, you do not provide an identifier for the `Font`, as in this example:

```
this.label1.Font = new
    System.DrawingFont("Courier New", 12.5F);
```

>> **NOTE**
If you don't provide an identifier for a `Font`, you can't reuse it. You will have to create it again to use it with additional `Control`s.

USING A `LinkLabel`

A **`LinkLabel`** is similar to a `Label`; it is a child of `Label`. Therefore, you can use it like a `Label`, but it provides the additional capability to link the user to other sources, such as Web pages or files. Table 11-4 summarizes the properties and lists the default event method for a `LinkLabel`. The **default event** for a `Control` is:

» The method whose shell is automatically created when you double-click the `Control` while designing a project in the IDE
» The method that you are most likely to alter when you use the `Control`
» The event that users most likely expect to generate when they encounter the `Control` in a working application

USING CONTROLS

With many `Control`s, including a `LinkLabel`, a mouse click by the user triggers the default event. When designing a program, you can double-click a `Control` in the IDE to generate a method shell, and then write any necessary statements within the shell.

Property or Method	Description
`ActiveLinkColor`	The color of the link when it is clicked
`LinkColor`	The original color of links before they have been visited; usually blue by default
`LinkVisited`	If `true`, the link's color is changed to the `VisitedLinkColor`
`VisitedLinkColor`	The color of a link after it has been visited; usually purple by default
`LinkClicked()`	Default event that is generated when the link is clicked by the user

Table 11-4 Commonly used `LinkLabel` properties and default event

>> **NOTE** The default event for many `Control`s, such as `Button`s and `LinkLabel`s, occurs when the user clicks the `Control`. However, the default event for a `Form` is the `Load()` method. In other words, if you double-click a `Form` in the IDE, you generate this method. In it, you can place statements that execute as soon as a `Form` is loaded.

When you create a `LinkLabel`, it appears as underlined text. The text is blue by default, but you can change the color in the `LinkLabel` Properties list in the IDE. When you pass the mouse pointer over a `LinkLabel`, the pointer changes to a hand; you have seen similar behavior while using hyperlinks in Web pages. When a user clicks a `LinkLabel`, it generates a click event, just as clicking a `Button` does. When a click event is fired from a `LinkLabel`, a `LinkClicked()` method is executed, similar to how clicking a `Button` can execute a `Click()` method.

>> **NOTE** You can create a program so that a user generates an event by clicking many types of objects. For example, for a `Label` named `label1`, you could write statements in a `label1_Click()` method. However, users do not usually expect to click `Label`s, but they do expect to click `LinkLabel`s.

Figure 11-6 shows a `Form` onto which two `LinkLabel`s have been dragged from the Toolbox in the IDE. The `Text` properties of the `LinkLabel`s have been changed to "Course Technology Website" and "Read our policy".

CHAPTER ELEVEN

Figure 11-6 A Form with two LinkLabels

If you double-click a LinkLabel in the IDE, a method shell is created for you in the format xxx_LinkClicked(), where xxx is the value of the Name property assigned to the LinkLabel. (This corresponds to what happens when you double-click a Button in the IDE.) For example, Figure 11-7 shows the two generated methods for the Form in Figure 11-6 when the default LinkLabel identifiers linkLabel1 and linkLabel2 are used. In Figure 11-7, all the code was automatically generated except for the two shaded lines. The programmer added those lines to indicate which actions should occur when a user clicks the corresponding LinkLabel in a running application.

```
public partial class Form1 : Form
{
    public Form1()
    {
        InitializeComponent();
    }

    private void linkLabel1_LinkClicked(object sender,
       LinkLabelLinkClickedEventArgs e)
    {
        System.Diagnostics.Process.Start("IExplore",
           "http://www.course.com");
    }

    private void linkLabel2_LinkClicked(object sender,
       LinkLabelLinkClickedEventArgs e)
    {
        System.Diagnostics.Process.Start
           (@"C:\C#\Chapter.11\Policy.txt");
    }
}
```

Figure 11-7 Two LinkClicked() methods

In each of the `LinkClicked()` methods in Figure 11-7, the programmer has added a call to `System.Diagnostics.Process.Start()`. This method allows you to run other programs from within an application. The `Start()` method has two overloaded versions:

» When you use one `string` argument, you open the named file.
» When you use two arguments, you open an application and provide its needed arguments.

In the `linkLabel1_LinkClicked()` method, the two arguments open Internet Explorer ("`IExplore`") and pass it the address of the Course Technology Web site. If an Internet connection is active, control transfers to the Web site.

In the `linkLabel2_LinkClicked()` method, only one argument is provided. It opens a file stored on the local disk. Figure 11-8 shows the text file that opens when the user clicks the link. By default, Notepad opens to display the policy because Notepad is the default application for a file with a .txt extension. Alternatively, you could code the following, which explicitly names Notepad as the application:

```
System.Diagnostics.Process.Start("Notepad",
    @"C:\C#\Chapter.11\Policy.txt");
```

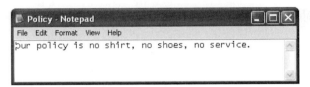

Figure 11-8 Text file opened by `linkLabel2_LinkClicked()` method

> **NOTE** In the `linkLabel2_LinkClicked()` method, an at sign (@) appears in front of the filename to be opened. This symbol indicates that all characters in the string should be interpreted literally. Therefore, the backslashes in the path are not interpreted as escape sequence characters.

The `LinkVisited` property can be set to `true` when you determine that a user has clicked a link, as shown in Figure 11-9. This setting indicates that the link should be displayed in a different color so the user can see the link has been visited. By default, the visited link color is purple, but you can change this setting in the Properties list for the `LinkLabel`.

```
private void linkLabel1_LinkClicked(object sender,
    LinkLabelLinkClickedEventArgs e)
{
    System.Diagnostics.Process.Start("IExplore",
        "http://www.course.com");
    linkLabel1.LinkVisited = true;
}
```

Figure 11-9 Setting the `LinkVisited` property

CHAPTER ELEVEN

ADDING COLOR TO A Form

The `Color` class contains a wide variety of predefined `Color`s that you can use with your `Control`s (see Table 11-5).

> **NOTE** C# also allows you to create custom colors. If no color in Table 11-5 suits your needs, search for "custom color" in the Visual Studio Help to obtain more information.

AliceBlue	DarkKhaki	GreenYellow	Linen
AntiqueWhite	DarkMagenta	Honeydew	Magenta
Aqua	DarkOliveGreen	HotPink	Maroon
Aquamarine	DarkOrange	IndianRed	MediumAquamarine
Azure	DarkOrchid	Indigo	MediumBlue
Beige	DarkRed	Ivory	MediumOrchid
Bisque	DarkSalmon	Khaki	MediumPurple
Black	DarkSeaGreen	Lavender	MediumSeaGreen
BlanchedAlmond	DarkSlateBlue	LavenderBlush	MediumSlateBlue
Blue	DarkSlateGray	LawnGreen	MediumSpringGreen
BlueViolet	DarkTurquoise	LemonChiffon	MediumTurquoise
Brown	DarkViolet	LightBlue	MediumVioletRed
BurlyWood	DeepPink	LightCoral	MidnightBlue
CadetBlue	DeepSkyBlue	LightCyan	MintCream
Chartreuse	DimGray	LightGoldenrodYellow	MistyRose
Chocolate	DodgerBlue	LightGray	Moccasin
Coral	Firebrick	LightGreen	NavajoWhite
CornflowerBlue	FloralWhite	LightPink	Navy
Cornsilk	ForestGreen	LightSalmon	OldLace
Crimson	Fuchsia	LightSeaGreen	Olive
Cyan	Gainsboro	LightSkyBlue	OliveDrab
DarkBlue	GhostWhite	LightSlateGray	Orange
DarkCyan	Gold	LightSteelBlue	OrangeRed
DarkGoldenrod	Goldenrod	LightYellow	Orchid
DarkGray	Gray	Lime	PaleGoldenrod
DarkGreen	Green	LimeGreen	PaleGreen

Table 11-5 `Color` properties (*continued*)

PaleTurquoise	RoyalBlue	Snow	White
PaleVioletRed	SaddleBrown	SpringGreen	WhiteSmoke
PapayaWhip	Salmon	SteelBlue	Yellow
PeachPuff	SandyBrown	Tan	YellowGreen
Peru	SeaGreen	Teal	
Pink	SeaShell	Thistle	
Plum	Sienna	Tomato	
PowderBlue	Silver	Transparent	
Purple	SkyBlue	Turquoise	
Red	SlateBlue	Violet	
RosyBrown	SlateGray	Wheat	

Table 11-5 (*continued*)

When you are designing a `Form`, you can choose colors from a list next to the `BackColor` and `ForeColor` properties in the IDE's Properties list. The statements created will be similar to the following:

```
this.label1.BackColor = System.Drawing.Color.Blue;
this.label1.ForeColor = System.Drawing.Color.Gold;
```

>> **NOTE** If you add `using System.Drawing;` at the top of your file, you can eliminate the references in the preceding lines and refer to the colors simply as `Color.Blue` and `Color.Gold`.

>> **NOTE** For professional-looking results when you prepare a resume or most other business documents, business executives recommend that you only use one or two fonts and colors, even though your word-processing program allows many such selections. The same is true when you design interactive GUI applications. Although many fonts and colors are available, you probably should stick with a few choices in a single project.

USING CheckBox AND RadioButton OBJECTS

In Chapter 10, you placed `Button` objects on a `Form`. The `Button` class derives from the `ButtonBase` class. The `ButtonBase` class has two other descendants: `CheckBox` and `RadioButton`.

CheckBox objects are GUI widgets the user can click to select or deselect an option. When a `Form` contains multiple `CheckBoxes`, any number of them can be checked or unchecked at the same time. **RadioButtons** are similar to `CheckBoxes`, except that when they are placed on a `Form`, only one `RadioButton` can be selected at a time—selecting any `RadioButton` automatically deselects the others. Table 11-6 contains commonly used `CheckBox` properties

CHAPTER ELEVEN

and the default event for which a method shell is generated when you double-click a `CheckBox` in the IDE. Table 11-7 contains the properties and default event for `RadioButton`s.

Property or Method	Description
Checked	Indicates whether the `CheckBox` is checked
CheckState	Indicates whether the `CheckBox` is checked, with a value for the `CheckState` enumeration (`Checked`, `Unchecked`, or `Indeterminate`)
Text	The text displayed to the right of the `CheckBox`
CheckedChanged()	Default event that is generated when the `Checked` property changes

Table 11-6 Commonly used `CheckBox` properties and default event

> **NOTE** If you precede a letter in the `Text` property value of a `ButtonBase` object with an ampersand (&), that letter acts as an access key. For example, if a `Button`'s text is defined as `&Press`, then typing Alt + P has the same effect as clicking the `Button`. Access keys are also called hot keys.

Property or Method	Description
Checked	Indicates whether the `RadioButton` is checked
Text	The text displayed to the right of the `RadioButton`
CheckedChanged()	Default event that is generated when the `Checked` property changes

Table 11-7 Commonly used `RadioButton` properties and default event

> **NOTE** You can place multiple groups of `RadioButton`s on a `Form` by using a `GroupBox` or `Panel`. For example, if you place several `GroupBox` `Control`s on a `Form` and you place several `RadioButton`s in each `GroupBox`, then one `RadioButton` can be selected from each `GroupBox` at any point in time; in other words, each `GroupBox` operates independently. You will learn more about `GroupBox`es and `Panel`s later in this chapter.

Figure 11-10 shows an example of a `Form` that contains four `CheckBox` objects and three `RadioButton` objects. It makes sense for the pizza topping choices to be displayed using `CheckBox`es because a user might select multiple toppings. However, options for delivery, pick-up, and dining in the restaurant are mutually exclusive, so they are presented using `RadioButton` objects.

USING CONTROLS

Figure 11-10 A Form with CheckBoxes and RadioButtons

Both CheckBox and RadioButton objects have a Checked property whose value is true or false. For example, if you create a CheckBox named extraToppings and you want to add $1.00 to a pizzaPrice value when the user checks the box, you can write the following:

```
if(extraToppings.Checked)
   pizzaPrice = pizzaPrice + 1.00;
```

Both CheckBox and RadioButton objects also have a CheckedChanged() method that is called when a user clicks any CheckBox or RadioButton.

Suppose the total price of a pizza should be altered based on a user's selections. In this example, the base price for a pizza is $12.00, and $1.25 is added for a topping. You can declare constants for the BASE_PRICE and TOPPING_PRICE of a pizza and declare a variable that is initialized to the pizza base price as follows:

```
private const double BASE_PRICE = 12.00;
private const double TOPPING_PRICE = 1.25;
private double price = BASE_PRICE;
```

Figure 11-11 shows some of the code you would add to the Form.cs file for the application. The checkBox1_CheckedChanged() method changes the pizza price. The shaded statements in the method were written by a programmer; the unshaded statements were generated by the IDE. If a change occurs because the checkBox was checked, then the TOPPING_PRICE is added to the price. If the change to the checkBox was to uncheck it, the TOPPING_PRICE is subtracted from the price. Either way, the Text property of a Label is changed to reflect the new price. Figure 11-12 shows the Form after the user has checked a box, checked another box, and then unchecked a box. Figure 11-13 shows the entire Form.cs file.

CHAPTER ELEVEN

```
private void checkBox1_CheckedChanged(object sender, EventArgs e)
{
    if (cheeseCheckBox.Checked)
        price += TOPPING_PRICE;
    else
        price -= TOPPING_PRICE;
    totalLabel.Text = "Total is " + price.ToString("C");
}
```

Figure 11-11 The checkBox1_CheckedChanged() method

Figure 11-12 Execution of CheckBoxAndRadioButtonDemo program

```
using System;
using System.Collections.Generic;
using System.ComponentModel;
using System.Data;
using System.Drawing;
using System.Text;
using System.Windows.Forms;

namespace CheckBoxAndRadioButtonDemo
{
    public partial class Form1 : Form
    {
        private const double BASE_PRICE = 12.00;
        private const double TOPPING_PRICE = 1.25;
        private double price = BASE_PRICE;
        public Form1()
        {
            InitializeComponent();
        }
```

Figure 11-13 The Forms.cs file of the CheckBoxAndRadioButtonDemo application (*continued*)

USING CONTROLS

```csharp
        private void checkBox1_CheckedChanged(object sender, EventArgs e)
        {
            if (cheeseCheckBox.Checked)
                price += TOPPING_PRICE;
            else
                price -= TOPPING_PRICE;
            totalLabel.Text = "Total is " + price.ToString("C");
        }

        private void checkBox2_CheckedChanged(object sender, EventArgs e)
        {
            if (sausageCheckBox.Checked)
                price += TOPPING_PRICE;
            else
                price -= TOPPING_PRICE;
            totalLabel.Text = "Total is " + price.ToString("C");
        }

        private void checkBox3_CheckedChanged(object sender, EventArgs e)
        {
            if (pepperoniCheckBox.Checked)
                price += TOPPING_PRICE;
            else
                price -= TOPPING_PRICE;
            totalLabel.Text = "Total is " + price.ToString("C");
        }

        private void checkBox4_CheckedChanged(object sender, EventArgs e)
        {
            if (onionCheckBox.Checked)
                price += TOPPING_PRICE;
            else
                price -= TOPPING_PRICE;
            totalLabel.Text = "Total is " + price.ToString("C");
        }
    }
}
```

Figure 11-13 (*continued*)

CHAPTER ELEVEN

> **NOTE** When you place RadioButtons on a Form, one is selected by default. If you want to start an application with no RadioButtons selected, you can add an extra "dummy" RadioButton to the Form, set its Visible property to false, and then set the dummy RadioButton's Checked property to true in the Form_Load() method.

ADDING A PictureBox TO A Form

A **PictureBox** is a Control in which you can display graphics from a bitmap, icon, JPEG, GIF, or other image file type. Just as with a Button or a Label, you can easily drag a PictureBox Control onto a Form in the Visual Studio IDE. Table 11-8 shows the common properties and default event for a PictureBox.

Property or Method	Description
Image	Sets the image that appears in the PictureBox
SizeMode	Controls the size and position of the image in the PictureBox; values are Normal, StretchImage (which resizes the image to fit the PictureBox), AutoSize (which resizes the PictureBox to fit the image), and CenterImage (which centers the image in the PictureBox)
Click()	Default event that is generated when the user clicks the PictureBox

Table 11-8 Commonly used PictureBox properties and default event

Figure 11-14 shows a new project in the IDE. The following tasks have been completed:

» The project was started.
» The Form Text property was changed to "Save money".
» The Form BackColor property was changed to White.
» A Label was dragged onto the Form, and its Text and Font were changed.
» A PictureBox was dragged onto the Form.

433

USING CONTROLS

> **NOTE**
> Your title bar or other features might be slightly different if you are using a different edition of Microsoft Visual Studio.

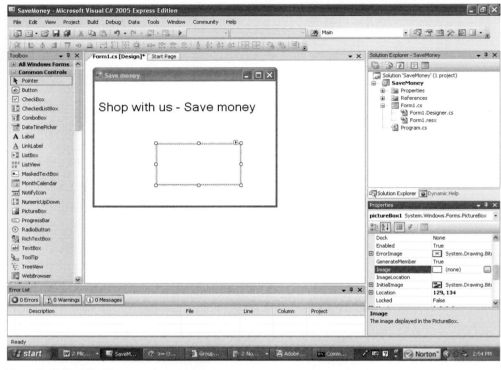

Figure 11-14 The IDE with a `Form` that contains a `PictureBox`

In Figure 11-14, in the Properties list at the right of the screen, the Image property is set to *none*. If you click the button with the ellipsis, a Select Resource window appears, as shown on the left in Figure 11-15. When you click the button, you can browse for stored images. When you select one, you see a preview in the Select Resource window, as shown on the right in Figure 11-15.

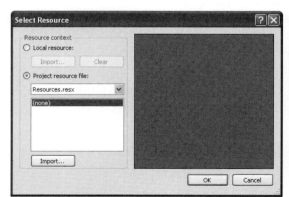 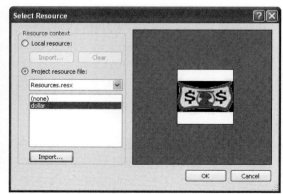

Figure 11-15 Select Resource window before and after image is selected

CHAPTER ELEVEN

After you click OK, the image appears in the `PictureBox`, as in Figure 11-16. In the Solution Explorer on the right side of the IDE, notice that the dollar.jpg file has been added to the project.

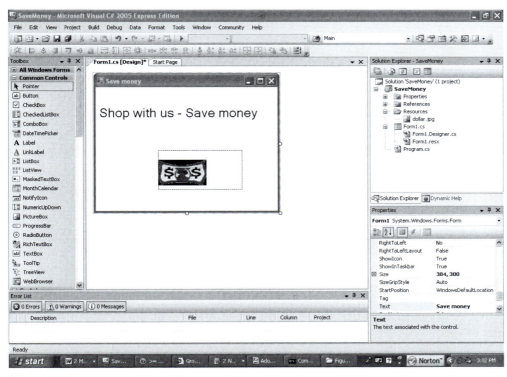

Figure 11-16 The `SaveMoney` project with an inserted image

If you examine the generated code, you can find the statements that instantiate a `PictureBox` (named `pictureBox1` by default) and statements that set its properties, such as `Size` and `Location`.

ADDING `ListBox`, `CheckedListBox`, AND `ComboBox` Controls TO A Form

`Button`s, `RadioButton`s, and `CheckBox`es represent a GUI family because they all descend from the `ButtonBase` class and they all share certain characteristics. Similarly, `ListBox`, `ComboBox`, and `CheckedListBox` objects descend from the same family—they all are list-type widgets that descend from `ListControl`. Of course, they are also `Control`s and so inherit properties such as `Text` and `BackColor` from the `Control` class. Other properties are more specific to list-type objects. Table 11-9 describes some commonly used `ListBox` properties.

USING CONTROLS

Property or Method	Description
Items	The collection of items in the ListBox; frequently, these are strings, but they can also be other types of objects
MultiColumn	Indicates whether display can be in multiple columns
SelectedIndex	Returns the index of the selected item. It no item has been selected, the value is −1. Otherwise, it is a value from 0 through $n-1$, where n is the number of items in the ListBox.
SelectedIndices	Returns a collection of all the selected indices (when SelectionMode is more than One)
SelectedItem	Returns a reference to the selected item
SelectedItems	Returns a collection of the selected items (when SelectionMode is more than One)
SelectionMode	Determines how many items can be selected (see Table 11-10)
Sorted	Sorts the items when set to true
SelectedIndexChanged()	Default event that is generated when the selected index changes

Table 11-9 Commonly used ListBox properties and default event

Figure 11-17 shows a typical ListBox on a Form. The **ListBox** Control enables you to display a list of items that the user can select by clicking. After you drag a ListBox onto a Form, you can select its Items property and type a list into a String Collection Editor, as shown on the right in Figure 11-17.

Figure 11-17 The String Collection Editor filling a ListBox and the completed ListBox on a Form

When you fill the String Collection Editor with the strings in Figure 11-17, the following code is generated in the `InitializeComponent()` method:

```
this.listBox1.Items.AddRange(new object[] {
        "English",
        "Math",
        "Biology",
        "Chemistry",
        "Spanish",
        ""});
```

With a `ListBox`, you allow the user to make a single selection or multiple selections by setting the `SelectionMode` property appropriately. For example, when the `SelectionMode` property is set to `One`, the user can make only a single selection from the `ListBox`. When the `SelectionMode` is set to `MultiExtended`, pressing Shift and clicking the mouse or pressing Shift and one of the arrow keys (up, down, left, or right) extends the selection to span from the previously selected item to the current item. Pressing Ctrl and clicking the mouse selects or deselects an item in the list. Table 11-10 lists the possible `SelectionMode` values.

> **NOTE** When the `SelectionMode` property is set to `SelectionMode.MultiSimple`, click the mouse or press the spacebar to select or deselect an item in the list.

Member Name	Description
MultiExtended	Multiple items can be selected, and the user can press the Shift, Ctrl, and arrow keys to make selections
MultiSimple	Multiple items can be selected
None	No items can be selected
One	Only one item can be selected

Table 11-10 `SelectionMode` enumeration list

For example, within a `Form`'s `Load()` method (the one that executes when a `Form` is first loaded), you could add the following:

```
this.listBox1.SelectionMode =
    System.Windows.Forms.SelectionMode.MultiExtended;
```

When you size a `ListBox` so that all the items cannot be displayed at the same time, a scroll bar is provided automatically on the side. The `ListBox` also provides the Boolean `MultiColumn` property, which you can set to display items in columns instead of a straight vertical list. This approach allows the control to display more items and avoids the need for the user to scroll down to an item.

USING CONTROLS

The SelectedItem property of a ListBox contains the value of the item a user has selected. For example, if you add a Label with the Text property "You selected: " in Figure 11-17, you can modify the label's Text property in the listBox1_SelectedIndexChanged method with a statement such as the following:

```
private void listBox1_SelectedIndexChanged
    (object sender, EventArgs e)
{
    label2.Text += listBox1.SelectedItem;
}
```

The SelectedItem is appended to the label. Figure 11-18 shows a typical result.

> **NOTE** With this code, the user's selection is appended to the text. If the user continues to make selections, the Text for label2 will continue to grow longer. Depending on your application, you might prefer to replace the Text for the label instead of adding to it.

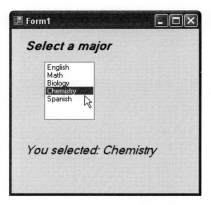

Figure 11-18 PickAMajor application after user has chosen *Chemistry*

The Items.Count property of a ListBox object holds the number of items in the ListBox. The GetSelected() method accepts an integer argument representing the array position of an item in the list. The method returns true if an item is selected and false if it is not. Therefore, code like the following could be used to count the number of selections a user makes from listbox1:

```
int count = 0;
for(int x = 0; x < listBox1.Items.Count; ++x)
    if(listBox1.GetSelected(x))
        ++count;
```

CHAPTER ELEVEN

The `SetSelected()` method can be used to set a `ListBox` item to be automatically selected by default. For example, the following statement causes the first item in `listBox1` to be the selected one:

```
listBox1.SetSelected(0, true);
```

A **ComboBox** is similar to a `ListBox`, except that it displays an additional editing field to allow the user to select from the list or to enter new text. The default `ComboBox` displays an editing field with a hidden list box. A **CheckedListBox** is also similar to a `ListBox`, with check boxes appearing to the left of each desired item.

ADDING MonthCalendar AND DateTimePicker ControlS TO A Form

The **MonthCalendar** and **DateTimePicker** Controls allow you to retrieve date and time information. Figure 11-19 shows a `MonthCalendar` that has been placed on a `Form`. The current date is contained in a rectangle by default, and the date that the user clicked is shaded. Controls at the top of the calendar allow the user to go forward or back one month at a time. Table 11-11 describes common `MonthCalendar` properties and the default event.

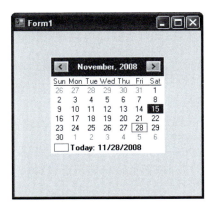

Figure 11-19 A typical `MonthCalendar`

USING CONTROLS

Property or Method	Description
`MaxDate`	Sets the last day that can be selected (the default is 12/31/9998)
`MaxSelectionCount`	Sets the maximum number of dates that can be selected at once (the default is 7)
`MinDate`	Sets the first day that can be selected (the default is 1/1/1753)
`MonthlyBoldedDates`	An array of dates that appear in boldface in the calendar; for example, holidays
`SelectionEnd`	The last of a range of dates selected by the user
`SelectionRange`	The dates selected by the user
`SelectionStart`	The first of a range of dates selected by the user
`ShowToday`	If `true`, the date displays in text at the bottom of the calendar
`ShowTodayCircle`	If `true`, today's date is circled (the "circle" appears as a square)
`DateChanged()`	Default event that is generated when the user selects a date

Table 11-11 Commonly used `MonthCalendar` properties and default event

>> **NOTE** If you set the `MinDate` value to the `MonthCalendar`'s `TodayDate` property, the user cannot select a date before today. For example, you cannot make appointments or schedule deliveries to happen in the past, so you might code the following:
>
> ```
> monthCalendar1.MinDate = monthCalendar1.TodayDate;
> ```
>
> Conversely, you might want to prevent users from selecting a date in the future—for example, if the user is entering the date he placed an outstanding order. In that case, you could code a statement similar to the following:
>
> ```
> monthCalendar1.MaxDate = monthCalendar1.TodayDate;
> ```

You can use several useful methods with the `SelectionStart` and `SelectionEnd` properties of `MonthCalendar`, including the following:

- » `ToShortDateString()`, which displays the date in the format 2/13/2009
- » `ToLongDateString()`, which displays the date in the format Friday, February 13, 2009
- » `AddDays()`, which takes a `double` argument and adds a specified number of days to the date
- » `AddMonths()`, which takes an `int` argument and adds a specified number of months to the date
- » `AddYears()`, which takes an `int` argument and adds a specified number of years to the date

>> **NOTE** The `AddDays()` method accepts a `double` argument because you can add fractional days to `SelectionStart` and `SelectionEnd`.

CHAPTER ELEVEN

> **NOTE** `SelectionStart` and `SelectionEnd` are structures of the `DateTime` type. Chapter 13 contains additional information about using `DateTime` objects to determine when files were created, modified, or accessed.

Many business and financial applications use `AddDays()`, `AddMonths()`, and `AddYears()` to calculate dates for events, such as payment for a bill (perhaps due in 10 days from an order) or scheduling a salesperson's callback to a customer (perhaps two months after initial contact). The default event for `MonthCalendar` is `DateChanged()`. For example, Figure 11-20 shows a method that executes when the user clicks a `MonthCalendar` named `cal`. A string is created from the literal text "You selected " and the start of the user's selection is converted to a short `string`. Figure 11-21 shows the output when the user selects February 27, 2008. The date that is 10 days in the future is correctly calculated as March 8.

```
private void cal_DateChanged(object sender,
   DateRangeEventArgs e)
{
   string newDate = "You selected " +
      cal.SelectionStart.ToShortDateString();
   label1.Text = newDate + "\nTen days from now is " +
      cal.SelectionStart.AddDays(10).ToShortDateString();
}
```

Figure 11-20 CalendarDemo application `cal_DateChanged()` method

Figure 11-21 Typical execution of `CalendarDemo`

The `DateTimePicker Control` displays a month calendar when the down arrow is selected. For example, Figure 11-22 shows a `DateTimePicker` before and after the user clicks the down arrow.

USING CONTROLS

Figure 11-22 The `DateTimePicker` Control

When you use the `CustomFormat` property, the date displayed in a `DateTimePicker Control` is more customizable than the one in a `MonthCalendar`. Table 11-12 describes some commonly used `DateTimePicker` properties and the default event.

Property or Method	Description
`CalendarForeColor`	Sets the calendar text color
`CalendarMonthBackground`	Sets the calendar background color
`CustomFormat`	A string value that uses codes to set a custom date and time format. For example, to display the date and time as `02/13/2009 12:00 PM - Friday`, set this property to "MM' /' dd' /' yyyy hh' :' mm tt - dddd". See the C# documentation for a complete set of format string characters.
`Format`	Sets the format for the date or time. Options are `Long` (for example, Friday, November 28, 2008), `Short` (11/28/2008), and `Time` (for example, 3:15:01 PM). You can also create a `CustomFormat`.
`Value`	The data selected by the user
`ValueChanged()`	Default event that is generated when the `Value` property changes

Table 11-12 Commonly used `DateTimePicker` properties and default event

CHAPTER ELEVEN

WORKING WITH A Form'S LAYOUT

When you place Controls on a Form in the IDE, you can drag them to any location to achieve the effect you want.

When you drag multiple Controls onto a Form, blue **snap lines** appear and help you align new Controls with others already in place. Figure 11-23 shows two snap lines that you can use to align a second label below the first one. Snap lines also appear when you place a control closer to the edge of a container than is recommended.

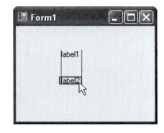

Figure 11-23 Snap lines in the Visual Studio Designer

You also can use the Location property in the Properties list to specify a location. With either technique, code like the following is generated:

```
this.label1.Location = new System.Drawing.Point(23, 19);
```

Several other properties can help you to manage the appearance of a Form (or other ContainerControl).

For example, setting the **Anchor property** causes a Control to remain at a fixed distance from the side of a container when the user resizes it. Figure 11-24 shows the Properties window for a Label that has been placed on a Form. The Anchor property has a drop-down window that lets you select or deselect the sides to which the label should be anchored. For most Controls, the default setting for Anchor is Top, Left.

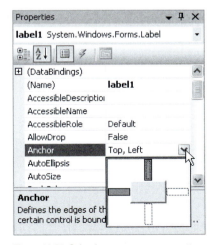

Figure 11-24 Selecting an Anchor property

443

Figure 11-25 shows a `Form` with two `Label`s. On the `Form`, `label1` has been anchored to the top left and `label2` has been anchored to the bottom right. The left side of the figure shows the `Form` as it first appears to the user, and the right side shows the `Form` after the user has resized it. Anchoring is useful when users expect a specific control to always be in the same general location in a container.

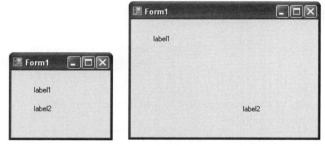

Figure 11-25 A `Form` with two `Label`s anchored to opposite corners

Setting the **Dock property** attaches a `Control` to the side of a container so that the `Control` stretches when the container's size is adjusted. Figure 11-26 shows the drop-down `Dock` Properties window for a `Button`. You can select any region in the window. Figure 11-27 shows a `Button` docked to the bottom of a `Form` before and after the `Form` has been resized.

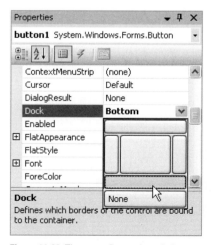

Figure 11-26 The `Dock` Properties window

Figure 11-27 A `Form` with a docked `Button`

A `Form` has a **Padding property** that specifies the distance between docked `Controls` and the edges of the `Form`. The `Padding` property has four values—one for each side of the `Form` (left, top, right, and bottom). They are set to 0 by default. Figure 11-28 shows the docked button from Figure 11-27 when the padding values have been set to 0, 0, 10, and 20.

Figure 11-28 A docked button with padding

A `Form` also has a **MinimumSize property** and a **MaximumSize property**. Each has two values—`Width` and `Height`. If you set these properties, the user cannot make the `Form` smaller or larger than you have specified. If you do not want the user to be able to adjust a `Form`'s size at all, set the `MinimumSize` and `MaximumSize` properties to be equal.

UNDERSTANDING GroupBoxES AND PanelS

Many types of `ContainerControls` are available to hold `Controls`. For example, you can use a **GroupBox** or **Panel** to group related `Controls` on a `Form`. When you move a `GroupBox` or `Panel`, all its `Controls` are moved as a group. To create either of these `Controls`, you drag it from the Toolbox in the IDE, and then drag the `Controls` you want on top of it. `GroupBoxes` can display a caption, but `Panels` cannot. `Panels` can include a scroll bar that the user can manipulate to view `Controls`; `GroupBoxes` do not have scroll bars. You can anchor or dock `Controls` inside a `GroupBox` or `Panel`, and you can anchor or dock a `GroupBox` or `Panel` inside a `Form`. Doing this provides `Control` groups that easily can be arranged.

ADDING A MenuStrip TO A Form

Most programs you use in a Windows environment contain a **menu strip**, which is a horizontal list of general options that appears under the title bar of a `Form` or `Window`. When you click an item in a menu strip, you might initiate an action. More frequently, you see a list box that contains more specific options. Each of these might initiate an action, or it might lead to another menu. For example, the Visual Studio IDE contains a horizontal main menu strip that begins with the options File, Edit, and View. You have used word-processing, spreadsheet, and even game programs with similar menus.

You can add a **MenuStrip** `Control` object to any `Form` you create. Using the Visual Studio IDE, you can add a `MenuStrip` to a `Form` by dragging it onto the `Form`. This creates a menu bar horizontally across the top of the `Form`, just below the title bar. Figure 11-29 shows a `MenuStrip` dragged onto a `Form`. The strip extends across the width of the `Form` and contains a "Type Here" text box. When you click the text box, you can enter a menu item. New text boxes appear below and to the right of the first one. Each time you add a menu item, new boxes are created so you can see where your next options will go.

USING CONTROLS

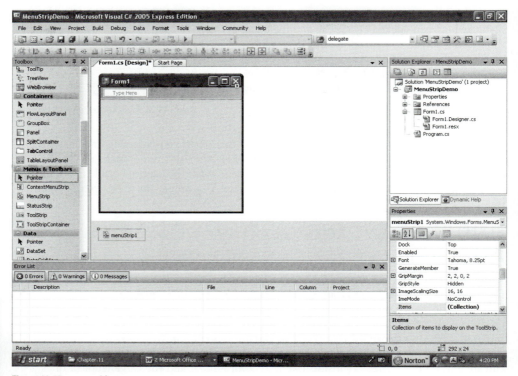

Figure 11-29 Form with MenuStrip

> **NOTE**
> Click the MenuStrip icon at the bottom of the design screen to view and change the properties for the MenuStrip. For example, you might want to change the Font or BackColor for the MenuStrip.

Figure 11-30 shows a MenuStrip in which the programmer has typed *Font*, and beneath it, *Large* and *Small*. New boxes are available to the right of Font and beneath Small. Figure 11-31 shows that the programmer continued by entering *Color* and three choices beneath it.

Figure 11-30 Form that contains MenuStrip with a few entries

Figure 11-31 Form that contains MenuStrip with more entries

446

CHAPTER ELEVEN

When you double-click an entry in the `MenuStrip`, a `Click()` method is generated. For example, if you click Large in the menu shown in Figure 11-31, the method generated is `largeToolStripMenuItem_Click()`, as follows:

```
private void largeToolStripMenuItem_Click
    (object sender, EventArgs e)
{
}
```

>> **NOTE**
If possible, your main menu selections should be single words. That way, a user will not mistakenly think that a single menu item represents multiple items.

As with all the other controls you have learned about, you can write any code statements you like within the method. For example, suppose a `Label` named `label1` has been dragged onto the `Form`. If choosing the Large menu option should result in a larger font for the label, you might code the method as follows:

```
private void largeToolStripMenuItem_Click
   (object sender, EventArgs e)
{
    label1.Font = new Font("Courier", 34);
}
```

>> **NOTE**
If you create each main menu item with an ampersand (&) in front of a unique letter, then the user can press Alt and the initial letter to activate the menu choice, besides clicking it with the mouse.

With the addition of this method, the `Form` operates as shown in Figure 11-32. If the `Label` appears in a small font and the user clicks the Large menu option, the font changes.

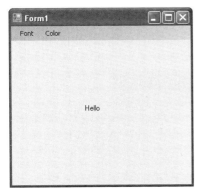
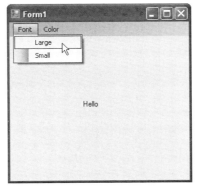

Figure 11-32 Executing the `MenuStripDemo` program

>> **NOTE** Users expect menu options to appear in conventional order. For example, users expect the far-left option on the main menu to be File, and they expect the Exit option to appear under File. Similarly, if an application contains a Help option, users expect to find it at the right side of the main menu. You should follow these conventions when designing your own main menus.

>> **NOTE**
You can work with the other menu items in this program in an exercise at the end of this chapter.

447

USING CONTROLS

USING OTHER Controls

If you examine the Visual Studio IDE or search through the Visual Studio documentation, you will find many other Controls that are not covered in this chapter. If you click **Project** on the main menu and click **Add New Item**, you can add extra Forms, Files, Controls, and other elements to your project. New controls and containers will be developed in the future, and you might even design new controls of your own. Still, all controls will contain properties and methods, and your solid foundation in C# will prepare you to use new controls effectively.

YOU DO IT

ADDING Labels TO A Form AND CHANGING THEIR PROPERTIES

>> **NOTE** The screen images in the next steps represent a typical Visual Studio environment. Based on options you selected in your installation, your screen might look different.

In the next steps, you will begin to create an application for Bailey's Bed and Breakfast. The main Form allows the user to select one of two suites and discover the amenities and price associated with each choice. You will start by placing two Labels on a Form and setting several of their properties.

To create a Form with Labels:

1. Open Microsoft Visual Studio. You might be able to use a desktop shortcut, or you might click **Start** on the taskbar, point to **All Programs**, and click the version of C# you have installed (for example, **Microsoft Visual C# Express Edition**).

2. Click **File** on the menu bar and click **New Project**. A New Project window appears. In the window under Templates, click **Windows Application**. Near the bottom of the New Project window, click in the **Name** text box and replace the default name with **BedAndBreakfast**. See Figure 11-33.

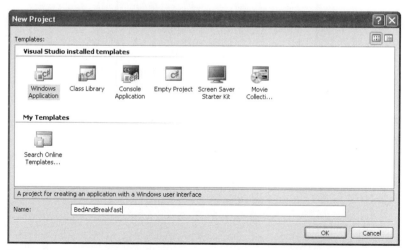

Figure 11-33 The New Project window for the BedAndBreakfast application

448

CHAPTER ELEVEN

3. Click **OK**. The design screen appears. The blank Form in the center of the screen has an empty title bar. Click the Form. The lower-right corner of the screen contains a Properties window that lists the Form's properties. In Figure 11-34, you can see that the Text property is set to **Form 1**.

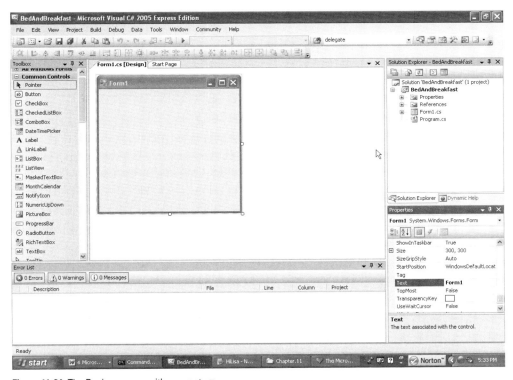

Figure 11-34 The Design screen with an empty Form

4. In the Properties list, click the description **Form 1** in the Settings box for the Text property. Delete **Form 1** and type **Bailey's Bed and Breakfast**. Press **Enter**; the title of the Form in the center of the screen changes to *Bailey's Bed and Breakfast*.

5. On the left side of the design screen, the Toolbox contains a list of components that can be added to a Form, including Buttons, CheckBoxes, Labels, and many others. Click **Label** and drag a Label onto the Form. When you release your mouse button, the Label appears on the Form and contains the default text "label1". On the right side of the screen under Properties, make sure the list box shows that you are viewing the properties for label1. If not, click label1 on the Form on the design screen.

449

USING CONTROLS

6. Change the Text property of label1 to **Welcome to Bailey's**, then press **Enter**; the text of the Label on the Form changes. Drag and resize the Label so it is close to the position of the Label in Figure 11-35. (If you prefer to set the Label's Location property manually in the Properties list, the Location should be **60, 30**.)

Figure 11-35 A Label placed on the Form in the BedAndBreakfast project

7. Make sure the Properties list still shows the properties for label1; if not, click the Label on the design screen. Locate the Font property in the Properties list. Currently, it lists the default font: Microsoft Sans Serif, 8.25 pt. Notice the ellipsis (three dots) at the right of the Font property name. (You might have to click in the Property to see the button.) Click the ellipsis to display the Font dialog box. Make selections to change the font to **Microsoft Sans Serif**, **18 point**, and **Italic**. Click **OK**. When you enlarge the Font for the Label, it is too close to the right edge of the Form. Drag it or change its Location property to approximately **32, 25**.

8. Drag a second Label onto the Form beneath the first one, and then set its Text property to **Check our rates**. Change its Location to approximately **76, 82** and its Font to **Microsoft Sans Serif, 12 point, Regular**.

9. Change the Name properties of the two labels so they are more descriptive. Change label1's Name to **mainLabel** and label2's Name to **checkRatesLabel**.

10. Save the project using one of the following methods: Click **File** on the menu bar and then click **Save All**, click the **Save All** button (which resembles a stack of diskettes), or press **Ctrl+Shift+S**. The project name and solution name (BedAndBreakfast) should already appear in the dialog box. You can browse for the location where you want to save the project. For example, you can choose the Chapter.11 folder on your Student Disk.

11. Click **Debug** on the menu bar and then click **Start Without Debugging**, or press **Ctrl+F5**. The Form appears, as shown in Figure 11-36.

12. Dismiss the Form by clicking the **Close** button in its upper-right corner.

Figure 11-36 The BedAndBreakfast Form

CHAPTER ELEVEN

EXAMINING THE CODE GENERATED BY THE IDE

In the next steps, you will examine the code generated by the IDE for at least two reasons:

- » To gain an understanding of the types of statements created by the IDE.
- » To lose any intimidation you might have about the code generated. You will recognize many of the C# statements.

To examine the generated code:

1. Click **View** on the menu bar and then click **Code** (or press **F7**) to view the code. As shown in Figure 11-37, you see the constructor for Form1 that calls the InitializeComponent() method.

```
using System;
using System.Collections.Generic;
using System.ComponentModel;
using System.Data;
using System.Drawing;
using System.Text;
using System.Windows.Forms;

namespace BedAndBreakfast
{
    public partial class Form1 : Form
    {
        public Form1()
        {
            InitializeComponent();
        }
    }
}
```

Figure 11-37 The Form1.cs code

2. In the Solution Explorer at the right side of the screen, double-click the **Form1.Designer.cs** filename. Scroll to the bottom of the exposed code. As Figure 11-38 shows, mainLabel and checkRatesLabel objects have been declared as Labels using the names you provided for them.

451

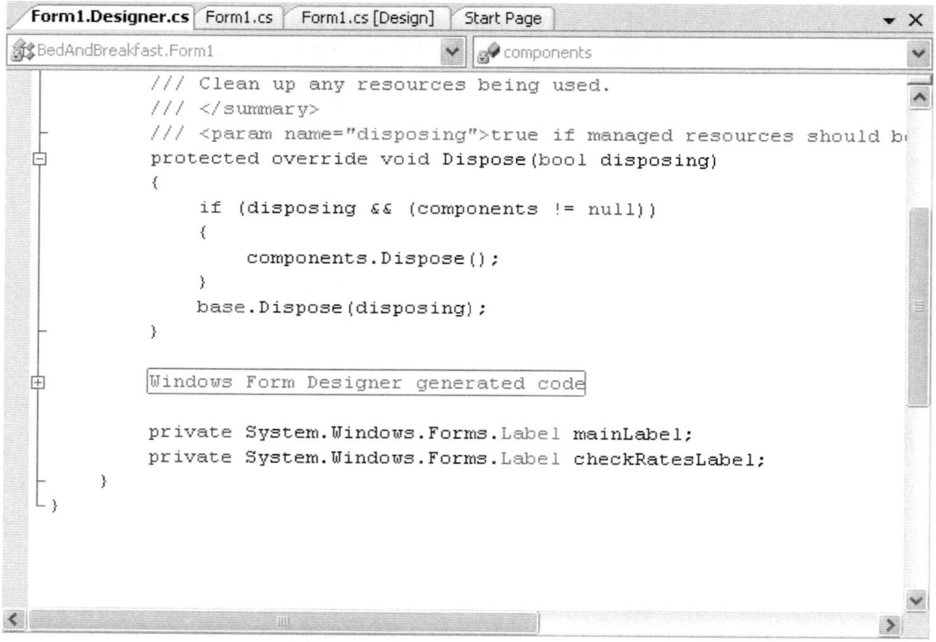
Form1.Designer.cs
Form1.cs
Form1.cs [Design]
Start Page
BedAndBreakfast.Form1
components
/// Clean up any resources being used.
/// </summary>
/// <param name="disposing">true if managed resources should b
protected override void Dispose(bool disposing)
{
if (disposing && (components != null))
{
components.Dispose();
}
base.Dispose(disposing);
}
Windows Form Designer generated code
private System.Windows.Forms.Label mainLabel;
private System.Windows.Forms.Label checkRatesLabel;
}
}

Figure 11-38 The bottom of the Form1.Designer.cs file

3. Click the method node represented by the plus (+) sign next to the box that contains `Windows Form Designer generated code`. The automatically generated lines of code expand. Scroll through the exposed code and identify the statements that define the `Font`, `Size`, `Location`, and `Text` of each `Label` you created. The statements that set the `Labels`' properties are easily identifiable because they are preceded with a comment that includes the name of each `Control`. Also locate the statements that set the `Text` and `Size` for the `Form`. Notice that the `Name` of the `Form` is `form1` because you have not assigned a new `Name` to it.
4. In the Solution Explorer, double-click the **Program.cs** filename to view the `Main()` method for the application.
5. Click the **Form1.cs design tab** to return to the Design view for the `Form`.
6. Click the **`Form`**. In the Properties list, change the name of the `Form` to **`welcomeForm`**. Return to view the code in the Form1.Designer file. Notice that the section that sets the `Form`'s properties has been modified to show the new `Name` you just assigned.
7. Next, change the `BackColor` property of the Bailey's Bed and Breakfast `Form`. Return to the Design view and click the **`Form`**. In the Properties list, click the **`BackColor`** property to see its list of choices. Choose the **Custom** tab and select the brightest **Yellow** in the third row of available colors. Click the **`Form`**, notice the color change, and then view the code in the Form1.Designer.cs file. Locate the statement that changes the `BackColor` of the `Form` to `Yellow`. As you continue to design `Forms`, periodically check the code to confirm your changes and better learn C#.

CHAPTER ELEVEN

8. Save the project.
9. If you want to take a break at this point, close Visual Studio.

ADDING CheckBoxES TO A Form

In the next steps, you will add two CheckBoxes to the BedAndBreakfast Form. These controls allow the user to select an available room and view information about it.

To add CheckBoxes to a Form:

1. Open the BedAndBreakfast project in Visual Studio, if it is not still open on your screen.

2. In the Design view of the Bed And Breakfast project in the Visual Studio IDE, drag a CheckBox onto the Form below the "Check our rates" Label. (See Figure 11-39 for its approximate placement.) Change the Text property of the CheckBox to **BelleAire Suite**. Change the Name of the property to **belleAireBox**.

Figure 11-39 BedAndBreakfast Form with one CheckBox

3. Drag a second CheckBox onto the Form beneath the first one. Change its Text property to **Lincoln Room** and its Name to **lincolnBox**. See Figure 11-40.

Figure 11-40 BedAndBreakfast Form with two CheckBoxes

453

USING CONTROLS

4. Next, you will create two new Forms: one that appears when the user selects the BelleAire CheckBox and one that appears when the user selects the Lincoln CheckBox. Click **Project** on the menu bar, then click **Add New Item**. In the Add New Item window, click **Windows Form**. In the Name text box at the bottom of the window, type **BelleAireForm**. See Figure 11-41.

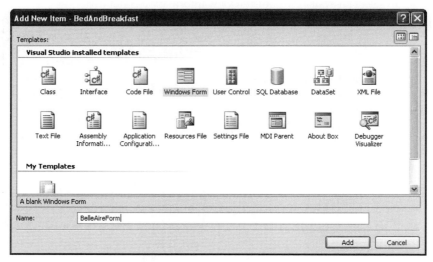

Figure 11-41 The Add New Item window

5. Click the **Add** button. A new Form is added to the project, as shown in Figure 11-42. Save the project (and continue to do so periodically).

Figure 11-42 The BelleAireForm added to the project

6. Change the Text property of the second Form to **BelleAire Suite**. Change its BackColor to Yellow to match the welcomeForm.

7. Drag a Label onto the Form, using Figure 11-43 as a guide to approximate its placement. Change the Text property of the Label to contain the following: **The BelleAire Suite has two bedrooms, two baths and a private balcony**. Click the arrow on the text property to type the long label message on two lines. Adjust the size of the Label if necessary to resemble Figure 11-43. Drag a second Label onto the Form and type the price as the Text property: **$199.95 per night**.

Figure 11-43 BelleAireSuite Form with two Labels

8. Select the **Pointer** tool from the Toolbox at the left of the screen. Drag it to encompass both Labels. In the Properties list, select the **Font** property to change the Font for both Controls at once. Choose a pleasing Font. Figure 11-44 shows 10-point Papyrus; you might choose a different font. Adjust the positions of the Labels if necessary to achieve a pleasing effect.

Figure 11-44 Font changed for the Labels

USING CONTROLS

9. In the Solution Explorer at the right side of the screen, double-click **Form1.cs**. Alternatively, click the **Form1** tab at the top of the Designer screen. Double-click the **BelleAire Suite CheckBox**. The program code (the method shell for the default event of a CheckBox) appears in the IDE main window. Within the belleAireBox_CheckedChanged() method, add an if statement that determines whether the BelleAire CheckBox is checked. If it is checked, create a new instance of BelleAireForm and display it.

    ```
    private void belleAireBox_CheckedChanged(object sender,
        EventArgs e)
    {
        if (belleAireBox.Checked)
        {
            BelleAireForm belleAireForm = new BelleAireForm();
            belleAireForm.ShowDialog();
        }
    }
    ```

10. Save and then execute the program by selecting **Debug** from the main menu, then **Start Without Debugging**. The main Bed and Breakfast Form appears. Click the **BelleAire Suite CheckBox**. The BelleAire Form appears. Dismiss the Form. Click the **Lincoln Room CheckBox**. Nothing happens because you have not yet written event code for this CheckBox. When you click the **BelleAire Suite CheckBox** again, the BelleAire form reappears. Dismiss the BelleAire Form.

11. When you dismiss the BelleAire Form, the BelleAire CheckBox remains checked. To see it appear as unchecked after its Form is dismissed, add a third statement within the if block in the CheckedChanged() message as follows:

    belleAireBox.Checked = false;

12. Save the project, then execute it again. When you select the BelleAire CheckBox, view the Form, and dismiss it, the CheckBox appears unchecked and is ready to check again. Dismiss the BedAndBreakfast Form.

13. Click **Project** on the menu bar and then click **Add New Item**. Click **Windows Form** and enter its Name: **LincolnForm**. When the new Form appears, change its Text property to **Lincoln Room**. Then add two Labels to the Form. The first should say: **Return to the 1850s in this lovely room with private bath**. The second should say: **$110.00 per night**. Change the Form's BackColor property to **White**. Change the Font to match the Font on the BelleAire Form. See Figure 11-45.

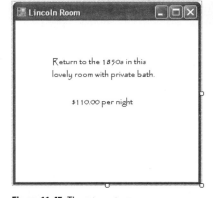

Figure 11-45 The LincolnForm

CHAPTER ELEVEN

14. From the Toolbox, drag a `PictureBox` onto the `Form`. Select its **Image** property. A dialog box allows you to browse for an image. Find the AbeLincoln file on your Student Disk and select **Import**. Adjust the size and positions of the labels and picture box so that everything looks attractive on the `Form`. See Figure 11-46.

Figure 11-46 `LincolnForm` with `Image` in `PictureBox`

15. In the Solution Explorer, choose `Form1`, double-click the Lincoln Room `CheckBox`, and add the following `if` statement to the `lincolnBox_CheckedChanged()` method:

    ```
    private void lincolnBox_CheckedChanged(object sender,
       EventArgs e)
    {
        if (lincolnBox.Checked)
        {
            LincolnForm lincolnForm = new LincolnForm();
            lincolnForm.ShowDialog();
            lincolnBox.Checked = false;
        }
    }
    ```

    >> **NOTE**
    The AbeLincoln file was obtained at *www.free-graphics.com*. You can visit the site and download other images to use in your own applications.

16. Save the project and then execute it. When the Bed and Breakfast `Form` appears, click either `CheckBox`—the appropriate informational `Form` appears. Close it and then click the other `CheckBox`. Again, the appropriate `Form` appears.

17. Close all forms. If you are taking a break, exit Visual Studio.

ADDING `RadioButtons` TO A `Form`

Next you will add more `Control`s to the Bed And Breakfast `Form`. You generally use `RadioButtons` when a user must select from mutually exclusive options.

To add `RadioButtons` to the project:

1. Open the `BedAndBreakfast` project if it is not still open. In the Design view of the main `Form`, add a `Label` and `Button` to the `Form`, using Figure 11-47 as a general guide to

457

USING CONTROLS

locations. Change the `Label`'s Text to **Make a reservation now** and the `Button`'s Text to **Make Reservation**. Change the `Button`'s Name property to `reservationButton`.

Figure 11-47 Developing the `BedAndBreakfast` project

2. From the main menu, select **Project**, click **Add New Item**, and click **Windows Form**. Name the `Form` **ReservationForm** and click **Add**. On the new `Form`, make the following changes:

   » Drag a `Label` onto the `Form`. Set its Text to **Select your breakfast option**.
   » Drag three `RadioButtons` onto the `Form`. Set their respective Text properties to **Continental**, **Full**, and **Deluxe**. Set their respective Names to **breakfast1Button**, **breakfast2Button**, and **breakfast3Button**.
   » Drag a `Label` onto the `Form`, then set its Text to **Price:** and its Name to **priceLabel**.

   See Figure 11-48 for approximate placement of all these `Control`s.

Figure 11-48 Developing the `ReservationForm`

458

3. Double-click the title bar of the `ReservationForm`. You generate a method named `ReservationForm_Load()`. Within this method, you can type statements that execute each time the `Form` is created. Add the following statements within the `ReservationForm` class, which declare three constants representing prices for different breakfast options. Within the `ReservationForm_Load()` method, set the `priceLabel` `Text` to the lowest price by default when the `Form` loads.

```
public partial class ReservationForm : Form
{
    private const double CONT_BREAKFAST_PRICE = 6.00;
    private const double FULL_BREAKFAST_PRICE = 9.95;
    private const double DELUXE_BREAKFAST_PRICE = 16.50;
    public ReservationForm()
    {
        InitializeComponent();
    }

    private void ReservationForm_Load(object sender,
       EventArgs e)
    {
        priceLabel.Text = "Total: " +
           CONT_BREAKFAST_PRICE .ToString("C");
    }
}
```

4. Return to the Design view for the Reservation `Form` and double-click the **Continental breakfast** `CheckBox`. When you see the generated `CheckedChanged()` method, add a statement that sets `priceLabel` to the continental breakfast price when the user makes that selection:

```
private void breakfast1Button _CheckedChanged
       (object sender, EventArgs e)
{
    priceLabel.Text = "Price: " +
       CONT_BREAKFAST_PRICE .ToString("C");
}
```

5. Return to the Design view for the Reservation `Form`, double-click the **Full breakfast** `CheckBox`, and add a statement to the generated method that sets the `priceLabel` to the full breakfast price when the user makes that selection:

```
private void breakfast2Button_CheckedChanged
       (object sender, EventArgs e)
{
    priceLabel.Text = "Price: " +
       FULL_BREAKFAST_PRICE .ToString("C");
}
```

USING CONTROLS

6. Return to the Design view for the Reservation Form, double-click the **Deluxe breakfast CheckBox**, and add a statement to the generated method that sets the priceLabel to the deluxe breakfast price when the user makes that selection:

```
private void breakfast3Button_CheckedChanged
    (object sender, EventArgs e)
{
    priceLabel.Text = "Price: " +
        DELUXE_BREAKFAST_PRICE.ToString("C");
}
```

7. In the Solution Explorer, double-click the **Form1.cs file** to view the original Form. Double-click the **Make Reservation Button**; when the Click() method is generated, add the following code so that the Reservation Form is loaded when a user clicks the Button.

```
private void reservationButton_Click(object sender,
    EventArgs e)
{
    ReservationForm resForm = new ReservationForm();
    resForm.ShowDialog();
}
```

8. Save the project and execute it. When the BedAndBreakfast Form appears, confirm that the BelleAire Suite and Lincoln Room CheckBoxes still work correctly, displaying their information Forms when they are clicked. Then click the **Make Reservation** Button. By default, the Continental Breakfast option is chosen, as shown in Figure 11-49, so the price is $6.00. Click the other RadioButton options to confirm that each correctly changes the breakfast price.

Figure 11-49 The ReservationForm with Continental breakfast RadioButton selected

9. Dismiss all the Forms.

CHAPTER ELEVEN

ADDING A MonthCalendar TO A Form

Next, you will add a MonthCalendar to a Form so guests can plan a stay at Bailey's Bed and Breakfast. Bailey's requires guests who arrive on a Friday to stay for two nights; otherwise, they accept reservations for a one-night stay. After you add the MonthCalendar, you can use Visual Studio's automatic statement completion feature to make an intelligent guess as to how to write the appropriate code.

To add a calendar to a form:

1. Open the Design view for the ReservationForm.cs file.

2. Drag a MonthCalendar onto the Form. Add two Labels above it. Set the left Label's Text property to **No date selected yet** and name it **minLabel**. Set the right Label's Text to **Pick your arrival date** and name it **arrivalLabel**. Adjust the size of the Form to accommodate all the Controls, as shown in Figure 11-50.

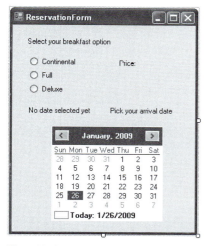

Figure 11-50 ReservationForm including MonthCalendar

3. Double-click the **MonthCalendar**. The default method generated is monthCalendar1_DateChanged(). Within the method shell, you want to type an if statement that changes the minimum stay Label from its original value to one of the following messages:

   » If the user selects a Friday, display "Two night stay minimum".
   » Otherwise, display "One night stay is okay".

   You want to make a decision (write an if statement) that compares the user's selection on the MonthCalendar object to "Friday". Position your insertion point between the method's curly braces and type the following:

   `if(m`

USING CONTROLS

As soon as you type the "m," a list box appears, as shown in Figure 11-51. Error messages appear at the bottom of the screen because the statement is incomplete at the moment.

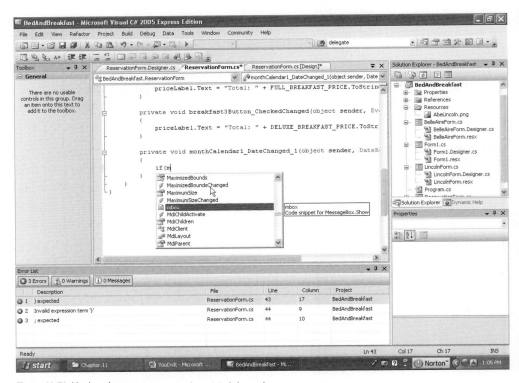

Figure 11-51 List box that appears as you type `if` statement

4. Scroll through the alphabetical list to find the name of the MonthCalendar object, monthCalendar1. Double-click it, then type a dot. A list of options appears, as shown in Figure 11-52.

CHAPTER ELEVEN

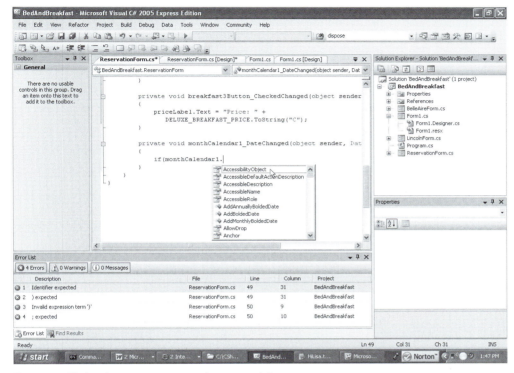

Figure 11-52 List box that appears as you continue to type `if` statement

5. Scroll through the list of available options. Because you are testing for dates the user has selected, `SelectionStart` seems to be an appropriate choice. Double-click it and type another dot; another list appears. `Day` seems to be an appropriate choice because you are interested in the day the selection starts. Type another dot; one of the choices is `Equals()`. Double-click it. The statement so far is:

`if(monthCalendar1.SelectionStart.DayOfWeek.Equals`

6. You have used the `Equals()` method many times before, so you know it needs parentheses and an argument to which to compare the calendar's selection. Because you will compare your `Start.DayOfWeek` selection to a specific `DayOfWeek`, you might guess that you should type `DayOfWeek` within the parentheses of the `Equals()` method. When you type a dot, the list box in Figure 11-53 appears. For this comparison, it makes sense to select `Friday`. Then close the parentheses. The entire `if` clause is:

```
if(monthCalendar1.SelectionStart.DayOfWeek.Equals
   (DayOfWeek.Friday)
```

USING CONTROLS

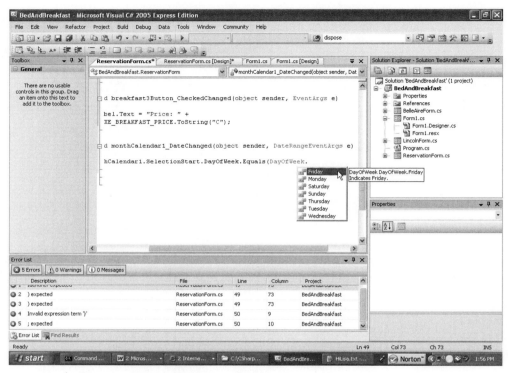

Figure 11-53 List box that appears with the `DayOfWeek` values

7. Complete the `if` statement as follows so that one message is displayed for Friday selections and a different message is displayed for any other day:

```
private void monthCalendar1_DateChanged_1
   (object sender, DateRangeEventArgs e)
{
    if(monthCalendar1.SelectionRange.Start.DayOfWeek.Equals
       (DayOfWeek.Friday))
          minLabel.Text = "Two night stay minimum";
    else
       minLabel.Text = "One night stay is okay";
}
```

8. Save the project, then execute it. Be sure to test all the available options. When you load the `ReservationForm` that contains the `MonthCalendar`, confirm that it shows the correct date as set on your system, and experiment with moving ahead or back several months. For example, Figure 11-54 shows the `Form` that appears after the user clicks the Make Reservation `Button` on the original `Form` and chooses the Deluxe breakfast and an arrival date of Friday, February 13, 2009. Because a Friday is selected, the `mainLabel` message is "Two night stay minimum".

CHAPTER ELEVEN

Figure 11-54 Reservation Form with Deluxe breakfast and Friday arrival chosen

9. Dismiss the Forms and close Visual Studio.

CHAPTER SUMMARY

» The Control class provides definitions for GUI objects such as Forms and Buttons. There are 26 direct descendants of Control and additional descendants of those classes. Each Control has more than 80 public properties and 20 protected ones. For example, each Control has a Font and a ForeColor that dictate how its text is displayed, and each Control has a Width and Height.

» A Label is one of the simplest GUI Control objects you can place on a Form. The Label class descends directly from Control. Typically, you use a Label to provide descriptive text for another Control object or to display other text information on a Form. You can create a Label by writing code or by using the Visual Studio IDE.

» You use the Font class to change the appearance of printed text on your Forms. When designing a Label or other Control on a Form, it is easiest to select a Font from the Properties list. The Font class includes a number of overloaded constructors.

» A LinkLabel is similar to a Label; it is a child of Label, but it provides the additional capability to link the user to other sources, such as Web pages or files.

» The Color class contains a wide variety of predefined Colors that you can use with your Controls.

» CheckBox objects are GUI widgets the user can click to select or deselect an option. When a Form contains multiple CheckBoxes, any number of them can be checked or unchecked at the same time. RadioButtons are similar to CheckBoxes, except that when they are placed on a Form, only one RadioButton can be selected at a time—selecting any RadioButton automatically deselects the others. CheckBox and RadioButton objects both have a Checked property whose value is true or false.

USING CONTROLS

» A `PictureBox` is a `Control` in which you can display graphics from a bitmap, icon, JPEG, GIF, or other image file type. Just as with a `Button` or a `Label`, you can easily add a `PictureBox` by dragging its `Control` onto the `Form` in the Visual Studio IDE.

» `ListBox`, `ComboBox`, and `CheckedListBox` objects descend from `ListControl`. The `ListBox Control` enables you to display a list of items that the user can select by clicking. With a `ListBox`, you allow the user to make a single selection or multiple selections by setting the `SelectionMode` property appropriately. A `ComboBox` is similar to a `ListBox`, except that it displays an additional editing field to allow the user to select from the list or to enter new text. A `CheckedListBox` is also similar to a `ListBox`, with check boxes appearing to the left of each desired item.

» The `MonthCalendar` and `DateTimePicker Controls` allow you to retrieve date and time information.

» When you place `Controls` on a `Form` in the IDE, you can drag them to any location to achieve the effect you want. When you drag multiple `Controls` onto a `Form`, blue snap lines appear and help you align new `Controls` with others already in place. You also can use the `Location` property in the Properties list to specify a location. `Anchor`, `Dock`, and `Padding` properties help you determine a `Control`'s size and position in the `Form`. A `Form` also has a `MinimumSize` property and a `MaximumSize` property. Each has two values—`Width` and `Height`.

» Many types of `ContainerControls` are available to hold `Controls`. For example, you can use a `GroupBox` or `Panel` to group related `Controls` on a `Form`. When you move a `GroupBox` or `Panel`, all its `Controls` are moved as a group.

» Most programs you use in a Windows environment contain a menu strip, which is a horizontal list of general options that appears under the title bar of a `Form` or `Window`. When you click an item in a menu strip, you might initiate an action. More frequently, you see a list box that contains more specific options. Each of these might initiate an action, or it might lead to another menu. You can add a `MenuStrip Control` object to any `Form` you create.

» If you examine the Visual Studio IDE or search through the Visual Studio documentation, you will find many other `Controls` you can use. If you click **Project** on the main menu and click **Add New Item**, you can add extra `Forms`, `Files`, `Controls`, and other elements to a project.

KEY TERMS

Widgets—short for "windows gadgets"—are interactive controls such as labels, scroll bars, check boxes, and radio buttons.

The **Control** class provides the definitions for GUI objects.

The **Component** class provides containment and cleanup for other objects.

A **Label** is a `Control` object that typically provides descriptive text for another `Control` object or displays other text information on a `Form`.

In Visual Studio, a **method node** is a small box that appears to the left of code; you use it to expand or collapse code.

CHAPTER ELEVEN

The **Font** class is used to change the appearance of printed text on Forms.

A **LinkLabel** is similar to a Label, but it provides the additional capability to link the user to other sources, such as Web pages or files.

The **default event** for a Control is the one generated when you double-click it while designing it in the IDE. It is the method you are most likely to alter when you use the Control, as well as the event that users most likely expect to generate when they encounter the Control in a working application.

The **Color** class contains a wide variety of predefined colors to use with Controls.

CheckBox objects are GUI widgets the user can click to select or deselect an option. When a Form contains multiple CheckBoxes, any number of them can be checked or unchecked at the same time.

RadioButtons are similar to CheckBoxes, except that when they are placed on a Form, only one RadioButton can be selected at a time—selecting any RadioButton automatically deselects the others.

A **PictureBox** is a Control in which you can display graphics from a bitmap, icon, JPEG, GIF, or other image file type.

The **ListBox** Control enables you to display a list of items that the user can select by clicking.

A **ComboBox** is similar to a ListBox, except that it displays an additional editing field that allows a user to select from the list or enter new text.

A **CheckedListBox** is also similar to a ListBox, with check boxes appearing to the left of each desired item.

The **MonthCalendar** and **DateTimePicker** Controls allow you to retrieve date and time information.

Snap lines appear in a design environment to help you align new Controls with others already in place.

Setting the **Anchor property** causes a Control to remain at a fixed distance from the side of a container when the user resizes it.

Setting the **Dock property** attaches a Control to the side of a container so that the Control stretches when the container's size is adjusted.

A Form has a **Padding property** that specifies the distance between docked Controls and the edges of the Form.

A Form also has a **MinimumSize property** and a **MaximumSize property**. Each has two values—Width and Height.

A **GroupBox** or **Panel** can be used to group related Controls on a Form.

A **menu strip** is a horizontal list of general options that appears under the title bar of a Form or Window. When you click an item in a menu strip, you might initiate an action. More frequently, you see a list box that contains more specific options.

You can add a **MenuStrip** Control object to any Form you create.

467

USING CONTROLS

REVIEW QUESTIONS

1. `Labels`, `Buttons`, and `CheckBoxes` are all _____.
   a. GUI objects
   b. `Controls`
   c. widgets
   d. all of these

2. All `Control` objects descend from _____.
   a. `Form`
   b. `Component`
   c. `ButtonBase`
   d. all of these

3. Which of the following is most like a `RadioButton`?
   a. `ListControl`
   b. `CheckedListBox`
   c. `PictureBox`
   d. `Button`

4. Which of the following is not a commonly used `Control` property?
   a. `BackColor`
   b. `Language`
   c. `Location`
   d. `Size`

5. The `Control` you frequently use to provide descriptive text for another `Control` object is a _____.
   a. `Form`
   b. `Label`
   c. `CheckBox`
   d. `MessageBox`

6. Which of the following creates a `Label` named `firstLabel`?
   a. `firstLabel = new firstLabel();`
   b. `Label = new firstLabel();`
   c. `Label firstLabel = new Label();`
   d. `Label firstLabel = Label();`

7. The property that determines what the user reads on a `Label` is the _____ property.
   a. `Text`
   b. `Label`
   c. `Phrase`
   d. `Setting`

8. Which of the following correctly creates a `Font`?
   a. `Font myFont = new Font("Arial", 14F, FontStyle.Bold);`
   b. `Font myFont = new Font("Courier", 13.6);`
   c. `myFont = Font new Font("TimesRoman", FontStyle.Italic);`
   d. `Font myFont = Font(20, "Helvetica", Underlined);`

9. The default event for a Control is the one that _____.
   a. occurs automatically whether a user manipulates the Control or not
   b. is generated when you double-click the Control while designing it in the IDE
   c. requires no parameters
   d. occurs when a user clicks the Control with a mouse

10. Assume you have created a Label named myLabel. Which of the following sets myLabel's background color to green?
    a. myLabel = BackColor.System.Drawing.Color.Green;
    b. myLabel.BackColor = System.Drawing.Color.Green;
    c. myLabel.Green = System.DrawingColor;
    d. myLabel.Background = new Color.Green;

11. A difference between CheckBox and RadioButton objects is _____.
    a. RadioButtons descend from ButtonBase; CheckBoxes do not
    b. only one RadioButton can be selected at a time
    c. only one CheckBox can appear on a Form at a time
    d. RadioButtons cannot be placed in a GroupBox; CheckBoxes can

12. The Checked property of a RadioButton can hold the values _____.
    a. true and false   c. 0 and 1
    b. Checked and Unchecked   d. Yes, No, and Undetermined

13. The Control in which you can display a bitmap or JPEG image is a(n) _____.
    a. DisplayModule   c. BitmapControl
    b. ImageHolder   d. PictureBox

14. ListBox, ComboBox, and CheckedListBox objects descend from the same family: _____.
    a. ListControl   c. ButtonBase
    b. List   d. ListBase

15. Which of the following properties is associated with a ListBox but not a Button?
    a. BackColor   c. Location
    b. SelectedItem   d. IsSelected

16. With a ListBox you can allow the user to choose _____.
    a. only a single option   c. either of these
    b. multiple selections   d. none of these

17. You can add items to a `ListBox` by using the _____ method.
    a. `Add()`
    b. `Append()`
    c. `List()`
    d. `AddRange()`

18. A `ListBox`'s `SelectedItem` property contains _____ .
    a. the position of the currently selected item
    b. the value of the currently selected item
    c. a Boolean value indicating whether an item is currently selected
    d. a count of the number of currently selected items

19. When you create a `ListBox`, by default its `SelectionMode` is _____ .
    a. `Simple`
    b. `MultiExtended`
    c. `One`
    d. `false`

20. A horizontal list of general options that appears under the title bar of a `Form` or `Window` is a _____ .
    a. task bar
    b. subtitle bar
    c. menu strip
    d. list box

EXERCISES

Save the programs that you create in these exercises in the Chapter.11 folder on your Student Disk.

1. Create a `Form` that contains two `Button`s, one labeled Stop and one labeled Go. Add a `Label` telling the user to click a button. When the user clicks Stop, change the `BackColor` of the `Form` to `Red`; when the user clicks Go, change the `BackColor` of the `Form` to `Green`. Save the project as **StopGo**.

2. Create a `Form` that contains at least five `Button` objects, each labeled with a color. When the user clicks a `Button`, change the `BackColor` of the `Form` appropriately. Save the project as **FiveColors**.

3. Create a `Form` that contains at least five `RadioButton` objects, each labeled with a color. When the user clicks a `RadioButton`, change the `BackColor` of the `Form` appropriately. Save the project as **FiveColors2**.

4. Create a `Form` for a video store that contains a `ListBox` with the titles of at least eight videos available to rent. Provide directions that tell users they can choose as many videos as they want by holding down the Ctrl key while making selections. When the user clicks a `Button` to indicate the choices are final, display the total rental price, which is $2.50

per video. If the user selects or deselects items and clicks the button again, make sure the total is updated correctly. Save the project as **Video**.

5. Create a `Form` with two `ListBox`es—one contains at least four `Font` names and the other contains at least four `Font` sizes. Let the first item in each list be the default selection if the user fails to make a selection. Allow only one selection per `ListBox`. After the user clicks a `Button`, display "Hello" in the selected `Font` and size. Save the project as **FontSelector**.

6. Create a `Form` for a car rental company. Allow the user to choose a car style (compact, standard, or luxury) and a number of days (1 through 7). After the user makes selections, display the total rental charge, which is $19.95 per day for a compact car, $24.95 per day for a standard car, and $39 per day for a luxury car. Use the `Control`s that you think are best for each function. Label items appropriately and use fonts and colors to achieve an attractive design. Save the project as **CarRental**.

7. Create a `Form` for a restaurant. Allow the user to choose one item from at least three options in each of the following categories—appetizer, entrée, and dessert. Assign a different price to each selection and display the total when the user clicks a `Button`. Use the `Control`s that you think are best for each function. Label items appropriately and use fonts and colors to achieve an attractive design. Save the project as **Restaurant**.

8. Create a `Form` for an automobile dealer. Include options for at least three car models. After users make a selection, proceed to a new `Form` that contains information about the selected model. Use the `Control`s that you decide are best for each function. Label items on the `Form` appropriately and use fonts and colors to achieve an attractive design. Save the project as **CarDealer**.

9. Create a spreadsheet and then include a few numbers in it that represent an annual budget. Create a `Form` that includes two `LinkLabel`s. One opens the spreadsheet for viewing, and the other visits your favorite Web site. Include `Label`s on the `Form` to explain each link. Save the project as **AnnualBudget**.

10. Create a `Form` for Nina's Cookie Source. Allow the user to select from at least three types of cookies, each with a different price per dozen. Allow the user to select $\frac{1}{2}$, 1, 2, or 3 dozen cookies. Adjust the final displayed price as the user chooses cookie types and quantities. Also allow the user to select an order date from a `MonthCalendar`. Assuming that shipping takes three days, display the estimated arrival date for the order. Include as many labels as necessary so the user understands how to use the `Form`. Save the project as **NinasCookieSource**.

11. Using the `MenuStripDemo` project on your Student Disk (see Figure 11-32), add appropriate functionality to the currently unprogrammed menu options (Small in the Font menu and the three options in the Color menu). Add at least three other menu options to the program, either vertically, horizontally, or both. Save the modified project as **MenuStripDemo2**.

DEBUGGING EXERCISES

Each of the following projects in the Chapter.11 folder on your Student Disk has syntax and/or logical errors. In each case, determine the problem and fix the program. After you correct the errors, save each project using the same name preceded with *Fixed*. For example, DebugEleven1 will become FixedDebugEleven1.

- a. DebugEleven1
- b. DebugEleven2
- c. DebugEleven3
- d. DebugEleven4

UP FOR DISCUSSION

1. Making exciting, entertaining, professional-looking GUI applications becomes easier once you learn to include graphics images, as you did when you learned about `PictureBox` objects in this chapter. You can copy graphics images from many locations on the Web. Should there be any restrictions on what graphics you use? Does it make a difference if you are writing programs for your own enjoyment, as opposed to putting them on the Web where others can see them? Should restrictions be different for using photographs versus using drawings? Does it matter if the photographs contain recognizable people? Would you impose any restrictions on images posted to your organization's Web site?

2. Should you be allowed to store computer games on your computer at work? If so, should you be allowed to play the games at work? If so, should there be any restrictions on when you can play them?

3. Suppose you discover a way to breach security in a Web site so that visitors might access information that belongs to the company. Should you be allowed to publish your findings? Should you notify the organization? Should the organization pay you a reward for discovering the breach? If they do, would this encourage you to search for more potential security violations? Suppose the newly available information on the Web site is relatively innocuous—for example, office telephone numbers of company executives. Suppose it is not—for example, home telephone numbers for the same executives. Does this make a difference?

CHAPTER TWELVE

12

HANDLING EVENTS

In this chapter you will:

- Learn about event handling
- Learn about delegates
- Create composed delegates
- Declare your own events and handlers
- Use the built-in `EventHandler`
- Handle `Control` component events
- Handle mouse events
- Handle keyboard events
- Manage multiple `Control`s
- Learn how to continue your exploration of `Control`s and `Event`s

HANDLING EVENTS

Throughout this book, you have learned how to create C# programs that perform a variety of tasks. In the last few chapters, you expanded your repertoire from creating functional but dull-looking command-line applications to creating attractive and interactive GUI windows.

The aspect of Windows widgets that makes them useful is their ability to cause events when a user interacts with them. In the last two chapters, you have seen Controls that respond to a user-initiated event—for example, a mouse click. In those chapters, you provided actions for Controls' default events. In this chapter, you will expand your understanding of the event-handling process. You will learn more about the object that triggers an event and the object that captures and responds to that event. You also will learn about delegates—objects that act as intermediaries in transferring messages from senders to receivers. You will create delegates and manage interactive events. You will learn to manage multiple events for a single Control and to manage multiple Controls for a project.

EVENT HANDLING

In C#, an event occurs when something interesting happens to an object. When you create a class, you decide exactly what is considered "interesting." For example, when you create a Form, you might decide to respond to a user clicking a Button but ignore a user who clicks a Label—clicking the Label is just not "interesting" to the Form.

You use an event to notify a client program when something happens to a class object the program is using. Events are used frequently in GUI programs—for example, you notify a program when the user clicks a Button or chooses an option from a ListBox. In addition, you can use events with ordinary classes that do not represent GUI controls. When an object's client might want to know about any changes that occur in the object, events enable the object to signal the client.

In Chapter 10, you learned that when a user interacts with a GUI object, an event is generated that causes the program to perform a task. GUI programs are **event driven**—an event such as a button click "drives" the program to perform a task. Programmers also say that a button click **raises an event**, **fires an event**, or **triggers an event**. A method that performs a task in response to an event is an **event handler**.

For example, Figure 12-1 shows a Form that contains a Label and a Button. The following changes are the only ones that have been made to the default Form in the IDE:

» The Size property has been adjusted to 400, 115.
» A Label has been dragged onto the Form, its Text property has been set to "Hello", and its Font has been increased to 9.75.
» A Button has been dragged onto the Form and its Text has been set to "Change Label".

Figure 12-1 A Form with a Label and a Button

CHAPTER TWELVE

If you double-click the button on the form in the IDE, you generate the following empty method in the program code:

```
private void button1_Click(object sender, EventArgs e)
{
}
```

The `button1_Click()` method is an event handler. Conventionally, event handlers are named using the identifier of the `Control` (in this case, `button1`), an underscore, and the name of the event (in this case, `Click`). You can create your own methods to handle events and provide any names for them, but the names should follow these conventions.

Suppose that when a user clicks the button, you want the text on the label to change from "Hello" to "Goodbye". You can write the following code within the event handler:

```
private void button1_Click(object sender, EventArgs e)
{
    label1.Text = "Goodbye";
}
```

The event-handler method is also known as an **event receiver**. The control that generates an event is an **event sender**. The first parameter in the list for the event receiver method is an object named `sender`; it is a reference to the object that generated the event. For example, if you code the event handler as follows, the output appears as in Figure 12-2.

```
private void button1_Click(object sender, EventArgs e)
{
    label1.Text = sender.ToString();
}
```

Figure 12-2 `FormWithButton` application displaying sender information

The label in Figure 12-2 shows that the sender of the event is an instance of `System.Windows.Forms.Button`, whose `Text` property is "Change Label".

The second parameter in the event-handler parameter list is a reference to an event argument object of type `EventArgs`; in this method, the `EventArgs` argument is named e. **EventArgs** is a C# class designed for holding event information. If you change the code in the event handler to the following, then run the program and click the button, you see the output in Figure 12-3.

```
private void button1_Click(object sender, EventArgs e)
{
    label1.Text = e.ToString();
}
```

475

HANDLING EVENTS

Figure 12-3 `FormWithButton` application displaying `EventArgs` information

In Figure 12-3, you can see that the e object is a `MouseEventArgs` object. That makes sense, because the user used the mouse to click the `Button`.

As you learned in Chapter 10, you can examine all of the code generated for the application that creates the `Form` shown in Figure 12-3. When you open the Designer.cs file in the IDE, you see comments as well as statements that set the `Controls`' properties. For example, the code generated for `button1` appears in Figure 12-4. You can recognize that such features as the button's `Location`, `Name`, and `Size` have been set.

The most unusual statement in the section of `button1` code is shaded; this statement concerns the **Click event**, which is generated when `button1` is clicked. This statement is necessary because `button1` does not automatically "know" what method will handle its events—C# and all other .NET languages allow you to choose your own names for event-handling methods for events generated by GUI objects. In other words, there is no requirement that the event-handling method be named `button1Click()`. You *could* create your program so that when the user clicks `button1`, the event-handling method is named `calculatePayroll()`, `changeLabel()`, or any other identifier for a method you could then write. Of course, you do not want to make such a change; it is clearest if the method that executes when `button1` is clicked is named `button1_Click()`. However, that convention is not required by the compiler, so the shaded statement in Figure 12-4 is necessary to identify the method that will handle the `Click` event. The shaded statement indicates that, for this program, the method name `button1_Click()` is the receiver for `button1`'s `Click` event. Programmers say the shaded method creates a delegate, or more specifically, a composed delegate. You will learn about these terms in the next two sections of this chapter.

```
//
// button1
//
this.button1.Location = new System.Drawing.Point(242, 46);
this.button1.Name = "button1";
this.button1.Size = new System.Drawing.Size(126, 23);
this.button1.TabIndex = 1;
this.button1.Text = "Change Label";
this.button1.UseVisualStyleBackColor = true;
this.button1.Click += new System.EventHandler(this.button1_Click);
```

Figure 12-4 Code involving `button1` generated by Visual Studio

> **NOTE** The code generated in Design mode in the IDE is not meant to be altered by typing. You should modify `Control` properties through the Properties window in the IDE, not by typing in the Designer.cs file.

CHAPTER TWELVE

UNDERSTANDING DELEGATES

A **delegate** is an object that contains a reference to a method; object-oriented programmers would say that a delegate encapsulates a method. In government, a delegate is a representative that you authorize to make choices for you. For example, you select a delegate to a presidential nominating convention. When human delegates arrive at a convention, they are free to make choices based on current conditions. Similarly, C# delegates provide a way for a program to take alternative courses when running. When you write a method, you don't always know which actions will occur, so you give your delegates authority to run the correct methods.

> **» NOTE** In Chapter 1, you learned that encapsulation is a basic feature of object-oriented programming. Recall that encapsulation is the technique of packaging an object's attributes and methods into a cohesive unit that can then be used as an undivided entity.

After you have instantiated a C# delegate, you can pass this object to a method, which then can call the method referenced within the delegate. In other words, a delegate provides a way to pass a reference to a method as an argument to another method. For example, if del is a delegate that contains a reference to the method M1(), you can pass del to a new method named MyMethod(). Alternatively, you could create a delegate named del that contains a reference to a method named M2() and then pass this version to MyMethod(). When you write MyMethod(), you don't have to know whether it will call M1() or M2(); you only need to know that it will call whatever method is referenced within del.

> **» NOTE** A C# delegate is similar to a function pointer in C++. A function pointer is a variable that holds a method's memory address. In the C++ programming language, you pass a method's address to another method using a pointer variable. Java does not allow function pointers because they are dangerous—if the program alters the address, you might inadvertently execute the wrong method. C# provides a compromise between the dangers of C++ pointers and the Java ban on passing functions. Delegates allow flexible method calls but remain secure because you cannot alter the method addresses.

You declare a delegate using the keyword delegate, followed by an ordinary method declaration that includes a return type, method name, and argument list. For example, by entering the following statement, you can declare a delegate named GreetingDelegate(), which accepts a string argument and returns nothing:

```
delegate void GreetingDelegate(string s);
```

The GreetingDelegate can encapsulate any method as long as it has a void return type and a single string argument. If you declare the delegate and then write a method with the same return type and argument list, you can assign it to the delegate. For example, the following Hello() method is a void method that takes a string argument:

```
public static void Hello(string s)
{
    Console.WriteLine("Hello, {0}!", s);
}
```

HANDLING EVENTS

Because the `Hello()` method matches the `GreetingDelegate` definition, you can assign a reference to the `Hello()` method to a new instance of `GreetingDelegate`, as follows:

```
GreetingDelegate myDel = new GreetingDelegate(Hello);
```

Once the reference to the `Hello()` method is encapsulated in the delegate `myDel`, each of the following statements will result in the same output: "Hello, Kim!".

```
Hello("Kim");
myDel("Kim");
```

In this example, the ability to use the delegate `myDel` does not seem to provide any benefits over using a regular method call to `Hello()`. If you have a program in which you pass the delegate to a method, however, the method becomes more flexible; you gain the ability to send a reference to an appropriate method you want to execute at the time.

For example, Figure 12-5 shows a `Greeting` class that contains `Hello()` and `Goodbye()` methods. The `Main()` method declares two delegates named `firstDel` and `secondDel`. One is instantiated using the `Hello()` method and the other is instantiated using the `Goodbye()` method. When the `Main()` method calls `GreetMethod()` two times, it passes a different method and string each time. Figure 12-6 shows the output.

```
using System;
delegate void GreetingDelegate(string s);
class Greeting
{
   public static void Hello(string s)
   {
      Console.WriteLine("Hello, {0}!", s);
   }
   public static void Goodbye(string s)
   {
      Console.WriteLine("Goodbye, {0}!", s);
   }
   public static void Main()
   {
      GreetingDelegate firstDel, secondDel;
      firstDel = new GreetingDelegate(Hello);
      secondDel = new GreetingDelegate(Goodbye);
      GreetMethod(firstDel, "Cathy");
      GreetMethod(secondDel, "Bob");
   }
   public static void GreetMethod
      (GreetingDelegate gd, string name)
   {
      Console.WriteLine("The greeting is:");
      gd(name);
   }
}
```

Figure 12-5 The `Greeting` program

Figure 12-6 Output of the Greeting program

CREATING COMPOSED DELEGATES

You can assign one delegate to another using the = operator. You also can use the + and += operators to combine delegates into a **composed delegate** that calls the delegates from which it is built. As an example, assume that you declare three delegates (with the same argument lists) named del1, del2, and del3, and that you assign a reference to the method M1() to del1 and a reference to method M2() to del2. When the statement del3 = del1 + del2 executes, del3 becomes a delegate that executes both M1() and M2(), in that order. Only delegates with the same argument list can be composed, and the delegates used must have a void return value. Additionally, you can use the - and -= operators to remove a delegate from a composed delegate.

Figure 12-7 shows a program that contains a composed delegate. This program contains only two changes from the Greeting program in Figure 12-5—the class name (Greeting2) and the shaded statement that creates the composed delegate. The delegate firstDel now executes two methods, Hello() and Goodbye(), whereas secondDel still executes only Goodbye(). Figure 12-8 shows the output; "Cathy" is used with two methods, but "Bob" is used with only one.

```
using System;
delegate void GreetingDelegate(string s);
class Greeting2
{
   public static void Hello(string s)
   {
      Console.WriteLine("Hello, {0}!", s);
   }
   public static void Goodbye(string s)
   {
      Console.WriteLine("Goodbye, {0}!", s);
   }
```

Figure 12-7 The Greeting2 program (*continued*)

HANDLING EVENTS

```
public static void Main()
{
    GreetingDelegate firstDel, secondDel;
    firstDel = new GreetingDelegate(Hello);
    secondDel = new GreetingDelegate(Goodbye);
    firstDel += secondDel;
    GreetMethod(firstDel, "Cathy");
    GreetMethod(secondDel, "Bob");
}
public static void GreetMethod
   (GreetingDelegate gd, string name)
{
    Console.WriteLine("The greeting is:");
    gd(name);
}
}
```

Figure 12-7 (*continued*)

Figure 12-8 Output of the `Greeting2` program

DECLARING YOUR OWN EVENTS AND HANDLERS

To declare your own event, you use a delegate. An event provides a way for a class's clients to dictate methods that should execute when an event occurs. The clients identify methods to execute by providing delegates. When an event occurs, any delegate that a client has given or passed to the event is invoked. Just like the event handlers automatically created in the IDE, each of your own event handler `delegates` requires two arguments—the object where the event was initiated (the sender) and an `EventArgs` argument. You can create an `EventArgs` object that contains event information, or you can use the `EventArgs` class static field named `Empty`, which represents an event that contains no event data. In other words, using the `Empty` field simply tells the client that an event has occurred without specifying details. For example, you can declare a `delegate` event handler named `ChangedEventHandler`, as shown in Figure 12-9. The shaded identifier `ChangedEventHandler` can be any legal identifier you choose. This delegate defines the set of arguments that will be passed to the method that handles the event. It can be used in a program that handles events.

> **NOTE**
> The value of `Empty` is a read-only instance of `EventArgs`. You can pass it to a method that accepts an `EventArgs` parameter.

CHAPTER TWELVE

```
public delegate void ChangedEventHandler
    (object sender, EventArgs e);
```

Figure 12-9 Declaring a delegate

For example, Figure 12-10 contains a simple Student class that is similar to many classes you already have created. The Student class contains just two data fields and will generate an event when the data in either field changes.

```
public class Student
{
    private int idNum;
    private double gpa;
    public event ChangedEventHandler Changed;
    public int IdNum
    {
        get
        {
            return idNum;
        }
        set
        {
            idNum = value;
            OnChanged(EventArgs.Empty);
        }
    }
    public double Gpa
    {
        get
        {
            return gpa;
        }
        set
        {
            gpa = value;
            OnChanged(EventArgs.Empty);
        }
    }
    public void OnChanged(EventArgs e)
    {
        Changed(this, e);
    }
}
```

Figure 12-10 The Student class

The Student class in Figure 12-10 contains fields that will hold an ID number and grade point average (GPA) for a Student. The first shaded statement in the figure defines a third Student

481

HANDLING EVENTS

> **NOTE**
> Events usually are declared as `public`, but you can use any accessibility modifier.

class attribute—an event named `Changed`. The declaration for an event looks like a field, but instead of being an `int` or a `double`, it is a `ChangedEventHandler`, as defined in Figure 12-9.

The `Student` class event (`Changed`) looks like an ordinary field. However, you cannot assign values to the event field as easily as you can to ordinary data fields. You can take only two actions on an event field: you can compose a new delegate onto the field using the `+=` operator, and you can remove a delegate from the field using the `-=` operator. For example, to add `StudentChanged` to the `Changed` field of a `Student` object named `stu`, you would write the following:

```
stu.Changed += new ChangedEventHandler(StudentChanged);
```

In the `Student` class, each `set` accessor assigns a value to the appropriate class instance field. However, when either the `idNum` or the `gpa` changes, the method in the `Student` class named `OnChanged()` is also called, using `EventArgs.Empty` as the argument. The `OnChanged()` method calls `Changed()` using two arguments—a reference to the `Student` object that was changed and the empty `EventArgs` object. Calling `Changed()` is also known as **invoking the event**.

> **NOTE** If no client has hooked up a delegate to the event, the `Changed` field will be `null`, rather than referring to the delegate that should be called when the event is invoked. Therefore, programmers often check for `null` before invoking the event, as in the following example:
> ```
> if(Changed != null)
>    Changed(this, e);
> ```
> For simplicity, the example in Figure 12-10 does not bother checking for `null`.

Figure 12-11 shows an `EventListener` class that listens for `Student` events. This class contains a `Student` object that is assigned a value using the parameter to the `EventListener` class constructor. The `StudentChanged()` method is added to the `Student`'s event delegate using the `+=` operator. The `StudentChanged()` method displays a message and `Student` data.

```
class EventListener
{
    private Student stu;
    public EventListener(Student student)
    {
        stu = student;
        stu.Changed += new ChangedEventHandler
            (StudentChanged);
    }
    private void StudentChanged(object sender, EventArgs e)
    {
        Console.WriteLine("The student has changed.");
        Console.WriteLine("   ID# {0}   GPA {1}",
           stu.IdNum, stu.Gpa);
    }
}
```

Figure 12-11 The `EventListener` class

Figure 12-12 shows a program that demonstrates the Student and EventListener classes. The program contains a single Main() method, which declares one Student and registers the program to listen for events from the Student class. Then three assignments are made. Because this program is registered to listen for events from the Student, each change in a data field triggers an event. That is, each assignment not only changes the value of the data field, it executes the StudentChanged() method that displays two lines of explanation. In Figure 12-13, the program output shows that an event occurs three times—once when the ID becomes 2345 (and the GPA is still 0), again when the ID becomes 4567 (and the GPA still has not changed), and a third time when the GPA becomes 3.2.

```
using System;
class DemoStudentEvent
{
    public static void Main()
    {
        Student oneStu = new Student();
        EventListener listener = new EventListener(oneStu);
        oneStu.IdNum = 2345;
        oneStu.IdNum = 4567;
        oneStu.Gpa = 3.2;
    }
}
```

Figure 12-12 The DemoStudentEvent program

Figure 12-13 Output of the DemoStudentEvent program

USING THE BUILT-IN EventHandler

The C# language allows you to create events using any delegate type. However, the .NET Framework provides guidelines you should follow if you are developing a class that others will use. These guidelines indicate that the delegate type for an event should take exactly two parameters: a parameter indicating the source of the event, and an EventArgs parameter that encapsulates any additional information about the event. For events that do not use additional information, the .NET Framework has already defined an appropriate type named **EventHandler**.

HANDLING EVENTS

Figure 12-14 shows all the code necessary to demonstrate an `EventHandler`. Note the following changes from the classes used in the `DemoStudentEvent` program:

» No delegate named `ChangedEventHandler` is declared.
» In the first statement with shading in the `Student` class, the event is declared to be of the built-in type `EventHandler`.
» In the second statement with shading, which appears in the `EventListener` class, the delegate composition uses `EventHandler`.

```
using System;
public class Student
{
    private int idNum;
    private double gpa;
    public event EventHandler Changed;
    public int IdNum
    {
        get
        {
            return idNum;
        }
        set
        {
            idNum = value;
            OnChanged(EventArgs.Empty);
        }
    }
    public double Gpa
    {
        get
        {
            return gpa;
        }
        set
        {
            gpa = value;
            OnChanged(EventArgs.Empty);
        }
    }
    public void OnChanged(EventArgs e)
    {
        Changed(this, e);
    }
}
```

Figure 12-14 The `Student`, `EventListener`, and `DemoStudentEvent2` classes (*continued*)

CHAPTER TWELVE

```
class EventListener
{
   private Student stu;
   public EventListener(Student student)
   {
      stu = student;
      stu.Changed += new EventHandler(StudentChanged);
   }
   private void StudentChanged(object sender, EventArgs e)
   {
      Console.WriteLine("The student has changed.");
      Console.WriteLine("   ID# {0}   GPA {1}",
         stu.IdNum, stu.Gpa);
   }
}
class DemoStudentEvent2
{
   public static void Main()
   {
      Student oneStu = new Student();
      EventListener listener = new EventListener(oneStu);
      oneStu.IdNum = 2345;
      oneStu.IdNum = 4567;
      oneStu.Gpa = 3.2;
   }
}
```

Figure 12-14 (*continued*)

When you compile and execute the program in Figure 12-14, the output is identical to that in Figure 12-13.

HANDLING Control COMPONENT EVENTS

When you want to handle events generated by GUI Controls, you use the same techniques as when you handle events that are not generated by Controls. The major difference is that when you create your own classes, like Student, you must define both the data fields and events you want to generate; but existing Control components, like Buttons and ListBoxes, already contain fields and public properties, like Text, as well as events with names, like Click. Table 12-1 lists just some of the more commonly used Control events.

> **NOTE** You can consult the Visual Studio Help feature to discover additional Control events, as well as more specific events assigned to individual Control child classes.

HANDLING EVENTS

Event	Description
BackColorChanged	Occurs when the value of the BackColor property has changed
Click	Occurs when a control is clicked
ControlAdded	Occurs when a new control is added
ControlRemoved	Occurs when a control is removed
CursorChanged	Occurs when the Cursor property value has changed
DragDrop	Occurs when a drag-and-drop operation is completed
DragEnter	Occurs when an object is dragged into a control's bounds
DragLeave	Occurs when an object has been dragged into and out of a control's bounds
DragOver	Occurs when an object has been dragged over a control's bounds
EnabledChanged	Occurs when the Enabled property value has changed
Enter	Occurs when a control is entered
FontChanged	Occurs when the Font property value has changed
ForeColorChanged	Occurs when the ForeColor property value has changed
GotFocus	Occurs when a control receives focus
HelpRequested	Occurs when a user requests help for a control
KeyDown	Occurs when a key is pressed while a control has focus
KeyPress	Occurs when a key is pressed while a control has focus
KeyUp	Occurs when a key is released while a control has focus
Leave	Occurs when a control is left
LocationChanged	Occurs when the Location property value has changed
LostFocus	Occurs when a control loses focus
MouseDown	Occurs when the mouse pointer hovers over a control and a mouse button is pressed
MouseEnter	Occurs when the mouse pointer enters a control
MouseHover	Occurs when the mouse pointer hovers over a control
MouseLeave	Occurs when the mouse pointer leaves a control
MouseMove	Occurs when the mouse pointer moves over a control
MouseUp	Occurs when the mouse pointer hovers over a control and a mouse button is released
MouseWheel	Occurs when the mouse wheel moves while a control has focus
Move	Occurs when a control is moved
Resize	Occurs when a control is resized changed
TextChanged	Occurs when the Text property value has changed
VisibleChanged	Occurs when the Visible property value has changed

Table 12-1 Some Control class public instance events

CHAPTER TWELVE

You have already used the IDE to create some event-handling methods. These methods have been the default events generated when you double-click a Control in the IDE. For example, in Chapter 10 you created a Click() method for a Button, and in Chapter 11 you created a LinkClicked() method for a LinkLabel. A Form can contain any number of Controls that might have events associated with them. Additionally, a single Control might be able to raise any number of events. For example, besides creating a Button's default Click event, you might want to define various actions when the user's mouse rolls over the button. Table 12-1 lists only a few of the many events available with Controls; any Control could conceivably raise many of those events.

Suppose you want to create a project that takes a different set of actions when the mouse is over a Button than when the mouse is clicked. Figure 12-15 shows a project that has been started in the IDE. The following actions have been taken:

» A Button was dragged onto the Form and its Text was set to "Click Me".
» A Label was added to the Form, its Text was set to "Hello", and its Font was increased.

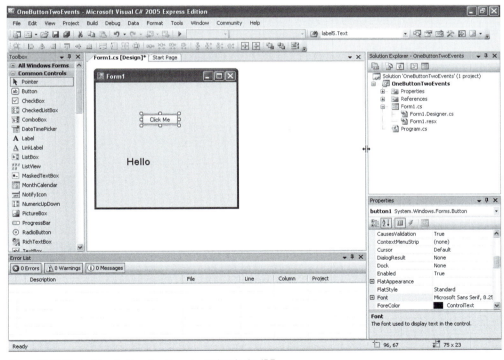

> **NOTE**
> Your title bar or other features might be slightly different if you are using a different edition of Microsoft Visual Studio.

Figure 12-15 Start of OneButtonTwoEvents project in the IDE

HANDLING EVENTS

When you double-click the `Button` on the `Form` in the IDE, you generate the shell of a `Click` method into which you can type a command to change the `Label`'s text and its color, as follows:

```
private void button1_Click(object sender, EventArgs e)
{
    label1.Text = "Button was clicked";
    label1.BackColor = Color.CornflowerBlue;
}
```

> **NOTE** `Color.CornflowerBlue` is one of C#'s predefined `Color` properties. A complete list appears in Table 11-5 in Chapter 11.

With the `Button` selected on the design `Form`, you can click the Events icon in the Properties window at the right side of the screen. The Events icon looks like a lightning bolt. Figure 12-16 shows that the Properties window displays events instead of properties and that the `Click` event has an associated method.

Figure 12-16 Properties window displaying events

> **NOTE** When you are viewing events in the Properties window, you can return to the list of properties by clicking the Properties icon. This icon is to the immediate left of the Events icon.

If you scroll through the `Events` listed in the Properties window, you can see a wide variety of `Event` choices. If you scroll down to `MouseEnter` and double-click, you can see the code for an event handler as follows:

```
private void button1_MouseEnter(object sender, EventArgs e)
{
}
```

You can type any statements you want within this method. For example:

```
private void button1_MouseEnter(object sender, EventArgs e)
{
    label1.Text = "Go ahead";
    button1.BackColor = Color.Red;
}
```

CHAPTER TWELVE

When you run the program with the two new methods, two different events can occur:

» When you enter the button with the mouse (that is, pass the mouse over it), the `Label`'s `Text` changes to "Go ahead" and the button turns red, as shown on the left in Figure 12-17.
» After the button is clicked, the `Label`'s `Text` changes again and the `Label` becomes blue, as shown on the right in Figure 12-17.

Figure 12-17 `OneButtonTwoEvents` program when mouse enters button and after button is clicked

If you examine the code generated by the Windows Form Designer, you will find the following two statements:

```
this.button1.Click += new System.EventHandler(this.button1_Click);
this.button1.MouseEnter += new System.EventHandler
   (this.button1_MouseEnter);
```

These `EventHandler` statements are similar to those in the `Student` class in Figure 12-14. The `Click` and `MouseEnter` delegates have been set to handle events appropriately for this application. You could have used the IDE to create these events just by selecting them from the Properties list and writing the action statements that you wanted. The IDE saves you time by automatically entering the needed statement correctly. However, by knowing how to manually create a GUI program that contains events, you gain a greater understanding of how event handling works. This knowledge helps you troubleshoot problems, and helps you create your own new events and handlers when necessary.

HANDLING MOUSE EVENTS

Mouse events include all the actions a user takes with a mouse, including clicking, pointing, and dragging. Mouse events can be handled for any `Control` through an object of the class `MouseEventArgs`. The delegate used to create mouse event handlers is `MouseEventHandler`. Every mouse event-handling method must have two parameters: an object representing the sender and an object representing the event. Depending on the event, the type of the second

HANDLING EVENTS

parameter is `EventArgs` or `MouseEventArgs`. Table 12-2 describes several common mouse events, and Table 12-3 lists some properties of the `MouseEventArgs` class.

Mouse event	Description	Event argument type
`MouseClick`	Occurs when the user clicks the mouse within the `Control`'s boundaries	`MouseEventArgs`
`MouseDoubleClick`	Occurs when the user double-clicks the mouse within the `Control`'s boundaries	`MouseEventArgs`
`MouseEnter`	Occurs when the mouse cursor enters the `Control`'s boundaries	`EventArgs`
`MouseLeave`	Occurs when the mouse cursor leaves the `Control`'s boundaries	`EventArgs`
`MouseDown`	Occurs when a mouse button is pressed while the mouse is within the `Control`'s boundaries	`MouseEventArgs`
`MouseHover`	Occurs when the mouse cursor is within the `Control`'s boundaries	`MouseEventArgs`
`MouseMove`	Occurs when the mouse is moved while within the `Control`'s boundaries	`MouseEventArgs`
`MouseUp`	Occurs when a mouse button is released while the mouse is within the `Control`'s boundaries	`MouseEventArgs`

Table 12-2 Common mouse events

`MouseEventArgs` property	Description
`Button`	Specifies which mouse button triggered the event; the value can be `Left`, `Right`, `Middle`, or none
`Clicks`	Specifies the number of times the mouse was clicked
`X`	The x-coordinate where the event occurred on the control that generated the event
`Y`	The y-coordinate where the event occurred on the control that generated the event

Table 12-3 Properties of the `MouseEventArgs` class

> **NOTE** `MouseClick` and `Click` are separate events. The `Click` event takes an `EventArgs` parameter, but `MouseClick` takes a `MouseEventArgs` parameter. For example, if you define a `Click` event, you do not have the `MouseEventArgs` class properties.

Figure 12-18 contains a `Form` with a single `Label` that changes as the user continues to click the mouse on it. Initially, the `Label` is empty, but the following code was added to the Form.cs file. Every time the mouse is clicked with this event handler, the label is appended with the words "Clicked at" and the x- and y-coordinate position where the click occurred on the `Form`.

```
private void Form1_MouseClick(object sender, MouseEventArgs e)
{
    label1.Text += "\nClicked at " + e.X + ", " + e.Y;
}
```

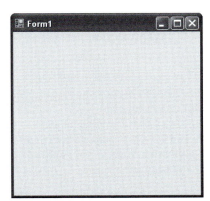
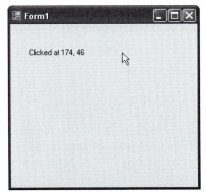
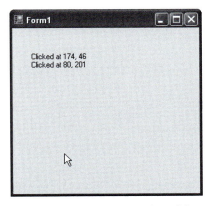
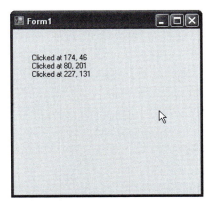

Figure 12-18 A `Form` that responds to clicks

When the programmer selects the `MouseClick()` event for `Form1` from the Event list in the IDE, the following code is generated in the Designer.cs file. This code instantiates the `MouseClick` delegate.

```
this.MouseClick += new System.Windows.Forms.MouseEventHandler
    (this.Form1_MouseClick);
```

HANDLING KEYBOARD EVENTS

Keyboard events, also known as **key events**, occur when a user presses and releases keyboard keys. Table 12-4 lists some common keyboard events. Similar to the way mouse events work, every keyboard event-handling method must have two parameters: an object representing the sender and an object representing the event. Depending on the event, the delegate used to create the keyboard event handler is either `KeyEventHandler` or `KeyPressEventHandler`, and the type of the second parameter is `KeyEventArgs` or `KeyPressEventArgs`.

Keyboard event	Description	Event argument type
KeyDown	Occurs when a key is first pressed	KeyEventArgs
KeyUp	Occurs when a key is released	KeyEventArgs
KeyPress	Occurs when a key is pressed	KeyPressEventArgs

Table 12-4 Keyboard events

Table 12-5 describes `KeyEventArgs` properties and Table 12-6 describes `KeyPressEventArgs` properties. An important difference is that `KeyEventArgs` objects include data about helper keys or modifier keys that are pressed with another key. For example, if you need to distinguish between a user pressing *A* and pressing *Alt+A* in your application, then you must use a keyboard event that uses an argument of type `KeyEventArgs`.

Property	Description
Alt	Indicates whether the Alt key was pressed
Control	Indicates whether the Control (Ctrl) key was pressed
Shift	Indicates whether the Shift key was pressed
KeyCode	Returns the code for the key
KeyData	Returns the key code along with any modifier key
KeyValue	Returns a numeric representation of the key (this number is known as the Windows virtual key code)

Table 12-5 Some properties of `KeyEventArgs` class

Property	Description
KeyChar	Returns the ASCII character for the key pressed

Table 12-6 A property of `KeyPressEventArgs` class

For example, suppose you create a `Form` with an empty `Label`, like the first `Form` in the series in Figure 12-18, and that you insert the `KeyUp()` method in Figure 12-19 into the Form.cs file. When the user releases a key, the `Label` is filled with information about the key. Figure 12-20 shows four executions of this modified program. During the first execution, the user typed *a*.

You can see on the form that the `KeyCode` is "A" (not "a"), but you also can see that the user did not press the Shift key.

```
private void Form1_KeyUp(object sender, KeyEventArgs e)
{
    label1.Text += "Key Code " + e.KeyCode;
    label1.Text += "\nAlt " + e.Alt;
    label1.Text += "\nShift " + e.Shift;
    label1.Text += "\nControl " + e.Control;
    label1.Text += "\nKey Data " + e.KeyData;
    label1.Text += "\nKey Value " + e.KeyValue;
}
```

Figure 12-19 `KeyUp()` method

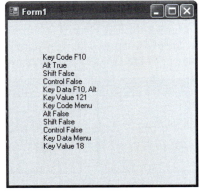

Figure 12-20 Four executions of `KeyDemonstration` program

HANDLING EVENTS

In the second execution in Figure 12-20, the user held down the Shift key, pressed *a*, and then released the Shift key. This causes two separate `KeyUp` events. The first has `KeyCode` "A" with Shift `true`, and the second has `KeyCode ShiftKey`. Notice that the `Key` values generated after typing *a*, *A*, and *Shift* are all different.

In the third execution in Figure 12-20, the user pressed the number 1, whose code is D1. In the final execution, the user pressed *Alt+F10* and released the F10 key first.

> **NOTE** When you view the Designer.cs file for the `KeyDemonstration` program, you see the following automatically created statement, which defines the composed delegate:
>
>   this.KeyUp += new System.Windows.Forms.KeyEventHandler
>   (this.Form1_KeyUp);

MANAGING MULTIPLE Controls

When `Forms` contain multiple `Controls`, you often want several actions to have a single consequence. For example, you might want the same action to occur whether the user clicks a button or presses the Enter key, or you might want multiple buttons to achieve the same result.

DEFINING FOCUS

> **NOTE** Setting two or more `Controls`' `TabIndex` values to 0 does not cause an error. Only one `Control` will receive focus, however.

When users encounter multiple GUI `Controls` on a `Form`, usually one `Control` has **focus**. That is, if the user presses the Enter key, the `Control` will raise an event.

`TabStop` is a Boolean property of a `Control` that identifies whether the `Control` will serve as a stopping place in a sequence of Tab key presses. `TabIndex` is a numeric property that indicates the order in which the `Control` will receive focus when the user presses the Tab key. Programmers typically use small numbers for `TabIndex` values, beginning with 0. When a `Control` has a `TabIndex` of 0, it receives focus when the `Form` is initialized.

Figure 12-21 shows a `Form` that contains three `Buttons` and a `Label`. The `Button` labeled "1" has focus because the `TabStop` value has been set to `true` for each of the `Buttons`, and they have been assigned `TabIndex` values in ascending order. When the application starts, the first `Button` has focus; whether the user clicks that button or presses Enter, the message appears as shown on the right side of the figure. The user can select the other `Buttons` by clicking them as usual, or by pressing Tab until the desired button has focus and then pressing Enter.

Figure 12-21 The `TabStopDemo` application

FIRING A SINGLE EVENT FROM MULTIPLE CONTROLS

When a `Form` contains multiple `Controls`, you can create a separate event for each `Control`. However, you can also associate the same event with multiple `Controls`. For example,

CHAPTER TWELVE

Figure 12-22 shows a `Form` that contains two `Button`s and a `Label`. In the IDE, you can double-click the first `Button` and create a method such as the following:

```
private void button1_Click(object sender, EventArgs e)
{
    label1.Text += " a letter button";
}
```

Figure 12-22 `Form` displayed by `TwoButtonsOneEvent` program

If you click the second button so its properties are displayed in the IDE's Properties list, you can click the Events icon to see a list of events associated with the second button. In Figure 12-23, no `Click` event has been chosen yet, but a list box is available. This list contains all the existing events that have the correct signature to be the event handler for the event. The list shows that the `button1_Click()` handler can also handle a `button2_Click` event, so you can select it. When you run the program, clicking either button produces the output shown in Figure 12-24.

Figure 12-23 `Event` properties for `button2`

Figure 12-24 Output of `TwoButtonsOneEvent` program after either button is clicked

495

> **NOTE** When two or more `Control`s generate the same event, many programmers prefer to generalize the event method name. For example, if `button1` and `button2` call the same method when clicked, it makes sense to name the event method `button_Click()` instead of `button1_Click()`.

> **NOTE** Perhaps you have shopped online at a site that offers multiple ways to "buy now." For example, you might click a grocery cart icon, choose "Buy now" from a menu, or click a button. If you want to encourage a user's behavior, it makes sense to provide multiple ways to accommodate it.

CONTINUING TO LEARN ABOUT `Control`S AND `Event`S

If you examine the Visual Studio IDE, you will discover many additional `Control`s that contain hundreds of properties and events. No single book or programming course can demonstrate all of them for you. However, if you understand good programming principles and the syntax and structure of C# programs, learning about each new C# feature becomes progressively easier. When you encounter a new control in the IDE, you probably can use it without understanding all the code generated in the background, but when you do understand the background, your knowledge of C# is more complete.

Continue to explore the Help facility in the Visual Studio IDE. Particularly, read the brief tutorials there. Also, you should search the Internet for C# discussion groups. C# is a new, dynamic language, and programmers pose many questions to each other online. Reading these discussions can provide you with valuable information and suggest new approaches to resolving problems.

YOU DO IT

CREATING DELEGATES

To demonstrate how delegates work, you will create two delegate instances in the next steps and assign different method references to them.

To demonstrate delegates:

1. Open a new file in your text editor. Type the necessary `using` statement, then create a delegate that encapsulates a `void` method that accepts a `double` argument:

   ```
   using System;
   delegate void DiscountDelegate(ref double saleAmount);
   ```

2. Begin creating a `Discount` class that contains a `StandardDiscount()` method. The method accepts a reference parameter that represents an amount of a sale. If the sale amount is at least $1000.00, a discount of 5% is calculated and subtracted from the sale amount; if the sale amount is not at least $1000, nothing is subtracted.

```
class Discount
{
   public static void StandardDiscount
      (ref double saleAmount)
   {
      const double DISCOUNT_RATE = 0.05;
      const double CUTOFF = 1000.00;
      double discount;
      if(saleAmount >= CUTOFF)
         discount = saleAmount * DISCOUNT_RATE;
      else
         discount = 0;
      saleAmount -= discount;
   }
```

3. Add a `PreferredDiscount()` method. The method also accepts a reference parameter that represents the amount of a sale and calculates a discount of 10% on every sale.

```
public static void PreferredDiscount(ref double saleAmount)
{
   const double SPECIAL_DISCOUNT = 0.10;
   double discount = saleAmount * SPECIAL_DISCOUNT;
   saleAmount -= discount;
}
```

4. Start a `Main()` method that declares variables whose values will be supplied by the user—a sale amount and a code. Declare two `DiscountDelegate` objects named `firstDel` and `secondDel`. Assign a reference to the `StandardDiscount()` method to one `DiscountDelegate` object and a reference to the `PreferredDiscount()` method to the other `DiscountDelegate` object.

```
public static void Main()
{
   double saleAmount;
   char code;
   DiscountDelegate firstDel, secondDel;
   firstDel = new DiscountDelegate(StandardDiscount);
   secondDel = new DiscountDelegate(PreferredDiscount);
```

5. Continue the `Main()` method with prompts to the user to enter a sale amount and a code indicating whether the standard or preferred discount should apply. Then, depending on the code, use the appropriate delegate to calculate the correct new value for `saleAmount`. Display the value and add closing curly braces for the `Main()` method and the class.

```
         Console.Write("Enter amount of sale ");
         saleAmount = Convert.ToDouble(Console.ReadLine());
         Console.Write("Enter S for standard discount, " +
            "or P for preferred discount ");
```

HANDLING EVENTS

```
        code = Convert.ToChar(Console.ReadLine());
        if(code == 'S')
            firstDel(ref saleAmount);
        else
            secondDel(ref saleAmount);
        Console.WriteLine("New sale amount is {0}",
            saleAmount.ToString("C2"));
    }
}
```

6. Save the file as **DiscountDelegateDemo.cs**, then compile and execute it. Figure 12-25 shows the results when the program is executed several times.

Figure 12-25 Sample executions of DiscountDelegateDemo program

CREATING A COMPOSED DELEGATE

When you compose delegates, you can invoke multiple method calls using a single statement. In the next steps, you will create a composed delegate to demonstrate how composition works.

To create a composed delegate:

1. Open the **DiscountDelegateDemo.cs** file in your text editor. Immediately save it as **DiscountDelegateDemo2.cs**.

2. Within the Main() method, add a third DiscountDelegate object to the statement that declares the two existing versions, as follows:

   ```
   DiscountDelegate firstDel, secondDel, thirdDel;
   ```

3. After the statements that assign values to the existing DiscountDelegate objects, add statements that assign the firstDel object to thirdDel and then add secondDel to it through composition.

   ```
   thirdDel = firstDel;
   thirdDel += secondDel;
   ```

CHAPTER TWELVE

4. Change the prompt for the code, as follows, to reflect three options. The standard and preferred discounts remain the same, but the extreme discount (supposedly for special customers) provides both types of discounts, first subtracting 5% for any sale equal to or greater than $1000, and then providing a discount of 10% more.

   ```
   Console.Write("Enter S for standard discount, " +
       "P for preferred discount, " +
       "\nor X for eXtreme discount ");
   ```

5. Change the `if` statement so that if the user does not enter *S* or *P*, then the extreme discount applies.

   ```
   if(code == 'S')
       firstDel(ref saleAmount);
   else
       if(code == 'P')
           secondDel(ref saleAmount);
       else
           thirdDel(ref saleAmount);
   ```

6. Save the program, then compile and execute it. For reference, Figure 12-26 shows the complete program. Figure 12-27 shows the output when the program is executed several times. When the user enters a sale amount of $1000 and an *S*, a 5% discount is applied. When the user enters a *P* for the same amount, a 10% discount is applied. When the user enters *X* with the same amount, a 5% discount is applied, followed by a 10% discount, which produces a net result of a 14.5% discount.

```
using System;
delegate void DiscountDelegate(ref double saleAmount);
class Discount
{
    public static void StandardDiscount(ref double saleAmount)
    {
        const double DISCOUNT_RATE = 0.05;
        const double CUTOFF = 1000.00;
        double discount;
        if(saleAmount >= CUTOFF)
            discount = saleAmount * DISCOUNT_RATE;
        else
            discount = 0;
        saleAmount -= discount;
    }
    public static void PreferredDiscount(ref double saleAmount)
    {
        const double SPECIAL_DISCOUNT = 0.10;
        double discount = saleAmount * SPECIAL_DISCOUNT;
        saleAmount -= discount;
    }
```

Figure 12-26 `DiscountDelegateDemo2` program (*continued*)

HANDLING EVENTS

```
public static void Main()
{
    double saleAmount;
    char code;
    DiscountDelegate firstDel, secondDel, thirdDel;
    firstDel = new DiscountDelegate(StandardDiscount);
    secondDel = new DiscountDelegate(PreferredDiscount);
    thirdDel = firstDel;
    thirdDel += secondDel;
    Console.Write("Enter amount of sale ");
    saleAmount = Convert.ToDouble(Console.ReadLine());
    Console.Write("Enter S for standard discount, " +
        "P for preferred discount, " +
        "\nor X for eXtreme discount ");
    code = Convert.ToChar(Console.ReadLine());
    if(code == 'S')
        firstDel(ref saleAmount);
    else
        if(code == 'P')
            secondDel(ref saleAmount);
        else
            thirdDel(ref saleAmount);
    Console.WriteLine("New sale amount is {0}",
        saleAmount.ToString("C2"));
}
```

Figure 12-26 (*continued*)

Figure 12-27 Three executions of DiscountDelegateDemo2 program

> **»NOTE** For static methods, like StandardDiscount and PreferredDiscount, a delegate object encapsulates the method to be called. When creating a class that contains instance methods, you create delegate objects that encapsulate both an instance of the class and a method of the instance. You will create this type of delegate in the next section.

CHAPTER TWELVE

CREATING A DELEGATE THAT ENCAPSULATES INSTANCE METHODS

In the next set of steps, you will create a simple `BankAccount` class that is similar to many classes you already have created. The `BankAccount` class will contain just two data fields—an account number and a balance. It also will contain methods to make withdrawals and deposits. An event will be generated after any withdrawal or deposit.

To create the `BankAccount` class:

1. Open a new file in your text editor. Type the `using System;` statement, then begin a class named `BankAccount`. The class contains an account number, a balance, and an event that executes when an account's balance is adjusted.

   ```
   using System;
   public class BankAccount
   {
       private int acctNum;
       private double balance;
       public event EventHandler BalanceAdjusted;
   ```

2. Add a constructor that accepts an account number parameter and initializes the balance to 0.

   ```
   public BankAccount(int acct)
   {
       acctNum = acct;
       balance = 0;
   }
   ```

3. Add read-only properties for both the account number and the account balance.

   ```
   public int AcctNum
   {
       get
       {
           return acctNum;
       }
   }
   public double Balance
   {
       get
       {
           return balance;
       }
   }
   ```

4. Add two methods. One makes account deposits by adding the parameter to the account balance and the other makes withdrawals by subtracting the parameter value from the bank balance. Each uses the `OnBalanceAdjusted` event handler that reacts to all deposit and withdrawal events by displaying the new balance.

HANDLING EVENTS

```
    public void MakeDeposit(double amt)
    {
       balance += amt;
       OnBalanceAdjusted(EventArgs.Empty);
    }
    public void MakeWithdrawal(double amt)
    {
       balance -= amt;
       OnBalanceAdjusted(EventArgs.Empty);
    }
```

5. Add the `OnBalanceAdjusted()` method that accepts an `EventArgs` parameter and calls `BalanceAdjusted`, passing it a reference to the current `BankAccount` object that was adjusted and to the `EventArgs` object. Include a closing curly brace for the class.

```
    public void OnBalanceAdjusted(EventArgs e)
    {
       BalanceAdjusted(this, e);
    }
}
```

> **NOTE** Earlier in the chapter, you learned that calling a method such as `OnBalanceAdjusted()` is also known as invoking the event.

6. Save the file as **DemoBankEvent.cs**.

CREATING AN EVENT LISTENER

When you write an application that declares a `BankAccount`, you might want the client program to listen for `BankAccount` events. To do so, you create an `EventListener` class.

To create an `EventListener` class:

1. After the closing curly brace of the `BankAccount` class, type the following `EventListener` class that contains a `BankAccount` object. When the `EventListener` constructor executes, the `BankAccount` field is initialized with the constructor parameter. Using the += operator, add the `BankAccountBalanceAdjusted()` method to the event delegate. Next, write the `BankAccountBalanceAdjusted()` method to display a message and information about the `BankAccount`.

```
class EventListener
{
   private BankAccount acct;
   public EventListener(BankAccount account)
   {
      acct = account;
      acct.BalanceAdjusted += new EventHandler
         (BankAccountBalanceAdjusted);
   }
```

```
        private void BankAccountBalanceAdjusted(object sender,
            EventArgs e)
        {
            Console.WriteLine
                ("The account balance has been adjusted.");
            Console.WriteLine("    Account# {0}   balance {1}",
                acct.AcctNum, acct.Balance.ToString("C2"));
        }
    }
```

2. Create a class to test the `BankAccount` and `EventListener` classes. Below the closing curly brace for the `EventListener` class, start a `DemoBankAccountEvent` class that contains a `Main()` method. Declare an integer to hold the number of transactions that will occur in the demonstration program. Also declare two variables: one can hold a code that indicates whether a transaction is a deposit or withdrawal, and one is the amount of the transaction.

```
class DemoBankAccountEvent
{
    public static void Main()
    {
        const int TRANSACTIONS = 5;
        char code;
        double amt;
```

3. Declare a `BankAccount` object that is assigned an arbitrary account number and declare an `EventListener` object so this program is registered to listen for events from the `BankAccount`. Each change in the `BankAccount` balance will not only change the balance data field, it will execute the `BankAccountBalanceAdjusted()` method that displays two lines of explanation.

```
        BankAccount acct = new BankAccount(334455);
        EventListener listener = new EventListener (acct);
```

4. Add a loop that executes five times (the value of `TRANSACTIONS`). On each iteration, prompt the user to indicate whether the current transaction is a deposit or withdrawal and to enter the transaction amount. Call the `MakeDeposit()` or `MakeWithdrawal()` method accordingly. At the end of the `for` loop, add a closing curly brace for the `Main()` method and another one for the class.

```
        for(int x = 0; x < TRANSACTIONS; ++x)
        {
            Console.Write
                ("Enter D for deposit or W for withdrawal ");
            code = Convert.ToChar(Console.ReadLine());
            Console.Write("Enter dollar amount ");
            amt = Convert.ToDouble(Console.ReadLine());
            if(code == 'D')
                acct.MakeDeposit(amt);
```

HANDLING EVENTS

```
            else
                acct.MakeWithdrawal(amt);
        }
    }
}
```

5. Save the file, then compile and execute it. For reference, Figure 12-28 shows a typical execution in which five transactions modify the account. The output shows that an event occurs five times—twice for deposits and three times for withdrawals.

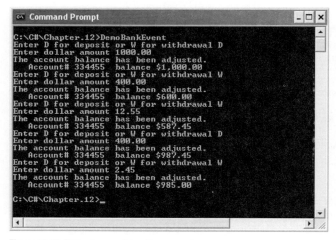

Figure 12-28 Typical execution of DemoBankEvent program

USING TabStop AND TabIndex

In the next steps, you will create a Form in the Visual Studio IDE and add three Buttons so you can demonstrate how to manipulate the TabStop and TabIndex properties.

To demonstrate TabStop and TabIndex:

1. Open the Visual Studio IDE and start a new project. Define it to be a **Windows Application** named **ManyButtons**.

2. Change the Text property of Form1 to **Many Buttons**.

3. Drag three Buttons onto the Form and place them as close as possible to the positions shown in Figure 12-29. Change the Text on the three Buttons to **Red**, **White**, and **Blue**, respectively.

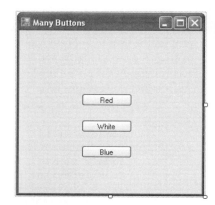

Figure 12-29 Three Buttons on the Many Buttons Form

504

CHAPTER TWELVE

4. Examine the Properties list for the Red button. The `TabStop` property has been set to `True` and the `TabIndex` is 0. Examine the properties for the White and Blue buttons. The IDE has set their `TabIndex` values to 1 and 2, respectively.

5. Click the **Save All** button and then run the program. When the `Form` appears, the Red button has focus. Press the **Tab** key, and notice that focus changes to the White button. When you press **Tab** again, focus changes to the Blue button. Press **Tab** several more times and observe that the focus rotates among the `Button`s.

6. Dismiss the `Form`.

7. Change the `TabIndex` property of the Blue button to **0**, and change the `TabIndex` of the Red button to **2**. (The `TabIndex` of the White button remains 1.) Save the program again and then run it. This time, the Blue button begins with focus. When you press **Tab**, the order in which the `Button`s receive focus is Blue, then White, then Red. (Clicking the `Button`s or pressing Enter raises no event because you have not assigned events to the `Button`s.)

8. Dismiss the `Form`. Select the White button and change its `TabStop` property to **False**. Save the program and then execute it. This time, the Blue button has focus when the `Form` appears. When you press **Tab**, focus alternates between the Blue and Red buttons, bypassing the White button, which is no longer part of the tabbing sequence.

9. Change the White button's `TabStop` value back to **True**. Change the `TabIndex` property for the Red button back to **0** and the `TabIndex` property for the Blue button back to **2**. Click the **Save All** button.

ASSOCIATING ONE METHOD WITH MULTIPLE EVENTS

In the next steps, you will add a single method to the Many Buttons `Form` and cause this method to execute no matter which `Button` the user clicks.

To associate one method with multiple events:

1. If it is not still open, open the **Many Buttons** project in the Visual Studio IDE. Drag a `Label` onto the `Form` and place it at the approximate location of the `Label` in Figure 12-30. Change the `Label`'s `Text` property to **Click a button**.

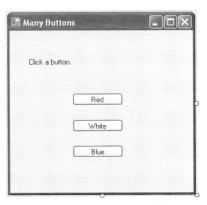

Figure 12-30 Many Buttons `Form` with `Label`

HANDLING EVENTS

2. Double-click the **Red** button on the Form to view the code for the shell of a `button1_Click()` method. Between the method's curly braces, insert a statement that will display the `ToString()` value of the object that generates the `button1_Click()` method:

    `label1.Text = sender.ToString();`

3. Click the **Save All** button and then execute the program. When the Form appears, the Label displays "Click a button." If you click the White or Blue button, nothing happens (because you have not yet assigned an event to those Buttons). When you click the Red button, however, the Label changes to show the `ToString()` representation of the sender object within the `button1_Click()` method. See Figure 12-31. The `ToString()` method for the object contains the object type (System.Windows.Forms.Button), a comma, and the object's Text property (Text: Red).

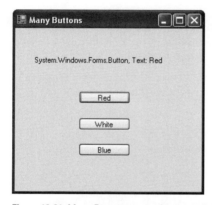

Figure 12-31 Many Buttons Form after user clicks Red button

4. Dismiss the Form. Within the IDE, return to Designer view.
5. Select the **White** button. In its Properties list, click the **Events** button (the lightning bolt). Select the **Click** event. From the list box next to the Click event, select **button1_Click()** as the method to associate with a click on button2.
6. On the Form, select the **Blue** button. In its **Events** list, select its **Click** event and associate it with the `button1_Click()` method.
7. Click the **Save All** button and then execute the program. No matter which button you click, an appropriate string appears within the Label, proving that a different object becomes the sender each time the method executes.

USING THE sender OBJECT IN AN EVENT

When a Form contains multiple widgets that you can manipulate, you can write event-handling methods for each one. Alternatively, you can write a single event-handling method that can take appropriate action based on which Control generated the event. The Control that

CHAPTER TWELVE

causes an event is represented as a generic object in the object sender argument to an event method.

Every object has an Equals() method that returns a Boolean value indicating whether two objects are the same object at the same memory location—that is, whether one object name is an alias for the other. Within the button1_Click() method, you can use the sender's Equals() method to determine which object (button1, button2, or button3) raised the event.

To determine which object raised an event:

1. With the **ManyButtons** program still open in the Visual Studio IDE, view the code for the Form and locate the button1_Click() method. After the statement that changes the Label's Text property, but before the closing curly brace of the method, add a nested if statement. This statement compares the sender object first to button1 (in which case you set the Form's BackColor to red), then to button2 (setting the Form's BackColor to white). By default, the statement assumes that the sender is button3 (setting the Form's color to blue).

```
if(sender.Equals(button1))
   this.BackColor = Color.Red;
else
   if(sender.Equals(button2))
       this.BackColor = Color.White;
   else
       this.BackColor = Color.Blue;
```

2. Click the **Save All** button and then execute the program. As you select Buttons, both the Label's text and the Form's background color change appropriately.

3. Exit Visual Studio.

CHAPTER SUMMARY

» You use an event to notify a client program when something happens to a class object the program is using. GUI programs are event driven—an event such as a button click "drives" the program to perform a task. Programmers also say a button click raises an event, fires an event, or triggers an event. A method that performs a task in response to an event is an event handler. The Click event is the event generated when a button is clicked.

» A delegate is an object that contains a reference to a method. C# delegates provide a way for a program to take alternative courses when running; a delegate provides a way to pass a reference to a method as an argument to another method.

» You can assign one delegate to another using the = operator. You also can use the + and += operators to combine delegates into a composed delegate that calls the delegates from which it is built.

» To declare your own event, you use a delegate. An event provides a way for a class's clients to dictate methods that should execute when an event occurs. The clients identify methods to execute by providing delegates. When an event occurs, any delegate that a client has given or passed to the event is invoked.

507

HANDLING EVENTS

» The .NET Framework provides guidelines you should follow if you are developing a class that others will use. These guidelines indicate that the delegate type for an event should take exactly two parameters: a parameter indicating the source of the event, and an `EventArgs` parameter that encapsulates any additional information about the event. For events that do not use additional information, the .NET Framework has already defined an appropriate type named `EventHandler`.

» When you use existing `Control` components like `Button`s and `ListBox`es, they contain fields and `public` properties like `Text`, as well as events with names like `Click`. A `Form` can contain any number of `Control`s that might have events associated with them. Additionally, a single control might be able to raise any number of events.

» Mouse events include all the actions a user takes with a mouse, including clicking, pointing, and dragging. Mouse events can be handled for any `Control` through an object of the class `MouseEventArgs`. The delegate used to create mouse event handlers is `MouseEventHandler`. Every mouse event-handling method must have two parameters: an object representing the sender and an object representing the event. Depending on the event, the type of the second parameter is `EventArgs` or `MouseEventArgs`.

» Keyboard events, also known as key events, occur when a user presses and releases keyboard keys. Every keyboard event-handling method must have two parameters: an object representing the sender and an object representing the event. Depending on the event, the type of the second parameter is either `KeyEventArgs` or `KeyPressEventArgs`.

» When users encounter multiple GUI `Control`s on a `Form`, usually one `Control` has focus. That is, if the user presses Enter, the `Control` will raise an event. When a `Form` contains multiple `Control`s, you can create a separate event for each `Control`. However, you can also associate the same event with multiple `Control`s.

» When you encounter a new control in the IDE, you probably can use it without understanding all the code generated in the background. However, when you do understand the background, your knowledge of C# is more complete.

KEY TERMS

Event-driven programs contain code that causes an event such as a button click to drive the program to perform a task.

A button click **raises an event**, **fires an event**, or **triggers an event**.

An **event handler** is a method that performs a task in response to an event.

An **event receiver** is another name for an event handler.

An **event sender** is the control that generates an event.

`EventArgs` is a C# class designed for holding event information.

The `Click` **event** is the event generated when a `Control` is clicked.

A **delegate** is an object that contains a reference to a method.

A **composed delegate** calls the delegates from which it is built.

CHAPTER TWELVE

Invoking the event occurs when you call an event method.

`EventHandler` is an appropriate type for events that do not use any information besides the source of the event and the `EventArgs` parameter.

Key events are keyboard events that occur when a user presses and releases keyboard keys.

When a `Control` has **focus** and the user presses Enter, the `Control` will raise an event.

REVIEW QUESTIONS

1. A delegate is an object that contains a reference to a(n) _____.
   a. object
   b. class
   c. method
   d. `Control`

2. C# delegates provide a way for a program to _____.
   a. take alternative courses when running
   b. include multiple methods
   c. include methods from other classes
   d. include multiple `Control`s that use the same method

3. Which of the following correctly declares a `delegate` type?
   a. `void aDelegate(int num);`
   b. `delegate void aDelegate(num);`
   c. `delegate void aDelegate(int num);`
   d. `delegate aDelegate(int num);`

4. If you have declared a `delegate` instance, you can assign it a reference to a method as long as the method has the same _____ as the `delegate`.
   a. return type
   b. identifier
   c. argument list
   d. two of the above

5. You can combine two delegates to create a(n) _____ delegate.
   a. assembled
   b. classified
   c. artificial
   d. composed

6. To combine two delegates using the + operator, the `delegate` objects must _____.
   a. have the same argument list
   b. have the same return type
   c. both of these
   d. neither of these

HANDLING EVENTS

7. In C#, a(n) _____ occurs when something interesting happens to an object.
   a. delegate
   b. event
   c. notification
   d. instantiation

8. In C#, an event provides a way for a class to allow clients to provide _____.
   a. GUI objects that other classes can use
   b. delegates to methods
   c. arguments to other classes
   d. widgets to `Forms`

9. An event handler `delegate` requires _____ arguments.
   a. zero
   b. one
   c. two
   d. any number greater than zero

10. Using an event handler, the sender is the _____.
    a. delegate associated with the event
    b. method called by the event
    c. object where the event was initiated
    d. class containing the method that the event invokes

11. The `EventArgs` class contains a static field named _____.
    a. `Empty`
    b. `Text`
    c. `Location`
    d. `Source`

12. When creating events, you can use a predefined delegate type named _____ that is automatically provided by the .NET Framework.
    a. `EventArgs`
    b. `EventHandler`
    c. `EventType`
    d. `Event`

13. Which of the following is not a predefined `Control` event?
    a. `MouseEnter`
    b. `Click`
    c. `Destroy`
    d. `TextChanged`

14. A single `Control` can raise _____ event(s).
    a. one
    b. two
    c. five
    d. any number of

15. When you create Forms with Controls that raise events, an advantage to creating the code by hand over using the Visual Studio IDE is _____ .

    a. you are less likely to make typing errors

    b. you save a lot of repetitious typing

    c. you are less likely to forget to set a property

    d. you gain a clearer understanding of the C# language

16. When a Form contains three Controls and one has focus, you can raise an event by _____ .

    a. clicking any Control

    b. pressing Enter

    c. either of these

    d. none of these

17. The TabStop property of a Control is a(n) _____ .

    a. integer value indicating the tab order

    b. Boolean value indicating whether the Control has a position in the tab sequence

    c. string value indicating the name of the method executed when the Control raises an event

    d. delegate name indicating the event raised when the user tabs to the Control

18. The TabIndex property of a Control is a(n) _____ .

    a. integer value indicating the tab order

    b. Boolean value indicating whether the Control has a position in the tab sequence

    c. string value indicating the name of the method executed when the Control raises an event

    d. delegate name indicating the event raised when the user tabs to the Control

19. The Control that causes an event is the _____ argument to an event method.

    a. first   c. third

    b. second   d. fourth

20. Which of the following is true?

    a. You can generate a single event from multiple Controls.

    b. You can generate multiple events from a single Control.

    c. Both of the above are true.

    d. None of the above are true.

EXERCISES

Save the programs that you create in these exercises in the Chapter.12 folder on your Student Disk.

1. Create a `Form` that contains three `Label`s that hold famous quotes of your choice. When the program starts, the background color of the `Form` and each `Label` should be black. When the user passes a mouse over a `Label`, change its `BackColor` to white, revealing the text of the quote. Save the project as **DisplayQuotes**.

2. Create a `Form` with a list of three `LinkLabel`s that link to any three Web sites you choose. When a user clicks a `LinkLabel`, link to that site. When a user's mouse hovers over a `LinkLabel`, display a brief message that explains the site's purpose. After a user clicks a link, move the most recently selected link to the top of the list and move the other two links down, making sure to retain the correct explanation with each link. Save the project as **RecentlyVisitedSites**.

3. Create a `Form` with a `ListBox` that lists at least four sports teams of your choice. When the user places the mouse over the `ListBox`, display a `Label` that contains single-game ticket prices for each team. The `Label` disappears when the user's mouse leaves the `ListBox` area. When the user clicks a team name in the `ListBox`, display another `Label` that contains the correct ticket price. Also change the `BackColor` of the `Form` to the selected team's color. Save the project as **TeamSelector**.

4. Locate an animated .gif file on the Web or use the one stored in the Chapter.12 folder on your Student Disk. Create a `Form` that contains a `PictureBox`. Display three different messages on a `Label`—one when the user's mouse is over the `PictureBox`, one when the mouse is not over the `PictureBox`, and one when the user clicks the `PictureBox`. Save the project as **Animated**.

5. The Sunshine Subdivision allows users to select siding for their new homes, but they allow only specific trim colors with each siding color. Create a `Form` for Sunshine Subdivision that allows a user to choose one of three siding colors from a `ListBox`—white, gray, or blue. When the user selects a siding color, the program should display a second `ListBox` that contains only the following choices:

   » White siding—black, red, green, or dark blue trim
   » Gray siding—black or white trim
   » Blue siding—white or dark blue trim

   After the user selects a trim color, the program should display a congratulatory message on a `Label` indicating that the choice is a good one. The trim `ListBox` also becomes invisible. If the user makes a new selection from the siding `ListBox`, the congratulatory message is invisible until the user selects a complementary trim.

Hint: You can remove the entire contents of a `ListBox` using the `Items.Clear()` method, as in `this.listBox2.Items.Clear();`. Save the project as **SunshineSubdivision**.

6. Create a `Form` that contains a guessing game with five `RadioButton`s numbered 1 through 5. Randomly choose one of the `RadioButton`s as the winning button. When the user clicks a `RadioButton`, display a message indicating whether the user is right.

   Add a `Label` to the `Form` that provides a hint. When the user's mouse hovers over the label, notify the user of one `RadioButton` that is incorrect. After the user makes a selection, disable all the `RadioButton`s. Save the project as **GuessANumber**.

> **NOTE** You can create a random number that is at least min but less than max using the following statements:
> ```
> Random RandomClass = new Random();
> int randomNumber;
> randomNumber = RandomClass.Next(min, max);
> ```

7. Create a `Form` that contains two randomly generated arrays, each containing 100 numbers. Include two `Button`s labeled "1" and "2". Starting with position 0 in each array, ask the user to guess which of the two arrays contains the higher number and to click one of the two buttons to indicate the guess. After each button click, the program displays the values of the two compared numbers, as well as running counts of the number of correct and incorrect guesses. After the user makes a guess, disable the `Button`s while the user views the results. After clicking a Next `Button`, the user can make another guess using the next two array values. If the user makes more than 100 guesses, the program should reset the array subscript to 0 so the comparisons start over, but continue to keep a running score. Save the project as **PickLarger**.

DEBUGGING EXERCISES

Each of the following files in the Chapter.12 folder on your Student Disk has syntax and/or logical errors. In each case, determine the problem and fix the program. After you correct the errors, save each file using the same filename preceded with *Fixed*. For example, DebugTwelve1.cs will become FixedDebugTwelve1.cs.

a. DebugTwelve1.cs
b. DebugTwelve2.cs
c. DebugTwelve3.cs
d. DebugTwelve4.cs

UP FOR DISCUSSION

1. Programming is a job that can be done from a remote location. For example, as a professional programmer, you might be able to work from home. Does this appeal to you? What are the advantages and disadvantages? If you have other programmers working for you, would you allow them to work from home? Would you require any "face time"—that is, time in the office with you or other workers?

2. Programming is a job that can be done from a remote location. For example, your organization might contact programmers who live in another country where wages are considerably lower than in the United States. Do you have any objections to employers using these workers? If so, what are they? If not, what objections might others have?

3. Suppose your organization hires programmers to work in another country. Suppose you also discover that working conditions there are not the same as in your country. For example, the buildings in which the workers do their jobs might not be subject to the same standards for ventilation and fire codes as the building where you work. Is your company under any obligation to change the working conditions?

4. Would you ever participate in a computer dating site? Would you go on a date with someone you met over the Web? What precautions would you take before such a date?

CHAPTER THIRTEEN

13

FILES AND STREAMS

In this chapter you will:

Understand computer files and how they are stored
Use the `File` and `Directory` classes
Understand data organization within a file
Understand streams
Write to a sequential access text file
Read from a sequential access text file
Search a sequential file
Understand serialization and deserialization

FILES AND STREAMS

In the early chapters of this book, you learned that storing values in variables provides programs with flexibility—a program that uses variables to replace constants can manipulate different values each time the program executes. However, when data values in a program are stored in variables, they are lost when the program ends. To retain data values for future use, you must store them in files. In this chapter, you will learn to create and manage files in C#.

UNDERSTANDING COMPUTER FILES AND HOW THEY ARE STORED

When data items are stored in a computer system, they can be stored for varying periods of time—temporarily or permanently.

Temporary storage is usually called computer memory or **random access memory** (RAM). When you write a C# program that stores a value in a variable, you are using temporary storage; the value you store is lost when the program ends or the computer loses power. This type of storage is **volatile**.

Permanent storage, on the other hand, is not lost when a computer loses power; it is **nonvolatile**. When you write a program and save it to a disk, you are using permanent storage.

> **»NOTE** When discussing computer storage, *temporary* and *permanent* refer to volatility, not length of time. For example, a *temporary* variable might exist for several hours in a large program or one that the user forgets to end, but a *permanent* piece of data might be saved and then deleted within a few seconds.

A **computer file** is a collection of information stored on a nonvolatile device in a computer system. Files exist on **permanent storage devices**, such as hard disks, floppy disks, Zip disks, USB drives, reels or cassettes of magnetic tape, and compact discs. Some files are **data files** that contain facts and figures, such as a payroll file that contains employee numbers, names, and salaries; some files are **program files** or **application files** that store software instructions. (You have created many such files throughout this book.) Other files can store graphics, text, or operating system instructions (such as the files with an .exe extension that your compiler has created for every .cs class you compile). Although their contents vary, files have many common characteristics—each file occupies space on a section of a storage device, and each has a name and a specific time of creation.

When you use data, you never directly use the copy that is stored in a file. Instead, you use a copy that is in memory. Especially when data items are stored on a hard disk, their location might not be clear to you—data just seems to be "in the computer." However, when you work with stored data, you must transfer a copy from the storage device into memory. When you store data in a computer file on a persistent storage device, you **write to the file**. This means you copy data from RAM to the file. When you copy data from a file on a storage device into RAM, you **read from the file**.

CHAPTER THIRTEEN

> **NOTE** Because you can erase data from files, some programmers prefer the term *persistent* storage to permanent storage. In other words, you can remove data from a file stored on a device such as a disk drive, so it is not technically permanent. However, the data remains in the file even when the computer loses power, so, unlike RAM, the data persists, or perseveres.

Computer files are the electronic equivalent of paper documents stored in file cabinets. In a physical file cabinet, the easiest way to store a document is to toss it into a drawer without a folder. When storing computer files, this is the equivalent of placing a file in the main or **root directory** of your storage device. However, for better organization, most office clerks place documents in folders; most computer users also organize their files into **folders** or **directories**. Users also can place folders within folders to form a hierarchy. The combination of the disk drive plus the complete hierarchy of directories in which a file resides is its **path**. For example, in the Windows operating system, the following line would be the complete path for a file named Data.txt on the C drive in a folder named Chapter.13 within the C# folder:

```
C:\C#\Chapter.13\Data.txt
```

> **NOTE** The terms *directory* and *folder* are used synonymously to mean an entity that is used to organize files. *Directory* is the more general term; the term *folder* came into use in graphical systems. For example, Microsoft began calling directories *folders* with the introduction of Windows 95.

C# provides built-in classes named `File` and `Directory` that contain methods to help you manipulate files and their directories, respectively.

USING THE `File` AND `Directory` CLASSES

The **File class** contains methods that allow you to access information about files. Some of the methods are listed in Table 13-1.

Method	Description
Create()	Creates a file
CreateText()	Creates a text file
Delete()	Deletes a file
Exists()	Returns true if the specified file exists
GetCreationTime()	Returns a DateTime object specifying when a file was created
GetLastAccessTime()	Returns a DateTime object specifying when a file was last accessed
GetLastWriteTime()	Returns a DateTime object specifying when a file was last modified
Move()	Moves a file to the specified location

Table 13-1 Selected `File` class methods

517

FILES AND STREAMS

> **NOTE** `DateTime` is a structure that contains data about a date and time. In Chapter 11, you used the date data from `DateTime` structures with `MonthCalendar` and `DateTimePicker` GUI objects. `DateTime` values can be expressed using Coordinated Universal Time (UTC), which is the internationally recognized name for Greenwich Mean Time (GMT). By default, `DateTime` values are expressed using the local time set on your computer. The property `DateTime.Now` returns the current local time. The property `DateTime.UtcNow` returns the current UTC time.

The `File` class is contained in the `System.IO` namespace. So, to use the `File` class, you can use its fully qualified name, `System.IO.File`, or you can add the statement `using System.IO;` at the top of your file. Figure 13-1 shows a program that includes the `using` statement and demonstrates several of the `File` class methods. The program prompts the user for a filename and then tests the file's existence. If the file exists, the last creation time, write time, and access time are displayed. If the file does not exist, a message is displayed. Figure 13-2 shows two executions of the program. In the first execution, the user enters a filename that is found, and the three significant dates are displayed. In the second execution, the entered filename does not exist.

> **NOTE** The `System.IO.FileInfo` class also allows you to access information about a file. See the Microsoft documentation at *http://msdn2.microsoft.com* for more information.

```
using System;
using System.IO;
public class FileStatistics
{
    public static void Main()
    {
        string fileName;
        Console.Write("Enter a filename ");
        fileName = Console.ReadLine();
        if(File.Exists(fileName))
        {
            Console.WriteLine("File exists");
            Console.WriteLine("File was created " +
                File.GetCreationTime(fileName));
            Console.WriteLine("File was last accessed " +
                File.GetLastAccessTime(fileName));
            Console.WriteLine("File was last written to " +
                File.GetLastWriteTime(fileName));
        }
        else
        {
            Console.WriteLine("File does not exist");
        }
    }
}
```

> **NOTE** In the `FileStatistics` program in Figure 13-1, the file must be in the same directory as the program that is running.

Figure 13-1 The `FileStatistics` program

518

CHAPTER THIRTEEN

Figure 13-2 Two typical executions of the `FileStatistics` program

The **Directory class** provides you with information about directories or folders. Table 13-2 lists some available methods in the Directory class.

Method	Description
CreateDirectory()	Creates a directory
Delete()	Deletes a directory
Exists()	Returns true if the specified directory exists
GetCreationTime()	Returns a DateTime object specifying when a directory was created
GetDirectories()	Returns a string array that contains the names of the subdirectories in the specified directory
GetFiles()	Returns a string array that contains the names of the files in the specified directory
GetLastAccessTime()	Returns a DateTime object specifying when a directory was last accessed
GetLastWriteTime()	Returns a DateTime object specifying when a directory was last modified
Move()	Moves a directory to the specified location

Table 13-2 Selected Directory class methods

Figure 13-3 contains a program that prompts a user for a directory and then displays a list of the files stored within it. Figure 13-4 shows two typical executions of the program.

519

FILES AND STREAMS

```
using System;
using System.IO;
public class DirectoryInformation
{
    public static void Main()
    {
        string directoryName;
        string[] listOfFiles;
        Console.Write("Enter a folder ");
        directoryName = Console.ReadLine();
        if(Directory.Exists(directoryName))
        {
            Console.WriteLine("Directory exists");
            listOfFiles = Directory.GetFiles(directoryName);
            for(int x = 0; x < listOfFiles.Length; ++x)
                Console.WriteLine(listOfFiles[ x] );
        }
        else
        {
            Console.WriteLine("Directory does not exist");
        }
    }
}
```

Figure 13-3 The DirectoryInformation program

Figure 13-4 Two typical executions of the DirectoryInformation program

UNDERSTANDING DATA ORGANIZATION WITHIN A FILE

Most businesses generate and use large quantities of data every day. You can store data in variables within a program, but this type of storage is temporary. When the application ends, the variables no longer exist, and the data is lost. Variables are stored in the computer's main or primary memory (RAM). When you need to retain data for any significant amount of time, you must save the data on a permanent, secondary storage device, such as a hard drive, USB storage device, or compact disc (CD).

Businesses store data in a relationship known as the **data hierarchy**, as shown in Figure 13-5. The smallest useful piece of data to most people is the character. A **character** is any one of the letters, numbers, or other special symbols (such as punctuation marks) that comprise data. Characters are made up of bits (the zeros and ones that represent computer circuitry), but people who use data do not care whether the internal representation for an 'A' is 01000001 or 10111110; rather, they are concerned with the meaning of 'A'—for example, it might represent a grade in a course, a person's initial, or a company code.

>> **NOTE**
C# uses Unicode to represent its characters. You first learned about Unicode in Chapter 1.

>> **NOTE** In computer terminology, a character can be any group of bits, and it does not necessarily represent a letter or number. Some of these do not correspond to characters in natural language; for example, some "characters" produce a sound or control your display. You also have used the '\n' character to start a new line.

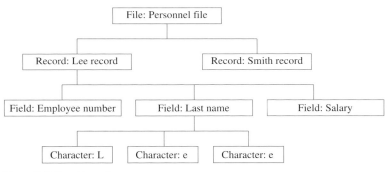

Figure 13-5 Data hierarchy

>> **NOTE**
You can think of a character as a unit of information instead of data with a particular appearance. For example, the mathematical character *pi* (π) and the Greek letter *pi* look the same, but have two different Unicode values.

When businesses use data, they group characters into fields. A **field** is a character or group of characters that has some meaning. For example, the characters *T*, *o*, and *m* might represent your first name. Other data fields might represent items such as last name, Social Security number, zip code, and salary.

>> **NOTE**
The set of all the characters used to represent data on a particular computer is that computer's **character set**.

Fields are grouped together to form records. A **record** is a collection of fields that contain data about an entity. For example, a person's first and last names, Social Security number, zip code, and salary represent that person's record. When programming in C#, you have created many classes, such as an Employee class or a Student class. You can think of the data typically stored in each of these classes as a record. These classes contain individual variables that represent data fields. A business's data records usually represent a person, item, sales transaction, or some other concrete object or event.

Records are grouped to create files. **Data files** consist of related records, such as a company's personnel file that contains one record for each company employee. Some files have only a few records; perhaps your professor maintains a file for your class with 25 records—one record for each student. Other files contain thousands or even millions of records. For example, a large insurance company maintains a file of policyholders, and a mail-order catalog company

FILES AND STREAMS

> **NOTE**
> The field used to control the order of records in a sequential file is the **key field**.

maintains a file of available items. A data file is used as a **sequential access file** when each record is stored in order based on the value in some field; for example, employees might be stored in Social Security number order, or inventory items might be stored in item number order.

Before an application can use a data file, it must open the file. A C# application **opens a file** by creating an object and associating a stream of bytes with that object. Similarly, when you finish using a file, the program should **close the file**—that is, the file is no longer available to your application. If you fail to close an input file (a file from which you are reading data), there usually are no serious consequences; the data still exists in the file. However, if you fail to close an output file (a file to which you are writing data), the data might become inaccessible. You should always close every file you open, and you should close the file as soon as you no longer need it. When you leave a file open for no reason, you use computer resources and your computer's performance suffers. Also, particularly within a network, another program might be waiting to use the file.

> **NOTE**
> When records are not used in sequence, the file is used as a random access file, which means that records can be accessed in any order.

UNDERSTANDING STREAMS

Whereas people view files as a series of records, with each record containing data fields, C# views files as just a series of bytes. When you perform an input operation in an application, you can picture bytes flowing into your program from an input device through a **stream**, which functions as a pipeline or channel. When you perform output, some bytes flow out of your application through another stream to an output device, as shown in Figure 13-6. A stream is an object, and like all objects, streams have data and methods. The methods allow you to perform actions such as opening, closing, and flushing (clearing) the stream.

Figure 13-6 File streams

When a file is opened, an object is created and a stream is associated with that object. When a C# program executes, three stream objects are created:

» `Console.In` refers to the standard input stream object, which accepts data from the keyboard.
» `Console.Out` refers to the standard output stream object, which allows a program to produce output on the screen.
» `Console.Error` refers to the standard error stream object, which allows a program to write error messages to the screen.

You have been using `Console.Out` and its `WriteLine()` and `Write()` methods throughout this book. However, you may have forgotten about the `Out` reference because in Chapter 1

CHAPTER THIRTEEN

you learned to eliminate it by including using System; at the top of your program files. Likewise, you have used Console.In with the ReadLine() and Read() methods.

Most streams flow in only one direction; each stream is either an input or output stream. You might open several streams at once within an application. For example, an application that reads a data disk and separates valid records from invalid ones might require three streams. The data arrives via an input stream, and as the program checks the data for invalid values, one output stream writes some records to a file of valid records, and another output stream writes other records to a file of invalid records.

Many file processing classes are available to you, including:

- » StreamReader for text input from a file
- » StreamWriter for text output to a file
- » FileStream for both input from and output to a file

> **»NOTE** StreamReader and StreamWriter inherit from TextReader and TextWriter, respectively. Console.In and Console.Out are properties of TextReader and TextWriter, respectively.

When you write a program that stores data in a file, you create a FileStream object. Table 13-3 lists some FileStream properties.

Property	Description
CanRead	Gets a value indicating whether current FileStream supports reading
CanSeek	Gets a value indicating whether current FileStream supports seeking
CanWrite	Gets a value indicating whether current FileStream supports writing
Length	Gets the length of the FileStream in bytes
Name	Gets the name of the FileStream
Position	Gets or sets the current position of the FileStream

Table 13-3 Selected FileStream properties

The FileStream class has 15 overloaded constructors. One that is used frequently includes the filename (or complete path), mode, and type of access. For example, you might construct a FileStream object using the following statement:

```
FileStream outFile = new FileStream("SomeText.txt",
    FileMode.Create, FileAccess.Write);
```

In this example, the filename is "SomeText.txt" and the mode is Create, which means a new file will be created even if one with the same name already exists. Also, the access is Write, which means you can write data to the file, but not read from it. Table 13-4 describes the available file modes and Table 13-5 describes the access types.

> **»NOTE** Another of FileStream's overloaded constructors requires only a filename and mode. If you use this version and the mode is set to Append, then the default access is Write; otherwise, the access is set to ReadWrite.

> **»NOTE** Programmers say FileStream **exposes** a stream around a file.

FILES AND STREAMS

Member	Description
Append	Opens the file if it exists and seeks the end of the file to append new data
Create	Creates a new file; if the file already exists, it is overwritten
CreateNew	Creates a new file; if the file already exists, an IOException is thrown
Open	Opens an existing file; if the file does not exist, a System.IO.FileNotFoundException is thrown
OpenOrCreate	Opens an existing file; if the file does not exist, it is created
Truncate	Opens an existing file; once opened, the file is truncated so its size is zero bytes

Table 13-4 FileMode enumeration

Member	Description
Read	Data can be read from the file.
ReadWrite	Data can be read from and written to the file.
Write	Data can be written to the file.

Table 13-5 FileAccess enumeration

When you create a FileStream object, you associate the object with a StreamWriter. Then you use WriteLine() or Write() with the StreamWriter object in much the same way you use it with Console.Out. For example, Figure 13-7 shows an application in which a FileStream object named outFile is created, then associated with a StreamWriter named writer in the first shaded line. The writer object then uses WriteLine() to send a string to the FileStream file instead of sending it to the Console. Figure 13-8 shows a typical execution and Figure 13-9 shows the file as it appears in Notepad.

```
using System;
using System.IO;
public class WriteSomeText
{
   public static void Main()
   {
      FileStream outFile = new
         FileStream("SomeText.txt", FileMode.Create,
            FileAccess.Write);
      StreamWriter writer = new StreamWriter(outFile);
      Console.Write("Enter some text ");
      string text = Console.ReadLine();
      writer.WriteLine(text);
      // Error occurs if the next two statements are reversed
      writer.Close();
      outFile.Close();
   }
}
```

Figure 13-7 WriteSomeText program

CHAPTER THIRTEEN

> **NOTE** Although the `WriteSomeText` application uses `Console.ReadLine()` to accept user input, you could also create a GUI `Form` to accept input. You will create an application that writes to and reads from files using a GUI environment in the "You Do It" exercises at the end of this chapter.

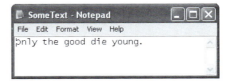

Figure 13-8 Typical execution of `WriteSomeText` program

Figure 13-9 File created by `WriteSomeText` program

WRITING TO A SEQUENTIAL ACCESS TEXT FILE

Although people think of data files as consisting of records that contain fields, C# uses files only as streams of bytes. Therefore, when you write a program to store a data file, you must dictate the form the file will take.

For example, suppose you want to store `Employee` data in a file. Assume an `Employee` contains an ID number, a name, and a salary. You could write stand-alone data for each of the three types to a file, or you could create an `Employee` class that is similar to many you have seen throughout this book. Figure 13-10 shows a typical `Employee` class that contains three fields and properties for each.

```
public class Employee
{
    private int empNum;
    private string name;
    private double salary;
    public int EmpNum
    {
        get{ return empNum;}
        set{ empNum = value;}
    }
    public string Name
    {
        get{ return name;}
        set{ name = value;}
    }
    public double Salary
    {
        get{ return salary;}
        set{ salary = value;}
    }
}
```

Figure 13-10 An `Employee` class

> **NOTE** In the `Employee` class in Figure 13-10, each `get` and `set` accessor has been written on a single line to save space. Except for the absence of extra whitespace, the code is identical to the multiline format you have seen earlier in this book.

FILES AND STREAMS

To store `Employee` data to a persistent storage device, you declare a `FileStream` object. For example:

```
FileStream outFile = new FileStream(FILENAME,
    FileMode.Create, FileAccess.Write);
```

The object is then associated with a `StreamWriter` object. For example:

```
StreamWriter writer = new StreamWriter(outFile);
```

> **NOTE**
> A comma is a commonly used delimiter, but a delimiter can be any character that is not needed as part of the data in a file.

After the `outFile` is associated with the `writer` object, `Employee` data can be written to the `writer` object using the `WriteLine()` method. When you write `Employee` data to a file, the fields should be separated by a delimiter. A **delimiter** is a character used to specify the boundary between characters in text files. Without a delimiter, the process of separating and interpreting data fields on a storage device is more difficult. For example, suppose you define a delimiter as follows:

```
const string DELIM = ",";
```

> **NOTE**
> A block of text within a string that represents an entity or field is a **token**.

Then, when you write data to a file, you can separate the fields with a comma using a statement such as the following:

```
writer.WriteLine(emp.EmpNum + DELIM + emp.Name + DELIM + emp.Salary);
```

Figure 13-11 contains a complete program that opens a file and continuously prompts the user for `Employee` data. When all three fields have been entered for an employee, the fields are written to the file, separated by commas. When the user enters the sentinel value 999 for an `Employee` ID number, the data entry loop ends and the file is closed. Figure 13-12 shows a typical execution and Figure 13-13 shows the contents of the sequential data file that is created.

```
using System;
using System.IO;
public class WriteSequentialFile
{
    public static void Main()
    {
        const int END = 999;
        const string DELIM = ",";
        const string FILENAME = "EmployeeData.txt";
        Employee emp = new Employee();
        FileStream outFile = new FileStream(FILENAME,
            FileMode.Create, FileAccess.Write);
        StreamWriter writer = new StreamWriter(outFile);
        Console.Write("Enter employee number or " + END + " to quit ");
        emp.EmpNum = Convert.ToInt32(Console.ReadLine());
```

Figure 13-11 `WriteSequentialFile` class (*continued*)

```
        while(emp.EmpNum != END)
        {
            Console.Write("Enter last name ");
            emp.Name = Console.ReadLine();
            Console.Write("Enter salary ");
            emp.Salary = Convert.ToDouble(Console.ReadLine());
            writer.WriteLine(emp.EmpNum + DELIM + emp.Name +
               DELIM + emp.Salary);
            Console.Write("Enter next employee number or " +
               END + " to quit ");
            emp.EmpNum = Convert.ToInt32(Console.ReadLine());
        }
        writer.Close();
        outFile.Close();
    }
}
```

Figure 13-11 (*continued*)

>> **NOTE** In the WriteSequentialFile class, the delimiter is defined to be a string instead of a char to force the composed argument to WriteLine() to be a string. If the first data field sent to WriteLine() was a string, then DELIM could have been declared as a char.

>> **NOTE** In the WriteSequentialFile program in Figure 13-11, the constant END is defined to be 999 so it can be used to check for the sentinel value. You first learned to use named constants in Chapter 2. Defining a named constant eliminates using a magic number in a program. The term **magic number** refers to the bad programming practice of hard-coding numbers (unnamed, literal constants) in code without explanation. In most cases, this makes programs harder to read, understand, and maintain.

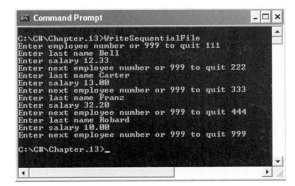

Figure 13-12 Typical execution of WriteSequentialFile program

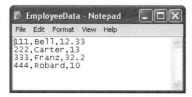

Figure 13-13 Contents of file created by `WriteSequentialFile` program

READING FROM A SEQUENTIAL ACCESS TEXT FILE

A program that reads from a sequential access data file contains many similar components to one that writes to a file. For example, a `FileStream` object is created, as in a program that writes a file. However, the access must be `FileAccess.Read` (or `ReadWrite`), as in the following statement:

```
FileStream inFile = new FileStream(FILENAME,
    FileMode.Open, FileAccess.Read);
```

Then, as when data is being written, the `FileStream` object is associated with a `StreamReader` object, as in the following statement:

```
StreamReader reader = new StreamReader(inFile);
```

After the `StreamReader` has been defined, the `ReadLine()` method can be used to retrieve one line at a time from the data file. For example, the following statement gets one line of data from the file and stores it in a string named `recordIn`:

```
string recordIn = reader.ReadLine();
```

If the value of `recordIn` is `null`, then no more data exists in the file. Therefore, a loop that begins `while(recordIn != null)` can be used to control the data entry loop.

After a record (line of data) is read in, the `Split()` method can be used to separate the data fields into an array of strings. The `Split()` method takes a character parameter and separates a string into substrings at each occurrence of the character delimiter. For example, the following code splits `recordIn` into the `fields` array at each `DELIM` occurrence. Then the three array elements can be stored as an `int`, `string`, and `double`, respectively.

```
string[] fields;
fields = recordIn.Split(DELIM);
emp.EmpNum = Convert.ToInt32(fields[0]);
emp.Name = fields[1];
emp.Salary = Convert.ToDouble(fields[2]);
```

Figure 13-14 contains a complete `ReadSequentialFile` application that uses the data file created in Figure 13-12. The records stored in the EmployeeData.txt file are read in one at a time, split into their `Employee` record components, and displayed. Figure 13-15 shows the output.

```
using System;
using System.IO;
public class ReadSequentialFile
{
    public static void Main()
    {
        const char DELIM = ',';
        const string FILENAME = "EmployeeData.txt";
        Employee emp = new Employee();
        FileStream inFile = new FileStream(FILENAME,
            FileMode.Open, FileAccess.Read);
        StreamReader reader = new StreamReader(inFile);
        string recordIn;
        string[] fields;
        Console.WriteLine("\n{0,-5}{1,-12}{2,8}\n",
            "Num", "Name", "Salary");
        recordIn = reader.ReadLine();
        while(recordIn != null)
        {
            fields = recordIn.Split(DELIM);
            emp.EmpNum = Convert.ToInt32(fields[0]);
            emp.Name = fields[1];
            emp.Salary = Convert.ToDouble(fields[2]);
            Console.WriteLine("{0,-5}{1,-12}{2,8}",
                emp.EmpNum, emp.Name, emp.Salary.ToString("C"));
            recordIn = reader.ReadLine();
        }
        reader.Close();
        inFile.Close();
    }
}
```

Figure 13-14 ReadSequentialFile program

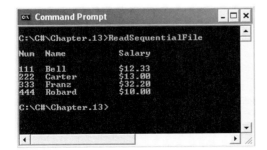

Figure 13-15 Output of ReadSequentialFile program

SEARCHING A SEQUENTIAL FILE

When you read data from a sequential file, as in the `ReadSequentialFile` program in Figure 13-14, the program starts at the beginning of the file and reads each record in turn until all the records have been read. Subsequent records are read in order because a file's **file position pointer** holds the byte number of the next byte to be read. For example, if each record in a file is 32 bytes long, then the file position pointer holds 0, 32, 64, and so on in sequence during the execution of the program.

Sometimes it is necessary to process a file multiple times from the beginning during a program's execution. For example, suppose you want to continue to prompt a user for a minimum salary and then search through a file for `Employees` who make at least that salary. You can compare the user's entered minimum with each salary in the data file and list those employees who meet the requirement. However, after one list is produced, the file pointer is at the end of the file and no more records can be read. To reread the file, you could close it and reopen it, but that requires unnecessary overhead. Instead, you can just reposition the file pointer using the `Seek()` method and the `SeekOrigin` enumeration. For example, the following statement repositions the pointer of a file named `inFile` to 0 bytes away from the `Begin` position of the file:

```
inFile.Seek(0, SeekOrigin.Begin);
```

Table 13-6 lists the values in the `SeekOrigin` enumeration that you can use.

Member	Description
Begin	Specifies the beginning of a stream
Current	Specifies the current position of a stream
End	Specifies the end of a stream

Table 13-6 The `SeekOrigin` enumeration

Figure 13-16 contains a program that repeatedly searches a file to produce lists of employees who meet a minimum salary requirement. The shaded portions of the program represent differences from the `ReadSequentialFile` application in Figure 13-14. In this program, each time the user enters a minimum salary that does not equal 999, the file position pointer is set to the beginning of the file, and then each record is read and compared to the minimum. Figure 13-17 shows a typical execution of the program.

CHAPTER THIRTEEN

```
using System;
using System.IO;
public class FindEmployees
{
    public static void Main()
    {
        const char DELIM = ',';
        const int END = 999;
        const string FILENAME = "EmployeeData.txt";
        Employee emp = new Employee();
        FileStream inFile = new FileStream(FILENAME,
           FileMode.Open, FileAccess.Read);
        StreamReader reader = new StreamReader(inFile);
        string recordIn;
        string[] fields;
        double minSalary;
        Console.Write("Enter minimum salary to find or " +
            END + " to quit ");
        minSalary = Convert.ToDouble(Console.ReadLine());
        while(minSalary != END)
        {
            Console.WriteLine("\n{0,-5}{1,-12}{2,8}\n",
                "Num", "Name", "Salary");
            inFile.Seek(0, SeekOrigin.Begin);
            recordIn = reader.ReadLine();
            while (recordIn != null)
            {
                fields = recordIn.Split(DELIM);
                emp.EmpNum = Convert.ToInt32(fields[0]);
                emp.Name = fields[1];
                emp.Salary = Convert.ToDouble(fields[2]);
                if(emp.Salary >= minSalary)
                    Console.WriteLine("{0,-5}{1,-12}{2,8}",
                        emp.EmpNum, emp.Name,
                         emp.Salary.ToString("C"));
                recordIn = reader.ReadLine();
            }
            Console.Write("\nEnter minimum salary to find or " +
                END + " to quit ");
            minSalary = Convert.ToDouble(Console.ReadLine());
        }
        reader.Close();   // Error occurs if
        inFile.Close();   //these two statements are reversed
    }
}
```

Figure 13-16 FindEmployees program

531

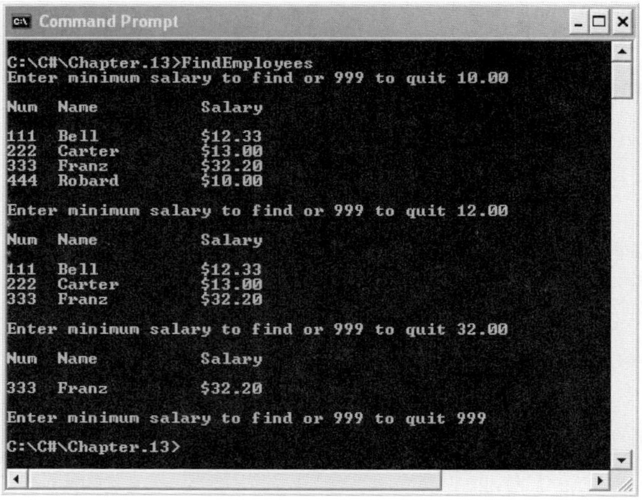

FILES AND STREAMS

```
C:\C#\Chapter.13>FindEmployees
Enter minimum salary to find or 999 to quit 10.00
Num  Name        Salary

111  Bell        $12.33
222  Carter      $13.00
333  Franz       $32.20
444  Robard      $10.00

Enter minimum salary to find or 999 to quit 12.00
Num  Name        Salary

111  Bell        $12.33
222  Carter      $13.00
333  Franz       $32.20

Enter minimum salary to find or 999 to quit 32.00
Num  Name        Salary

333  Franz       $32.20

Enter minimum salary to find or 999 to quit 999
C:\C#\Chapter.13>
```

Figure 13-17 Typical execution of `FindEmployees` program

>> **NOTE** When you seek beyond the length of the file, you do not cause an error. Instead, the file size grows. In Microsoft Windows NT and later, any data added to the end of a file is set to zero. In Microsoft Windows 98 or earlier, any data added to the end of the file is not set to zero. This means that previously deleted data might become visible to the stream.

UNDERSTANDING SERIALIZATION AND DESERIALIZATION

Writing to a text file allows you to store data for later use. However, there are two disadvantages to writing to a text file:

» Data in a text file is easily readable in a text editor such as Notepad. Although this feature is useful to developers when they test programs, it is not a very secure way to store data.

» When a record in a data file contains many fields, it is cumbersome to convert each field to text and combine the fields with delimiters before storing the record on a disk. Similarly, when you read a text file, it is somewhat unwieldy to eliminate the delimiters, split the text into tokens, and convert each token to the proper data type. It would be more convenient to write an entire object to a file at once.

C# provides a technique called serialization that can be used for writing objects to and reading objects from data files. **Serialization** is the process of converting objects into streams of bytes. **Deserialization** is the reverse process; it converts streams of bytes back into objects.

To create a class that can be serialized, you mark it with the [Serializable] attribute, as shown in the shaded statement in Figure 13-18. The Employee class in the figure is identical to the one in Figure 13-10 except for the [Serializable] attribute.

```
[Serializable]
public class Employee
{
    private int empNum;
    private string name;
    private double salary;
    public int EmpNum
    {
        get{ return empNum;}
        set{ empNum = value;}
    }
    public string Name
    {
        get{ return name;}
        set{ name = value;}
    }
    public double Salary
    {
        get{ return salary;}
        set{ salary = value;}
    }
}
```

Figure 13-18 Serializable `Employee` class

In a class marked with the `[Serializable]` attribute, every instance variable must also be serializable. By default, all C# simple data types are serializable, including `string`s. However, if your class contains fields that are more complex data types, you must check the declaration of those classes to ensure they are serializable. By default, array objects are serializable. However, if the array contains references to other objects, such as `Date`s or `Student`s, those objects must be serializable.

>> **NOTE** If you want to be able to write class objects to a file, you can implement the `ISerializable` interface instead of marking a class with the `[Serializable]` attribute. When you use this approach, you must write a method named `GetObjectData()`. Marking the class with the attribute is the simpler format.

>> **NOTE** Attributes provide a method of associating information with C# code. They are always contained in square brackets. The C# documentation at *http://msdn2.microsoft.com* provides more details.

Two namespaces are included in programs that employ serialization:

» `System.Runtime.Serialization.Formatters.Binary;`
» `System.Runtime.Serialization;`

When you create a program that writes objects to files, you declare an instance of the `BinaryFormatter` class with a statement such as the following:

`BinaryFormatter bFormatter = new BinaryFormatter();`

FILES AND STREAMS

Then, after you fill a class object with data, you can write it to an output file named `outFile` with a statement such as the following:

```
bFormatter.Serialize(outFile, objectFilledWithData);
```

The `Serialize()` method takes two arguments—the name of the file and a complete object that might contain any number of data fields. The entire object is written to the data file with this single statement.

Similarly, when you read an object from a data file, you use a statement like the following:

```
objectInstance = (TypeOfObject)bFormatter.Deserialize(inFile);
```

This statement uses the `Deserialize()` method with a `BinaryFormatter` object to read in one object from the file. The object is cast to the appropriate type and can be assigned to an instance of the object. Then you can access individual fields. An entire object is read with this single statement, no matter how many data fields it contains.

Figure 13-19 shows a program that writes `Employee` class objects to a file and later reads them in. After the `FileStream` is declared for an output file, a `BinaryFormatter` is declared in the first shaded statement. The user enters an ID number, name, and salary for an `Employee`, and the completed object is written to a file in the second shaded statement. When the user enters 999, the output file is closed.

```
using System;
using System.IO;
using System.Runtime.Serialization.Formatters.Binary;
using System.Runtime.Serialization;
public class SerializableDemonstration
{
   public static void Main()
   {
      const int END = 999;
      const string FILENAME = "Data.ser";
      Employee emp = new Employee();
      FileStream outFile = new FileStream(FILENAME,
         FileMode.Create, FileAccess.Write);
      BinaryFormatter bFormatter = new BinaryFormatter();
      Console.Write("Enter employee number or " + END +
         " to quit ");
      emp.EmpNum = Convert.ToInt32(Console.ReadLine());
      while(emp.EmpNum != END)
      {
         Console.Write("Enter last name ");
         emp.Name = Console.ReadLine();
         Console.Write("Enter salary ");
```

Figure 13-19 `SerializableDemonstration` program (*continued*)

```
            emp.Salary = Convert.ToDouble(Console.ReadLine());
            bFormatter.Serialize(outFile, emp);
            Console.Write("Enter employee number or " + END +
                " to quit ");
            emp.EmpNum = Convert.ToInt32(Console.ReadLine());
         }
         outFile.Close();
         FileStream inFile = new FileStream(FILENAME,
            FileMode.Open, FileAccess.Read);
         Console.WriteLine("\n{0,-5}{1,-12}{2,8}\n",
            "Num", "Name", "Salary");
         while(inFile.Position < inFile.Length)
         {
            emp = (Employee)bFormatter.Deserialize(inFile);
            Console.WriteLine("{0,-5}{1,-12}{2,8}",
               emp.EmpNum, emp.Name, emp.Salary.ToString("C"));
         }
         inFile.Close();
      }
   }
```

Figure 13-19 (continued)

After the output file closes in the SerializableDemonstration program in Figure 13-19, it is reopened for reading. A loop is executed while the Position property of the input file is less than its Length property. In other words, the loop executes while there is more data in the file. The last shaded statement in the figure deserializes data from the file and casts it to an Employee object, where the individual fields can be accessed. Figure 13-20 shows a typical execution of the program.

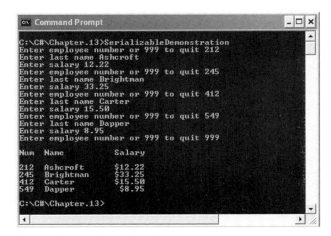

Figure 13-20 Typical execution of SerializableDemonstration program

The file created by the SerializableDemonstration program is not as easy to read as the text file created by the WriteSequentialFile program earlier in the chapter (in Figure 13-11). Figure 13-21 shows the file contents displayed in Notepad. If you examine the file carefully, you can discern the string names and some Employee class information, but the rest of the file is not easy to read.

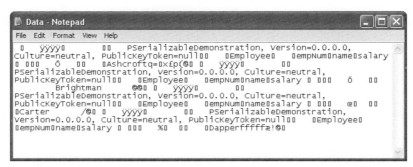

Figure 13-21 Data file created using SerializableDemonstration program

YOU DO IT
CREATING A FILE
In the next steps, you will create a file that contains a list of names.

To create a file:

1. Open a new file in your editor and write the first lines needed for a program that creates a file of names.

   ```
   using System;
   using System.IO;
   public class CreateNameFile
   {
   ```

2. Start a Main() method that declares a FileStream you can use to create a file named Names.txt that is open for writing. Also create a StreamWriter to which you associate the file.

   ```
   public static void Main()
   {
      FileStream file = new FileStream("Names.txt",
         FileMode.Create, FileAccess.Write);
      StreamWriter writer = new StreamWriter(file);
   ```

CHAPTER THIRTEEN

3. Add an array of names as follows. Each name is 10 characters long.

   ```
   string[] names = {"Anthony   ",
                     "Belle     ",
                     "Carolyn   ",
                     "David     ",
                     "Edwin     ",
                     "Frannie   ",
                     "Gina      ",
                     "Hannah    ",
                     "Inez      ",
                     "Juan      "};
   ```

   >>**NOTE**
   Add spaces to make each new name the same length so that they can demonstrate the `Seek()` method in a later exercise.

4. Declare a variable to use as an array subscript, then write each name to the output file.

   ```
   int x;
   for(x = 0; x < names.Length; ++x)
       writer.WriteLine(names[x]);
   ```

5. Close the `StreamWriter` and the `FileStream`. Also add two closing curly braces—one for the `Main()` method and one for the class.

   ```
       writer.Close();
       file.Close();
     }
   }
   ```

6. Save the file as **CreateNameFile.cs**. Compile and execute it. Using My Computer or Windows Explorer, open the file in a text editor. The file contents appear in Figure 13-22.

Figure 13-22 File created by `CreateNameFile` program

READING FROM A FILE

In the next steps, you will read the text from the file created by the CreateNameFile program.

To read text from a file:

1. Start a new file in your text editor as follows:

   ```
   using System;
   using System.IO;
   public class ReadNameFile
   {
   ```

2. Start a Main() method that declares a FileStream that uses the same filename as the one created by the CreateNameFile program. Declare the file mode to be Open and the access to be Read. Declare a StreamReader with which to associate the file. Also declare an integer that counts the names read and a string that holds the names.

   ```
   public static void Main()
   {
      FileStream file = new FileStream("Names.txt",
         FileMode.Open, FileAccess.Read);
      StreamReader reader = new StreamReader(file);
      int count = 1;
      string name;
   ```

3. Display a heading and read the first line from the file. While a name is not null, display a count and a name, and increment the count.

   ```
   Console.WriteLine("Displaying all names");
   name = reader.ReadLine();
   while(name != null)
   {
      Console.WriteLine("" + x + " " + name);
      name = reader.ReadLine();
      ++count;
   }
   ```

4. Close the StreamReader and the File, and add closing curly braces for the method and the class.

   ```
          reader.Close();
          file.Close();
       }
   }
   ```

5. Save the file as **ReadNameFile.cs**. Compile and execute it. The output appears in Figure 13-23.

CHAPTER THIRTEEN

```
Command Prompt
C:\C#\Chapter.13>ReadNameFile
Displaying all names
1 Anthony
2 Belle
3 Carolyn
4 David
5 Edwin
6 Frannie
7 Gina
8 Hannah
9 Inez
10 Juan

C:\C#\Chapter.13>
```

Figure 13-23 Output produced by `ReadNameFile` program

USING THE Seek() METHOD

In the next steps, you will use the `Seek()` method to reposition a file pointer so you can access a file from any location. The user will be prompted to enter a number representing a starting point to list the names in the Names.txt file. Names from that point forward will be listed, and then the user will be prompted for another selection.

To demonstrate the Seek() method:

1. Open a new file in your editor and start a program that will demonstrate how to access certain names from the Names.txt file. You created this file in the `CreateNameFile` application.

   ```
   using System;
   using System.IO;
   public class AccessSomeNames
   {
       public static void Main()
       {
           FileStream file = new FileStream("Names.txt",
               FileMode.Open, FileAccess.Read);
           StreamReader reader = new StreamReader(file);
   ```

2. Declare a constant named END that represents an input value that allows the user to exit the program. Then declare other variables that the program will use.

   ```
   const int END = 999;
   int count = 0;
   int num;
   int size;
   string name;
   ```

539

3. Read a line from the input file. While names are available, continue to read and count them. Then compute the size of each name by dividing the file length by the number of strings stored in it.

   ```
   name = reader.ReadLine();
   while(name != null)
   {
       ++count;
       name = reader.ReadLine();
   }
   size = (int)file.Length / count;
   ```

4. Prompt the user for the number of the first record to read, and read the value from the `Console`.

   ```
   Console.Write("\nWith which number do you want to start? ");
   num = Convert.ToInt32(Console.ReadLine());
   ```

5. As long as the user does not enter the sentinel END value, display the number and then use the `Seek()` method to position the file pointer at the correct file location. Because users enter numbers starting with 1, you calculate the file position by first subtracting 1 from the user's entry. For example, when a user enters 1 as the number of the first record to view, the file should start at position 0. The calculated record number is then multiplied by the size of each name in the file. For example, if each name is 12 bytes long, then the calculated starting position should be 0, 12, 24, 36, or some other multiple of the record size. Read and write the name at the calculated location. Then, in a loop, read and write all the remaining names until the end of the file. Finally, prompt the user for the next starting value for a new list.

   ```
   while(num != END)
   {
       Console.WriteLine("Starting with name " + num + " : ");
       file.Seek((num - 1) * size, SeekOrigin.Begin);
       name = reader.ReadLine();
       Console.WriteLine("   " + name);
       while(name != null)
       {
           name = reader.ReadLine();
           Console.WriteLine("   " + name);
       }
       Console.Write("\nWith which number do you " +
           "want to start? ");
       num = Convert.ToInt32(Console.ReadLine());
   }
   ```

6. Close the `StreamReader` and `File` objects and add closing braces for the method and the class.

   ```
   reader.Close();
   file.Close();
   }
   }
   ```

CHAPTER THIRTEEN

7. Save the file as **AccessSomeNames.cs**. Compile and execute it. Figure 13-24 shows a typical execution during which the user displays three sets of names starting at a different point each time.

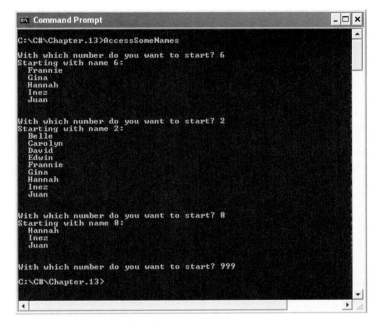

Figure 13-24 Typical execution of `AccessSomeNames` program

CREATING A FILE IN A GUI ENVIRONMENT

The file writing and reading examples in this chapter have used console applications so that you could concentrate on the features of files in the simplest environment. However, you can write and read files in GUI environments as well. In the next steps, you will create two applications. The first allows a user to enter invoice records using a `Form` and to store them in a file. The second application allows a user to view stored records using a `Form`.

To write a GUI application that creates a file:

1. Open the Visual Studio IDE and start a new Windows project named **EnterInvoices**.

2. Create a `Form` like the one shown in Figure 13-25 by making the following changes:
   » Change the `Text` property of the `Form` to **Invoice Data**.
   » Drag a `Label` onto the `Form` and change its `Text` property to **Enter invoice data**.
   » Drag three more `Label`s onto the `Form` and change their `Text` properties to **Invoice number**, **Last name**, and **Amount**, respectively.

FILES AND STREAMS

» Drag three TextBoxes onto the Form next to the three descriptive Labels. Change the Name properties of the three TextBoxes to **invoiceBox**, **nameBox**, and **amountBox**, respectively.

» Drag a Button onto the Form and change its Text to **Enter record**.

Figure 13-25 Designing the EnterInvoices Form

3. View the code for the Form. At the start of the class, before the Form1() constructor, add the shaded code shown in Figure 13-26. The new code contains statements that perform the following:

» Declare a delimiter that will be used to separate records in the output file.

» Declare a path and filename. You can change the path if you want to store the file in a different location on your system.

» Declare variables for the number, name, and amount of each invoice.

» Open the file and associate it with a StreamWriter.

```
namespace EnterInvoices
{
    public partial class Form1 : Form
    {
        const string DELIM = ",";
        const string FILENAME =
            @"C:\C#\Chapter.13\Invoices.txt";
        int num;
        string name;
        double amount;
        static FileStream outFile = new
            FileStream(FILENAME, FileMode.Create,
            FileAccess.Write);
        StreamWriter writer = new StreamWriter(outFile);
        public Form1()
        {
            InitializeComponent();
        }
```

Figure 13-26 Partial code for EnterInvoices program with typed statements shaded

CHAPTER THIRTEEN

> **»NOTE** In Chapter 11, you learned that placing an at sign (@) in front of a filename indicates that all characters in the string should be interpreted literally. This means that the backslashes in the path will not be interpreted as escape sequence characters.

4. At the top of the file, with the other `using` statements, add the following so that the `FileStream` can be declared:

   using System.IO

5. Return to Design view and double-click the **Enter record** button. As shown in the shaded portions of Figure 13-27, add statements within the method to accept data from each of the three `TextBoxes` and convert each field to the appropriate type. Then write each field to a text file, separated by delimiting commas. Finally, clear the `TextBox` fields to be ready for the user to enter a new set of data.

```
private void button1_Click(object sender, EventArgs e)
{
    num = Convert.ToInt32(invoiceBox.Text);
    name = nameBox.Text;
    amount = Convert.ToDouble(amountBox.Text);
    writer.WriteLine(num + DELIM + name + DELIM + amount);
    invoiceBox.Clear();
    nameBox.Clear();
    amountBox.Clear();
}
```

Figure 13-27 Code for `button1_Click()` method of `EnterInvoices` program

6. Locate the `Dispose()` method, which executes when the user clicks the Close button to dismiss the `Form`. A quick way to locate the method in the Visual Studio IDE is to select **Edit** from the main menu, click **Find and Replace**, click **Quick Find**, and type **Dispose**. The method appears on the screen. Add two statements to close `writer` and `outFile`, as shown in the shaded statements in Figure 13-28.

```
protected override void Dispose(bool disposing)
{
    writer.Close();
    outFile.Close();
    if (disposing && (components != null))
    {
        components.Dispose();
    }
    base.Dispose(disposing);
}
```

Figure 13-28 The `Dispose()` method in the `EnterInvoices` program

543

FILES AND STREAMS

7. Click **Save All**. Execute the program. When the `Form` appears, enter data in each `TextBox` and then click the **Enter record** button when you finish. The `TextBoxes` clear in preparation for you to enter another record. Enter at least three records before dismissing the `Form`. Figure 13-29 shows data entry in progress.

Figure 13-29 Entering data in the `EnterInvoices` application

READING DATA FROM A FILE INTO A Form
In the next steps, you will create a `Form` that you can use to read records from a `File`.

To read data into a `Form`:

1. Open a new Windows project in Visual Studio and name it **ViewInvoices**.

2. Create a `Form` like the one shown in Figure 13-30 by making the following changes:

    » Change the `Text` of `Form1` to **Invoice Data**.
    » Add four `Labels` with the text and approximate locations shown in Figure 13-30.
    » Add a `Button` with the `Text` **View record**.
    » Add three `TextBoxes`. Name them `numBox`, `nameBox`, and `amountBox`, respectively.

3. In the IDE, double-click the **View Record** `Button` to view the code.

Figure 13-30 The `ViewInvoices` Form

4. Add the shaded statements in Figure 13-31. They include:

    » A `using System.IO` statement
    » Constants for the file delimiter character and the filename

544

CHAPTER THIRTEEN

» A string into which records can be read and an array of strings into which to separate the string read in
» A FileStream and StreamReader to handle the input file
» Within the button1_Click() method, statements to read in a line from the file and split it into three components

> **NOTE**
> If you used a different path for the Invoices.txt file in the EnterInvoices program, then change this file's path accordingly.

```
using System;
using System.Collections.Generic;
using System.ComponentModel;
using System.Data;
using System.Drawing;
using System.Text;
using System.Windows.Forms;
using System.IO;

namespace ViewInvoices
{
    public partial class Form1 : Form
    {
        const char DELIM = ',';
        const string FILENAME = @"C:\C#\Chapter.13\Invoices.txt";
        string recordIn;
        string[] fields;
        static FileStream file = new FileStream(FILENAME,
            FileMode.Open, FileAccess.Read);
        StreamReader reader = new StreamReader(file);
        public Form1()
        {
            InitializeComponent();
        }

        private void button1_Click(object sender, EventArgs e)
        {
            recordIn = reader.ReadLine();
            fields = recordIn.Split(DELIM);
            numBox.Text = fields[0];
            nameBox.Text = fields[1];
            amountBox.Text = fields[2];
        }
    }
}
```

Figure 13-31 Partial code for the ViewInvoices application

FILES AND STREAMS

5. Add two `Close()` statements to the `Dispose()` method, as shown in Figure 13-32.

```
protected override void Dispose(bool disposing)
{
    reader.Close();
    file.Close();
    if (disposing && (components != null))
    {
        components.Dispose();
    }
    base.Dispose(disposing);
}
```

Figure 13-32 The `Dispose()` method for the `ViewInvoices` program

6. Save the project and then execute it. When the Form appears, click the Button to view records. You see the data for the first record you entered when you ran the EnterInvoices application; your Form should look like the one in Figure 13-33. Click the Button again to display the next record.

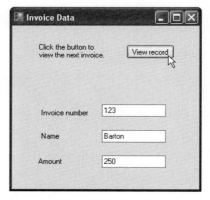

Figure 13-33 Typical execution of `ViewInvoices` program

7. Continue to click the Button to view each record. After you view the last record you entered, click the Button again. An unhandled exception is generated, as shown in Figure 13-34, because you attempted to read data past the end of the input file.

Figure 13-34 Error message window displayed after user attempts to read past the end of the file

CHAPTER THIRTEEN

8. Click the **Details** button in the UnhandledException window to view details of the error. Figure 13-35 shows that a System.NullReferenceException was thrown and not handled.

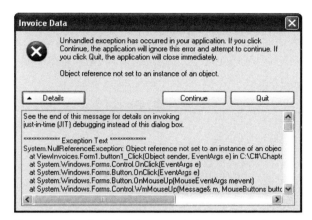

Figure 13-35 Details displayed by unhandled exception window

9. Click **Quit** to close the unhandled exception window.
10. To remedy the unhandled exception problem, you could take any number of actions. Depending on the application, you might want to do one or more of the following:
    » Display a message.
    » Disallow any more button clicks.
    » End the program.
    » Reposition the file pointer to the file's beginning so the user can view the records again.

    For this example, you will take the first two actions: display a message and disallow further button clicks. Return to Visual Studio and locate the code for the button1_Click() method. Add a try...catch block, as shown in Figure 13-36. Place all the record-handling code in a try block, and if an exception is thrown, change the Text in label1 and disable the View record Button.

FILES AND STREAMS

```
private void button1_Click(object sender, EventArgs e)
{
    try
    {
        recordIn = reader.ReadLine();
        fields = recordIn.Split(DELIM);
        numBox.Text = fields[ 0];
        nameBox.Text = fields[ 1];
        amountBox.Text = fields[ 2];
    }
    catch (SystemException)
    {
        label1.Text = "You have viewed\nall the records";
        button1.Enabled = false;
    }
}
```

> **» NOTE**
> You learned about exception handling and `try...catch` pairs in Chapter 9.

Figure 13-36 The `button1_Click()` method modified to handle an exception

11. Save the project and then execute it. This time, after you have viewed all the available records, an appropriate message is displayed and the button is disabled, as shown in Figure 13-37.

Figure 13-37 `ViewInvoices Form` after user has viewed last record

12. Dismiss the `Form`. Close Visual Studio.

CHAPTER THIRTEEN

CHAPTER SUMMARY

» Temporary storage is usually called computer memory or random access memory (RAM). This type of storage is volatile. Permanent storage, on the other hand, is non-volatile. A computer file is a collection of information stored on a nonvolatile device in a computer system. Files exist on permanent storage devices. When you store data in a computer file on a persistent storage device, you write to the file. When you copy data from a file on a storage device into RAM, you read from the file. Computer users organize their files into folders or directories.

» The `File` class contains methods that allow you to access information about files. The `Directory` class provides you with information about directories or folders.

» A character can be any one of the letters, numbers, or other special symbols (such as punctuation marks) that comprise data. A field is a group of characters that has some meaning. Fields are grouped together to form records. A record is a collection of fields that contain data about an entity. Records are grouped to create files. A data file is used as a sequential access file when each record is stored in order based on the value in some field. Before an application can use a data file, it must open the file by creating an object and associating a stream of bytes with that object. When you close a file, it is no longer available to your application.

» C# views files as a series of bytes that flow into a program from an input device or out of a program to an output device through an object called a stream, which functions as a pipeline or channel. When a C# program executes, three stream objects are created: `Console.In`, `Console.Out`, and `Console.Error`. When you write a program that stores data in a file, you create a `FileStream` object.

» Data can be written to a `StreamWriter` object using the `WriteLine()` method. Fields should be separated by a delimiter, which is a character used to specify the boundary between characters in text files.

» Data can be read from a `StreamReader` object using the `ReadLine()` method. The return value is a string. If the value of the returned string is `null`, then no more data exists in the file. After a record (line of data) is read in, the `Split()` method can be used to separate the data fields into an array of strings. The `Split()` method takes a character parameter and separates a string into substrings at each occurrence of the character delimiter.

» When you read data from a sequential file, subsequent records are read in order because a file's position pointer holds the byte number of the next byte to be read. To reread a file, you could close it and reopen it, or you can just reposition the file pointer using the `Seek()` method and the `SeekOrigin` enumeration.

» Serialization is the process of converting objects into streams of bytes. Deserialization is the reverse process; it converts streams of bytes back into objects. To create a class that can be serialized, you mark it with the `[Serializable]` attribute. An entire object can be written to or read from a data file with a single statement.

KEY TERMS

Random access memory (RAM) is temporary storage in a computer.

Volatile storage is the type that is lost when power is lost.

Nonvolatile storage is permanent storage; it is not lost when a computer loses power.

A **computer file** is a collection of information stored on a nonvolatile device in a computer system.

Permanent storage devices, such as hard disks, floppy disks, Zip disks, USB drives, reels or cassettes of magnetic tape, and compact discs, are used to store files.

Data files contain facts and figures.

Program files or **application files** store software instructions.

When you store data in a computer file on a permanent storage device, you **write to the file**.

When you copy data from a file on a storage device into RAM, you **read from the file**.

Persistent storage is nonvolatile storage.

The **root directory** is the main directory of a storage device.

Folders or **directories** are structures used to organize files on a storage device.

A **path** is composed of the disk drive in which a file resides plus the complete hierarchy of directories.

The `File` **class** contains methods that allow you to access information about files.

The `Directory` **class** provides information about directories or folders.

The **data hierarchy** is the relationship of characters, fields, records, and files.

A **character** is any one of the letters, numbers, or other special symbols (such as punctuation marks) that comprise data.

A computer's **character set** is the group of all the characters used to represent data on a particular computer.

A **field** is a character or group of characters that has some meaning.

A **record** is a collection of fields that contain data about an entity.

Data files consist of related records.

A **sequential access file** is a data file in which each record is stored in order based on the value in some field.

The **key field** is the field used to control the order of records in a sequential file.

Opening a file involves creating an object and associating a stream of bytes with it.

Closing a file means it is no longer available to an application.

A **stream** is a pipeline or channel though which bytes are input from and output to a file.

Programmers say `FileStream` **exposes** a stream around a file.

CHAPTER THIRTEEN

A **delimiter** is a character used to specify the boundary between characters in text files.

A **token** is a block of text within a string that represents an entity or field.

The term **magic number** refers to the bad programming practice of hard-coding numbers in code without explanation.

A file's **file position pointer** holds the byte number of the next byte to be read.

Serialization is the process of converting objects into streams of bytes.

Deserialization is the process of converting streams of bytes back into objects.

REVIEW QUESTIONS

1. Random access memory is _____ .
   - a. persistent
   - b. volatile
   - c. permanent
   - d. sequential

2. A collection of facts and figures stored on a nonvolatile device in a computer system is a(n) _____ .
   - a. data file
   - b. application file
   - c. operating system
   - d. memory map

3. Which of the following is not permanent storage?
   - a. RAM
   - b. a hard disk
   - c. a USB drive
   - d. all of these

4. When you store data in a computer file on a persistent storage device, you are _____ .
   - a. reading
   - b. directing
   - c. writing
   - d. rooting

5. Which of the following is not a `File` class method?
   - a. `Create()`
   - b. `Delete()`
   - c. `Exists()`
   - d. `End()`

6. In the data hierarchy, a group of characters that has some meaning, such as a last name or ID number, is a _____ .
   - a. byte
   - b. field
   - c. file
   - d. record

FILES AND STREAMS

7. When each record stored in a file is accessed in order based on the value in some field, the file is a(n) _____ file.
   a. random access
   b. application
   c. formatted
   d. sequential

8. When you open a file, you create an object and associate a _____ of bytes with it.
   a. path
   b. folder
   c. stream
   d. directory

9. Which of the following is not part of a `FileStream` constructor?
   a. the file size
   b. the file mode
   c. the filename
   d. the type

10. When a file's mode is `Create`, a new file will be created _____.
    a. even if one with the same name already exists
    b. only if one with the same name does not already exist
    c. only if one with the same name already exists
    d. only if the access is `Read`

11. Which of the following is not a `FileStream` property?
    a. `CanRead`
    b. `CanExist`
    c. `CanSeek`
    d. `CanWrite`

12. Which of the following is not a file `Access` enumeration?
    a. `Read`
    b. `Write`
    c. `WriteRead`
    d. `ReadWrite`

13. A character used to specify the boundary between characters in text files is a _____.
    a. sentinel
    b. stopgap
    c. delimiter
    d. margin

14. Which character can be used to specify a boundary between characters in text files?
    a. a comma
    b. a semicolon
    c. either of these
    d. neither of these

15. After a `StreamReader` has been defined and associated with a file, the `ReadLine()` method can be used to _____ .
    a. retrieve one line at a time from the file
    b. retrieve one character at a time from the file
    c. store one line at a time in a file
    d. split a `string` into tokens

16. The argument to the `Split()` method is _____ .
    a. `void`
    b. the number of fields into which to split a record
    c. the character that identifies a new field in a `string`
    d. a `string` that can be split into tokens

17. The `Split()` method stores its results in _____ .
    a. a `string`
    b. an array of `strings`
    c. an appropriate data type for each token
    d. an array of bytes

18. A file's _____ holds the byte number of the next byte to be read.
    a. index indicator
    b. position pointer
    c. header file
    d. key field

19. The process of converting objects into streams of bytes is _____ .
    a. extrication
    b. splitting
    c. mapping
    d. serialization

20. Which of the following is serializable?
    a. an `int`
    b. an array of `ints`
    c. a `string`
    d. all of the above

FILES AND STREAMS

EXERCISES

1. Create a program that allows a user to continually enter directory names until the user types "end". If the directory name exists, display a list of the files in it; otherwise, display a message indicating the directory does not exist. If the directory exists and files are listed, prompt the user to enter one of the filenames. If the file exists, display its creation date and time; otherwise, display a message indicating the file does not exist. Save the program as **TestFileAndDirectory.cs**. Create as many test directories and files as necessary to test your program. Figure 13-38 shows a typical execution.

Figure 13-38 Typical execution of `TestFileAndDirectory` program

2. Create a file that contains your favorite movie quote. Use a text editor such as Notepad and save the file as **Quote.txt**. Copy the file contents and paste them into a word-processing program such as Word. Save the file as **Quote.doc**. Write an application that displays the sizes of the two files as well as the ratio of their sizes to each other. To discover a file's size, you can create a `System.IO.FileInfo` object using a statement such as the following, where FILE_NAME is a string that contains the name of the file:

   ```
   FileInfo wordInfo = new FileInfo(FILE_NAME);
   ```

   Save the file as **FileComparison.cs**.

3. Using Visual Studio, create a `Form` like the one shown in Figure 13-39. Specify a directory on your system, and when the `Form` loads, list the files it contains in a `CheckedListBox`. Allow the user to click a file's check box and display the file's creation date and time. (Each time the user checks a new filename, display its creation date in place of the original selection.) Save the project as **TestFileAndDirectory2**. Create as many files as necessary to test your program. Figure 13-39 shows a typical execution.

CHAPTER THIRTEEN

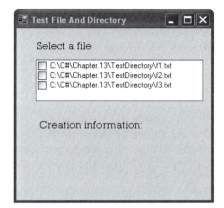 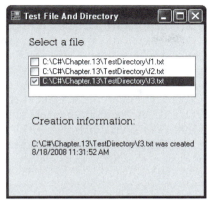

Figure 13-39 Typical execution of `TestFileAndDirectory2` program before and after user makes selection

4. a. Create a `Friend` class in which you can store your friends' first and last names, phone numbers, and the month and day of your friends' birthdays. Write a program that prompts you to enter friends' data and saves each record to a file. Save the program as **WriteFriendRecords.cs**.

   b. Create a program that reads the file created in Exercise 4a and displays each friend's data to the screen. Save the programs as **ReadFriendRecords.cs**.

   c. Create a program that prompts you for a birth month, reads the file created in Exercise 4a, and displays data for each friend who has a birthday in the specified month. Save the programs as **FriendBirthdayReminder.cs**.

5. a. In the Visual Studio IDE, design a `Form` that allows a user to select options for the background color and size and to give the `Form` a title. The `Form` should look like the one shown in Figure 13-40. Change each feature of the `Form` as the user makes selections. After the user clicks the "Save form settings" `Button`, save the color, size, and title as strings to a file and disable the button. Save the project as **CustomizeAForm**.

   b. In the Visual Studio IDE, design a `Form` like the one in Figure 13-40, except include a `Button` to retrieve the `Form` settings. When the user clicks the "Retrieve form settings" `Button`, read the settings from the file saved in the CustomizeAForm project, and set the `Form`'s color, size, and title to the values that were saved previously. Save the project as **RetrieveCustomizedForm**.

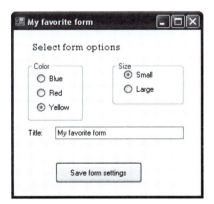

Figure 13-40 Form in `CustomizeAForm` project

FILES AND STREAMS

6. Using the Visual Studio IDE, create a Form that contains a game in which the computer randomly selects one of three letters (A, B, or C) 10 times, and the user tries to guess which letter was selected. At the start of the game, read in the previous high score from a data file. (Create this file to hold "0" the first time the game is played.) Display the previous high score on the Form to show the player the score to try to beat. As the player makes each guess, show the player's guess and the computer's choice, and award a point if the player correctly guesses the computer's choice. Keep a running count of the number of correct guesses. After 10 random selections and guesses, disable the game controls and create a file that holds the new high score, which might be the same as before the game or a new higher number. When the player begins a new game, the high score will be displayed on the Form as the new score to beat. Save the project as **HighScore**.

DEBUGGING EXERCISES

Each of the following files in the Chapter.13 folder on your Student Disk has syntax and/or logical errors. In each case, determine the problem and fix the program. After you correct the errors, save each file using the same filename preceded with *Fixed*. For example, save DebugThirteen1.cs as **FixedDebugThirteen1.cs**.

a. DebugThirteen1.cs
b. DebugThirteen2.cs
c. DebugThirteen3.cs
d. DebugThirteen4.cs

UP FOR DISCUSSION

1. In Exercise 2 earlier in this chapter, what did you discover about the size difference between files that hold the same contents but were created using different software (such as Word and Notepad)? Why do you think the file sizes are so different, even though the files contain the same data?

2. Suppose your employer asks you to write a program that lists all the company's employees, their salaries, and their ages. You are provided with the company personnel file to use as input. You decide to take the file home so you can create the program over the weekend. Is this acceptable? What if the file contained only employees' names and departments, but not more sensitive data such as salaries and ages?

APPENDIX A

OPERATOR PRECEDENCE AND ASSOCIATIVITY

OPERATOR PRECEDENCE AND ASSOCIATIVITY

When an expression contains multiple operators, their **precedence** controls the order in which the individual operators are evaluated. For example, multiplication has a higher precedence than addition, so the expression 2 + 3 * 4 evaluates as 14 because the value of 3 * 4 is calculated before adding 2. Table A-1 summarizes all operators in order of precedence from highest to lowest.

Category	Operators	Associativity
Primary	x.y f(x) a[x] x++ x-- new typeof checked unchecked	left
Unary	+ - ! ~ ++x --x (T)x	right
Multiplicative	* / %	left
Additive	+ -	left
Shift	<< >>	right
Relational	< > <= >= is as and type testing	left
Equality	== !=	left
Logical AND	&	left
Logical XOR	^	left
Logical OR	|	left
Conditional AND	&&	left
Conditional OR	||	left
Conditional	?:	right
Assignment	= *= /= %= += -= <<= >>= &= ^= |=	right

Table A-1 Operator precedence

When you use two operators with the same precedence, the **associativity** of the operators controls the order in which the operations are performed:

» Except for the assignment and conditional operators, all binary operators (those that take two arguments) are **left-associative**, meaning that operations are performed from left to right. For example, 5 + 6 + 7 is evaluated first as 5 + 6, or 11; then 7 is added, bringing the value to 18.

» The assignment operators and the conditional operator (? :) are **right-associative**, meaning that operations are performed from right to left. For example, x = y = z is evaluated as y = z first, and then x is set to the result.

» All unary operators (those that take one argument) are right-associative. If b is 5, the value of - ++b is determined by evaluating ++b first (6), then taking its negative value (–6).

APPENDIX A

You can control precedence and associativity by using parentheses. For example, a + b * c first multiplies b by c and then adds the result to a. The expression (a + b) * c, however, forces the sum of a and b to be calculated first; then the result is multiplied by c.

KEY TERMS

The **precedence** of operators controls the order in which individual operators are evaluated in an expression.

The **associativity** of operators controls the order in which operations of equal precedence are performed in an expression.

With **left-associative** operators, operations are performed from left to right.

With **right-associative** operators, operations are performed from right to left.

APPENDIX B

CREATING A MULTIFILE ASSEMBLY

When you write a program that contains a `Main()` method and other methods, you can contain all the methods in a single file, as shown in the program in Figure B-1.

```
using System;
public class ProgramThatCallsAMethod
{
    public static void Main()
    {
        DisplayMessage();
    }
    public static void DisplayMessage()
    {
        Console.WriteLine("Hello");
    }
}
```

Figure B-1 A class that contains a `Main()` method and a `DisplayMessage()` method

CREATING A MULTIFILE ASSEMBLY

Instead of including the `DisplayMessage()` method in the `ProgramThatCallsAMethod` class, as shown in Figure B-1, you might want to write the method in its own class. That way, it can more easily be used by any application. To be able to use `DisplayMessage()` from its own class, you can create a multifile assembly. In the Microsoft .NET Framework, an **assembly** is a partially compiled code library; a **multifile assembly** is one composed from multiple files. As you become more proficient using C#, you will find additional reasons to create multifile assemblies besides including methods stored in separate files. Probably the most common reason is to combine modules written in different languages, such as Visual C++ or Visual Basic.

To create a multifile assembly, you need to create a namespace and use some additional command-line options when you compile your program.

> **NOTE**
> You first learned about namespaces when you used the `System` namespace in Chapter 1. A namespace is a scheme that provides a way to group similar classes.

Suppose you want to include the `DisplayMessage()` method in its own class. Figure B-2 shows how the class should be constructed. The `DisplayMessage()` method has been copied from Figure B-1, and the shaded statements have been added.

```
namespace MessageNamespace
{
    using System;
    class Message
    {
        public static void DisplayMessage()
        {
            Console.WriteLine("Hello");
        }
    }
}
```

Figure B-2 The `MessageNamespace` namespace, stored in a file named DisplayMessage.cs

A namespace is created, using any identifier you choose. In Figure B-2, the name is `MessageNamespace`. Normally, you do not include *Namespace* within the name of a namespace; a more conventional name would be *Message*. This example uses *MessageNamespace* to help you remember that the name refers to a namespace rather than a class or a file. The `using System;` command is used in the DisplayMessage.cs file because the method uses `Console.WriteLine()`. The `DisplayMessage()` method is enclosed in its own class. The class might have any legal C# identifier; in this case, it is named `Message`.

When the file in Figure B-2 is saved as DisplayMessage.cs and compiled using the `csc` command, an error message is issued, as shown in Figure B-3. The message indicates that the file does not have a `Main()` method and cannot be compiled as a regular program. Your intention is not to have the class act as a stand-alone program; rather, you want the class to contain a method that other programs can use. To compile the class file, you must use a command that tells the compiler to create a **netmodule file**—that is, a file that contains modules to be used as part of another program rather than one that contains an executable program. When you compile the program that contains the `Main()` method for

APPENDIX B

the multifile assembly, you must include a command that adds the netmodule to the `Main()` program.

Figure B-3 Error message issued when DisplayMessage.cs is compiled using the `csc` command

To compile the DisplayMessage.cs file as a netmodule, use the following command:

```
csc /t:module DisplayMessage.cs
```

This command creates a file named DisplayMessage.netmodule. The file can now be used by a client program. For example, Figure B-4 shows a class named `Test`. Because the shaded statement `using MessageNamespace;` is included at the top of the file, the program has access to the methods stored in the `MessageNamespace` namespace. The method there can be called with the class-dot-method command `Message.DisplayMessage()`, as shown in the second shaded line.

```
using MessageNamespace;
public class Test
{
    public static void Main()
    {
        Message.DisplayMessage();
    }
}
```

Figure B-4 The `Test` class

After the client program in Figure B-4 is stored in a file named Test.cs, you can use the `addmodule` command to associate the netmodule file with the program:

```
csc Test.cs /addmodule:DisplayMessage.netmodule
```

Figure B-5 shows the command that compiles the program and the subsequent execution. The output "Hello" comes from the `DisplayMessage()` method within the `MessageNamespace` namespace.

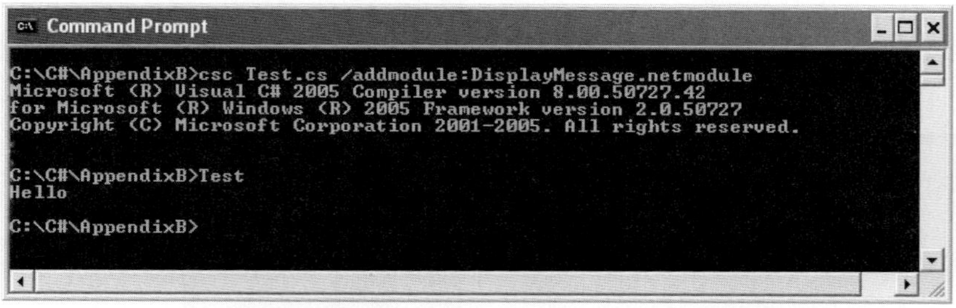

CREATING A MULTIFILE ASSEMBLY

Figure B-5 Compiling and executing Test.cs

KEY TERMS

An **assembly** is a partially compiled code library.

A **multifile assembly** is an assembly composed from multiple files.

A **netmodule file** contains modules to be used as part of another program rather than containing an executable program.

APPENDIX C

C

USING THE IDE EDITOR

The Visual C# Code Editor is like a word processor for writing source code. Just as a word-processing program provides support for spelling and grammar, the C# Code Editor helps ensure your C# syntax is free of spelling and grammar errors. This support can be grouped into five main categories:

- » IntelliSense
- » Refactoring
- » Code snippets
- » Wavy underlines
- » Readability aids

INTELLISENSE

IntelliSense is Microsoft's name for the set of features designed to minimize the time you spend looking for help and to help you enter code more accurately and efficiently. The IntelliSense features provide basic information about C# language keywords, .NET

USING THE IDE EDITOR

Framework types, and method signatures as you type them in the editor. The information is displayed in ToolTips, list boxes, and Smart Tags. Features of IntelliSense include:

- » Providing completion lists
- » Providing quick information
- » Listing members
- » Providing parameter information
- » Adding `using` statements

PROVIDING COMPLETION LISTS

As you enter source code in the editor, IntelliSense displays a list box that contains all the C# keywords, .NET Framework classes, and names you have defined in your program that fit the current circumstances. For example, Figure C-1 shows a list box that makes suggestions based on what the programmer has typed in the Code Editor. If you find a match in the list box for the name you intend to type, you can select the item. Alternatively, you can press the Tab key to have IntelliSense finish entering the name or keyword for you.

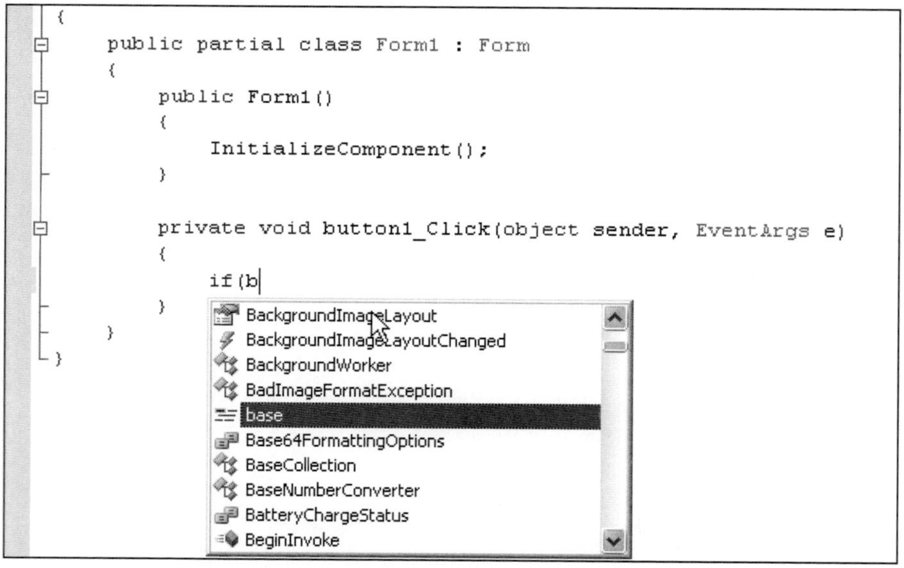

```
{
    public partial class Form1 : Form
    {
        public Form1()
        {
            InitializeComponent();
        }

        private void button1_Click(object sender, EventArgs e)
        {
            if(b|
        }
    }
}
```

```
BackgroundImageLayout
BackgroundImageLayoutChanged
BackgroundWorker
BadImageFormatException
base
Base64FormattingOptions
BaseCollection
BaseNumberConverter
BatteryChargeStatus
BeginInvoke
```

Figure C-1 A list displayed by IntelliSense

PROVIDING QUICK INFORMATION

When you hover the cursor over a .NET Framework type, IntelliSense displays a Quick Info ToolTip that contains basic documentation about that type.

APPENDIX C

LISTING MEMBERS

When you enter a .NET Framework type or an identifier of a specific type into the Code Editor, and then type the dot operator (.), IntelliSense displays a list box that contains the members of that type. When you make a selection and then press the Tab key, IntelliSense enters the member's name. For example, Figure C-2 shows the list displayed when the user types button1, which is an identifier of type Button. When you don't know what method or property you want for an object, typing its identifier and a dot can direct you to the appropriate choice. This technique sometimes teaches you about features you did not even realize were available.

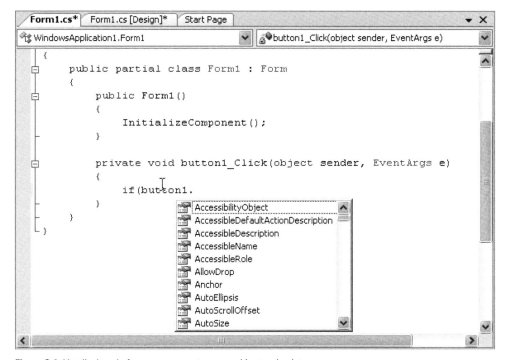

Figure C-2 List displayed after programmer types an object and a dot

PROVIDING PARAMETER INFORMATION

When you enter a method name in the Code Editor and then type an opening parenthesis, IntelliSense displays a Parameter Info ToolTip that shows the method's parameter list. If the method is overloaded, multiple method signatures are displayed and you can scroll through them.

ADDING using STATEMENTS

If you attempt to create an instance of a .NET Framework class without a sufficiently qualified name, IntelliSense displays a Smart Tag after the unresolved identifier. When you click the Smart Tag, IntelliSense displays a list of using statements to help you resolve the identifier. When you select one from the list, IntelliSense adds the directive to the top of your source code file, and you can continue coding at your current location.

REFACTORING

As a project grows during development, you sometimes need to make changes to make it more readable, better organized, or more portable. For example, you might want to divide methods into smaller methods, change the number or types of a method's parameters, or rename identifiers. **Refactoring** is the process of rewriting a computer program to improve its structure, readability, or performance without changing its function. The IDE's refactoring tool is accessible by right-clicking in the Code Editor. The tool helps you restructure code much more conveniently and thoroughly than traditional approaches, such as searching and replacing every instance of a variable name. For more information, see the C# documentation.

CODE SNIPPETS

Code snippets are small units of commonly used C# source code that you can enter accurately and quickly with only a couple of keystrokes. To access the code snippet menu, right-click in the Code Editor. You can browse from among the many snippets provided with Visual C#, and you can also create your own.

WAVY UNDERLINES

Wavy underlines give you instant feedback about errors in your code as you type. A red wavy underline identifies a syntax error, such as a missing semicolon or mismatched braces. A green wavy underline identifies a potential compiler warning, and blue identifies an Edit and Continue issue. In Figure C-3, two wavy underlines appear because the code in the last statement is not yet complete.

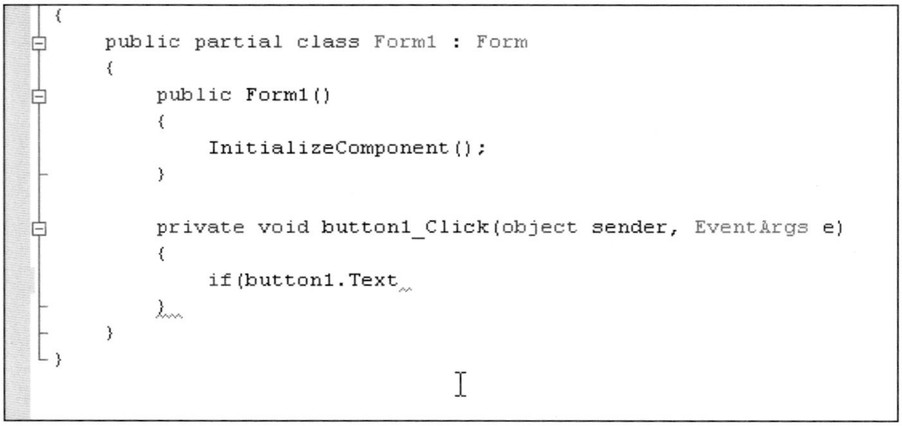

```
{
    public partial class Form1 : Form
    {
        public Form1()
        {
            InitializeComponent();
        }

        private void button1_Click(object sender, EventArgs e)
        {
            if(button1.Text
        }
    }
}
```

Figure C-3 Wavy underlines in Code Editor

APPENDIX C

READABILITY AIDS

The editor assigns different colors to various categories of identifiers in a C# source code file to make the code easier to read. For example, C# keywords are bright blue, classes are blue-green, and comments are green.

KEY TERMS

IntelliSense is Microsoft's name for the set of features designed to minimize the time you spend looking for help and to help you enter code more accurately and efficiently.

Refactoring is the process of rewriting a computer program to improve its structure, readability, or performance without changing its function.

Code snippets are small units of commonly used C# source code that you can enter accurately and quickly with only a couple of keystrokes.

INDEX

* (asterisk)
. (dot)
: (colon)
{ } (curly braces)
" (double quotes)
= (equal sign)
! (exclamation point)
> (greater than)
< (less than)
- (minus)
( ) (parentheses)
&& (ampersands, AND operator)
|| (pipes, OR operator)
[ ] (square brackets)

A

abstract classes, using, 295–298, 311
abstract methods, 296, 312
access, public, protected internal, 205
access modifiers
   class, 260
   usage of, 10, 32, 258
access specifiers, `protected`, 278–281
accessibility for methods, 172, 205
accessing
   array elements using subscripts, 143–144
   base class methods from derived classes, 285–286
accessors
   and classes, 261
   `set`, `get`, 221
accumulated totals, programming, 126–127, 133
actual parameters
   within method calls, 179
   for methods, 205
add and assign operator (+=), 51–52, 71
`AddDays()`, `AddMonths()`, `AddYears()` methods, 441
adding comments to programs, 12–14, 29–30

addition operator (+), 50
`AddRange()` method, 381
aliases
   and variable declarations, 42
   and classes, 16, 33
   described, 70, 206
   and intrinsic types, 40
   reference and output parameters, 191
aligning controls on forms, 443
ambiguous methods
   avoiding, 196–198
   described, 206
ampersands (&)
   and form menu choices, 447
   and AND operator, 104, 105
ancestors of subclasses, 275, 311
`Anchor` property, 443, 467
AND operator
   combining with OR, 91–92
   described, 105
   using, 88–89, 99–100, 104
angle brackets (<>) and XML-documentation format comments, 14
application files, 516, 550
application programs
   and class concepts, 214–216
   terminating, 337
`ApplicationException` class, 322, 347–350
`Application.Run()` method, 378–380
applications, fault-tolerant, 358
arguments
   and methods, 172, 203
   usage of, 8–9, 32
   used with `MessageBox.Show()` (table), 366–372
   writing methods that require multiple, 180–182
   writing methods that require single, 177–180
arithmetic operators
   binary, 69
   numeric type conversions, 54–55

   overloading, 239–244
   using shortcut, 51–52, 69
   using standard binary, 50–51
arithmetic statements, using in programs, 65–66
array elements
   assigning values to, 140–142
   described, 141, 164
   using subscripts to access, 143–144
arrays
   creating, 159–160
   declaring, assigning values to elements, 140–142
   described, 164
   initializing, 142–143, 160
   jagged, 189
   multidimensional, using, 155–158, 165
   of objects, creating, 255–258
   of objects, declaring, 244–250
   parameter, 206
   parameter, using, 193–194
   passing by reference, 187
   passing to methods, 185–189
   searching for exact match, 146–150
   searching for range matches, 150–151
   using `BinarySearch()` method, 151–153
   using `for` loop with, 160
   using `foreach` to control access, 145
   using `Sort()` method, 153–154
ascending order and `Sort()` method, 153–154
assemblers, 3
assemblies, multifile, 177, 561–564
assigning
   an alias to a class, 15
   delegates, 479, 507
   names to memory locations, 2
   values to array elements, 140–142
   values to constants, 60
   values to variables, 41–43
assignment operator (=), 42, 70
assignments described, 42, 70

associativity, and operator precedence, 71, 558–559
asterisks (*)
   and code comments, 33
   multiplication operator, 50
at sign (@) and verbatim identifiers, 11
attributes of objects, 5–6, 32, 533

B

backslashes (\)
   and escape sequences, 72
   usage in C#, 14
base 16, 57, 72
base class methods
   accessing from derived classes, 285–286
   overriding, 282–284
base classes
   adding constructors to, 309–310
   with constructors, using, 293–295
   derived class objects and, 286–287
   described, 274, 311
   members, using in derived classes, 306–308
`base` keyword, 294, 295, 312
binary operators, 50, 69, 71
`BinarySearch()` method, 151–153, 164–165, 245–250
black box devices
   described, 32, 205
   and encapsulation, 6
   and implementation hiding, 177
bloat, code, 173, 204
block comments, 14, 33
blocking statements, 104
blocks
   See also specific block type
   and curly braces ({ }), 120, 122, 143
   described, 85, 105
   unreachable, 335
body, method, 9, 32
`bool` data type, 69, 53–54
Boolean logical AND operator, 90–91, 105
Boolean logical inclusive OR operator, 90–91, 105
Boolean variables, 53–54, 66–67, 71
braces, curly. *See* curly braces

brackets
   angle (<>). *See* angle brackets
   square ([ ]). *See* square brackets
`break` keyword, 94, 106
bugs, 3
button clicks, raising, firing, triggering events, 474, 508
`button1_Click()` method, 475
buttons
   adding functionality to, 402–403
   adding functionality to `MessageBox`, 372–374
`Buttons` described, 380, 407
buttons
   focus, described, 372, 407
   on forms, adding functionality to, 390–392

C

C#
   case-sensitivity of, 9, 11
   class names in, 12–13
   data types (table), 41
   procedure names, 4
   programming language described, 2, 7, 32
   programs, C# programs
   selected `Exceptions` (table), 323
   Visual C# key features, 382–385
C# compiler
   compiling and executing program using Visual Studio IDE, 24–29
   and garbage values, 126
call stacks, 343–347, 358
called methods, 172, 204
calling methods, 172, 198–199, 204
calls
   nested method, 205
   program, 4, 32
camel casing, 4, 32
capitalization of properties, 222
`case` keyword, 94, 106
`case` labels, 93–95, 106
case-sensitivity
   character data in C#, 120
   of C#, 9, 11
casing, camel and Pascal, 4, 32

`catch` blocks
   catching multiple `Exceptions`, 331–334
   described, 358
   in exception handling, 326–329
   and `finally` blocks, 336–338
cd command, 23
changing
   directories in path, 23
   program's culture, 49
`char` data type, 55–57, 72
character data, case-sensitivity in C#, 120
character sets, 521, 550
characters
   described, 521, 549, 550
   storing in `char` variable, 56
   string data type, 33
`CheckBox`
   adding to `Form`, 453–457
   described, 465, 467
   and `RadioButton` objects, 428–432
`Checked` property, 430
`CheckedChanged()` method, 430
`CheckedListBox`, 435–439, 467
child classes, 275–278, 311
class access modifiers, 216, 260
class clients, 215, 260
class definitions, 216, 260
class headers, 216, 260
class users, 215, 260
classes
   See also specific class
   concepts about, 214–216
   constructors. *See* constructors
   creating, 251–254, 258
   creating instance variables and methods, 217–218
   derived from `System.Windows.Forms.Control`, 416–417
   described, 5, 32
   destructors, 250–251
   extending, 276–278, 305–306
   identifiers, selecting, 11
   inheritance. *See* inheritance
   instantiation of, 215, 260
   names in C#, legal and illegal, 5, 12–13

INDEX

storing, organizing, 224–225
types of, 311–312
from which objects can be instantiated, 216
`class` keyword, 11
click events, 391
`Click` events, 407, 476, 490, 508
`Click()` method, 392
clients
  class, 215, 260
  of methods, 205
closing files, 550
code
  adding comments to programs, 12–14
  alignment of `while` and `do`, 123
  appearance in this book, 8
  bloat described, 173, 204
  blocks, 85, 105
  compiling from command prompt, 17–19
  created by Visual Studio IDE, 385–390, 451–453, 565–569
  dead, 335, 358
  hash, 312
  and pseudocode, 105
  refactoring, 391, 568
  snippets, and Code Editor, 568
  source. See source code
Code Editor
  and collapsing regions, 389–390
  described, 382, 407, 565–569
colons (:) and conditional operators, 96
`Color` class, 465, 467
colors, adding to controls, 427–428
combining AND and OR operators, 91–92
`ComboBox` control, 439, 467
command line
  compiling and executing programs from, 23–24
  compiling from, 30
  described, 5, 32
  operating systems, 4
command prompt
  compiling code from, 17–19
  described, 32
commands. See specific command

commas
  and delimiters, 526
  and initialized variables, 121
commenting out statements, 14, 33
comments
  adding to programs, 12–14, 29–30
  commenting out statements, 33
  example of, 387–388
  program, described, 32
`Compare()` method, `String` class, 57–59, 72
`CompareTo()` method, 57–59, 72, 245, 248, 260, 261
comparison operators, 57–59, 69, 71
compilers
  described, 3, 32
  errors and warnings, 18
  just in time (JIT), 33
compiling
  C# programs, 16–21
  code from command prompt, 17–19
  code from within Visual Studio IDE, 19
  and executing programs from command line, 23–24
  and executing programs using Visual Studio IDE, 24–29
`Component` class, 414, 466
components, dismissing, 407
composed delegates
  creating, 479–480, 498–500
  described, 507, 508
composition technique described, 261
compound expressions, using in `if` statements, 88–92
computer files, storage, 516–517, 550
computer programs. See programs
concatenating strings, 46, 70
concrete classes, 295, 312
conditional AND operator, 88–89, 105
conditional operators
  described, 90, 104, 106
  making decisions using, 96
console input, accepting, 61–63
`Console.In`, `Console.Out`, `Console.Error` stream objects, 522–525, 549
`Console.ReadLine()` method, 61, 72

constants
  declaring, 40
  defining named, 60–61, 72
  described, 69, 70
constructor initializers, 236–238, 261
constructors
  adding to base, derived classes, 309–310
  base classes with, using, 293–295
  described, 261
  overloading, 234–236, 254–255
  parameterless, 234, 261
  passing parameters to, 233–234
  throwing `Exceptions` from, 350
  understanding, 232–233, 259
  using, 220, 311
  using constructor initializers, 236–238
contextual keywords, 261
`Control` class
  described, 466
  some `public` instance events (table), 486
  summary, 465
controls
  See also specific control
  adding colors to, 427–428
  adding to forms, 375
  checkboxes and radiobuttons, 428–432
  described, 407
Controls
  default event for, 423
  focus, and raising events, 509
  handling component events, 485–489
  learning about, 496
  managing multiple, 494–496
  understanding, 414–417
conversions, implicit, implicit reference, 312
counted loops, 132
.cs files, 26
`csc` command, 17
cultures, usage of, 49, 71
curly braces ({ })
  and accessors, 221–222
  and blocks, 105, 116, 120, 122, 143
  and method declarations, 203

573

curly braces ({ }) (*continued*)
  and placeholders, 44
  usage of, 10
cutting and deleting text, 26

D

data
  constants, 69
  organization within files, 520–522
  passed by reference, 205
  primitive, 7
data files, 516, 521, 550
data hierarchy, 521, 550
data items
  and methods, 178
  variables and constants, 40
data types
  C# (table), 41
  described, 40, 70
  float, 71
  floating-point, 47–48, 69
  `int`, and C#, 21
  integral, 47, 70
  Java vs. C#, 7
  in method's `return` statement, 184
  `string`, 20, 33
databases, primary keys in, 225, 261
`DateTimePicker`, 439–442, 467
dead code, 335, 358
debugging
  See also exception handling
  described, 3, 32
  with `StackTrace` property, 344–347
`decimal` data type, 47
decimal data type, 71
decision structures, 82–83
decisions
  avoiding common errors when making, 97–100
  decision structures, 105
  dual-alternative, 104, 105
  making using `if-else` statements, 86–88
  making using `if` statements, 83–86
  making using `switch` statements, 92–96

short-circuit evaluations, 89, 105
using compound expressions in `if` statements, 88–92
using conditional operator, 96
using programs to make, 82–83
declarations
  method, 172, 205
  variable, 40, 70
declaring
  arrays, 140–142, 260
  arrays of objects, 244–250
  delegates, 477
  events, event handlers, 480–483, 507–508
  objects, 218–221
  variables, 40–43, 63–64
decrement operator (--), 52, 71
decrementing variables, 118, 132
default constructors, 232, 261
`default` keyword, 94, 106
default value of objects, 232, 261
defining named constants, 60–61
definite loops, 120, 132
`delegate` keyword, 477
delegates
  composed. *See* composed delegates
  creating, 496–498
  described, 507, 508
  understanding, 477–479
delimiters, usage of, 526, 551
derived classes
  accessing base class methods from, 285–286
  adding constructors to, 309–310
  benefits of, 302–303
  described, 274, 311
  objects as instances of base class, 286–287
  using base class members in, 306–308
deserialization, serialization and, 532–536, 549, 551
designing `Form` with Visual Studio IDE, 382–385
destructors
  described, 261
  using, 250–251, 260
dialog boxes, modal, 372, 407
`DialogResult` enumeration, 372, 407
directives, `using`, 15–16

directories
  changing, 23
  root, 517, 550
  usage of, 517
`Directory` class, 517–520, 549, 550
dismissing components, 372, 407
displaying variable values, 43–46
`Dispose()` method, 388
division operator (/), 50
`do` loops, using, 122–124, 129–132
`Dock` property, 443, 467
`double` data type, 47, 71
double quotation marks ("") and string values, 57
downloading C# standards, 7
dual-alternative decisions, 86, 104, 105
Dynamic Help, Visual Studio C#, 393

E

Ecma International C# standards, 7
editors
  Code Editor, 382, 407, 565–569
  entering programs into, 22
empty body, 118, 132
encapsulation
  described, 6, 32, 477
  of instance methods, creating delegate for, 501–502
`enum`, 106
enumerations
  described, 106, 372, 407
  `DialogResult`, 407
`Equals()` method, 57–59, 72, 290
equals sign (=)
  assigning values with, 51
  assignment operator, 42, 70
error-handling
  object-oriented. *See* exception handling
  traditional methods, 325–326
error lists in IDE, 383, 407
error messages
  See also specific message
  instantiating from abstract classes, 296
  troubleshooting, 18

INDEX

errors
  exception handling. *See* exception handling
  program, troubleshooting, 18
  semantic, 3, 32
  wavy underlines, and Code Editor, 568
escape sequences
  newline, 177
  usage of, 67, 72
evaluations, short-circuit, 89, 105
event-driven programs, 474, 508
event handlers, declaring, 474, 480–483, 508
event handling described, 474–476
event listeners, creating, 502–504
event receivers, 475, 508
event senders, 475, 508
EventArgs class, 475–476, 480, 508
EventHandler
  described, 509
  using built-in, 483–485
events
  associating one method with multiple, 505–506
  and button-clicks, 508
  click, 391. *See* click events
  declaring, 480–483
  default, for Control, 423, 467
  described, 391, 407
  handling, 474–476
  key, described, 492, 509
  keyboard, handling, 492–494
  usage of, 507
  using sender objects in, 506–507
  viewing in Properties window, 488
Events
  and Controls, 496
  learning about, 496
exception handling
  catching multiple Exceptions, 331–335
  creating your own Exception class, 347–350
  described, 322, 358
  handling exceptions with loops, 338–340
  object-oriented methods, 326–329
  rethowing Exceptions, 350–352
  summary, 356–357

throwing Exceptions between methods, 340–343
tracing Exceptions through call stack, 343–347
traditional error-handling, 325–326
using finally block, 336–338
using ToString() method and Message property, 329–331
exceptions
  See also exception handling
  catching multiple, 331–335
  described, 322, 356, 358
  generating SystemException, 324–325
  understanding, 322–324
Exceptions
  rethrowing, 350–352, 358
  throwing between methods, 340–343
  tracing through call stack, 343–347
exclamation point (!) and NOT operator, 97, 106
executing programs from command line, 23–24
explicit cast, 55
explicit numeric type conversions, 55
extended classes, 274, 276–278, 302–306, 311

F

fault-tolerant applications, 358
fields
  class object attributes, 215
  described, 260, 521, 550
  public, and private methods, 226–229
File class, 517–520, 549, 550
file extensions, naming by text editors, 22
file position pointers, 530, 551
file streams, 522–525
files
  See also specific file type
  computer, data, program, described, 516, 550
  creating, 536–537
  creating in GUI environment, 541–544

data organization within, 520–522
netmodule, 562, 564
placing methods in their own, 175
reading from, writing to, 516, 525–529, 538–539, 550
FileStream class, 523–525, 550
finally blocks
  described, 358
  using, 336–338
float data type, 47, 71
floating-point numbers and data types, 47–48, 69, 71
flowcharts
  described, 104, 105
  of do loops, 123
  and pseudocode, 82–83
focus
  of buttons, 372, 407
  of Controls on forms, 494–496, 509
folders, usage of, 517, 550
Font class, 421–423, 467
for loops
  described, 132
  searching arrays using, 146–147
  using, 120–122, 129–131, 132
  using with arrays, 160
foreach statements, 145, 164
Form Designer described, 382, 407
formal parameters within methods, 179, 205
format specifiers, 48, 71
format strings
  described, 44, 70
  standard numeric, 71
Forms
  adding buttons to, 403–405
  adding CheckBox to, 453–457
  adding functionality to Button on, 390–392
  adding ListBox, CheckedListBox, ComboBox controls to, 435–439
  adding menustrip to, 445–447
  adding MonthCalendar and DateTimePicker controls to 439–442
  adding MonthCalendar to, 461–465
  adding PictureBox to, 433–435
  adding radiobuttons to, 457–460

575

Forms (*continued*)
  creating, 374–378
  creating for program's main window, 378–380
  creating with `Label`, 417–421
  described, 407
  designing with Visual Studio IDE, 382–385, 406
  managing multiple `Controls`, 494–496
  reading data from file into, 544–548
  setting label's font, 421–423
  working with layout of, 443–445
forward slashes (//) and code comments, 14, 31, 33
fragile classes, 281, 311

G

garbage values, 126
`get` accessors, 221, 261
`GetHashCode()` method, 290–292
`GetType()` method, 289
governing types in `switch` statements, 106
graphical user interface. *See* GUI
`GroupBox`, 445, 467
GUI `Controls`. *See* `Controls`
GUI (graphical user interface)
  adding functionality to buttons on forms, 390–392
  creating file in, 541–544
  creating `Form` for program's main window, 378–380
  C#'s, 7
  described, 4, 366, 407
  forms. *See* Forms

H

handling
  `Control` component events, 485–489
  events, 474–476
  keyboard events, 492–494
  mouse events, 489–492

has-a relationships, 261
hash code, 312
headers
  class, 216, 260
  method, 32, 172, 205
help, Visual Studio, 392–393
hexadecimal, 57, 72
hiding
  classes, 283, 311
  information, 217, 261
  method implementation, 176–177, 176–177, 203
high-level programming languages, 2, 31

I

`IComparable` interface, 246–249, 260, 261
ID numbers, verifying (program), 128–131
identifiers, selecting, 3, 11, 32
IDEs (Integrated Development Environments)
  compiling code from within, 22
  compiling from command prompt, 17
  Visual Studio. *See* Visual Studio IDE
`if-else` statements
  described, 86, 105
  making decisions using, 86–88
  using nested, 100–102
`if` statements
  described, 105
  making decisions using, 83–86, 104
  nested, 85–86, 88
  and range checks, 98–99, 106
  using compound expressions in, 88–92
immutable strings, 59, 72
implementation hiding, 176–177, 203, 205
implicit cast, 54, 72
implicit conversion, 286–287, 312
implicit parameters, 222–223, 261
implicit reference conversion, 312
implicitly described, 54, 72
incrementing variables, 118, 132

indefinite loops, 118, 132
indexes described, 141, 164
"IndexOutOfRangeException" error message, 144
infinite loops, 116, 132
information hiding, 217, 261
inheritance
  abstract classes, using, 295–298
  accessing base class methods from derived classes, 285–287
  base classes with constructors, 293–295
  benefits of, 302–303
  `Control` class hierarchy, 414
  derived class objects as instance of base class, 286–287
  described, 6–7, 32, 311
  example of, 303–305
  extending classes, 276–278, 305–306
  interfaces, creating and using, 298–302
  multiple, 298, 312
  `Object` class, using, 288–292
  overriding base class methods, 282–284
  summary, 310–311
  terminology, 274–275
  understanding, 272–274
initialization of variables, 42, 70, 121
`InitializeComponent()` method, 389, 437
initializer, constructor, 261
initializer lists and arrays, 143, 164
initializing arrays, 142–143, 147, 160
inner loops, 124, 133
input, accepting console, 61–63
instance methods
  creating, 217–218
  creating delegate for encapsulation of, 501–502
  described, 261
instance variables
  creating, 217–218
  described, 215, 260
instances of classes, 5, 32
instantiating arrays, 142–143
instantiation of class, 215, 260
`int` data type, 21, 47

INDEX

integers
  described, 71
  and integral data types, 47, 70
  using standard binary arithmetic operators, 50–51
integral data types, 47, 70
integral variables, 63–64
Integrated Development Environments. *See* IDEs
IntelliSense features
interactive programs, accepting console input, 61–63, 72
interfaces
  creating, using, 298–302, 311
  described, 32, 246, 261
  forms. *See* Forms
  graphical user interface. *See* GUI
GUI (graphical user interface), 4
  in object-oriented programs, 6
interfacing with systems, 177, 205
intermediate languages (ILs), 17, 33
internal access for methods, 174, 205
`internal` class access modifiers, 216
internal class access modifiers, 260
interpreters, 3
intrinsic types, 40–41, 70
invoked methods, 172, 204
invoking events, 509
invoking objects, 248, 261
is-a relationships, 215, 260
iteration variables, 145
iterations of loops, 116, 132

J

jagged arrays, 158, 164, 189
Java
  and C#, 7
  reserved keywords (table), 12
JIT (just in time) compiler, 17, 33

K

key events, 492, 508, 509
key fields, 550
keyboard events, handling, 492–494, 508
keys, primary, 225, 261

keywords
  See also specific keyword
  contextual, 261
  described, 10, 32
  readability aids (color), 569

L

`Labels`
  adding to `Form` and changing properties, 448–450
  creating `Form` with, 417–421
  described, 465, 466
  setting fonts, 421–423
labels, `case`, 93–94, 95, 106
languages, programming. *See* programming languages
layout of forms, 443–445
left-associative, operator precedence, 558, 559
`Length` property, using with arrays, 144–145, 161, 164
lexically, and comparison operators, 58, 72
line comments, usage of, 14, 33
`LinkClicked()` method, 424, 425, 426
`LinkLabel`, 423–426, 465, 467
`LinkVisited` property, 426
`ListBox` control
  adding to `Form`, 435–439
  described, 467
literal constants, 40, 70
literal strings, 8
`Load()` method, 437
local variables and methods, 179, 205
logic, program
  using AND and OR, 102–104
  described, 3, 32
logical AND, OR operators, 90–91
loop body, 116, 132
loop control variables, 117, 132
loop statements, nesting, 124–126
loop structures
  accumulated totals, 126–127
  usage of, 116–126
loops
  See also loop statements, loop structures

  `for`, 120–122
  described, 116, 131, 132
  exception handling using, 338–340
  improving performance, 128
  nested, 124–125
  `while`, 116–120

M

machine language, 2, 31
magic numbers, 527, 551
`Main()` method
  alternate ways to write, 20–21
  and alternative methods, 172
  classes using, 214, 258
  in Solution Explorer projects, 390
  in multifile assemblies, 561–564
  usage of, 10–11
managing multiple events, 494–496
matrix (two-dimensional array), 155, 164
`MaximizeSize` property, 445, 467
memory
  See also storage
  locations in programs, 3
  RAM (random access memory), 516, 550
  of rectangular, two-dimensional arrays, 155
menu strips, adding to `Form`, 445–447, 467
`MenuStrip` control, 445–447, 467
`Message` property, 329–331
`MessageBox`
  adding functionality to buttons, 372–374
  creating, 366–372
  described, 406, 407
`MessageBox.Show()` method, 366–372
method body, 9
method calls
  nested, 185
  and `this` reference, 230–232
method declarations, headers, definitions, 205
method headers, 9, 32
method mode, Visual Studio, 418, 466
method signatures, 206

methods
See also specific method
  abstract, 296, 312
  accessibility modifiers for, 173–175
  ambiguous, avoiding, 196–198, 205
  associating with multiple events, 505–506
  calling, 198–199
  of class objects, 215
  containing Exceptions, 357
  deciding which to use in C# program, 29
  described, 32, 203, 204
  hiding implementation, 176–177
  instance, 217, 217–218, 261
  and overloaded operators, 240
  overloading, 195–196, 202–203
  overriding methods, 246, 261
  passing arrays to, 185–189
  passing objects to, 238–239
  properties, creating, 221–224
  public fields and private, 226–229
  reference parameters, 191–193, 201–202
  return type, 183, 205
  static, nonstatic, 174, 205
  that require multiple arguments, 180–182
  that require single argument, 177–180
  that return a value, 183–185
  throwing Exceptions between, 340–343
  understanding, 172–173
  using ref, out, and params parameters within, 189–194
  using reference parameters, 201–202
  value parameter, using, 189–190
  virtual, 312
  writing that receive parameters and returns a value, 199–200
  writing with no parameters, no return value, 173–176
Microsoft Visual Studio 2005 and C# programming language, 7
MinimizeSize property, 445, 467
minus sign (-)
  decrement operator (--), 71, 52
  subtraction operator, 50

mission critical processes, exception handling in, 323, 358
modal dialog boxes, 372, 407
modifiers, access. *See* access modifiers
MonthCalendar
  adding to Form, 439–442, 461–465
  described, 467
mouse events, handling, 489–492, 508
MouseClick() events, 490, 491
MouseEventArgs class, 489–491
MSDN Library, installing, 392
multidimensional arrays, 155–158, 164, 165
multifile assembly, 177, 205, 561–564
multiple inheritance, 298, 312
multiplication operator (*), 50

N

named constants, defining, 60–61, 72
namespaces
  See also specific namespace
  described, 9, 32
  naming, 562
naming
  class objects, 219
  classes, 5, 11
  interfaces, 299
  memory location, 2
  projects, 24–25, 383
  variables, 40
nested
  if-else statements, 100–102
  if statements, 85–86, 88, 105
  loops, using, 124–125
  method calls, 185, 205
netmodule files, 562, 564
.NET
  environment and Visual Studio, 366
  Framework types, and IDE editor, 565–568
new operator, creating objects using, 141, 164
newline escape sequences, 177
nonstatic methods, 174, 205
nonvolatile and volatile storage, 516

nonvolatile storage, 550
NOT operator, using, 97, 100, 106
notation, scientific, floating-point variables, 48
Notepad, using as code editor, 22, 24
numbers, magic, 527, 551
numeric type conversions, 54–55

O

Object class
  type in System namespace, 312
  using, 288–292
object-oriented exception handling, 326–329
object-oriented programming, 32
objects
  attributes, states, properties, 5, 32
  classes and, 214–216
  creating arrays of, 255–258
  creating class and, 251–254
  declaring, 218–221
  declaring arrays of, 244–250
  default value of, 232, 261
  described, 32
  GUI. *See* GUI
  invoking, 248, 261
  in object-oriented programming, 4
  passing to methods, 238–239
  properties, creating, 221–224
  serialization of, 551
one-dimensional arrays, 155, 164
opening files, 550
operands, 50, 71
operating systems, command line, 4
operator precedence, 50–51, 71, 558–559
operators
  See also specific operator
  overloading, 195, 239–244, 259
OR operator
  combining with AND, 91–92
  described, 105
  using, 90, 99–100, 104
order of operations described, 71
organizing classes, 224–225
outer loops, 124, 133

INDEX

output
  displaying variable values, 43–46
  eliminating reference to Out by using System namespace, 15–16
  writing C# programs that produce, 8–11
output parameters, using, 191–193, 206
overloading
  constructors, 234–236, 294
  constructors to a class, 254–255
  described, 206
  methods, 195–196, 202–203
  operators, 239–244
override keyword, 312
overriding base class methods, 282–284
overriding methods, 261

P

Padding property, 467
Panel, 445, 467
parallel arrays, 146–147, 164
parameter arrays, 206
parameterless constructors, 234, 261
parameters
  of arguments, described, 8, 32
  formal, actual, value, reference, 205
  implicit, 222–223, 261
  in Java, 7
  methods that can accept, 20, 203
params keyword, 193, 194, 206
parent classes, 275–278, 311
parentheses (( ))
  around expressions, 92
  C# procedure names, 4
  and methods, 172, 174
  AND and OR operators, 91
partial keyword, 386
Pascal casing, 4, 32
passing
  arrays to methods, 185–189
  multiple arguments to methods, 180
  parameters to constructors, 233–234
path commands, setting, 18

paths
  changing to root directory, 23
  described, 550
  and file organization, 517
percent sign (%), modulus operator, 50
permanent storage devices, 516, 550
persistent storage, 517, 550
PictureBox
  adding to Form, 433–435
  described, 467
pipe symbol (|) and OR operator, 90–91, 105
placeholders, 44, 70
planning programs using pseudocode, 82–83
plus sign (+)
  addition operator, 50, 239
  and concatenation, 46
  and overloaded operators, 195
  prefix, postfix increment operator (++), 71
pointers
  file position, 530, 551
  use in C#, 7
polymorphism
  described, 6, 32
  and inheritance, 283
positioning buttons on windows, 380
postfix increment operator (++), 52, 71
posttest loops, 124, 133
precedence
  operator, 50–51, 71, 558–559
  type, 72
precision specifiers, 48, 71
prefix increment operator (++), 52, 71
preprocessor directives, 389–390
pretest loops, 124, 133
primary keys, 225, 261
primitive data, 7
private access for methods, 205
private access modifiers, 10, 32, 174
private class access modifiers, 216, 260
private methods, 229
procedural programs, 3, 31
procedures
  described, 32
  names, and parentheses (( )), 4
program comments, 12–14, 32
program files, 516, 550
program logic, 32

programming, object-oriented, 3–7, 32
programming languages
  C#. See C#
  high-level, 31
  intermediate languages (ILs), 17, 33
  usage of, 2–3
programs
  See also specific program, program type
  adding comments to, 12–14, 29–30
  calling, invoking procedures, 4, 32
  compiling and executing from command line, 23–24
  compiling and executing using Visual Studio IDE, 24–29
  debugging, 3, 32
  delivery charge, creating, 102–104
  described, 2, 31
  entering into editors, 22
  event-driven, 474, 508
  exception handling. See exception handling
  fault-tolerant applications, 358
  Form as main window, 378–380
  interactive, 72
  making decisions using, 82–83
  shell, 12
  stopping, terminating, 337
  writing and compiling C#, 16–21
projects, forms, 384
prompt
  command, 32
  and interactive programs, 61
prompts described, 72
properties
  accessors, 221–222
  of classes, 259, 261
  creating, 221–224
  of Forms, 376–377
  of objects, 5, 32
Properties window, IDE, 383
protected access for methods, 174
protected access specifiers, 216, 278–281
protected class internal access, 260
protected internal access, 174, 205
pseudocode, usage of, 82–83, 105
public access for methods, 205
public access modifiers, 10, 32, 172, 173
public class access modifiers, 216, 260

`public` fields and `private` methods, 226–229
`Public` class, 12

Q

question marks (?) and conditional operators, 96
quotation marks (" ") around filenames, 22

R

`RadioButtons`
  and `Checkbox`, 428–432
  usage of, 457–460, 467
RAM (random access memory), 516, 550
range checks, performing accurate, efficient, 98–99, 106
range matches, searching arrays for, 150–151, 164
read-only property and `get` accessors, 221, 261
reading
  data from file into `Form`, 544–548
  from files, 516, 538–539, 550
  from sequential access files, 528–529
records described, 521, 550
rectangular arrays, 155, 164
recursive methods, 312
refactoring, 391, 568
reference equality, 312
reference parameters to methods, 191–193, 201–202, 205
reference, passed by, 187, 205
reference types, 261
relationships
  has-a, 261
  is-a, 215, 260
rethrowing `Exceptions`, 350–352, 358
`return` statements, 94, 183–184, 205
return type of methods, 174, 183, 205
`Reverse()` method, using, 154, 161–165

right-associative, operator precedence, 558, 559
robustness described, 358
root directory, 517, 550

S

scope
  classes, and destructors, 250
  of variables, 175, 205
searching
  arrays for exact matches, 146–150
  arrays for range matches, 150–151
  sequential access files, 530–532
  Visual Studio help, 392–393
`Seek()` method, 539–541
self-documenting program elements, 60, 72
semantic errors described, 3, 32
semicolons (;) and variable declarations, 40, 42
`sender` objects, using in events, 506–507
sentinel values, 119, 132
sequence structures, 82–83, 105
sequential access files, 522, 550
  reading from, 528–529
  searching, 530–532
  writing to, 525–528
serialization and deserialization, 532–536, 549, 551
`set` accessors, 221, 261
shell programs, 12
short-circuit evaluations, 89, 105
shortcut, arithmetic operators, 51–52, 69
`Show()` method and `MessageBox`, 366–372
`ShowDialog()` method, 378
side effects, and conditional AND and OR operators, 90–91, 106
signatures, method, 206
significant digits, 47, 71
single-dimensional arrays, 155, 164
slashes (/)
  division operator, 50
  forward and comments, 14, 31, 33
Smart Tags, IntelliSense and .NET Framework classes, 567–568

snap lines, 443, 467
Solution Explorer, 383, 384, 407
`Sort()` method, 153–154, 161–165, 245–250
source code, 17, 33, 569
square brackets ([ ]) around subscripts, 141
`StackTrace` property, 344–347
standard numeric format strings, 48, 71
`StartsWith()` method, 59, 72
state of an object, 5, 32
statements
  See also specific statement
  arithmetic, using in programs, 65–66
  automatic statement completion feature, 29
  blocks, 105
  commenting out, 14, 33
  self-documenting, 60
states
  of class objects, 215
  of objects, 5, 32
static access modifiers, 10, 32
`static` keyword
static methods, 174, 205, 218, 228
storage
  of computer files, 516–517
  permanent devices, 550
  persistent, 517, 550
  of variables, 520
  volatile and nonvolatile, 516, 550
storing
  classes, 224–225
  object properties, 229–231
`StreamReader` class, 523, 549
streams, usage of, 522–525, 550
`StreamWriter` class, 523, 549
`string` data type, 20, 33, 57–59, 72
strings
  concatenating, 46, 70
  format, 44, 70
  immutable, 59, 72
  literal, 8
structures
  See also specific structure
  decision, 82–83, 105
  loop, 116–126
  sequence, 82–83, 105
subclasses, 275, 311

INDEX

subscripts
  accessing array elements with, 143–144
  in arrays, 141
  described, 164
subtraction operator (-), 50
superclasses, 275, 311
switch expressions, 94, 106
switch keyword, 94, 106
switch statements, making decisions using, 92–96, 104
switch structures, using, 93–95, 106
syntax
  described, 32
  errors, passing arguments in reverse, 181
  high-level programming language, 2–3
System namespace
  described, 9, 32, 40
  eliminating reference to Out by using, 15–16
  Object class in, using, 288–292
System.Array class, 145, 164
System.Drawing.Size(), 378
SystemException, generating, 324–325, 357
System.IO namespace, 518
System.Windows.Forms.Control class, 381

T

tables (two-dimensional arrays), 155, 164
TabStop, TabIndex, 504–505
ternary operators, 106
text, cutting vs. deleting in Visual Studio IDE, 26
text editors. See editors
this reference, 229–232, 259, 261
tilde (~), and destructors, 250
tokens, 526, 551
Toolbox (of IDE), 407
Toolbox, Visual Studio IDE, 382, 384, 398
ToString() method, 48, 179, 289–290, 329–331, 357

totals, accumulating, in programs, 126–128
tracing Exceptions through call stack, 343–347
transitive inheritance, 275, 311
translater, language, 3
troubleshooting
  common errors in decision-making, 97–100
  csc command, 18
true-false as expression operators, 240
try blocks
  catching multiple Exceptions, 331–334
  described, 358
  in exception handling, 326–329
  and finally blocks, 336–338
two-dimensional arrays, 164
type precedence, 54, 72

U

unary operators, 52, 71
underscore (_) and identifiers, 11
Unicode characters, 41, 57, 521
unifying type, 54, 72
unreachable blocks, 335, 358
uppercase
  and named constants, 60
  properties, 222
  usage of in C#, 11
user, class, 215, 260
user input
  accepting console input, 61–63
  with forms. See Forms
  writing program to, 68–69
using clause, 15–16, 567–568

V

value parameters of methods 179, 189–190, 205
value types described, 261
values
  assigning to array elements, 140–142

default, of objects, 232, 261
displaying variable, 43–46
formatting floating-point, 48–49
garbage, 126
sentinel, 119, 132
writing methods that return, 183–185
variable declarations, 40–42, 70
variables
  aliases, using, 191
  Boolean, 66–67
  declaring and using, 40–43, 63–64
  described, 3, 32, 70
  displaying values, 43–46
  floating-point, 47–48
  incrementing, decrementing, 132
  instance, 260
  iteration, 145
  local, 205
  loop control, 117, 132
  scope of, 175, 205
  storage of, 520
  temporary iteration, 164
  usage of, 6
verbatim identifiers, 11, 32
verifying ID numbers (program for), 128–131
versions of C#, 7
viewing events in Properties window, 488
virtual methods, 312
visible classes, 312
Visual Basic and C# programming language, 7
Visual C#. See C#
Visual C# key features, 382–385
Visual C# Code Editor, using, 565–569
Visual Studio 2005 and C# programming language, 7
Visual Studio IDE
  code created by, 385–390, 451–453
  compiling and executing program using, 24–29
  compiling code from within, 19
  designing Form using, 382–385, 406
  editors in, 22, 565–569
  Help, 392–393
  method mode, 418
  Visual C# key features, 382–385
  working with, 395–402

void keyword, 20, 32
void methods, 174
volatile and nonvolatile storage, 516, 550

warnings, responding to compiler, 18
while loops
  described, 132
  searching arrays using, 148–150
  using, 116–120, 128–129
whitespace and arithmetic operators, 10, 32, 53
widgets described, 414, 466
windows
  creating Form for program's main, 378–380
  placing buttons on, 380–382
  vs. MessageBox, 406
WordPad, using as code editor, 22
Write() method, 43–46
WriteLine() method, 9, 15–16, 32, 43–46, 69
writing
  C# programs that produces output, 8–11
  C# programs, 31
  and compiling C# programs, 16–21
  to files, 516, 550
  Main() method, alternatives, 20–21
  method that receives parameters and returns a value, 199–200
  methods that require multiple arguments, 180–182
  methods that require single arguments, 177–180
  methods that return a value, 183–185
  methods with no parameters, no return value, 173–176
  to sequential access files, 525–528

XML-documentation format comments, 14, 33

Z

zero variable, 353